The IDG Books Bible Advantage

The *Excel 97 Bible* is part of the Bible series brought to you by IDG Books Worldwide. We designed Bibles to meet your growing need for quick access to the most complete and accurate computer information available.

Bibles work the way you do: They focus on accomplishing specific tasks — not learning random functions. These books are not long-winded manuals or dry reference tomes. In Bibles, expert authors tell you exactly what you can do with your software and how to do it. Easy to follow, step-by-step sections; comprehensive coverage; and convenient access in language and design — it's all here.

The authors of Bibles are uniquely qualified to give you expert advice as well as insightful tips and techniques not found anywhere else. Our authors maintain close contact with end users through feedback from articles, training sessions, e-mail exchanges, user group participation, and consulting work. Because our authors know the realities of daily computer use and are directly tied to the reader, our Bibles have a strategic advantage.

Bible authors have the experience to approach a topic in the most efficient manner, and we know that you, the reader, will benefit from a "one-on-one" relationship with the author. Our research shows that readers make computer book purchases because they want expert advice on a product. Readers want to benefit from the author's experience, so the author's voice is always present in a Bible series book.

You will find what you need in this book whether you read it from cover to cover, section by section, or simply one topic at a time. As a computer user, you deserve a comprehensive resource of answers. We at IDG Books Worldwide are proud to deliver that resource with the *Excel 97 Bible*.

Brenda McLaughlin
Senior Vice President and Group Publisher
Internet: YouTellUs@idgbooks.com

Excel 97
Bible

Excel 97 Bible

by John Walkenbach

IDG Books Worldwide, Inc.
An International Data Group Company

Foster City, CA ✦ Chicago, IL ✦ Indianapolis, IN ✦ Southlake, TX

Excel 97 Bible

Published by
IDG Books Worldwide, Inc.
An International Data Group Company
919 E. Hillsdale Blvd.
Suite 400
Foster City, CA 94404
http://www.idgbooks.com (IDG Books Worldwide Web site)
http://www.dummies.com (Dummies Press Web site)

Library of Congress Catalog Card No.: 96-78773

ISBN: 0-7645-3036-4

Printed in the United States of America

12 11 10 9 8

1B/SS/QT/QR/IN

Distributed in the United States by IDG Books Worldwide, Inc.

Distributed by Macmillan Canada for Canada; by Transworld Publishers Limited in the United Kingdom and Europe; by WoodsLane Pty. Ltd. for Australia; by WoodsLane Enterprises Ltd. for New Zealand; by Longman Singapore Publishers Ltd. for Singapore, Malaysia, Thailand, and Indonesia; by Simron Pty. Ltd. for South Africa; by Toppan Company Ltd. for Japan; by Distribuidora Cuspide for Argentina; by Livraria Cultura for Brazil; by Ediciencia S.A. for Ecuador; by Addison-Wesley Publishing Company for Korea; by Ediciones ZETA S.C.R. Ltda. for Peru; by WS Computer Publishing Company, Inc., for the Philippines; by Unalis Corporation for Taiwan; by Contemporanea de Ediciones for Venezuela. Authorized Sales Agent: Anthony Rudkin Associates for the Middle East and North Africa.

For general information on IDG Books Worldwide's books in the U.S., please call our Consumer Customer Service department at 800-762-2974. For reseller information, including discounts and premium sales, please call our Reseller Customer Service department at 800-434-3422.

For information on where to purchase IDG Books Worldwide's books outside the U.S., please contact our International Sales department at 415-655-3172 or fax 415-655-3295.

For information on foreign language translations, please contact our Foreign & Subsidiary Rights department at 415-655-3021 or fax 415-655-3281.

For sales inquiries and special prices for bulk quantities, please contact our Sales department at 415-655-3200 or write to the address above.

For information on using IDG Books Worldwide's books in the classroom or for ordering examination copies, please contact our Educational Sales department at 800-434-2086 or fax 817-251-8174.

For press review copies, author interviews, or other publicity information, please contact our Public Relations department at 415-655-3000 or fax 415-655-3299.

For authorization to photocopy items for corporate, personal, or educational use, please contact Copyright Clearance Center, 222 Rosewood Drive, Danvers, MA 01923, or fax 508-750-4470.

is a trademark under exclusive license to IDG Books Worldwide, Inc., from International Data Group, Inc.

IDG
BOOKS
WORLDWIDE

About the Author

John Walkenbach is one of the country's leading authorities on spreadsheet software. He holds a Ph.D. from the University of Montana and has worked as an instructor, programmer, and market research manager. He finally found a job he's good at: principal of JWalk and Associates Inc., a one-person San Diego-based consulting firm that specializes in spreadsheet application development. John is also a shareware developer, and his most popular product is the Power Utility Pak add-in for Excel — which is used by thousands of people throughout the world. John started writing about spreadsheets in 1984, and he has since written more than 250 articles and reviews for publications such as *PC World, InfoWorld, Windows,* and *PC/Computing.* In addition, he's the author of a dozen other spreadsheet books, including *Excel 95 For Windows Power Programming With VBA, Excel Programming For Windows 95 For Dummies,* and *Excel 97 For Windows For Dummies Quick Reference* (all from IDG Books). In his spare time, John enjoys composing and playing music in a variety of styles, including blues, bluegrass, and new age. Currently, his toys include a multi-synthesizer MIDI system, a growing collection of acoustic and electric guitars, and a made-in-Montana Flatiron mandolin. You can reach John on the Internet at john@j-walk.com, or visit his Web site (The Spreadsheet Page) at http://www.j-walk.com/ss/.

ABOUT IDG BOOKS WORLDWIDE

Welcome to the world of IDG Books Worldwide.

IDG Books Worldwide, Inc., is a subsidiary of International Data Group, the world's largest publisher of computer-related information and the leading global provider of information services on information technology. IDG was founded more than 25 years ago and now employs more than 8,500 people worldwide. IDG publishes more than 275 computer publications in over 75 countries (see listing below). More than 60 million people read one or more IDG publications each month.

Launched in 1990, IDG Books Worldwide is today the #1 publisher of best-selling computer books in the United States. We are proud to have received eight awards from the Computer Press Association in recognition of editorial excellence and three from *Computer Currents'* First Annual Readers' Choice Awards. Our best-selling *...For Dummies®* series has more than 30 million copies in print with translations in 30 languages. IDG Books Worldwide, through a joint venture with IDG's Hi-Tech Beijing, became the first U.S. publisher to publish a computer book in the People's Republic of China. In record time, IDG Books Worldwide has become the first choice for millions of readers around the world who want to learn how to better manage their businesses.

Our mission is simple: Every one of our books is designed to bring extra value and skill-building instructions to the reader. Our books are written by experts who understand and care about our readers. The knowledge base of our editorial staff comes from years of experience in publishing, education, and journalism — experience we use to produce books for the '90s. In short, we care about books, so we attract the best people. We devote special attention to details such as audience, interior design, use of icons, and illustrations. And because we use an efficient process of authoring, editing, and desktop publishing our books electronically, we can spend more time ensuring superior content and spend less time on the technicalities of making books.

You can count on our commitment to deliver high-quality books at competitive prices on topics you want to read about. At IDG Books Worldwide, we continue in the IDG tradition of delivering quality for more than 25 years. You'll find no better book on a subject than one from IDG Books Worldwide.

John Kilcullen
President and CEO
IDG Books Worldwide, Inc.

Eighth Annual
Computer Press
Awards ≥1992

Ninth Annual
Computer Press
Awards ≥1993

Tenth Annual
Computer Press
Awards ≥1994

XI WINNER

Eleventh Annual
Computer Press
Awards ≥1995

Dedication

This one's for Pat, Ken, Kim, and Steve.

Credits

**Senior Vice President
and Group Publisher**
Brenda McLaughlin

Publishing Director
Walt Bruce

Acquisitions Manager
Gregory S. Croy

Acquisitions Editor
Ellen L. Camm

Software Acquisitions Editor
Tracy Lehman Cramer

Marketing Manager
Melisa M. Duffy

Marketing Coordinator
Julie Bastian

Managing Editor
Andy Cummings

Administrative Assistant
Laura J. Moss

Editorial Assistant
Timothy J. Borek

Production Director
Beth Jenkins

**Supervisor of Project
Coordination, Production
Proofreading, and Indexing**
Cindy L. Phipps

Supervisor of Page Layout
Kathie S. Schutte

Supervisor of Graphics and Design
Shelley Lea

Production Systems Specialist
Debbie J. Gates

Supervisor of Reprints and Blueline
Tony Augsburger

Development Editor
Barbra Guerra

Copy Editors
John Edwards
Mary Ann Faughnan
Nate Holdread
Kelly Oliver
Jeannie Smith

Technical Reviewer
Forrest Houlette

Project Coordinator
Sherry Gomoll

Layout and Graphics
Brett Black, Elizabeth
Cárdenas-Nelson, J Tyler Connor,
Angela F. Hunckler, Todd Klemme,
Drew Moore, Brent Savage,
Kathie S. Schutte

Production Administration
Todd Klemme
Jacalyn L. Pennywell
Leslie Popplewell
Theresa Sanchez-Baker
Melissa Stauffer
Bryan Stephenson

Proofreaders
Christine Langin-Faris,
Rachel Garvey, Nancy Price, Robert
Springer, Carrie Voorhis

Indexer
Rebecca Plunkett

Book Design
Drew Moore

Acknowledgements

Thanks to everyone at IDG Books who played a part in getting this book into your hands, especially Barb Guerra, Nate Holdread, and John Edwards. Without their able assistance, I'd still be pounding away at my keyboard.

Much of the inspiration for this book came from two sources: the comp.apps.spreadsheets Usenet newsgroup and the Excel Forum on CompuServe. Thanks to all the participants in these groups whose problems and questions gave me ideas for topics in the book.

Finally, thanks to all the people throughout the world who have taken the time to let me know that my books have made an impact. My goal is to write books that go well beyond the material found in competing books. Based on the feedback that I've received, I think I'm succeeding. Writing software books may not be the most glamorous job — but I can't think of anything else that I'd rather be doing.

John Walkenbach

La Jolla, California

(The Publisher would like to give special thanks to Patrick J. McGovern, without whom this book would not have been possible.)

Contents at a Glance

Table of Contents

Part II: Introductory Concepts   53

Chapter 4: Navigating through Excel 55

Part III: Advanced Features   361

Part V: Other Topics 631

Introduction

Thanks for purchasing the *Excel 97 Bible* — your complete guide to a powerful and easy-to-use spreadsheet product.

I think that Excel 97 is the best spreadsheet program on the market (trust me — I've used them all). Excel has been around in various incarnations for almost a decade, and each subsequent release pushes the spreadsheet envelope a bit further — in some cases, a *lot* further. My goal in writing this book is to share with you some of what I know about Excel, and in the process make you more efficient on the job.

The book contains everything that you need to know to learn the basics of Excel and then move on to more advanced topics at your own pace. You find many useful examples as well as some of the tips and slick techniques that I've accumulated over the years. The book is an excellent alternative to the printed material that's included with Excel (which is skimpier than ever) and is *much* more comprehensive. And, with all due respect to Microsoft's documentation department, I think that you are going to find this book a lot more interesting than the manuals.

Is This Book for You?

The Bible series from IDG Books Worldwide is designed for beginning, intermediate, and advanced users. This book covers all the essential components of Excel and provides clear and practical examples that you can adapt to your own needs.

Excel can be used at many levels — from the simple to the extremely complex. I think I've drawn a good balance here, focusing on the topics that are most useful to most users. The following can help you decide whether this book is for you.

Yes — If you have no spreadsheet experience

If you're new to the world of spreadsheets, welcome to the fold. This book has everything that you need to get started with Excel and then advance to other topics as the need arises.

Yes — If you have used previous versions of Excel

If you've used Excel 5 or Excel 95, you're going to feel right at home with Excel 97. If you're skipping a few upgrades and moving up from Excel 3 or Excel 4, you have lots to learn, because Microsoft has made many improvements in the past few years. In any case, this book can get you up to speed quickly.

Yes — If you have used Excel for the Macintosh

The Macintosh versions of Excel are very similar to the Windows versions. If you're moving over from the Mac platform, you find some good background information as well as specific details to make your transition as smooth as possible.

Yes — If you have used DOS versions of 1-2-3 or Quattro Pro

If you're abandoning a text-based spreadsheet such as 1-2-3 or Corel's Quattro Pro in favor of a more modern graphical product, this book can serve you well. You have a head start because you already know what spreadsheets are all about, and you discover some great new ways of doing things.

Yes — If you have used Windows versions of 1-2-3 or Quattro Pro

If you've tried the others and are convinced that Excel is the way to go, this book quickly teaches you what Excel is all about and why it has such a great reputation. Because you're already familiar with Windows *and* spreadsheets, you can breeze through many introductory topics.

No — If you are an Excel expert who wants to learn some powerful customization techniques using the Visual Basic for Applications (VBA) programming language

I had to draw the line somewhere. Although I cover VBA programming in this book and provide examples at this book's Web site, I don't go into the depth that advanced users may require. Rather, I refer you to my *Excel For Windows 95 Power Programming Techniques,* 2nd Edition (IDG Books Worldwide, Inc.).

No — If you want to learn all about Windows

Although I tell you enough about Windows to get by, this book is not intended to be a Windows manual. Try Brian Livingston's *Windows 95 Secrets* (IDG Books Worldwide, 1995), Alan Simpson's *Windows 95 Uncut* (IDG Books Worldwide, 1995), or *Windows 95 For Dummies* (IDG Books Worldwide, 1995) by Andy Rathbone.

Maybe — If you want just enough to get by

This book certainly tells you just enough to get by, but if that's all you want, it's probably overkill. Check out Greg Harvey's *Excel For Windows 97 For Dummies* (IDG Books Worldwide, 1996). It's cheaper and has fewer pages. Even if you don't consider yourself a dummy, you may enjoy the way he presents the material — very lighthearted, with a definite de-emphasis on technical matters.

Software Versions

This book was written for Excel 97 (also known as Excel 8), but most of the information also applies to Excel 5 and Excel 95. If you use any version of Excel prior to Version 5, this book doesn't do you much good, because the earlier versions are drastically different from the current version.

Conventions in This Book

Take a minute to scan this section to learn some of the typographical conventions that are used in this book.

Excel commands

In Excel, as in all Windows programs, you select commands from the pull-down menu system. In this book, such commands appear in normal typeface but are distinguishable because the commands have a single letter underlined, just as the commands appear in the menus. The underlined letter represents the *hot-key letter*. For example, if I mention the File⇨Save command, note that the *F* and *S* are underlined. These correspond to the single-letter keys that you can use to access the commands from the keyboard. In this example, you would press Alt+F and then S to issue the File⇨Save command.

Filenames, named ranges, and your input

Input that you make from the keyboard appears in **bold**. Filenames and named ranges may appear in `a different font`. Lengthy input usually appears on a separate line. For instance, I may instruct you to enter a formula such as the following:

```
="Part Name: " &VLOOKUP(PartNumber,PartList,2)
```

Key names

Names of the keys on your keyboard appear in normal type. When two keys should be pressed simultaneously, they are connected with a plus sign, like this: Press Alt+E to select the Edit menu. Here are the key names as I refer to them throughout the book:

Alt	down arrow	Num Lock	right arrow
Backspace	End	Pause	Scroll Lock
Caps Lock	Home	PgDn	Shift
Ctrl	Insert	PgUp	Tab
Delete	left arrow	Print Screen	up arrow

Functions

Excel's built-in worksheet functions appear in uppercase, like this: Enter a SUM formula in cell C20.

Mouse conventions

I assume that you're using a mouse or some other pointing device. You come across some of the following mouse-related terms:

Mouse pointer: The small graphic figure that moves on-screen when you move your mouse. The mouse pointer is usually an arrow, but it changes shape when you move to certain areas of the screen or when you're performing certain actions.

Point: Move the mouse so that the mouse pointer is on a specific item. For example, "Point to the Save button on the toolbar."

Press: Press the left mouse button once and keep it pressed. Normally, this is used when dragging.

Click: Press the left mouse button once and release it immediately.

Right-click on: Press the right mouse button once and release it immediately. The right mouse button is used in Excel to pop up shortcut menus that are appropriate for whatever is currently selected.

Double-click on: Press the left mouse button twice in rapid succession. If your double-clicking doesn't seem to be working, you can adjust the double-click sensitivity using the Windows Control Panel icon.

Drag: Press the left mouse button and keep it pressed while you move the mouse. Dragging is often used to select a range of cells or to change the size of an object.

What the Icons Mean

Throughout the book, you see special graphic symbols, or *icons,* in the left margin. These call your attention to points that are particularly important or relevant to a specific group of readers. The icons in this book are as follows:

Excel 97 This symbol denotes features that are new to Excel 97. If you've upgraded from Excel 95, this cues you in on the new features. If you're still using Excel 95, this icon warns you of features that aren't available in your version.

Note This icon signals the fact that something is important or worth noting. This may alert you to a concept that helps you master the task at hand, or it may denote something that is fundamental to understanding subsequent material.

Tip This icon marks a more efficient way of doing something that may not be obvious.

Web site This indicates that the material uses an example file located at this book's Web site (see "This Book Has a Web Site," later in this Introduction).

Caution I use this symbol when there is a possibility that the operation I'm describing could cause problems if you're not careful.

Cross Reference This icon indicates that a related topic is discussed elsewhere in this book.

How This Book Is Organized

Notice that the book is divided into seven main parts.

Part I: "Getting Started" — This part consists of three chapters that provide background about Excel. Chapter 2 describes the new features in Excel 97. Chapter 3 is a hands-on guided tour of Excel, which gives new users an opportunity to get their feet wet immediately.

Part II: "Introductory Concepts" — The chapters in Part II cover the basic concepts with which all Excel users should be familiar.

Part III: "Advanced Features" — This part consists of six chapters dealing with topics that are sometimes considered advanced. Many beginning and intermediate users may find this information useful as well.

Part IV: "Analyzing Data" — The broad topic of data analysis is the focus of the chapters in Part IV. Users of all levels can find some of these chapters of interest.

Part V: "Other Topics" — This part consists of four chapters that didn't quite fit into any other part. The chapters deal with using Excel with other applications, auditing and proofing your work, and exploring the fun side of Excel (yes, Excel *does* have a fun side).

Part VI: "Customizing Excel" — Part VI is for those who want to customize Excel for their own use or who are designing workbooks or add-ins that are to be used by others. I briefly discuss the XLM macro system, but I focus primarily on Visual Basic for Applications.

Part VII: "Appendixes" — The appendixes consist of supplemental and reference material that may be useful to you.

How to Use This Book

This book is not intended to be read cover-to-cover. Rather, it's a reference book that you can consult when

- ✦ You're stuck while trying to do something.
- ✦ You need to do something that you've never done before.
- ✦ You have some time on your hands, and you're interested in learning something new.

The index is quite comprehensive, and each chapter typically focuses on a single broad topic. If you're just starting out with Excel, I recommend that you read the first three chapters to gain a basic understanding of the product and then do some experimenting on your own. After you've become familiar with Excel's environment, you can refer to the chapters that interest you most. Some users, however, may prefer to follow the chapters in order. Part II was designed with these users in mind.

Don't be discouraged if some of the material is over your head. Most users get by just fine using only a small subset of Excel's total capabilities. In fact, the 80/20 rule applies here: 80 percent of Excel users use only 20 percent of its features. However, using only 20 percent of Excel's features still gives you *lots* of power at your fingertips.

This Book Has a Web Site

You find that my writing style emphasizes examples. I know that I learn more from a well-thought-out example than from reading a dozen pages. I've found that this is true for many other people. Consequently, I spent a lot of time developing the examples in this book. You can download the example files from the World Wide Web at the IDG Books Web Site. The URL is:

```
http://www.idgbooks.com
```

Appendix D further describes the material that is available for download.

 When you see this icon, you can open the example file and try out the example for yourself.

Power Utility Pak Coupon

Toward the back of the book, you find a coupon that you can redeem for a copy of my Power Utility Pak software — a collection of useful Excel utilities and new worksheet functions. This product normally sells for $39.95, but I'm making it available to readers of this book for only $9.95, plus shipping and handling. I developed this package using VBA exclusively, and the complete source files are also available for those who want to learn slick VBA techniques.

I think that the Power Utility Pak is extremely useful in your day-to-day work with Excel, and I urge you to take advantage of this offer.

Contacting the Author

I'm always happy to hear from readers of my books. The best way to contact me is by e-mail at the following Internet address:

```
author@j-walk.com
```

If you don't have access to electronic mail, you can send snail mail to me in care of IDG Books Worldwide, Inc.

Visit The Spreadsheet Page

For even more information on Excel, be sure to check out The Spreadsheet Page on the World Wide Web. The URL is

```
http://www.j-walk/ss/
```

Getting Started

T he three chapters in this part fill you in on background about Excel 97. They also give new users a
chance to sample some of Excel's features.

A Bit of Background

Every book has to start somewhere. This chapter starts
from square one and introduces you to the concept of a
spreadsheet. I include lots of interesting background information on Excel and Windows.

What Is Excel?

Excel is a software product that falls into the general category
known as *spreadsheets*. Excel is one of several spreadsheet
products that you can run on your PC. Others include 1-2-3
and Quattro Pro.

A spreadsheet (including Excel) is a highly interactive computer program that consists of a collection of rows and
columns that are displayed on-screen in a scrollable window.
The intersection of each row and column is called a *cell*, and a
cell can hold a number, a text string, or a formula that performs a calculation using one or more other cells. It's easy to
copy cells, move cells, and modify any formulas you create.
A spreadsheet can be saved in a file for later use or discarded
after it has served its intended purpose. The cells in a spreadsheet can be formatted in any number of ways and printed for
hard-copy reference. In addition, groups of numerical cells
can be used to generate charts and maps.

The most significant advantage of an electronic spreadsheet
is that the formulas recalculate their results if you change any
of the cells they use. As a result, once you get your spreadsheet set up by defining formulas, you can use this "model" to
explore different possibilities with little additional effort on
your part. Excel is currently the best-selling Windows spreadsheet — and I hope to explain why in the pages of this book.

Windows Makes It Happen

Windows is now installed on virtually all new PCs and is easily the most popular operating system. However, it wasn't always that way. In the early days of personal computing, all software was text-based (no graphics), and you could run only one program at a time. Even worse, just about every program you used had an entirely different look and feel. For example, depending on which program you were running, pressing the F1 function key might bring up a help display, save your file, erase characters, or give you a quick exit from the program. Back in the old days, you had to be on your toes.

Microsoft Windows evolved gradually and the early versions were much different from today's Windows. (Figure 1-1 shows what Windows 95 looks like on a computer screen.) The big turning point in the story of Windows occurred in May 1990. This is when Microsoft released Windows 3.0 — the first version that really made it feasible to use Windows. In the summer of 1995 (after many delays) Microsoft released Windows 95. This was a major upgrade — actually, a new product — that is a complete operating system. Microsoft also sells Windows NT, a 32-bit operating system that's more advanced than Windows 95. Excel 97 also runs under Windows NT.

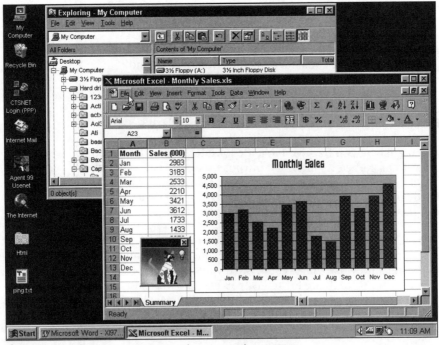

Figure 1-1: Windows 95 is a complete operating system.

Today, almost all PC software is developed for Windows. So, what makes Windows so special? I think that five aspects of Windows are responsible for its success.

Common user interface

By *user interface,* I'm referring to the methods by which the user (you) interacts with the software. A user interface consists of a number of components, including menus, toolbars, and shortcut keys. You've probably noticed that all the programs you run under Windows tend to look pretty much the same. For example, they all have a menu along the top, most of them use toolbars, and they almost always use the same shortcut keys for basic operations such as copying and pasting. This consistency is important because it enhances overall productivity. In short, if you learn to use one Windows program, you have a head start on learning others.

Multitasking

As the term implies, *multitasking* is the capability to perform more than one task at a time. In this case, a *task* is a program. You probably already know that you can run more than one program at a time when you use Windows and that you can easily switch among programs. For example, you may be running Excel and remember that you need to whip off a quick memo to your staff. There's no need to close down Excel; you can just open your word processor in another window.

Say that you're downloading a humongous file from the Internet and the process takes 20 minutes. Rather than sit and stare at the bytes-transferred message, you can jump to another program and do something more productive. It gets even better. Some programs (but not many, yet) also support *multithreading.* This means that the program can be working on one thing while you're doing another thing in the same program. The current version of Excel doesn't support such multithreading, but I expect that a future version will.

Shared resources

In the pre-Windows days, every program had to provide its own separate support for things such as printers and video drivers. In other words, every time you installed a program, you had to go through a tedious process of choosing the proper printer and video-display driver. In many cases, your printer wasn't actually supported, so you had to figure out which one to "emulate." If you acquired a new printer, you had to go through another tedious process of changing the printer setting for all your software.

Windows eliminates this by handling all this information centrally. For example, Windows keeps track of which printer(s) you have, so every Windows software program simply calls on Windows to do the actual printing.

WYSIWYG

WYSIWYG, as nearly everyone on the planet knows, stands for What You See Is What You Get. This term aptly describes most Windows programs. The formatting that you apply appears on-screen and also prints looking exactly the same. You may take this for granted, but we old-timers wasted far too much paper trying to get our printouts to look right.

The fun factor

Finally, most people agree that Windows is fun to use. The capability to personalize your system with wallpaper and sounds and to play with slick screen savers helps make Windows popular.

The Evolution of Excel

Excel 97 is actually Excel 8 in disguise. A bit of rational thinking might lead you to think that this is the eighth version of Excel. Think again! Microsoft may be a successful company, but their version-naming techniques can be quite confusing. As you'll see, Excel 97 is actually the sixth version of Excel.

Excel 2

This was the original version of Excel for Windows, which first appeared in late 1987. It was labeled Version 2 to correspond to the Macintosh version (which was the original Excel). Because Windows wasn't in widespread use at the time, this version included a *run-time* version of Windows — a special version with just enough features to run Excel and nothing else. This version was quite crude by today's standards and was actually quite ugly.

Excel 3

At the end of 1990, Microsoft released Excel 3 for Windows. This was a significant improvement in both appearance and features. It included toolbars, drawing capabilities, worksheet outlining, add-in support, 3D charts, workgroup editing, and lots more.

Excel 4

Excel 4 hit the streets in the spring of 1992. This version made quite an impact in the marketplace because Windows was becoming more popular. It had lots of new features, many of which made it easier for beginners to get up to speed quickly.

Excel 5

In early 1994, Excel 5 appeared on the scene. This version introduced tons of new features, including multisheet workbooks and the new Visual Basic for Applications (VBA) macro language. Like its predecessor, Excel 5 took top honors in just about every spreadsheet comparison published in the trade magazines.

Excel 7

Technically, this version was called Excel for Windows 95 (there was no Excel 6). It began shipping in the summer of 1995. On the surface, it doesn't seem that much different from Excel 5 (there were only a few major new features). But Excel 7 was significant because it was the first version to use more advanced 32-bit code. Excel 7 and Excel 5 use the same file format.

Excel 8

Excel 8 (officially known as Excel 97) is the topic of this book. This is probably the most significant upgrade yet. The toolbars and menus have a great new look, online help has taken a dramatic step forward, and it's packed with many new features that are a direct result of user feedback. And if you're a developer, you'll find that Excel's programming language (VBA) has moved up several notches on the scale. In Chapter 2, I provide a list of the new features in Excel 97.

Excel's Competitors

Although Excel is usually considered the best spreadsheet available, it's not without its competitors. Its two main competitors are 1-2-3 and Quattro Pro.

The three leading spreadsheets are similar in their basic capabilities. For example, they all let you work with multiple worksheets in a single file; they all support a wide variety of charts; and they all have macro capabilities to help you automate or customize your work.

Many users, myself included, find that Excel is superior to the other products in terms of both power and ease of use.

What Excel Has to Offer

Excel is a feature-rich product that can be used at many different levels. Chances are that you won't need all of Excel's features, but it's a good idea to be familiar with what they can do. For example, you may be tempted to seek out another software product and not even realize that Excel has a feature that can accomplish a particular task. Or, you could be spending lots of time performing a task that Excel can handle automatically.

The following is a quick overview of what Excel can do for you. All these topics, of course, are discussed in subsequent chapters of this book.

Multisheet files

Excel's files (called *workbooks*) can consist of any number of separate sheets. The sheets can be worksheets, chart sheets, macro sheets, or custom dialog boxes. This feature makes it easy to organize your work. For example, you can keep all your budgeting spreadsheets in a single workbook.

Multiple document interface

Excel enables you to work with many files at once; it's not necessary to close down a file even if you need to consult another (see Figure 1-2). This capability makes it easy to transfer information between worksheets in different workbooks.

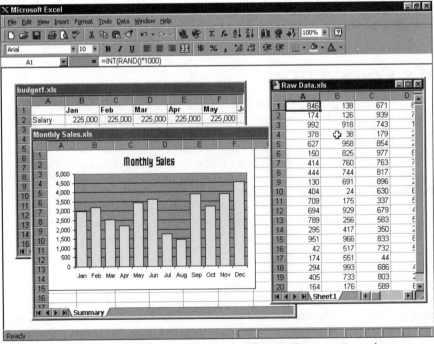

Figure 1-2: Excel lets you work with as many different files as you need.

File compatibility

Excel has its own file format, identifiable by the XLS file extension. In addition, Excel can read files produced by other spreadsheet programs (such as 1-2-3 and Quattro Pro) and it also can read text files, dBASE files, and HTML documents.

Interactive help

Computer documentation keeps getting better. In the past, users were lucky if the manual that accompanied a software product accurately covered all the features. Nowadays, the trend is away from written manuals and towards online help. Almost all applications, including Excel, emphasize *online help* — in other words, you can get help on-screen while working in Excel. Excel's online help is excellent and extremely detailed.

Excel 97 Excel 97, as well as all the other Office 97 products, introduces a new way of providing help. The Office Assistant, shown in Figure 1-3, serves several purposes in Excel:

✦ It observes your actions and stores up a series of tips, which can save you time. You can choose to view these tips whenever you want.

✦ It provides specific help with certain aspects of the program (for example, creating charts).

✦ If you enter an invalid formula, it will often make a suggestion on how to correct it.

✦ It provides an easy way to search for help on a particular topic. Just enter your question in natural language, and the Office Assistant displays a list of relevant help topics.

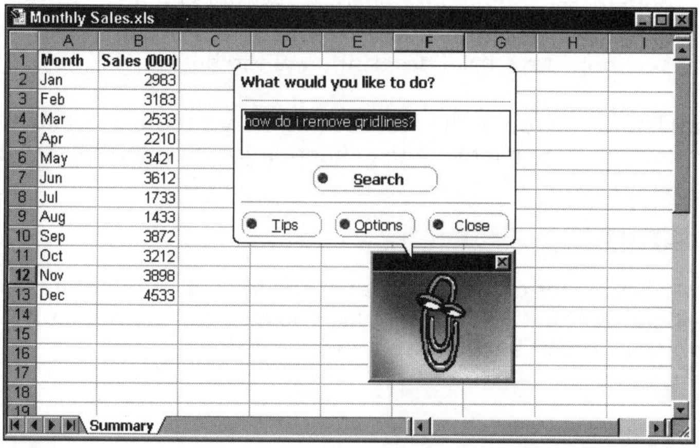

Figure 1-3: The Office Assistant pops up to provide help when needed.

Easy-to-use features

Excel may well be the easiest-to-use spreadsheet available. It includes many features designed specifically to make commonly used tasks straightforward and fast for both beginners and experts. The program walks you step-by-step through several procedures, and basic editing and formatting commands are intuitive and efficient. For example, a single dialog box lets you change any aspect of formatting a cell or range, and right-clicking on anything brings up a context-sensitive short-cut menu.

List management

One of Excel's most significant strengths is how it works with lists stored in a worksheet. This feature makes it easy to sort, filter, summarize, and manipulate data stored in your worksheet.

Built-in functions

Excel includes an enormous collection of built-in functions that you can use in your formulas. In addition to common functions such as SUM and AVERAGE, you can choose functions that perform sophisticated operations that are difficult or impossible to do otherwise. For example, the CORREL function calculates the correlation coefficient for two sets of data. You also can develop other functions by using the Visual Basic for Applications (VBA) macro language (it's not as difficult as you may think).

Customizable toolbars

Excel's *toolbars* — groups of buttons representing commands — are real time-savers, enabling you to perform common commands without using the menu. You can customize your toolbars by adding buttons for tasks that you do most often. To find out what a button does, drag the mouse over a toolbar button and pause for about a second. Excel pops up a brief description of the button.

Excel 97 In Excel 97, the menu bar at the top of the screen is actually a toolbar. As such, you can easily customize it or even move it to a different location on the screen.

Flexible text handling

Although Excel's forte is number crunching, it's not too shabby at handling text. You can format or orient text that you put in cells. You also can insert text boxes (which you can move and resize) anywhere on your worksheet.

Rich text formatting

Excel is the only spreadsheet that enables you to easily format individual characters within a cell. For example, if a cell contains text, you can make one letter bold or a different color.

Great charts

Excel's charting features — among the best available in any spreadsheet — enable you to modify and augment a wide assortment of graph types. You can insert a chart anywhere in a worksheet or place it on a special chart sheet.

Integrated mapping

Excel's mapping feature lets you display your data in terms of a geographic map (see Figure 1-4). For example, you can easily create an attractive map that shows your company's sales volume by state.

Figure 1-4: This map was generated with only a few mouse clicks.

Drawing tools

Excel includes an excellent set of drawing tools that let you create attractive diagrams and basic drawings directly on your worksheet or chart. For example, you can include a simple flow diagram along with your numerical analysis.

Worksheet outlining

Spreadsheet outlining, introduced way back in Version 3, enables you to collapse hierarchical information to show any level of detail. People who work with multi-level budgets will find this feature particularly valuable.

Pivot tables

A pivot table makes it easy to change how you view a table of data. It can quickly summarize a list or database, and you can use drag-and-drop techniques to change the layout of the table. If you work with multidimensional data, you should check out this powerful feature — which I consider to be one of Excel's major strengths.

Advanced analytical tools

Analytical types will get particularly excited about Excel, whose unique *array* feature enables you to do things that are impossible in other spreadsheets. Excel also includes goal seeking, a powerful Solver feature, and the Analysis ToolPak add-in, which provides extensive statistical, financial, engineering, and scientific functions and procedures.

Flexible printing and print preview

When it's time to put your work on paper, you'll be pleased to see how easy it is. Besides normal WYSIWYG formatting, Excel provides the best print previewer I've seen. From the preview window, you can easily make last-minute adjustments, including new column widths and margins. In addition, a new Page Break Preview mode lets you adjust the page breaks by using simple dragging techniques.

Worksheet auditing and annotation

No one's perfect, but Excel can help you get closer to that goal. Excel provides a variety of auditing tools to help you track down errors and potential errors in your worksheet formulas.

A feature in Excel automatically displays comments attached to cells when the user drags the mouse over a cell that contains a comment. This is an excellent way to remind others (or yourself) what a particular cell represents.

Scenario management

Spreadsheets are often used for *what-if analysis* — change one or more assumptions and observe the effects on dependent formulas. Excel simplifies this process with its scenario manager. You can name scenarios, switch among scenarios (with just a few mouse clicks), and generate reports that summarize the results of your scenarios.

Spell checking and AutoCorrect

An integrated spell checker spots spelling errors in your worksheets and charts. You need not ever again display a chart titled "Bugdet Review" in a crowded boardroom.

Excel has borrowed a handy feature, AutoCorrect, from Microsoft Word. This corrects many types of input errors as you type. For example, if you enter *BUdget* into a cell, Excel automatically changes the second letter to a lowercase *u*. You can also use this feature to develop your own shorthand. For example, you can instruct Excel to replace IWC with International Widget Corporation.

Templates

If your work tends to fall into a few specific categories, it may be worth your time to set up custom spreadsheet *templates*, which are preconfigured shells that include text, row, and column headings, formats, column widths, macros, and so on. You can use these templates to help create similar spreadsheets.

Excel has a Template Wizard that walks you through the steps required to create a custom template. Excel also includes several handy templates that you may find useful. An example of such a template is shown in Figure 1-5.

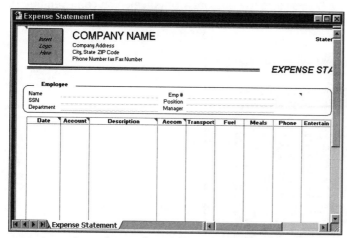

Figure 1-5: One of several templates included with Excel 97.

Database management

You can work with spreadsheet data as if Excel were a database. Excel not only features all the standard database commands but also enables you to work with databases stored in external files.

XLM macro compatibility

In previous Excel versions, you could create macros using special macro functions in XLM documents. Although Visual Basic for Applications is a much better macro language, Excel 97 still supports XLM macros. This means that you can continue to run macros developed for previous versions of Excel.

Visual Basic for Applications (VBA)

VBA is a powerful programming language built right into Excel (as well as several other Microsoft products). After you learn VBA's ropes, you can do magic with your Excel workbooks.

Custom dialog boxes

Excel makes it very easy to create custom dialog boxes (also known as user forms). Custom dialogs are usually used in conjunction with VBA macros that you write.

Worksheet controls

Excel lets you insert functional "dialog box" controls (such as buttons, scrollbars, list boxes, and check boxes) directly on your worksheet. You can even link them to cells without using macros. See Figure 1-6 for an example of such controls.

Figure 1-6: You can add functional controls directly to your worksheet to make it easier to use.

Protection options

If you need to keep others (or yourself) from modifying your worksheet, you'll find that Excel offers a variety of protection techniques. For example, you can protect cells that contain formulas to eliminate the possibility of accidentally deleting an important formula.

Add-in capability

Although Microsoft didn't originate the concept of spreadsheet add-ins, it has implemented the feature well in Excel. When you load an add-in, you enhance the program's functionality. Excel includes several add-ins, and you can even use VBA to create your own add-ins.

Data exchange

Excel can access all normal Windows features, such as copying and pasting between different applications, as well as the powerful Dynamic Data Exchange (DDE) facility, which creates data links between different applications.

OLE 2 support

Excel supports Microsoft's Object Linking and Embedding (OLE 2) technology, which makes data sharing easier than ever. For example, you can embed a Word for Windows document in a worksheet and then access all WinWord features — right in your worksheet.

Internet support

Excel 97 includes a variety of new features that make it easy to access Internet documents, save documents as HTML files, and even create hyperlinks directly in your spreadsheet documents.

Cross-platform consistency

Excel runs on the Macintosh and the PC (in Windows); in fact, the versions are virtually identical across the two platforms. If you learn the Windows version, you can move to a Mac and feel right at home.

Summary

In this chapter, I introduce the concept of a spreadsheet and presented a brief history of Excel. I also discuss why Microsoft Windows is important and examine Excel's evolution within the Microsoft environment. The bulk of the chapter provides an overview of Excel's key features — all of which will be covered in subsequent chapters.

✦   ✦   ✦

What's New in Excel 97?

Every new release of Excel is a big event among Excel fans, and Excel 97 is certainly no exception. In my opinion, this is the most significant upgrade yet. In this chapter I provide an overview of what's new, what's gone, and what's changed compared to Excel 95.

Toolbars and Menus

When you load Excel 97 for the first time, you'll notice that it looks different. Look a little closer and you'll see that the toolbar buttons no longer look like buttons. It may not be immediately apparent, but the menu has also changed. In fact, the menu is now a toolbar. That's right. With Excel 97 there is no difference between a toolbar button and a menu item.

You'll find that you can drag the "menu" toolbar to any position you want. And, you can customize the toolbars by adding menu commands. Or, you can add toolbar buttons to the menu toolbar.

Cross Reference Refer to Chapter 33 for more information about customizing menus and toolbars.

The Excel toolbars, by the way, have been changed quite a bit. You'll find many new toolbars, and several old toolbars are no longer available.

Office Assistant

One feature that you can't help but notice is the new Office Assistant, which replaces both the Answer Wizard and the Tip Wizard found in Excel 95. The Office Assistant is displayed in a floating window, and it can take the form of any of nine "characters" that provide assistance when you need it (and sometimes even when you don't need it).

The Office Assistant provides pop-up balloons that make it easy to search for answers. For example, you can enter a question in natural language, such as *How do I generate random numbers?* Figure 2-1 shows the options presented by the Office Assistant. In many cases, you'll be able to jump directly to a help topic that answers your question.

The Office Assistant character is animated — and even makes sounds if you like. The animations are great, but they quickly get old and can even be distracting. Fortunately, you can control how the Assistant behaves by right-clicking on its window.

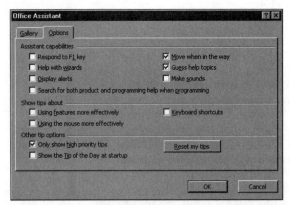

Figure 2-1 The Office Assistant provides a list of topics that may (or may not) answer your question.

Note When you install Excel 97, there is an option to omit the Office Assistant feature.

Cross Reference For more information about the Office Assistant, refer to Appendix A.

File Format

Excel 97 uses a new file format (but it still uses the .XLS extension), so earlier versions of Excel cannot read the files it saves. You can, of course, save your work in a format that's readable by previous versions of Excel. If you need to share your files with those who still use a previous version of Excel, you can specify the default file format that will be used when you save your files.

Increased Capacity

Excel users often ask how they can increase the number of rows in a worksheet. With Excel 97, I think that question won't come up as often. An Excel 97 worksheet has 65,536 rows — four times as many as previous versions.

Cell capacity has also been increased, from 255 to a whopping 32,767 characters. Unfortunately, formulas still must adhere to the existing 1,024-character limit.

In the past, a chart series was limited to 4,000 points. That limit has been upped to 32,000 points.

Multilevel Undo and Redo

Multilevel undo lets you backtrack through the past 16 operations you performed. For example, if you realize that you made a big mistake, you can undo your actions one at a time until you get back to the point you were at before you made the mistake.

Formulas

Excel 97 includes some new features that help you create and edit formulas.

Formula Palette

When you're creating or editing a formula, the new Formula Palette can help you insert functions and show you the formula's result as it's being constructed. This tool normally appears directly below the edit line, but you can drag it to any location. Access the Formula Palette by clicking the Edit Formula button (=) on the edit line.

The Formula Palette includes all the functionality of the Function Wizard, which is no longer available.

Range finders

The new range finder feature is very helpful. When you edit a formula, each range used by the formula is outlined in a different color (and the color corresponds to the range reference in the formula). You can drag the colored outline to change the range references. You can use this same technique to change the range used in a chart.

Natural language formulas

Excel 97 has the ability to recognize row and column labels in your tables — and you can use these headers in your formulas without creating any names. Simply use a space to separate the row header from the column header, as in the following formula.

```
=Jan Income - Jan Expenses
```

Formula AutoCorrect

If you enter an incorrect formula, Excel may suggest a correction for you. Excel 97 recognizes 15 common formula-building errors. Figure 2-2 shows an example of Excel trying to be helpful.

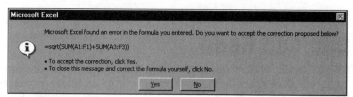

Figure 2-2: If you enter an incorrect formula, Excel may suggest a correction.

Page Break Preview

Excel 97 augments its print preview feature with another tool that lets you adjust page breaks dynamically. The new Page Break Preview mode displays the worksheet in a special view that lets you adjust the print range and the page breaks by dragging with your mouse. In this mode, you also have complete access to all of Excel's commands.

Pivot Tables

Excel's pivot table feature has always been great. Microsoft made many improvements in Excel 97.

✦ The data caching is more efficient. If you make multiple pivot tables from the same data, only one copy of the data is cached.

✦ Formatting now stays put when the pivot table is refreshed.

✦ You can create calculated fields and calculated items by building formulas. This is great, but it could be better. For example, you can't use worksheet functions in your formulas.

✦ You can choose from three different ways to select data as you navigate through the pivot table (structured selection), giving you visual cues to help identify relationships in the pivot table.

✦ Dates in pivot tables are handled correctly (this was a problem in previous versions).

✦ An AutoShow feature hides irrelevant data. You can display only the five highest values, for example.

Data Validation

Many spreadsheet models contain input cells that are used by formulas. With previous versions of Excel, there was no easy way to ensure that data entered into cells was of the proper type. Excel 97's new data validation feature lets you specify the type of data that is valid.

Track Changes

If you've ever used the "revisions" feature in Microsoft Word, you'll feel right at home with the new Track Changes feature. Turn it on, and all changes are tracked and monitored. You can then choose to accept or reject the changes selectively.

New Wizards

Excel 97 includes several new wizards, most of which are add-ins.

✦ **Conditional Sum Wizard:** Creates a formula that sums data in a list if the data matches criteria you specify.

✦ **File Conversion Wizard:** Converts a group of files to Excel workbook format.

✦ **Lookup Wizard:** Creates a formula to look up data in a list using another known value in the list.

✦ **Web Form Wizard:** Sets up a form on a Web server so that data entered in the form is added to a database.

✦ **Microsoft Excel Internet Assistant:** Converts ranges of worksheet data and charts to HTML Web page files (including GIF conversion).

✦ **Query Wizard:** Excel 97 still uses Microsoft Query to access external database files, but it now includes a wizard to help you create the queries.

Cell Formatting

Excel 97 provides some great new formatting features that can make your worksheets look better than ever.

Cross Reference These features are described in Chapter 11.

Conditional formatting

One of the questions I hear most frequently from users is *How can I set things up so a cell's formatting changes, depending on the value in the cell?* Before Excel 97, the solution to that problem involved a rather complex macro, but now, conditional formatting is built right into Excel (see Figure 2-3).

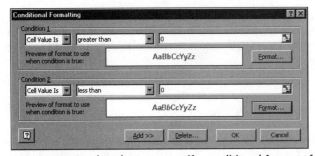

Figure 2-3 Excel 97 lets you specify conditional formats for a cell or range.

Merging cells

The new "merge cells" feature is something that I never thought of before, but now I wonder how I ever lived without it. Excel 97 lets you merge two or more cells into one larger cell. Merging cells doesn't merge the *contents* of cells; rather, it merges the actual cells and creates a single larger cell from any number of other cells.

This is a very useful new feature — great for creating forms and tables. Figure 2-4 shows an example of eight cells (B3:10) that have been merged into a single cell. This merged cell holds a single value.

Cell orientation

Previous versions of Excel supported vertical text in a cell, but Excel 97 lets you rotate the text at any angle.

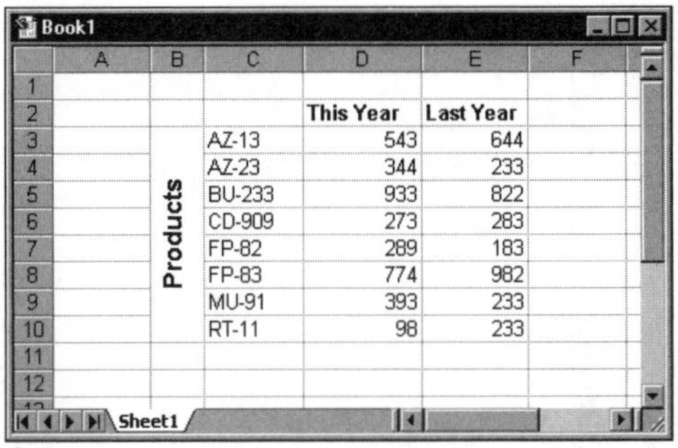

Figure 2-4: Excel 97 offers a unique new feature: merging cells.

Cell indenting

In the past, if you wanted to display hierarchical information, the common solution was to create a series of narrow columns to "indent" at various levels. With Excel 97 you can specify the number of characters to indent within a cell, letting you create a hierarchical list in a single column.

Shrink to fit

No, Excel doesn't come with a pair of Levi's. Rather, "shrink to fit" is a new formatting option that automatically shrinks the contents of a cell so that it displays in the allotted column width. Sounds great in theory. In practice, the shrunken text almost always appears too small to me.

New border options

Excel 97 includes an option to insert diagonal "borders" in a cell or range. A diagonal border gives the effect of a cell or range being crossed out.

Cell comments

Previous versions of Excel supported cell note — comments that were attached to a cell. Microsoft scrapped the cell note feature and replaced it with cell comments. This feature is much more flexible. For example, you can choose to display all cell comments at once, and even apply custom formatting to the comments. Figure 2-5 shows an example of a cell comment.

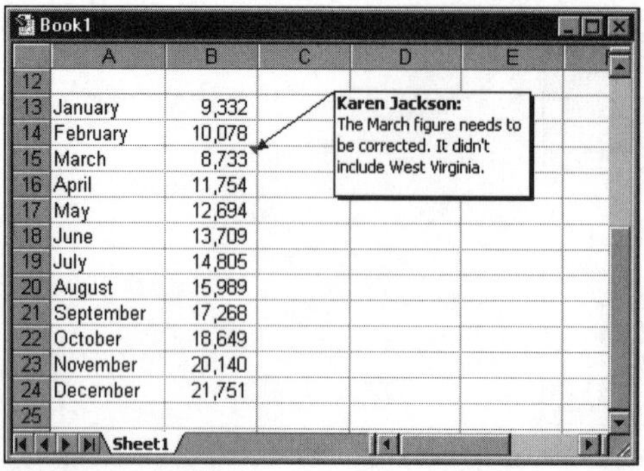

Figure 2-5:Cell comments are more flexible than the former cell notes feature.

Charting

If charts are your thing, you'll find lots to like in Excel 97. The charting feature has been completely redesigned — but it's so well done that you won't have to do much relearning. The result is that it's easier than ever to create and customize your charts.

Cross Reference I discuss basic charting-making in Chapter 13 and advanced charting in Chapter 16.

New chart types

Excel 97 includes the following new chart types:

◆Bubble charts

◆Pie of pie (show the detail of one pie slice using another pie)

◆Bar of pie (show the detail of one pie slice using a bar)

◆Cylinder charts (3D)

◆Pyramid charts (3D)

◆Cone charts (3D)

The concept of chart autoformats has been replaced with chart subtypes. Excel 97 offers 14 basic chart types, and each chart type has two or more subtypes. In addition, it provides several built-in custom chart types and you can easily create your own custom chart types.

New Chart Wizard

The old Chart Wizard has been replaced with a new 4-step Chart Wizard (with tabbed dialog boxes). It lets you adjust virtually every aspect of the chart while you create it.

Single-click activation

In the past, activating an embedded chart required a double-click. With Excel 97, a single click not only activates the chart but also selects a chart element within the chart.

Chart element selector

In the past, it was sometimes difficult to select a specific element in a chart. For example, it often took several attempts to select a particular axis. A new tool on the Chart toolbar lets you select a chart element by choosing from a drop-down list.

Range finders

In Excel 97, when you select a data series in a chart, the range that is used by the series is outlined in the worksheet. You can easily drag the outline to change the data range — add more data to the chart or remove some data from the chart. Excellent idea and it works well.

Time-scaled axes

If you use dates or times in an axis, you'll notice some major improvements. For example, it's now possible to display the first day of each month on a category axis.

Relocatable charts

Charts can now be easily changed from an embedded chart to a chart sheet chart (and vice versa).

Chart tips

Move the mouse pointer over a data point in a chart, and a small box appears that tells you the name of the point and its value.

Data tables

Another new addition to the charting arena is data tables. As you can see in Figure 2-6, you have the option of displaying the data directly in the chart.

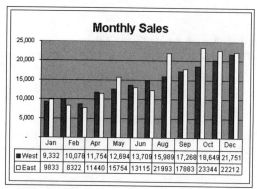

Figure 2-6: Charts can now display a data table.

Fill effects

Now there's no excuse for drab charts. Excel 97 provides some great new fill effects for charts items (chart walls, floors, columns, bars, and so on). Besides the standard fill patterns, you can now choose from:

✦ Multi-color gradient fills (get some very cool effects)

✦ Pictures (fill a bar with a GIF file, for example)

✦ Textures (choose from a variety of supplied textures, or provide your own)

Drawing Objects

The Excel drawing feature has been completely revamped. The new Drawing toolbar in Excel 97 is jam-packed with all sorts of new objects, called AutoShapes. All told, you can pick from about 150 different shapes.

Cross Reference I discuss the drawing tools in Chapter 14

In addition, you now have direct access to:

✦ **Word Art:** Create attractive 3D text effects.

✦ **Shadow effects:** Add any of a number of shadows to an object.

✦ **3D effects:** Manipulate the perspective effects of any object.

✦ **Lines and arrows:** Control line width and arrow shapes.

✦ **Rotation:** Rotate any object to any angle.

✦ **Alignment:** Automatically align objects.

✦ **Distribute:** Evenly space objects.

If you insert a graphic on a worksheet, you can use the new Picture toolbar to adjust the image using basic imaging tools (contrast, brightness, cropping, for example).

Drawn objects can also be set as semi-transparent, which allows the underlying cells to show through faintly.

Internet Features

Excel 97 has several new features that deal with the Internet.

✦ **Web toolbar:** Contains tools to work with Web documents in a browser-like fashion.

✦ **HyperLinks:** You can include hyperlinks in your worksheets. These links can open WWW documents or other Excel documents.

✦ **FindFast Web Query:** Use this tool to search Excel or HTML documents on an intranet. Search results appear in an HTML document with links to the found documents.

✦ **Open HTML document:** Excel can import HTML files and does a reasonable job of formatting the document, including text formatting, graphics, and hyperlinks.

✦ **Save file as an HTML document:** An add-in lets you create an HTML file from a document — including charts (which are converted to GIF files).

✦ **Use URLs in formulas:** A new way to get up-to-date information by linking to a URL on a Web server.

 Cross Reference I discuss these features in Chapter 30.

IntelliMouse Support

If your system is equipped with a Microsoft IntelliMouse, you can use the middle wheel to scroll vertically through the worksheet. Or, you can set the wheel to zoom in and out.

Programmability

Excel 97, like all the applications in Office 97, uses VBA as its macro language. Creating macro-driven applications is a bit different, compared to Excel 5. For starters, you use the new Visual Basic Editor — a separate application that works seamlessly with Excel. Creating custom dialog boxes also occurs in the Visual Basic Editor.

Summary

This chapter provides a brief overview of the new features in Excel 97.

✦   ✦   ✦

Getting Acquainted with Excel

New users are sometimes overwhelmed when they first fire up Excel. They're greeted with an empty workbook, lots of strange buttons, and unfamiliar commands on the menus. This chapter helps you feel more at home with Excel, explains its main parts, and even gives you a chance to do a few things to get better acquainted.

Starting Excel

Before you can use Excel, it must be installed on your system. And before you can install Excel, Microsoft Windows must be installed on your system. Excel 97 requires a 32-bit operating system such as Windows 95 or Windows NT. With any luck, Excel is already installed and ready to run.

Excel's Parts

When Excel starts up, your screen looks something like Figure 3-1. This figure identifies the major parts of Excel's window, which are explained in the following paragraphs.

This figure shows Excel running in VGA mode (640 × 480 pixels). Your screen may look different if you're running Windows in a different video mode that displays more pixels on-screen.

Title bar

All Windows programs have a title bar. This identifies the name of the program and also holds some control buttons that you can use to modify the window.

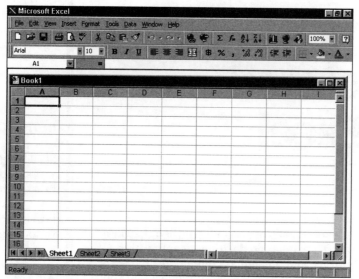

Figure 3-1: Excel runs in a window, which in this case is maximized so that it occupies the full screen.

Window Control menu button

This button is actually Excel's icon. When you click on it, you get a menu that lets you manipulate Excel's window.

Minimize button

Clicking on this button minimizes Excel's window and displays it in the Windows taskbar.

Restore button

Clicking on this button "unmaximizes" Excel's window so that it no longer fills the entire screen. If Excel isn't maximized, this button is replaced by a Maximize button.

Close button

Clicking on this button closes Excel. If there are any unsaved files, you're prompted to save them.

Menu bar

This is Excel's main menu. Clicking on a word on the menu drops down a list of menu items, which is one way for you to issue a command to Excel.

Excel 97 The menu bar in Excel 97 is not fixed in place. In fact, it's actually a toolbar. You can drag it to any of the sides of the window or even make it free-floating if you like.

Toolbars

The toolbars hold buttons that you click on to issue commands to Excel. Some of the buttons expand to show additional buttons or commands.

Formula bar

When you enter information or formulas into Excel, they appear in this line.

Name box

This displays the name of the active cell in the current workbook. When you click on the arrow, the list drops down to display all named cells and named ranges (if any) in the active workbook. You also can use the Name box to quickly give a name to the selected cell or range.

The Name box also displays the name of a selected object, such as charts or drawing objects. However, you cannot use the Name box to select an object or change the name of an object.

Status bar

This bar displays various messages, as well as the status of the Num Lock, Caps Lock, and Scroll Lock keys on your keyboard.

Parts of a Workbook Window

When you work with Excel, you work is stored in workbooks. Each workbook appears in a separate window within Excel's workspace.

Figure 3-2 shows a typical workbook window. The major parts are described in the following paragraphs. Notice that a workbook window has many parts in common with Excel's window.

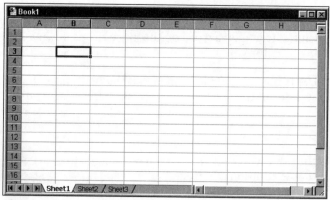

Figure 3-2: An empty Excel workbook, named Book1.

Title bar

This identifies the name of the workbook and also holds some control buttons that you can use to modify the window.

Window Control menu button

Clicking on this button (actually an icon) displays a menu that lets you manipulate the workbook window.

Minimize button

Clicking on this button minimizes the workbook window so that only the title bar shows.

Maximize button

Clicking on this button maximizes the workbook window to fill Excel's complete workspace. If the window is already maximized, a Restore button appears in its place.

Close button

Clicking on this button closes the workbook. If the workbook hasn't been saved, you're prompted to save it.

Select All button

Clicking on the intersection of the row and column headers selects all cells on the active worksheet of the active window.

Active cell indicator

This dark outline indicates the currently active cell (one of the 16,777,216 cells on each worksheet).

Row headings

Numbers ranging from 1 to 65,536 — one for each row in the worksheet. You can click on a row heading to select an entire row of cells.

Column headings

Letters ranging from A to IV — one for each of the 256 columns in the worksheet. After column Z comes column AA, which is followed by AB, AC, and so on. After column AZ comes BA, BB, and so on until you get to the last column, labeled IV. You can click on a column heading to select an entire column of cells.

Tab scroll buttons

These buttons let you scroll the sheet tabs to display tabs that aren't visible.

Sheet tabs

Each of these notebook-like tabs represents a different sheet in the workbook. A workbook can have any number of sheets, and each sheet has its name displayed in a sheet tab.

Tab split bar

This lets you increase or decrease the area devoted to displaying sheet tabs. When you show more sheet tabs, the horizontal scrollbar's size is reduced.

Horizontal scrollbar

Lets you scroll the sheet horizontally.

Vertical scrollbar

Lets you scroll the sheet vertically.

Excel 97 If you have a Microsoft IntelliMouse, you can use the mouse wheel to scroll vertically.

A Hands-on Excel Session

The remainder of this chapter consists of an introductory session with Excel. If you've never used Excel, you may want to follow along on your computer to get a feel for how this program works. Don't be alarmed if you don't understand all the steps — that's what the rest of this book is for.

This example assumes that you've been asked to prepare a one-page report that shows your company's quarterly sales broken down by the two sales regions (North and South). This section walks you through the steps required to do the following:

1. Enter a table of data (the sales figures) into a worksheet.

2. Create and copy a formula (to calculate totals).

3. Format the data so that it looks good.

4. Create a chart from the data.

5. Save the workbook to a file.

6. Print the data and chart (the one-page report).

When you're finished, you'll have a worksheet that looks like the one in Figure 3-3.

Web site   This section is quite detailed and provides every step that you need to reproduce the worksheet shown in Figure 3-3. If you already have experience with a spreadsheet, you may find this section to be a bit *too* detailed. Don't worry. You'll find that the pace picks up in the remainder of the book.

Getting ready

As a first step, you start Excel and maximize its window to fill the entire screen. Then you maximize the blank workbook named Book1.

1. If Excel isn't running, start it. You're greeted with a blank window named Book1. If Excel is already running, click on its Close button to exit Excel. Then restart it so that you see the empty window named Book1.

2. If Excel doesn't fill the entire screen, maximize Excel's window by clicking on the Maximize button in Excel's title bar.

3. Maximize the workbook window so that you can see as much of the workbook as possible. Do this by clicking on the Maximize button in Book1's title bar.

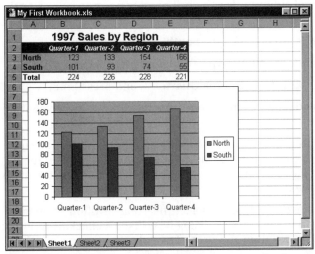

Figure 3-3: This is the worksheet that you create in the step-by-step session.

Entering the headings

In this step, you enter the row and column headings into the worksheet named Sheet1 in Book1. When you're finished, the worksheet will look like Figure 3-4.

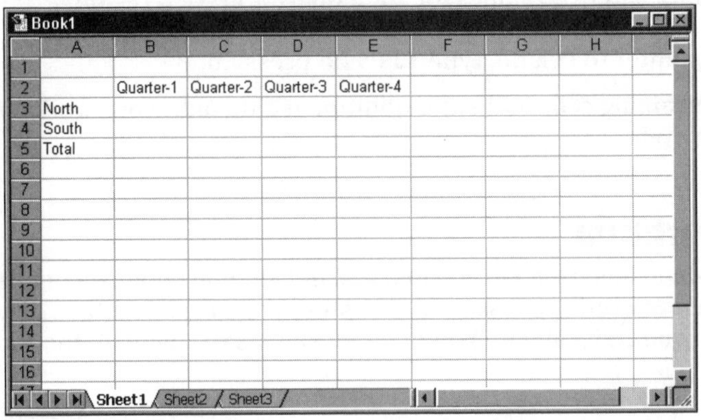

Figure 3-4: The worksheet after entering headings for the data.

1. Move the cell pointer to cell A3 using the direction keys. The Name box displays the cell's address.

2. Enter **North** into cell A3. Just type the text and then press Enter. Depending on your setup, Excel either moves the cell pointer down to cell A4 or the pointer remains in cell A3.

3. Move the cell pointer to cell A4, type **South**, and press Enter.

4. Move the cell pointer to cell A5, type **Total**, and press Enter.

5. Move the cell pointer to cell B2, type **Quarter 1**, and press Enter.

Note

At this point, you could enter the other three headings manually, but we'll let Excel do the work.

6. Move the cell pointer to cell B2 if it's not already there. Notice the small square at the lower-right corner of the cell pointer. This is called the *fill handle*. When you move the mouse pointer over the fill handle, the mouse pointer changes to a dark cross.

Note

If the cell doesn't have a fill handle, select the Tools⇨Options command and click on the Edit tab in the Options dialog box. Place a checkmark next to the option labeled Allow cell drag and drop. Then click on OK to close the Options dialog box.

7. Move the mouse pointer to the fill handle until the mouse pointer changes to a cross. Then click on and drag to the right until you select the three cells to the right (C2, C3, and C4). Release the mouse button, and you'll see that Excel filled in the three remaining headings for you. This is an example of AutoFill.

Entering the data

In this step, you simply enter the values for each quarter in each region.

1. Move the cell pointer to cell B3, type **123**, and press Enter.

2. Move to the remaining cells and enter additional data until your worksheet looks like Figure 3-5.

Creating a formula

So far, what you've done has been fairly mundane. In fact, you could accomplish the same effect with any word processor. In this step, you take advantage of what a spreadsheet is known for: formulas. You create formulas to calculate the total for each region.

1. Move the cell pointer to cell B5.

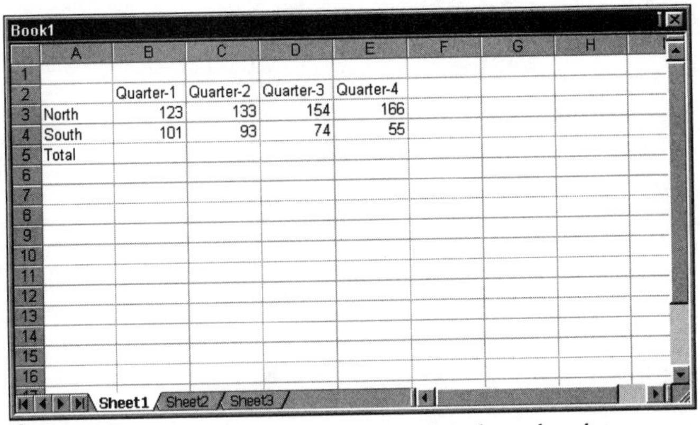

Figure 3-5: The worksheet after entering the sales data.

2. Locate the AutoSum button the toolbar below the menu and click on it once. The AutoSum button has a Greek sigma on it. The toolbar below the menu is called the Standard toolbar. Notice that Excel inserts the following into the cell:

```
=SUM(B3:B4)
```

This is a formula that calculates the sum of the values in the range B3 through B4.

3. Because this formula is exactly what you want (Excel guessed correctly), press Enter to accept the formula. You see that the sum of the two values is displayed in the cell. You could repeat this step for the remaining three quarters, but it's much easier to simply copy the formula to the three cells to the right.

4. Move the cell pointer to cell B5 if it's not already there.

5. Move the mouse pointer to the fill handle. When it changes to a cross, click and drag three cells to the right. Release the mouse button and discover that Excel copied the formula to the cells that you selected.

At this point, your worksheet should look like Figure 3-6. To demonstrate that these are actual "live" formulas, try changing one or two of the values in rows 3 or 4. You'll see that the cells with the formulas change also. In other words, the formulas are recalculating and displaying new results using the modified data.

Formatting the table

The table looks fine, but it could look even better. In this step, you use Excel's automatic formatting feature to spiff it up a bit.

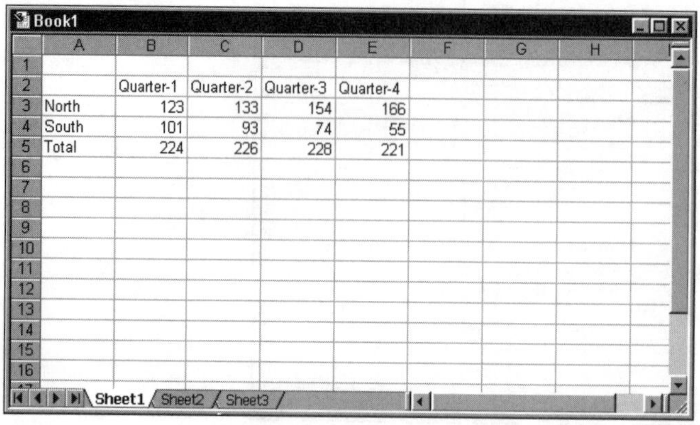

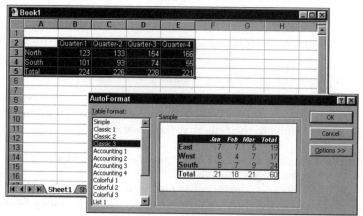

Figure 3-6: The worksheet after inserting a formula and copying it.

1. Move the cell pointer to any cell in the table (it doesn't matter which one because Excel will figure out that table's boundaries).

2. Click on the Format menu; it drops down to display its menu items.

3. Select AutoFormat from the list of menu items. Two things happen: Excel determines the table boundaries and highlights the entire table, and it displays the AutoFormat dialog box. Figure 3-7 shows how this looks.

Figure 3-7: Excel's AutoFormat dialog box makes it easy to quickly format a table.

4. The AutoFormat dialog box has 16 "canned" formats from which to choose. Click on the table format named Classic 3. You see an example of this format in the right side of the dialog box.

5. Click on the OK button. Excel applies the formats to your table.

Your worksheet should look like Figure 3-8. Note that Excel made the following formatting changes for you automatically:

✦ It changed some of the cell background colors.

✦ It changed some of the cell foreground colors.

✦ It made the column headings italic.

✦ It made the row labels bold.

✦ It added borders.

You could have performed all these formatting operations yourself, but it probably would have taken several minutes. The AutoFormat feature can save you lots of time.

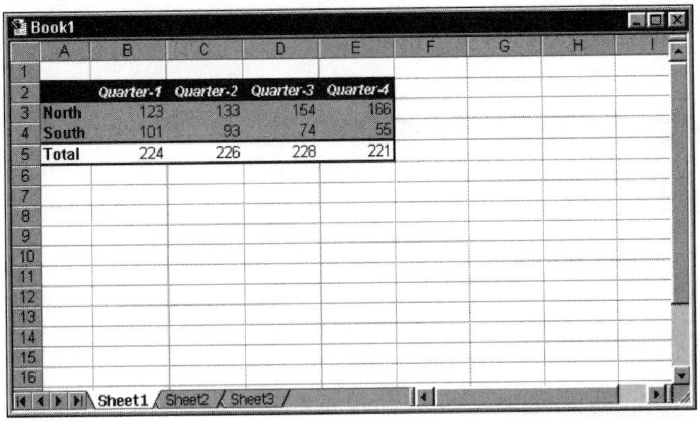

Figure 3-8: Your worksheet after applying automatic formatting.

Adding a title

In this step, you simply add a title to the table, make the title bold, and adjust it so that it's centered across the five columns of the table.

1. Move the cell pointer to cell A1.

2. Enter **1997 Sales by Region** and press Enter.

3. Move the cell pointer back to cell A1 if it's not there and click on the Bold button on the Formatting toolbar (the Bold button has a large *B*). This makes the text bold.

4. Click on the Font Size arrow (see Figure 3-9) on the Formatting toolbar and select 14 from the list. This makes the text larger.

5. Click in cell A1 and drag to the right until you select A1, B1, C1, D1, and E1 (that is, the range A1:E1). Don't drag the cell's fill handle. You want to select the cells — not make a copy of cell A1.

6. Click on the Merge and Center button (see Figure 3-9) on the Formatting toolbar. The text in cell A1 is centered across the selected cells. In fact, clicking on that button merged the five cells into one larger cell.

Merging cells is a new feature in Excel 97.

Your worksheet should look like Figure 3-10.

Figure 3-9: The Font Size arrow (left) and the Merge and Center button (right) appear on the Formatting toolbar.

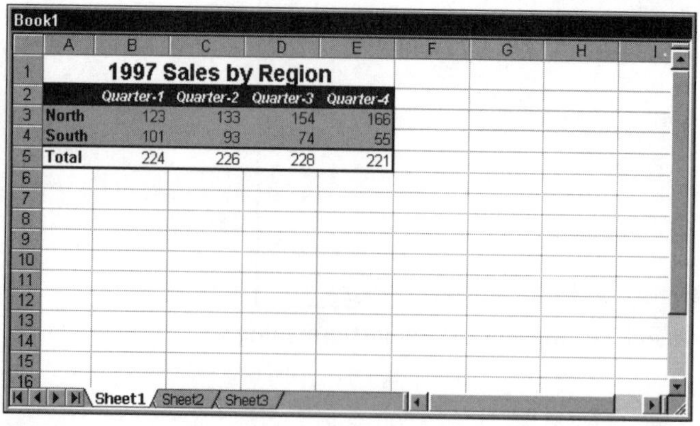

Figure 3-10: Your worksheet after adding a title and formatting it.

Creating a chart

In this step, you create a chart from the data in the table. The chart is placed on the worksheet directly below the table.

1. Move the cell pointer to cell A2.

2. Click and drag until you've selected all the cells in the rectangle with A2 at the upper left and E4 at the lower right (15 cells in all). Notice that you're not selecting the cells in the row that displays the totals; you don't want the totals to appear in the chart.

3. With the range A2:E4 selected, click on the Chart Wizard button on the Standard toolbar (the ChartWizard button has an image of a column chart). Excel displays the first in a series of dialog boxes that will help you create the chart you want. Refer to Figure 3-11.

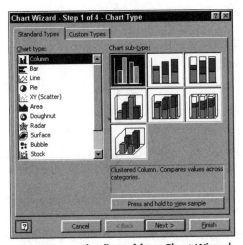

Figure 3-11: The first of four Chart Wizard dialog boxes that help you create a chart.

4. The first step is to choose the chart type. The default chart, a Column chart, is highlighted. This is a good choice for this particular data. At this point, you could click on the Next button and specify lots of additional options for the chart. Or, you can simply click on Finish and accept all of Excel's default choices. Click on the Finish button.

Excel creates the chart and displays it on the worksheet. It also displays its Chart toolbar just in case you want to modify the chart. To get rid of the toolbar, just click on the X in its title bar. Your worksheet should look like Figure 3-12. If you want, you can:

✦ Resize the chart by dragging on any of the eight handles on its borders (the handles appear only when the chart is selected).

✦ Move the chart by clicking on and dragging any of its borders.

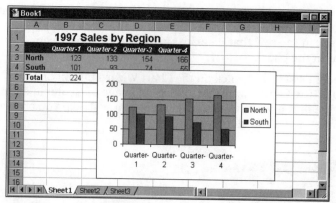

Figure 3-12: The Chart Wizard inserts the chart on the worksheet.

Saving the workbook

Up until now, everything that you've done has occurred in your computer's memory. If the power should fail, all would be lost. It's time to save your work to a file. Call this workbook `My first workbook`.

1. Click on the Save button on the Standard toolbar. The Save button looks like a disk. Excel responds with the Save As dialog box.

2. In the box labeled File name, enter **My first workbook** and press Enter (see Figure 3-13).

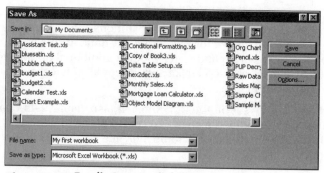

Figure 3-13: Excel's Save As dialog box.

Excel saves the workbook as a file. The workbook remains open so that you can work with it some more.

Printing the report

As the final step, you print this report. I'm assuming that you have a printer attached and that it works properly. To print the worksheet, just click on the Print button the Standard toolbar (this button has an image of a printer on it). The worksheet (including the chart) is printed using the default settings.

Quitting Excel

As the final step, click on the Close button in Excel's title bar to exit Excel. Because no changes were made to the workbook since it was last saved, Excel closes down without asking whether you want to save the file.

Summary

If this was your first time using Excel, you probably have lots of questions about what you've just done in the preceding exercise. Those questions are answered in the next few chapters.

If you're the adventurous type, you may have answered some of your own questions by trying out various buttons or menu items. If so, congratulations! Experimenting is the best way to get to know Excel. Just remember, the worst thing that can happen is that you mess up a workbook file. And if you do your experimentation unimportant files, you have absolutely nothing to lose. And, don't forget about the Office Assistant. You can click on the Office Assistant at any time and type a question (using natural language). There's an excellent chance that the Assistant will steer you to a help topic that answers your question.

✦   ✦   ✦

Introductory Concepts

T he chapters in Part II discuss the basic concepts of Excel — topics with which all Excel users should be familiar.

◆   ◆   ◆   ◆

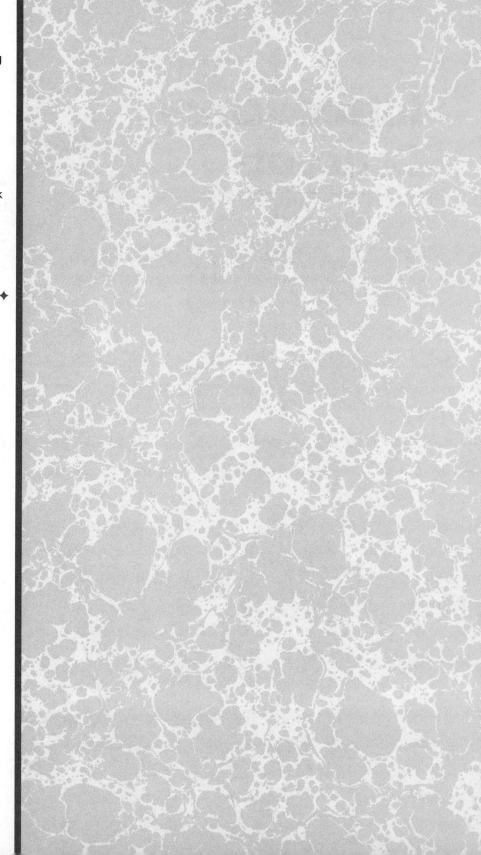

Navigating through Excel

Because you'll spend lots of time working in Excel, it's important that you understand the basics of navigating through workbooks and how to best utilize Excel's user interface. If you're an experienced Windows user, some of this information may already be familiar to you, so this is your chance to learn even more.

If you're new to Excel, some of the information in this chapter may not make much sense. It will become clearer as you progress through the other chapters, however.

Working with Excel's Windows

The files that Excel uses are known as *workbooks*. A workbook can hold any number of sheets, and these sheets can be either worksheets (the most common type) or chart sheets (a sheet that holds a single chart). A *worksheet* is what people usually think of when they think of a spreadsheet. A worksheet has rows and columns that intersect at a cell.

Figure 4-1 shows Excel with four workbooks open, each in a separate window. One of the windows is minimized and appears at the bottom of the screen (when a workbook is minimized, only its title bar is visible). Note that worksheet windows can overlap, and the title bar of one window is a different color. That's the window that contains the *active workbook*.

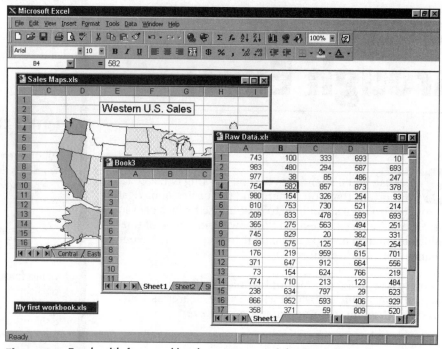

Figure 4-1: Excel, with four workbooks open, one of them minimized.

The workbook windows that Excel uses work much like the windows in any other Windows program. Excel's windows can be one of the following:

✦ Maximized to fill Excel's entire workspace. A maximized window does not have a title bar, and the worksheet's name appears in Excel's title bar. To maximize a window, click on its Maximize button.

✦ Minimized to appear as a small window with only a title bar. To minimize a window, click on its Minimize button.

✦ Restored to a nonmaximized size. To restore a maximized or minimized window, click on its Restore button. Restored windows can be moved and resized to your liking.

If you work with more than one workbook at a time (which is quite common), you have to learn how to move, resize, and switch among the workbook windows.

As you're probably aware, Excel itself is contained in a window. Excel's window also can be maximized, minimized, or displayed in a nonmaximized size. When Excel's window is maximized, it fills the entire screen. You can activate other programs by using the Windows taskbar (usually located at the bottom of your screen).

Moving and resizing windows

To move or resize a workbook window, it can't be maximized. You *can* move a minimized window, but doing so will have no effect on its position when it is subsequently restored.

To move a window, click on and drag its title bar with your mouse. Note that the windows can extend off-screen in any direction, if you like.

To resize a window, click on and drag any of its borders until it's the size you want it to be. When you position the mouse pointer on a window's border, the mouse pointer changes shape to let you know that you can then click on and drag. To resize a window horizontally and vertically at the same time, click on and drag any of its corners.

If you would like all your workbook windows to be visible (that is, not obscured by another window), you can fiddle around moving and resizing them manually, or you can let Excel do it for you automatically. The Window⇨Arrange command displays the dialog box shown in Figure 4-2. This dialog box has four window-arrangement options. Just select the one you want and click on OK.

Figure 4-2: The Arrange Windows dialog box makes it easy to arrange the windows of all open workbooks.

Switching among windows

As I mentioned, at any given time, one (and only one) workbook window is the active window. This is the window that accepts your input, and it is the window on which your commands work. The active window's title bar is a different color, and the window appears at the top of the stack of windows.

There are several ways to make a different window the active workbook:

✦ Click on another window if it's visible. The window you click on moves to the top and becomes the active window.

✦ Press Ctrl+Tab to cycle through all open windows until the window that you want to work with appears on top. Shift+Ctrl+Tab cycles through the windows in the opposite direction.

✦ Click on the Window menu and select the desired window from the bottom part of the pull-down menu. The active window has a check mark next to it, as shown in Figure 4-3. This shows up to nine windows. If you have more than nine workbook windows open, choose More Windows (which appears below the nine window names).

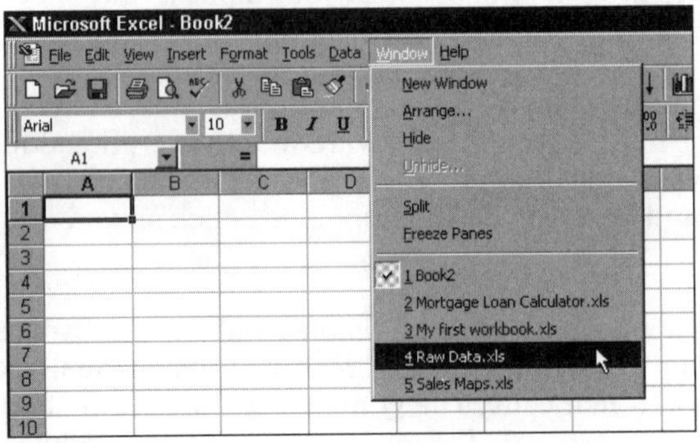

Figure 4-3: You can activate a different window by selecting it from the pull-down Window menu.

Many users (myself included) prefer to do most of their work with maximized workbook windows. This lets you see more cells and eliminates the distraction of other workbook windows getting in the way. And besides, it's easy to activate another workbook window when you need to use it.

When you maximize one window, all the other windows are maximized, too (but you can't see them). Therefore, if the active window is maximized and you activate a different window, the new active window is maximized also. If the active workbook window is maximized, you can't select another window by clicking on it (because other windows aren't visible). You must use either Ctrl+Tab or the Window menu to activate another window.

When would you *not* want to work exclusively with maximized worksheet windows? As I discuss in Chapter 8, Excel has some handy drag-and-drop features. For example, you can drag a range of cells from one workbook window to another. To do any of this dragging and dropping, both windows must be visible (that is, not maximized).

Another point to keep in mind is that a single workbook can be displayed in more than one window. For example, if you have a workbook with two worksheets, you may want to display each worksheet in a separate window. All the window manipulation procedures described previously still apply.

Closing windows

When you close a workbook window, Excel checks to see whether any changes have been made since the last time the file was saved. If not, the window is closed without a prompt from Excel. If you've made any changes, Excel prompts you to save the file before closing the window. You learn more about working with files in the next chapter.

To close a window, simply click on the Close button on the title bar.

Mouseless window manipulation

Although using a mouse to manipulate Excel's windows is usually the most efficient route, you also can perform these actions using the keyboard. Table 4-1 summarizes the key combinations that manipulate workbook windows.

Table 4-1 Keystrokes Used to Manipulate Windows	
Key Combination	**Action**
Ctrl+F4	Close a window
Ctrl+F5	Restore a window
Ctrl+F6	Activate the next window
Ctrl+Shift+F6	Activate the previous window
Ctrl+Tab	Activate the next window
Ctrl+Shift+Tab	Activate the previous window
Ctrl+F7	Move a window*
Ctrl+F8	Resize a window*
Ctrl+F9	Minimize a window
Ctrl+F10	Maximize a window
Alt+W[n]	Activate the nth window

* Use the direction keys to make the change, and then press Enter.

Moving Around a Worksheet

You'll be spending a lot of time moving through your worksheets, so it pays to learn all the tricks.

Every worksheet consists of rows (numbered 1 through 65,536) and columns (labeled A through IV). After column Z comes column AA, after column AZ comes column BA, and so on. The intersection of a row and a column is a single cell. At any given time, one cell is the *active cell*. The active cell is indicated by a darker border, as shown in Figure 4-4. Its *address* (that is, its column letter and row number) appears in the Name box. Depending on the technique you use to navigate through a workbook, you may or may not change the active cell when you navigate.

Excel 97 In Excel 97, the row and column headings of the active cell are displayed in bold — making it easier to identify the active cell.

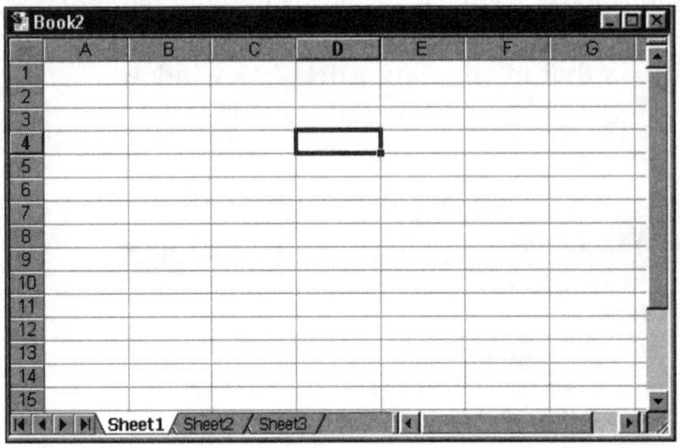

Figure 4-4: The active cell is the cell with the dark border; in this case, cell D4.

How big is a worksheet?

It's interesting to stop and think how big a worksheet really is. There are 256 columns and 65,536 rows. Do the arithmetic and you'll see that this works out to 16,777,216 cells. Remember, this is in just one worksheet. A single workbook can hold more than one worksheet — hundreds, if necessary.

If you're using the standard VGA video mode with the default row heights and column widths, you can see 9 columns and 18 rows (or 162 cells) at a time. This works out to less than 0.001 percent of the entire worksheet. Put another way, there are more than 100,000 screenfulls of information in a single worksheet.

If you started entering a single digit into each cell at a relatively rapid clip of one cell per second, it would take you about 194 days, nonstop, to fill up a worksheet. To print the results of your efforts would require more than 36,000 sheets of paper.

By the way, don't even think about actually using all of the cells in a worksheet. Unless your system is equipped with an unusually large amount of memory, things will slow to a crawl as Windows churns away swapping information to disk.

Using the keyboard

As you probably already know, you can use the standard navigational keys on your keyboard to move around a worksheet. These keys work just as you would expect: down arrow moves the active cell down one row, right arrow moves it one column to the right, and so on. PgUp and PgDn move the active cell up or down one full window (the actual number of rows moved depends on the number of rows displayed in the window).

Tip   When Scroll Lock is turned on, you can scroll through the worksheet without changing the active cell. This can be useful if you need to view another area of your worksheet and then quickly return to your original location. Just press Scroll Lock and then use the direction keys to scroll through the worksheet. When you want to return to the original position (the active cell), press Ctrl+Backspace. Then, press Scroll Lock again to turn it off. When Scroll Lock is turned on, Excel displays SCRL in the status bar at the bottom of the window.

The Num Lock key on your keyboard controls how the keys on the numeric keypad behave. When Num Lock is on, Excel displays NUM in the status bar. When this indicator is on, the keys on your numeric keypad generate numbers. Most keyboards have a separate set of navigational keys located to the left of the numeric keypad. These keys are not affected by the state of the Num Lock key.

Table 4-2 summarizes all the worksheet movement keys available in Excel.

Table 4-2 Excel's Worksheet Movement Keys	
Key	*Action*
Up arrow	Moves the active cell up one row
Down arrow	Moves the active cell down one row
Left arrow	Moves the active cell one column to the left
Right arrow	Moves the active cell one column to the right
PgUp	Moves the active cell up one screen
PgDn	Moves the active cell down one screen
Alt+PgDn	Moves the active cell right one screen
Alt+PgUp	Moves the active cell left one screen
Ctrl+Backspace	Scrolls to display the active cell
Up arrow*	Scrolls the screen up one row (active cell does not change)
Down arrow*	Scrolls the screen down one row (active cell does not change)
Left arrow*	Scrolls the screen left one column (active cell does not change)
Right arrow*	Scrolls the screen right one column (active cell does not change)

* With Scroll Lock on

The actions for some of the keys in the preceding table may be different, depending on the transition options that you've set. Select the Tools⇨Options command and then click on the Transition tab in the Options dialog box. If the Transition Navigation Keys option is checked, the navigation keys correspond to those used in older versions of Lotus 1-2-3. Generally, it's better to use the standard Excel navigation keys than those for 1-2-3.

Tip   If you know either the cell address or the name of the cell that you want to activate, you can get there quickly by pressing F5 (the shortcut key for the Edit⇨GoTo command). This command displays a dialog box. Just enter the cell coordinate in the Reference box (or choose a named cell from the list), press Enter, and you're there.

Using a mouse

Navigating through a worksheet with a mouse also works just as you would expect. To change the active cell, click on a cell and it becomes the active cell. If the cell that you want to activate is not visible in the workbook window, you can use the scrollbars to scroll the window in any direction. To scroll one cell, click on either of the arrows on the scrollbar. To scroll by a complete screen, click on either side of the scrollbar's scroll box. You also can drag the scroll box for faster scrolling. Working with the scrollbars is more difficult to describe than to do, so if scrollbars are new to you, I urge you to play around with them for a few minutes. You'll have it figured out in no time.

When you drag the scrollbar's button, a small yellow box appears that tells you which row or column you will scroll to when you release your finger from the mouse.

 If you have a Microsoft IntelliMouse, you can use the mouse wheel to scroll vertically. The wheel scrolls three lines per click at the default rate. Also, if you click the wheel and move the mouse in any direction, the worksheet scrolls automatically in that direction. The more you move the mouse, the faster the scrolling. If you would prefer to use the mouse wheel to zoom the worksheet, select the Tools⇨Options command, click on the General tab, and place a check mark next to the option labeled Zoom on roll with IntelliMouse.

Using the scrollbars or scrolling with the Intellimouse doesn't change the active cell. It simply scrolls the worksheet. To change the active cell, you must click on a new cell after scrolling.

Notice that only the active workbook window has scrollbars. When you activate a different window, the scrollbars appear.

Giving Commands to Excel

Excel is designed to take orders from you. You give these orders by issuing commands. You can give commands to Excel using the following methods:

✦ Menus

✦ Shortcut menus

✦ Toolbar buttons

✦ Shortcut key combinations

In many cases, you have a choice as to how to issue a particular command. For example, if you want to save your workbook to disk, you can use the menu (the File⇨Save command), a shortcut menu (right-click on the workbook's title bar and click on Save), a toolbar button (the Save button on the Standard toolbar), or a shortcut key combination (Ctrl+S). The particular method you use is up to you.

The following sections provide an overview of the four methods of issuing commands to Excel.

Using Excel's Menus

Excel, like all other Windows programs, has a menu bar located directly below the title bar (see Figure 4-5). This menu is always available and ready for your command. Excel's menus change, depending on what you're doing. For example, if you're working with a chart, Excel's menus change to give you options that are appropriate for a chart. This all happens automatically, so you don't even have to think about it.

Figure 4-5: Excel's menu bar.

Note Technically, Excel 97's menu bar is just another toolbar. In Excel 97, toolbars and menu bars are functionally identical. However, I'll continue to discuss menu bars as if they are something different.

Using a mouse

Accessing the menu with a mouse is quite straightforward. Click on the menu that you want and it drops down to display menu items, as in Figure 4-6. Click on the menu item to issue the command.

Changing Your Mind

When you issue a command to Excel using any of the available methods, Excel carries out your command. However, just about every command can be reversed using the Edit➪Undo command. Select this command after issuing a command, and it's as if you never issued the command.

Excel 97 greatly extends the Undo feature by adding 15 additional levels of Undo. This means that you can reverse the effects of the last 16 commands that you executed! You may not fully appreciate this feature until you realize that you made a major error (such as deleting a column of formulas) and didn't discover it until quite a bit later. You can use the Edit➪Undo command repeatedly until your worksheet reverts to the point before you made your error.

Rather than use the Edit➪Undo command, you may prefer to use the Undo button on the Standard toolbar. If you click on the arrow on the right side of the button, you can see a description of the commands that are "undoable" (see the accompanying figure). The Redo button performs the opposite way: it repeats commands that have been undone.

So, as you're working away in Excel, don't forget about Undo. It can be a real lifesaver.

Figure 4-6: Accessing Excel's Edit menu causes it to display its menu items.

Some menu items lead to an additional *submenu;* when you click on the menu item, the submenu appears to the right. Menu items that have a submenu display a small triangle. For example, the Edit⇨Clear command has a submenu, shown in Figure 4-7. Excel's designers incorporated submenus primarily to keep the menus from becoming too lengthy and overwhelming to users.

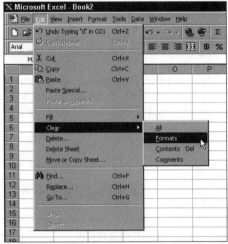

Figure 4-7: The submenu of the Edit⇨Clear command.

Some menu items also have shortcut keys associated with them. If so, they usually display the key combination next to the menu item. For example, the Edit⇨Find command's shortcut key combination is Ctrl+F.

Sometimes, you'll notice that a menu item appears *grayed out.* This simply means that the menu item isn't appropriate for what you're doing. Nothing happens if you select such a menu item.

Menu items that are followed by an ellipsis (three dots) always display a dialog box. Menu commands that don't have an ellipsis are executed immediately. For example, the Insert⇨Cells command results in a dialog box because Excel needs more information about the command. The Insert⇨Rows command doesn't need a dialog box, and this command is issued immediately when you choose the command.

Using the keyboard

You can issue menu commands using the mouse or the keyboard. Although most users tend to prefer a mouse, others find that accessing the menus with the keyboard is more efficient. This is especially true if you're entering data into a worksheet. Using a mouse means that you have to move your hand from the keyboard, locate the mouse, move it and click on it, and then move your hand back to the keyboard. Although this takes only a few seconds, those seconds add up.

To issue a menu command from the keyboard, press Alt and the menu's *hot key* at the same time (the hot key is the underlined letter in the menu). This displays the menu's menu items. Then press the appropriate hot key for the menu item.

For example, to issue the Data➪Sort command, press Alt+D, followed by S. You can keep the Alt key pressed while you press S, or not — it doesn't matter.

You also can press Alt alone, or F10. This selects the first menu (the File menu). Then you can use the direction keys to highlight the menu that you want and press Enter. Then use the direction keys to choose the appropriate menu item and press Enter again.

Moving the menu

Excel 97 As I mentioned, in Excel 97 a menu bar is the same as a toolbar. Because it's a toolbar, you can move the menu to a new location, if you like. To move the menu, just click on it and drag it to its new location. This can be a bit tricky, because you must click on the menu in a location that doesn't contain a menu item. Clicking to the right of the Help menu is the best place to click on You can drag the menu to any of the window borders, or leave it free-floating. Figure 4-8 shows the menu after relocating it to the left side of the window.

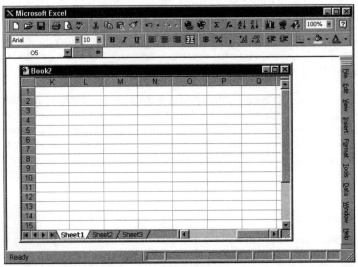

Figure 4-8: You can move Excel's menu to a new location if you like.

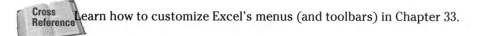

Cross Reference: Learn how to customize Excel's menus (and toolbars) in Chapter 33.

Using Shortcut Menus

Besides the omnipresent menu bar, discussed in the preceding section, Excel features a slew of what are known as *shortcut menus*. A shortcut menu is context sensitive — its contents depend on what you're doing at the time. Shortcut menus don't contain *all* the relevant commands, just those that are most commonly used for whatever is selected. You can display a shortcut by right-clicking just about anything in Excel.

As an example, examine Figure 4-9, which shows the shortcut menu, called a *context menu* in Windows 95, that appears when you right-click on a cell. The shortcut menu appears at the mouse pointer position, which makes it fast and efficient to select a command.

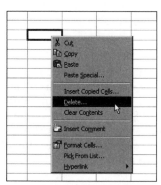

Figure 4-9: Right-clicking on a cell displays this shortcut menu.

The shortcut menu that appears depends on what is currently selected. For example, if you're working with a chart, the shortcut menu that appears when you right-click on a chart part contains commands that are pertinent to what is selected.

Tip: Although shortcut menus were invented with mouse users in mind, you also can display a shortcut menu by pressing Shift+F10.

Instant help for commands

Excel's menus and toolbars can be a bit daunting at times, especially for newcomers. One approach — the best approach, in my opinion — is to simply try things out and see what happens. If you're not that adventurous, there's an easy way to find what a particular menu command or toolbar button is used for.

Drag the mouse pointer over a menu item or toolbar button (but don't click on it). A small box appears that tells you the name of the button or menu command. Often, this provides enough information for you to determine if the command or button is what you want.

For context-sensitive help on a menu command or toolbar button, choose the Help➪What's This? command (or, press Shift+F1). The mouse pointer turns into an arrow with a question mark beside it. Now, just select any menu command or toolbar button, and Excel displays a lengthy description of the item. Note that the command itself won't be issued when you click on a menu item or toolbar button.

Excel's Toolbars

Excel, like all leading applications, includes convenient graphical toolbars. Clicking on a button on a toolbar is just another way of issuing commands to Excel. In many cases, a toolbar button is simply a substitute for a menu command. For example, the Copy button is a substitute for the Edit➪Copy command. Some toolbar buttons, however, don't have any menu equivalent. One example is the AutoSum button, which automatically inserts a formula to calculate the sum of a range of cells. This button does not have a menu equivalent.

Excel 97 The toolbars in Excel 97 are greatly enhanced, compared to previous versions. There are more toolbars than before, and many new toolbar tools. Toolbars can be customized to include menu commands as well as buttons.

By default, Excel displays two toolbars (named *Standard* and *Formatting*). Technically, it displays three toolbars, since the menu bar is actually a toolbar named *Worksheet menu Bar*. All told, Excel has 22 built-in toolbars. You have complete control over which toolbars are displayed and where they are located. In addition, you can even create custom toolbars made up of buttons that you find most useful.

Cross Reference
Learn how to customize toolbars and create new toolbars in Chapter 33.

Table 4-3 lists all of Excel's built-in toolbars.

Table 4-3
Excel's Built-In Toolbars

Toolbar	Use
Standard	Issuing commonly used commands
Formatting	Changing how your worksheet or chart looks
Pivot Table	Working with pivot tables
Chart	Manipulating charts
Reviewing	Tools for using workbooks in groups
Forms	Adding controls (buttons, spinners, and so on) to a worksheet
Stop Recording	Recording macros
External Data	Performing queries on external database files
Auditing	Identifying errors in your worksheet
Full Screen	Toggles in and out of full-screen view (one tool only)
Circular Reference	Assistance in identifying circular references in formulas
Visual Basic	Writing macros in Visual Basic for Applications
Web	Accessing the Internet from Excel
Control Toolbox	Adding ActiveX controls to a workbook or form
Exit Design Mode	Toggle in and out of design mode (one tool only)
Worksheet Menu Bar	The menu that appears when a worksheet is active
Chart Menu Bar	The menu that appears when a chart is selected
Drawing	Insert or edit drawings on a worksheet
Word Art	Insert or edit a picture composed of words
Picture	Insert or edit graphic images
Shadow Settings	Insert or edit shadows that appear behind objects
3D Settings	Add 3D effects to objects

Sometimes, Excel automatically pops up a toolbar to help you with a particular task. For example, if you're working with a chart, Excel displays its Chart toolbar.

Hiding or showing toolbars

To hide or display a particular toolbar, choose the View⇨Toolbars command, or right-click on any toolbar. Either of these actions displays a list of common toolbars (but not all toolbars). The toolbars that have a check mark next to them are currently visible. To hide a toolbar, click on it to remove the check mark. To display a toolbar, click on it to add a check mark.

If the toolbar that you want to hide or show does not appear on the menu list, select the Customize command from the View➪Toolbars menu (or from the shortcut menu that appears when you right-click on a toolbar). Excel displays its Customize dialog box, shown in Figure 4-10. This dialog box shows a list of all toolbars that are available — the built-in toolbars plus any custom toolbars. The toolbars that have a check mark next to them are currently visible. To hide a toolbar, click on it to remove the check mark. To display a toolbar, click on it to add a check mark. When you're finished, click on the Close button.

Figure 4-10: Choose which toolbars to display in the Customize dialog box.

The Customize dialog box has some other options with which you may want to experiment. Click on the Options tab to display these options (see Figure 4-11). If you prefer larger buttons, check the Large icon check box. And if you find those pop-up screen tips distracting, uncheck the Show ScreenTips on toolbars check box. You can also specify what type of animation you prefer for the menus.

Figure 4-11: The Options tab of the Customize dialog box provides some options for toolbars.

Cross Reference I discuss the Commands tab of the Customize dialog box in Chapter 33.

Moving toolbars

Toolbars can be moved to any of the four sides of Excel's window or be free-floating. A free-floating toolbar can be dragged anywhere you want. You also can change its size simply by dragging any of its borders. To hide a free-floating toolbar, click on its Close button.

Excel 97 Because Excel 97 menu bars are actually toolbars, this discussion also applies to the menu bars.

When a toolbar isn't free-floating, it's said to be *docked*. A docked toolbar is stuck to the edge of Excel's window and doesn't have a title bar. Therefore, a docked toolbar can't be resized.

To move a toolbar (docked or free-floating), click the mouse anywhere on the background of the toolbar (that is, anywhere except on a button) and drag it. When you drag it toward the window's edge, it automatically docks itself there. When a toolbar is docked, its shape changes to a single row or single column.

Excel 97 In previous versions of Excel, some toolbars could not be docked on the left or right side of the window because they contained "nonbutton" buttons (such as the Zoom or Font controls). With Excel 97, *all* toolbars can be docked in any position. However, if the toolbar contains one of these nonbutton controls, the control will not appear if it doesn't fit.

Tip Double-clicking on the background of a toolbar displays the Customize dialog box.

Learning more about toolbars

It would take many pages to describe all the toolbar buttons available, so I won't even try. I leave it up to you to discover this handy feature on your own. But throughout the rest of the book, I point out toolbar buttons that may be useful in particular situations.

Chapter 33 discusses toolbars in more detail, including how to customize toolbars.

Shortcut Keys

Earlier in this chapter, I mentioned that some menu commands have equivalent shortcut keys. Usually, the shortcut key combination is displayed next to the menu item — providing a built-in way for you to learn the shortcuts as you select the commands.

Throughout the book, I point out the relevant shortcut keys as I discuss a particular topic.

Appendix C lists all the shortcut keys available in Excel.

Working with Dialog Boxes

Earlier in this chapter, I pointed out that menu items that end with an ellipsis (three dots) result in a dialog box. All Windows programs use dialog boxes, so you may already be familiar with the concept.

About dialog boxes

You can think of a dialog box as Excel's way of getting more information from you about the command you selected. For example, if you choose the View⇨Zoom command (which changes the magnification of the worksheet), Excel can't carry out the command until it finds out from you what magnification level you want. Dialog boxes can be simple or much more complicated. Dialog boxes are made up of several items, known as *controls*.

When a dialog box appears in response to your command, you make additional choices in the dialog box by manipulating the controls. When you're finished, click on the OK button (or press Enter) to continue. If you change your mind, click on the Cancel button (or press Escape) and nothing further happens — it's as if the dialog box never appeared.

If a dialog box obscures an area of your worksheet that you need to see, you can simply click on the dialog's title bar and drag it to another location. The title bar in a dialog box has two controls: a Help button (Question-mark icon) and a Close button. When you click on the Help button, the mouse pointer displays a question mark. You can click on any part of the dialog box to get a description of what that part is used for. Clicking on the Close button is the same as clicking on the Cancel button or pressing Escape.

Although a dialog box looks like just another window, it works a little differently. When a dialog box is displayed, you can't do anything in the workbook until the dialog box is closed. In other words, you must dismiss the dialog box before you can do anything.

Dialog box controls

Most people find working with dialog boxes to be quite straightforward and natural. The controls usually work just as you would expect, and they can be manipulated with your mouse or directly from the keyboard.

The following sections describe the most common dialog box controls and show some examples.

Navigating dialog boxes using the keyboard

Although dialog boxes were designed with mouse users in mind, some users prefer to use the keyboard at times. With a bit of practice, you'll find that navigating a dialog box directly from the keyboard may be more efficient in some cases.

Every dialog box control has text associated with it, and this text always has one underlined letter (known as a *hot key* or an *accelerator key*). You can access the control from the keyboard by pressing the Alt key along with the underlined letter. You also can use Tab to cycle through all of the controls on a dialog box. Shift+Tab cycles through the controls in reverse order.

When a control is selected, it appears with a darker outline. You can use the spacebar to activate a selected control.

Buttons

A button control is about as simple as it gets. Just click on it, and it does its thing. Most dialog boxes have at least two buttons. The OK button closes the dialog box and executes the command. The Cancel button closes the dialog box with no further action. If the text on a button is followed by an ellipsis, it means that clicking on the button leads to another dialog box.

Pressing the Alt key along with the button's underlined letter is equivalent to clicking on the button. Pressing Enter is the same as clicking on the OK button, and pressing Esc is the same as clicking on the Cancel button.

Option buttons

Option buttons are sometimes known as radio buttons because they work like the preset station buttons on an old-fashioned car radio. Like these car radios, only one option button at a time can be "pressed." An option button is like choosing a single item on a multiple-choice test. When you click on an option button, the previously selected option button is unselected.

Option buttons are usually enclosed in a group box, and a single dialog box can have several sets of option buttons. Figure 4-12 shows an example of a dialog box with option buttons.

Figure 4-12: This dialog box has seven option buttons.

Check boxes

A check box control is used to indicate whether an option is on or off. This is similar to responding to an item on a true-false test. Figure 4-13 shows a dialog box with several check boxes. Unlike option buttons, each check box is independent of the others. Clicking on a check box toggles the check mark on and off.

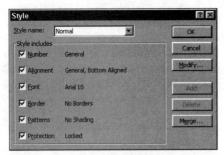

Figure 4-13: An example of check boxes in a dialog box.

Range selection boxes

 A range selection box lets you specify a worksheet range by dragging inside the worksheet. A range selection box has a small button that, when clicked on, collapses the dialog box to make it easier for you to select the range by dragging in the worksheet. When you've selected the range, click on the button again to restore the dialog box. Figure 4-14 shows a dialog box with two range selection box controls. The control in the middle is a standard edit box.

Figure 4-14: A range selection box lets you specify a worksheet range by dragging in the worksheet.

Spinners

A spinner control makes it easy to specify a number. You can click on the arrows to increment or decrement the displayed value. A spinner is almost always paired with an edit box. You can enter the value directly into the edit box or use the spinner to change it to the desired value. Figure 4-15 shows a dialog box with several spinner controls.

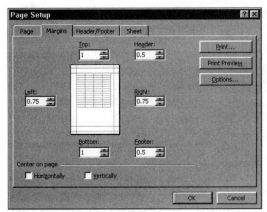

Figure 4-15: This dialog box has several spinner controls.

List boxes

A list box control contains a list of options from which you choose. If the list
is longer than will fit in the list box, you can use its vertical scrollbar to scroll
through the list. Figure 4-16 shows an example of a dialog box that contains two
list box controls.

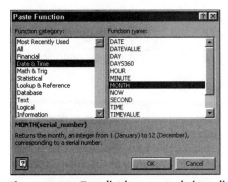

Figure 4-16: Two list box controls in a dialog box.

Drop-down boxes

Drop-down boxes are similar to list boxes, but they show only a single option at a
time. When you click on the arrow on a drop-down box, the list drops down to
display additional choices. Figure 4-17 shows an example of a drop-down box
control.

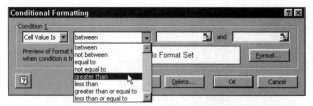

Figure 4-17: A drop-down box control in a dialog box.

Tabbed dialog boxes

Many of Excel's dialog boxes are "tabbed" dialog boxes. A tabbed dialog box includes notebook-like tabs, each of which is associated with a different panel. When you click on a tab, the dialog box changes to display a new panel, which has a new set of controls. The Format Cells dialog box, which appears in response to the Format⊃ Cells command, is a good example. This dialog box is shown in Figure 4-18. Notice that it has six tabs, which makes it functionally equivalent to six different dialog boxes.

Tabbed dialog boxes are quite convenient because you can make several changes in a single dialog box. When you've made all your setting changes, click on OK or press Enter.

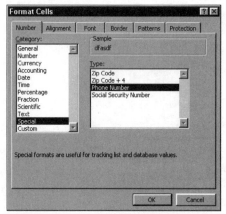

Figure 4-18: The Format Cells dialog box is an example of a tabbed dialog box.

Tip   To select a tab using the keyboard, use Ctrl+PgUp or Ctrl+PgDn, or simply press the first letter of the tab that you wish to activate.

Summary

This chapter covers background information that is essential to using Excel efficiently. I discuss methods to manipulate windows (which hold workbooks), as well as several techniques to move around within a worksheet using the mouse or the keyboard. I also discuss the various methods used to issue commands to Excel: menus, shortcut menus, toolbar buttons, and shortcut key combinations. I conclude with a general discussion of dialog boxes — an element common to all Windows programs.

✦   ✦   ✦

Working with Files and Workbooks

◆ ◆ ◆ ◆

In This Chapter

Basic information
about files

Descriptions of the
files used by Excel

Workbook file
operations that you
must know about

Tips on protecting
your files from
disaster

◆ ◆ ◆ ◆

Computer users won't get too far without understanding the concept of files. Every computer program uses files, and a good understanding of how to manage files stored on your hard drive will make your job easier. In this chapter, I discuss how Excel uses files and what you need to know about files in order to use Excel.

Some Background on Files

A *file* is an entity that stores information a disk. A hard disk is usually organized into directories (or folders) to facilitate the organization of files. For example, all the files that comprise Excel are stored in a separate folder on your computer. And, your system probably has a directory named My Documents which is used as the default location for storing Excel workbooks.

Files can be manipulated in several ways. They can be copied, renamed, deleted, or moved to another disk or folder. These types of file operations are usually performed using the tools in Windows (although you also can perform these operations without leaving Excel).

Computer programs are stored in files, and programs also store information that they use in files. Some programs (such as Excel) use files by loading them into memory. Others (such as database programs) access selective parts of a file directly from the disk and don't read the entire file into memory.

Windows makes it easy to access *properties* of files. Properties include information such as file type, size, when it was created, and so on. Excel lets you access some additional custom properties of files that can help you locate and categorize your files. For example, you can store information that lets you quickly locate all workbook files that apply to a particular client.

How Excel Uses Files

When you installed Excel on your system, the Setup program copied a number of files to your hard disk and also created several new folders to hold the files. These files consist of the files that are needed to run Excel, plus some sample files and Help files. The Setup program also made (or modified) some entries in the Windows *Registry*. The Registry is a master database of sorts, which keeps track of all configuration information for the operating system and the software installed on your system and also associates Excel's data files with Excel.

Excel's data files

Excel's primary file type is called a workbook file. When you open a workbook in Excel, the entire file is loaded into memory, and any changes that you make occur only in the copy of the file that's in memory. If the workbook is large, your system may not have enough memory to hold the file. In such a case, Windows uses disk-based virtual memory to simulate actual memory (this slows things down considerably). When you save the workbook, Excel saves the copy in memory to your disk, overwriting the previous copy of the file.

Table 5-1 lists the various types of files that Excel supports directly.

Table 5-1 Data Files Used by Excel	
File Type	**Description**
BAK	Backup file
XLA	Excel add-in file. Several add-ins are supplied with Excel, and you also can create your own add-ins.
XLB	Excel toolbar configuration file
XLC	Excel 4 chart file*
XLL	Excel link library file
XLM	Excel 4 macro file*
XLS	Excel workbook file
XLT	Excel template file
XLW	Excel workspace file

* These files became obsolete beginning with Excel 5. However, Excel can still read and write these files for compatibility with previous versions.

Foreign file formats supported

Although Excel's default file format is an XLS workbook file, it also can open files generated by several other applications. In addition, Excel can save workbooks in several different formats. Table 5-2 contains a list of file formats that Excel can read and write.

Cross Reference Chapter 22 covers file importing and exporting in detail.

Table 5-2
File Formats Supported by Excel

File Type	Description
WKS	1-2-3 Release 1 spreadsheet format**
WK1	1-2-3 Release 2 spreadsheet format***
WK3	1-2-3 Release 3 spreadsheet format***
WK4	1-2-3 for Windows spreadsheet format
WQ1	Quattro Pro for DOS spreadsheet format
WB1	Quattro Pro for Windows spreadsheet format**
DBF	dBASE database format
SLK	SYLK spreadsheet format
WB1	Quattro Pro for Windows spreadsheet format
HTM, HTML	Hypertext Markup Language files
CSV	Comma-separated value text file format
TXT	Text file format
PRN	Text file format
DIF	Data interchange format

** Excel can open files in this format, but not save them.

*** When you open one of these files, Excel searches for the associated formatting file (either FMT or FM3) and attempts to translate the formatting.

Essential Workbook File Operations

This section describes the operations that you perform with workbook files: opening, saving, closing, deleting, and so on. As you read through this section, keep in mind that you can have any number of workbooks open at any time, and that at any given time only one workbook is the active workbook. The workbook's name is displayed in its title bar (or in Excel's title bar if the workbook is maximized).

Creating a new workbook

When you start Excel, it automatically creates a new (empty) workbook called Book1. This workbook exists only in memory and has not been saved to disk. By default, this workbook consists of three worksheets named Sheet1, Sheet2, and Sheet3. If you're starting a new project from scratch, you can use this blank workbook.

You can always create another new workbook in either of three ways:

✦ Use the File➪New command.

✦ Click on the New Workbook button on the Standard toolbar (this button has an image of a sheet of paper).

✦ Press the Ctrl+N shortcut key combination.

If you choose the File➪New command, you're greeted with a dialog box named New (see Figure 5-1). This is a tabbed dialog box that lets you choose a template for the new workbook. If you don't have any custom templates defined, the General tab displays only one option: Workbook. Clicking on this gives you a plain workbook. Templates that are included with Excel are listed in the Spreadsheet Solutions tab. If you choose one of these templates, your new workbook is based on the selected template file.

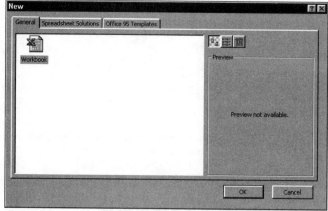

Figure 5-1: The New dialog box lets you choose a template upon which to base the new workbook.

Cross Reference I discuss templates later on in this chapter, and Chapter 34 discusses this topic in detail.

Pressing Ctrl+N or clicking on the New button on the Standard toolbar bypasses the New dialog box and creates a new default workbook immediately. If you want to create a new workbook based on a template, you must use the File⇨New command.

Tip If you find that you almost always end up closing the default Book1 workbook that appears when you start Excel, you can set things up so that Excel starts without an empty workbook. To do so, you need to edit the command line that you use to start Excel. For example, if you start Excel using a shortcut on your Windows desktop, right-click on the shortcut icon and choose Properties from the menu. Click on the Shortcut tab and add **/e** after the command line listed in the Target field. Here's an example of a command line modified in this manner (the actual drive and path may vary on your system):

```
C:\MICROSOFT OFFICE\EXCEL\EXCEL.EXE /e
```

Opening an existing workbook

There are several ways to open a workbook that has been saved on your disk:

✦ Use the File⇨Open command.

✦ Click on the Open button on the Standard toolbar (the Open button has an image of a file folder opening up).

✦ Press the Ctrl+O shortcut key combination.

All these methods result in the Open dialog box, shown in Figure 5-2.

You also can open an Excel workbook by double-clicking on its icon in any folder window. If Excel isn't running, it starts automatically. Or, you can drag a workbook icon into the Excel window to load the workbook.

If you want to open a file that you've used recently, it may be listed at the bottom of the drop-down File menu. This menu shows a list of files you've worked on recently. Just click on the filename and the workbook opens for you (bypassing the Open dialog box).

Excel 97 In previous versions of Excel, the recent file list showed only four files. Excel 97 lets you select the number of files to display — from none up to nine. To change this setting, use the Tool⇨Options command. In the Options dialog box, click on the General tab and make the change to the Recently used file list setting.

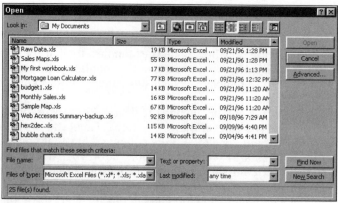

Figure 5-2: The Open dialog box.

To open a workbook from the Open dialog box, you must provide two pieces of information: the name of the workbook file (specified in the File name field) and its folder (specified in the Look in field).

This dialog box may be a bit overwhelming at first. You can ignore most of it because many of the controls deal with locating files. If you know what folder the file is in, it's simply a matter of specifying the folder and then selecting the filename. Click on OK and the file opens. You also can just double-click on the filename to open it.

Tip   You can hold down the Ctrl key and select multiple workbooks. When you click on OK, all the selected workbook files will open.

Right-clicking on a filename in the Open dialog box displays a shortcut menu with many extra choices. For example, you can copy the file, delete it, modify its properties, and so on.

Specifying a folder
The Look in field is actually a drop-down box. Click on the arrow and the box expands to show your system components. You can select a different drive or directory from this list. The Up One Level icon (a file folder with an upward arrow) moves up one level in the folder hierarchy.

Filtering by file type
At the bottom of the Open dialog box, the drop-down list is labeled Files of type. When this dialog box is displayed, it shows Microsoft Excel Files (*.xl*, *.xls, *.xla). This means that the files displayed are filtered, and you see only files that have an extension beginning with the letters XL. In other words, you see only standard Excel files: workbooks, add-ins, and templates.

If you want to open a file of a different type, click on the arrow in the drop-down list and select the file type that you want to open. This changes the filtering and displays only files of the type you specify.

Favorite places

Your hard disk probably has dozens of folders, and you can store your Excel workbooks in any folder. If you keep your workbooks in one folder, they will be easy to find. If you have many workbook files, however, you'll probably want to organize them into more folders. For example, you may have a folder for business files and a folder for personal files.

Excel helps you locate workbooks quickly by keeping track of your "favorite places" — folders that you specify to hold your workbook files. Two icons in the Open dialog box are relevant here (see Figure 5-3):

> **Look in Favorites:** This button displays the folders and files that you have designated as favorites.
>
> **Add to Favorites:** This button lets you add a folder or file to your list of favorites.

This feature can be quite handy, because it eliminates the need to traverse nested folders to find a particular file. If you store your Excel workbooks in more than one folder, it's a good idea to add all these additional folders to your favorites list. Then, you can just click on the Look in Favorites icon to display a list of those folders.

Figure 5-3: These two icons let you set up your favorite places to store your workbooks.

File display preferences

The Open dialog box can display your workbook filenames in four different styles:

✦ **List:** As a list of filenames only, displayed in multiple columns

✦ **Details:** As a list of filenames with details about each file (its size, file type, and when it was last modified)

✦ **Properties:** As a list of filenames with file properties displayed in a separate panel for the selected file

✦ **Preview:** As a list of filenames with a preview screen displayed in a separate panel for the selected file

You control the style by clicking on any of the four icons in the upper part of the Open dialog box (see Figure 5-4). The style that you choose is entirely up to you.

Tip   If you display the files using the Details style, you can sort the file list by any of the columns displayed (name, size, type, or date). To sort the file list, click on the appropriate column heading.

Figure 5-4: These four icons change the way files are listed in the Open dialog box.

Commands and settings

Commands and Settings, the last icon in the Open dialog box, is a bit unusual because clicking on it displays a shortcut menu. Here are the menu items and what they do:

Open Read Only: Opens the selected file in read-only mode. This is equivalent to checking the Read Only check box and opening the file.

Open as Copy: Opens a copy of the selected file. If the file is named budget.xls, the workbook that gets opened is named copy of budget.xls.

Print: Opens the selected file, prints it, and then closes it.

Properties: Displays the Properties dialog box for the selected file. This lets you examine or modify the file's properties without actually opening it.

Sorting: Opens the Sort By dialog box that lets you change the order in which the files are listed. You can sort the file list by name, size, file type, or date.

Search Subfolders: This option displays all matching files in all folders beneath the current folder. If the current folder is your hard drive, selecting this option shows you all matching files on the entire drive.

Group Files by Folder: Shows the files organized by folders. If this option is not checked, the files are displayed without their identifying folder. This is relevant only if the Search Subfolders option is selected.

Map Network Drive: Displays a dialog box that lets you map a network directory to a drive designator.

Add/Modify FTP Locations: Lets you add an Internet FTP site. An FTP site stores files that can be downloaded or opened directly by Excel.

Saved Searches: Lets you recall a file search that you previously saved.

Searching for files

A common problem among computer users is "losing" a file. You know you saved a file, but you don't remember the folder that you saved it in. Fortunately, Excel makes it fairly easy to locate such lost files using the Open dialog box. This is a rather complex subject, and I address it in detail later in this chapter.

Tip   You may find it more efficient to use the Windows file find feature. Click on the Windows Start menu and then select _HYPERLINK mailto: Find⇨Files _Find⇨Files_ or Folders. Enter the file specification and click on the Find Now button. For example, you can enter **bud*.xls** to locate all Excel files that begin with "bud." Files that match the file specification will be listed in the Find: All File list. To open a file, select it from the list and drag it to the Excel window.

Opening a file as read-only

You may have a workbook that you don't want to modify in any way. If so, you can open the file as read-only to ensure that the original copy is not modified. A read-only file can't be overwritten. You can, however, save the workbook with a different name. To open a file as read-only, click on the Read Only check box in the Open dialog box. Or, as mentioned previously, you can use the shortcut menu that appears when you click on the Commands and Settings icon.

Opening workbooks automatically

Many people find that they work on the same workbooks day after day. If this describes you, you'll be happy to know that you can have Excel open specific workbook files automatically whenever you start Excel.

The XLStart folder is located within the Microsoft Office folder. Any workbook files (excluding template files) that are stored in this folder open automatically when Excel starts. If one or more files open automatically from this folder, Excel won't start up with a blank workbook.

You can specify an alternate startup folder in addition to the XLStart folder. Choose the Tools⇨Options command and select the General tab. Enter a new folder name in the field labeled Alternate Startup File Location. After you do that, Excel automatically opens all workbook files in both the XLStart folder and the alternate folder that you specified.

Saving workbooks

When you're working on a workbook, it's vulnerable to day-ruining events such as power failures and system crashes. Therefore, you often should save your work to disk. Saving a file takes only a few seconds, but re-creating four hours of lost work takes about four hours.

Excel provides four ways to save your workbook:

✦ Use the File⇨Save command.

✦ Click on the Save button the Standard toolbar.

✦ Press the Ctrl+S shortcut key combination.

✦ Press the Shift+F12 shortcut key combination.

If your workbook has already been saved, it's saved again using the same filename. The original version of the file is overwritten. If you want to save the workbook to a new file, use the File⇨Save As command (or press F12).

If your workbook has never been saved, its title bar displays a name such as Book1 or Book2. Although Excel lets you use these generic workbook names for filenames, it's not recommended. Therefore, the first time that you save a new workbook, Excel displays the Save As dialog box (see Figure 5-5) to let you provide a more meaningful name.

The Save As dialog box is somewhat similar to the Open dialog box. Again, you need to specify two pieces of information: the workbook's name and the folder in which to store it. If you want to save the file to a different folder, select the desired folder in the Save in field. If you want to create a new folder, click on the Create New Folder icon in the Save As dialog box. The new folder is created within the folder that's displayed in the Save in field.

File naming rules

Excel's workbook files are subject to the same rules that apply to other Windows 95 (or later) files. A filename can be up to 255 characters, including spaces. This lets you (finally) give meaningful names to your files. You can't, however, use any of the following characters in your filenames:

\ (slash)

? (question mark)

: (colon)

* (asterisk)

" (quote)

< (less than)

> (greater than)

| (vertical bar)

You can use uppercase and lowercase letters in your names to improve readability. The filenames aren't case sensitive, however. If you have a file named My 1997 Budget and try to save another file with the name MY 1997 BUDGET, Excel asks whether you want to overwrite the original file.

If you plan to share your files with others who use a previous version of Excel, you should make sure that the filename is no longer than eight characters with no spaces. Otherwise, the filename will appear rather strange. For example, a file named My 1997 Budget will appear as MY1997~1.XLS. This is because Windows assigns every file an eight-character filename to be compatible with pre-Windows 95 operating systems.

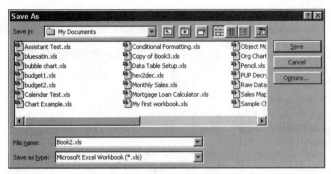

Figure 5-5: The Save As dialog box.

After you've selected the folder, enter the filename in the File name field. There is no need to specify a file extension. Excel adds it automatically, based on the file type specified in the Save as type field.

If a file with the same name already exists in the folder you specified, Excel asks whether you want to overwrite the file with the new file. Be careful with this because there is no way to recover the previous file if you overwrite it.

Caution   It's important to remember that saving a file overwrites the previous version of the file on disk. If you open a workbook and then completely mess it up, don't save the file! Instead, close the workbook without saving it, and then open the good copy on disk.

The default file location

When you save a workbook file for the first time, the Save As dialog box proposes a folder in which to save it. Normally, this is the My Documents folder. If you want, you can change the default file location. To do so, choose the Tools⇨Options command and click on the General tab in the Options dialog box. Then enter the folder's path into the field labeled Default File Location. After doing so, the Save As dialog box defaults to this folder.

Note, however, that if you override the default folder in the Save As dialog box, the new folder becomes the default. So, if you use the File⇨Save As command to save another workbook, Excel proposes the new default folder.

File save options

The Save As dialog box has a button labeled Options. When you click on this button, Excel displays its Save Options dialog box, shown in Figure 5-6. This dialog box lets you set the following several options.

Saving your work automatically

If you're the type who gets so wrapped up in your work that you forget to save your file, you may be interested in Excel's AutoSave feature. AutoSave automatically saves your workbooks at a prespecified interval. Using this feature requires that you load an add-in file. This add-in is included with Excel, but it's not normally installed. To load the AutoSave add-in, select the Tools⇨Add-Ins command. This displays a dialog box. Click on AutoSave in the list of add-ins and then click on OK. The add-in will be loaded every time you run Excel. If you no longer want to use AutoSave, repeat the process and uncheck the AutoSave add-in.

When AutoSave is loaded, the Tools menu has a new menu item: AutoSave. Selecting the Tools⇨AutoSave command displays the dialog box shown in the accompanying figure.

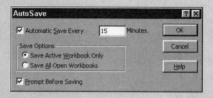

This dialog box lets you specify the time interval for saving. In general, you should specify a time interval equal to the maximum amount of time that you're willing to lose. For example, if you don't mind losing 15 minutes of work, set the interval for 15 minutes.

Option buttons let you choose between saving all open workbooks or just the active workbook. Another option lets you specify whether you want to be prompted before the save takes place. If you choose to be prompted, you have the opportunity to cancel the save if you're right in the middle of something important.

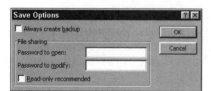

Figure 5-6: The Save Options dialog box.

Always Create Backup: If this option is set, the existing version of the workbook is renamed as a BAK file before the workbook is saved. Doing this makes it possible to go back to the previously saved version of your workbook. Some users like to use this option because it adds another level of safety. Just be aware that your worksheet files will take up about twice as much disk space, so it's a good idea to delete the backup files occasionally.

Password to Open: If you enter a password, the password is required before anyone can open the workbook. You're asked to enter the password a second time to confirm it. Passwords can be up to 15 characters long and are case sensitive.

Be careful with this option because it is impossible to open the workbook (using normal methods) if you forget the password.

Password to Modify: This is the password required to save changes to the workbook under the same filename. Use this option if you want to make sure that changes aren't made to the original version of the workbook. In other words, the workbook can be saved with a new name, but a password is required to overwrite the original version.

Read-Only Recommended: If this option is checked, the file can't be saved under its original name. This is another way to ensure that a workbook file isn't overwritten.

Caution Saving a workbook with a password is not a foolproof method of protecting your work. Several utilities exist that are designed to "crack" passwords in Excel files.

Workbook summary information

When you save a file for the first time by closing the Save As dialog box, Excel may prompt you for summary information by displaying the Properties dialog box shown in Figure 5-7. This lets you specify lots of descriptive information about the workbook and also displays some details about the file.

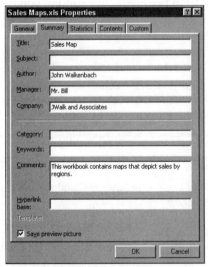

Figure 5-7: You can provide all sorts of information about your workbook in the Properties dialog box.

The Properties dialog box may or may not appear, depending on how Excel is configured. To specify whether to display the Properties dialog box automatically, select the Tools⇨Options command, click on the General tab, and adjust the setting of the Prompt for File Properties check box.

The Properties dialog box has five tabs:

General: This panel displays general information about the file — its name, size, location, when it was created, and so on. You can't change any of the information in this panel.

Summary: This panel appears by default when you first save the file. It contains nine fields of information that you can enter and modify. You can use the information in this panel to quickly locate workbooks that meet certain criteria. This is discussed later in the chapter.

Statistics: This panel shows additional information about the file, and it can't be changed.

Contents: This panel displays the names of the sheets in the workbook, arranged by sheet type.

Custom: This panel can be quite useful if you use it consistently. Basically, it lets you store a variety of information about the file in a sort of database. For example, if the workbook deals with a client named Smith and Jones Corp., you can keep track of this bit of information and use it to help locate the file later.

You also can access the Properties dialog box for the active workbook at any time by selecting the File⇨Properties command from the menu. In addition, you can view the properties of a workbook from the Open dialog box. Right-click on the file in which you're interested and choose Properties from the shortcut menu.

Saving files in older formats

If your colleagues also use Excel, you may find yourself exchanging workbook files. If so, it's important that you know which version of Excel they use. Excel 97 uses a new file format, and older versions of Excel cannot open these files.

If you send a workbook to someone who uses an earlier version of Excel, however, you must remember to save the file in a format that the earlier version can read.

Note If the file will be used by someone who doesn't use Windows 95, make sure that you use a filename with eight or fewer characters.

Excel 5 was the first version to use multisheet workbooks. Prior to Excel 5, worksheets, chart sheets, and macro sheets were stored in separate files. Consequently, if you share a multisheet workbook with someone who still uses one of these older versions, you must save each sheet separately — and in the proper format.

The Save As dialog box has a field labeled Save as type. This lets you choose the format in which to save the file. The Excel file formats are listed in Table 5-3.

Table 5-3
Excel File Formats

Format	What it does
Microsoft Excel Workbook	This saves the file in the standard Excel 97 file format.
Microsoft Excel 5/95 Workbook	This saves the file in a format that can be read by both Excel 5 and Excel 95.
Microsoft Excel 4.0 Worksheet*	This saves the file in a format that can be read by Excel 4.
Microsoft Excel 3.0 Worksheet*	This saves the file in a format that can be read by Excel 3.
Microsoft Excel 2.1 Worksheet*	This saves the file in a format that can be read by Excel 2.1

* These file formats do not support multisheet workbooks.

If you need to send a workbook with three worksheets in it to a colleague who uses Excel 4, you must save it as three separate files and make sure that you select the Microsoft Excel 4.0 Worksheet option from the Save as type drop-down box (see Figure 5-8).

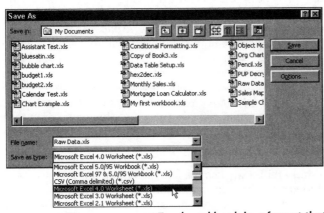

Figure 5-8: You can save an Excel workbook in a format that is readable with previous versions of Excel.

Excel 97 Excel 97 has a new option that lets you specify the default format for saved workbooks. To change the default setting, select the Tools⇨Options command, click on the Transition tab, and choose the file type from the drop-down list labeled Save Excel files as.

Closing workbooks

When you're finished with a workbook, you should close it to free the memory it uses. You can close a workbook using any of the following methods:

✦ Use the File➪Close command.

✦ Click on the Close button in the workbook's title bar.

✦ Double-click on the Control icon in the workbook's title bar.

✦ Press the Ctrl+F4 shortcut key.

✦ Press the Ctrl+W shortcut key.

If you've made any changes to your workbook since it was last saved, Excel asks whether you want to save the workbook before closing it.

Tip   To close all open workbooks, press the Shift key and choose the File➪Close All command. This command appears only when you hold down the Shift key while you click on the File menu. Excel closes each workbook, prompting you for each unsaved workbook.

Using workspace files

As you know, you can work with any number of workbook files at a time. For example, you may have a project that uses two workbooks, and you like to arrange the windows in a certain way to make it easy to access them both. Fortunately, Excel lets you save your entire workspace to a file. *Workspace,* as used here, means all the workbooks and their screen positions and window sizes — sort of a snapshot of Excel's current state. Then, you can open the workspace file and Excel is set up exactly as it was when you saved your workspace.

To save your workspace, use the File➪Save Workspace command. Excel proposes the name resume.xlw for the workspace file. You can use this name or enter a different name in the File name field. Click on the Save button, and the workspace will be saved to disk.

Caution   It's important to understand that a workspace file doesn't include the workbook files themselves. It includes only the information needed to recreate the workspace. The workbooks in the workspace are saved in standard workbook files. Therefore, if you distribute a workspace file to a coworker, make sure that you also include the workbook files to which the workspace file refers.

Tip   If you save your workspace file in the XLStart folder, Excel opens the workspace file automatically when it starts up. This is handy if you tend to work with the same files everyday, because you can essentially pick up where you left off the previous day.

Deleting a workbook

When you no longer need a workbook file, you may want to delete it from your disk. Doing so will free disk space and reduce the number of files displayed in the Open dialog box.

There are many ways to delete a file using Windows, and you can even delete files directly from Excel. You can right-click on a filename in the Open dialog box and choose Delete from the shortcut menu (see Figure 5-9).

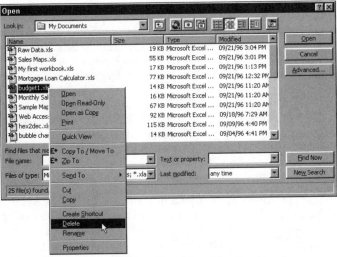

Figure 5-9: You can delete a file without leaving Excel.

If your system is set up to use the Recycle Bin (which is the default setting for Windows), you may be able to recover a deleted file later if you discover that it was deleted accidentally.

Finding a workbook

The ability to use Excel's comprehensive tools for cataloging and locating workbook files, along with the capability to use long filenames, should help put an end to the perennial problem of "losing" files.

Using Excel's Find feature can be a bit confusing at first, but once you get the hang of it you'll discover its advantages. The searching takes place from the Open dialog box. You can search for files based on

✦ The name of the file

✦ The type of file

✦ Text contained in the file

✦ Properties associated with the file

✦ When the file was last modified

In the following sections, I describe the types of searches that you can perform.

Identifying the search scope

Before beginning your search for a file, you must identify the scope of the search. This can be very broad (My Computer) or quite narrow (a single folder). You specify the search scope in the Look in field of the Open dialog box. You can choose My Computer to search all local devices, Network Neighborhood to search network devices, or select a particular folder either locally or on a network.

Most of the time you'll want to search all subfolders also. To specify this, click on the Commands and Settings button and select Search Subfolders. If you want the list of found files to be organized by folder, also select the Group files by folder option.

Searching by filename

If you know the filename (or approximate filename), enter it in the File name field. If you aren't sure of the exact filename, you can use wildcard characters to specify an approximate match. Use a question mark (?) as a placeholder for a single character and an asterisk (*) as a placeholder for any number of characters. For example, if you know that the file has the word *Budget* in it, you can enter ***Budget*** to find all filenames that contain the word *budget*. To start the search, click on the Find Now button.

Some searches may take quite a long time. To stop a search, click on the Stop button. The Stop button replaces the Find Now button when a search is in progress.

Searching by file type

The Files of type field lets you specify the type of files to locate. Normally, this will be the default, Microsoft Excel Files. But you can search for other file types by clicking on the drop-down arrow and choosing from the list of file types that Excel can open. To start the search, click on the Find Now button.

Searching for text in a file

Often, you won't be able to remember the filename, but you will remember a particular piece of information in the file. For example, you may have prepared a report that dealt with company benefits. If your search for a filename that contains *Benefits* fails, you can try a text search for the word *Benefits*. After all, it's quite likely that your worksheet includes this word at least once.

To perform a text search, enter the word or phrase that you're looking for in the field labeled Text or property. Then click on the Find Now button to start the search.

Searching by properties

Excel workbooks have a set of properties. Some properties can't be changed, but many can. For example, one of a file's properties is the date and time that it was last accessed. You can't change this property directly — it's automatically updated by the operating system. You can set or examine properties for workbooks using the File⇨Properties command.

To search for files with a particular property, enter the property into the Text or property field and click on the Find Now button to begin the search.

Searching by file modification date

You can also search for files based on the date they were last modified. Click on the Last modified drop-down arrow, and you get a list that represents times: today, last week, this week, and so on. Select the time that matches your needs and click on the Find Now button to begin the search.

Combining searches

As you can see, Excel offers some powerful search capabilities. It's even more powerful than you may think, because you can combine these different types of searches. For example, you can search for a file that contains specific text *and* was last modified yesterday. You set up these combined searches by entering criteria into more than one of the fields discussed above.

The Open dialog box has another button, labeled Advanced. This button brings up a dialog box called Advanced Find. This box has several additional search features that let you define more specific criteria. Most users will have no need for such sophisticated file searches.

Sharing workbooks with others

If your system is connected to a network, there are some other issues related to workbook files of which you should be aware. I devote an entire chapter (Chapter 21) to workgroup issues.

Using Template Files

In this section I discuss template files. You may be able to save yourself a lot of work by using a template instead of creating a new workbook from scratch.

A template is basically a worksheet that's all set up with formulas and is ready for you to enter data. The templates distributed with Excel are nicely formatted and relatively easy to customize. When you open a new workbook based on the template, you save the workbook to a new file. In other words, you don't overwrite the template.

Figure 5-10 shows one of the Spreadsheet Solutions templates.

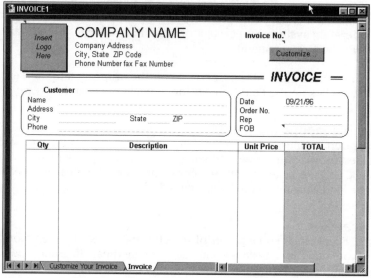

Figure 5-10: Excel includes several templates, designed to perform common tasks.

Following is a list of the templates that are included with Excel 97. These templates are located in the Spreadsheet Solutions folder.

Note   Not all these templates may be installed on your system. To install templates that aren't available, re-run the Excel (Or Office 97) Setup program.

Business Planner: Helps you create an income statement, balance sheet, and cash flow summary.

Car Lease Manager: Helps you decide how to negotiate a car lease.

Change Request: Helps you track problems and request fixes to products or processes.

Expense Statement: Helps you create expense report forms and a log to track them.

Invoice: Helps you create invoices.

Loan Manager: Helps you understand the cost of borrowing money and how to save money doing it.

Personal Budgeter: Helps you create a personal budget to track spending and plan savings.

Purchase Order: Helps you create purchase orders to send to vendors.

Sales Quote: Helps you create sales quotes for prospective customers.

Timecard: Helps you create a schedule for managing hourly employees.

The Spreadsheet Solutions templates are handy, but be aware that they include a lot of overhead — several worksheets, dialog sheets, and a custom toolbar. Consequently, the workbooks that you generate using these templates may be larger than you would expect. On the positive side, studying how these templates are designed can provide advanced users with some great tips.

Tip   You can download additional templates from Microsoft's Web site (http://www.microsoft.com).

If any of these templates appear to be useful, I urge you to check them out and work with them a while. They may seem a bit overwhelming at first, but they can save you many hours of work. Each template includes online help that describes how to use it.

Cross Reference   Chapter 33 discusses templates in more detail and describes how to create your own template files.

Protecting Your Work

The final topic in this chapter offers a few words on backing up your work to protect yourself from disaster — or at least save yourself the inconvenience of repeating your work. Earlier in the chapter, you learned how to make Excel create a backup copy of your workbook when you saved the file. That's a good idea, but it certainly isn't the only backup protection you should use.

If you've been around computers for a while, you probably know that hard disks aren't perfect. I've seen many hard disks fail for no apparent reason and with absolutely no advance warning. In addition, files can get corrupted — which usually makes them unreadable and essentially worthless. If a file is truly important, you need to take extra steps to ensure its safety. There are several backup options for ensuring the safety of individual files:

Keep a backup copy of the file on the same drive. This is essentially what happens when you select the Always Create A Backup option when you save a workbook file. Although this offers some protection if you create a mess from the worksheet, it won't do you any good if the entire hard drive crashes.

Keep a backup copy on a different hard drive. This assumes, of course, that your system has more than one hard drive. This offers more protection than the preceding method because it's quite unlikely that both hard drives would fail. If the entire system is destroyed or stolen, however, you're out of luck.

Keep a backup copy on a network server. This assumes that your system is connected to a server on which you can write files. This method is fairly safe. If the network server is located in the same building, however, you're at risk if the entire building burns down or is otherwise destroyed.

Keep a backup copy on a removable medium. This is the safest method. Using a removable medium, such as a floppy disk or tape, lets you physically take the backup to another location. So, if your system (or the entire building) is damaged, your backup copy remains intact.

Most people with good backup habits acquired them because they've been burned in the past (myself included).

Windows comes with software that you can use to back up your entire system. Consult your Windows manual or online help for details.

Summary

This chapter covers the rather broad topic of files. I start with an overview of how computers use files and narrow the scope to cover how Excel uses files. The chapter includes a discussion of the essential file operations you perform from Excel, including creating new workbook files, opening existing files, saving files, and closing files. I also discuss Excel's handy file-searching features that let you locate files quickly, no matter where they are stored. I conclude with an introduction to the template files that are included with Excel.

✦   ✦   ✦

Entering and Editing Worksheet Data

✦   ✦   ✦   ✦

In This Chapter

An overview of
Excel's data types

Entering and
formatting values,
dates, and times

Entering text

Basic stylistic
formatting

Data entry tips

✦   ✦   ✦   ✦

People use spreadsheets primarily to store data and
perform calculations. This chapter discusses the various
types of data that you can enter into Excel.

Types of Worksheet Data

As you know, an Excel workbook can hold any number of
worksheets, and each worksheet is made up of cells. A cell
can hold any of three types of data:

✦   A value

✦   Text

✦   A formula

Note A worksheet also can hold charts, maps, drawings, pictures,
buttons, and other objects. These objects actually reside on
the worksheet's *draw layer,* which is an invisible layer on top
of each worksheet. I discuss the draw layer in Chapter 14.
This chapter is concerned only with data you enter into
worksheet cells.

Values

Values, also known as numbers, represent a quantity of some
type: sales, number of employees, atomic weights, test scores,
and so on. Values that you enter into cells can be used in
formulas or provide the data used to create a chart. Values
also can be dates (such as 6/9/97) or times (such as 3:24 a.m.),
and you'll see that you can manipulate these types of values
quite efficiently.

Figure 6-1 shows a worksheet with some values entered in it.

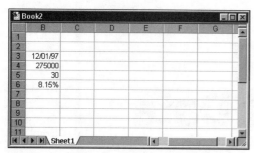

Figure 6-1: Values entered in a worksheet.

Text

Most worksheets also include non-numeric text in some of their cells. You can insert text to serve as labels for values, headings for columns, or to provide instructions about the worksheet. Text that begins with a number is still considered text. For example, if you enter an address such as **1425 Main St.** into a cell, Excel considers this to be text rather than a value.

Figure 6-2 shows a worksheet with text in some of the cells. In this case, the text is used to clarify what the values mean.

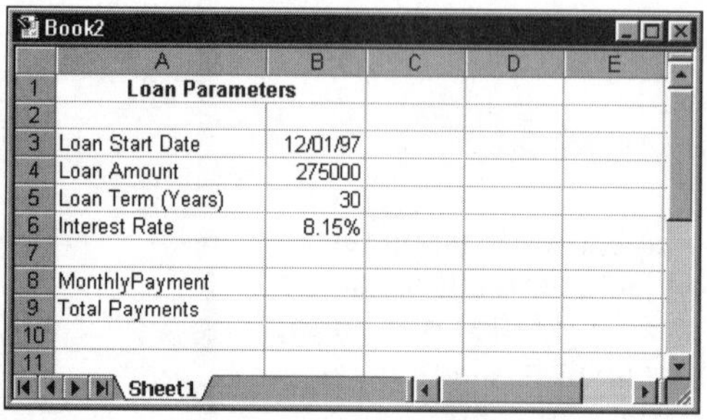

Figure 6-2: This worksheet consists of text and values.

Excel's numerical limitations

New users often are curious about the types of values that Excel can deal with. In other words, how large can numbers be? And how accurate are large numbers?

Excel's numbers are precise up to 15 digits. For example, if you enter a large value such as 123,123,123,123,123,123 (18 digits), Excel actually stores it with only 15 digits of precision: 123,123,123,123,123,000. This may seem quite limiting, but in practice it rarely causes any problems.

Here are some of Excel's other numericjal limits:

Largest positive number: 9.9E+307

Smallest negative number: −9.9E+307

Smallest positive number: 1E−307

Largest negative number: −1E−307

These numbers are expressed in scientific notation. For example, the largest positive number is "9.9 times 10 to the 307th power."

Formulas

Formulas are what make a spreadsheet a spreadsheet — otherwise, you'd just have a strange word processor that was good at working with tables. Excel lets you enter powerful formulas that use the values (or even text) in cells to calculate a result. When you enter a formula into a cell, the formula's result appears in the cell. If you change any of the values used by a formula, the formula recalculates and shows the new result. Figure 6-3 shows a worksheet with values, text, and formulas.

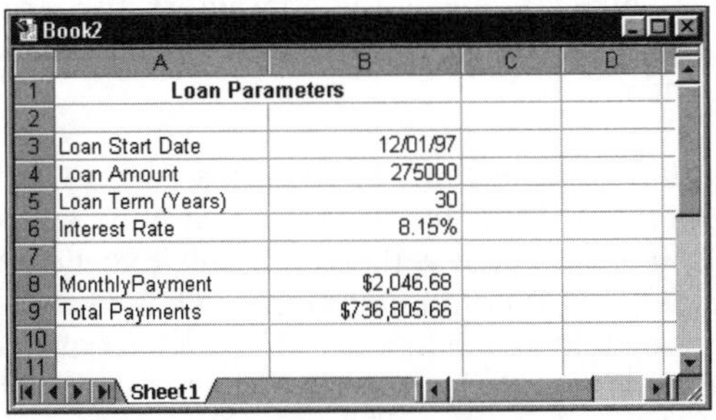

Figure 6-3: Cells B8 and B9 contain formulas that use the other values.

Cross Reference Chapter 9 discusses formulas in detail.

Entering Values

Entering values into a cell is quite easy. Just move the cell pointer to the appropriate cell (this makes it the active cell), enter the value, and press Enter. The value is displayed in the cell, and it also appears in Excel's formula bar. You can, of course, include decimal points when entering values and dollar signs; plus signs, minus signs, and commas also are allowed. If you precede a value with a minus sign or enclose it in parentheses, Excel considers it to be a negative number.

Note   Sometimes, the value that you enter won't be displayed exactly as you enter it. More specifically, if you enter a large number, it may be converted to scientific notation. Notice, however, that the formula bar displays the value that you entered originally. Excel simply reformatted the value so that it would fit into the cell. If you make the column wider, the number is displayed as you entered it.

Later in this chapter I discuss the various ways to format values so that they appear differently.

Entering Text

Entering text into a cell is just as easy as entering a value: activate the cell, type the text, and press Enter. A cell can contain a maximum of about 32,000 characters.

Excel 97   The 32,000 character limit in a cell is a dramatic increase over the maximum allowed in previous versions — a paltry 255 characters. To give you an idea of how much text can fit into a single cell, consider the fact that this entire chapter has approximately 32,000 characters!

If you type an exceptionally long text entry into a cell, the characters appear to wrap around when they reach the right edge of the window, and the formula bar expands so that the text wraps around.

What happens when you enter text that's longer than its column's current width? If the cells to the immediate right are blank, Excel displays the text in its entirety, spilling the entry into adjacent cells. If an adjacent cell is not blank, Excel displays as much of the text as possible (the full text is contained in the cell; it's just not displayed). If you need to display a long text string in a cell that's adjacent to a non-blank cell, you can edit your text to make it shorter, increase the width of the column, use a smaller font, wrap the text within the cell so that it occupies more than one line, or use Excel's new "shrink to fit" option (see Chapter 11 for details).

Dates and Times

Often, you need to enter dates and times into your worksheet. To Excel, a date or a time is simply treated as a value — but it's formatted to appear as a date or a time.

Working with date values

If you work with dates and times, you need to understand Excel's date and time system. Excel handles dates using a serial number system. The earliest date that Excel can understand is January 1, 1900. This date has a serial number of 1. January 2, 1900, has a serial number of 2, and so on. This system makes it easy to deal with dates in formulas. For example, you can enter a formula to calculate the number of days between two dates.

Most of the time, you don't have to be concerned with Excel's serial number date system. You can simply enter a date in a familiar date format, and Excel takes care of the details behind the scenes. For example, if you need to enter June 1, 1997, you can simply enter the date by typing **June 1, 1997** (or any of a number of different date formats). Excel interprets your entry and stores the value 35582 — which is the date serial number for that date.

Here is a sampling of the date formats that Excel recognizes. After entering a date, you can format it to appear in a different date format. (I discuss such formatting later in the chapter.)

Entered into a Cell	Excel's Interpretation
6-1-97	June 1, 1997
6-1-1997	June 1, 1997
6/1/97	June 1, 1997
6/1/1997	June 1, 1997
6-1/97	June 1, 1997
June 1, 1997	June 1, 1997
Jun 1	June 1 of the current year
June 1	June 1 of the current year
6/1	June 1 of the current year
6-1	June 1 of the current year

Caution As you can see, Excel is rather smart when it comes to recognizing dates that you enter into a cell. It's not perfect, however. For example, Excel does *not* recognize any of the following entries as dates: June 1 1997, Jun-1 1997, and Jun-1/1997. Rather, it interprets these entries as text. If you plan to use dates in formulas, make sure that the date you enter is actually recognized as a date; otherwise, your formulas will produce incorrect results.

Tip After you enter a date, check the formula bar. If the formula bar displays exactly what you entered, Excel didn't interpret the date you entered as a date. If the formula bar displays your entry in a format like mm/dd/yyyy, that means Excel correctly interpreted your entry as a date.

Working with time values

When working with times, you simply extend Excel's date serial number system to include decimals. In other words, Excel works with times by using fractional days. For example, the date serial number for June 1, 1997, is 35582. Noon (halfway through the day) is represented internally as 35582.5.

Again, you normally don't have to be concerned with these serial numbers (or fractional serial numbers for times). Just enter the time into a cell in a recognized format.

Here are some examples of time formats that Excel recognizes.

Entered into a Cell	Excel's Interpretation
11:30:00 am	11:30 a.m.
11:30:00 AM	11:30 a.m.
11:30 pm	11:30 p.m.
11:30	11:30 a.m.

The preceding samples don't have a day associated with them. You also can combine dates and times, however, as follows:

Entered into a Cell	Excel's Interpretation
6/1/97 11:30	11:30 a.m. on June 1, 1997

Changing or Erasing Values and Text

It should come as no surprise that you can change the contents of a cell after the fact. After you enter a value or text into a cell, you can modify it in a number of ways:

✦ Erase the cell's contents.

✦ Replace the cell's contents with something else.

✦ Edit the cell's contents.

Erasing the contents of a cell

To erase the value, text, or formula in a cell, just activate the cell and press Delete. To erase more than one cell, select all the cells that you want to erase, and then press Delete. Pressing the Delete key removes the cell's contents but doesn't remove any formatting (such as bold, italic, or a different number format) that you may have applied to the cell.

For more control over what gets deleted, you can use the Edit⇨Clear command. This menu item leads to a submenu with four additional choices (see Figure 6-4). These choices are described as follows:

All: Clears everything from the cell

Formats: Clears only the formatting and leaves the value, text, or formula

Contents: Clears only the cell's contents and leaves the formatting

Comments: Clears the comment (if one exists) attached to the cell

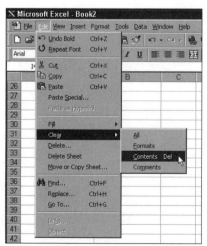

Figure 6-4: Excel provides several options for clearing cells.

Replacing the contents of a cell

To replace the contents of a cell with something else, just activate the cell and type in your new entry. It replaces the previous contents. Any formatting that you applied to the cell remains.

Editing the contents of a cell

If the cell contains only a few characters, it's often easier to simply replace it by typing in new data. But if the cell contains lengthy text or a complex formula and you need to make a slight modification, you probably want to edit the cell rather than reenter information.

When you want to edit the contents of a cell, you can use one of three ways to get into cell edit mode:

✦ Double-click on the cell. This lets you edit the cell contents directly in the cell.

✦ Press F2. This lets you edit the cell contents directly in the cell.

✦ Activate the cell that you want to edit, and then click in the formula bar. This lets you edit the cell contents in the formula bar.

You can use whichever method you prefer. Some people find it easier to edit directly in the cell; others prefer to use the formula bar for editing a cell. All these methods cause the formula bar to display two new mouse icons, as shown in Figure 6-5. The X icon cancels editing, and the cell's contents aren't changed (Esc has the same effect). The Check Mark icon completes the editing and enters the modified contents into the cell (Enter has the same effect).

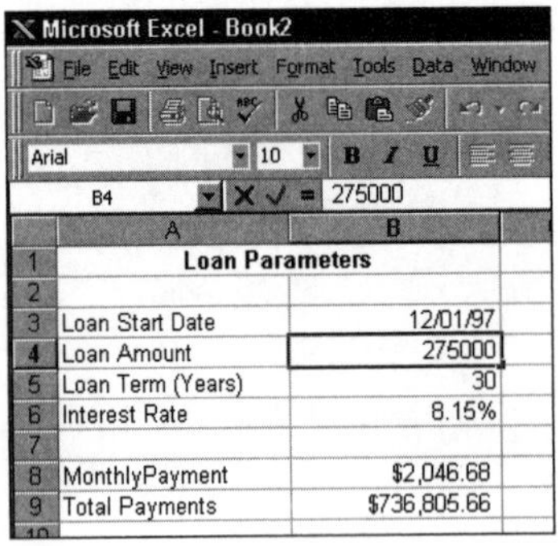

Figure 6-5: The formula bar displays two new icons when you begin editing a cell.

Excel 97 If the cell contains a formula, you can edit the formula using any of the techniques listed previously. Or, you can take advantage of a new feature: the Formula Palette. To activate the formula palette, click on the "=" icon in the formula bar. I discuss the Formula Palette in Chapter 9.

Editing a cell's contents works pretty much as you might expect. When you begin editing a cell, the cursor changes to a vertical bar, and you can move the vertical bar by using the direction keys. You can add new characters at the cursor location. After you're in edit mode, you can use any of the following keys to move through the cell contents:

Left/right arrow: The left- and right-arrow keys move the cursor left and right one character, respectively, without deleting any characters.

Ctrl+left/right arrow: Moves the cursor one group of characters to the left and right, respectively. A group of characters is defined by a space characters.

Backspace: Erases the character to the immediate left of the cursor.

Delete: Erases the character to the right of the cursor, or all selected characters.

Insert: When you're editing, pressing the Insert key places Excel in OVR (Overwrite) mode. Rather than add characters to the cell, you *overwrite*, or replace, existing characters with new ones, depending on the position of the cursor. If the cursor is above a character and you type in OVR mode, Excel replaces the old character with the character you type.

Home: Moves the cursor to the beginning of the cell entry.

End: Moves the cursor to the end of the cell entry.

Enter: Accepts the edited data.

While editing a cell, you can use the following key combination to select characters in the cell.

Shift+left/right arrow: Selects characters to the left or right of the cursor.

Shift+Home: Selects all characters from the beginning of the cell to the cursor.

Shift+End: Selects all characters from the cursor to the end of the cell.

Tip   You also can use the mouse to select characters while you're editing a cell. Just click on and drag the mouse pointer over the characters that you want to select.

Formatting Values

Values that you enter into cells are normally unformatted. In other words, they simply consist of a string of numerals. In many cases, you want to format the numbers so that they are easier to read or are more consistent in terms of the number of decimal places shown.

Figure 6-6 shows two columns of values. The first column consists of unformatted values. The cells in the second column have been formatted to make the values easier to read. If you move the cell pointer to a cell that has a formatted value, you find that the formula bar displays the value in its unformatted state. This is because the formatting affects only how the value is displayed in the cell.

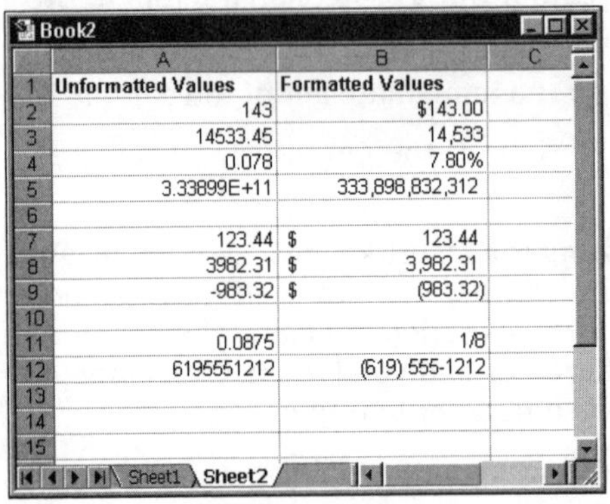

Figure 6-6: Unformatted values (left column) and the same values formatted.

Automatic number formatting

Excel is smart enough to perform some formatting for you automatically. For example, if you enter **12.2%** into a cell, Excel knows that you want to use a percentage format and applies it for you automatically. If you use commas to separate thousands (such as **123,456**) Excel applies comma formatting for you. And if you precede your value with a dollar sign, the cell will be formatted for currency.

Formatting numbers using the toolbar

The Formatting toolbar, which is displayed by default, contains several buttons that let you quickly apply common number formats. When you click on one of these buttons, the active cell takes on the specified number format. You also can select a range of cells (or even an entire row or column) before clicking on these buttons. If more than one cell is selected, the number format is applied to all the selected cells. Table 6-1 summarizes the formats that these Formatting toolbar buttons perform.

Table 6-1
Number-Formatting Buttons on the Formatting Toolbar

Button Name	Formatting Applied
Currency Style	Adds a dollar sign to the left, separates thousands with a comma, and displays the value with two digits to the right of the decimal point
Percent Style	Displays the value as a percentage with no decimal places
Comma Style	Separates thousands with a comma and displays the value with two digits to the right of the decimal place
Increase Decimal	Increases the number of digits to the right of the decimal point by one
Decrease Decimal	Decreases the number of digits to the right of the decimal point by one

Cross Reference These five toolbar buttons actually apply predefined "styles" to the selected cells. These styles are similar to those used in word processing programs. Chapter 11 describes how to modify existing styles and create new styles.

Formatting numbers using shortcut keys

Table 6-2 summarizes some shortcut key combinations that you can use to apply common number formatting to the selected cells or range.

Table 6-2
Number-Formatting Keyboard Shortcuts

Key Combination	Formatting Applied
Ctrl+Shift+~	General number format (that is, unformatted values)
Ctrl+Shift+$	Currency format with two decimal places (negative numbers appear in parentheses)
Ctrl+Shift+%	Percentage format with no decimal places
Ctrl+Shift+^	Scientific notation number format with two decimal places
Ctrl+Shift+#	Date format with the day, month, and year
Ctrl+Shift+@	Time format with the hour, minute, and a.m. or p.m.
Ctrl+Shift+!	Two decimal places, 1000 separator, and hyphen for negative values

Other number formats

In some cases, the number formats accessible from the Formatting toolbar (or using the shortcut key combination) are just fine. More often, however, you want more control over how your values appear. Excel offers a great deal of control over number formats.

Figure 6-7 shows Excel's Format Cells dialog box. This is a tabbed dialog box. For formatting numbers, you need to use the tab labeled Number.

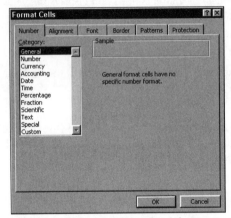

Figure 6-7: The Number tab of the Format Cells dialog box lets you format numbers in just about any way imaginable.

There are several ways to bring up the Format Cells dialog box. Start by selecting the cell or cells that you want to format, and then

- ✦ Select the Format⇨Cells command.
- ✦ Right-click and choose Format Cells from the shortcut menu.
- ✦ Press the Ctrl+1 shortcut key.

The Number tab of the Format Cells dialog box displays 12 categories of number formats from which to choose. When you select a category from the list box, the right side of the panel changes to display appropriate options. For example, Figure 6-8 shows how the dialog box looks when you click on the Number category.

When numbers appear to add up incorrectly

It's important to understand that applying a number format to a cell doesn't change the value in any way — formatting changes only how the value looks. For example, if a cell contains .874543, you might format it to appear as 87%. If that cell is used in a formula, the formula uses the full value (.87453), not the displayed value (.87).

In some situations, formatting may cause Excel to display calculation results that appear incorrect, such as when totaling numbers with decimal places (see the accompanying figure). In this example, the values are formatted to display two decimal places. This formatting displays the values rounded. But because Excel uses the full precision in its formula, the sum of these two values appears to be incorrect (10.00 + 10.10 = 20.11). The actual values that are summed are 10.004 and 10.103.

There are several solutions to this problem. You could format the cells to display more decimal places. Or, you can use the ROUND function individual numbers and specify the number of decimal places Excel should round to. I discuss this and other built-in functions in Chapter 10.

Another solution is to instruct Excel to change the worksheet values to match their displayed format. To do this, use the Tools⇨Options command, select the Calculation tab, and check the Precision as Displayed check box. Excel warns you that the underlying numbers will be permanently changed to match their appearance on-screen. If you want to select this option, it's a good idea to backup the worksheet on disk first in case you change your mind.

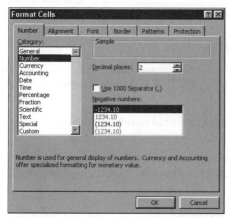

Figure 6-8: Options for the Number category.

The Number category has three options that you can control: the number of decimal places displayed, whether to use a comma for the thousand separator, and how you want negative numbers displayed. Notice that the Negative Numbers list box has four choices (two of which display negative values in red), and the choices change depending on the number of decimal places and your choice for a comma. Also, notice that the top of the panel displays a sample of how the active cell will appear with the selected number format. After you've made your choices, click on OK to apply the number format to all the selected cells.

Here is a list of the number format categories, along with some general comments.

General: The General number format is the default format. It displays numbers as integers, decimals, or in scientific notation if the value is too wide to fit in the cell.

Number: This format lets you specify the number of decimal places, whether to use a comma to separate thousands, and how to display negative numbers (with a minus sign, in red, in parentheses, or in red and in parentheses).

Currency: This format lets you specify the number of decimal places, whether to use a dollar sign, and how to display negative numbers (with a minus sign, in red, in parentheses, or in red and in parentheses). This format always uses a comma to separate thousands.

Accounting: This format differs from the Currency format in that the dollar signs always line up vertically.

Date: This category lets you choose from 11 date formats.

Time: This category lets you choose from six time formats.

Percentage: This category lets you choose the number of decimal places and always displays a percent sign.

Fraction: This category lets you choose from among nine fraction formats.

Scientific: This format always displays with an E. You can choose the number of decimal places to display.

Text: Applying the Text number format to a value causes Excel to treat the value as text (even if it looks like a value). This feature is useful for items such as part numbers.

Special: This category contains four additional number formats (Zip Code, Zip Code +4, Phone Number, and Social Security Number).

Custom: This category lets you define custom number formats that aren't included in any of the other categories. I describe custom number formats in the next section.

Figure 6-9 shows an example from each category.

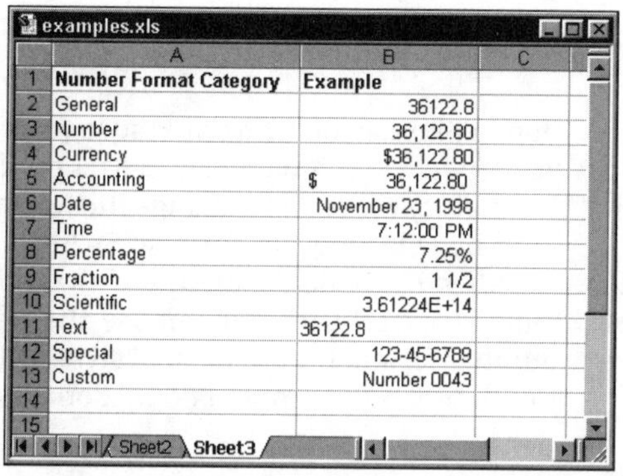

examples.xls

	A	B	C
1	Number Format Category	Example	
2	General	36122.8	
3	Number	36,122.80	
4	Currency	$36,122.80	
5	Accounting	$ 36,122.80	
6	Date	November 23, 1998	
7	Time	7:12:00 PM	
8	Percentage	7.25%	
9	Fraction	1 1/2	
10	Scientific	3.61224E+14	
11	Text	36122.8	
12	Special	123-45-6789	
13	Custom	Number 0043	
14			
15			

Sheet2 Sheet3

Figure 6-9: Examples of values with various number formats.

The best way to learn about number formats is to experiment. Enter some values on a worksheet and practice applying number formats.

Note If the cell displays a series of pound signs (such as #########), it means that the column is not wide enough to display the value using the number format that you selected. The solution is either to make the column wider or to change the number format.

Custom number formats

As I mentioned in the previous section, the Custom number format category lets you create number formats that aren't included in any of the other categories. Excel gives you a great deal of flexibility in creating custom number formats, but it can be rather tricky. You construct a number format by specifying a series of codes. You enter this code sequence in the Type field when the Custom category is selected in the Number panel of the Format Cells dialog box. Here's an example of a simple number format code:

```
0.000
```

This code consists of placeholders and a decimal point. The code tells Excel to display the value with three digits to the right of the decimal place.

Here's another example:

```
00000
```

Preformatting cells

Most of the time, you'll apply number formats to cells that already contain values. You also can preformat cells with a specific number format. Then, when you enter a value, it takes on the format that you specified. You can preformat specific cells, entire rows or columns, or even the entire worksheet.

Rather than preformat an entire worksheet, however, it's a better idea to change the number format for the Normal style (unless you specify otherwise, all cells use the Normal style). You can change the Normal style by selecting the Format⇨Style command. In the Style dialog box, click on the Modify button and then choose the new number format for the Normal style. Refer to Chapter 11 for more information about styles.

This custom number format has five placeholders and displays the value with five digits (no decimal point). This is a good format to use when the cell will hold a zip code (in fact, this is the code actually used by the Zip Code format in the Special category). When you format the cell with this number format and then enter a zip code such as 06604 (Bridgeport, CT), the value is displayed with the leading zero. If you enter this number into a cell with the General number format, it displays as 6604 (no leading zero).

If you scroll through the list of number formats in the Custom category in the Format Cells dialog box, you see many more examples. Most of the time, you'll be able to use one of these codes as a starting point, and only slight customization will be needed.

Excel also makes it possible to specify different format codes for positive numbers, negative numbers, zero values, and text. You do so by separating the codes with a semicolon. The codes are arranged in the following structure:

```
Positive format; Negative format; Zero format; Text format
```

Here's an example of a custom number format that specifies a different format for each of these types:

```
[Green]General;[Red]General;[Black]General;[Blue]General
```

This example takes advantage of the fact that there are special codes for colors. A cell formatted with this custom number format displays its contents in a different color, depending on the value. In this case, positive numbers are green, negative numbers are red, zero is black, and text is blue.

Cross Reference If you want to automatically apply cell formatting such as text or background color based on the cell's contents, a better solution is to use Excel's new Conditional Formatting feature. I discuss this feature in Chapter 11.

The number format that follows (three semicolons) consists of no format codes for each part of the format structure — essentially hiding the contents of the cell:

```
; ; ;
```

Table 6-2 lists the formatting codes available for custom formats, along with brief descriptions. These codes are further described in Excel's online help.

Table 6-2	
Codes Used in Creating Custom Number Formats	
Code	**Comments**
General	Displays the number in General format
#	Digit placeholder
0 (zero)	Digit placeholder
?	Digit placeholder
.	Decimal point
%	Percentage
,	Thousands separator
E- E+ e— e+	Scientific notation
$ — + / ( ) : space	Displays this character
\	Displays the next character in the format
*	Repeats the next character to fill the column width
_	Skips the width of the next character
"text"	Displays the text inside the double quotation marks
@	Text placeholder
[color]	Displays the characters in the color specified
[COLOR n]	Displays the corresponding color in the color palette, where n is a number from 0 to 56
[condition value]	Lets you set your own criteria for each section of a number format

Table 6-3 lists the codes used in creating custom formats for dates and times.

Table 6-3
Codes Used in Creating Custom Formats for Dates and Times

Code	Comments
m	Displays the month as a number without leading zeros (1–12)
mm	Displays the month as a number with leading zeros (01–12)
mmm	Displays the month as an abbreviation (Jan–Dec)
mmmm	Displays the month as a full name (January–December)
d	Displays the day as a number without leading zeros (1–31)
dd	Displays the day as a number with leading zeros (01–31)
ddd	Displays the day as an abbreviation (Sun–Sat)
dddd	Displays the day as a full name (Sunday–Saturday)
yy or yyyy	Displays the year as a two-digit number (00–99), or as a four-digit number (1900–2078)
h or hh	Displays the hour as a number without leading zeros (0–23), or as a number with leading zeros (00–23)
m or mm	Displays the minute as a number without leading zeros (0–59), or as a number with leading zeros (00–59)
s or ss	Displays the second as a number without leading zeros (0–59), or as a number with leading zeros (00–59)
[]	Displays hours greater than 24, or minutes or seconds greater than 60
AM/am/A/a/PM/pm/P/p	Displays the hour using a 12-hour clock; if no AM/PM indicator is used, the hour uses a 24-hour clock

Note   Custom number formats are stored with the worksheet. To make the custom format available in a different workbook, you must copy a cell that uses the custom format to the other workbook.

Web   Figure 6-10 shows several examples of custom number formats, and the workbook
site   is available at this book's Web site. Studying these examples will help you understand the concept and may give you some ideas for your own custom number formats.

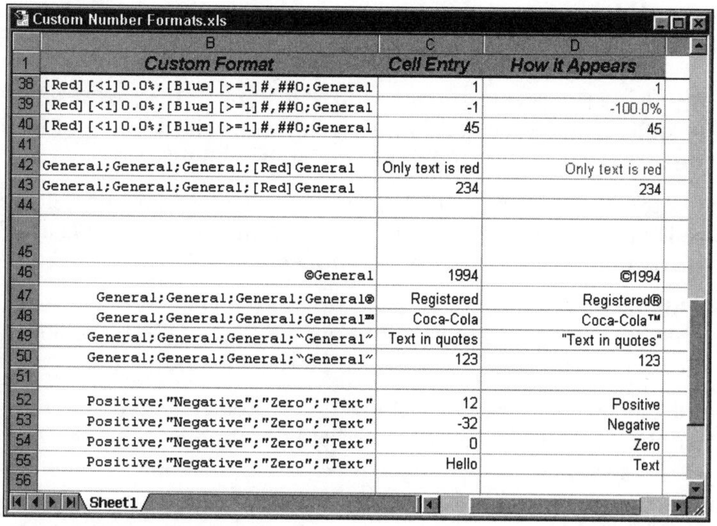

	B	C	D
	Custom Format	**Cell Entry**	**How it Appears**
38	[Red][<1]0.0%;[Blue][>=1]#,##0;General	1	1
39	[Red][<1]0.0%;[Blue][>=1]#,##0;General	-1	-100.0%
40	[Red][<1]0.0%;[Blue][>=1]#,##0;General	45	45
41			
42	General;General;General;[Red]General	Only text is red	Only text is red
43	General;General;General;[Red]General	234	234
44			
45			
46	©General	1994	©1994
47	General;General;General;General®	Registered	Registered®
48	General;General;General;General™	Coca-Cola	Coca-Cola™
49	General;General;General;"General"	Text in quotes	"Text in quotes"
50	General;General;General;"General"	123	123
51			
52	Positive;"Negative";"Zero";"Text"	12	Positive
53	Positive;"Negative";"Zero";"Text"	-32	Negative
54	Positive;"Negative";"Zero";"Text"	0	Zero
55	Positive;"Negative";"Zero";"Text"	Hello	Text
56			

Custom Number Formats.xls — Sheet1

Figure 6-10: Examples of custom number formats.

Basic Cell Formatting

The preceding section discussed number formatting. This section discusses some of the basic *stylistic* formatting options available to you. These formatting techniques apply to values, text, and formulas. The options I discuss in this section are available from the Formatting toolbar. Complete formatting options are available in the Format Cells dialog box, which appears when you choose the Format⇨Cells command.

Cross Reference
The concept of worksheet stylistic formatting is discussed in detail in Chapter 11.

It's important to remember that the formatting you apply works with the selected cell or cells. Therefore, you need to select the cell (or range of cells) before applying the formatting.

Alignment

When you enter text in a cell, it's normally left-justified in the cell. Values, on the other hand, are displayed right-aligned in the cell.

To change the alignment of a cell's contents, select the cell and then click on the appropriate button on the Formatting toolbar. The relevant buttons are as follows:

Align Left: Aligns the text to the left side of the cell. If the text is wider than the cell, it spills over to the cell to the right. If the cell to the right is not empty, the text is truncated and not completely visible.

Center: Centers the text in the cell. If the text is wider than the cell, it spills over to cells on either side if they are empty. If the adjacent cells aren't empty, the text is truncated and not completely visible.

Align Right: Aligns the text to the right side of the cell. If the text is wider than the cell, it spills over to the cell to the left. If the cell to the left is not empty, the text is truncated and not completely visible.

Merge and Center: Centers the text in the selected cells and also merges the cells into one cell. This is a new feature that I describe in detail in Chapter 11.

Font and text size

To change the font and the size of the contents of a cell or range, select the cells and then use the Font and Font Size tools on the Formatting toolbar. These tools are drop-down lists. Click on the arrow on the tool to display a list of fonts or font sizes (see Figure 6-11). Then choose the font or size that you want.

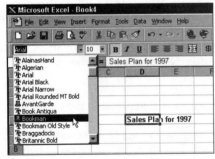

Figure 6-11: Selecting a font from the Font tool.

Attributes

The Formatting toolbar also has buttons that let you make the selected cells bold, italic, or underlined. As you might expect, clicking on the appropriate tool makes the change. These buttons actually are toggles. So, if the cell is already bold, clicking on the Bold button takes the bold off.

Borders

Another type of formatting is borders — lines drawn around all or part of selected cells or ranges. When you click on the Borders button on the Formatting toolbar, it expands to display 12 border choices in a miniature toolbar. You can drag the toolbar's title bar and move it anywhere you want (see Figure 6-12).

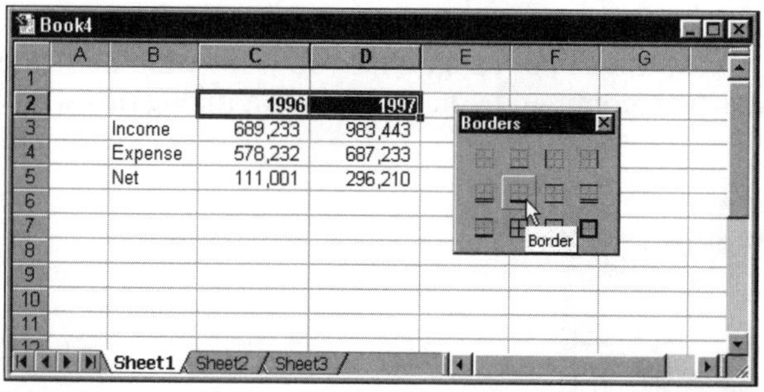

Figure 6-12: The Borders tool on the Formatting toolbar can be dragged anywhere on-screen.

To add a border to the selected cell or cells, just click on the icon that corresponds to the type of border you want. The upper-left icon removes all borders from the selected cells.

Note   Normally, Excel displays gridlines in the worksheet to delineate cells. If you add border formatting, you probably want to turn off the gridline display. To do so, choose the Tools⇨Options command, click on the View tab, and uncheck the Gridlines check box. This makes it easier to see the effects of borders.

Colors

The Fill Color tool lets you quickly change the background color of the cell, and the Font Color tool lets you change the text color. These tools are similar to the Borders tool and also can be moved to a different location.

Data Entry Tips

I wrap up this chapter with some useful tips and techniques that can make your data entry more efficient.

Validating data entry

Excel 97   A new feature in Excel 97 lets you specify the type of data that a cell or range should hold. For example, you might develop a spreadsheet that will be used by others. Assume that the worksheet has an input cell that is used in a formula. This particular cell might require a value between 1 and 12 in order to produce valid results in the formula. You can use the data validation feature to display a message if the user enters a value that does not fall between 1 and 12.

To set up data validation, select the cell or range that you want validated, and then choose the Data⇨Validation command. Excel displays a dialog box with three tabs (see Figure 6-13).

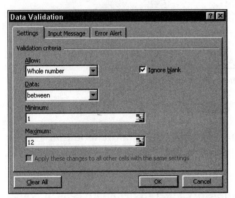

Figure 6-13: The Data Validation dialog box lets you specify the type of data that will be entered in a cell.

    ✦ Click on the Settings tab and specify the type of data that the cell should have. The dialog box changes, depending on your choice in the Allow box.

    ✦ Click on the Input Message tab and specify a message that will appear when the cell is selected (optional). The message will appear from the Office Assistant (if it's displayed), or it will appear in a small pop-up box.

    ✦ Click on the Error Alert tab and specify the message that will appear in a dialog box if invalid data is entered (optional).

You can set up data validation for as many cells as you want.

Caution   Using this technique isn't foolproof. The validation does not occur if the user pastes invalid data into a cell that is set up for validation.

Move the cell pointer after entering data?

Depending on how Excel is configured, pressing the Enter key after entering data into a cell may automatically move the cell pointer to another cell. Some users (like myself) find this annoying; others like it. To change this setting, choose the Tools⇨Options command and click on the Edit tab. The check box that controls this behavior is labeled Move Selection after Enter.

You can also specify the direction in which the cell pointer moves (down, left, up, or right). This also is controlled in the Edit panel of the Options dialog box.

Use arrows instead of Enter

Throughout this chapter, I've mentioned several times that you use the Enter key when you're finished making a cell entry. Well, that's only part of the story. You can use any of the direction keys instead of Enter. And, not surprisingly, these direction keys send you in the direction that you indicate. For example, if you're entering data in a row, press the right-arrow key rather than Enter. The other arrow keys work as expected, and you can even use PgUp and PgDn.

Selecting cells before entering data

Here's a tip that most Excel users don't know about. If you preselect a range of cells, Excel automatically moves the cell pointer to the next cell when you press Enter. If the selection consists of multiple rows, Excel moves down the column; when it reaches the end of the column, it moves to the top of the next column. To skip a cell, just press Enter without entering anything. To go backward, use Shift+Enter. If you prefer to enter the data by rows rather than by columns, use Tab rather than Enter.

If you have lots of data to enter, this technique can save you a few keystrokes — and also ensure that the data you enter winds up in the proper place.

Use Ctrl+Enter for repeated information

If you need to enter the same data into multiple cells, your first inclination may be to enter it once and then copy it to the remaining cells. Here's a better way: Select all the cells that you want to contain the data, enter the value, text, or formula, and then press Ctrl+Enter. The single entry will be inserted into each cell in the selection.

Automatic decimal points

If you're entering lots of numbers with a fixed number of decimal places, you may be interested in this tip that makes Excel work like some adding machines. Select the Tools⇨Options command and click on the Edit tab. Check the check box labeled Fixed Decimal and make sure that it's set for two decimal places. When the Fixed Decimal option is set, Excel supplies the decimal points for you automatically. For example, if you enter **12345** into a cell, Excel interprets it as 123.45 (it adds the decimal point). To restore things back to normal, just uncheck the Fixed Decimal check box in the Options dialog box.

Note

Changing this setting doesn't affect any values that you have already entered.

Using AutoFill

Excel's AutoFill feature makes it easy to insert a series of values or text items in a range of cells. It uses the AutoFill handle (the small box at the lower left of the active cell). You can drag the AutoFill handle to copy the cell or automatically complete a series.

Using AutoComplete

AutoComplete lets you type the first few letters of a text entry into a cell, and Excel automatically completes the entry based on other entries that you've already made in the column. If your data entry task involves repetitious text, this feature is for you.

Here's how it works. Say that you're entering product information in a column. One of your products is named *Widgets*. The first time that you enter *Widgets* into a cell, Excel remembers it. Later, when you start typing *Widgets* in that same column, Excel recognizes it by the first few letters and finishes typing it for you. Just press Enter and you're done. It also changes the case of letters for you automatically. If you start entering *widget* (with a lowercase *w*), Excel makes the *w* uppercase to be consistent with the previous entry in the column.

Besides reducing typing, this feature also ensures that your entries are spelled correctly and are consistent.

Tip

You also can access a mouse-oriented version of this feature by right-clicking on the cell and selecting Pick from List from the shortcut menu. With this method, Excel displays a drop-down box with all the entries in the current column. Click on the one that you want, and it's entered automatically.

If you find the AutoComplete feature distracting, you can turn it off in the Edit panel of the Options dialog box. Just remove the check mark from the check box labeled Enable AutoComplete for Cell Values.

Entering the current date or time into a cell

Sometimes, you need to date-stamp or time-stamp your worksheet. Excel provides two shortcut keys that do this for you:

Current date: Ctrl+; (semicolon)

Current time: Ctrl+Shift+; (semicolon)

Forcing a new line in a cell

If you have lengthy text in a cell, you can force Excel to display it in multiple lines within the cell. Use Alt+Enter to start a new line in a cell. Figure 6-14 shows an example of text in a cell that is displayed in multiple lines. When you add a line break, Excel automatically changes the cell's format to Wrap Text. More about the Wrap Text formatting feature in Chapter 11.

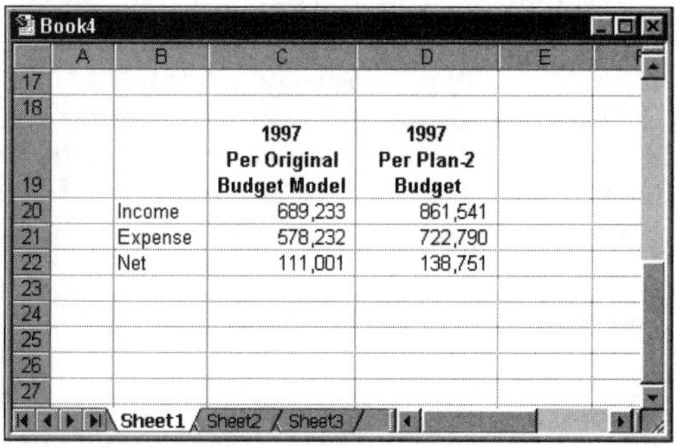

Figure 6-14: Alt+Enter lets you force a line break in a cell.

Entering fractions

If you want Excel to enter a fraction into a cell, leave a space between the whole number part and the fractional part. For example, to enter the decimal equivalent of 6 7/8, enter **6 7/8** and press Enter. Excel enters 6.875 into the cell and automatically formats the cell as a fraction. If there is no whole number part (for example, 1/8), you must enter a zero first, like this: **0 1/8**.

Using a data entry form

If you're entering data that is arranged in rows, you may find it easier to use Excel's built-in data form for data entry. Figure 6-15 shows an example of this.

Figure 6-15: Excel's built-in data form can simplify many data entry tasks.

Start by defining headings for the columns in the first row of your data entry range. You can always erase these entries later if you don't need them. Excel needs headings for this command to work, however. Select any cell in the header row and choose the Data⇨Form command. Excel asks whether you want to use that row for headers (answer Yes). It then displays a dialog box with edit boxes and several buttons. You can use Tab to move between the edit boxes. When you complete the data for a row, click on the New button. Excel dumps the data into the worksheet and clears the dialog box for the next row.

This data form feature has many other useful buttons; I discuss it further in Chapter 23.

Using AutoCorrect for data entry

You can use Excel's AutoCorrect feature to create shortcuts for commonly used words or phrases. For example, if you work for a company named Consolidated Data Processing Corporation, you can create an AutoCorrect entry for an abbreviation, such as cdp. Then, whenever you type *cdp*, Excel automatically changes it to *Consolidated Data Processing Corporation.*

You can customize the AutoCorrect feature by using the Tools⇨AutoCorrect command. Check the option labeled Replace text as you type, and then enter your custom entries (Figure 6-16 shows an example). You can set up as many as you like.

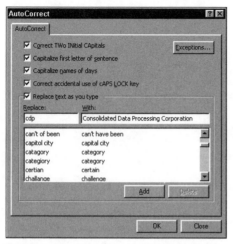

Figure 6-16: You can use Excel's AutoCorrect feature to set up keyboard shortcuts.

Summary

A worksheet cell can contain a value, text, or a formula. This chapter focuses on the task of entering values and formulas. I explain Excel's method of dealing with dates and times and also introduce the concept of number formatting — which makes numbers appear differently but doesn't affect their actual value. I also discuss common editing techniques and basic stylistic formatting. I conclude with a series of general data entry tips.

✦　　　✦　　　✦

Essential Spreadsheet Operations

In this chapter I discuss the common spreadsheet
operations that you need to know. A thorough knowledge
of these procedures will make you work more efficiently.

Working with Worksheets

When you open a new workbook in Excel, the workbook has
some number of worksheets in it. You can specify how many
sheets each new workbook will contain. By default, this
number of worksheets is three. Although empty worksheets
really don't use much additional memory or disk storage
space, they just get in the way. And besides, it's easy to add a
new worksheet when you need one. I strongly recommend
that you change the default value to one worksheet. To do so,
issue the Tools⇨Options command, select the General tab,
and change the Sheets in new workbook setting to one. After
doing this, all new workbooks will have only a single
worksheet.

It may be helpful to think of a workbook as a notebook and
worksheets as pages in the notebook. As with a notebook, you
can activate a particular sheet, add new sheets, remove
sheets, copy sheets, and so on. The remainder of this section
discusses the operations that you perform with worksheets.

Activating worksheets

At any given time, one workbook is the active workbook, and
one sheet in the active workbook is the active sheet. To
activate a different sheet, just click on its sheet tab located at
the bottom of the workbook window. You also can use the
following shortcut keys to activate a different sheet:

Ctrl+PgUp: Activates the previous sheet, if there is one

Ctrl+PgDn: Activates the next sheet, if there is one

If your workbook has several sheets, all tabs may not be visible. You can use the tab scrolling buttons (see Figure 7-1) to scroll the sheet tabs.

Figure 7-1: The tab scrolling buttons let you scroll the sheet tabs to display tabs that are not visible.

The sheet tabs share space with the worksheet's horizontal scrollbar. You also can drag the tab split box (see Figure 7-2) to display more or fewer tabs. Dragging the tab split box simultaneously changes the number of tabs and the size of the horizontal scrollbar.

Figure 7-2: Dragging the tab split box lets you see more (or fewer) sheet tabs.

Tip   When you right-click on any of the tab-scrolling buttons, Excel displays a list of all sheets in the workbook. You can quickly activate a sheet by selecting it from the list.

Adding a new worksheet

There are three ways to add a new worksheet to a workbook:

✦ Select the Insert➪Worksheet command.

✦ Press Shift+F11.

✦ Right-click on a sheet tab, choose the Insert command from the shortcut menu, and then select Worksheet from the Insert dialog box.

Any of these methods cause Excel to insert a new worksheet before the active worksheet, and the new worksheet becomes the active worksheet. The new worksheet, of course, has a sheet tab that displays its name.

Tip   To add additional worksheets after inserting a worksheet, press Ctrl+Y (the shortcut for the Edit➪Repeat command) once for each additional sheet that you want to add.

In Chapter 34 I discuss how to create and use worksheet templates. This feature allows you to add specially formatted or customized worksheets to an existing workbook.

Deleting a worksheet

If you no longer need a worksheet, or if you want to get rid of an empty worksheet in a workbook, you can delete it. There are two ways to do this:

✦ Select the Edit⇨Delete Sheet command.

✦ Right-click on the sheet tab and choose the Delete command from the shortcut menu.

Excel asks you to confirm the fact that you want to delete the sheet.

Tip You can delete multiple sheets with a single command by selecting the sheets that you want to delete. To do so, press Ctrl while you click on the sheet tabs that you want to delete. Then, use either of the preceding methods. To select a group of contiguous sheets, click on the first sheet tab, press Shift, and then click on the last sheet tab.

Caution When you delete a worksheet, it's gone for good. This is one of the few operations in Excel that can't be undone.

Changing a worksheet's name

Worksheets, by default, are named Sheet1, Sheet2, and so on. It's usually a good idea to provide more meaningful names to your worksheets. To change a sheet's name, use any of the following methods:

✦ Choose the Format⇨Sheet⇨Rename command.

✦ Double-click on the sheet tab.

✦ Right-click on the sheet tab and choose the Rename command from the shortcut menu.

In any of these cases, Excel highlights the sheet tab so that you can edit the name or replace it with a new name.

Sheet names can be up to 31 characters, and spaces are allowed. You can't use the following characters in sheet names:

[]   square brackets

:   colon

/	slash
\	backslash
?	question mark
*	asterisk

Keep in mind that the name you give will be displayed on the tab and that a longer name results in wider tabs. Therefore, if you use lengthy sheet names, you'll be able to see fewer sheet tabs without scrolling.

Moving a worksheet

Sometimes, you want to rearrange the order of worksheets in a workbook. If you have a separate worksheet for each sales region, for example, it might be helpful to arrange the worksheets in alphabetical order or by total sales. You also may want to move a worksheet from one workbook to another.

To move a worksheet to a different workbook, both workbooks must be open. There are two ways to move a worksheet:

✦ Select the Edit⇨Move or Copy Sheet command. This command is also available when you right-click on a sheet tab.

✦ Click on the sheet tab and drag it to its desired location (either in the same workbook or in a different workbook). When you drag, the mouse pointer changes to a small sheet and a small arrow guides you.

Dragging is often the easiest method, but if the workbook has many sheets, you may prefer to use the menu command. This command displays the dialog box shown in Figure 7-3. This dialog box lets you select the workbook and the new location.

Figure 7-3: The Move or Copy dialog box.

If you move a worksheet to a workbook that already has a sheet with the same name, Excel changes the name to make it unique. For example, Sheet1 becomes Sheet1 (2).

Tip
You also can move multiple sheets at once by selecting them: Press Ctrl while you click on the sheet tabs that you want to move.

Copying a worksheet

You can make an exact copy of a worksheet — either in its original workbook or in a different workbook. The procedures are similar to those for moving a workbook:

✦ Select the Edit⇨Move or Copy Sheet command. Select the location for the copy and make sure that the check box labeled Create a copy is checked. (The Move or Copy command is also available when you right-click on a sheet tab.)

✦ Click on the sheet tab, press Ctrl, and drag it to its desired location (either in the same workbook or in a different workbook). When you drag, the mouse pointer changes to a small sheet with a plus sign on it.

If necessary, Excel changes the name of the copied sheet to make it unique within the workbook.

Hiding and unhiding a worksheet

In some cases, you may want to hide a worksheet. Hiding a worksheet is useful if you don't want others to see it, or if you just want to get it out of the way. When a sheet is hidden, its sheet tab is hidden also.

To hide a worksheet, choose the Format⇨Sheet⇨Hide command. The active worksheet (or selected worksheets) will be hidden from view. Every workbook must have at least one visible sheet, so Excel won't allow you to hide all sheets in a workbook.

To unhide a hidden worksheet, choose the Format⇨Sheet⇨Unhide command. Excel pops up a dialog box that lists all hidden sheets. Chose the sheet that you want to unhide and click on OK. You can't select multiple sheets from this dialog box, so you need to repeat the command for each sheet that you want to unhide.

Zooming worksheets

Excel lets you scale the size of your worksheets. Normally, everything you see onscreen is displayed at 100 percent. You can change the "zoom percentage" from 10 percent (very tiny) to 400 percent (huge). Using a small zoom percentage can help you get a bird's-eye view of your worksheet to see how it's laid out. Zooming in is useful if your eyesight isn't quite what it used to be and you have trouble deciphering those 8-point sales figures. Figure 7-4 shows a window zoomed to 10 percent and a window zoomed to 400 percent.

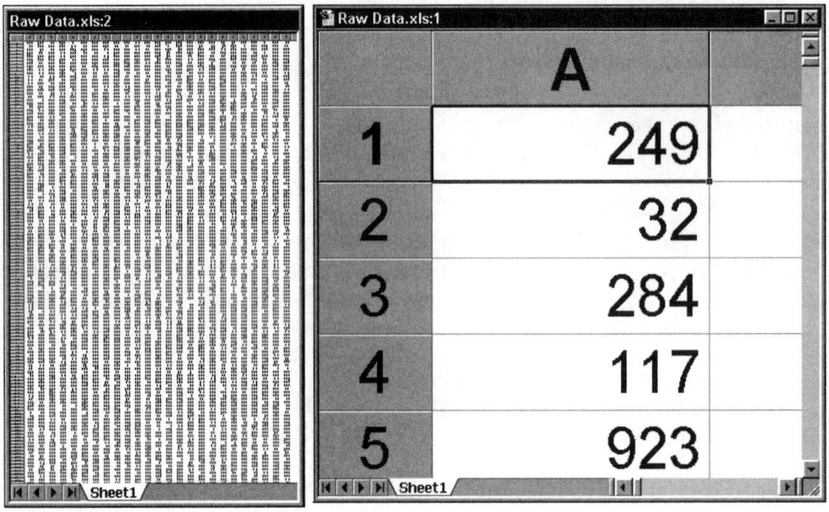

Figure 7-4: A window zoomed to 10 percent and a window zoomed to 400 percent.

The easiest way to change the zoom factor of the active worksheet is to use the Zoom tool on the Standard toolbar. Just click on the arrow and select the desired zoom factor. Your screen transforms immediately. You can also type a zoom percentage directly into the Zoom tool. The Selection pull-down list zooms the worksheet to display only the selected cells (useful if you want to view only a particular range).

Zooming only affects the active worksheet, so you can use different zoom factors for different worksheets.

If the Standard toolbar isn't displayed, you can set the zoom percentage by using the View➪Zoom command. This command displays the dialog box shown in Figure 7-5. You can select an option or enter a value between 10 and 400 into the edit box next to the Custom option.

Figure 7-5: The Zoom dialog box.

Note The zoom factor affects only how the worksheet is displayed on-screen. It has no effect on how it is printed. There are separate options for changing the size of your printed output (use the File⇨Page Setup command). See Chapter 12 for details.

Excel 97 If your worksheet uses named ranges (refer to Chapter 8), you'll find that zooming your worksheet down to 39 percent or less displays the name of the range overlaid on the cells. This is useful for getting an overview of how a worksheet is laid out.

Excel 97 If you're using a Microsoft IntelliMouse, you can change the zoom factor by pressing Ctrl while you spin the mouse wheel. Each spin changes the zoom factor by 15 percent (but you can't zoom out more than 100 percent). If you find that you do a lot of zooming in, you can change the default behavior for the mouse wheel from scrolling to zooming. To change the default, select the Tools⇨Options command, click on the General tab, and then select the Zoom on roll with IntelliMouse check box. After making this change, you can zoom by spinning the wheel and you won't have to press Ctrl.

Views, Split Sheets, and Frozen Panes

This section discusses a few additional worksheet options at your disposal.

Multiple views

Sometimes, you may want to view two different parts of a worksheet at once. Or, you may want to examine more than one sheet in the same workbook. You can accomplish either of these actions by opening a new view to the workbook. You do this by displaying your workbook in one or more additional windows.

To create a new view of the active workbook, choose the Window⇨New Window command. Excel displays a new window with the active workbook. Figure 7-6 shows an example of this. Notice the text in the windows' title bars: *Budget.xls:1* and *Budget.xls:2*.

To help you keep track of the windows, Excel appends a colon and a number to each window.

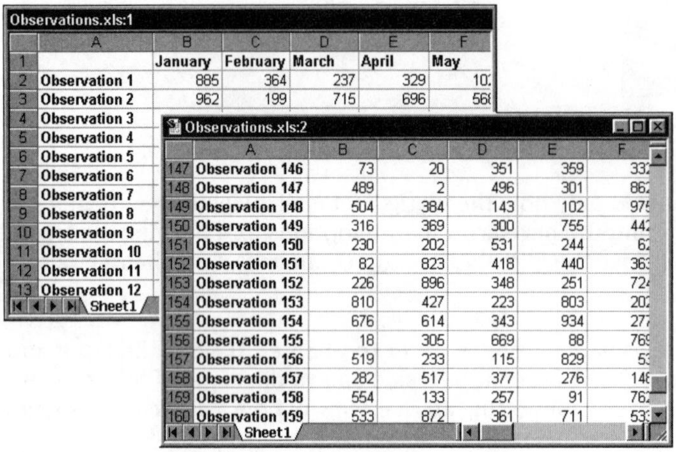

Figure 7-6: Two views of the same workbook.

A single workbook can have as many views (that is, separate windows) as you like. Each window is independent of the others. In other words, scrolling to a new location in one window doesn't cause scrolling in the other window(s). This also lets you display a different worksheet in a separate window. Figure 7-7 shows three views in the same workbook. Each view is displaying a different worksheet.

You can close these additional windows using the standard methods. For example, clicking on the Close button title bar closes the active window but doesn't close the other windows.

Cross Reference As I explain in Chapter 8, displaying multiple windows for a workbook also makes it easier to copy information from one worksheet to another. You can use Excel's drag-and-drop procedures to do this.

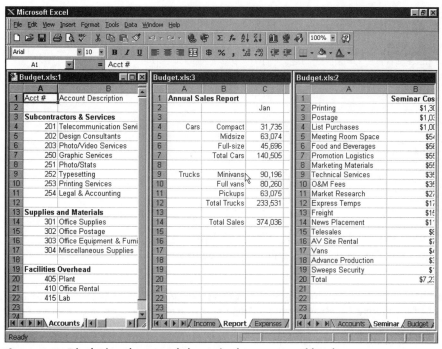

Figure 7-7: Displaying three worksheets in the same workbook.

Splitting panes

If you prefer not to clutter your screen with additional windows, Excel provides another option for viewing multiple parts of the same worksheet. The Window➪ Split command splits the active worksheet into two or four separate panes. The split occurs at the location of the cell pointer. You can use the mouse to drag the pane and make it the size you desire.

Figure 7-8 shows a worksheet split into four panes. Notice that row numbers and column letters aren't continuous. In other words, splitting panes lets you display widely separated areas of a worksheet in a single window. The two top-to-bottom stacked panes always have the same column headings, and the two side-by-side panes always have the same row headings. To remove the split panes, choose the Window➪Remove Split command.

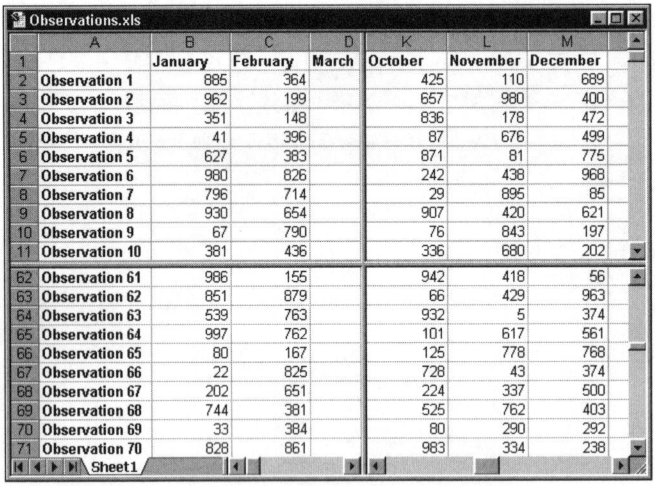

	A	B	C	D	K	L	M
1		January	February	March	October	November	December
2	Observation 1	885	364		425	110	689
3	Observation 2	962	199		657	980	400
4	Observation 3	351	148		836	178	472
5	Observation 4	41	396		87	676	499
6	Observation 5	627	383		871	81	775
7	Observation 6	980	826		242	438	968
8	Observation 7	796	714		29	895	85
9	Observation 8	930	654		907	420	621
10	Observation 9	67	790		76	843	197
11	Observation 10	381	436		336	680	202
62	Observation 61	986	155		942	418	56
63	Observation 62	851	879		66	429	963
64	Observation 63	539	763		932	5	374
65	Observation 64	997	762		101	617	561
66	Observation 65	80	167		125	778	768
67	Observation 66	22	825		728	43	374
68	Observation 67	202	651		224	337	500
69	Observation 68	744	381		525	762	403
70	Observation 69	33	384		80	290	292
71	Observation 70	828	861		983	334	238

Figure 7-8: This worksheet is split into four panes.

Tip

Another way to split and unsplit panes is to drag either the vertical or horizontal split bar. Figure 7-9 shows where these split bars are located. To remove split panes using the mouse, drag the pane separator all the way to the edge of the window, or just double-click on it.

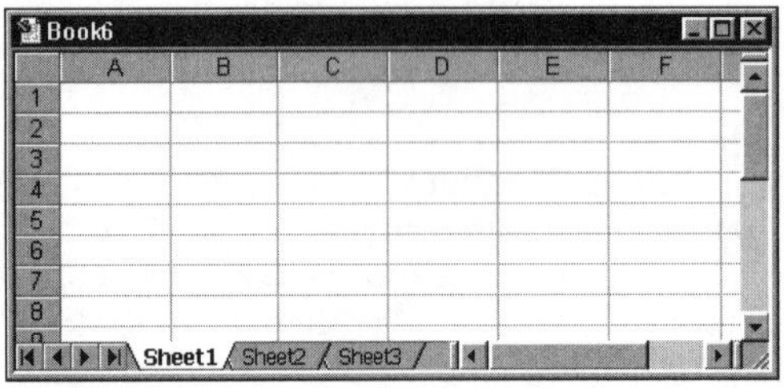

Figure 7-9: Drag these split bars to create panes.

Freezing panes

Many worksheets, such as the one shown in Figure 7-10, are set up with row and column headings.

When you scroll through such a worksheet, it's easy to get lost when the row and column headings scroll out of view, as you can see in Figure 7-11. Excel provides a handy solution to this problem: freezing panes.

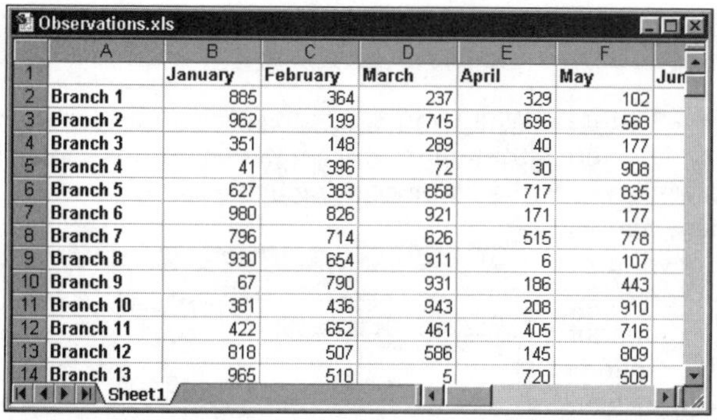

	A	B	C	D	E	F	
		January	February	March	April	May	Jun
2	Branch 1	885	364	237	329	102	
3	Branch 2	962	199	715	696	568	
4	Branch 3	351	148	289	40	177	
5	Branch 4	41	396	72	30	908	
6	Branch 5	627	383	858	717	835	
7	Branch 6	980	826	921	171	177	
8	Branch 7	796	714	626	515	778	
9	Branch 8	930	654	911	6	107	
10	Branch 9	67	790	931	186	443	
11	Branch 10	381	436	943	208	910	
12	Branch 11	422	652	461	405	716	
13	Branch 12	818	507	586	145	809	
14	Branch 13	965	510	5	720	509	

Observations.xls — Sheet1

Figure 7-10: A worksheet with row and column headings.

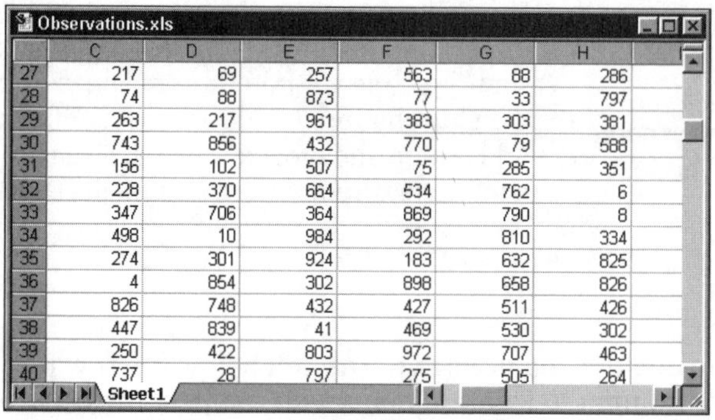

	C	D	E	F	G	H	
27	217	69	257	563	88	286	
28	74	88	873	77	33	797	
29	263	217	961	383	303	381	
30	743	856	432	770	79	588	
31	156	102	507	75	285	351	
32	228	370	664	534	762	6	
33	347	706	364	869	790	8	
34	498	10	984	292	810	334	
35	274	301	924	183	632	825	
36	4	854	302	898	658	826	
37	826	748	432	427	511	426	
38	447	839	41	469	530	302	
39	250	422	803	972	707	463	
40	737	28	797	275	505	264	

Observations.xls — Sheet1

Figure 7-11: It's easy to lose your bearings when the row and column headers scroll out of view.

Figure 7-12 shows the worksheet from the previous figure, but with frozen panes. In this case, row 1 and column A are frozen in place. This keeps the headings visible while scrolling through the worksheet.

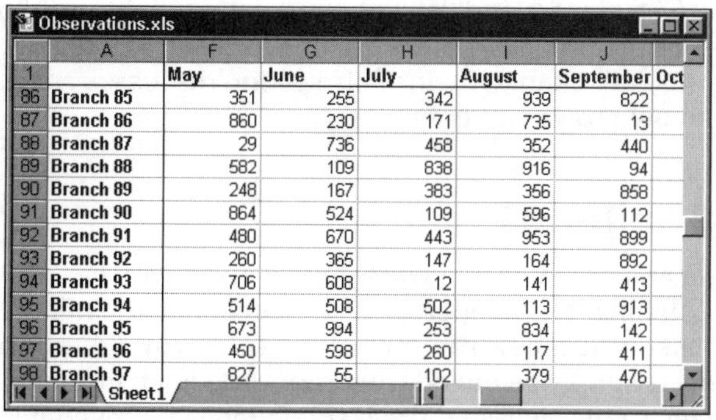

	A	F	G	H	I	J	
		May	June	July	August	September	Oct
86	Branch 85	351	255	342	939	822	
87	Branch 86	860	230	171	735	13	
88	Branch 87	29	736	458	352	440	
89	Branch 88	582	109	838	916	94	
90	Branch 89	248	167	383	356	858	
91	Branch 90	864	524	109	596	112	
92	Branch 91	480	670	443	953	899	
93	Branch 92	260	365	147	164	892	
94	Branch 93	706	608	12	141	413	
95	Branch 94	514	508	502	113	913	
96	Branch 95	673	994	253	834	142	
97	Branch 96	450	598	260	117	411	
98	Branch 97	827	55	102	379	476	

Observations.xls — Sheet1

Figure 7-12: A worksheet with the row and column headings frozen in place.

Naming views

Some users may be interested in a feature called *named views*. This feature lets you give names to various views of your worksheet and to switch quickly among these named views. A view includes settings for window size and position, frozen panes or titles, outlining, zoom factor, the active cell, print area, and many of the settings in the Options dialog box. Optionally, a view can include hidden print settings and hidden rows and columns. If you find that you're constantly fiddling with these settings and then changing them back, using named views can save you lots of effort.

In previous versions of Excel, the named view feature required an add-in. This feature is built into Excel 97.

When you select the View⇨Custom Views command, you get the dialog box shown in the accompanying figure.

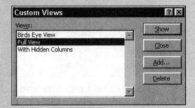

The Custom Views dialog box displays a list of all named views. To select a particular view, just select it from the list and click on the Show button. To add a view, click on the Add button and provide a name. To delete a named view from the list, click on the Delete button.

To freeze panes, start by moving the cell pointer to the cell below the row to freeze and to the right of the column to freeze. Then select the Window⇨Freeze Panes command. Excel inserts dark lines to indicate the frozen rows and columns. You'll find that these frozen rows and column remain visible as you scroll throughout the worksheet. To remove the frozen panes, select the Window⇨Unfreeze Panes command.

Working with Rows and Columns

Every worksheet has exactly 65,536 rows and 256 columns. Although it would be nice to be able to specify the number of rows and columns for each worksheet, these values are fixed and you can't change them. This section discusses some worksheet operations that involve rows and columns.

Inserting rows and columns

Although the number of rows and columns in a worksheet is fixed, you can still insert and delete rows and columns. These operations don't change the number of rows or columns. Rather, inserting a new row moves the other rows down to accommodate it. The last row is simply removed from the worksheet. Inserting a new column shifts the columns to the right and the last column is removed if it's empty.

Note If the last row (row 65,536) is not empty, you can't insert a new row. Similarly, if the last column (column IV) contains information, Excel won't let you insert a new column. You can use this to your advantage. For example, if you want to ensure that no one adds new rows or columns to your worksheet, simply enter something (anything) into cell IV65536. Attempting to add a row or column displays the dialog box shown in Figure 7-13.

To insert a new row or rows, you can use any of the following techniques:

✦ Select an entire row or multiple rows by clicking on the row numbers in the worksheet border. Select the Insert⇨Rows command.

✦ Select an entire row or multiple rows by clicking on the row numbers in the worksheet border. Right-click and choose Insert from the shortcut menu.

✦ Move the cell pointer to the row that you want to insert and select the Insert⇨Rows command. If you select multiple cells in the column, Excel inserts additional rows that correspond to the number of cells selected in the column.

The procedure for inserting a new column or columns is the same (but you use the Insert⇨Column command).

Figure 7-13: Excel's way of telling you that you can't add a new row or column.

You also can insert cells rather than just rows or columns. Select the range into which you want to add new cells and select the Insert⇨Cells command. To insert cells, the other cells must be shifted to the right or shifted down. Therefore, Excel displays the dialog box shown in Figure 7-14 to find out the direction that you want to shift the cells.

Figure 7-14: When you insert cells, Excel needs to know the direction to shift the cells to make room.

Caution Shifting cells around could cause problems in other places in your worksheet, so use caution with the Insert➪Cells command. Better yet, avoid it if you can and insert entire rows or columns. In fact, I've *never* used this command.

Deleting rows and columns

To delete a row or rows, use any of the following methods:

✦ Select an entire row or multiple rows by clicking on the row numbers in the worksheet border; then select the Edit➪Delete command.

✦ Select an entire row or multiple rows by clicking on the row numbers in the worksheet border. Right-click on and choose Delete from the shortcut menu.

✦ Move the cell pointer to the row that you want to delete and select the Edit➪Delete command. In the dialog box that appears, choose the Entire row option. If you select multiple cells in the column, Excel deletes all selected rows.

Deleting columns works the same way. If you discover that you accidentally deleted a row or column, select the Edit➪Undo command (or Ctrl+Z) to undo the action.

Changing column widths and row heights

Excel provides several different ways to change the widths of columns and the height of rows.

Changing column widths

Column width is measured in terms of the number of characters that will fit into the cell's width. By default, each column's width is 8.43. This is actually a rather meaningless measure because in most fonts the width of individual characters varies — the letter *i* is much narrower than the letter *W,* for example.

There are a number of ways to change the width of a column or columns. Before changing the width, you can select multiple columns so that the width will be the same for all selected columns. To select multiple columns, click and drag in the column border, or press Ctrl while you select individual columns. To select all columns, click on the Select All button in the upper-left corner of the worksheet border (or press Ctrl+Shift+spacebar).

✦ Drag the right column border with the mouse until the column is the desired width.

✦ Choose the Format➪Column➪Width command and enter a value in the Column Width dialog box.

✦ Choose the Format⇨Column⇨AutoFit Selection command. This adjusts the width of the selected column so that the widest entry in the column fits. If you want, you can just select cells in the column, and the column is adjusted based on the widest entry in your selection.

✦ Double-click on the right border of a column to automatically set the column width to the widest entry in the column.

Tip To change the default width of all columns, use the Format⇨Column⇨Standard Width command. This displays a dialog box into which you enter the new default column width. All columns that haven't been previously adjusted take on the new column width.

Changing row heights

Row height is measured in points (a standard unit of measurement in the printing trade). The default row height depends on the font defined in the Normal style. Excel adjusts row heights automatically to accommodate the tallest font in the row. So, if you change the font size of a cell to, say, 20 points, Excel makes the column taller so that the entire text is visible.

You can set the row height manually, however, using any of several techniques. As with columns, you can select multiple rows.

✦ Drag the lower row border with the mouse until the row is the desired height.

✦ Choose the Format⇨Row⇨Height command and enter a value (in points) in the Row Height dialog box.

✦ Double-click on the bottom border of a row to automatically set the row height to the tallest entry in the row. You also can use the Format⇨ Row⇨AutoFit command for this.

Changing the row height is useful for spacing out rows and is preferable to inserting empty rows between lines of data. Figure 7-15 shows a simple report that uses taller rows to produce a double-spaced effect.

Hiding rows and columns

Excel lets you hide rows and columns. This may be useful if you don't want users to see particular information.

Tip You can also hide the rows and columns that aren't used in your worksheet — effectively making your worksheet appear smaller.

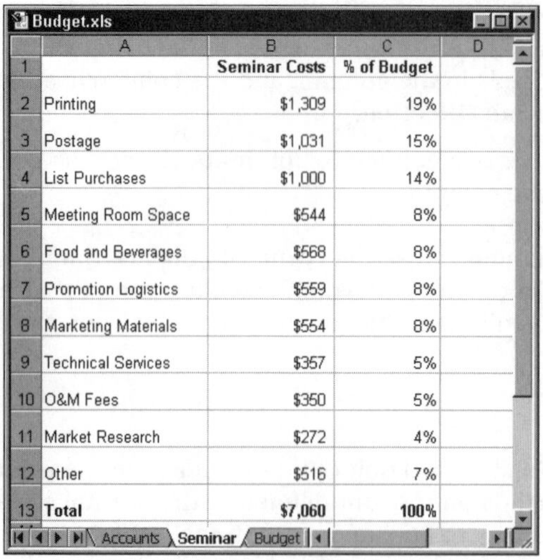
Budget.xls

	A	B	C	D
1		Seminar Costs	% of Budget	
2	Printing	$1,309	19%	
3	Postage	$1,031	15%	
4	List Purchases	$1,000	14%	
5	Meeting Room Space	$544	8%	
6	Food and Beverages	$568	8%	
7	Promotion Logistics	$559	8%	
8	Marketing Materials	$554	8%	
9	Technical Services	$357	5%	
10	O&M Fees	$350	5%	
11	Market Research	$272	4%	
12	Other	$516	7%	
13	**Total**	**$7,060**	**100%**	

Accounts | Seminar | Budget

Figure 7-15: Changing row heights is the best way to space out the rows in a report.

To hide a row or rows, select the row or rows and choose the Format➪RowHide command. To hide a column or columns, select the column or columns and choose the Format➪Column➪Hide command.

You also can drag the row or column's border to hide it. To hide a row, drag the bottom border upward. To hide a column, drag the column's right border to the left.

A hidden row is actually a row with its height set to zero. Similarly, a hidden column has a column width of zero. When you use the arrow keys to move the cell pointer, cells in hidden rows or columns are skipped. In other words, you can't use the arrow keys to move to a cell in a hidden row or column.

Unhiding a hidden row or column can be a bit tricky because it's difficult to select a row or column that's hidden. The solution is to select the columns or rows that are adjacent to the hidden column or row (select at least one column or row on either side). Then, select the Format➪Row➪Unhide or the Format➪Column➪Unhide command. Another method is to use the Edit➪Go To command (or its F5 equivalent) to activate a cell in a hidden row or column. For example, if column A is hidden, you can press F5 and specify cell A1 (or any other cell in column A). This moves the cell pointer to the hidden column. Then you can use the appropriate command to unhide the column.

Summary

This chapter delves into some important operations that all Excel users should know about. I cover topics dealing with adding and removing worksheets, renaming worksheets, and moving and copying worksheets. I also discuss topics that help you control the view of your worksheet: freezing panes and splitting panes. I conclude with a discussion of operations that involve entire rows or columns.

✦　　✦　　✦

Working with Cells and Ranges

◆ ◆ ◆ ◆

In This Chapter

Essential operations that involve cells and ranges: selecting, copying, moving, and so on

Naming cells and ranges (and why this is a good idea)

Deleting and redefining names

◆ ◆ ◆ ◆

This chapter discusses a variety of techniques that you use to work with cells and ranges.

Cells and Ranges

As you know, a cell is a single addressable element in a worksheet that can hold a value, text, or a formula. A cell is identified by an *address,* which is made up of its column letter and row number. For example, cell D12 is the cell in the fourth column and the twelfth row.

A group of cells is called a *range.* You designate a range address by specifying its upper-left cell address and its lower-right cell address, separated by a colon.

Here are some examples of range addresses:

A1:B1	Two cells that occupy one row and two columns
C24	A range that consists of a single cell
A1:A100	100 cells in column A
A1:D416	cells (four rows by four columns)
C1:C65536	An entire column of cells; this range also can be expressed as C:C
A6:IV6	An entire row of cells; this range also can be expressed as 6:6
A1:IV65536	All cells in a worksheet

Alternate cell addresses

Normally, you reference cells by their column letter and row number (cell D16 for the cell at the intersection of the fourth column and sixteenth row, for example). You may not know it, but Excel gives you a choice in this matter. You can select the Tools⇨Options command (General tab) and then choose the R1C1 reference style option. After selecting this option, the column borders in your worksheets are displayed as numbers rather than as letters. Furthermore, all cell references in your formulas use this different notation.

If you find RC notation confusing, you're not alone. RC notation isn't too bad when you're dealing with absolute references. But, when relative references are involved, the brackets can drive you batty.

The numbers in the brackets refer to the relative position of the reference. For example, R[−5]C[−3] specifies the cell that's five rows above and three columns to the left. On the other hand, R[5]C[3] references the cell that's five rows *below* and three columns to the *right*. If the brackets are omitted, it specifies the same row or column: R[5]C refers to the cell five rows below in the same column.

See the table for examples of how normal formulas would translate to RC notation. These formulas are in cell B1 (otherwise known as R1C1).

Formulas Using Column Lettersand Row Numbers	Formulas Using RC Notation
=$A$1	=R1C1
=A1+A2+A3	=RC[-1]+R[1]C[-1]+R[2]C[-1]
=(A1+A2)/$A$3	=(RC[-1]+R[1]C[-1])/R3C1

Note   When you're simply navigating through a worksheet or formatting cells, it's not all that important that you know the range address with which you're working. Understanding cell addresses is most important when creating formulas, as you'll see in the next chapter.

Selecting ranges

To perform an operation a range of cells in a worksheet, you must select the range of cells first. For example, if you want to make the text bold for a range of cells, you must select the range and then click on the Bold button on the Formatting toolbar (or, use any of several other methods to make the text bold).

When you select a range, the cells appear in reverse video. The exception is the active cell, which remains its normal color. Figure 8-1 shows an example of a selected range in a worksheet.

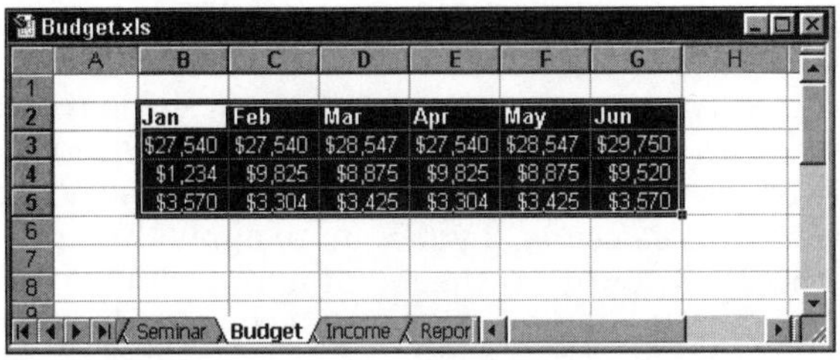

Figure 8-1: When you select a range, it appears highlighted. The active cell within the range is not highlighted.

You can select a range in several ways:

✦ Click on the mouse and drag to highlight the range. If you drag to the end of the screen, the worksheet will scroll.

✦ Press the Shift key while you use the direction keys to select a range.

✦ Press F8 and then move the cell pointer with the direction keys to highlight the range. Press F8 again to return the direction keys to normal movement.

✦ Use the Edit➪Go To command (or press F5) and enter a range's address manually into the Go To dialog box. When you click on OK, Excel selects the cells in the range that you specified.

Tip   As you're selecting a range, Excel displays the number of rows and columns in your selection the Name box (located on the left side of the formula bar).

Selecting complete rows and columns

You can select entire rows and columns much as you select ranges. There are several ways to do this:

✦ Click on the row or column border to select a single row or column.

✦ To select multiple adjacent rows or columns, simply click on a row or column border and drag to highlight additional rows or columns.

✦ To select multiple (nonadjacent) rows or columns, press Ctrl while you click on the rows or columns that you want.

✦ Press Ctrl+spacebar to select a column. The column of the active cell (or columns of the selected cells) will be highlighted.

✦ Press Shift+spacebar to select a row. The row of the active cell (or rows of the selected cells) will be highlighted.

✦ Click on the Select All button (or Ctrl+Shift+spacebar) to select all rows. Selecting all rows is the same as selecting all columns, which is the same as selecting all cells.

Selecting noncontiguous ranges

Most of the time, the ranges that you select will be *contiguous* — a single rectangle of cells. Excel also lets you work with noncontiguous ranges. A *noncontiguous range* consists of two or more ranges (or single cells), not necessarily next to each other. This is also known as a *multiple selection*. If you want to apply the same formatting to cells in different areas of your worksheet, one approach is to make a multiple selection. When the appropriate cells or ranges are selected, the formatting that you select is applied to them all. Figure 8-2 shows a noncontiguous range selected in a worksheet.

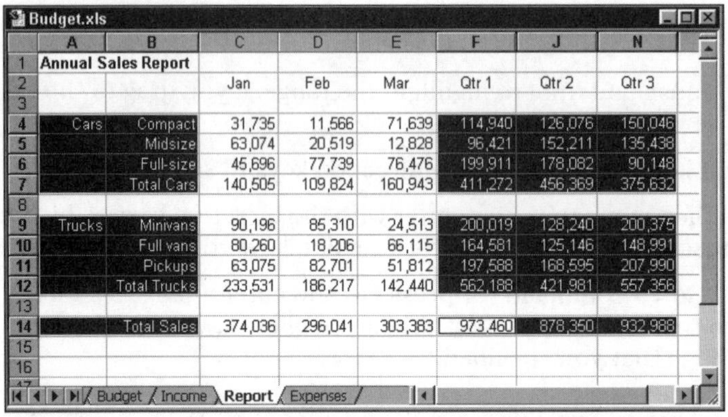

Figure 8-2: Excel lets you select noncontiguous ranges, as shown here.

You can select a noncontiguous range in several ways:

✦ Hold down Ctrl while you click the mouse and drag to highlight the individual cells or ranges.

✦ From the keyboard, select a range as described previously (using F8 or the Shift key). Then press Shift+F8 to select another range without canceling the previous range selections.

✦ Use the Edit⇨Go To command and enter a range's address manually into the Go To dialog box. Separate the different ranges with a comma. When you click on OK, Excel selects the cells in the ranges that you specified (see Figure 8-3).

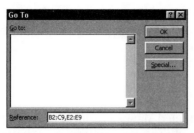

Figure 8-3: Enter a noncontiguous range by separating the ranges with a comma. This example will select a noncontiguous range made up of two ranges: B2:C9 and E2:E9.

Selecting multisheet ranges

So far, this discussion has focused on ranges on a single worksheet. As you know, an Excel workbook can contain more than one worksheet. And, as you might expect, ranges can extend across multiple worksheets. You can think of these as three-dimensional ranges.

Say that you have a workbook set up to track expenses by department. A common approach is to use a separate worksheet for each department. This approach makes it easy to organize the data, and you can click on a sheet tab to view the information for a particular department.

Figure 8-4 shows a workbook that has four sheets named Total, Marketing, Operations, and Manufacturing. The sheets are laid out identically. The only difference is the values. The Total sheet contains formulas that compute the sum of the corresponding items in the three departmental worksheets.

Department Budget Summary.xls

	A	B	C	D	E	F
1		Quarter 1	Quarter 2	Quarter 3	Quarter 4	
2	Salaries	120000	120000	120000	120000	
3	Travel	5000	6000	5000	6000	
4	Supplies	2500	2500	2500	2500	
5	Facility	3000	3000	3000	3000	
6	Total	130500	131500	130500	131500	
7						
8						
9						

Total \ Marketing \ Operations \ Manufacturing

Figure 8-4: A sample workbook that uses multiple worksheets.

The worksheets in the Department Budget Summary workbook aren't formatted in any way. If you want to apply number formats, for example, one (not so efficient) approach is to simply format the values in each worksheet separately. A better technique is to select a multisheet range and format the cells in all of the sheets at once. Here's a step-by-step example of multisheet formatting using the workbook shown in Figure 8-4.

1. Activate the Total worksheet.
2. Select the range that contains values: B2:E6.
3. Press Shift and click on the sheet tab labeled Manufacturing. This selects all worksheets between the active worksheet (Totals) and the sheet tab that you click on — in essence, a three-dimensional range of cells (see Figure 8-5). Notice that the workbook window's title bar displays *[Group]*. This is a reminder that you've selected a group of sheets and that you're in Group edit mode.
4. Click on the Comma Style button on the Formatting toolbar. This applies comma formatting to the selected cells.
5. Click one of the other sheet tabs. This selects the sheet and also cancels Group mode; *[Group]* is no longer displayed in the title bar.

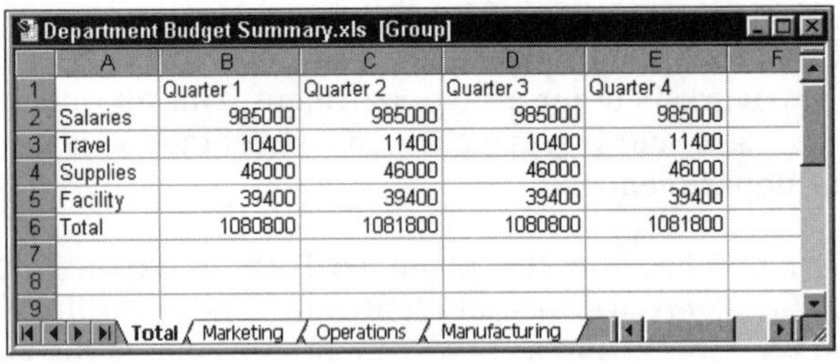

	A	B	C	D	E	F
1		Quarter 1	Quarter 2	Quarter 3	Quarter 4	
2	Salaries	985000	985000	985000	985000	
3	Travel	10400	11400	10400	11400	
4	Supplies	46000	46000	46000	46000	
5	Facility	39400	39400	39400	39400	
6	Total	1080800	1081800	1080800	1081800	
7						
8						
9						

Figure 8-5: Excel in Group mode. A three-dimensional range of cells is selected.

Comma formatting was applied to all of the values in the selected sheets.

In general, selecting a multisheet range is a simple two-step process: select the range one sheet and then select the worksheets to include in the range. You can press Shift to select a group of contiguous worksheets or hold down Ctrl to select individual worksheets. If all of the worksheets in a workbook aren't laid out the same, you can skip the sheets that you don't want to format. In either case, the selected sheet tabs appear in reverse video, and Excel displays *[Group]* in the title bar.

Tip To select all sheets in a workbook, right-click on any sheet tab and choose Select All Sheets from the shortcut menu.

Special selections

Earlier, I mentioned the Edit⇨Go To command (or F5) as a way to select (or go to) a cell or range. Excel also provides a way to select only "special" cells in the workbook or in a selected range. You do this by choosing the Edit⇨Go To command, which brings up the Go To dialog box. Clicking on the Special button displays the Go To Special dialog box shown in Figure 8-6.

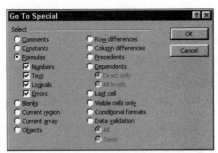

Figure 8-6: The Go To Special dialog box lets you select specific types of cells.

After making your choice in the dialog box, Excel selects the qualifying subset of cells in the current selection. Usually, this results in a multiple selection. If no cells qualify, Excel lets you know.

Note If you bring up the Go To Special dialog box with only one cell selected, Excel bases its selection on the entire active area of the worksheet.

Table 8-1 offers a description of the options available in this dialog box. Some of the options can be quite useful.

Table 8-1
Select Special Options

Option	What It Does
Comments	Selects only the cells that contain cell comments (see the next section). Ctrl+Shift+? is the shortcut for this.
Constants	Selects all nonempty cells that don't contain formulas. This option is useful if you have a model set up, and you want to clear out all input cells and enter new values. The formulas remain intact.
Formulas	Selects cells that contain formulas. Qualify this by selecting the type of result: numbers, text, logical values (TRUE or FALSE), or errors. These terms are described in the next chapter.

(continued)

Table 8-1 (continued)

Option	What It Does
Blanks	Selects all empty cells.
Current Region	Selects a rectangular range of cells around the active cell. This range is determined by surrounding blank rows and columns. Ctrl+* is the shortcut key for this.
Current Array	Selects the entire array. I discuss arrays in Chapter 20.
Objects	Selects all graphic objects on the worksheet.
Row Differences	Analyzes the selection and selects cells that are different from other cells in each row. Ctrl+\ is the shortcut for this.
Column Differences	Analyzes the selection and selects the cells that are different from other cells in each column. Ctrl+Shift+| is the shortcut for this.
Precedents	Selects cells that are referred to in the formulas in the active cell or selection. You can select either direct precedents or precedents at any level.
Dependents	Selects cells with formulas that refer to the active cell or selection. You can select either direct dependents or dependents at any level.
Last Cell	Selects the bottom-right cell in the worksheet that contains data or formatting. Ctrl+End is the shortcut for this.
Visible Cells Only	Selects only visible cells in the selection. This option is useful when dealing with outlines or an autofiltered list.
Conditional Formats	Selects cells that have a conditional format applied (using the Format⇨Conditional Formatting command).
Data Validation	Selects cells that are set up for data entry validation (using the Data⇨Validation command). The All option selects all such cells. The Same option selects only the cells that have the same validation rules as the active cell.

Annotating a Cell

Excel's cell comment feature lets you attach a comment to a cell. This feature is useful when you need to document a particular value. It's also useful to help you remember what a formula does.

Excel 97 In previous versions of Excel, cell comments were known as cell notes. Excel 97 not only changed the name of this feature, but added quite a bit of new functionality.

To add a comment to a cell, select the cell and choose the Insert⇨Comment command (or Shift+F2). Excel inserts a comment that points to the active cell, as shown in Figure 8-7. Initially, the comment consists of your name. Enter the text for the cell comment, and then click anywhere in the worksheet to hide the comment.

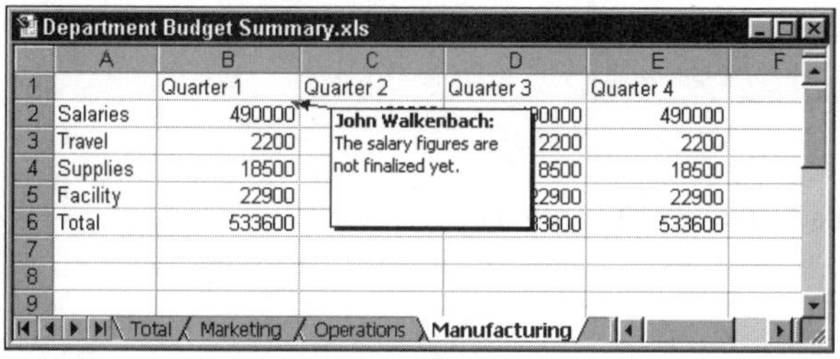

Figure 8-7: Excel lets you add a descriptive note to a cell.

Cells that have a comment attached display a small red triangle in the upper-right corner. When you move the mouse pointer over a cell that contains a comment the comment becomes visible.

Note Use the Tools⇨Options command (View tab) to control how cell comment indicators are displayed. You can turn these indicators off if you like.

Tip If you would like all cell comments to be visible (regardless of the location of the cell pointer), use the View⇨Comments command. This command is a toggle; select it again to hide all cell comments. To edit a comment, activate the cell, right-click, and choose Edit Comment from the shortcut menu

To delete a cell comment, activate the cell that contains the comment, right-click, and choose Delete Comment from the shortcut menu.

Deleting Cell Contents

To erase the contents of a cell or range, select the cell or range and press Delete. Or you can use the Edit⇨Clear command, which provides additional options.

Tip To erase cells using only the mouse, select the cell or range to be deleted. Then click on the fill handle — the small square at the lower right of the selection indicator (see Figure 8-8). When you move the mouse pointer over the fill handle, the pointer changes to a cross. As you drag up and/or to the left, Excel grays out the selection. Release the mouse button to erase the contents of the grayed selection.

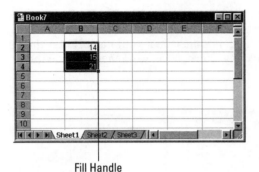

Fill Handle

Figure 8-8: Use the fill handle to erase cell contents using the mouse.

Copying a Range

Copying the contents of a cell is a very common operation. You can do any of the following:

✦ Copy a cell to another cell.

✦ Copy a cell to a range of cells. The source cell is copied to every cell in the destination range.

✦ Copy a range to another range. Both ranges must be the same size.

Note Copying a cell normally copies the cell contents, any formatting that was applied to the original cell, and the cell comment (if it has one). When you copy a cell that contains a formula, the cell references in the copied formulas are changed automatically to be relative to their new destination. More on this in the next chapter.

Copying consists of two steps (although there are shortcut methods, as you'll see later):

1. Select the cell or range to copy (the source range) and copy it to the Windows Clipboard.

2. Move the cell pointer to the range that will hold the copy (the destination range) and paste the Clipboard contents.

When you paste information, Excel overwrites — without warning — any cells that get in the way. If you find that some essential cells were overwritten by pasting, execute the Edit➪Undo command (or press Ctrl+Z).

Because copying is used so often, Excel provides many different methods. I discuss each method in the following sections.

About the Windows Clipboard

In several places throughout this chapter, I mention the Windows Clipboard. The Clipboard is an area of memory that stores information that has been cut or copied from a Windows program. The Clipboard can store data in a variety of formats. Because it is managed by Windows, information on the Clipboard can be pasted to other Windows applications, regardless of where it originated (I discuss the topic of interapplication copying and pasting in Chapter 29). Normally, you can't see information stored on the Clipboard (nor would you want to).

You can, however, run the Clipboard Viewer program, which comes with Windows, to view the Clipboard contents. This program may or may not be installed on your system (it is not installed by default). The accompanying figure shows an example of this program running.

I copied a range of cells from Excel, and the figure shows how it appears in the Clipboard Viewer. You can use the Clipboard Viewer's Display menu to view the data in different formats. You also can save the Clipboard contents in a file, which you can then open at a later time.

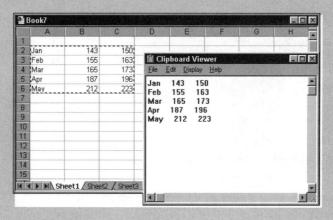

Copying by using toolbar buttons

The Standard toolbar has two buttons that are relevant to copying: the Copy button and the Paste button. Clicking on the Copy button transfers a copy of the selected cell or range to the Clipboard. After performing the copy part of this operation, activate the cell that will hold the copy and click on the Paste button.

If you're copying a range, you don't need to select an entire range before clicking on the Paste button. You need only activate the upper-left cell in the destination range.

Copying by using menu commands

If you prefer, you can use the following menu commands for copying and pasting:

Edit⇨Copy: Copies the selected cells to the Clipboard

Edit⇨Paste: Pastes the Clipboard contents to the selected cell or range

Copying by using shortcut menus

You also can use the Copy and Paste commands on the shortcut menu, as shown in Figure 8-9. Select the cell or range to copy, right-click on, and choose Copy from the shortcut menu. Then, activate the cell to copy to, right-click on, and choose Paste from the shortcut menu.

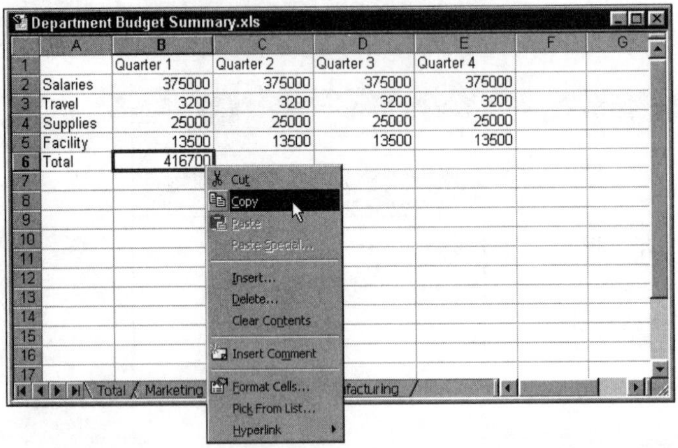

Figure 8-9: Right-clicking displays a shortcut menu, which contains Copy and Paste commands.

Copying by using shortcut keys

The copy and paste operations also have shortcut keys associated with them:

Ctrl+C: Copies the selected cells to the Clipboard

Ctrl+V: Pastes the Clipboard contents to the selected cell or range

Note

These shortcut keys also are used by most other Windows applications.

Copying by using drag and drop

Excel also lets you copy a cell or range by dragging. Select the cell or range that you want to copy and then move the mouse pointer to one of its four borders. When the mouse pointer turns into an arrow, press Ctrl; the mouse pointer will be augmented with a small plus sign. Then, simply drag the selection to its new location, keeping the Ctrl key pressed. The original selection remains behind, and Excel makes a new copy when you release the mouse button.

Note   If the mouse pointer doesn't turn into an arrow when you point to the border of a cell or range, you need to make a change to your settings. Select the Tools⇨ Options command, click on the Edit tab, and place a check mark on the option labeled Allow cell drag and drop.

Copying to adjacent cells

Often, you'll find that you need to copy a cell to an adjacent cell or range. This type of copying is quite common when working with formulas. For example, if you're working on a budget, you might create a formula to add up the values in column B. You can use the same formula to add up the values in the other columns. Rather than reenter the formula, you'll want to copy it to the adjacent cells.

Excel provides some additional options on its Edit menu for copying to adjacent cells. To use these commands, select the cell that you're copying plus the cells that you are copying to (see Figure 8-10). Then, issue the appropriate command for one-step copying.

Edit⇨Fill⇨Down (or Ctrl+D): Copies the cell to the selected range below

Edit⇨Fill⇨Right (or Ctrl+R): Copies the cell to the selected range to the right

Edit⇨Fill⇨Up: Copies the cell to the selected range above

Edit⇨Fill⇨Left: Copies the cell to the selected range to the left

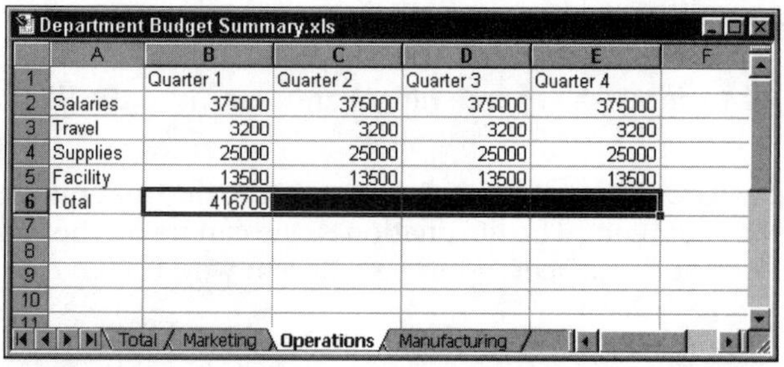

Figure 8-10: To copy to adjacent cells, start by selecting the cell to copy plus the cells that you want to copy to.

Yet another way to copy to adjacent cells is to drag the selection's fill handle. Excel copies the original selection to the cells that you highlight while dragging. This is an example of AutoFill. I discuss more uses for this feature in Chapter 9.

Copying a Range to Other Sheets

The copy procedures described previously also work as expected when you want to copy a cell or range to another worksheet, even if the worksheet is in a different workbook. The only difference is that you must activate the other worksheet before you select the location to copy to.

Excel offers a quicker way to copy a cell or range and paste it to other worksheets in the same workbook. Start by selecting the range to copy. Then, press Ctrl and click on the sheet tabs for the worksheets that you want to copy the information to (Excel will display *[Group]* in the workbook's title bar). Select the Edit➪Fill➪ Across Worksheet command, and you'll get a dialog box that asks what you want to copy (All, Contents, or Formats). Make your choice and click on OK. The selected range will be copied to the other selected worksheets and will occupy the same cells.

Caution Be careful with this command because Excel doesn't warn you if the destination cells are not empty. You can quickly overwrite lots of information with this command and not even realize it.

Moving a Cell or Range

Copying a cell or range doesn't modify the cell or range that was copied. If you want to relocate a cell or range to another location, you'll find that Excel is also quite accommodating.

Recall that the Edit➪Copy command makes a copy of the selected cell or range and puts the copy on the Clipboard. The Edit➪Cut command also places the selection the Clipboard, but it removes it from its original location as well. To move a cell or range, therefore, requires two steps:

1. Select the cell or range to copy (the source range) and "cut" it to the Windows Clipboard.

2. Activate the cell that will hold the moved cell or range (the destination range) and paste the Clipboard contents. The destination range can be on the same worksheet or in a diffesrent worksheet — or in a different workbook.

Tip You also can move a cell or range by dragging it. Select the cell or range to be copied and then move the mouse pointer to either of its four borders. When you do so, the mouse pointer turns into an arrow. Drag the selection to its new location and release the mouse button. This option is similar to copying a cell, except that you don't press Ctrl while dragging.

Other Cell and Range Operations

As you know, the Edit➪Paste command simply transfers the Clipboard contents to the selected location in your worksheet. You may be interested to know about a much more versatile version of this command: Edit➪Paste Special. In order for this command to be available, you need to copy a cell or range to the Clipboard (using Edit➪Cut won't work). Then select the cell where you want to paste. You'll get the dialog box shown in Figure 8-11. This dialog box has several options, which I explain in the following sections.

Figure 8-11: The Paste Special dialog box.

Pasting all

Selecting the All option in the Paste Special dialog box is equivalent to using the Edit➪Paste command. It copies the cell's contents, formats, and data validation.

Pasting formulas as values

Normally, when you copy a range that contains formulas, the formulas get copied, and Excel automatically adjusts the cell references. The Values option in the Paste Special dialog box lets you copy the *results* of formulas. The destination for the copy can be a new range or the original range. In the latter case, the original formulas will be replaced by their current values.

Pasting cell formats only

If you've applied formatting to a cell or range, you can copy only the formatting and paste it to another cell or range. Use the Formats option in the Paste Special dialog box. This can save a great deal of time if you've applied lots of formatting to a cell and want to duplicate the formatting elsewhere.

Pasting cell comments

If you want to copy only the cell comments from a cell or range, use the Comments option in the Paste Special dialog box. This option doesn't copy cell contents or formatting.

Pasting validation criteria

Excel 97 If you've created validation criteria for a particular cell (by using the Data➪ Validation command), you can copy the validation criteria to another cell or range. Use the Validation option in the Paste Special dialog box.

Performing mathematical operations without formulas

The option buttons in the Operation section of the Paste Special dialog box let you perform an arithmetic operation. For example, you can copy a range to another range and select the Multiply operation. Excel multiplies the corresponding values in the source range and the destination range and replaces the destination range with the new values.

Figure 8-12 shows another example of using a mathematical operation with the Paste Special dialog box. The objective is to increase the values in B4:B10 by ten percent (without using formulas). I copied the contents of cell B1 to the Clipboard. I then selected B4:B10 and issued the Edit➪Paste Special command. Choosing the Multiply operation will cause each cell in B4:B10 to be multiplied by the value on the Clipboard, effectively increasing the cell values by ten percent. You'll also need to select the Value option — otherwise the cells will take on the formatting of the pasted cell.

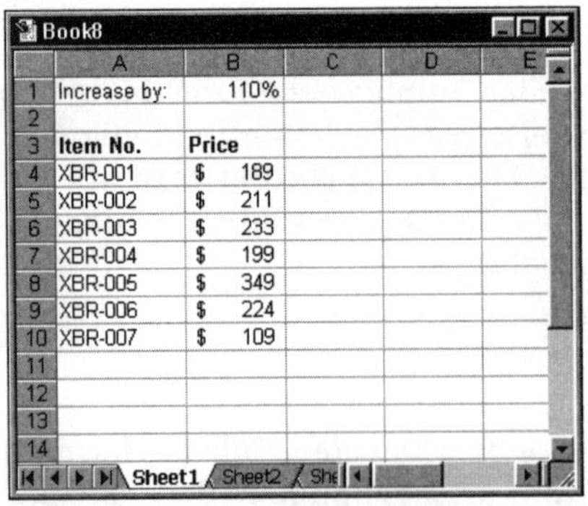

Figure 8-12: Using the Paste Special command to increase the values in a range by ten percent.

Skipping borders when pasting

Often, you'll want to avoid copying borders around a cell. For example, if you have a table with a border around it, copying a cell from one of the outer cells in the table will also copy the border. To avoid pasting the border, choose the All except borders option in the Paste Special dialog box.

Skipping blanks when pasting

The Skip Blanks option in the Paste Special dialog box prevents Excel from over-writing cell contents in your paste area with blank cells from the copied range. This option is useful if you're copying a range to another area, but you don't want the blank cells in the copied range to overwrite existing data.

Transposing a range

The Transpose option in the Paste Special dialog box changes the orientation of the copied range. Rows become columns and columns become rows. Any formulas in the copied range are adjusted so that they work properly when transposed. Note that this check box can be used with the other options in the Paste Special dialog box. Figure 8-13 shows an example of a horizontal range that was trans-posed to a vertical range.

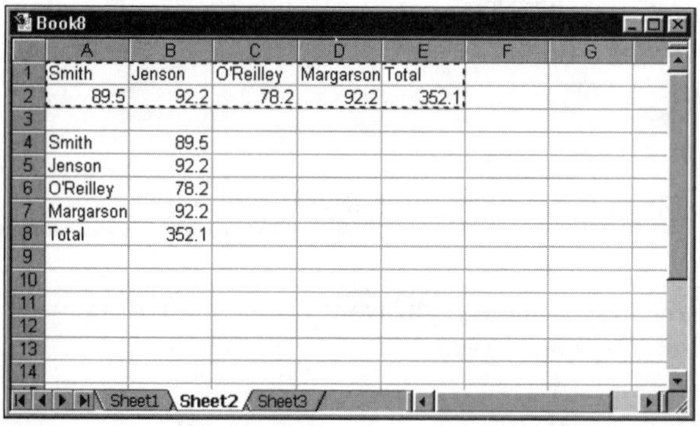

Figure 8-13: The range in A1:E2 was transposed to A4:B8.

Naming Cells and Ranges: The Basics

Dealing with cryptic cell and range addresses can sometimes be confusing (this will become even more apparent when you deal with formulas, which are covered in the next chapter). Fortunately, Excel lets you assign descriptive names to cells and ranges. For example, you can give a cell a name such as `Interest_Rate`, or you can name a range `JulySales`. Working with these names (rather than cell or range addresses) has several advantages.

Advantages of using names

Using names offers the following advantages:

✦ A meaningful range name (such as `Total_Income`) is much easier to remember than a cell address (such as AC21).

✦ Entering a name is less error-prone than entering a cell or range address.

✦ You can quickly move to areas of your worksheet by using the Name box, located at the left side of the formula bar (click on the arrow to drop down a list of defined names), or by choosing the Edit⇨Go To command (or F5) and specifying the range name.

✦ When you select a named cell or range, the name appears in the Name box.

✦ Creating formulas is easier. You can paste a cell or range name into a formula by using the Insert⇨Name⇨Paste command, or by selecting a name from the Name box.

✦ Names make your formulas more understandable and easier to use. A formula such as =Income–Taxes is more intuitive than =D20–D40.

✦ Macros are easier to create and maintain when you use range names rather than cell addresses.

✦ You can give a name to a value or formula — even when the value or formula doesn't exist on the worksheet. For example, you can create the name `Interest_Rate` for a value of .075. Then you can use this name in your formulas (more about this in the next chapter).

Valid names

Although Excel is quite flexible about the names that you can define, it does have some rules:

✦ Names can't contain any spaces. You might want to use an underscore or a period character to simulate a space (such as `Annual_Total` or `Annual.Total`).

✦ You can use any combination of letters and numbers, but the name must begin with a letter. A name can't begin with a number (such as `3rdQuarter`), or look like a cell reference (such as `Q3`).

✦ Symbols, except for underscore and period, aren't allowed. Although it's not documented, I've found that Excel also allows a backslash (\) and question mark (?).

✦ Names are limited to 255 characters. Trust me, using a name anywhere near this length is not a good idea.

✦ You can use single letters (except for R or C), but this is generally not recommended because it defeats the purpose of using meaningful names.

Excel also uses a few names internally for its own use. Although you can create names that override Excel's internal names, it's best to avoid doing so. To be on the safe side, avoid using the following for names: `Print_Area`, `Print_Titles`, `Consolidate_Area`, and `Sheet_Title`.

Excel 97 A new feature in Excel 97 lets you use labels that appear as row and column headings as names. The best part about this is that you don't have to actually define the names. This feature is most useful when you use formulas, so I discuss it in detail in Chapter 9.

Creating names manually

There are several ways to create names. This section discusses two methods to create names manually.

Using the Define Name dialog box

To create a range name, start by selecting the cell or range that you want to name. Then, select the Insert⇨Name⇨Define command (or press Ctrl+F3). Excel displays the Define Name dialog box, shown in Figure 8-14.

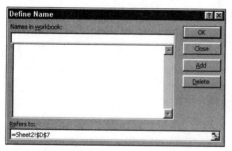

Figure 8-14: Create names for cells or ranges by using the Define Name dialog box.

Type a name in the edit box labeled Names in workbook (or use the name that Excel proposes, if any). The active or selected cell or range address appears in the Refers to box. Verify that the address listed is correct, then click on OK to add the name to your worksheet and close the dialog box. Or, you can click on the Add button to continue adding names to your worksheet. If you do this, you must specify the Refers to range by typing an address (make sure to begin with an equal sign) or by pointing to it in the worksheet. Each name appears in the list box.

Using the Name box

A faster way to create a name is to use the Name box. Select the cell or range to name, then click on the Name box and enter the name. Press Enter to create the name. If a name already exists, you can't use the Name box to change the reference that the name refers to. Attempting to do so simply selects the name that you enter.

Note   When you enter a name in the Name box, you *must* press Enter to actually register the name. If you type a name and then click on in the worksheet, Excel won't create the name.

The Name box is a drop-down list, and it shows all names in the workbook (see Figure 8-15). When you select a named cell or range, its name appears in the name box. To select a named cell or range, click on the Name box and select the name. Excel selects the named cell or range. Oddly enough, there is no way to access the Name box from the keyboard; a mouse is required. Once you click on the Name box, however, you can use the direction keys and Enter to select a name.

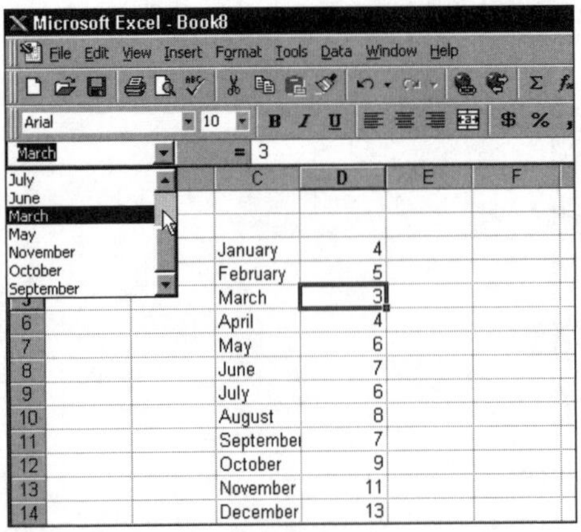

Figure 8-15: The Name box shows all names defined in the workbook.

Creating names automatically

You may have a worksheet that contains text that you want to use for names for adjacent cells or ranges. Figure 8-16 shows an example of such a worksheet. In this case, you might want to use the text in column A to create names for the corresponding values in column B. Excel makes this very easy to do.

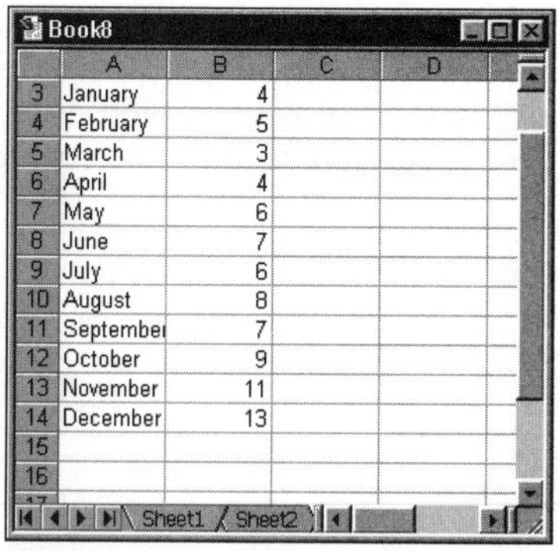

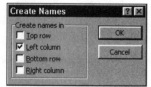

	A	B	C	D
3	January	4		
4	February	5		
5	March	3		
6	April	4		
7	May	6		
8	June	7		
9	July	6		
10	August	8		
11	September	7		
12	October	9		
13	November	11		
14	December	13		
15				
16				

Figure 8-16: Excel makes it easy to create names by using text in adjacent cells.

To create names using adjacent text, start by selecting the name text and the cells that you want to name (these can be individual cells or ranges of cells). The names must be adjacent to the cells you're naming (a multiple selection is allowed). Then choose the Insert⇨Name⇨Create command (or Ctrl+Shift+F3). Excel displays the Create Names dialog box, shown in Figure 8-17. The check marks in this dialog box are based on Excel's analysis of the selected range. For example, if it finds text in the first row of the selection, it proposes that you create names based on the top row. If Excel didn't guess correctly, you can change the check boxes. Click on OK and the names are created in a jiffy.

Create Names

Create names in
- [ ] Top row
- [✓] Left column
- [ ] Bottom row
- [ ] Right column

OK
Cancel

Figure 8-17: The Create Names dialog box.

Note If the text contained in a cell results in an invalid name, Excel modifies the name to make it valid. For example, if a cell contains the text *Net Income* (which is invalid for a name because it contains a space), Excel converts the space to an underscore character. If Excel encounters a value or a formula where text should be, however, it doesn't convert it to a valid name. It simply doesn't create a name.

Caution It's a good idea to double-check the names that Excel creates. Sometimes the Insert⇨Name⇨Create command works counterintuitively. Figure 8-18 shows a small table of text and values. If you select the entire table, choose the Insert⇨ Name⇨Create command, and accept Excel's suggestions (Top Row and Left Column options), you'll find that the name Products doesn't refer to A2:A5 as you would expect. Rather, it refers to B2:C5. If the upper-left cell of the selection contains text and you choose the Top Row and Left Column options, Excel uses that text for the name of the entire data — excluding the top row and left column. So, before you accept the names that Excel creates, take a minute to make sure that they refer to the correct ranges.

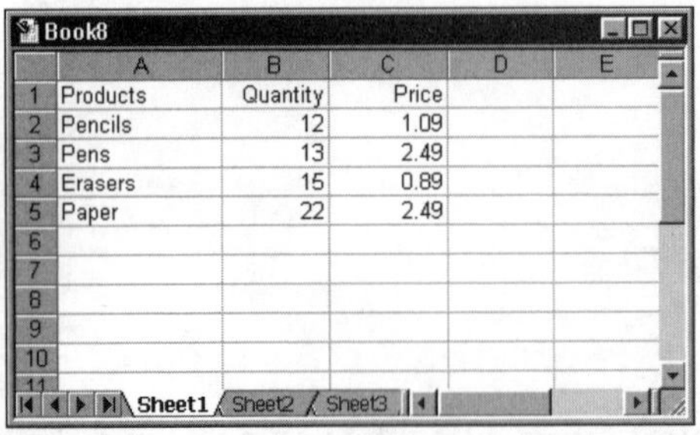

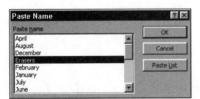

Figure 8-18: Creating names from the data in this table may produce unexpected results.

Creating a table of names

Excel lets you create a list of all names in the workbook, which is useful for tracking down errors or as a way to document your work. To create a table of names, first move the cell pointer to an empty area of your worksheet — the table is created at the active cell position. Use the Insert⇨Name⇨Paste command (or F3). Excel displays the Paste Name dialog box shown in Figure 8-19. This dialog box lists all of the defined names. To paste a list of names, click on the Paste List button.

Figure 8-19: The Paste Name dialog box.

Caution The list that Excel pastes will overwrite any cells that get in the way, so make sure that the active cell is located in an empty portion of the worksheet.

Deleting names

If you no longer need a defined name, you can delete it. Choose the Insert⇨Name⇨ Define command to display the Define Name dialog box. Choose the name that you want to delete from the list and click on the Delete button.

Caution   Be extra careful when deleting names. If the name is used in a formula, deleting the name causes the formula to become invalid (it will display #NAME?). However, deleting a name can be undone, so if you find that formulas return #NAME after you delete a name, select Edit⇨Undo to get the name back.

If you delete the rows or columns that contain named cells or ranges, the names contain an invalid reference. For example, if cell A1 on Sheet1 is named Interest and you delete row 1 or column A, Interest then refers to =Sheet1!#REF! (that is, an erroneous reference). If you use Interest in a formula, the formula displays #REF.

Redefining names

After you've defined a name, you may want to change the cell or range to which it refers. You can use the Define Name dialog box to do this. Select the Insert⇨ Name⇨Define command, click on the name that you want to change, and edit the cell or range address in the Refers to edit box. If you like, you can click on the edit box and select a new cell or range by pointing in the worksheet. Excel automatically adjusts the cells to which your names refer. For example, assume that cell A10 is named Summary. If you delete a row above row 10, Summary then refers to cell A9. This is just what you would expect to happen, so you don't need to be concerned about it.

Changing names

Excel doesn't have a simple way to change a name once the name is created. If you create a name and then realize that it's not the name you wanted — or, perhaps, that you spelled it incorrectly — you must create the new name and then delete the old name.

Learning more about names

Excel offers some additional features when it comes to using names — features unmatched in any of its competitors. These advanced naming features are most useful when working with formulas. I discuss these features in Chapter 9.

Summary

In this chapter I discuss the basic worksheet operations that involve cells and ranges. These operations include selecting, copying, moving, deleting, and working with ranges that extend across multiple worksheets in a workbook. I also introduce the topic of names. This is an important concept that can make your worksheets more readable and easier to maintain.

✦   ✦   ✦

Creating and Using Formulas

Formulas are what make a spreadsheet so useful. Without formulas, a spreadsheet would be nothing more than a word processor with a very powerful table feature (and not much else). A worksheet without formulas is essentially dead. Using formulas adds life and lets you calculate results from the data stored in the worksheet. This chapter introduces formulas and helps you get up to speed with this important element.

Introducing Formulas

To add a formula to a worksheet, you enter it into a cell. You can delete, move, and copy formulas just like any other item of data. Formulas use arithmetic operators to work with values, text, worksheet functions, and other formulas to calculate a value in the cell. Values and text can be located in other cells, which makes changing data easy and gives worksheets their dynamic nature. For example, Excel recalculates formulas if the value in a cell used by the formula changes. In essence, you can see multiple scenarios quickly by changing the data in a worksheet and letting formulas do the work.

A formula entered into a cell can consist of any of the following elements:

- ✦ Operators such as + (for addition) and * (for multiplication)
- ✦ Cell references (including named cells and ranges)
- ✦ Values
- ✦ Worksheet functions (such as SUM or AVERAGE)

A formula can consist of up to 1,024 characters. After you enter a formula into a cell, the cell displays the result of the formula. The formula itself appears in the formula bar when the cell is activated, however.

Here are a few examples of formulas:

=150*.05	Multiplies 150 times .05. This formula uses only values and isn't all that useful.
=A1+A2	Adds the values in cells A1 and A2.
=Income–Expenses	Subtracts the cell named `Expenses` from the cell named `Income`.
=SUM(A1:A12)	Adds the values in the range A1:A12.
=A1=C12	Compares cell A1 with cell C12. If they are identical, the formula returns TRUE, otherwise it returns FALSE.

Note   Notice that formulas always begin with an equal sign. This is how Excel distinguishes formulas from text.

Operators used in formulas

Excel lets you use a variety of operators in your formulas. Table 9-1 lists the operators that Excel recognizes. In addition to these, Excel has many built-in functions that let you perform more operations. These functions are discussed in detail in Chapter 10.

Table 9-1
Operators Used in Formulas

Operator	Name
+	Addition
-	Subtraction
*	Multiplication
/	Division
^	Exponentiation
&	Concatenation
=	Logical comparison (equal to)

Operator	Name
>	Logical comparison (greater than)
<	Logical comparison (less than)
>=	Logical comparison (greater than or equal to)
<=	Logical comparison (less than or equal to)
<>	Logical comparison (not equal to)

You can, of course, use as many operators as you need (formulas can be quite complex). Figure 9-1 shows a worksheet with a formula in cell B5. The formula is as follows:

```
=(B2-B3)*B4
```

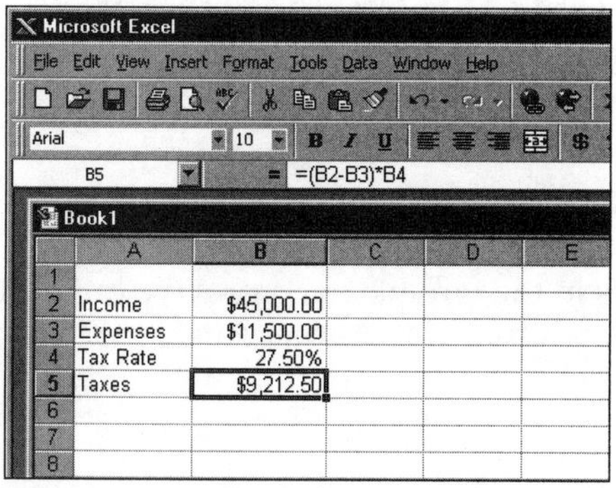

Figure 9-1: A formula that uses two operators.

In this example, the formula subtracts the value in B3 from the value in B2 and then multiplies the result by the value in B4. If the worksheet had names defined for these cells, the formula would be a lot more readable. Here's the same formula after naming the cells:

```
=(Income-Expenses)*TaxRate
```

Now are you beginning to understand why using names is such an important concept? Following are some additional examples of formulas that use various operators.

="Part-"&"23A"	Joins *(concatenates)* the two text strings to produce *Part-23A*.
=A1&A2	Concatenates the contents of cell A1 with cell A2. Concatenation works with values as well as text. If cell A1 contains 123 and cell A2 contains 456, this formula would return the value 123456.
=6^3	Raises 6 to the third power (216).
=216^(1/3)	Returns the cube root of 216 (6).
=A1<A2	Returns TRUE if the value in cell A1 is less than the value in cell A2. Otherwise, it returns FALSE. Logical comparison operators also work with text. If A1 contained *Bill* and A2 contained *Julia,* the formula would return TRUE because Bill comes before Julia in alphabetical order.
=A1<=A2	Returns TRUE if the value in cell A1 is less than or equal to the value in cell A2. Otherwise, it returns FALSE.
=A1<>A2	Returns TRUE if the value in cell A1 isn't equal to the value in cell A2. Otherwise, it returns FALSE.

Operator precedence

In an earlier example, I used parentheses in the formula to control the order in which the calculations occur. The formula without parentheses would look like this:

```
=Income-Expenses*TaxRate
```

If you enter the formula without the parentheses, you'll discover that Excel computes the wrong answer. To understand why this is so, you need to understand a concept called *operator precedence.* This is basically the set of rules that Excel uses to perform its calculation. Table 9-2 lists Excel's operator precedence. This table shows that exponentiation has the highest precedence (that is, it's performed first) and logical comparisons have the lowest precedence.

You use parentheses to override Excel's built-in order of precedence. Returning to the previous example, the formula that follows doesn't use parentheses and is therefore evaluated using Excel's standard operator precedence. Because multiplication has a higher precedence, the `Expense` cell is multiplied by the `TaxRate` cell. Then this result is subtracted from `Income`. This isn't what was intended.

```
=Income-Expenses*TaxRate
```

The correct formula, which follows, uses parentheses to control the order of operations. Expressions within parentheses are always evaluated first. In this case, `Expenses` is subtracted from `Income` and the result is multiplied by `TaxRate`.

```
=(Income-Expenses)*TaxRate
```

Table 9-2
Operator Precedence in Excel Formulas

Symbol	Operator	Precedence
^	Exponentiation	1
*	Multiplication	2
/	Division	2
+	Addition	3
-	Subtraction	3
&	Concatenation	4
=	Equal to	5
<	Less than	5
>	Greater than	5

You can also *nest* parentheses in formulas. Nesting means putting parentheses inside of parentheses. If you do so, Excel evaluates the most deeply nested expressions first and works its way out. Figure 9-2 shows an example of a formula that uses nested parentheses.

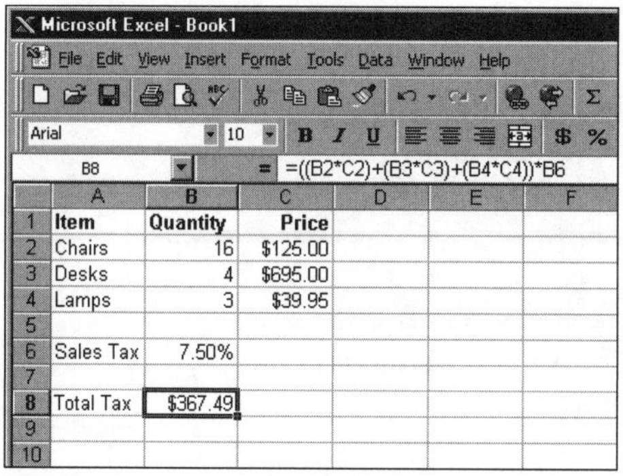

Figure 9-2: A formula with nested parentheses.

```
=((B2*C2)+(B3*C3)+(B4*C4))*B6
```

This formula has four sets of parentheses — three sets are nested inside the fourth set. Excel evaluates each nested set of parentheses and then adds up the three results. This sum is then multiplied by the value in B6.

Tip It's a good idea to make liberal use of parentheses in your formulas. I often use parentheses even when they aren't necessary to clarify the order of operations and make the formula easier to read. For example, if you want to add 1 to the product of two cells, the following formula will do it:

    =1+A1*A2

I find it much clearer, however, to use the following formula (with superfluous parentheses):

    =1+(A1*A2)

Every left parenthesis, of course, must have a matching right parenthesis. If you have many levels of nested parentheses, it can sometimes be difficult to keep them straight. If the parentheses don't match, Excel pops up a message telling you so and won't let you enter the formula. Fortunately, Excel lends a hand in helping you match parentheses. When you're entering or editing a formula that has parentheses, pay attention to the text. When the cursor moves over a parenthesis, Excel momentarily makes it and its matching parenthesis bold. This lasts for less than a second, so be alert.

Excel 97 In some cases, if your formula contains mismatched parentheses, Excel may propose a correction to your formula. Figure 9-3 shows an example of the Formula AutoCorrect feature. It's tempting to simply accept the proposed correction, but be careful. In many cases the proposed formula, although syntactically correct, isn't the formula that you want!

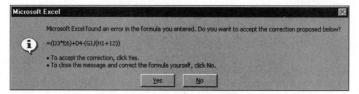

Microsoft Excel

Microsoft Excel found an error in the formula you entered. Do you want to accept the correction proposed below?

=(D3*E6)+D4-(G1/(H1+12))

• To accept the correction, click Yes.
• To close this message and correct the formula yourself, click No.

[Yes]   [No]

Figure 9-3: Excel 97's new Formula AutoCorrect feature often suggests a correction to an erroneous formula.

Excel's built-in functions

Excel provides a bewildering number of built-in worksheet functions that you can use in your formulas. These include common functions (such as SUM, AVERAGE, and SQRT) as well as functions designed for special purposes such as statistics or engineering. Functions can greatly enhance the power of your formulas. They can simplify your formulas and make them easier to read; in many cases, functions let you perform calculations that would not be possible otherwise. If you can't find a worksheet function that you need, Excel even lets you create your own custom functions.

Cross Reference

I discuss Excel's built-in functions in the next chapter, and Chapter 36 covers the basics of creating custom functions using VBA.

Entering Formulas

As I mentioned earlier, a formula must begin with an equal sign to let Excel know that the cell contains a formula rather than text. There are basically two ways to enter a formula into a cell: enter it manually or enter it by pointing to cell references. I discuss each of these methods in the following sections.

Entering formulas manually

Entering a formula manually involves, well, entering a formula manually. You simply type an equal sign (=) followed by the formula. As you type, the characters appear in the cell as well as in the formula bar. You can, of course, use all the normal editing keys when entering a formula.

Entering formulas by pointing

The other method of entering a formula still involves some manual typing, but you can simply point to the cell references instead of entering them manually. For example, to enter the formula =A1+A2 into cell A3, follow these steps:

1. Move the cell pointer to cell A3.

2. Type an equal sign (=) to begin the formula. Notice that Excel displays *Enter* in the status bar.

3. Press the up arrow twice. As you press this key, notice that Excel displays a faint moving border around the cell and that the cell reference appears in cell A3 and in the formula bar. Also notice that Excel displays *Point* in the status bar.

4. Type a plus sign (+). The faint border disappears and *Enter* reappears in the status bar.

5. Press the up arrow one more time. A2 is added to the formula.

6. Press Enter to end the formula.

Pointing to cell addresses rather than entering them manually is usually more accurate and less tedious.

Tip

When you create a formula that refers to other cells, the cell that contains the formula has the same number format as the first cell it refers to.

Excel 97 includes the Formula Palette feature that you can use when entering or editing formulas. To access the Formula Palette, click on the Edit Formula button in the edit line (it has an image of an equal sign). The Formula Palette lets you enter formulas manually or use the pointing techniques described previously. The advantage is that the Formula Palette displays the result of the formula as it's being entered. Figure 9-4 shows the Formula Palette at work. The Formula Palette normally appears directly below the edit line, but you can drag it to any convenient location (as you can see in the figure).

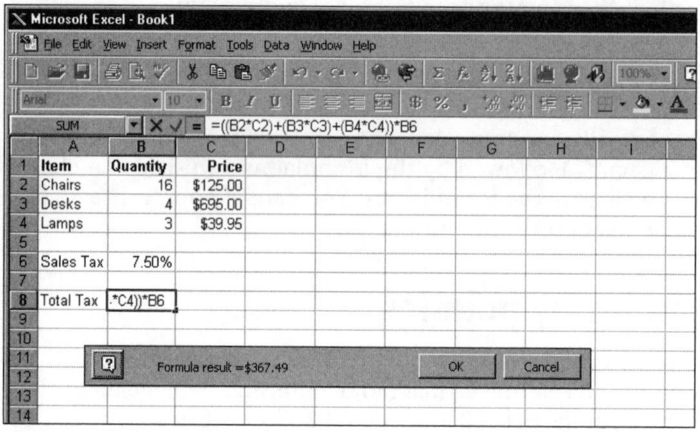

Figure 9-4: The Formula Palette, new to Excel 97, displays the result of the formula as it's being entered.

Pasting names

If your formula uses named cells or ranges, you can type the name in place of the address or choose the name from a list and have Excel insert the name for you automatically. There are two ways to insert a name into a formula:

✦ Select the Insert⇨Name⇨Paste command. Excel displays its Paste Name dialog box with all the names listed (see Figure 9-5). Select the name and click on OK. Or, you can double-click on the name, which inserts the name and closes the dialog box.

✦ Press F3. This also displays the Paste Name dialog box.

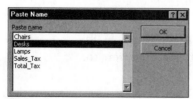

Figure 9-5: The Paste Name dialog box lets you insert a name into a formula.

Referencing Cells Outside the Worksheet

Formulas can refer to cells in other worksheets — and the worksheets don't even have to be in the same workbook. Excel uses a special type of notation to handle these types of references.

Cells in other worksheets

To use a reference to a cell in another worksheet in the same workbook, use the following format:

```
SheetName!CellAddress
```

In other words, precede the cell address with the worksheet name, followed by an exclamation point. Here's an example of a formula that uses a cell on the Sheet2 worksheet:

```
=A1*Sheet2!A1
```

This formula multiplies the value in cell A1 on the current worksheet by the value in cell A1 on Sheet2.

Note   If the worksheet name in the reference includes one or more spaces, you must enclose it in single quotation marks. For example, here's a formula that refers to a cell on a sheet named `All Depts`:

```
=A1*'All Depts'!A1
```

Cells in other workbooks

To refer to a cell in a different workbook, use this format:

```
=[WorkbookName]SheetName!CellAddress
```

In this case, the cell address is preceded by the workbook name (in square brackets), the worksheet name, and an exclamation point. Here's an example of a formula that uses a cell reference in the Sheet1 worksheet in a workbook named `Budget`:

```
=[Budget.xls]Sheet1!A1
```

If the workbook name in the reference includes one or more spaces, you must enclose it (and the sheet name) in single quotation marks. For example, here's a formula that refers to a cell on Sheet1 in a workbook named `Budget For 1997`:

```
=A1*'[Budget For 1997]Sheet1'!A1
```

When a formula refers to cells in a different workbook, the other workbook doesn't need to be open. If the workbook is closed, you must add the complete path to the reference. Here's an example:

```
=A1*'C:\ MSOffice\Excel\[Budget For 1997]Sheet1'!A1
```

Cross Reference I discuss the topic of file linking in detail in Chapter 19.

Entering references to cells outside the worksheet

The easiest way to create formulas that refer to cells not in the current worksheet is to use the pointing technique described earlier (refer to "Entering formulas by pointing"). Excel takes care of the details involving the workbook and worksheet references. The workbook that you're using in your formula must be open to use the pointing method.

Note If you point to a different worksheet or workbook when creating a formula, you'll notice that Excel always inserts absolute cell references. Therefore, if you plan to copy the formula to other cells, make sure that you change the cell references to relative. This concept of absolute versus relative cell references is discussed in the following section.

Absolute Versus Relative References

It's important to distinguish between *relative* and *absolute cell references.* By default, Excel creates relative cell references in formulas. The distinction becomes apparent when you copy a formula to another cell.

Relative references

Figure 9-6 shows a worksheet with a formula in cell D2. The formula, which uses the default relative references, is as follows:

```
=B2*C2
```

When you copy this formula to the two cells below it, Excel doesn't produce an exact copy of the formula; rather, it generates these formulas:

Cell D3:=B3*C3

Cell D4:=B4*C4

In other words, Excel adjusts the cell references to refer to the cells that are relative to the new formula. Think of it like this: The original formula contained instructions to multiply the value two cells to the left by the value one cell to the left. When you copy the cell, these instructions get copied, which results in the new formulas. Usually, this is exactly what you want. You certainly don't want to copy the formula verbatim; if you did, the new formulas would produce the same value as the original formula.

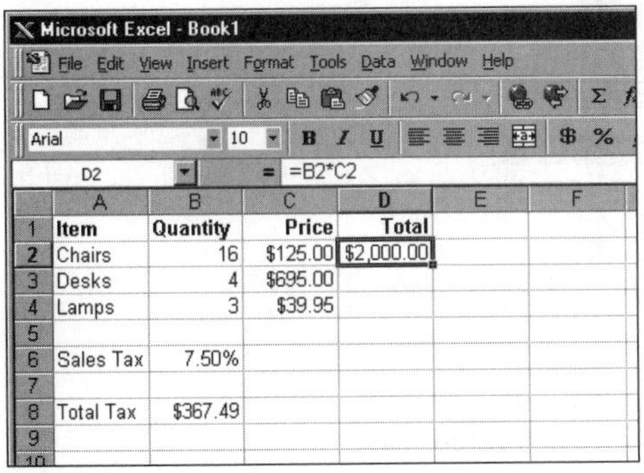

Figure 9-6: The formula in cell D2 will be copied to the cell below.

Note When you cut and paste a formula (move it to another location), the cell references in the formula aren't adjusted. Again, this is what you normally want to happen. When you move a formula, you generally want it to continue to refer to the original cells.

Absolute references

There are times, however, when you *do* want a cell reference to be copied verbatim. Figure 9-7 shows an example of a formula that contains an absolute reference.

In this example, cell B6 contains a sales tax rate. The formula in cell D2 is as follows:

```
=(B2*C2)*$B$6
```

Notice in this example that the reference to cell B6 has dollar signs before the column part and before the row part. These dollar signs make it an absolute cell reference. When you copy this formula to the two cells below, Excel generates the following formulas:

Cell D3: =(B3*C3)*$B$6

Cell D4: =(B4*C4)*$B$6

In this case, the relative cell references were changed, but the reference to cell B6 wasn't changed because it's an absolute reference.

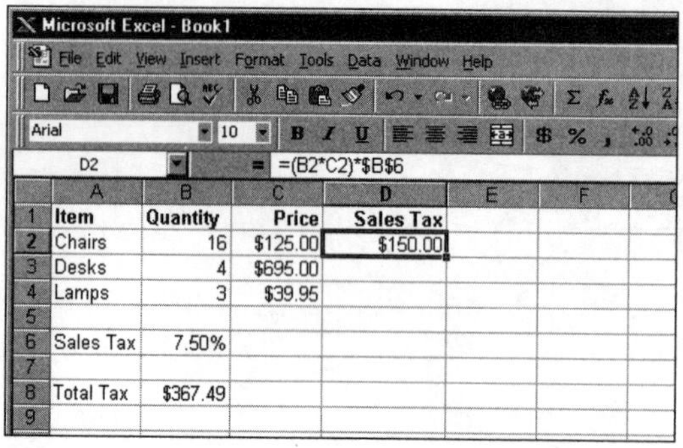

Figure 9-7: A formula that uses an absolute cell reference.

Mixed references

An absolute reference uses two dollar signs in its address: one for the column part and one for the row part. Excel also allows mixed references in which only one of the address parts is absolute. Table 9-3 summarizes all the possible types of cell references.

When would you use a mixed reference? Figure 9-8 shows an example of a situation in which a mixed reference is appropriate. This worksheet will contain a table of values in which each cell will consist of the value in column A multiplied by the value in row 1. The formula in cell B2 is as follows:

=B$1*$A2

	Table 9-3
	Types of Cell References

Example	Type
A1	Relative reference
$A$1	Absolute reference
$A1	Mixed reference (column part is absolute)
A$1	Mixed reference (row part is absolute)

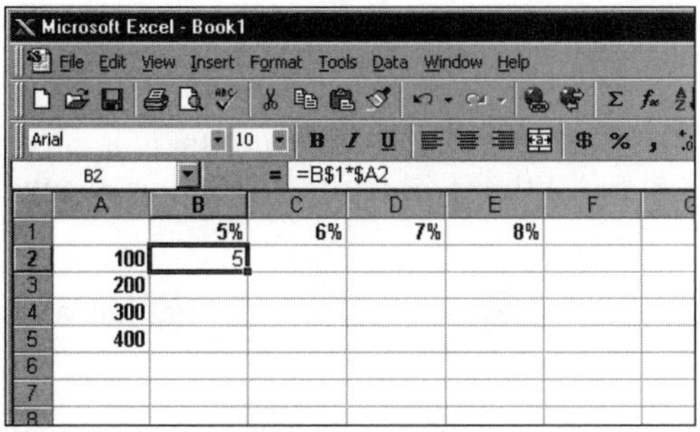

Figure 9-8: This formula uses a mixed reference.

This formula contains two mixed cell references. In the B$1 reference, the row part is absolute, but the column part is relative. In the $A2 reference, the row part is relative, but the column part is absolute. You can copy this formula to the range B2:E5 and each cell will contain the correct formula. For example, the formula in cell E5 would be as follows:

```
=E$1*$A5
```

Entering nonrelative references

You can enter nonrelative references (absolute or mixed) manually by inserting dollar signs in the appropriate positions. Or, you can use a handy shortcut: the F4 key. When you're entering a cell reference — either manually or by pointing — you can press F4 repeatedly to have Excel cycle through all four reference types.

For example, if you enter **=A1** to start a formula, pressing F4 converts the cell reference to +$A$1. Pressing F4 again converts it to +A$1. Pressing it again displays +$A1. Pressing it one more time returns to the original +A1. Keep pressing F4 until Excel displays the type of reference you want.

Note When you name a cell or range, Excel (by default) uses an absolute reference for the name. For example, if you give the name SalesForecast to A1:A12, the Refers to box in the Define Name dialog box lists the reference as $A$1:$A$12. This is almost always what you want. If you copy a cell that has a named reference in its formula, the copied formula contains a reference to the original name.

When a Formula Returns an Error

Sometimes when you enter a formula, Excel displays a value that begins with a pound sign (#). This is a signal that the formula is returning an error value. You'll have to correct the formula (or correct a cell that is referenced by the formula) to get rid of the error display.

As I noted previously in this chapter, Excel 97 often suggests a correction for an erroneous formula.

Note If the entire cell is filled with pound characters, this means that the column isn't wide enough to display the value. You can either widen the column or change the number format of the cell.

Table 9-4 lists the types of error values that may appear in a cell that has a formula.

Formulas may return an error value if a cell that they refer to has an error value. This is known as the ripple effect — a single error value can make its way to lots of other cells that contain formulas that depend on the cell.

Table 9-4
Excel Error Values

Error Value	Explanation
#DIV/0!	The formula is trying to divide by zero (an operation that's not allowed on this planet). This also occurs when the formula attempts to divide by a cell that is empty.
#NAME?	The formula uses a name that Excel doesn't recognize. This can happen if you delete a name that's used in the formula or if you have unmatched quotes when using text.
#N/A	The formula is referring (directly or indirectly) to a cell that uses the NA functions to signal the fact that data is not available.
#NULL!	The formula uses an intersection of two ranges that don't intersect (this concept is described later in the chapter).
#NUM!	There is a problem with a value; for example, you specified a negative number where a positive number is expected.
#REF!	The formula refers to a cell that isn't valid. This can happen if the cell has been deleted from the worksheet.
#VALUE!	The formula includes an argument or operand of the wrong type. An operand is a value or cell reference that a formula uses to calculate a result.

Editing Formulas

You can edit your formulas just like you can edit any other cell. You might need to edit a formula if you make some changes to your worksheet and you need to adjust the formula to accommodate the changes. Or, the formula may return one of the error values described in the previous section and you need to edit the formula to correct the error.

As I discuss in Chapter 6, there are four ways to get into cell edit mode:

✦ Double-click on the cell. This lets you edit the cell contents directly in the cell.

✦ Press F2. This lets you edit the cell contents directly in the cell.

✦ Activate the cell that you want to edit, and then click in the formula bar. This lets you edit the cell contents in the formula bar.

✦ Click on the Edit Formula button in the edit line to access the Formula Palette.

While you're editing a formula, you can select multiple characters by dragging the mouse over them or by holding down Shift while you use the direction keys.

You might have a lengthy formula that you can't seem to edit correctly — and Excel won't let you enter it because of the error. In this case, you can convert the formula to text and tackle it again later. To convert a formula to text, just remove the initial equal sign (=). When you're ready to try again, insert the initial equal sign to convert the cell contents back to a formula.

Changing When Formulas Are Calculated

You've probably noticed that the formulas in your worksheet get calculated immediately. If you change any cells that the formula uses, the formula displays a new result with no effort on your part. This is what happens when Excel's Calculation mode is set to Automatic. In this mode (which is the default mode), Excel follows these rules when calculating your worksheet:

✦ When you make a change — enter or edit data or formulas, for example — Excel calculates immediately those formulas that depend on new or edited data.

✦ If it's in the middle of a lengthy calculation, Excel temporarily suspends calculation when you need to perform other worksheet tasks; it resumes when you're finished.

✦ Formulas are evaluated in a natural sequence. In other words, if a formula in cell D12 depends on the result of a formula in cell D11, cell D11 is calculated before D12.

Sometimes, however, you may want to control when Excel calculates formulas. For example, if you create a worksheet with thousands of complex formulas, you'll find that things can slow to a snail's pace while Excel does its thing. In such a case, you would want to set Excel's calculation mode to Manual. You can do this in the Calculation panel of the Options dialog box (see Figure 9-9).

To select Manual calculation mode, click on the Manual option button. When you switch to Manual calculation mode, the Recalculate before save check box is automatically turned on. You can turn this off if you want to speed up file saving operations.

If your worksheet uses any data tables (described in Chapter 26), you may want to select the Automatic except tables option. Large data tables are notoriously slow to calculate.

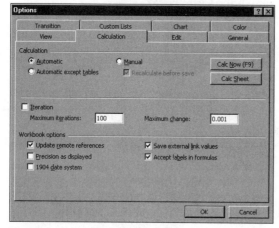

Figure 9-9: The Options dialog box lets you control when Excel calculates formulas.

When you're working in Manual calculation mode, Excel displays *Calculate* in the status bar when you have any uncalculated formulas. You can use the following shortcut keys to recalculate the formulas:

> **F9:** Calculates the formulas in all open workbooks
>
> **Shift+F9:** Calculates only the formulas in the active worksheet. Other worksheets in the same workbook won't be calculated.

Note Excel's Calculation mode isn't specific to a particular worksheet. When you change Excel's Calculation mode, it affects all open workbooks, not just the active workbook.

Handling Circular References

When you're entering formulas, you may occasionally see a message from Excel like the one shown in Figure 9-10. This indicates that the formula you just entered will result in a *circular reference.* A circular reference occurs when a formula refers to its own value — either directly or indirectly. For example, if you enter **=A1+A2+A3** into cell A3, this is a circular reference because the formula in cell A3 refers to cell A3. Every time the formula in A3 is calculated, it must be calculated again because A3 has changed. The calculation would go on forever — in other words, the answer will never be resolved.

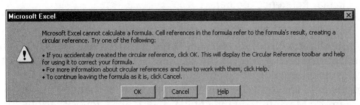

Figure 9-10: Excel's way of telling you that your formula contains a circular reference.

When you get the circular reference message after entering a formula, Excel gives you two options:

✦ Click on OK to attempt to locate the circular reference.

✦ Click on Cancel to enter the formula as is.

Normally, you'll want to correct any circular references, so you should choose OK. When you do so, Excel displays its Circular Reference toolbar (see Figure 9-11). On the Circular Reference toolbar, click on the first cell in the Navigate Circular Reference drop-down list box, and then examine the cell's formula. If you cannot determine whether the cell is the cause of the circular reference, click on the next cell in the Navigate Circular Reference box. Continue to review the formulas until the status bar no longer displays *Circular.*

If you ignore the circular reference message (by clicking on Cancel), Excel lets you enter the formula and displays a message in the status bar to remind you that a circular reference exists. In this case, the message would read *Circular: A3.* If you activate a different workbook, the message would simply display *Circular* (without the cell reference).

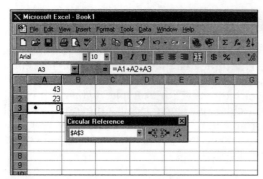

Figure 9-11: The Circular Reference toolbar.

Note Excel won't tell you about a circular reference if the Iteration setting is on. You can check this in the Options dialog box (in the Calculation panel). If Iteration is on, Excel performs the circular calculation the number of times specified in the Maximum iterations field (or until the value changes by less than .001 — or whatever value is in the Maximum change field). There are a few situations in which you would use a circular reference intentionally (see a following section). In these cases, the Iteration setting must be on. It's best, however, to keep the Iteration setting off so that you'll be warned of circular references. Most of the time, a circular reference indicates an error that must be corrected.

Indirect circular references

Usually, a circular reference is quite obvious and therefore easy to identify and correct. Sometimes, however, circular references are indirect. In other words, a formula may refer to a formula that refers to a formula that refers back to the original formula. In some cases, it may require a bit of detective work to get to the problem.

You may be able to get some assistance identifying a formula's dependents and precedents by using the tools on the Circular Reference toolbar. I discuss these tools in Chapter 31.

Intentional circular references

As I mentioned previously, you can use a circular reference to your advantage in some situations. Figure 9-12 shows a simple example. You can download this workbook from this book's home page.

In this example, a company has a policy of contributing five percent of its net profit to charity. The contribution itself, however, is considered an expense and is therefore subtracted from the net profit figure. This produces a circular reference — but this circular reference can be resolved if the Excel's Iteration setting is turned on.

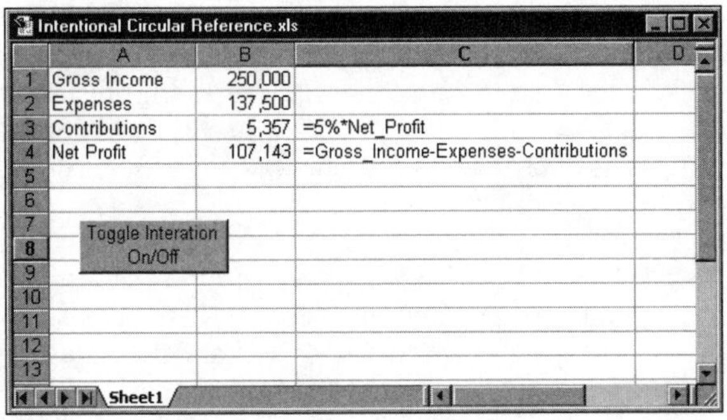

Figure 9-12: An example of an intentional circular reference.

The Contributions cell contains the following formula:

```
=5%*Net_Profit
```

The Net Profit cell contains the following formula:

```
=Gross_Income-Expenses-Contributions
```

These formulas produce a resolvable circular reference. Excel keeps calculating until the formula results don't change anymore. To get a feel for how this works, open the workbook and substitute various values for Gross Income and Expenses. If the Iteration setting is off, Excel displays its Circular Reference message and won't display the correct result. If the Iteration setting is on, Excel keeps calculating until the Contributions value is, indeed, five percent of Net Profit. In other words, the result gets increasingly accurate until it converges on the final solution.

For your convenience, I include a button on the worksheet that toggles the Iteration setting on and off by using a simple macro.

Note   Depending on your application, you may need to adjust the settings in the Maximum iterations field or the Maximum change field in the Options dialog box. For example, to increase accuracy, you can make the Maximum change field smaller. If the result doesn't converge after 100 iterations, you can increase the Maximum iterations field.

Using AutoFill rather than formulas

In Chapter 8, I discuss AutoFill as a quick way to copy a cell to adjacent cells. AutoFill also has some other uses, which may even substitute for formulas in some cases. I'm surprised to find that many experienced Excel users don't take advantage of the AutoFill feature — which can be a real timesaver.

Besides being a shortcut way to copy cells, AutoFill can quickly create a series of incremental values. For example, if you need a list of values from 1 to 100 to appear in A1:A100, you could do it with formulas. You would enter **1** in cell A1, the formula **=A1+1** into cell A2, and then copy the formula to the 98 cells below.

You also could use AutoFill to create the series for you without using a formula. To do so, enter **1** into cell A1 and **2** into cell A2. Select A1:A2 and drag the fill handle down to cell A100. When you use AutoFill in this manner, Excel analyzes the selected cells and uses this information to complete the series. If cell A1 contained 1 and cell A2 contained 3, Excel would recognize this pattern and fill in 5, 7, 9, and so on. This also works with decreasing series (10, 9, 8, and so on) and dates. If there is no discernible pattern in the selected cells, Excel performs a linear regression and fills in values on the calculated trend line.

Excel also recognizes common series names such as months and days of the week. If you enter Monday into a cell and then drag its fill handle, Excel fills in the successive days of the week. You also can create custom AutoFill lists using the Custom Lists panel of the Options dialog box. Finally, if you drag the fill handle with the right mouse button, Excel displays a shortcut menu to let you select an AutoFill option.

Advanced Naming Techniques

As promised in the preceding chapter, this section describes some additional techniques that involve names.

Sheet level names

Normally, a name that you create can be used anywhere within the workbook. In other words, names, by default, are "workbook level" names rather than "sheet level" names. But what if you have several worksheets in a workbook and you want to use the same name (such as Dept_Total) on each sheet? This is an example of when you would need to create sheet level names.

To define the name Dept_Total in more than one worksheet, activate the worksheet where you want to define the name, choose Insert⇨Name⇨Define and precede the name with the worksheet name and an exclamation point in the Names in workbook box. For example, to define the name Dept_Total on Sheet2, activate Sheet2 and enter the following in the Define Name dialog box:

```
Sheet2!Dept_Total
```

If the worksheet name contains at least one space, enclose the worksheet name in single quotation marks, like this:

```
'Adv Dept'!Dept_Total
```

You also can create a sheet level name by using the Name box (located at the left side of the formula bar). Select the cell or range, activate the Name box, and enter the name, preceded by the sheet's name and an exclamation point (as shown previously). Press Enter to create the name.

When you write a formula that uses a sheet level name on the sheet where it's defined, you don't need to include the worksheet name in the range name (the Name box won't display the worksheet name either). If you use the name in a formula on a different worksheet, however, you must use the entire name (sheet name, exclamation point, and name).

Note Only the sheet level names on the current sheet appear in the Name box. Similarly, only sheet level names in the current sheet appear in the list when you access the Paste Name or Define Name dialog boxes.

Using sheet level names can become complicated if you have an identical book level name and sheet level name (yes, Excel does allow this). In such a case, the sheet level name takes precedence over the book level name — but only in the worksheet in which the sheet level name is defined. For example, a cell might have a book level name of Total defined on Sheet1. You also can define a sheet level name of Total (in, say Sheet2). When Sheet1 is active, Total refers to the sheet level name. When any other sheet is active, Total refers to the book level name. You can refer to a sheet level name in a different worksheet, however, by preceding the name with the worksheet name and an exclamation point (such as Sheet1!Total). To make your life easier, just avoid using the same name at the book level and sheet level.

Using multisheet names

Names even can extend into the third dimension; that is, they can extend across multiple worksheets in a workbook. You can't simply select the multisheet range and enter a name in the Name box, however. Excel makes you do a little additional work to define a multisheet name.

You must use the Define Name dialog box to create a multisheet name, and you must enter the reference in the <u>R</u>efers to box manually. The format for a multisheet reference is as follows:

```
FirstSheet:LastSheet!RangeReference
```

In Figure 9-13, a multisheet name is being defined for A1:C12 that extends across Sheet1, Sheet2, and Sheet3.

After the name is defined, you can use it in formulas. This name won't appear in the Name box, however, or in the Go To dialog box. In other words, Excel lets you define the name, but it doesn't give you a way to automatically select the cells to which the name refers.

Figure 9-13: Creating a multisheet name.

Naming constants

Even many advanced Excel users don't realize that you can give a name to an item that doesn't even appear in a cell. For example, if formulas in your worksheet use a sales tax rate, you would probably insert the tax rate value into a cell and use this cell reference in your formulas. To make things easier, you would probably also give this cell a name such as SalesTax.

Here's another way to do it: Choose the Insert⇨Name⇨Define command (or press Ctrl+F3) to bring up the Define Name dialog box. Enter the name (in this case, SalesTax) into the Names in workbook field. Then click on the Refers to box and delete its contents and replace it with a value such as .075 (see Figure 9-14). Don't precede the constant with an equal sign. Click on OK to close the dialog box.

Figure 9-14: Defining a name that refers to a constant.

You've just created a name that refers to a constant rather than a cell or range. If you type **=SalesTax** into a cell, you'll see that this simple formula returns .075 — the constant that you defined. You also can use this constant in a formula such as =A1*SalesTax.

As with all names, named constants are stored with the workbook. They can be used on any worksheet in the workbook.

In the preceding example, the constant was a value. A constant also can be text, however. For example, you can define a constant for your company's name. If you work for Microsoft, you can define the name MS for Microsoft Corporation.

Note: Named constants don't appear in the Name box or in the Go To dialog box — which makes sense, because these constants don't reside anywhere tangible. They do appear in the Paste Names dialog box, however, which *does* make sense because you'll be using these names in formulas.

As you might expect, you can change the value of the constant by accessing the Define Name dialog box and simply changing the value in the Refers to box. When you close the dialog box, the formulas that use this name are recalculated using the new value.

Although this technique is useful in many situations, the main drawback is that the value is rather difficult to change. Having a constant located in a cell makes it much easier to modify. If the value is truly a "constant," however, you won't need to change it.

Naming formulas

This section takes the preceding section to the next logical level: naming formulas. Figure 9-15 shows an example of this. In this case, the name MonthlyRate refers to the following formula:

```
=Sheet3!$B$1/12
```

When you use the name MonthlyRate in a formula, it uses the value in B1 divided by 12. Notice that the cell reference is an absolute reference.

Naming formulas gets more interesting when you use relative references rather than absolute references. When you use the pointing technique to create a formula in the Refers to box, Excel always uses absolute cell references, which is unlike its behavior when you create a formula in a cell.

Figure 9-15: Excel lets you give a name to a formula that doesn't exist in the worksheet.

Figure 9-16 shows a name, Power, being created for the following formula:

```
=Sheet1!A1^Sheet1!B1
```

Notice that cell C1 is the active cell. This is very important. When you use this named formula in a worksheet, the cell references are always relative to the cell that contains the name. For example, if you enter **=POWER** into cell D12, cell D12 displays the result of B12 raised to the power of the value contained in cell C12.

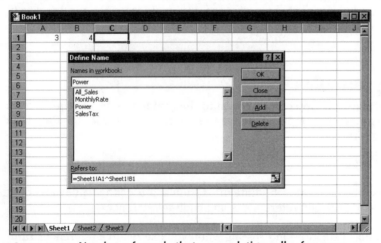

Figure 9-16: Naming a formula that uses relative cell references.

This book's home page contains a workbook that has additional examples of this technique.

Range intersections

This section describes an interesting concept that is unique to Excel: *range intersections*. Excel uses an intersection operator — a space — to determine the overlapping references in two ranges. Figure 9-17 shows a simple example. The formula in cell G5 is:

```
=B1:B7 A4:E4
```

and returns 180, the value in cell B4 — that is, the value at the intersection of the two ranges.

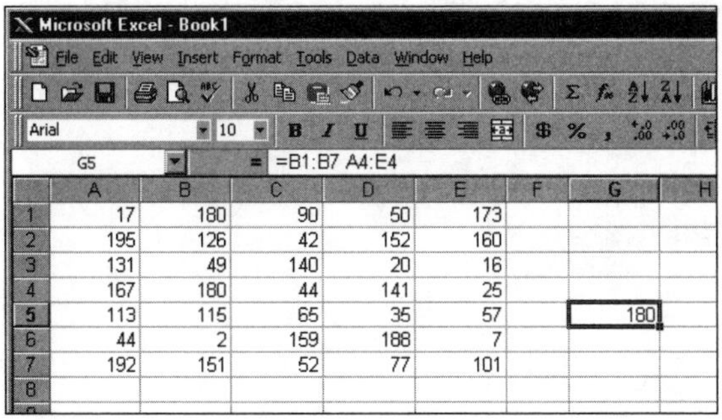

Figure 9-17: An example of an intersecting range.

The intersection operator is one of three *reference* operators for ranges. Table 9-5 lists these operators.

Table 9-5
Reference Operators for Ranges

Operator	What It Does
: (colon)	Specifies a range
, (comma)	Specifies the union of two ranges
(space)	Specifies the intersection of two ranges

The real value of knowing about range intersections is apparent when you use names. Examine Figure 9-18, which shows a table of values. I selected the entire table and then used the Insert⇨Name⇨Create command to create names automatically. Excel created the following names:

`North`	=Sheet1!$B$2:$E$2	`Qtr1`	=Sheet1!$B$2:$B$5
`South`	=Sheet1!$B$3:$E$3	`Qtr2`	=Sheet1!$C$2:$C$5
`West`	=Sheet1!$B$4:$E$4	`Qtr3`	=Sheet1!$D$2:$D$5
`East`	=Sheet1!$B$5:$E$5	`Qtr4`	=Sheet1!$E$2:$E$5

With these names defined, you'll find that you can create formulas that are very easy to read. For example, to calculate the total for Quarter 4, just use this formula:

```
=SUM(Qtr4)
```

But it really gets interesting when you use the intersection operator. Move to any blank cell and enter the following formula:

```
=Qtr1 West
```

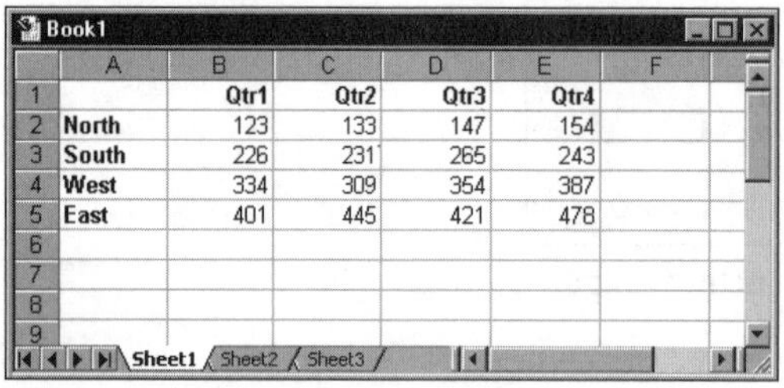
Book1

	A	B	C	D	E	F
1		Qtr1	Qtr2	Qtr3	Qtr4	
2	North	123	133	147	154	
3	South	226	231	265	243	
4	West	334	309	354	387	
5	East	401	445	421	478	
6						
7						
8						
9						

Sheet1 Sheet2 Sheet3

Figure 9-18: This table demonstrates how to use range intersections.

You'll find that this formula returned the value for the first quarter for the West region. In other words, it returned the value where the `Qtr1` range intersects with the `West` range. Naming ranges in this manner can help you create very readable formulas.

Applying names to existing references

When you create a new name for a cell or a range, Excel doesn't automatically use the name in place of existing references in your formulas. For example, assume that you have the following formula in cell F10: =A1–A2.

If you define a name `Income` for A1 and `Expenses` for A2, Excel won't automatically change your formula to =Income–Expenses. It's fairly easy to replace cell or range references with their corresponding names, however.

Using row and column headings as "names"

Excel 97

If you like the idea of using meaningful names in your formulas — but don't like the idea of going through the trouble of creating the names — you'll like the Excel 97 feature that lets you use "names" without actually defining them.

To understand how it works, refer to the accompanying figure. The figure shows a typical table, with row and column headers. Excel 97 lets you use the row and column headers as names in your formulas (and you don't have to define the names). For example, to refer to the cell that holds February sales for the South region, use the following formula:

        =Feb South

In other words, the formula returns the cell that intersects the Feb column and the South row. You can also use this technique with functions. Here's a formula that returns the total sales for March:

        =SUM(March)

Excel handles all the details for you. If you change a row or column heading, all the formulas are changed automatically to use the new label.

	A	B	C	D	E	F
1		Jan	Feb	Mar	Total	
2	North	11	14	15	40	
3	South	31	34	44	109	
4	West	43	32	56	131	
5	East	109	89	65	263	
6						
7						
8						
9						

Sheet1 / Sheet2 / Sheet3 /

This technique has a few limitations. The labels are not "real" names — they don't appear in the Define Name dialog box, nor do they appear in the Name box. Because of this, you can use this method only when the formula refers to cells on the same sheet.

To apply names to cell references in formulas after the fact, start by selecting the range that you want to modify. Then, choose the Insert⇨Name⇨Apply command. Excel displays the Apply Names dialog box, shown in Figure 9-19. Select the names that you want to apply by clicking on them, and click on OK. Excel replaces the range references with the names in the selected cells.

The Apply Names dialog box has some options. If you click on the Options button, the dialog box expands to display even more options. Most of the time, the defaults will work just fine. For more control over the names that you apply, however, you may want to use one or more of its options. These are described in Excel's online Help.

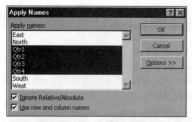

Figure 9-19: The Apply Names dialog box lets you replace cell or range references with names.

Tips for Working with Formulas

I conclude this chapter with a few additional tips and pointers relevant to formulas.

Don't hard code values

When you create a formula, think twice before using a value in the formula. For example, if your formula calculates sales tax (which is 6.5 percent), you may be tempted to enter a formula such as:

```
+A1*.065
```

A better approach is to insert the sales tax rate in a cell and use the cell reference. Or, you can define it as named constant using the technique presented earlier in this chapter. Doing so makes it easier to modify and maintain your worksheet. For example, if the sales tax range changed to 6.75 percent, you would have to modify every formula that uses the old value. If the tax rate is stored in a cell, you simply change one cell and all the formulas are updated.

Using the formula bar as a calculator

If you simply need to perform a calculation, you can use the formula bar as a calculator. For example, enter the following formula — but don't press Enter:

```
=(145*1.05)/12
```

If you press Enter, Excel enters the formula into the cell. But because this formula will always return the same result, you might prefer to store the formula's result rather than the formula. To do so, press F9 followed by Enter. Excel stores the formula's result (12.6875) rather than the formula. This also works if the formula uses cell references.

This is most useful when you use worksheet functions. For example, to enter the square root of 221 into a cell, enter **=SQRT(221)**, press F9, and press Enter. Excel enters the result: 14.8660687473185. You also can use this technique to evaluate just part of a formula. Consider this formula:

```
=(145*1.05)/A1
```

If you want to convert just the part in the parentheses to a value, get into edit mode and drag the mouse over the part that you want to evaluate (that is, select 145*1.05). Then, press F9 followed by Enter. Excel converts the formula to the following:

```
=152.25/A1
```

Making an exact copy of a formula

As you know, when you copy a formula, Excel adjusts its cell references when you paste it to a different location. Sometimes you may want to make an exact copy of the formula. One way to do this is to convert the cell references to absolute values, but this isn't always desirable. A better approach is to select the formula while you're in edit mode and then copy it to the Clipboard as text. There are several ways to do this. Here's a step-by-step example of how to make an exact copy of the formula in A1 and copy it to A2:

1. Double-click on A1 to get into edit mode.

2. Drag the mouse to select the entire formula. You can drag from left to right or from right to left.

3. Click on the Copy button the Standard toolbar. This copies the selected text to the Clipboard.

4. Press Enter to end edit mode.

5. Activate cell A2.

6. Click on the Paste button to paste the text into cell A2.

You also can use this technique to copy just *part* of a formula to use in another formula. Just select the part of the formula that you want to copy by dragging the mouse; then use any of the available techniques to copy the selection to the Clipboard. You can then paste the text to another cell.

Formulas (or parts of formulas) copied in this manner won't have their cell references adjusted when they are pasted to a new cell. This is because the formulas are being copied as text, not as actual formulas.

Converting formulas to values

If you have a range of formulas that will always produce the same result (that is, dead formulas), you may want to convert them to values. As discussed in the previous chapter, you can use the Edit➪Paste Special command to do this. Assume that range A1:A20 contains formulas that have calculated a result and that will never change. To convert these formulas to values:

1. Select A1:A20.
2. Click on the Copy button.
3. Select the Edit➪Paste Special command. Excel displays its Paste Special dialog box.
4. Click on the Values option button and then click on OK.
5. Press Enter or Esc to cancel paste mode.

Array formulas

Excel supports another type of formula called an *array formula*. Array formulas can be extremely powerful because they let you work with complete ranges of cells rather than individual cells. You'll find that you can perform some amazing feats using array formulas. This is a rather advanced concept, which I cover in Chapter 20.

Summary

This chapter introduces the concept of formulas. Formulas are entered into cells and use values found in other cells to return a result. I explain how to enter and edit formulas, when to use absolute cell references, how to identify errors in your formulas, and how to handle circular references (either accidental or intentional). I also explain how to set Excel to Manual recalculation mode — and why you would need to do so. I also discuss some additional naming techniques that can make your formulas even more powerful. I conclude with a series of tips that can help you get the most out of formulas.

✦   ✦   ✦

Using Worksheet Functions

In the preceding chapter, I discussed formulas. This chapter
continues with coverage of Excel's built-in worksheet
functions.

What Is a Function?

Functions, in essence, are built-in tools that are used in
formulas. They can make your formulas perform powerful
feats and save you a great deal of time. Functions can do the
following:

+ Simplify your formulas

+ Allow formulas to perform calculations that are otherwise impossible

+ Speed up some editing tasks

+ Allow "conditional" execution of formulas — giving them
  rudimentary decision-making capability

Function examples

Here's an example of how a built-in function can simplify a
formula. To calculate the average of the values in ten cells
(A1:A10) without using a function, you need to construct a
formula like this:

```
=(A1+A2+A3+A4+A5+A6+A7+A8+A9+A10)/10
```

Not very pretty, is it? Even worse, this formula would have to be changed if you added another cell to the range. You can replace this formula with a much simpler one that uses one of Excel's built-in worksheet functions:

```
=AVERAGE(A1:A10)
```

Next is an example of how using a function can let you perform calculations that would not be possible otherwise. What if you need to determine the largest value in a range? There's no way a formula could tell you the answer without using a function. Here's a simple formula that returns the largest value in the range A1:D100:

```
=MAX(A1:D100)
```

Functions can sometimes eliminate manual editing. Assume that you have a worksheet with 1,000 names, all in uppercase. Your boss sees the listing and informs you that the names will be mail merged with a form letter and that uppercase is not acceptable: JOHN F. CRANE must appear as John F. Crane. You *could* spend the next several hours reentering the list — or you could use a formula like this, which uses a function to convert the text in cell A1 to proper case:

```
=PROPER(A1)
```

Enter this formula once, and copy it down to the next 999 rows. Then use the Edit⇨Paste Special command (with the Values option) to convert the formulas to values. Delete the original column, and you've just accomplished several hours of work in less than a minute.

One last example should convince you of the power of functions. Suppose that you have a worksheet that calculates sales commissions. If the salesperson sold more than $100,000 of product, the commission rate is 7.5 percent; otherwise, the commission rate is 5.0 percent. Without using a function, you would have to create two different formulas and make sure that the correct formula is used for each sales amount. Here's a formula that uses the IF function to ensure that the correct commission is calculated, regardless of the sales amount:

```
=IF(A1<100000,A1*5%,A1*7.5%)
```

More about functions

All told, Excel comes with more than 300 functions. And if that's not enough, you can purchase additional specialized functions from third-party suppliers and even create your own custom functions (using VBA), if you're so inclined.

It's easy to be overwhelmed by the sheer number of functions, but you'll probably find that you use only a dozen or so functions on a regular basis. And as you'll see, Excel's Paste Function dialog box (described later in this chapter) makes it easy to locate and insert a function, even if it's not one you're familiar with.

Cross Reference Appendix B contains a complete listing of Excel's worksheet functions, with a brief description of each.

Function Arguments

In the preceding examples, you may have noticed that all the functions used parentheses. The information inside the parentheses is called an *argument*. Functions vary in how they use arguments. Depending on the function, a function may use:

✦ No arguments

✦ One argument

✦ A fixed number of arguments

✦ An indeterminate number of arguments

✦ Optional arguments

An example of a function that doesn't use an argument is RAND, which returns a random number between 0 and 1. Even if a function doesn't use an argument, however, you must still provide a set of empty parentheses, like this:

```
=RAND()
```

If a function uses more than one argument, each argument is separated by a comma. The examples at the beginning of the chapter used cell references for arguments. Excel is quite flexible when it comes to function arguments, however. Rather than consisting of a cell reference, the argument can consist of literal values, literal text strings, or expressions.

Accommodating former 1-2-3 users

If you've ever used any of the 1-2-3 spreadsheets (or any versions of Quattro Pro), you'll recall that these products require that functions be preceded with an "at" sign (@). Excel is smart enough to distinguish functions without having to flag them with a symbol.

Because old habits die hard, however, Excel accepts @ symbols when you enter functions in your formulas — but it removes them as soon as the formula is entered.

These competing products also use two dots (..) as a range operator — for example, A1..A10. Excel also lets you use this notation when you enter formulas, but it replaces it with its own range operator, a colon (:).

This accommodation goes only so far, however. Excel still insists that you use the standard Excel function names and doesn't recognize or translate those used in other spreadsheets. For example, if you enter the 1-2-3 @AVG function, Excel flags it as an error (Excel's name for this function is AVERAGE).

Using names as arguments

As you've seen, functions can use cell or range references for their arguments. When Excel calculates the formula, it simply uses the current contents of the cell or range to perform its calculations. The SUM function returns the sum of its argument(s). To calculate the sum of the values in A1:D20, you can use:

```
=SUM(A1:A20)
```

And, not surprisingly, if you've defined a name for A1:A20 (such as Sales), you can use the name in place of the reference:

```
=SUM(Sales)
```

Tip   In some cases, you may find it useful to use an entire column or row as an argument. For example, the formula that follows sums all values in column B:

```
=SUM(B:B)
```

This technique is particularly useful if the range that you're summing changes (if you're continually adding new sales figures, for instance). If you do use an entire row or column, just make sure that the row or column doesn't contain extraneous information that you don't want included in the sum. You might think that using such a large range (a column consists of 65,536 cells) might slow down calculation time — this isn't true. Excel's recalculation engine is quite efficient.

Excel 97 If you have a table of values that has row and column headings, you can use the heading text as a "name" without actually defining the name. Refer to Chapter 9 for details.

Literal arguments

A *literal argument* is a value or text string that you enter into a function. For example, the SQRT function takes one argument. Here's an example of a formula that uses a literal value for the function's argument:

```
=SQRT(225)
```

Using a literal argument with a simple function like this defeats the purpose of using a formula. This formula always returns the same value, so it could just as easily be replaced with the value 15. Using literal arguments makes more sense with formulas that use more than one argument. For example, the LEFT function (which takes two arguments) returns characters from the beginning of its first argument; the second argument specifies the number of characters. If cell A1 contains the text *Budget,* the following formula returns the first letter, or *B:*

```
=LEFT(A1,1)
```

Expressions as arguments

Excel also lets you use *expressions* as arguments. Think of an expression as a formula within a formula. When Excel encounters an expression as a function's argument, it evaluates the expression and then uses the result as the argument's value. Here's an example:

```
=SQRT((A1^2)+(A2^2))
```

This formula uses the SQRT function, and its single argument is the following expression:

```
(A1^2)+(A2^2)
```

When Excel evaluates the formula, it starts by evaluating the expression in the argument and then computes the square root of the result.

Other functions as arguments

Because Excel can evaluate expressions as arguments, it should not be surprising that these expressions can include other functions. Writing formulas that have functions within functions is sometimes known as *nesting* functions. Excel starts by evaluating the most deeply nested expression and works its way out. Here's an example of a nested function:

```
=SIN(RADIANS(B9))
```

The RADIANS function converts degrees to radians — which is the unit used by all of Excel's trigonometric functions. If cell B9 contains an angle in degrees, the RADIANS function converts it to radians, and then the SIN function computes the sine of the angle.

You can nest functions as deeply as you need, as long as you don't exceed the 1,024-character limit for a formula.

Ways to Enter a Function

There are two ways to enter a function into a formula: manually or by using the Paste Function dialog box.

Entering a function manually

If you're familiar with the function — you know how many arguments it takes and the types of arguments — you may choose to simply type the function and its arguments into your formula. Often this method is the most efficient.

Changeable range references

Many functions contain a range reference as an argument. For example, the function that follows uses the range A10:A20.

```
=SUM(A10:A20)
```

If you add a new row between rows 10 and 20, Excel expands the formula's range reference for you automatically. If you add a new row between rows 12 and 13, the formula changes to the following:

```
=SUM(A10:A21)
```

In most cases this is exactly what you want to happen. If you insert a new row at row 10, however, Excel does *not* include the new row in the range reference. If you insert a new row at the end of the range, this new row is not added to the function's reference either. This type of behavior often confuses new users, who think that Excel should be able to read their minds and change their formulas accordingly.

If you need to work with expandable ranges in your functions, there are a number of things you can do:

✦ Use a complete column or row as a reference. The following formula always returns the sum of every value in column A:

```
=SUM(A:A)
```

✦ Use an additional row in your range reference. If you have data in A1:A10 and you need to expand the range by adding new rows, change the reference to A1:A11 (and make sure that cell A11 is blank). Then you can insert a new row at row 11, and the range reference will include the new row.

Tip   When you enter a function, Excel always converts the function's name to uppercase. It's a good idea to use lowercase when entering functions. If Excel doesn't convert it to uppercase, it means that it doesn't recognize your entry as a function — you spelled it incorrectly.

Tip   If you omit the closing parenthesis, Excel adds it for you automatically. For example, if you enter =**SUM(A1:C12** and press Enter, Excel corrects the formula by adding the right parenthesis.

Pasting a function

Excel 97   Previous versions of Excel included the Function Wizard to assist with entering functions. In Excel 97, The Function Wizard has been replaced with the Formula Palette. This feature provides a way to enter a function and its arguments in a semiautomated manner. Using the Formula Palette ensures that the function is spelled correctly and has the proper number of arguments in the correct order.

To insert a function, the first step is to select the function from the Paste Function dialog box. You access this dialog box by any of the following methods:

✦ Choose the Insert⇨Function command from the menu.

✦ Click on the Paste Function button the Standard toolbar.

✦ Press Shift+F3.

Any of these options displays the Paste Function dialog box, shown in Figure 10-1.

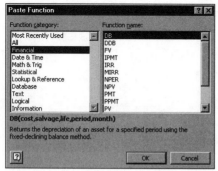

Figure 10-1: The Paste Function dialog box.

The dialog box shows the 11 function categories in the Function category list box (it may show more function categories if custom functions are available). When you select a category, the Function name list box displays the functions in the selected category.

The Most Recently Used category lists the functions you've used most recently. The All category lists all the functions available across all categories. Use this if you know a function's name but aren't sure of its category.

Tip A quick way to select a function in the Most Recently Used category is to click on the Edit Formula icon in the formula bar, and then select the function from the function list (which occupies the space normally used by the Name box).

When you select a function in the Function name list box, notice that the function (and its argument names) is displayed in the dialog box, along with a brief description of what the function does.

When you've located the function that you want to use, click on OK. Excel's Formula Palette appears, as in Figure 10-2. Use this tool to specify the arguments for the function.

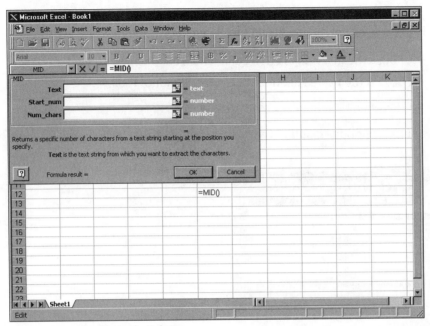

Figure 10-2: The Formula Palette.

Tip   The Formula Palette normally appears directly below the formula bar. You can move it to any other location by dragging it.

Inserting a function: An example

In this section, I present a step-by-step example that explains how to insert a function into a formula. The formula uses the AVERAGE function to compute the average of a range of cells.

1. Open a new workbook and enter values into H1:H6 (any values will do).

2. Activate cell H7. This cell will contain the formula.

3. Click on the Insert Function button the Standard toolbar. Excel displays its Paste Function dialog box.

4. Because the AVERAGE function is in the Statistical category, click on Statistical in the Function category list box. The Function name list box displays the statistical functions.

5. Click on AVERAGE in the Function name list box. The dialog box shows the function and its list of arguments. It also displays a brief description of the function.

6. Click on the OK button. Excel closes the Paste Function dialog box and displays the Formula Palette (see Figure 10-3). This tool prompts you for the function's arguments.

7. Activate the range box labeled Number1.

8. Select the range H1:H6 in the worksheet. This range address appears in the range box, and the Formula Palette shows the result.

9. Because you're finding the average of only one range, there's no need to enter any additional arguments. Click on the OK button.

Cell H7 now contains the following formula, which returns the average of the values in H1:H6:

```
=AVERAGE(H1:H6)
```

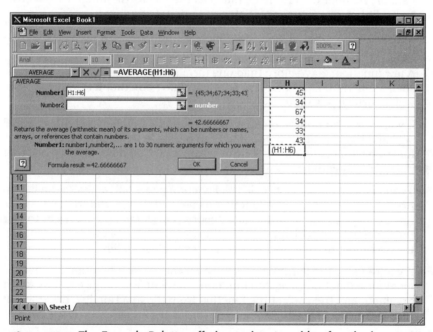

Figure 10-3: The Formula Palette, offering assistance with a function's arguments.

More about entering functions

Following are some additional tips to keep in mind when using the Formula Palette to enter functions:

✦ Click on the Help button at any time to get help about the function you selected.

✦ If you're starting a new formula, the Formula Palette automatically provides the initial equal sign for you.

✦ If the active cell is not empty when you invoke the Formula Palette, you will be able to edit the formula.

✦ You can use the Paste Function dialog box to insert a function into an existing formula. Just edit the formula and move the cursor to the location where you want to insert the function. Then invoke the Paste Function dialog box and select the function.

✦ If you change your mind about entering a function, you can click on the Cancel button.

✦ The number of range edit boxes displayed for a function is determined by the number of arguments used by the function you selected. If a function uses no arguments, there are no range edit boxes. If the function uses a variable number of arguments (such as the AVERAGE function), Excel adds a new edit box every time you enter an optional argument.

✦ The box to the right of each argument edit box displays the current value for each argument.

✦ A few functions have more than one form (INDEX is an example). If you select such a function, Excel displays another dialog box that lets you choose which form you want to use.

✦ If you only need help remembering a function's arguments, type an equal sign and the function's name, and then press Ctrl+Shift+A. Excel inserts the function with placeholders for the arguments. You'll need to replace these placeholders with actual arguments.

✦ To quickly locate a function in the Function name list, activate the list box, press the first letter of the function name, and then scroll to the desired function. For example, if the All category is selected and you want to insert the SIN function, click on the Function name list box and press S. This selects the first function that begins with S — very close to SIN.

✦ If you're using the Formula Palette and want to use a function for an argument for a function (a nested function), activate the range edit box for the argument and then select the function from the function list. Excel will insert the nested function and prompt you for its arguments.

✦ If the active cell contains a formula that uses one or more functions, the Formula Palette lets you edit each function. In the formula bar, click on the function that you want to edit. Figure 10-4 shows a formula with multiple functions.

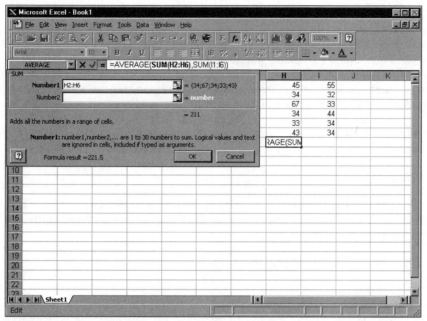

Figure 10-4: If the formula contains multiple functions, click on the function in the formula bar to edit it.

Function Examples

This section presents examples of formulas that use functions. I cover all categories listed in the Paste Function dialog box, but not every available function. For more information about a particular function, consult the online help. For a list of all functions by category, use the Paste Function dialog box (or see Appendix B).

Mathematical and trigonometric functions

Excel provides 50 functions in this category, more than enough to do some serious number crunching. The category includes common functions such as SUM and INT as well as plenty of esoteric functions — one of which may be just what you need.

INT
The INT function returns the integer (nondecimal) portion of a number by truncating all digits after the decimal point. The example that follows returns 412:

```
=INT(412.98)
```

RAND

The RAND function, which takes no arguments, returns a uniform random number that is greater than or equal to 0 and less than 1. Uniform means that all numbers have an equal chance of being generated. This function is often used in worksheets to simulate events that aren't completely predictable — such as winning lottery numbers or fourth-quarter sales. This function returns a new result whenever the worksheet is calculated.

In the example that follows, the formula returns a random number between 0 and 12 (but 12 will never be generated):

```
=RAND()*12
```

The following formula generates a random integer between two values. The cell named Lower contains the lower bound, and the cell named Upper contains the upper bound:

```
=INT((Upper-Lower+1)*RAND()+Lower)
```

Volatile functions

Some Excel functions belong to a special class of functions called *volatile*. No, these aren't functions that cause your worksheet to explode. Rather, a volatile function is recalculated whenever calculation occurs in the workbook — even if the formula that contains the function is not involved in the recalculation.

The RAND function is an example of a volatile function. This function generates a new random number every time the worksheet is calculated. Other volatile functions are as follows:

AREAS	INDEX	OFFSET
CELL	INDIRECT	ROWS
COLUMNS	NOW	TODAY

A side effect of using these volatile functions is that Excel always prompts you to save the workbook — even if no changes were made. For example, if you open a workbook that contains any of these volatile functions, scroll around a bit (but don't change anything), and then close the file, Excel asks whether you want to save the workbook.

You can circumvent this behavior by using Manual Recalculation mode, with the Recalculate before Save option turned off.

ROMAN

The ROMAN function converts a value to its Roman numeral equivalent (hey, I never said *all* the functions were useful). Unfortunately for old-movie buffs, there is no function to convert in the opposite direction. The function that follows returns MCMXCVII:

```
=ROMAN(1997)
```

ROUND

The ROUND function rounds a value to a specified digit to the left or right of the decimal point. This function is often used to control the precision of your calculation. ROUND takes two arguments: the first is the value to be rounded; the second is the digit. If the second argument is negative, the rounding occurs to the left of the decimal point. Table 10-1 demonstrates, with some examples, how this works.

Table 10-1
Examples of Using the ROUND Function

Function	Result
=ROUND(123.457,2)	123.46
=ROUND(123.457,1)	123.50
=ROUND(123.457,0)	123.00
=ROUND(123.457,-1)	120.00
=ROUND(123.457,-2)	100.00
=ROUND(123.457,-3)	0.00

Caution   Don't confuse rounding a value with number formatting applied to a value. When a formula references a cell that has been rounded with the ROUND function, the formula uses the rounded value. If a number has been formatted to *appear* rounded, formulas that refer to that cell use the actual value stored.

Note   If your work involves rounding, also check out the ROUNDUP and ROUNDDOWN functions. In addition, the FLOOR and CEILING functions let you round to a specific multiple — for example, you can use FLOOR to round a value down to the nearest multiple of 10 (124.5 would be rounded to 130).

PI

The PI function returns the value of π significant to 14 decimal places. It doesn't take any arguments and is simply a shortcut for the value 3.14159265358979. In the example that follows, the formula calculates the area of a circle (the radius is stored in a cell named Radius):

```
=PI()*(Radius^2)
```

SIN

The SIN function returns the sine of an angle. The *sine* is defined as the ratio between the opposite side and the hypotenuse of a triangle. SIN takes one argument — the angle expressed in radians. To convert degrees to radians, use the RADIANS function (there's also a DEGREES function to do the opposite conversion). For example, if cell F21 contains an angle expressed in degrees, the formula that follows returns the sine:

```
=SIN(RADIANS(F21))
```

Note Excel contains the full complement of trigonometric functions. Consult the online Help for details.

SQRT

The SQRT function returns the square root of its argument. If the argument is negative, this function returns an error. The example that follows returns 32:

```
=SQRT(1024)
```

To compute a cube root, raise the value to the 1/3 power. The example that follows returns the cube root of 32768 — which is 32. Other roots can be calculated in a similar manner.

```
=32768^(1/3)
```

SUM

If you analyzed a random sample of workbooks, it's a safe bet that you would discover that SUM is the most widely used function. It's also among the simplest. The SUM function takes from one to 30 arguments. To calculate the sum of three ranges (A1:A10, C1:10, and E1:E10), you would use three arguments, like this:

```
=SUM(A1:A10,C1:10,E1:E10)
```

The arguments don't have to be all the same type. For example, you can mix and match single cell references, range references, and literals, as follows:

```
=SUM(A1,C1:10,125)
```

Because the SUM function is so popular, the Excel designers made it very accessible — automatic, in fact. To insert a formula that uses the SUM function, just click on the AutoSum button the Standard toolbar. Excel analyzes the context and suggests a range for an argument. If it suggests correctly (which it usually does), press Enter or click on the AutoSum button again. If Excel's guess is not correct, just drag the mouse and make the selection yourself. To insert a series of SUM formulas — to add up several columns of numbers, for example — select the entire range and then click on AutoSum. In this case, Excel knows exactly what you want, so it doesn't ask you to confirm it.

SUMIF

The SUMIF function is useful for calculating conditional sums. Figure 10-5 displays a worksheet with a table that shows sales by month and by region. I used the SUMIF function in the formulas in column F. For example, the formula in F2 is as follows:

```
=SUMIF(B:B,E2,C:C)
```

	A	B	C	D	E	F	G	H
1	Month	Region	Sales		Regional Summary			
2	Jan	North	16,491		North	54,485		
3	Jan	South	14,557		South	55,089		
4	Jan	West	3,522		West	45,668		
5	Jan	East	22,041		East	61,846		
6	Feb	North	2,061		TOTAL	217,088		
7	Feb	South	21,813					
8	Feb	West	1,169		Monthly Summary			
9	Feb	East	12,486		Jan	56,611		
10	Mar	North	33,956		Feb	37,529		
11	Mar	South	18,318		Mar	79,155		
12	Mar	West	13,500		Apr	43,793		
13	Mar	East	13,381		TOTAL	217,088		
14	Apr	North	1,977					
15	Apr	South	401					
16	Apr	West	27,477					
17	Apr	East	13,938					
18								
19								

Figure 10-5: The SUMIF function returns the sum of values if the values meet specified criteria.

SUMIF takes three arguments. The first argument is the range you're using in the selection criteria — in this case, the entire column B. The second argument is the selection criteria, a region name in the example. The third argument is the range of values to sum if the criteria is met. In this example, the formula in F2 adds the values in column C only if the corresponding text in column B matches the region in column E.

The figure also shows the data summarized by month. The formula in F9 is:

```
=SUMIF(A:A,E9,C:C)
```

Cross Reference You also can use Excel's pivot table feature to perform these operations. I cover pivot tables in Chapter 25.

Text functions

Although Excel is primarily known for its numerical prowess, it has 23 built-in functions that are designed to manipulate text. I demonstrate a few of them in this section.

CHAR

The CHAR function returns a single character that corresponds to the ANSI code specified in its argument (these codes range from 1 to 255). The CODE function performs the opposite conversion. The formula that follows returns the letter *A*:

```
=CHAR(65)
```

This function is most useful for returning symbols that are difficult or impossible to enter from the keyboard. For example, the formula that follows returns the copyright symbol (©):

```
=CHAR(169)
```

Figure 10-6 shows the characters returned by the CHAR function for arguments from 1 to 255 (using the Arial font).

Note Not all codes produce printable characters, and the characters may vary depending on the font used.

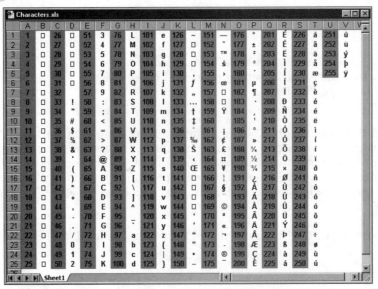

Figure 10-6: Characters returned by the CHAR function.

LEFT

The LEFT function returns a string of characters of a specified length from another string, beginning at the leftmost position. This function uses two arguments. The first argument is the string and the second argument (optional) is the number of characters. If the second argument is omitted, Excel extracts the first character from the text. In the example that follows, the formula returns the letter *B*:

```
=LEFT("B.B. King")
```

The formula that follows returns the string *Albert*:

```
=LEFT("Albert King",5)
```

Note Excel also has a RIGHT function that extracts characters from the right of a string of characters and a MID function (described after the next section) that extracts characters from any position.

LEN

The LEN function returns the number of characters in a string of text. For example, the following formula returns 12:

```
=LEN("Stratocaster")
```

If you don't want to count leading or trailing spaces, use the LEN function with a nested TRIM function. For example, if you want to know the number of characters in the text in cell A1 (without any extraneous spaces), use this formula:

```
=LEN(TRIM(A1))
```

MID

The MID function returns characters from a text string. It takes three arguments. The first argument is the text string. The second argument is the position where you want to begin extracting. The third argument is the number of characters you want to extract. If cell A1 contains the text *Joe Louis Walker,* the formula that follows returns *Louis:*

```
=MID(A1,5,5)
```

REPLACE

The REPLACE function replaces characters with other characters. The first argument is the text containing the string you're replacing. The second argument is the character position where you want to start replacing. The third argument is the number of characters to replace. The fourth argument is the new text that will replace the existing text. In the example that follows, the formula returns *Albert Collins:*

```
=REPLACE("Albert King",8,4,"Collins")
```

SEARCH

The SEARCH function lets you identify the position in a string of text in which another string occurs. The function takes three arguments. The first argument is the text you're looking for. The second argument is the string you're searching in. The third argument (optional) is the position to start looking at. If it's omitted, Excel starts searching from the beginning of the text.

In the example that follows, assume that cell A1 contains the text *John Lee Hooker*. The formula returns 5 because the first space character was found at the fifth character position.

```
=SEARCH(" ",A1,1)
```

To find the second space in the text, use a nested SEARCH function that uses the result of the first search (incremented by one character) as its third argument. Here it is:

```
=SEARCH(" ",A1,SEARCH(" ",A1,1)+1)
```

The following formula uses the LEFT function to return the characters to the left of the first space in the text in cell A1. For example, if A1 contains *Jimmy Dawkins,* the formula would return the first name *Jimmy*.

```
=LEFT(A1,SEARCH(" ",A1))
```

The preceding formula has a slight flaw: if the text in cell A1 contains no spaces, the formula results in an error. Here's an improved version that returns the entire string in A1 if it doesn't contains a space:

```
=IF(ISERROR(SEARCH(" ",A1)),A1,LEFT(A1,SEARCH(" ",A1)))
```

UPPER

The UPPER function converts characters to uppercase. If cell A1 contains the text *Lucille*, the formula that follows returns *LUCILLE*.

```
=UPPER(A1)
```

Note Excel also has a LOWER function (to convert to lowercase) and a PROPER function (to convert to proper case). In proper case, the first letter of each word is capitalized.

Logical functions

The Logical category contains only six functions (although several other functions could, arguably, be placed in this category). In this section, I discuss three of these functions.

IF

The IF function is one of the most important of all functions. This function can give your formulas decision-making capability.

The IF function takes three arguments. The first argument is a logical test that must return either TRUE or FALSE. The second argument is the formula's result if the first argument is TRUE. The third argument is the formula's result if the first argument is FALSE.

In the example that follows, the formula returns *Positive* if the value in cell A1 is greater than zero, and returns *Negative* otherwise:

```
=IF(A1>0,"Positive","Negative")
```

Notice that the first argument (A1>0) evaluates to logical TRUE or FALSE. This formula has a problem in that it returns the text *Negative* if the cell is blank or contains 0. The solution is to use a nested IF function to perform another logical test. The revised formula is as follows:

```
=IF(A1>0,"Positive",IF(A1<0,"Negative","Zero"))
```

The formula looks complicated, but when you break it down, you see that it's rather simple. Here's how the logic works. If A1 is greater than 0, the formula displays *Positive* and nothing else is evaluated. If A1 is not greater than zero, however, the second argument is evaluated. The second argument is as follows:

```
IF(A1<0,"Negative","Zero")
```

This is simply another IF statement that performs the test on A1 again. If it's less than 0, the formula returns *Negative*. Otherwise, it returns *Zero*. You can nest IF statements as deeply as you need to — although it can get very confusing after three or four levels.

Using nested IF functions is quite common, so it's in your best interest to understand how this concept works. Mastering it will definitely help you create more powerful formulas.

Figure 10-7 shows an example of using the IF function to calculate sales commissions. In this example, the normal commission rate is 5.5 percent of sales. If the sales rep exceeds the sales goal, the commission rate is 6.25 percent. The formula in cell C6, shown below, uses the IF function to make a decision regarding which commission rate to use based on the sales amount:

```
=IF(B6>=SalesGoal,B6*BonusRate,B6*CommissionRate)
```

AND

The AND function returns a logical value (TRUE or FALSE) depending on the logical value of its arguments. If all its arguments return TRUE, then the AND function returns TRUE. If at least one of its arguments returns FALSE, then AND returns FALSE.

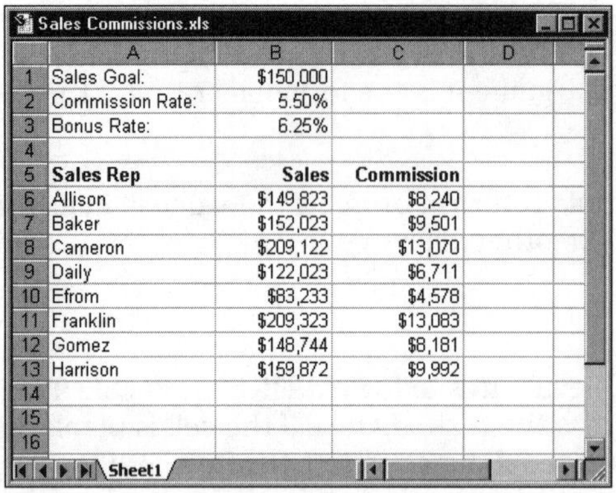

Sales Commissions.xls

	A	B	C	D
1	Sales Goal:	$150,000		
2	Commission Rate:	5.50%		
3	Bonus Rate:	6.25%		
4				
5	**Sales Rep**	**Sales**	**Commission**	
6	Allison	$149,823	$8,240	
7	Baker	$152,023	$9,501	
8	Cameron	$209,122	$13,070	
9	Daily	$122,023	$6,711	
10	Efrom	$83,233	$4,578	
11	Franklin	$209,323	$13,083	
12	Gomez	$148,744	$8,181	
13	Harrison	$159,872	$9,992	
14				
15				
16				

Sheet1

Figure 10-7: Using the IF statement to calculate sales commissions.

In the example that follows, the formula returns TRUE if the values in cells A1:A3 are all negative:

```
=AND(A1<0,A2<0,A3<0)
```

The formula that follows uses the AND function as the first argument for an IF function. If all three cells in A1:A3 are negative, this formula displays *All Negative.* If at least one is not negative, the formula returns *Not All Negative:*

```
=IF(AND(A1<0,A2<0,A3<0),"All Negative","Not All Negative")
```

OR

The OR function is similar to the AND function, but it returns TRUE if at least one of its arguments is TRUE; otherwise, it returns FALSE. In the example that follows, the formula is TRUE if either A1, A2, or A3 is negative.

```
=OR(A1<0,A2<0,A3<0)
```

Information functions

Excel's 15 functions in the Information category return a variety of information about cells. Many of these functions return logical TRUE or FALSE.

CELL

The CELL function returns information about a particular cell. It takes two arguments. The first argument is a code for the type of information to display. The second argument is the reference to the cell in which you're interested.

The example that follows uses the "type" code, which returns information about the type of data in the cell. It returns *b* if the cell is blank, *l* if it contains text (a label), or *v* if the cell contains a value or formula. For example, if cell A1 contains text, the following formula returns *l*.

```
=CELL("type",A1)
```

If the second argument contains a range reference, Excel uses the upper-left cell in the range.

Note

Excel has other functions that let you determine the type of data in a cell. The following functions may be more useful: ISBLANK, ISERR, ISERROR, ISLOGICAL, ISNA, ISNONTEXT, ISNUMBER, ISREF, ISTEXT, and TYPE.

Table 10-2 lists the possible values for the first argument of the CELL function. When using the CELL function, make sure that you enclose the first argument in quotation marks.

Table 10-2
Codes for the CELL Function Info_Type Argument

Type	What It Returns
address	The cell's address
col	Column number of the cell
color	1 if the cell is formatted in color for negative values — otherwise, 0
contents	The contents of the cell
filename	Name and path of the file that contains the cell (returns empty text if the workbook has not been saved)
format	Text value corresponding to the number format of the cell
prefix	Text value corresponding to the label prefix of the cell; this is provided for 1-2-3 compatibility
protect	0 if the cell is not locked; 1 if the cell is locked
row	Row number of the cell
type	Text value corresponding to the type of data in the cell
width	Column width of the cell rounded off to an integer

INFO

The INFO function takes one argument — a code for information about the operating environment. In the example that follows, the formula returns the path of the current folder (that is, the folder that Excel displays when you choose the File⇨Open command).

```
=INFO("directory")
```

Table 10-3 lists the valid codes for the INFO function. The codes must be enclosed in quotation marks.

Table 10-3 Codes for the INFO Function	
Code	**What It Returns**
directory	Path of the current folder
memavail	Amount of memory available, in bytes
memused	Amount of memory being used, in bytes
numfile	Number of worksheets in all open workbooks (including hidden work-books and add-ins)
origin	Returns the cell reference of the top- and leftmost cell visible in the window based on the current scrolling position
osversion	Current operating system version, as text
recalc	Current recalculation mode — Automatic or Manual
release	Version of Excel
system	Name of the operating environment — mac (for Macintosh) or pcdos (for Windows)
totmem	Total memory available on the system, in bytes

ISERROR

The ISERROR function returns TRUE if its argument returns an error value. Otherwise, it returns FALSE. This function is useful for controlling the display of errors in a worksheet.

Figure 10-8 shows a worksheet set up to track monthly sales. Each month, the worksheet is updated with two figures: the number of sales reps on staff and the total sales for the month. Formulas in columns E and F calculate the percentage of the sales goal (Actual Sales divided by Sales Goal) and the average sales per sales rep. Notice that the formulas in column F display an error when the data is missing. Cell F2 contains a simple formula:

```
=D2/C2
```

To avoid displaying an error for missing data, change the formula to the following and copy it to the cells that follow. If the division results in an error, the formula displays nothing. Otherwise, it displays the result.

```
=IF(ISERROR(D2/C2),"",D2/C2)
```

	A	B	C	D	E	F	G	H
	Month	Sales Goal	Sales Reps	Actual Sales	Pct. Of Goal	Avg. Per Rep		
2	January	500,000	9	510,233	102%	56,693		
3	February	525,000	10	518,733	99%	51,873		
4	March	550,000	10	569,844	104%	56,984		
5	April	575,000	10	560,923	98%	56,092		
6	May	600,000	11	601,923	100%	54,720		
7	June	625,000			0%	#DIV/0!		
8	July	650,000			0%	#DIV/0!		
9	August	675,000			0%	#DIV/0!		
10	September	700,000			0%	#DIV/0!		
11	October	725,000			0%	#DIV/0!		
12	November	750,000			0%	#DIV/0!		
13	December	775,000			0%	#DIV/0!		
14								
15								

Figure 10-8: This worksheet is displaying an error for formulas that refer to missing data.

Note

Excel offers several other functions that let you trap error values: ERROR.TYPE, ISERR, and ISNA. Also, note that the preceding formula could have used the ISBLANK function to test for missing data.

Date and time functions

If you use dates or times in your worksheets, you owe it to yourself to check out Excel's 14 functions that work with these types of values. In this section, I demonstrate a few of these functions.

Cross Reference

To work with dates and times, you should be familiar with Excel's serial number date-and-time system. Refer to Chapter 6.

TODAY

The TODAY function takes no argument. It returns a date that corresponds to the current date — that is, the date set in the system. If you enter the following formula into a cell on June 16, 1997, the formula returns 6/16/97:

```
=TODAY()
```

Note

Excel also has a NOW function that returns the current system date and the current system time.

DATE

The DATE function displays a date based on its three arguments: year, month, and day. This function is useful if you want to create a date based on information in your worksheet. For example, if cell A1 contains 1997, cell B1 contains 12, and cell C1 contains 25, the following formula returns the date for December 25, 1997:

```
=DATE(A1,B1,C1)
```

DAY

The DAY function returns the day of the month for a date. If cell A1 contains the date 12/25/97, the following formula returns 25:

```
=DAY(A1)
```

Note Excel also includes the YEAR and MONTH functions that extract from a date the year part and month part, respectively.

WEEKDAY

The WEEKDAY function returns the day of the week for a date. It takes two arguments: the date and a code that specifies the type of result (the second argument is optional). The codes are listed in Table 10-4.

Table 10-4	
Codes for the WEEKDAY Function	
Code	**What It Returns**
1 or omitted	Numbers 1-7, corresponding to Sunday through Saturday
2	Numbers 1-7, corresponding to Monday through Sunday
3	Numbers 0-6, corresponding to Monday through Sunday

If cell A1 contains 12/25/97, the formula that follows returns 5 — which indicates that this date is a Thursday:

```
=WEEKDAY(A1)
```

Tip You also can format cells that contain dates to display the day of the week as part of the format. Use a custom format code of ddd (for abbreviated days of the week) or dddd (for fully spelled days of the week).

TIME

The TIME function displays a time based on its three arguments: hour, minute, and second. This function is useful if you want to create a time based on information in your worksheet. For example, if cell A1 contains 8, cell B1 contains 15, and cell C1 contains 0, the following formula returns 8:15:00 AM:

```
=TIME(A1,B1,C1)
```

HOUR

The HOUR function returns the hour for a time. If cell A1 contains the time 8:15:00 AM, the following formula returns 8:

```
=HOUR(A1)
```

Note   Excel also includes the MINUTE and SECOND functions, which extract the minute part and second part, respectively, from a time.

Financial functions

The Financial function category includes 15 functions designed to perform calculations that involve money.

Depreciation functions

Excel offers five functions to calculate depreciation of an asset over time. The function you choose depends on the type of depreciation you use. Figure 10-9 shows a chart that depicts how an asset is depreciated over time, using each of the five depreciation functions.

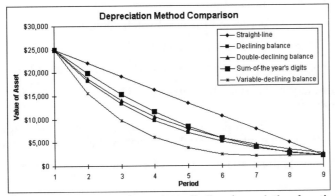

Figure 10-9: A comparison of Excel's five depreciation functions.

Table 10-5 summarizes the depreciation functions and the arguments used by each. For complete details, consult the online Help system.

Table 10-5 Excel's Depreciation Functions		
Function	**Depreciation Method**	**Arguments***
SLN	Straight-line	Cost, Salvage, Life
DB	Declining balance	Cost, Salvage, Life, Period, [Month]
DDB	Double-declining balance	Cost, Salvage, Life, Period, Month, [Factor]
SYD	Sum-of-the year's digits	Cost, Salvage, Life, Period
VDB	Variable-declining balance	Cost, Salvage, Life, Start Period, End Period, [Factor], [No Switch]

* Arguments in brackets are optional

The arguments for the depreciation functions are described as follows:

Cost: Original cost of the asset

Salvage: Salvage cost of the asset after it has been fully depreciated

Life: Number of periods over which the asset will be depreciated

Period: Period in the Life for which the calculation is being made

Month: Number of months in the first year; if omitted, Excel uses 12

Factor: Rate at which the balance declines; if omitted, it is assumed to be 2 (that is, double-declining)

Rate: Interest rate per period. If payments are made monthly, for example, you must divide the annual interest rate by 12.Loan and annuity functions

Table 10-6 lists the functions that can help you perform calculations related to loans and annuities.

Notice that these functions all use pretty much the same arguments — although the exact arguments used depend on the function. To use these functions successfully, you must understand how to specify the arguments correctly. The following list explains these arguments:

Nper: Total number of payment periods. For a 30-year mortgage loan with monthly payments, Nper would be 360.

Pmt: Fixed payment made each period for an annuity or a loan. This usually includes principal and interest (but not fees or taxes).

FV: Future value (or a cash balance) after the last payment is made. The future value for a loan is 0. If FV is omitted, Excel uses 0.

Type: Either 0 or 1, and indicates when payments are due. Use 0 if the payments are due at the end of the period and 1 if they are due at the beginning of the period.

Guess: Used only for the RATE function. It's your best guess of the internal rate of return. The closer your guess, the faster Excel can calculate the exact result.

Table 10-6
Loan and Annuity Functions

Function	Calculation	Arguments*
FV	Future Value	Rate, Nper, Pmt, [PV], [Type]
PV	Present Value	Rate, Nper, Pmt, [PV], [Type]
PMT	Payment	Rate, Nper, PV, [FV], [Type]
PPMT	Principal Payment	Rate, Per, Nper, PV, [FV], [Type]
IPMT	Interest Payment	Rate, Per, Nper, PV, [FV], [Type]
RATE	Interest Rate per Period	Nper, Pmt, PV, [FV], [Type], [Guess]
NPER	Number of Periods	Rate, Pmt, PV, [FV], [Type]

* Arguments in brackets are optional

This book's Web site contains an example workbook that demonstrates the use of the PMT, PPMT, and IPMT functions to calculate a fixed-interest amortization schedule.

Lookup and Reference functions

The 15 functions in the Lookup and Reference category are used to perform table lookups and obtain other types of information. I demonstrate some of these functions in this section.

VLOOKUP

The VLOOKUP function can be quite useful when you need to use a value from a table, such as a table of tax rates. This function retrieves text or a value from a table, based on a specific key in the first column of the table. The retrieved result is at a specified horizontal offset from the first row of the table.

Figure 10-10 shows an example of a lookup table (named `PartsList`) in range D2:F9. The worksheet is designed so that a user can enter a part number into cell B2 (which is named `Part`), and formulas in cells B4 and B5 return the appropriate information for the part by using the lookup table. The formulas are as follows:

Cell B4: `=VLOOKUP(Part,PartsList,2,FALSE)`

Cell B5: `=VLOOKUP(Part,PartsList,3,FALSE)`

The formula in B4 looks up the value in the cell named `Part` in the first column of the table named `PartsList`. It returns the value in the column that corresponds to its third argument (column 2). The fourth argument tells Excel that it must find an exact match. If the fourth argument is TRUE (or omitted), Excel returns the next largest value that is less than the lookup value (the values in the first column must be in ascending order). Using an inexact match is useful for income-tax tables in which an income may fall into a range of values. In other words, there won't be a line in the table for every possible income.

If you enter a value that is not found in the table, the formula returns #N/A. You can change the formula to produce a more user-friendly error message by using the ISNA function. The revised formula is as follows:

`=IF(ISNA(VLOOKUP(Part,PartsList,2,FALSE)),"NotFound",VLOOKUP(Part,PartsList,2,FALSE))`

If you enter a part that is not in the list, this formula returns *Not Found* rather than #N/A.

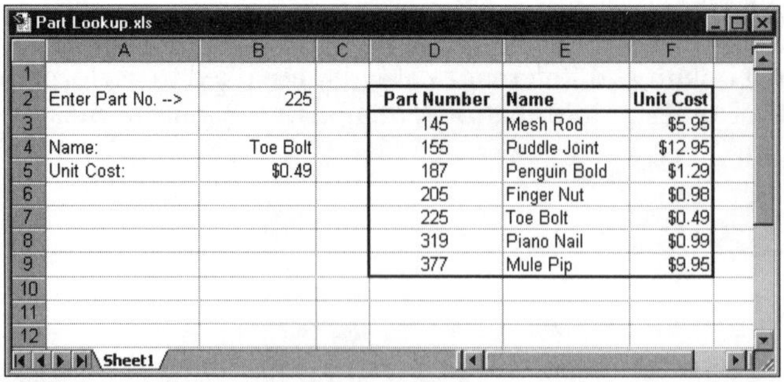

	A	B	C	D	E	F
1						
2	Enter Part No. -->	225		**Part Number**	**Name**	**Unit Cost**
3				145	Mesh Rod	$5.95
4	Name:	Toe Bolt		155	Puddle Joint	$12.95
5	Unit Cost:	$0.49		187	Penguin Bold	$1.29
6				205	Finger Nut	$0.98
7				225	Toe Bolt	$0.49
8				319	Piano Nail	$0.99
9				377	Mule Pip	$9.95
10						
11						
12						

Part Lookup.xls — Sheet1

Figure 10-10: A vertical lookup table.

Note The HLOOKUP function works exactly like VLOOKUP except that it looks up the value horizontally in the table's first row.

MATCH

The MATCH function searches a range for a value or text and returns the relative row or column in which the item was found. Figure 10-11 shows a simple example. The worksheet contains the month names in A1:A12. Cell D2 contains the following formula:

```
=MATCH(D1,A1:A12,0)
```

The formula returns 7 because cell D1 contains *July,* and July is the seventh element in the range A1:A12.

The third argument for the MATCH function specifies the type of match you want (0 means an exact match). Values of 1 and –1 are used when you'll accept an inexact match.

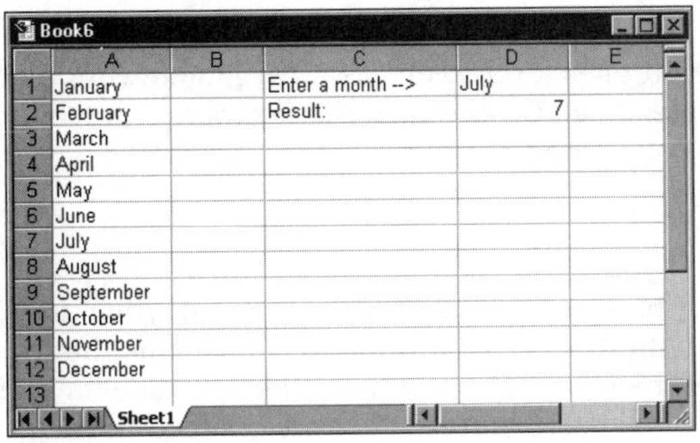

Figure 10-11: Using the MATCH function to return a relative position in a range.

INDEX

The INDEX function returns a value from a range using a row index (for a vertical range), column index (for a horizontal range), or both (for a two-dimensional range). The formula that follows returns the value in A1:J10 that is in its fifth row and third column:

```
=INDEX(A1:J10,5,3)
```

You can download a workbook that demonstrates the INDEX function and the MATCH function. The workbook, shown in Figure 10-12, displays the mileage between selected U.S. cities.

The OFFSET function performs a similar function.

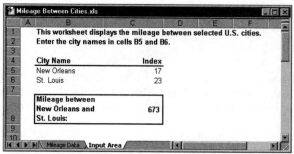

Figure 10-12: This workbook uses the INDEX and MATCH
functions to look up the mileage between selected U.S. cities.

INDIRECT

The INDIRECT function returns the value in a cell specified by its text argument. For example, the following formula returns the value (or text) in cell A1:

    =INDIRECT("A1")

This function is most useful when it uses a reference as its argument (not a literal, as shown previously). For example, if cell C9 contains the text *Sales,* the following formula returns the value in the cell named Sales:

    =INDIRECT(C9)

This concept can be a bit difficult to grasp but, after you master it, you can put it to good use. Figure 10-13 shows a multisheet workbook with formulas that use the INDIRECT function to summarize the information in the other worksheets in the workbook. Cell B2 contains the following formula, which was copied to the other cells:

    =INDIRECT("'"&$A2&"'"&"!"&B$1)

This formula builds a cell reference by using text in row 1 and column A. The argument is evaluated as follows:

    'Denver'!Sales

The Denver sheet has a range named Sales. Therefore, the indirect function returns the value in the cell named Sales on the Denver worksheet.

This file is available at the book's Web site.

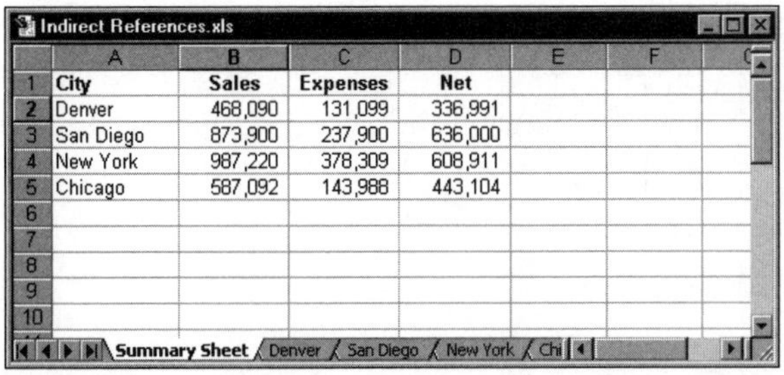

Figure 10-13: These formulas use the INDIRECT function to summarize values contained in the other workbooks.

Statistical functions

The Statistical category contains a whopping 71 functions that perform various calculations. Many of these are quite specialized, but several are useful for nonstatisticians.

AVERAGE

The AVERAGE function returns the average (arithmetic mean) of a range of values. This is equivalent to the sum of the range divided by the number of values in the range. The formula that follows returns the average of the values in the range A1:A100:

```
=AVERAGE(A1:A100)
```

If the range argument contains blanks or text, these cells aren't included in the average calculation. As with the SUM formula, you can supply any number of arguments.

Note Excel also provides the MEDIAN function (which returns the middle-most value in a range) and the MODE function (which returns the value that appears most frequently in a range).

COUNTIF

The COUNTIF function is useful if you want to count the number of times a specific value occurs in a range. This function takes two arguments: the range that contains the value to count and a criteria used to determine what to count. Figure 10-14 shows a worksheet set up with student grades. I used the COUNTIF function in the formulas in column E. For example, the formula in E2 is as follows:

```
=COUNTIF(B:B,D2)
```

Notice that the first argument consists of a range reference for the entire column B. This makes it easy to insert new names without having to change the formulas.

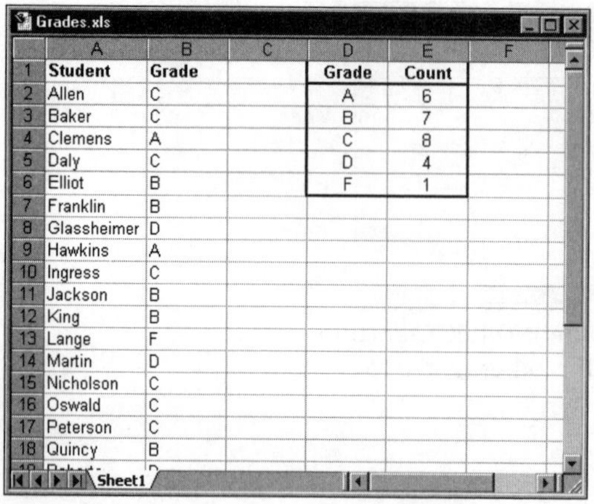

	A	B	C	D	E	F
1	Student	Grade		Grade	Count	
2	Allen	C		A	6	
3	Baker	C		B	7	
4	Clemens	A		C	8	
5	Daly	C		D	4	
6	Elliot	B		F	1	
7	Franklin	B				
8	Glassheimer	D				
9	Hawkins	A				
10	Ingress	C				
11	Jackson	B				
12	King	B				
13	Lange	F				
14	Martin	D				
15	Nicholson	C				
16	Oswald	C				
17	Peterson	C				
18	Quincy	B				

Figure 10-14: Using the COUNTIF function to create a distribution of grades.

Note
You also can use the Analysis ToolPak add-in to create frequency distributions. See Chapter 28 for details.

COUNT and COUNTA

The COUNT function returns the number of values in a range. The COUNTA function returns the number of nonblank cells in a range. For example, the following formula returns the number of nonempty cells in column A:

```
=COUNTA("A:A")
```

MAX and MIN

Use the MAX function to return the largest value in a range and the MIN function to return the smallest value in a range. The following formula displays the largest and smallest values in a range named Data; using the concatenation operator causes the result to appear in a single cell:

```
="Smallest: "&MIN(Data)&" Largest: "&MAX(Data)
```

For example, if the values in Data range from 12 to 156, this formula returns *Smallest: 12 Largest: 156*.

LARGE and SMALL

The LARGE function returns the *n*th-largest value in a range. For example, to display the second-largest value in a range named Data, use the following formula:

```
=LARGE(Data,2)
```

The SMALL function works just as you would expect: it returns the *n*th-smallest value in a range.

Database functions

Excel's Database function category consists of a dozen functions that are used when working with database tables (also known as lists) stored in a worksheet. These functions all begin with the letter *D,* and they all have nondatabase equivalents. For example, the DSUM function is a special version of the SUM function that returns the sum of values in a database that meet a specified criteria. A database table is a rectangular range with field names in the top row. Each subsequent row is considered a record in the database.

Cross Reference To use a database function, you must specify a special criteria range in the worksheet. This type of criteria range is the same one that is used with Excel's Data⇨Filter⇨Advanced Filter command. I discuss this topic in Chapter 23.

The DSUM function calculates the sum of the values in a specified field, filtered by the criteria table. For example, to calculate the total sales for the North region, enter **North** under the Region field in the criteria range. Then enter the following formula into any cell (this assumes that the database table is named Data and that the criteria range is named Criteria):

```
=DSUM(Data,"Sales",Criteria)
```

The formula returns the sum of the Sales field, but only for the records that meet the criteria in the range named Criteria. You can change the criteria, and the formula displays the new result. For example, to calculate the sales for January, enter **Jan** under the Month field in the Criteria range (and delete any other entries).

Web site If you want to use several DSUM formulas, you can have each of them refer to a different criteria range (you can use as many criteria ranges as you like).

Excel's other database functions work exactly like the DSUM function.

Analysis ToolPak functions

When you begin to feel familiar with Excel's worksheet functions, you can explore those that are available when the Analysis ToolPak is loaded. This add-in provides you with dozens of additional worksheet functions.

When this add-in is loaded, the Paste Function dialog box displays a new category, Engineering. It also adds new functions to the following function categories: Financial, Date & Time, Math & Trig, and Information.

Cross Reference I discuss the Analysis ToolPak in Chapter 28. See Appendix B for a summary of the Analysis ToolPak function.

Creating Megaformulas

Often, spreadsheets require intermediate formulas to produce a desired result. After you get the formulas working correctly, it's often possible to eliminate the intermediate formulas and use a single *megaformula* instead (this term is my own — there is no official name for such a formula). The advantages? You use fewer cells (less clutter) and recalculation takes less time. Besides, people in the know will be impressed with your formula-building abilities. The disadvantage? The formula may be impossible to decipher or modify.

Here's an example: imagine a worksheet with a column of people's names. And suppose that you've been asked to remove all middle names and middle initials from the names — but not all names have a middle name or initial. Editing the cells manually would take hours, so you opt for a formula-based solution. Although this task is not a difficult one, it normally involves several intermediate formulas. Also assume that you want to use as few cells as possible in the solution.

Figure 10-15 shows the solution, which requires six intermediate formulas. The names are in column A; the end result is in column H. Columns B through G hold the intermediate formulas. Table 10-7 shows the formulas used in this worksheet, along with a brief description of each.

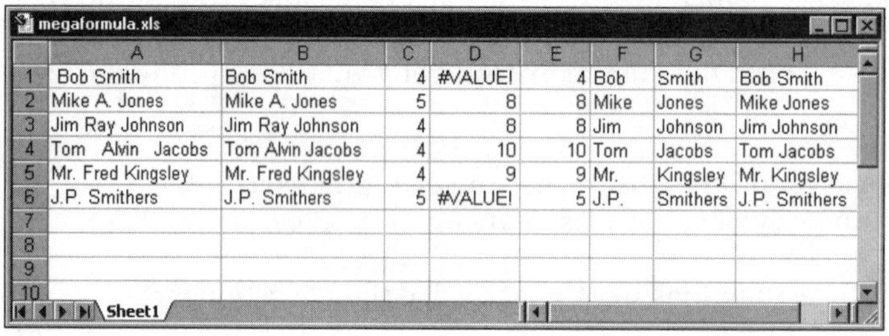

	A	B	C	D	E	F	G	H
1	Bob Smith	Bob Smith	4	#VALUE!	4	Bob	Smith	Bob Smith
2	Mike A. Jones	Mike A. Jones	5	8	8	Mike	Jones	Mike Jones
3	Jim Ray Johnson	Jim Ray Johnson	4	8	8	Jim	Johnson	Jim Johnson
4	Tom Alvin Jacobs	Tom Alvin Jacobs	4	10	10	Tom	Jacobs	Tom Jacobs
5	Mr. Fred Kingsley	Mr. Fred Kingsley	4	9	9	Mr.	Kingsley	Mr. Kingsley
6	J.P. Smithers	J.P. Smithers	5	#VALUE!	5	J.P.	Smithers	J.P. Smithers
7								
8								
9								
10								

Figure 10-15: Removing the middle names and initials requires six intermediate formulas.

Table 10-7
Intermediate Formulas

Cell	*Intermediate Formula*	*What It Does*
B1	=TRIM(A1)	Removes excess spaces
C1	=FIND(" ",B1,1)	Locates first space
D1	=FIND(" ",B1,C1+1)	Locates second space (returns an error if there is no second space)

Cell	Intermediate Formula	What It Does
E1	=IF(ISERROR(D1),C1,D1)	Uses the first space if no second space
F1	=LEFT(B1,C1)	Extracts the first name
G1	=RIGHT(B1,LEN(B1)-E1)	Extracts the last name
H1	=F1&G1	Concatenates the two names

You can eliminate all the intermediate formulas by creating a huge formula (what I call a megaformula). You do so by starting with the end result and then replacing each cell reference with a copy of the formula in the cell referred to (but don't copy the equal sign). Fortunately, you can use the Clipboard to copy and paste. Keep repeating this process until cell H1 contains nothing but references to cell A1. You end up with the following megaformula in one cell:

```
=LEFT(TRIM(A1),FIND("",TRIM(A1),1))&RIGHT(TRIM(A1),LEN(TRIM(A1))-
    IF(ISERROR(FIND(" ",TRIM(A1),FIND("
    ",TRIM(A1),1)+1)),FIND(" ",TRIM(A1),1),FIND("
    ",TRIM(A1),FIND(" ",TRIM(A1),1)+1)))
```

When you're satisfied that the megaformula is working, you can delete the columns that hold the intermediate formulas because they are no longer used.

The megaformula performs exactly the same task as all the intermediate formulas — although it's virtually impossible for anyone (even the original author) to figure out. If you decide to use megaformulas, make sure that the intermediate formulas are performing correctly before you start building a megaformula. Even better, keep a copy of the intermediate formulas somewhere in case you discover an error or need to make a change.

Web site This workbook is available at this book's Web site.

Your only limitation is that Excel's formulas can be no more than 1,024 characters. Because a megaformula is so complex, you may think that using one would slow down recalculation. Actually, the opposite is true. As a test, I created a worksheet that used a megaformula 20,000 times. Then I created another worksheet that used six intermediate formulas rather than the megaformula. As you can see in Table 10-8, the megaformula recalculated faster and also resulted in a much smaller file.

Table 10-8
Intermediate Formulas Versus Megaformula

Method	Recalc Time (seconds)	File Size
Intermediate formulas	9.2	7.1MB
Megaformula	5.1	2.5 MB

Creating Custom Functions

Although Excel offers more functions than you'll ever need, it's likely that you'll eventually search for a function you need and you won't be able to find it. The solution is to create your own.

If you don't have the skills to create your own functions, you may be able to purchase custom Excel functions from a third-party provider that specializes in your industry. Or you can hire a consultant to develop functions that meet your needs.

To create a custom function, you must be well-versed in Visual Basic for Applications (VBA). When you create a custom function, you can use it in your worksheet, just like the built-in functions.

 Cross Reference I cover custom worksheet functions in Chapter 36.

Learning More about Functions

This chapter has just barely skimmed the surface. Excel has hundreds of functions I haven't mentioned. To learn more about the functions available to you, I suggest that you browse through them by using the Paste Function dialog box and click on the Help button when you see something that looks useful. The functions are thoroughly described in Excel's online Help system. Figure 10-16 shows an example of the help available for a function.

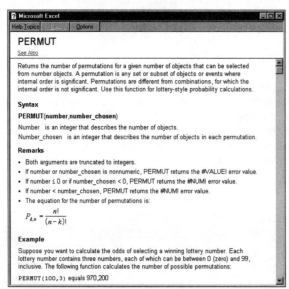

Figure 10-16: All of Excel's worksheet functions are described in the online Help system.

Summary

This chapter discusses the built-in worksheet functions available in Excel. These functions are arranged by category, and you can enter them into your formulas manually (by typing them) or by using the Paste Function dialog box and the Formula Palette. Many examples of functions across the various categories are also discussed.

✦　　✦　　✦

Worksheet Formatting

In Chapter 6, I discussed number formatting, which lets you change the way that values are displayed in their cells. This chapter covers what I refer to as *stylistic* formatting, which is purely cosmetic.

Overview of Stylistic Formatting

The stylistic formatting that you apply to worksheet cells doesn't affect the actual content of the cells. Rather, the goal of such formatting is to make your work easier to read or more attractive. The types of formatting I discuss in this chapter consist of the following:

♦Using different type fonts, sizes, and attributes

♦Changing the way cells contents are aligned within cells

♦Using colors in the background or foreground in cells

♦Using patterns for cell background

♦Using borders around cells

♦Using a graphic background for your worksheet

Web site — This book's Web site contains a file that demonstrates many of the techniques used in this chapter.

Why bother with formatting?

Some users tend to shy away from formatting. After all, it doesn't do anything to make the worksheet more accurate, and formatting just takes valuable time.

I'll be the first to admit that stylistic formatting isn't essential for every workbook you develop. If no one except you will ever see it, you may not want to bother. If anyone else will use your workbook, however, I strongly suggest that you spend some time applying simple formatting. Figure 11-1 shows an example of how even simple formatting can significantly improve a worksheet's readability.

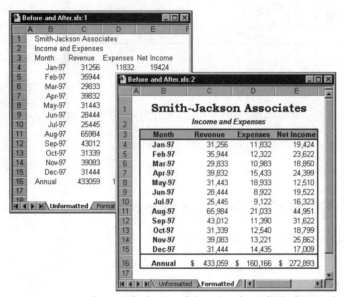

Figure 11-1: Before and after applying simple stylistic formatting.

On the other hand, some users go overboard with formatting. I've downloaded many Excel worksheets from the Internet and online services such as CompuServe. Some of these worksheets are hideous and don't convey a professional image. The main problems are too many different fonts and sizes and overuse of color and borders.

Eventually you'll strike a happy medium with your stylistic formatting: not too much, but enough to clarify what you're trying to accomplish.

When to format

When you're developing a worksheet, you can apply stylistic formatting at any time. Some people prefer to format their work as they go along (I'm in this group). Others wait until the workbook is set up and then apply the formatting as the final step (the icing on the cake). The choice is yours.

The Formatting toolbar

In Chapter 6, I introduce the Formatting toolbar, which is a quick way to apply simple stylistic formatting. Figure 11-2 shows this toolbar.

Figure 11-2: The Formatting toolbar contains many tools to apply formats.

In many cases, this toolbar may contain all the formatting tools you need. But some types of formatting require using the Format Cells dialog box. This chapter covers the finer points of stylistic formatting, including options not available on the Formatting toolbar.

The Format Cells dialog box

Throughout this chapter, I refer to the Format Cells dialog box. This is a tabbed dialog box from which you can apply nearly any type of stylistic formatting (as well as number formatting). The formats selected in the Format Cells dialog box apply to the current selection of cells.

After selecting the cell or range to format, you can bring up the Format Cells dialog box by using any of the following methods:

◆ Choose the Format➪Cells command.

◆ Press Ctrl+1.

◆ Right-click on the selected cell or range and choose Format Cells from the shortcut menu.

The Format Cells dialog box contains six tabs. When you first access this dialog box, the Number panel is displayed. You can choose another panel by clicking on any of the other tabs. When you display this dialog box again, Excel displays it with the panel you were last using.

Working with Fonts

One of the elements that distinguishes a graphical user interface (GUI) such as Windows from a character-based interface (such as plain old DOS) is fonts. A GUI can display different fonts in different sizes and with different attributes (bold, italic, underline). A character-based display typically shows one font of the same size and may be able to handle different font attributes.

Tip   You can use different fonts, sizes, or attributes in your worksheets to make various parts stand out — as in the headers for a table. You also can adjust the font size to make more information appear on a single page.

Reducing the font size so that your report fits on a certain number of pages isn't always necessary. Excel has a handy option that automatically scales your printed output to fit on a specified number of pages. I discuss this option in Chapter 12.

About fonts

When you select a font, Excel displays only the fonts that are installed on your system. Windows includes several fonts, and Microsoft Office 97 includes many additional fonts that you can install on your system. In addition, you can acquire fonts from a variety of other sources such as the Internet and online services. For best results, you should use TrueType fonts. These fonts can be displayed and printed in any size, without the "jaggies" that characterize nonscalable fonts.

If you plan to distribute a workbook to other users, you should stick with the fonts that are included with Windows. If you open a workbook and your system doesn't have the font with which the workbook was created, Windows attempts to use a similar font. Sometimes this works, and sometimes it doesn't. To be on the safe side, use only the fonts that follow if you plan to share your workbook with others:

✦ Arial
✦ Courier New
✦ Symbol
✦ Times New Roman
✦ Wingdings

The default font

By default, the information you enter into an Excel worksheet uses the 10-point Arial font. A font is described by its typeface (Arial, Times New Roman, Courier New, and so on) as well as by its size, measured in points (there are 72 points in one inch). Excel's row height is, by default, 12.75 points. Therefore, 10-point type entered into 12.75-point rows leaves a small amount of blank space between the characters in adjacent rows.

Note If you have not manually changed a row's height, Excel automatically adjusts the row height based on the tallest text you enter into the row. You can, of course, override this adjustment and change the row height to any size you like. Excel's row height must be in 0.25-point increments. For example, if you enter a row height of 15.35, Excel makes the row 15.5 points high (it always rounds up).

The default font is the font specified by the Normal style for the workbook. All cells have the Normal style unless you specifically apply a different style. If you want to change the font for all cells that have the Normal style, you simply change the font used in the Normal style. Here's how to do it:

1. Choose the Format⇨Style command. Excels displays the Style dialog box.

2. Make sure that Normal appears in the drop-down box labeled Style, and click on the Modify button. Excel displays the Format Cells dialog box.

3. Choose the font and size you want as the default, and click on OK to return to the Style dialog box.

4. Click on OK again to close the Style dialog box.

The font for all cells that use the Normal style changes to the font you specified. Changing the font for the Normal style can be done at any time. I discuss Excel's style feature later in this chapter.

Tip If you want to change the default font permanently, create a template named book.xlt that uses a different font for the Normal style. I discuss templates in Chapter 34.

Changing fonts

The easiest way to change the font or size for selected cells is to use the Font and Font Size tools on the Formatting toolbar. Just select the cells, click on the appropriate tool, and choose the font or size from the drop-down list.

You also can use the Font panel in the Format Cells dialog box, as shown in Figure 11-3. This panel lets you control several other attributes of the font from a single dialog box. Notice that you also can change the font style (bold, italic), underlining, color, and effects (strikethrough, superscript, or subscript). If you click on the check box labeled Normal Font, Excel displays the selections for the font defined for the Normal style.

Note Notice that Excel provides four different underlining styles. For the two accounting underline styles, dollar signs and percent signs aren't underlined. In the two nonaccounting underline styles, the entire cell contents are always underlined.

Figure 11-3: The Font panel in the Format Cells dialog box.

Figure 11-4 shows examples of font formatting.

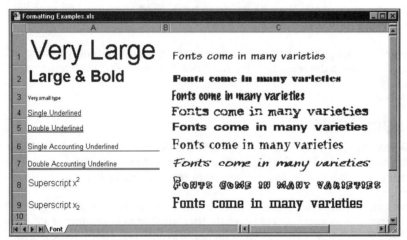

Figure 11-4: Examples of font formatting.

Using multiple formatting in one cell

If a cell contains text (not a formula or a value), Excel also lets you format individual characters in the cell. To do so, get into edit mode and then select the characters you want to format. You can select characters by dragging the mouse over them or by holding down the Shift key as you press the left- or right-arrow key. Then use any of the standard formatting techniques. The changes apply to only the selected characters in the cell. This technique doesn't work with cells that contain values or formulas.

Selecting fonts and attributes with shortcut keys

If you prefer to keep your hands on the keyboard, you can use the following shortcut keys to quickly format a selected range:

Ctrl+B   Bold

Ctrl+I   Italic

Ctrl+U   Underline

Ctrl+5   Strikethrough

These shortcut keys act as a toggle. For example, you can turn bold on and off by repeatedly pressing Ctrl+B.

Figure 11-5 shows a few examples of using different fonts, sizes, and attributes in a cell.

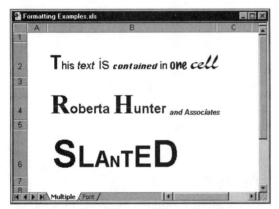

Figure 11-5: You can use different fonts, sizes, or attributes for selected characters in text.

Changing Cell Alignment

Cell alignment refers to how a cell's contents are situated in the cell. The contents of a cell can be aligned both vertically and horizontally in the cell. The effect you see depends on the cell's height and width. For example, if the row uses standard height, you may not be able to notice any changes in the cell's vertical alignment (but if you increase the row's height, these effects are apparent).

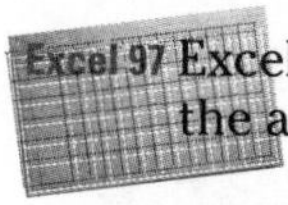

Excel 97 Excel 97 also allows you to display text at a specified orientation — you choose the angle.

Figure 11-6 shows some examples of cells formatted with the various horizontal, and vertical alignment options.

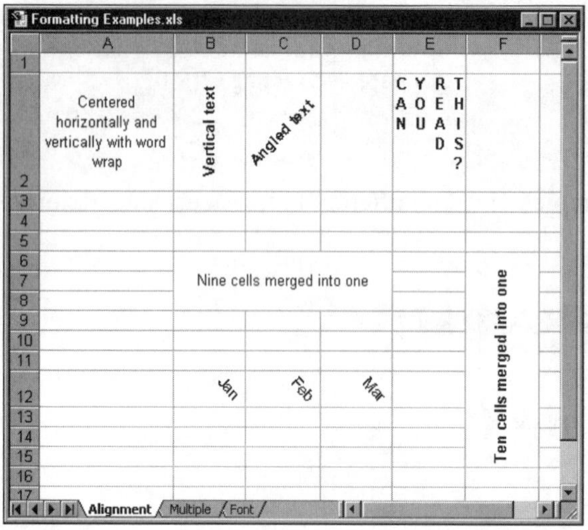

Figure 11-6: Examples of Excel's alignment options.

Horizontal alignment options

You can apply most of the horizontal alignment options by using the tools on the Formatting toolbar. Or you can use the Alignment panel in the Format Cells dialog box, as shown in Figure 11-7.

The horizontal alignment options are as follows:

✦ **General:** Aligns numbers to the right and text to the left and centers logical and error values. This option is the default alignment.

✦ **Left:** Aligns the cell contents to the left side of the cell. If the text is wider than the cell, it spills over to the cell to the right. If the cell to the right is not empty, the text is truncated and not completely visible.

✦ **Center:** Centers the cell contents in the cell. If the text is wider than the cell, it spills over to cells on either side if they are empty. If the adjacent cells aren't empty, the text is truncated and not completely visible.

✦ **Right:** Aligns the cell contents to the right side of the cell. If the text is wider than the cell, it spills over to the cell to the left. If the cell to the left isn't empty, the text is truncated and not completely visible.

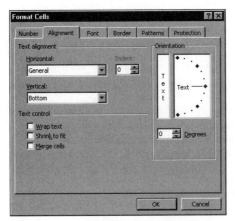

Figure 11-7: The Alignment panel in the Format Cells dialog box.

  ◆ **Fill:** Repeats the contents of the cell until the cell's width is filled. If cells to the right also are formatted with Fill alignment, they also are filled.

  ◆ **Justify:** Justifies the text to the left and right of the cell. This option is applicable only if the cell is formatted as wrapped text and uses more than one line.

  ◆ **Center across selection:** Centers the text over the selected columns. This option is useful for precisely centering a heading over a number of columns.

Excel 97   Excel 95's Center Across Selection tool on the formatting toolbar has been replaced in Excel 97 with a tool called Merge and Center. Although the new tool has the same image as the Center Across Selection tool, it does not perform the same formatting.

Vertical alignment options

To change the vertical alignment, you must use the Alignment tab of the Format Cells dialog box (these options are not available on the Formatting toolbar). The vertical alignment options are as follows:

  ◆ **Top:** Aligns the cell contents to the top of the cell.

  ◆ **Center:** Centers the cell contents vertically in the cell.

  ◆ **Bottom:** Aligns the cell contents to the bottom of the cell.

  ◆ **Justify:** Justifies the text vertically in the cell; this option is applicable only if the cell is formatted as wrapped text and uses more than one line.

Text control options

The Alignment tab of the Format Cells dialog box offers three additional options — two of them are new with Excel 97.

Wrap text

The Wrap text option displays the text on multiple lines in the cell, if necessary. This option is useful for column headings because it enables you to display lengthy headings without having to make the columns too wide.

Shrink to fit

Excel 97 includes a Shrink to fit option. This reduces the size of the text so it fits into the cell without spilling over to the next cell.

If you apply wrap text formatting to a cell you cannot use the shrink to fit formatting.

Merging Cells

Excel 97 introduces a unique feature: merged cells. Merging cells doesn't combine the contents of cells. Rather, it lets you combine a group of cells that occupy the same space into a single cell. Figure 11-8 shows two sets of merged cells. Range C3:G3 has been merged into a single cell that holds the table's title. Range B5:B9 has also been merged, and it holds a title for the table's rows.

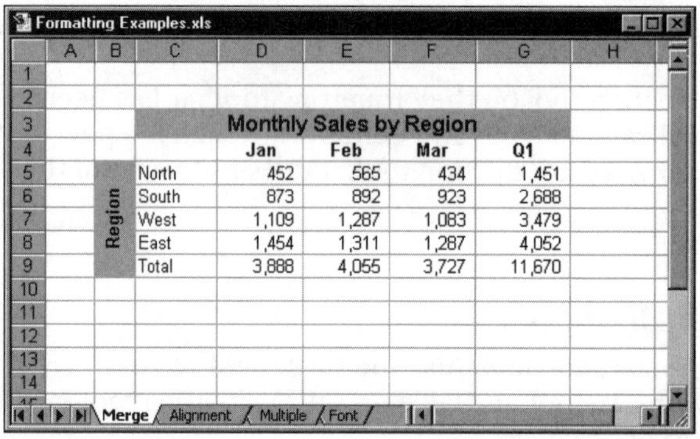

Figure 11-8: The titles for this table consist of merged cells.

You can merge any number of cells, occupying any number of rows and columns. However, the range to be merged should be empty except for the upper left cell. If any of the other cells to be merged are not empty, Excel will display a warning.

To merge cells, select the cells to be merged, then click on the Merge and Center tool on the Formatting toolbar. The only way to "unmerge" cells is to use the Format Cells dialog box.

Changing a cell's orientation

Excel 97 Previous versions of Excel could display text horizontally or vertically. Excel 97 now lets you specify any angle. To change the orientation, select the cell or range, access the Format Cells dialog box, and select the Alignment tab. Use the gauge to specify an angle between -90 and +90 degrees.

Figure 11-9 shows an example of text displayed at a 45 degree angle.

Figure 11-9: An example of rotated text.

Another type of justification

Excel provides another way to justify text, using its Edit⇨Fill⇨Justify command. This command has nothing to do with the alignment options discussed in this chapter. The Edit⇨Fill⇨Justify command is useful for rearranging text in cells so that it fits in a specified range. For example, you may import a text file that has very long lines of text.

You easily can justify this text so that it's displayed in narrower lines. The accompanying figures show a range of text before and after I used this command.

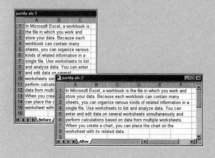

This command works with text in a sinjle column. It essentially redistributes the text in the cells so that it fits into a specified range. You can make the text either wider (so that it uses fewer rows) or narrower (so that it uses more rows).

Select the cells to be justified (all in one column) and then extend the selection to the right so that the selection is as wide as you want the end result to be. Choose the Edit⇨Fill⇨Justify command, and Excel redistributes the text.

Blank rows serve as paragraph markers. If the range you select isn't large enough to hold all the text, Excel warns you and allows you to continue or abort. Be careful, because justified text overwrites anything that gets in its way.

Colors and Shading

Excel provides the tools to create some very colorful worksheets. I've known people who avoid using color because they are uncertain of how the colors will translate when printed on a black-and-white printer. With Excel, that's not a valid reason. You can instruct Excel to ignore the colors when you print. You do this by checking the Black and White check box in the Sheet panel of the Page Setup dialog box (choose the File⇨Page Setup command to display this dialog box).

You control the color of the cell's text in the Font panel of the Format Cells dialog box, and you control the cell's background color in the Patterns panel. You can also use tools on the Formatting toolbar (Font Color and Fill Color) to change the color of these items.

A cell's background can be solid (one color) or consist of a pattern that uses two colors. To select a pattern, click on the Pattern drop-down list in the Format Cells dialog box. It expands as shown in Figure 11-10. Choose a pattern from the top part of the box and a second color from the bottom part. The first pattern in the list is "None" — use this option if you want a solid background. The Sample box to the right shows how the colors and pattern will look. If you plan to print the worksheet, you need to experiment to see how the color patterns translate to your printer.

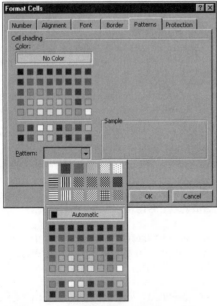

Figure 11-10: Choosing a pattern for a cell background.

You might want to use a background color to make a large table of data easier to read. You're undoubtedly familiar with computer printer paper that has alternating green-and-white horizontal shading. You can use background colors to simulate this effect in Excel. See Figure 11-11 for an example.

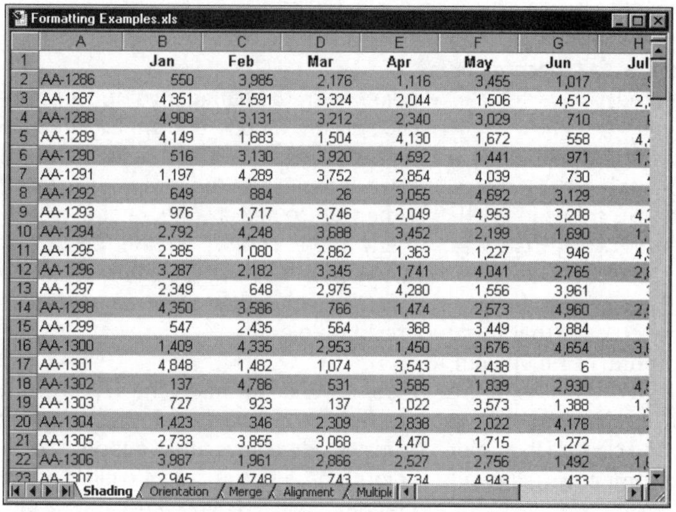

	A	B	C	D	E	F	G	H
1		Jan	Feb	Mar	Apr	May	Jun	Jul
2	AA-1286	550	3,985	2,176	1,116	3,455	1,017	
3	AA-1287	4,351	2,591	3,324	2,044	1,506	4,512	2,
4	AA-1288	4,908	3,131	3,212	2,340	3,029	710	
5	AA-1289	4,149	1,683	1,504	4,130	1,672	558	4,
6	AA-1290	516	3,130	3,920	4,592	1,441	971	1,
7	AA-1291	1,197	4,289	3,752	2,854	4,039	730	
8	AA-1292	649	884	26	3,055	4,692	3,129	
9	AA-1293	976	1,717	3,746	2,049	4,953	3,208	4,
10	AA-1294	2,792	4,248	3,688	3,452	2,199	1,690	1,
11	AA-1295	2,385	1,080	2,862	1,363	1,227	946	4,
12	AA-1296	3,287	2,182	3,345	1,741	4,041	2,765	2,
13	AA-1297	2,349	648	2,975	4,280	1,556	3,961	
14	AA-1298	4,350	3,586	766	1,474	2,573	4,960	2,
15	AA-1299	547	2,435	564	368	3,449	2,884	
16	AA-1300	1,409	4,335	2,953	1,450	3,676	4,654	3,
17	AA-1301	4,848	1,482	1,074	3,543	2,438	6	
18	AA-1302	137	4,786	531	3,585	1,839	2,930	4,
19	AA-1303	727	923	137	1,022	3,573	1,388	1,
20	AA-1304	1,423	346	2,309	2,838	2,022	4,178	
21	AA-1305	2,733	3,855	3,068	4,470	1,715	1,272	
22	AA-1306	3,987	1,961	2,866	2,527	2,756	1,492	1,
23	AA-1307	2,945	4,748	743	734	4,943	433	2,

Figure 11-11: Shading alternate lines can make a lengthy table easier to read.

Tip Here's a quick way to apply shading to every other row. This technique assumes that you want to shade every odd-numbered row in the range A1:F100. Start by shading A1:F1 with the color you want. Then select A1:F2 and copy it to the Clipboard. Next select A3:F100 and choose Edit➪Paste Special (with the Formats option).

Tip To quickly hide the contents of a cell, make the background color the same as the font color. The cell contents are still visible in the formula bar when the cell is selected, however.

Borders and Lines

Borders often are used to group a range of similar cells or simply to delineate rows or columns. Excel offers 13 different styles of borders, as you can see in the Border panel in the Format Cells dialog box (see Figure 11-12). This dialog box works with the selected cell or range and lets you specify which border style to use for each border of the selection.

Excel 97 Excel 97 offers five new border styles.

About the color palette

Excel gives you 56 colors from which to choose. These colors are known as the palette. You can examine the colors in the palette by clicking on the Color or Font Color tool on the Formatting toolbar. You may notice that these colors aren't necessarily unique (some are repeated).

Chances are, you're running Windows in a video mode that supports at least 256 colors. So why can you use only 56 colors in Excel? Good question. That's just the way Excel was designed.

You're not limited to the 56 colors that some unknown techie in Redmond came up with, however. You can change the colors in the palette to whatever you like. To do so, access the Options dialog box and click on the Color tab, as shown in the accompanying figure.

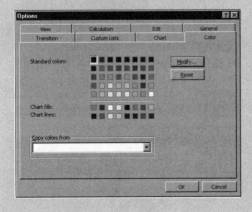

You'll see that there seems to be some rationale for the colors in the palette. For example, the first 40 are designated standard colors. These are followed by 8 chart fill colors, and 8 chart line colors.

If you want to change a color, select it and click on the Modify button. Excel responds with a dialog box named Colors. This dialog box has two tabs: Standard and Custom. Use either tab to select a new color (you have many more choices in the Custom tab). When you've select the color, click on OK, and the color you selected replaces the previous color.

If your worksheet uses the replaced color, the new color takes over. If your system is using a video driver that supports only 16 colors, some of the colors will be made by blending two colors (*dithering*). Dithered colors can be used for cell backgrounds, but text and lines are displayed using the nearest solid color. If you want to revert back to Excel's standard colors, click on the Reset button.

Each workbook stores its own copy of the color palette, and you even can copy color palettes from another workbook (which must be open). Use the Options dialog box's drop-down box labeled Copy Colors From.

Before you invoke this dialog box, select the cell or range to which you want to add borders. First choose a line style and then choose the border position for the line style by clicking one of the icons.

Notice that there are three "presets," which can save you some clicking on. If you want to remove all borders from the selection, click on None. To put an outline around the selection, choose Outline preset. To put borders inside the selection, click on Inside preset.

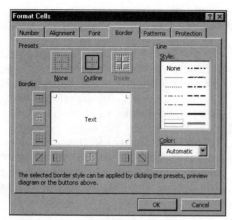

Figure 11-12: The Border panel of the Format Cells dialog box.

Excel displays the selected border style in the dialog box. You can choose different styles for different border positions. You also can choose a color for the border. Using this dialog box may require some trial and error, but you'll get the hang of it. Figure 11-13 shows examples of borders in a worksheet.

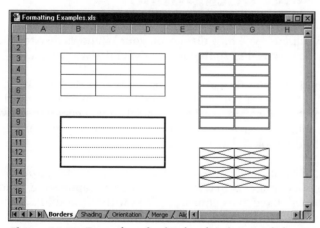

Figure 11-13: Examples of using borders in a worksheet.

Excel 97 Excel 97 offers two new border options: diagonal lines through the cell. This type of border gives the appearance that the cell or range has been crossed out.

Tip   If you use border formatting in your worksheet, you might want to turn off the grid display to make the borders more pronounced. Use the View panel of the Options dialog box to do this.

Producing 3D effects

You can use a combination of borders and background shading to produce attractive 3D effects on your worksheet. These 3D effects resemble raised or depressed panels, as shown in the accompanying figure.

For the best results, use a light gray background color. To produce a raised effect, apply a white border to the top and left side of the range and a dark gray border on the bottom and right side.

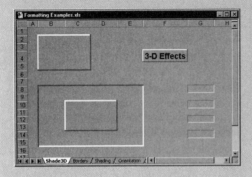

To produce a sunken effect, use a dark gray border on the top and left side and a white border on the bottom and right side. You can vary the line thickness to produce different effects.

You can download the 3D Shading utility, which is part of the Power Utility Pak, from this book's Web site.

Adding a Worksheet Background

Excel also lets you choose a graphics file to serve as a background for a worksheet — similar to the wallpaper you may display on your Windows desktop. The graphic image you choose is repeated so that it tiles the entire worksheet.

Tip   Thousands of background graphics files are available on the World Wide Web. Many web sites use graphic files for backgrounds, and these files are designed to "tile" nicely. In addition, these files are usually very small. If you encounter a web site that uses a good graphic background, you can save the file to your hard drive and use it in your Excel workbooks.

To add a background to a worksheet, choose the Format⯈Sheet⯈Background command. Excel displays a dialog box that lets you choose a graphics file. When you locate a file, click on OK. Excel tiles your worksheet with the graphic. Some backgrounds make it difficult to view text, so you may want to use a background color for cells that contain text (see Figure 11-14). You'll also want to turn off the gridline display because the gridlines show through the graphic.

Note   The graphic background on a worksheet is for display only — it doesn't get printed when you print the worksheet.

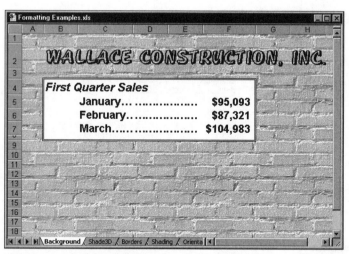

Figure 11-14: This worksheet has a graphic background. Cells that contain text use a white background, which overrides the graphic.

AutoFormatting

So far, this chapter has described the individual formatting commands and tools at your disposal. Excel also has a feature known as *AutoFormatting* that can automatically perform many types of formatting for you. Figure 11-15 shows an unformatted table in worksheet and the same table that was formatted using one of Excel's AutoFormats.

Copying formats by painting

If you want to copy the formats from a cell to another cell or range, you can use the Edit⇨Paste Special command and click on the Formats option. Another option is to use the Format Painter button the Standard toolbar (it's the button with the paintbrush image).

Start by selecting the cell or range that has the formatting attributes you want to copy. Then click on the Format Painter button. Notice that the mouse pointer appears as a paintbrush. Next, click on and drag (paint)

the cells to which you want to apply the formats. Release the mouse button, and the painting is finished (and you don't have to clean the brush).

Double-clicking on the Format Painter button causes the mouse pointer to remain a paintbrush after you release the mouse button. This lets you paint other areas of the work-sheet with the same formats. To get out of paint mode, click on the Format Painter button again (or press Esc).

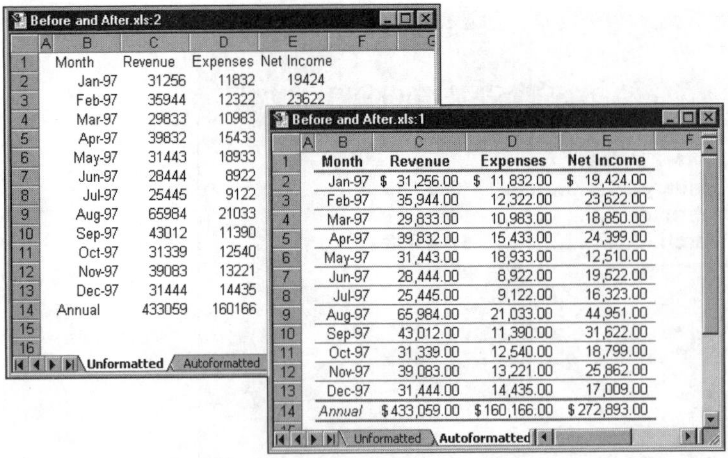

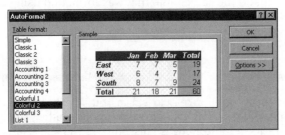

Figure 11-15: A worksheet table before and after using AutoFormat.

Using AutoFormats

To apply an AutoFormat, move the cell pointer anywhere within a table you want to format (Excel determines the table's boundaries automatically). Then choose the Format⇨AutoFormat command. Excel responds with the dialog box shown in Figure 11-16. Choose one of the 17 AutoFormats from the list and click on OK. Excel formats the table for you.

Figure 11-16: The AutoFormat dialog box.

Excel's AutoFormatting is smarter than it may appear on the surface. For example, it analyzes the data contained in the table and formats the table to handle items such as subtotals. Figure 11-17 shows an example of a table that contains a subtotal line for each department. When I applied an AutoFormat, the formatting took these subtotals into account and produced an attractive table in about one second.

	A	B	C	D	E	F
1						
2		**Region**	**State**	*Sales*		
3		West	California	872,982.00		
4		West	Washington	498,232.00		
5		West	Oregon	198,355.00		
6		**West Total**		1,569,569.00		
7		East	New York	733,209.00		
8		East	New Jersey	507,816.00		
9		East	Massachusetts	450,982.00		
10		**East Total**		1,692,007.00		
11		Midwest	Missouri	322,484.00		
12		Midwest	Illinois	598,329.00		
13		**Midwest Total**		920,813.00		
14		*Grand Total*		4,182,389.00		
15						
16						

Figure 11-17: AutoFormatting even accommodates subtotals in a table.

Controlling AutoFormats

I would have wagered good money that Excel 97 would allow user-defined AutoFormats. But I would have lost the bet. Although you can't define your own AutoFormats, you can control the type of formatting that is applied. When you click on the Options button in the AutoFormat dialog box, the dialog box expands to show six options (see Figure 11-18).

Initially, the six check boxes are all checked — which means that Excel will apply formatting from all six categories. If you want it to skip one or more categories, just uncheck the appropriate box before you click on OK. For example, when I use AutoFormats, I hardly ever want Excel to change the column widths, so I turn off the Width/Height option. If you've already formatted the numbers, you may want to turn off the Number option.

Figure 11-18: The AutoFormat dialog box expanded to show its options.

Using Conditional Formatting

Excel 97 One of the most common requests among Excel users is a way to change the formatting of a cell, based on its contents. For example, if the cell contains a negative number, make the cell bold with a red background. Microsoft responded to this request by including a new conditional formatting feature in Excel 97.

To apply conditional formatting to a cell or range, select the range and then choose the Format⇨Conditional Formatting command. You'll get the dialog box shown in Figure 11-19. This dialog box lets you specify up to three conditions for the selected cells.

Figure 11-19: Excel 97 lets you specify formats that are displayed, based on the cell's value.

The condition can be based on the cell's value, or it can be based on a formula that you specify (the formula must be a logical formula and return either True or False).

1. In the drop-down list, choose either Cell Value Is or Formula Is.

2. If you chose Cell Value Is in Step 1, specify the conditions by using the controls in the dialog box. For example, you can specify between 0 and 100. You can enter values or cell references.

3. If you chose Formula Is in Step 1, specify a reference to the formula. Remember, the formula must return either True or False.

4. Click on the Format button and specify the formatting that will be used when the condition is true.

5. If you want to specify another conditional format for the selection, click on the Add button. The dialog box will expand so you can repeat Steps 1–4 for another condition.

6. When you're finished, click on OK.

Note Conditional formatting is a great feature, but it's not foolproof. If you copy a value and paste it into a cell that has conditional formatting, the formatting will not be applied. In fact, copying a value to a cell that has conditional formatting wipes out the conditional formatting information. In other words, the feature works only for data that is entered into a cell manually or calculated by a formula.

Using Named Styles

Perhaps one of the most underutilized features in Excel is its *named style* feature — something that was borrowed from the word processing genre. As a side note, named styles may also be the most underutilized feature in word processors.

If you find yourself continually applying the same combination of fonts, lines, and shading in your worksheets, it's to your advantage to create and use named styles. Named styles save time and reduce formatting errors by applying formats you specify in a single step. This feature also is useful for helping you to apply consistent formats across your worksheets.

The real advantage of styles, however, is that you can change a component of a style and then all the cells using that named style automatically incorporate the change. Suppose that you apply a particular style to a dozen cells scattered throughout your worksheet. Later you realize that these cells should have a font size of 14 points rather than 12 points. Rather than change each one, simply edit the style. All cells with that particular style change automatically. This can be a significant timesaver.

A style can consist of settings for six different attributes, although a style doesn't have to use all the attributes. You may recognize these attributes; they correspond to the six panels in the Format Cells dialog box. The attributes that make up a style are as follows:

- ✦ Number format
- ✦ Font (type, size, and color)
- ✦ Alignment (vertical and horizontal)
- ✦ Borders
- ✦ Pattern
- ✦ Protection (locked and hidden)

By default, all cells have the Normal style. In addition, Excel provides five other built-in styles — all of which control only the cell's number format. The styles available in every workbook are listed in Table 11-1.

If these styles don't meet your needs (and they probably don't), you can easily create new styles.

Table 11-1
Excel's Built-In Styles

Style Name	Description	Number Format Example
Normal	Excel's default style	1234
Comma*	Comma with two decimal places	1,234.00
Comma[0]	Comma with no decimal places	1,234
Currency*	Left-aligned dollar sign with two decimal places	$ 1,234.00
Currency[0]	Left-aligned dollar sign with no decimal places	$ 1,234
Percent*	Percent with no decimal places	12%

* This style can be applied by clicking on a button on the Standard toolbar.

Applying styles

This section discusses the methods you can use to apply existing styles to cells or ranges.

Toolbar buttons

As mentioned in the preceding section, three buttons on the Standard toolbar are used to attach a particular style to a cell or range. It's important to understand that when you use these buttons to format a value, you're really changing the cell's style. Consequently, if you later want to change the Normal style, cells formatted with any of these buttons won't be affected by the change.

Using the Style tool

If you plan to work with named styles, you might want to make an addition to one of your toolbars. In fact, I strongly suggest that you do so. Excel has a handy Style tool available. But (oddly) it's not on any of the built-in toolbars — maybe this is why the named style feature is underutilized. To add the Style tool to a toolbar (the Formatting toolbar is a good choice), follow these steps:

1. Right-click on any toolbar and choose Customize from the shortcut menu. Excel displays its Customize dialog box.

2. In the Categories list box, click on Formatting. The Buttons box displays all available tools in the Formatting category.

3. Click on the Style tool (it's labeled *Style*) and drag it to your Formatting toolbar. If you drag it in the middle of the toolbar, the other tools scoot over to make room for it.

4. If the formatting toolbar is too wide to show all the tools, you can make two of them (the Zoom tool and the new Style tool) narrower by clicking on and dragging their right border. You also can get rid of any tools you never use by simply dragging them away (don't worry, you can always reset the toolbar to its original state).

5. When the toolbar looks the way you want it, click on the Close button in the Customize dialog box.

The new Style tool displays the style of the selected cell and also lets you quickly apply a style — or even create a new style. To apply a style by using the Style tool, just select the cell or range, click on the Style tool, and choose the style you want to apply.

Using the Format⇨Style command

You also can apply a style by using the Format⇨Style command. Excel will display its Style dialog box. Just choose the style you want to apply from the Style Name drop-down list. Using the Style tool, as described in the previous section, is a much quicker way to apply a style.

The Web site for this book contains a workbook in which I've defined several styles. You may want to download this workbook and experiment with them.

Creating new styles

There are two ways to create a new style: using the Format⇨Style command or using the Style tool. To create a new style, first select a cell and apply all the formatting that will be included in the new style. You can use any of the formatting available in the Format Cells dialog box.

When the cell is formatted to your liking, choose the Format⇨Style command. Excel displays its Style dialog box, shown in Figure 11-20. The name displayed in the Style Name drop-down list is the current style of the cell (probably Normal). This box is highlighted, so you can simply enter a new style name by typing it. When you do so, Excel displays the words *By Example* to indicate that it's basing the style on the current cell.

The check boxes display the current formats for the cell. By default, all check boxes are checked. If you don't want the style to include one or more format categories, uncheck the appropriate box(es). Click on OK to create the style.

You also can create a style from scratch in the Style dialog box. Just enter a style name and then click on the Modify button to select the formatting.

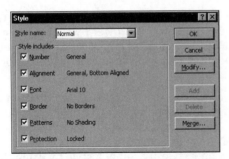

Figure 11-20: You can create a new style by using the Style dialog box.

Tip   If you followed my advice and added the Style tool to one of your toolbars, you can create a new style without using the Style dialog box. Just format a cell, activate the Style tool, and type the name. The only disadvantage to this method is that you can't specify which format categories to omit from the style. But as you'll see next, it's easy to modify an existing style.

Overriding a style

After you apply a style to a cell, you can apply additional formatting to it by using any formatting method discussed in this chapter. Formatting modifications you make to the cell don't affect other cells that use the same style.

Modifying a style

To change an existing file, call up the Style dialog box. Choose from the drop-down box the style you want to modify. You can make changes to the check boxes to include or exclude any of the format categories. Or you can click on the Modify button. Excel displays the familiar Format Cells dialog box. Make the changes you want and click on OK. Click on OK again to close the Style dialog box. All the cells with the selected style are modified with the new formatting.

Tip   You also can change a style by modifying the formatting of a cell that uses the style. After doing so, activate the Style tool and reselect the style name. Excel asks whether you want to redefine the style based on the selection. Respond in the affirmative to change the style — and all of the cells that use the style.

Deleting a style

If you no longer need a style, you can delete it. To do so, activate the Style dialog box, choose the style from the list, and click on Delete. All the cells that had the style revert back to the Normal style.

Note If you applied additional formatting to a cell that had a style applied to it and then you delete the style, the cell retains all its additional formatting.

Merging styles from other workbooks

You may create one or more styles you use frequently. Although you could go through the motions and create these styles for every new workbook, a better approach is to merge the styles from a workbook that already has them created.

To merge styles from another workbook, the workbook that contains the styles to be merged must be open. Choose the Format⇨Style command and click on the Merge button. Excel displays a list of all open workbooks, as shown in Figure 11-21. Select the workbook and click on OK. The active workbook then contains all styles from the other workbook.

Figure 11-21: Merging styles from another workbook is a good way to make your workbooks look consistent.

When you're merging styles, colors are based on the palette stored with the workbook. If the workbook from which you're merging has a different color palette, the colors used in the merged styles may not look the same.

Controlling Styles with Templates

When you start Excel, it loads with a number of default settings, including the settings for stylistic formatting. If you find that you spend a great deal of time changing the default elements, you should know about templates.

Here's an example. You may prefer to use 12-point Arial rather than 10-point Arial as the default font. And maybe you prefer that Wrap Text be the default setting for alignment. Changing defaults is easy to do when you know about templates.

The trick is to create a workbook with the Normal style modified to the way you want it. Then save the workbook as a template in your XLStart folder. After doing so, selecting the File⇨New command displays a dialog box from which you can choose the template for the new workbook. Template files also can store other named styles. This is an excellent way to give your workbooks a consistent look.

Cross Reference Chapter 34 discusses templates in detail.

Summary

This chapter explores all topics related to stylistic formatting: different fonts and size, alignment options, applying colors and shading, and using borders and lines. I discuss Excel's AutoFormat feature, which can format a table of data automatically. The chapter concludes with a discussion of named styles, an important concept that can save you time and also make your worksheets look more consistent.

✦   ✦   ✦

Printing Your Work

◆ ◆ ◆ ◆

In This Chapter

Excel's printer defaults and how to change the print settings

Using print preview to see your output before sending it to the printer

Using the new page break preview mode to adjust the print range and page breaks dynamically

Using custom views for multiple print jobs in a single workbook

Printing tips and techniques

◆ ◆ ◆ ◆

Many worksheets that you develop with Excel are designed to serve as printed reports. You'll find that printing from Excel is quite easy, and you can generate attractive, well-formatted reports with minimal effort. But, as you'll see, Excel has plenty of printing options, which are explained in this chapter.

One-Step Printing

The Print button on the Standard toolbar is a quick way to print the current worksheet using the default settings. Just click on the button, and Excel sends the worksheet to the printer. If you've changed any of the default print settings, Excel uses the new settings; otherwise, it uses the following default settings:

- ◆ Prints the active worksheet (or all selected worksheets), including any embedded charts or drawing objects
- ◆ Prints one copy
- ◆ Prints the entire worksheet
- ◆ Prints in portrait mode
- ◆ Doesn't scale the printed output
- ◆ Uses 1-inch margins for the top and bottom and .75-inch margins for the left and right
- ◆ Prints with no headers or footers
- ◆ For wide worksheets that span multiple pages, it prints down and then across

As you might suspect, you can change any of these default print settings.

When you print a worksheet, Excel prints only the *active area* of the worksheet. In other words, it won't print all four million cells — just those that have data in them. If the worksheet contains any embedded charts or drawing objects, they also are printed (unless you have modified the Print Object property of the object).

Note If you create a workbook based on a template, the template may contain different default print settings. I discuss templates in Chapter 34.

Adjusting Your Print Settings

The sections that follow discuss the various print settings that you can modify. You adjust these settings in two different dialog boxes:

✦ The Print dialog box (accessed with the File⇨Print command or Ctrl+P).

✦ The Page Setup dialog box (accessed with the File⇨Page Setup command). This is a tabbed dialog box with four panels.

Both of these dialog boxes have a Print Preview button that previews the printed output on-screen.

Settings in the Print Dialog Box

The following sections discuss the options available in the Print dialog box. The Print dialog box is where you actually start the printing (unless you used the Print button the Standard toolbar). After you've selected your print settings, click on OK from the Print dialog box to print your work.

Selecting a printer

Before printing, make sure that the correct printer is selected (applicable only if you have access to more than one printer). You do this in the Print dialog box, shown in Figure 12-1. You can select the printer from the drop-down list labeled Printer. This dialog box also lists information about the selected printer, such as its status and where it's connected.

Clicking on the Properties button displays a property box for the selected printer. The exact dialog box that you see depends on the printer. This dialog box lets you adjust printer-specific settings. In most cases, you won't have to change any of these settings, but it's a good idea to be familiar with the settings that you can change.

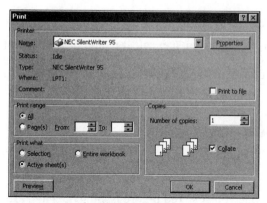

Figure 12-1: The Print dialog box.

If you check the Print to file check box, the output is sent to a file. Excel prompts you for a filename before it begins printing. The resulting file will *not* be a standard text file. Rather, it will include all the printer codes required to print your worksheet. Printing to a file is useful if you don't have immediate access to a printer. You can save the output to a file and then send this file to your printer at a later time.

Tip   If you want to save your workbook as a text file, use the File⇨Save As command, and select one of the text file formats from the drop-down list labeled Save as type.

Excel 97   Excel 97 offers a new way to view your worksheets: page break preview mode. To enter this mode, choose the View⇨Page Break Preview command. The worksheet display changes, and you can see exactly what will be printed and where the page breaks occur. To change the print range, drag any of the dark borders. I discuss this feature in more detail later in this chapter.

After you print a worksheet (or view it in page break preview mode), Excel displays dashed lines to indicate where the page breaks occur. This is a useful feature because the display adjusts dynamically. For example, if you find that your printed output is too wide to fit on a single page, you can adjust the column widths (keeping an eye on the page break display) until they are narrow enough to print one page.

Tip   If you don't want to see the page breaks displayed in your worksheet, access the Options dialog box, click on the View tab, and remove the check mark from the Automatic Page Breaks check box.

Printing selected pages

If your printed output uses multiple pages, you can select which pages to print in the Print dialog box. In the Page Range section, indicate the number of the first and last pages to print. You can use the spinner controls or type the page numbers in the edit boxes.

Specifying what to print

The Print What section of the Print dialog box lets you specify what to print. You have three options:

✦ **Selection:** Prints only the range you selected before issuing the File⇨Print command.

✦ **Selected sheet( ):** Prints the active sheet or sheets that you selected. You can select multiple sheets by pressing Ctrl and clicking on the sheet tabs. If multiple sheets are selected, each sheet begins printing on a new page.

✦ **Entire workbook:** Prints the entire workbook, including chart sheets.

Tip   You can also use the File⇨Print Area⇨Set Print Area command to specify the range or ranges to be printed. Before choosing this command, select the range or ranges that you want to print. To clear the print area, use the File⇨Print Area⇨ Clear Print Area command

Printing multiple copies

The Print dialog box also lets you select how many copies to print. The upper limit is 32,767 copies — not that anyone would ever need that many copies. You also can specify that you want the copies collated. If you choose this option, Excel prints the pages in order for each set of output. If you're printing only one page, the Collate setting is ignored.

Settings in the Page Setup Dialog Box

The following sections discuss the options available in the Page Setup dialog box.

Controlling page settings

Figure 12-2 shows the Page panel of the Page Setup dialog box. This panel lets you control the following settings:

✦ **Orientation:** This is either Portrait (tall pages) or Landscape (wide pages). Landscape orientation might be useful if you have a wide range that doesn't fit on a vertically oriented page.

✦ **Scaling:** You can set a scaling factor manually or let Excel scale the output automatically to fit on the desired number of pages. Scaling can range from 10 percent to 400 percent of normal size. If you want to return to normal scaling, enter 100 in the box labeled % Normal Size.

✦ **Paper Size:** This setting lets you select the paper size that you're using. Click on the box and see the choices.

✦ **Print Quality:** If the installed printer supports it, you can change the printer's resolution — which is expressed in dots per inch (dpi). The higher the number, the better the quality. Higher resolutions take longer to print.

✦ **First Page Number:** You can specify a page number for the first page. This is useful if the pages you're printing will be part of a larger document and you want the page numbering to be consecutive. Use Auto if you want the beginning page number to be 1 — or to correspond to the pages that you selected in the Print dialog box. If you're not printing page numbers in your header or footer, this setting is irrelevant.

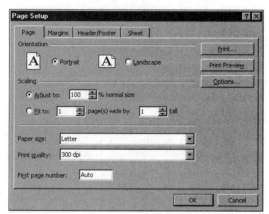

Figure 12-2: You control page settings in the Page panel of the Page Setup dialog box.

Adjusting margins

A margin is the blank space on the side of the page. The wider the margins, the less space that is available for printing. You can control all four page margins from Excel. Figure 12-3 shows the Margins tab of the Page Setup dialog box.

To change a margin, click on the appropriate spinner (or you can enter a value directly).

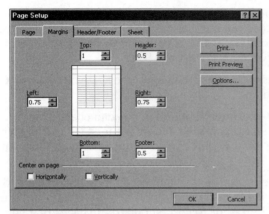

Figure 12-3: The Margins tab of the Page Setup dialog box.

Note The Preview box in the center of the dialog box is a bit deceiving because it doesn't really show you how your changes look in relation to the page. Rather, it simply displays a darker line to let you know which margin you're adjusting.

In addition to the page margins, you can adjust the distance of the header from the page's top and the distance of the footer from the page's bottom. These settings should be less than the corresponding margin; otherwise, the header or footer may overlap with the printed output.

Normally, Excel prints a page at the top and left margins. If you would like the output to be centered vertically or horizontally, check the appropriate check box.

You also can change the margins while you're previewing your output — ideal for last-minute adjustments before printing. I discuss print previewing later in the chapter.

Changing the header or footer

A header is a line of information that appears at the top of each printed page. A footer, on the other hand, is a line of information that appears at the bottom of each printed page. Headers and footers each have three sections: left, center, and right. For example, you can specify a header that consists of your name left justified, the worksheet name centered, and the page number right justified.

Excel 97 By default, new workbooks created by Excel 97 do not have any headers or footers. In previous versions of Excel, headers and footers were provided by default.

The Header/Footer tab of the Print Options dialog box is shown in Figure 12-4. This dialog box displays the current header and footer and gives you other header and footer options in the drop-down lists labeled Header and Footer.

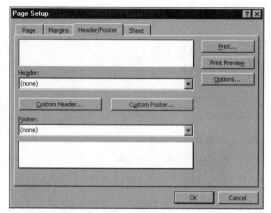

Figure 12-4: The Header/Footer tab of the Page Setup dialog box.

When you click on the Header (or Footer) drop-down, Excel displays a list of pre-defined headers. If you see one that you like, select it. You'll then be able to see how it looks in context — which part is left justified, centered, or right justified. If you don't want a header or footer, choose the option labeled (*none*).

If none of the predefined headers or footers is exactly what you want, you can define a custom header or footer. Start by selecting a header or footer that's similar to the one you want to create (you'll use the selected header or footer as the basis for the customized one). Click on the Custom Header or Custom Footer button, and Excel displays a dialog box like the one shown in Figure 12-5.

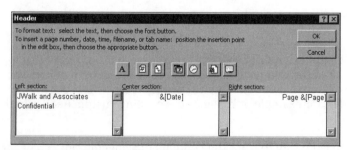

Figure 12-5: If none of the predefined headers or footers is satisfactory, you can define a custom header or custom footer.

This dialog box lets you enter text or codes in each of the three sections. To enter text, just activate the section and enter the text. To enter variable information, such as the current date or the page number, you can click on one of the buttons. Clicking on the button inserts a special code. The buttons and their functions are listed in Table 12-1.

Table 12-1 Custom Header/Footer Buttons and Their Functions		
Button	*Code*	*Function*
Font	Not applicable	Lets you choose a font for the selected text
Page Number	&[Page]	Inserts the page number
Total Pages	&[Pages]	Inserts the total number of pages to be printed
Date	&[Date]	Inserts the current date
Time	&[Time]	Inserts the current time
File	&[File]	Inserts the workbook name
Sheet	&[Tab]	Inserts the sheet's name

You can combine text and codes and insert as many codes as you like into each section. If the text you enter uses an ampersand (&), you must enter the ampersand twice (because an ampersand is used by Excel to signal a code). For example, to enter the text *Research & Development* into a section of a header or footer, enter **Research && Development**.

You also can use different fonts and sizes in your headers and footers. Just select the text that you want to change and click on the Font button. Excel displays its Fonts dialog box so that you can make your choice. If you don't change the font, Excel uses the font defined for the Normal style.

Tip   You can use as many lines as you like. Use Alt+Enter to force a line break for multiline headers or footers.

After you define a custom header or footer, it appears at the bottom of the appropriate drop-down list in the Header/Footer panel of the Page Setup dialog box. You can have only one custom header and one custom footer in a workbook. So, if you edit a custom header, for example, it replaces the existing custom header in the drop-down list.

Unfortunately, there is no way to print the contents of a specific cell in a header or footer. For example, you might want Excel to use the contents of cell A1 as part of a header. The only way to do this is to manually enter the cell's contents — or write a macro to perform this operation.

Controlling sheet options

The Sheet tab of the Page Setup dialog box (shown in Figure 12-6) contains several additional options.

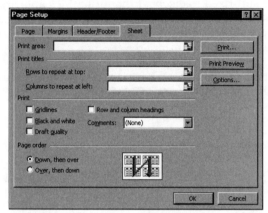

Figure 12-6: The Sheet tab of the Page Setup dialog box.

Print area

The Print Area box lists the range defined as the print area. If you select a range of cells and choose the Selection option in the Print dialog box, the selected range address appears in this box. Excel also defines this as the reference for the Print_Area name.

If the Print Area box is blank, it means that Excel prints the entire worksheet. You can activate this box and select a range (Excel will modify its definition of Print_Area), or you can enter a previously defined range name into the box.

Print titles

Many worksheets are set up with titles in the first row and descriptive names in the first column. If such a worksheet requires more than one page, you may find it difficult to read subsequent pages because the text in the first row and first column won't be printed. Excel offers a simple solution: *print titles*.

Note Don't confuse print titles with headers; these are two different concepts. Headers appear at the top of each page and contain information such as the worksheet name, date, or page number. Print titles describe the data being printed, such as field names in a database table or list.

You can specify rows to repeat at the top of every printed page, or columns to repeat at the left of every printed page. To do so, just activate the appropriate box and select the rows or columns in the worksheet. Or, you can enter these references manually. For example, to specify rows 1 and 2 as repeating rows, enter **1:2**.

Note In the old days, users often were surprised to discover that print titles appeared twice on the first page of their printouts. That's because they defined a print area that included the print titles. Excel now handles this automatically, however, and doesn't print titles twice if they are part of the print area.

Tip You can specify different print titles for each worksheet in the workbook. Excel remembers print titles by creating sheet-level names (Print_Titles).

Print

The section labeled Print contains five check boxes:

✦ **Gridlines:** If checked, Excel prints the gridlines to delineate cells. If you turned off the gridline display in the worksheet (in the View panel of the Options dialog box), Excel unchecks this box for you automatically. In other words, the default setting for this option is determined by the gridline display in your worksheet.

✦ **Black and white:** If checked, Excel ignores any colors in the worksheet and prints everything in black and white. This lets you format your worksheet for screen viewing yet still get readable print output.

✦ **Draft quality:** If checked, the printing is done in draft mode. In draft mode, Excel doesn't print embedded charts or drawing objects, cell gridlines, or borders. This usually reduces the printing time.

✦ **Row and column headings:** If checked, Excel prints the row and column headings on the printout. This makes it easy to identify specific cells from a printout.

✦ **Comments:** If checked, Excel prints cell notes using the option you specify: At the end of the sheet or As displayed on sheet.

Printer-specific options

You may have noticed that the Print dialog box has a button labeled Options. Clicking on this button displays another dialog box that lets you adjust properties specific to the selected printer. See Figure 12-7 for an example. You can also access this dialog box from the Page Setup dialog box (click on the Options button).

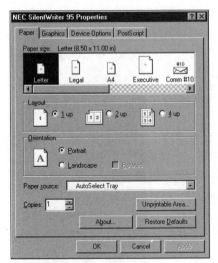

Figure 12-7: This dialog box lets you set printer-specific options.

Some of the printer settings can be set directly from Excel. Other settings may not be accessible from Excel, and you can change them here. For example, if your printer uses multiple paper trays, you can select which tray to use.

Using Print Preview

Excel's print preview feature displays an image of the printed output on your screen. This is a handy feature that lets you see the result of the options that you set before you actually send the job to the printer. It'll save you lots of time — not to mention printing supplies.

Accessing print preview

There are several ways to access the print preview feature:

✦ Select the File⇨Print Preview command.

✦ Click on the Print Preview button on the Standard toolbar. Or, you can press Shift and click on the Print button on the Standard toolbar (the Print button serves a dual purpose).

✦ Click on the Print Preview button in the Print dialog box.

✦ Click on the Print Preview button in the Page Setup dialog box.

Any of these methods changes Excel's window to a preview window, as shown in Figure 12-8.

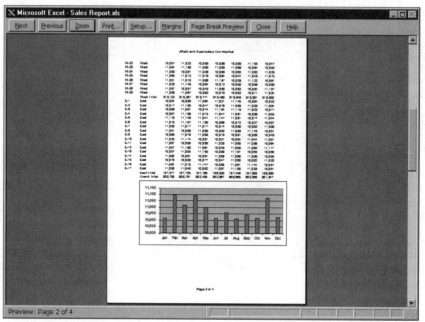

Figure 12-8: The print preview feature lets you see the printed output before you send it to the printer.

The preview window has several buttons along the top:

✦ **Next:** Displays an image of the next page.

✦ **Previous:** Displays an image of the previous page.

✦ **Zoom:** Zooms the display in or out. There are two levels of zooming, and this button toggles between them. You also can just click on the preview image to toggle between zoom modes.

✦ **Print:** Sends the job to the printer.

✦ **Setup:** Displays the Page Setup dialog box so that you can adjust some settings. When you close the dialog box, you return to the preview screen so that you can see the effects of your changes.

✦ **Margins:** Displays adjustable columns and margins. I describe this feature in the next section.

✦ **Page Break Preview:** Displays the worksheet in page break preview mode.

✦ **Close:** Closes the preview window.

✦ **Help:** Displays help for the preview window.

Making changes while previewing

When you click on the Margins button in the preview window, Excel adds markers to the preview that indicate column borders and margins (see Figure 12-9). You can drag the column or margin markers to make changes that appear on-screen.

For example, if you print a worksheet and discover that the last column is being printed on a second page, you can adjust the column widths or margins in the preview window to force the last column to print on a single page. After you drag one of these markers, Excel updates the display so that you can see what effect it had.

When you make changes to the column widths in the preview window, these changes also are made to your worksheet. Similarly, changing the margins in the preview window changes the settings that appear in the Margins panel of the Page Setup dialog box.

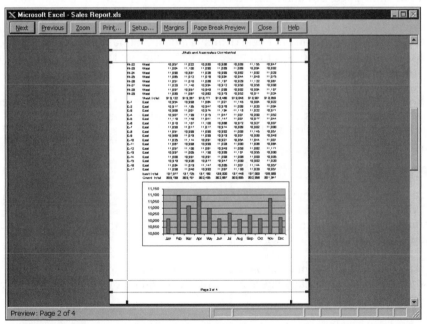

Figure 12-9: You can adjust column widths or margins directly from the print preview window.

Dealing with Page Breaks

If you print lengthy reports, you know that it's often important to have control over the page breaks. For example, you normally wouldn't want a row to print on a page by itself. Fortunately, Excel gives you superb control over page breaks.

As you may have discovered, Excel handles page breaks automatically. After you print or preview your worksheet, it even displays dashed lines to indicate where page breaks occur. Sometimes, however, you'll want to force a page break — either a vertical or a horizontal one. For example, if your worksheet consists of several distinct areas, you may want to print each area on a separate sheet of paper.

Inserting a page break

To insert a vertical manual page break, move the cell pointer to the cell that will begin the new page, but make sure that the pointer's in column A; otherwise, you'll insert a vertical page break and a horizontal page break. For example, if you want row 14 to be the first row of a new page, activate cell A14. Then choose the Insert⇨Page Break command. Excel displays a dashed line to indicate the page break. The dashed line for manual page breaks is slightly thinner than those for natural page breaks.

To insert a horizontal page break, move the cell pointer to the cell that will begin the new page, but in this case, make sure that it's in row one. Select the Insert⇨ Page Break command to create the page break.

Removing a page break

To remove a vertical manual page break, move the cell pointer anywhere in the first row beneath the manual page break and select the Insert⇨Remove Page Break command (this command appears only when the cell pointer is in the first row following a manual page break).

To remove a horizontal manual page break, perform the same procedure, but position the cell pointer anywhere in the first column following a horizontal page break.

Tip   To remove all manual page breaks in the worksheet, click on the Select All button (or press Ctrl+A); then choose the Insert⇨Remove Page Break command.

Using page break preview

Excel 97 A new feature in Excel 97, page break preview, makes it easier than ever to deal with page breaks. To use page break preview, choose the View⇨Page Break Preview command. The screen changes, as shown in Figure 12-10.

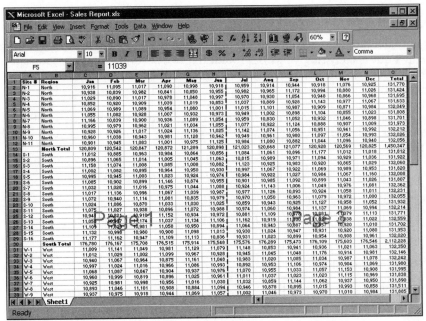

Figure 12-10: Page break preview mode gives you a bird's eye view of your worksheet and shows exactly where the page breaks occur.

When you enter page break preview, Excel

✦ changes the zoom factor so that you can see more of the worksheet.

✦ displays the page numbers overlaid on the pages.

✦ displays the current print range with a white background; non-printing data appears with a gray background.

✦ displays all page breaks.

When you're in page break preview, you can drag the borders to change the print range or the page breaks. When you change the page breaks, Excel automatically adjusts the scaling so that the information fits on the pages per your specifications.

Note In page break preview, you still have access to all of Excel's commands. You can change the zoom factor if you find the text to be too small.

To return to normal viewing, select the View➪Normal command.

Using Custom Views

It's not uncommon to create a workbook that is used to store a variety of information. It's quite likely that you would want to print several different reports from the workbook. If this sounds familiar, you need to know about Excel's custom views feature.

The custom views feature enables you to give names to various views of your worksheet, and you can quickly switch among these named views. A view includes settings for the following:

✦ Print settings as specified in the Page Setup dialog box (optional)

✦ Hidden rows and columns (optional)

✦ Display settings as specified in the Options Display dialog box

✦ Selected cells and ranges

✦ The active cell

✦ Window sizes and positions

✦ Frozen panes

For example, you might define a view that hides a few columns of numbers, another view with a print range defined as a summary range only, another view with the page setup set to landscape, and so on.

Excel 97   In previous versions of Excel, this feature was available by loading the View Manager add-in. This feature is now called custom views, and it's built into Excel 97.

To create a named custom view, first set up your worksheet with the view that you want to name. This can include any of the settings listed previously. For example, you might create a view that has a specific range of cells defined as the print range. Then select the View⇨Custom Views command. Excel displays a dialog box that lists all named views. Initially, this list will be empty, but you can click on the Add button to add a view in the Add View dialog box, shown in Figure 12-11.

Figure 12-11: The Add View dialog box lets you add a named custom view.

Enter a name for the view and make any adjustments to the check boxes. Click on OK and the view is saved. You can add as many views as you like and easily switch among them.

More about Printing

This section provides some additional information regarding printing.

Problems with fonts (when WYS isn't WYG)

Sometimes, you may find that the printed output doesn't match what you see on-screen. This is almost always due to a problem with the fonts that you use. If your printer doesn't have a font that you use to display your worksheet, Windows attempts to match it as best as it can. Often, it's not good enough.

This problem can almost always be solved simply by using TrueType fonts; these scalable fonts are designed for both screen viewing and printing.

Printing noncontiguous ranges on a single page

You may have discovered that Excel lets you specify a print area that consists of noncontiguous ranges (a multiple selection). For example, if you need to print, say, A1:C50, D20:F24, and M11:P16, you can press Ctrl while you select these ranges, and then issue the File⇨Print command and choose the Selection option. Better yet, give this multiple selection a range name so that you can quickly activate the same ranges the next time.

Printing multiple ranges is a handy feature, but you may not like the fact that Excel prints each range on a new sheet of paper — and there is no way to change this behavior.

One solution to this problem is to create live *snapshots* of the three ranges and paste these snapshots to an empty area of the worksheet. Then you can print this new area that consists of the snapshots, and Excel won't skip to a new page for each range.

To create a live snapshot of a range, select the range and copy it to the Clipboard. Then activate the cell where you want to paste the snapshot (an empty worksheet is a good choice) and choose the Edit⇨Paste Picture Link command to paste a live link (see the Note that follows). Repeat this procedure for the other ranges. After you've pasted them, you can rearrange the snapshots any way you like. You'll notice that these are truly live links: change a cell in the original range and the change appears in the linked picture. Figure 12-12 shows an example of snapshots made from several ranges.

Note The Edit⇨Paste Picture Link command is available only if you press Shift while you click on the Edit menu. You also can use the Camera tool to paste a linked picture, but you'll have to add this tool to a toolbar because it doesn't appear on any of the built-in toolbars (you can find it in the Utility category in the Customize dialog box). Apparently, Microsoft is trying to keep this useful technique to itself.

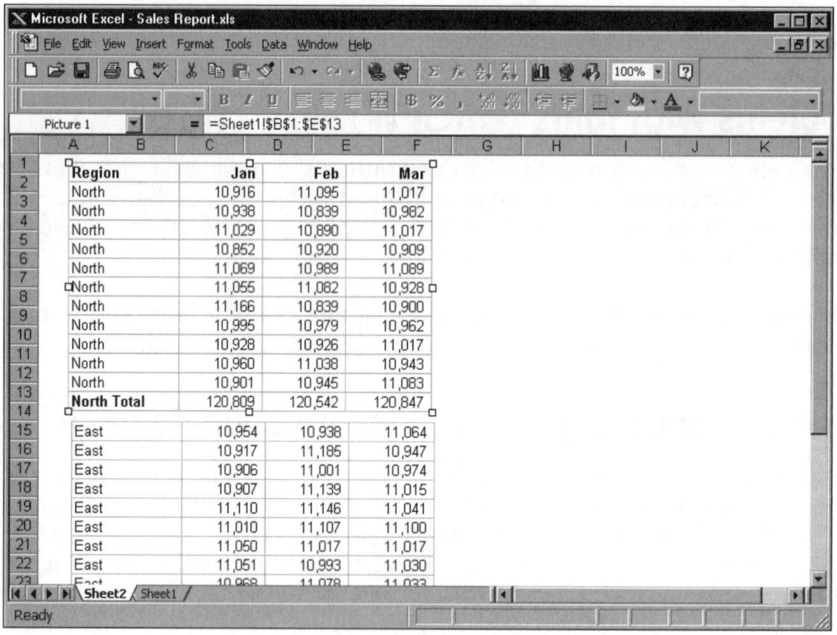

Figure 12-12: These two objects are linked pictures of ranges elsewhere in the workbook. This makes it possible to print nonadjacent ranges on a single sheet.

Hiding cells before printing

You may have a worksheet that contains confidential information. You may want to print the worksheet, but not the confidential parts. Several techniques prevent certain parts of a worksheet from printing.

✦ When you hide rows or columns, the hidden rows won't be printed.

✦ You can effectively hide cells or ranges by making the text color the same color as the background color.

✦ You also can hide cells by using a custom number format that consists of three semicolons (;;;).

✦ You can mask off a confidential area of a worksheet by covering it with a rectangle object. Click on the Rectangle tool on the Drawing toolbar and drag the rectangle to the proper size. For best results, you can make the rectangle white with no border.

✦ You can use a text box object, available using the Text Box tool on the Drawing toolbar, to mask off a range. The advantage to using a text box is that you can add text to it with information about the concealed data (see Figure 12-13).

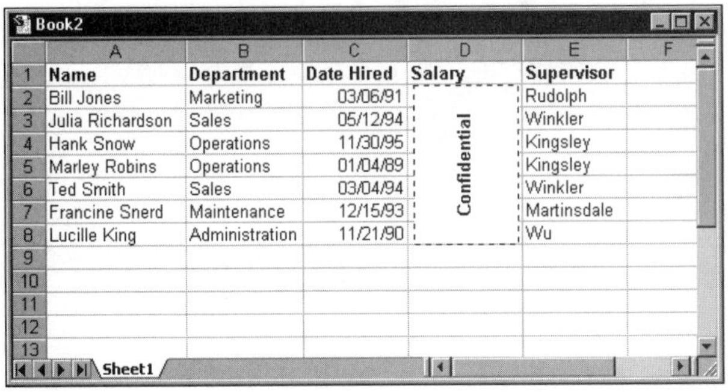

	A	B	C	D	E	F
1	Name	Department	Date Hired	Salary	Supervisor	
2	Bill Jones	Marketing	03/06/91		Rudolph	
3	Julia Richardson	Sales	05/12/94		Winkler	
4	Hank Snow	Operations	11/30/95		Kingsley	
5	Marley Robins	Operations	01/04/89		Kingsley	
6	Ted Smith	Sales	03/04/94		Winkler	
7	Francine Snerd	Maintenance	12/15/93		Martinsdale	
8	Lucille King	Administration	11/21/90		Wu	
9						
10						
11						
12						
13						

Figure 12-13: You can use a text box to hide confidential data so that it won't print.

If you find that you must regularly hide data before you print certain reports, consider using the custom views feature to create a named view that doesn't show the confidential information.

Using a template to change printing defaults

If you find that you're never satisfied with Excel's default print settings, you may want to create a template with the print settings that you use most often. After doing so, you can create a new workbook based on the template, and the workbook will have your own print settings for defaults.

I discuss template files in Chapter 34.

Summary

This chapter presents the basics and some fine points of printing in Excel. You learn how to use the Print dialog box and the Page Setup dialog box to control what gets printed and how. You also learn about the print preview feature that shows how the printed output will look before it hits the paper. The chapter covers features such as manual page breaks, custom views, page break preview mode, tips on printing noncontiguous ranges on a single sheet, and hiding cells that contain confidential information.

✦   ✦   ✦

Chart-Making Basics

◆   ◆   ◆   ◆

In This Chapter

An overview of
Excel's chart-making
capability

When to use an
embedded chart
and when to use a
separate chart sheet

Using the Chart
Wizard to walk you
through the steps to
create a chart

A discussion of
some basic chart
modifications

How to change
Excel's default chart
type

◆   ◆   ◆   ◆

Charts — also known as graphs — have been an integral part of spreadsheets since the early days of Lotus 1-2-3. Charting features have improved significantly over the years, and you'll find that Excel provides you with the tools to create a wide variety of highly customizable charts. In fact, there's so much capability here that *two* chapters present the information. This chapter presents the basic information you need to know to create charts and make simple modifications to them. Chapter 16 continues with a discussion of advanced options and a slew of chart-making tricks and techniques.

Overview of Charts

Basically, a chart is a way to present a table of numbers visually. Displaying data in a well-conceived chart can make it more understandable, and often you can make your point more quickly. Charts are particularly useful for getting a visual picture of a lengthy series of numbers and their relationships. Making a quick chart helps you spot trends and patterns that would be nearly impossible to identify in a range of numbers.

Charts are based on numbers that appear in a worksheet. Before you can create a chart, you have to enter some numbers. Normally, the data used by a chart resides in a single worksheet within one file — but that's not a strict requirement. A single chart can use data from any number of worksheets or even from different workbooks.

When you create a chart in Excel, you have two options for placing the chart:

✦ Insert the chart directly into a worksheet as an object. This is known as an *embedded* chart (see Figure 13-1 for an example).

✦ Create the chart as a new chart sheet in your workbook (see Figure 13-2). A chart sheet differs from a worksheet in that it can hold a single chart and doesn't have cells.

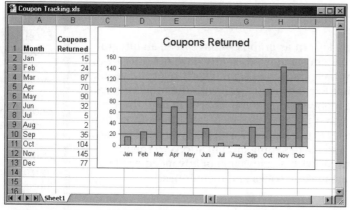

Figure 13-1: An embedded chart is inserted directly on a worksheet.

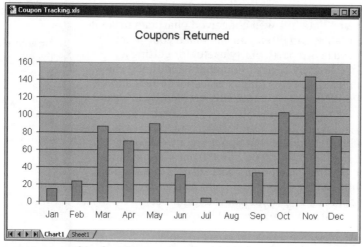

Figure 13-2: This chart is on a separate chart sheet.

Each method has its advantages, as you'll see later in this chapter. Regardless of which chart-making option you choose, you have complete control over the chart's appearance. You can change the colors, move the legend, format the numbers on the scales, add gridlines, and so on.

Converting a range of numbers into a chart is quite easy, and many people find this aspect of Excel to be rather fun. You can experiment with different chart types to determine the best way to make your case. If that isn't enough, you can make a variety of adjustments to your charts, such as adding annotations, clip art, and other bells and whistles. The real beauty of Excel's charts, however, is that they are linked to worksheet data. So if your numbers change, the charts reflect those changes instantly.

Chart types

You're probably aware that there are many chart types: bar charts, line charts, pie charts, and so on. Excel lets you create all the basic chart types and even some esoteric chart types such as radar charts and doughnut charts. Table 13-1 lists Excel's chart types and the number of subtypes associated with each.

Table 13-1 Excel's Chart Types	
Chart Type	*Subtypes*
Area	6
Bar	6
Column	7
Combination	6
Line	7
Pie	6
Doughnut	2
Radar	3
XY (Scatter)	5
Surface	4
Bubble	2
Stock	4
Cylinder	7
Cone	7
Pyramid	7

Note See the "Reference: Excel's Chart Types" section in this chapter for a complete listing of Excel's chart types.

Which chart type to use?

A common question asked by beginning chart makers is how to determine the most appropriate chart type for the data. The answer is that there is no answer. I'm not aware of any hard-and-fast rules for determining which chart type is best for your data. The best rule of thumb is to use the chart type that gets your message across in the simplest way.

Figures 13-3, 13-4, and 13-5 show the same data plotted using three chart different types. Although all three charts represent the same information, they look quite different.

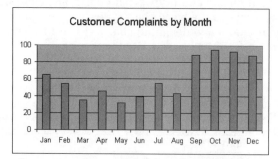

Figure 13-3: An example of a column chart.

Figure 13-4: An example of an area chart.

Figure 13-5: An example of a pie chart.

The column chart is probably the best choice for this particular set of data because it clearly shows the information for each month in discrete units. The area chart may not be appropriate because it seems to imply that the data series is continuous; that is, that there are points in between the 12 actual data points (this same argument could be made against using a line chart). The pie chart is simply too confusing. Pie charts are most appropriate for a data series in which you want to emphasize proportions. Too many data points make a pie chart impossible to interpret.

Fortunately, Excel makes it easy to change a chart's type after the fact. Experiment with various chart types until you find the one that represents your data accurately and clearly — and as simply as possible.

The ChartWizard

The easiest way to create a chart is to use the ChartWizard. The ChartWizard consists of a series of interactive dialog boxes that guide you through the process of creating the exact chart you need. Figure 13-6 shows the first of four Chart Wizard dialog boxes.

Chapter 3 presented a step-by-step introductory example that created a simple chart using the ChartWizard. If you're new to chart making, you may want to work through that example. I explain the ChartWizard in detail later in this chapter.

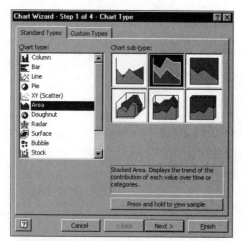

Figure 13-6: One of several dialog boxes displayed by the ChartWizard.

Creating a chart with one keystroke

For a quick demonstration of how easy it is to create a chart, follow these instructions. This example bypasses the ChartWizard and creates a chart on a separate chart sheet.

1. Enter data to be charted into a worksheet. Figure 13-7 shows an example of data that's appropriate for a chart.
2. Select the range of data you entered in Step 1.
3. Press F11. Excel inserts a new chart sheet (named Chart1) and displays the chart based on the selected data. Figure 13-8 shows the result.

	A	B	C	D	E
1		Region 1	Region 2		
2	January	89	85		
3	February	93	74		
4	March	75	31		
5					
6					
7					
8					

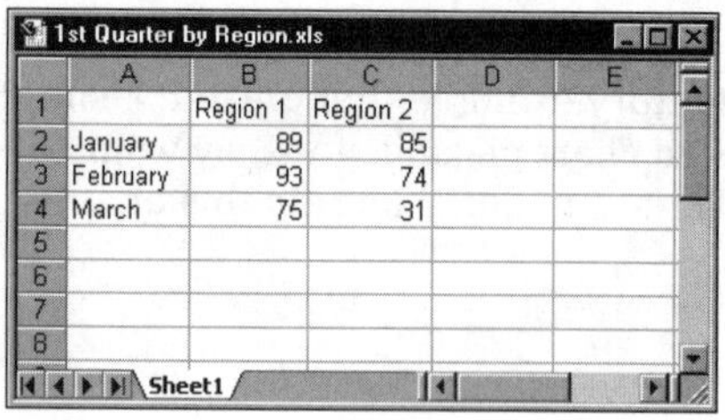

Figure 13-7: This range would make a good chart.

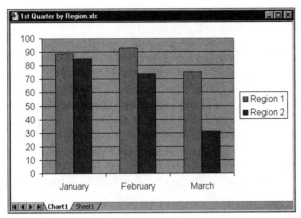

Figure 13-8: This chart was generated with one keystroke.

In this simple example, Excel created its default chart type (which is a two-dimensional column chart) by using the default settings. For more control over the chart-making process, you'll want to use the ChartWizard.

How Excel Handles Charts

A chart is essentially an object that Excel creates. This object is made up of one or more data series, and these data series are displayed graphically (how they are displayed depends on the selected chart type). For example, if you create a line chart that uses two data series, the chart contains two lines — each representing one data series. The lines are distinguishable from each other by thickness, color, or data markers used. The data series in the chart are linked to cells in the worksheet.

Most charts can have any number of data series (up to 255). The exception is a standard pie chart, which can display only one data series. If your chart uses more than one data series, you may want to use a legend to distinguish each series. Excel *does* place a limit on the number of categories (or data points) in a data series: 32,000 (4,000 for 3D charts). Most users never run up against this limit.

Excel 97 In previous versions of Excel, a data series was limited to 4,000 points.

One way to distinguish charts is by the number of axes they use:

✦ Common charts, such as column, line, and area charts, have a category axis and a value axis. The category axis is normally the horizontal axis, and the value axis is normally the vertical axis (this is reversed for bar charts, in which the bars extend from the left of the chart rather than from the bottom).

✦ Pie charts and doughnut charts have no axes (but they do have calories). A pie chart can display only one data series. A doughnut chart can display multiple data series.

✦ A radar chart is a special chart that has one axis for each point in the data series. The axes extend from the center of the chart.

✦ True 3D charts have three axes: a category, value, and series axis that extends into the third dimension. Refer to the sidebar, "3D or not 3D? That is the question," for a discussion about Excel's 3D charts.

After you create a chart, it's not stagnant. You can always change its type, add custom formatting, add new data series to it, or change an existing data series so that it uses data in a different range.

Before you create a chart, you need to determine whether you want it to be an embedded chart or a chart that resides on a chart sheet. I discuss this topic in the sections that follow.

Embedded charts

An embedded chart basically floats on top of a worksheet on the worksheet's draw layer. As with other drawing objects (such as a text box or a rectangle), you can move an embedded chart, resize it, change its proportions, adjust its borders, and perform other operations.

3D or not 3D? That is the question

Some of Excel's charts are referred to as 3D charts. This terminology can be a bit confusing, because some of these so-called 3D charts aren't technically 3D charts. Rather, they are 2D charts with a perspective look to them; that is, they appear to have some depth. The accompanying figure shows two "3D" charts.

The chart on the left isn't a true 3D chart. It's simply a 2D chart that uses perspective to add depth to the columns. The chart on the right is a true 3D chart because the data series extend into the third dimension.

A true 3D chart has three axes: a value axis (the height dimension), a category axis (the width dimension), and a series axis (the depth dimension).

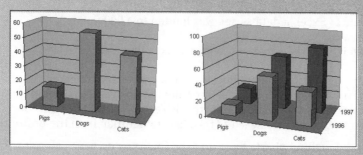

Cross Reference Chapter 14 discusses Excel's drawing objects and the draw layer.

To make any changes to the actual chart in an embedded chart object, you must click on it. This activates the chart; Excel's menus include commands appropriate for working with charts. The main advantage to using embedded charts is that you can print the chart next to the data it uses.

Excel 97 In previous version of Excel, you had to double-click on an embedded chart to activate it. With Excel 97, a single-click on is all it takes — and when you click on a chart you also select an object in the chart.

Figure 13-9 shows an example of a report that includes an embedded chart.

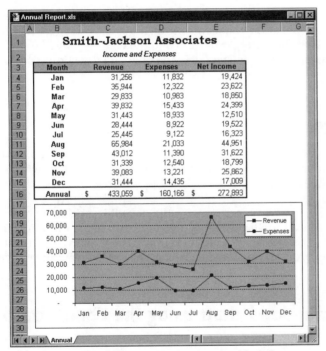

Figure 13-9: This report includes an embedded chart.

Chart sheets

When you create a chart on a chart sheet, the chart occupies the entire sheet. If you plan to print a chart on a page by itself, using a chart sheet is your best choice. If you have many charts to create, you may want to create each one on a separate chart sheet to avoid cluttering your worksheet. This technique also makes it easier to locate a particular chart, because you can change the names of the chart sheets' tabs to correspond to the chart that it contains.

When a chart sheet is active, Excel's menus change. For example, the <u>D</u>ata menu is replaced by a Chart menu, and other menus include commands appropriate for working with charts.

Normally, a chart in a chart sheet is displayed in WYSIWYG mode: the printed chart will look just like the image on the chart sheet. If the chart doesn't fit in the window, you can use the scrollbars to scroll it or adjust the zoom factor.

You also can specify that the chart in a chart sheet is sized according to the window size. Do this with the <u>V</u>iew⇨Sized with <u>W</u>indow command. When this setting is enabled, the chart adjusts itself when you resize the workbook window (it will always fit perfectly in the window). In this mode, the chart you're working on may or may not correspond to how it looks when printed.

Excel 97   If you create a chart on a chart sheet, you can easily convert it to an embedded chart. Choose the Chart⇨Location command and specify the worksheet that holds the embedded chart. The chart sheet is deleted and the chart is moved to the sheet you specify. This operation also works in the opposite direction: You can relocate an embedded chart to a new chart sheet.

Creating Charts

In this section, I discuss the methods you can use to create embedded charts as well as charts on chart sheets. Both chart types can be created with or without the assistance of the ChartWizard.

Note   Excel always has a default chart type. Normally, the default is a column chart (but you can change this type, as you'll see later). If you create a chart without using the ChartWizard, Excel creates the chart by using the default chart type. If you use the ChartWizard, Excel prompts you for the chart type, so the default chart type becomes irrelevant.

Creating an embedded chart using the ChartWizard

To invoke the ChartWizard to create an embedded chart:

1. Select the data to be charted (optional).
2. Choose the <u>I</u>nsert⇨C<u>h</u>art command (or, click on the ChartWizard tool on the Standard toolbar).
3. Make your choices in Steps 1 through 3 of the ChartWizard.
4. In Step 4 of the ChartWizard, select the option labeled As <u>o</u>bject in.

I explain the ChartWizard in detail later in this chapter.

Creating an embedded chart directly

To create an embedded chart without using the ChartWizard:

1. Make sure the Chart toolbar is displayed.

2. Select the data to be charted.

3. Click on the Chart Type tool on the Chart toolbar, and select a chart type from the displayed icons.

The chart is added to the worksheet using the default settings.

Note   The Chart Type tool on the Chart toolbar displays an icon for the last selected chart. This tool can be expanded, however, to display all 18 chart types (see Figure 13-10). Just click on the arrow to display the additional chart types.

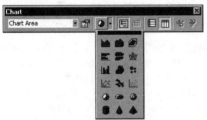

Figure 13-10: The Chart Type tool expands to let you create a chart of the type you want.

Creating a chart on a chart sheet using the ChartWizard

To invoke the ChartWizard to create an embedded chart:

1. Select the data to be charted (optional).

2. Choose the Insert⇨Chart command (or, click on the ChartWizard tool on the Standard toolbar).

3. Make your choices in Steps 1 through 3 of the ChartWizard.

4. In Step 4 of the ChartWizard, select the option labeled As new sheet.

To create a new chart on a chart sheet using the default chart type, select the data to be charted and press the F11 key. This command inserts a new chart sheet. The chart is created from the selected range without accessing the ChartWizard.

The Chart toolbar

The Chart toolbar appears whenever you click on an embedded chart or activate a chart sheet. This toolbar, shown in the accompanying figure, includes nine tools. You can use these tools to make some common chart changes:

Chart Objects: When a chart is activated, you can select a particular chart element using this drop-down list.

Format Selected Object: Displays the Format dialog box for the selected chart element.

Chart Type: This tool expands to display 18 chart types when you click on the arrow. After it's expanded, you can drag this tool to a new location — creating, in effect, a miniature floating toolbar.

Legend: Toggles the legend display in the selected chart.

Data Table: Toggles the display of the data table in a chart.

By Row: Plots the data by rows

By Column: Plots the data by columns

Angle Text (Downward): Displays the selected text at a -45 degree angle

Angle Text (Upward): Displays the selected text at a +45 degree angle

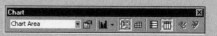

If you press Shift while you click on either of the Angle Text tools, the selected text will be returned to normal (no angle).

Excel includes several other chart-related tools that aren't on the Chart toolbar. You can customize the toolbar to include these additional tools. These tools are in the Charting category in the Customize dialog box.

In addition, several tools on the other toolbars also work with charts. Examples include the Color, Font Color, Bold, Italic, and Font.

Creating a Chart with the ChartWizard

Excel 97 The ChartWizard in Excel 97 is very different from previous versions of Excel. However, if you've used the ChartWizard in an earlier version of Excel, you should have no problems with the new version.

The ChartWizard consists of a series of four dialog boxes that prompt you for various settings for the chart. By the time you reach the last dialog box, the chart is usually just what you need.

Selecting the data

Before you invoke the ChartWizard, select the data that will be included in the chart. This step isn't necessary, but it makes things easier for you. If you don't select the data before invoking the ChartWizard, you can select it in the second ChartWizard dialog box.

When you select the data, include items such as labels and series identifiers. Figure 13-11 shows a worksheet with a range of data set up for a chart. This data consists of monthly sales for two regions. You would select the entire range, including the month names and region names.

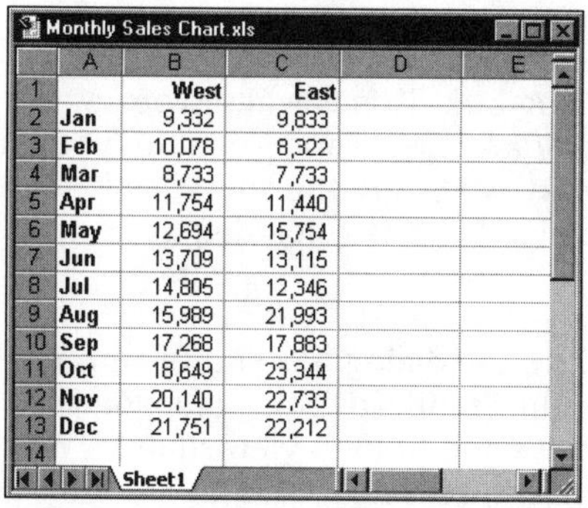

	A	B	C	D	E
1		West	East		
2	Jan	9,332	9,833		
3	Feb	10,078	8,322		
4	Mar	8,733	7,733		
5	Apr	11,754	11,440		
6	May	12,694	15,754		
7	Jun	13,709	13,115		
8	Jul	14,805	12,346		
9	Aug	15,989	21,993		
10	Sep	17,268	17,883		
11	Oct	18,649	23,344		
12	Nov	20,140	22,733		
13	Dec	21,751	22,212		
14					

Figure 13-11: Data to be charted.

The data you're plotting doesn't have to be contiguous. You can press Ctrl and make a multiple selection. Figure 13-12 shows an example of how to select noncontiguous ranges for a chart. In this case, Excel uses only the selected cells for the chart.

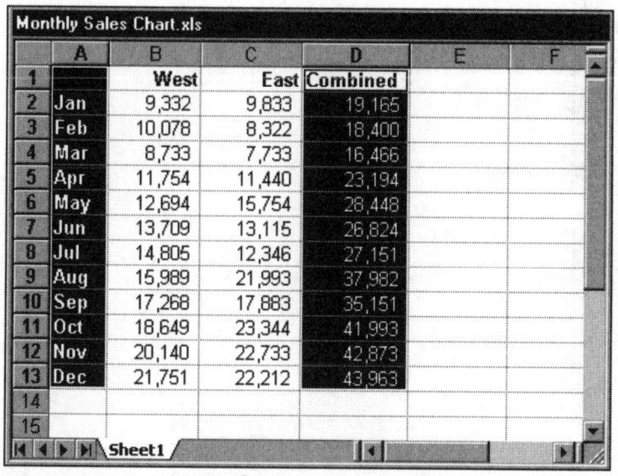

	A	B	C	D	E	F
1		West	East	Combined		
2	Jan	9,332	9,833	19,165		
3	Feb	10,078	8,322	18,400		
4	Mar	8,733	7,733	16,466		
5	Apr	11,754	11,440	23,194		
6	May	12,694	15,754	28,448		
7	Jun	13,709	13,115	26,824		
8	Jul	14,805	12,346	27,151		
9	Aug	15,989	21,993	37,982		
10	Sep	17,268	17,883	35,151		
11	Oct	18,649	23,344	41,993		
12	Nov	20,140	22,733	42,873		
13	Dec	21,751	22,212	43,963		
14						
15						

Figure 13-12: Selecting noncontiguous ranges to be charted.

After selecting the data, invoke the ChartWizard. You can click on the ChartWizard button on the Standard toolbar or use the Insert⇨Chart command. Excel displays the first of four ChartWizard dialog boxes.

At any time while using the ChartWizard, you can go back to the preceding step by clicking on the Back button. Or you can click on Finish to end the ChartWizard. If you end it early, Excel creates the chart by using the information you provided up to that point.

Don't be too concerned about creating the perfect chart. Every choice you make in the ChartWizard can be changed at any time after the fact.

ChartWizard Step 1 of 4

Figure 13-13 shows the first ChartWizard dialog box. This is where you select the chart type. This dialog box has two tabs: Standard Types and Custom Types. The Standard Types tab displays the 14 basic chart types and the subtypes for each. The Custom Types tab displays some customized charts (including user-defined custom charts).

Tip   When you're working in the Custom Types tab, the dialog box shows a preview of your data with the selected chart type. In the Standard Types tab, you get a preview by clicking on the button labeled Press and hold to view sample. When you click on this button, keep the mouse button pressed.

When you've decided on a chart type and subtype, then click on the Next button to move on to the next step.

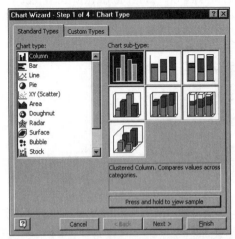

Figure 13-13: The first of four ChartWizard dialog boxes.

ChartWizard Step 2 of 4

In the second step of the ChartWizard (shown in Figure 13-14), you verify the data ranges and specify the orientation of the data (whether it's arranged in rows or columns). The orientation of the data will have a drastic effect on the look of your chart. Most of the time, Excel guesses the orientation correctly — but not always.

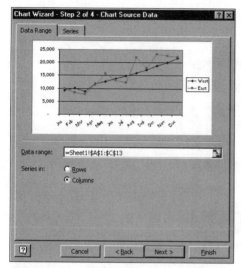

Figure 13-14: In the second ChartWizard dialog box, you verify the range and specify whether to plot by columns or rows.

If you select the Series tab, you'll be able to verify or change the data used for each series of the chart.

Click on the Next button to advance to the next dialog box.

ChartWizard Step 3 of 4

The third ChartWizard dialog box, shown in Figure 13-15, is where you specify most of the options for the chart. This dialog box has six tabs.

Titles: Add titles to the chart.

Axes: Turn axes display on or off, and specify the type of axes.

Gridlines: Specify gridlines, if any.

Legend: Specify whether to include a legend and where to place it.

Data Labels: Specify whether to show data labels and what type of labels.

Data Table: Specify whether to display a table of the data.

Note The options available depend on the type of chart you selected in Step 1 of the ChartWizard.

When you've selected the chart options, click on Next to move to the final dialog box.

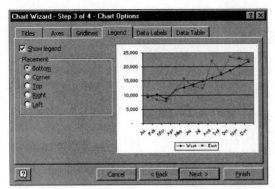

Figure 13-15: You specify the chart options in the third ChartWizard dialog box.

ChartWizard Step 4 of 4

Step 4 of the ChartWizard, shown in Figure 13-16, lets you specify where to place the chart. Make you choice and click on Finish.

The chart is created and activated. If you place the chart on a worksheet, it is centered in the worksheet window.

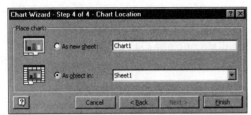

Figure 13-16: Step 4 of the ChartWizard asks you where to put the chart.

Basic Chart Modifications

After you create a chart, you can modify it at any time.

The modifications you can make to a chart are extensive. This section covers some of the more common chart modifications:

- ♦ Moving and resizing the chart
- ♦ Changing the chart type
- ♦ Moving chart elements
- ♦ Deleting chart elements

Other types of chart modifications are discussed in Chapter 16.

Activating a chart

Before you can modify a chart, it must be activated. To activate an embedded chart, click on it. This activates the chart and also selects the element that you click on.

To activate a chart on a chart sheet, just click on its sheet tab.

Excel 97 Previous versions of Excel required that you double-click on an embedded chart to activate it. With Excel 97, you can double-click on a chart element to display that element's Format dialog box. I discuss the various chart elements in Chapter 16.

Moving and resizing a chart

If your chart is on a chart sheet, you can't move it or resize it. You can, however, change the way it's displayed by selecting the View⇨Sized with Window command.

If your chart is an embedded chart, you can freely move and resize it. Click on the chart's border, and then drag the border to move the chart or drag any of the eight handles to resize the chart.

Changing the chart type

To change the chart type of the active chart, use either of the following methods:

- ♦ Choose the Chart Type button on the Chart toolbar. Click on the drop-down arrow, and this button expands to show 18 basic chart types.
- ♦ Choose the Chart⇨Chart Type command.

The Chart➪Chart Type command displays the dialog box shown in Figure 13-17. You may recognize this as the first of the ChartWizard dialog boxes. Click on the Standard Types tab to select one of the standard chart types (and a subtype), or click on the Custom Types tab to select a customized chart. After selecting a chart type, click on OK; the selected chart will be changed to the type you selected.

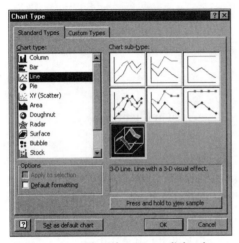

Figure 13-17: The Chart Type dialog box lets you change the chart's type.

Caution If you've customized some aspects of your chart, choosing a new chart type from the Custom Types tab may override some or all of the changes you've made. For example, if you've added gridlines to the chart and then select a custom chart type that doesn't use gridlines, your gridlines disappear. Therefore, it's a good idea to make sure that you're satisfied with the chart before you make too many custom changes to it. However, you can always use Edit➪Undo to reverse your actions.

In the Custom Types tab, if you click on the User-defined option, the list box displays the name of any user-defined custom formats. If you haven't defined any custom formats, this box shows MS Excel 4.0 — this is the default chart type for Excel 4.0. I suppose that Microsoft included this one for nostalgia buffs.

Cross Reference In Chapter 16, I explain how to create custom formats.

Moving and deleting chart elements

Some of the chart parts can be moved (any of the titles, the legend, or data labels). To move a chart element, simply click on it to select it, and then drag it to the desired location in the chart. To delete a chart element, select it and then press Delete.

Other modifications

When a chart is activated, you can select various parts of the chart to work with. Modifying a chart is similar to everything else you do in Excel. First, you make a selection (in this case, select a chart part). Then you issue a command to do something with the selection.

You can use the Fill Color tool on the Formatting toolbar to change colors. For example, if you want to change the color of a series, select the series and choose the color you want from the Fill Color tool. You'll find that many other toolbar tools work with charts. For example, you can select the chart's legend and then click on the Bold tool to make the legend text bold.

When you double-click on a chart element (or press Ctrl+1 after selecting it), its Formatting dialog box appears. The dialog box that appears varies, depending on the item selected. In most cases, the dialog box is of the tabbed variety. Many modifications are self-evident — for example, changing the font used in a title. Others, however, are a bit more tricky. Chapter 16 discusses these chart modifications in detail.

Changing the Default Chart Type

Throughout this chapter, I mention the default chart type many times. Excel's default chart type is a 2D column chart with a light gray plot area, a legend on the right, and horizontal gridlines.

If you don't like the looks of this chart or if you normally use a different type of chart, you can easily change the default chart in the following manner:

1. Select the Chart⇨Chart Type command.
2. Choose the chart type that you want to be the default. This can be a chart from either the Standard Types tab or the Custom Types tab.
3. Click on the button labeled Set as default chart type.

You are asked to verify your choice.

Tip   If you have many charts of the same type to create, it's more efficient to change the default chart format to the chart type with which you're working. Then you can create all your charts without having to select the chart type.

Printing Charts

There's nothing special about printing embedded charts; it works just like printing a worksheet (see Chapter 12). As long as the embedded chart is included in the range to be printed, the chart is printed as it appears on-screen.

Tip If an embedded chart is selected when you issue the File⇨Print command (or click on the Print button), the chart is printed on a page by itself, and the worksheet itself is not printed.

If you print in Draft mode, embedded charts aren't printed. Also, if you don't want a particular embedded chart to appear on your printout, right-click on the chart and choose Format Object from the shortcut menu. Activate the Properties tab in the Format Object dialog box and remove the check mark from the Print Object check box.

If the chart is on a chart sheet, it prints on a page by itself. If you access Excel's Page Setup dialog box when the chart sheet is active, the Sheet tab is replaced with a tab named Chart. Figure 13-18 shows the Chart panel of the Page Setup dialog box.

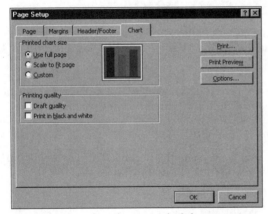

Figure 13-18: The Chart panel of the Page Setup dialog box.

This dialog box has several options:

Use full page: The chart is printed to the full width and height of the page margins. This choice is usually not a good one because the chart's relative proportions change and you lose the WYSIWYG advantage.

Scale to fit page: Expands the chart proportionally in both dimensions until one dimension fills the space between the margins. This option usually results in the best printout.

Custom: Prints the chart as it appears on your screen. Use the View➪Sized with Window command to make the chart correspond to the window size and proportions. The chart prints at the current window size and proportions.

The Printing quality options work just like those for worksheet pages. If you choose the Draft quality option for a chart sheet, the chart is printed, but its quality may not be high (the actual effect depends on your printer). Choosing the Print in black and white option prints the data series with black-and-white patterns rather than colors.

Tip   Because charts usually take longer to print than text, it's an especially good idea to use the print preview feature before printing a chart. This feature lets you see what the printed output will look like so that you can avoid surprises.

Reference: Excel's Chart Types

For your reference, I conclude this chapter with a discussion of Excel's chart types and a listing of the subtypes for each. This section may help you determine which chart type is best for your data.

Column charts

Column charts are one of the most common chart types. This type of chart is useful for displaying discrete data (as opposed to continuous data). You can have any number of data series, and the columns can be stacked on top of each other. Figure 13-19 shows an example of a column chart. Table 13-2 lists Excel's seven column chart subtypes.

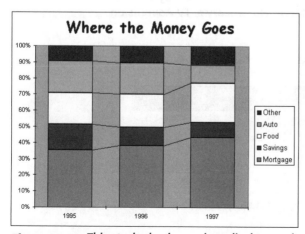

Figure 13-19: This stacked column chart displays each series as a percentage of the total. It may substitute for several pie charts.

Table 13-2 Column Chart Subtypes	
Chart Type	**Description**
Clustered Column	Standard Column chart
Stacked Column	Column chart with data series stacked
100% Stacked Column	Column chart with data series stacked and expressed as percentages
3-D Clustered Column	Standard Column chart with a perspective look
3-D Stacked Column	Column chart with a perspective look. Data series are stacked and expressed as percentages.
3-D 100% Stacked Column	Column chart with a perspective look. Data series are stacked and expressed as percentages.
3-D Column	A true 3D column chart with a third axis

Bar charts

A *bar chart* is essentially a column chart that has been rotated 90 degrees to the left. The advantage in using a bar chart is that the category labels may be easier to read (see Figure 13-20 for an example). Bar charts can consist of any number of data series. In addition, the bars can be stacked from left to right. Table 13-3 lists Excel's six bar chart subtypes.

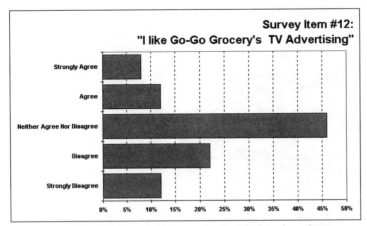

Figure 13-20: If you have lengthy category labels, a bar chart may be a good choice.

Table 13-3 **Bar Chart Subtypes**	
Chart Type	*Description*
Clustered Bar	Standard bar chart
Stacked Bar	Bar chart with data series stacked
100% Stacked Bar	Bar chart, with data series stacked and expressed as percentages
3-D Clustered Bar	Standard bar chart with a perspective look
3-D Stacked Bar	Bar chart with a perspective look. Data series are stacked and expressed as percentages.
3-D 100% Stacked Bar	Bar chart with a perspective look. Data series are stacked and expressed as percentages.

Line charts

Line charts are common. They are frequently used to plot data that is continuous rather than discrete. For example, plotting daily sales as a line chart may let you spot trends over time. See Figure 13-21 for an example.

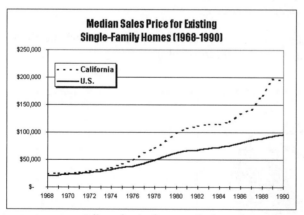

Figure 13-21: A line chart often can help you spot trends in your data.

Table 13-4 lists Excel's seven line chart subtypes.

Table 13-4 Line Chart Subtypes	
Chart Type	**Description**
Line	Standard line chart
Stacked Line	Line chart with stacked data series
100% Stacked Line	Line chart with stacked data series expressed as percentages
Line with Data Markers	Line chart with data markers
Stacked Line with Data Markers	Line chart with stacked data series and data markers
100% Stacked Line with Data Markers	Line chart with stacked data series, line markers, expressed as percentages
3-D Line	A true 3D line chart with a third axis

Pie charts

A *pie chart* is useful when you want to show relative proportions or contributions to a whole. Figure 13-22 shows an example of a pie chart. Generally, a pie chart should use no more than five or six data points; otherwise, it's difficult to interpret. A pie chart can use only one data series.

You can explode a slice of a pie chart. Activate the chart and select the slice you want to explode. Then drag it away from the center.

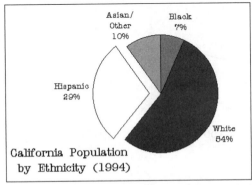

Figure 13-22: A pie chart with one slice exploded.

Table 13-5 lists Excel's six pie chart subtypes.

Table 13-5 Pie Chart Subtypes	
Chart Type	**Description**
Pie	Standard pie chart
3-D Pie	Pie chart with perspective look
Pie of Pie	Pie chart with one slice broken into another pie
Exploded Pie	Pie chart with one or more slices exploded
Exploded 3-D Pie	Pie chart with perspective look, with one or more slices exploded
Bar of Pie	Pie chart, with one slice broken into a column

Excel 97 The Pie of Pie and Bar of Pie charts are new to Excel 97. These two chart types let you display a second chart that clarifies one of the pie slices. You can use the Options tab of the Format Data Series dialog box to specify which data is assigned to the second chart. Refer to Chapter 16 for details.

XY (Scatter) charts

Another common chart type is *XY (Scatter) charts* (also known as *scattergrams*). An XY chart differs from the other chart types in that both axes display values (there is no category axis).

This type of chart often is used to show the relationship between two variables. Figure 13-23 shows an example of an XY chart that plots the relationship between sales calls and sales. The chart shows that these two variables are positively related: months in which more calls were made typically had higher sales volumes.

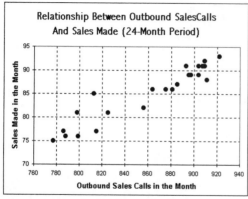

Figure 13-23: An XY (Scatter) chart.

Table 13-6 lists Excel's five XY (Scatter) chart subtypes.

Table 13-6 **XY (Scatter) Chart Subtypes**	
Chart Type	*Description*
Scatter	XY chart with markers and no lines
Scatter with Smoothed Lines	XY chart with markers and smoothed lines
Scatter with Smoothed Lines and No Data Markers	XY chart with smoothed lines and no markers
Scatter with Lines	XY chart with lines and markers
Scatter with Lines and No Data Markers	XY chart with lines and no markers

Area charts

An *area chart* is similar to a line chart that has been colored in. Figure 13-24 shows an example of a stacked area chart. Stacking the data series lets you clearly see the total plus the contribution by each series.

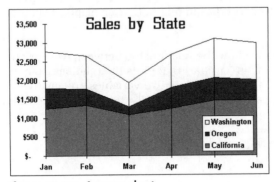

Figure 13-24: An area chart.

Table 13-7 lists Excel's six area chart subtypes.

Table 13-7 **Area Chart Subtypes**	
Chart Type	*Description*
Area	Standard area chart
Stacked Area	Area chart, data series stacked
100% Stacked Area	Area chart, expressed as percentages
3-D Area	A true 3D area chart with a third axis
3-D Stacked Area	Area chart with a perspective look, data series stacked
3-D 100% Stacked area	Area chart with a perspective look, expressed as percentages

Doughnut charts

A *doughnut chart* is similar to a pie chart, except that it has a hole in the middle. Unlike a pie chart, a doughnut chart can display more than one series of data. Figure 13-25 shows an example of a doughnut chart (I added the arrow and series descriptions manually; these items aren't part of a doughnut chart).

Notice that the data series are displayed as concentric rings. As you can see, a doughnut chart with more than one series to chart can be difficult to interpret. Sometimes a better choice is to use a stacked column chart for such comparisons.

Table 13-8 lists Excel's two doughnut chart subtypes.

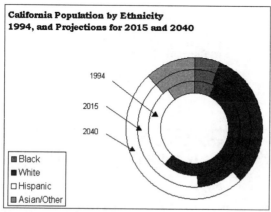

Figure 13-25: A doughnut chart.

Table 13-8 **Doughnut Chart Subtypes**	
Chart Type	*Subtype*
Doughnut	Standard doughnut chart
Exploded Doughnut	Doughnut chart with all slices exploded

Radar charts

You may not be familiar with radar charts. A *radar chart* has a separate axis for each category, and the axes extend out from the center. The value of the data point is plotted on the appropriate axis. If all data points in a series had an identical value, it would produce a perfect circle. See Figure 13-26 for an example of a radar chart.

Table 13-9 lists Excel's three radar chart subtypes.

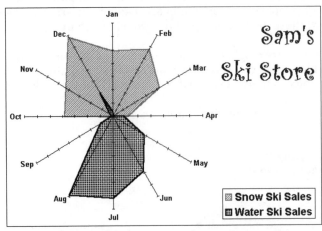

Figure 13-26: A radar chart.

Table 13-9 **Radar Chart Subtypes**	
Chart Type	*Subtype*
Radar	Standard radar chart (lines only)
Radar with Data Markers	Radar chart with lines data markers
Filled Radar	Radar chart with lines colored in

Surface charts

Surface charts display two or more data series on a surface. As you can see in Figure 13-27, these charts can be quite interesting. Unlike other charts, Excel uses color to distinguish values, not to distinguish the data series. The only way to change these colors is to modify the workbook's color palette by using the Color panel in the Options dialog box.

Table 13-10 lists Excel's four 3D surface chart subtypes.

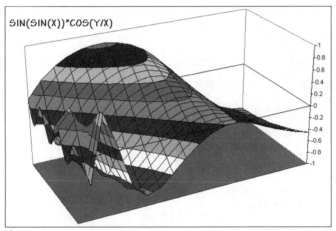

Figure 13-27: A surface chart.

Table 13-10	
Surface Chart Subtypes	
Chart Type	*Description*
3-D Surface	Standard 3D surface chart
3-D Surface (wireframe)	3D surface chart with no colors
Surface (top view)	3D surface chart as viewed from above
Surface (top view wireframe)	3D surface chart as viewed from above, no color

Bubble charts

Excel 97 Bubble charts are new to Excel 97. Think of a bubble chart as an XY (Scatter) chart that can display additional data series. That additional data series is represented by the size of the bubbles.

Figure 13-28 shows an example of a bubble chart. In this case the size the chart displays results of a weight loss program. The x-axis is original weight, the y-axis shows length of time in the program, and the size of the bubbles represents the amount of weight lost.

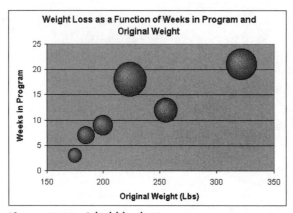

Figure 13-28: A bubble chart.

Table 13-11 lists Excel's two bubble chart subtypes.

Table 13-11	
Bubble Chart Subtypes	
Chart Type	*Subtype*
Bubble Chart	Standard bubble chart
Bubble with 3-D effect	Bubble chart with 3D bubbles

Stock charts

Stock charts are most useful for displaying stock market information. These charts require three to five data series, depending on the subtype.

Figure 13-29 shows an example of a stock chart. This chart uses the High-Low-Close subtype that requires three data series.

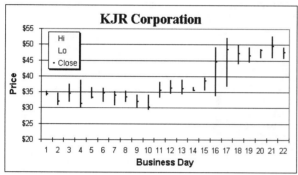

Figure 13-29: A stock chart.

Table 13-12 lists Excel's four stock chart subtypes.

Table 13-12 Stock Chart Subtypes	
Chart Type	**Subtype**
High-Low-Close	Displays the stock's high, low, and closing prices
Open-High-Low-Close	Displays the stock's opening, high, low, and closing prices
Volume-High-Low-Close	Displays the stock's volume, high, low, and closing prices
Volume-Open-High-Low-Close	Displays the stock's volume, open, high, low, and closing prices

Cylinder, Cone, and Pyramid charts

Excel 97 These three charts types are essentially the same — except for the shapes used. You can usually use these charts in place of a bar or column chart.

Figure 13-30 shows an example of a pyramid chart.

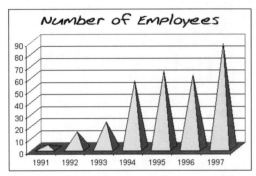

Figure 13-30: A pyramid chart.

Each of these chart types has seven subtypes, which are described in Table 13-13.

Table 13-13	
Cylinder, Cone, and Pyramid Chart Subtypes	

Chart Type	*Subtype*
Clustered Column	Standard column chart
Stacked Column	Column chart with data series stacked
100% Stacked Column	Column chart with data series stacked and expressed as percentages
Clustered Bar	Standard bar chart
Stacked Bar	Bar chart with data series stacked
100% Stacked Bar	Bar chart with data series stacked and expressed as percentages
3-D Column	A true 3D column chart with a third axis.

Summary

In this chapter, I introduce Excel's chart-making feature. Charts can be embedded on a worksheet or created in a separate chart sheet. You can use the ChartWizard to walk you through the chart-making process or create a default chart in a single step. I describe how to change the default chart type.

After a chart is created, you can make many types of modifications. I discuss a few simple modifications and present additional chart information in Chapter 16. Printing charts works much like printing worksheets, although you should be familiar with the page setup options when you're printing chart sheets. I conclude the chapter with a complete listing and description of Excel's chart types and subtypes.

✦ ✦ ✦

Enhancing Your Work with Pictures and Drawings

In Chapter 13, you learned how to create charts from the numbers in your worksheet. This chapter continues in the same vein and discusses pictures and drawings. Like charts, these objects can be placed on a worksheet's draw layer to add pizzazz to an otherwise boring report.

In this chapter, I discuss three major types of images:

✦ Bitmap and line-art graphics imported directly into a workbook or copied from the Clipboard

✦ Objects created using Excel's drawing tools

✦ Objects inserted using other Microsoft Office tools such as WordArt and Organization Chart

Note Excel also can create another type of graphic image: maps. But that's the topic of Chapter 17.

Importing Graphics Files

Excel can import a wide variety of graphics files into a worksheet. You have three choices:

✦ Use the Microsoft Clip Gallery to locate and insert an image.

✦ Directly import a graphic file.

✦ Copy and paste the image using the Windows Clipboard.

Using the Clip Gallery

The Clip Gallery is a shared application that is also accessible from other Microsoft Office products.

Note   Besides providing an easy way to locate and insert images, the Clip Gallery lets you insert sound and video files.

You access the Clip Gallery by selecting the Insert⇨Picture⇨Clip Art command. This displays the dialog box shown in Figure 14-1. Click on the Pictures or Clip Art tab. Then select a category and image and click on Insert. The image is embedded in your worksheet (this will be an OLE object). Excel also displays its Picture toolbar, which contains tools that let you adjust the image.

The Clip Art tab contains line images, and the Picture category contains bitmap images.

Figure 14-1: The Microsoft Clip Gallery dialog box lets you insert pictures, sounds, or video.

Tip   You also can add new files to the Clip Gallery. You might want to do this if you tend to insert a particular graphic file into your worksheets (such as your company logo). Use the Import Clips button to select the file and specify the category for the image.

Importing graphics files

If the graphic image that you want to insert is available in a file, you can easily import the file. Choose the Insert⇨Picture⇨From File command. Excel displays the Insert Picture dialog box, shown in Figure 14-2. This dialog box works just like the Open dialog box. By default, it displays only the graphics files that Excel can import. If you choose the Preview option, Excel displays a preview of the selected file in the right panel of the dialog box.

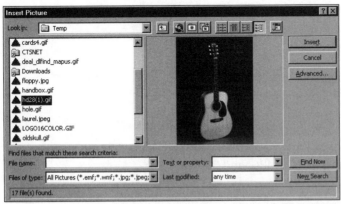

Figure 14-2: The Insert Picture dialog box lets you embed a picture in a worksheet.

About graphics files

Graphics files come in two main categories: *bitmap* and *vector* (picture). Bitmap images are made up of discrete dots. They usually look pretty good at their original size but often lose clarity if you increase or decrease the size. Vector-based images, on the other hand, retain their crispness, regardless of their size. Examples of common bitmap file formats include BMP, PCX, DIB, JPG, and GIF. Examples of common vector file formats include CGM, WMF, EPS, and DRW.

Bitmap files vary in the number of colors they use (even black-and-white images use multiple colors, because these are usually gray-scale images). If you view a high-color bitmap graphic using a video mode that displays only 256 colors, the image usually doesn't look very good.

You can find thousands of graphics files free for the taking on the Internet and on-line services such as CompuServe, America Online, and Prodigy.

Using bitmap graphics in a worksheet can dramatically increase the size of your work-book, resulting in more memory usage and longer load and save times.

Figure 14-3 shows an example of a graphic image in a worksheet.

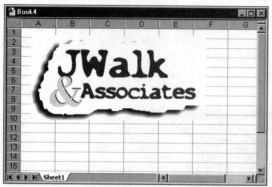

Figure 14-3: An example of a graphics file embedded in a worksheet.

Table 14-1 lists the graphics file types that Excel can import. The most common graphics file formats are GIF, JPG, and BMP.

Table 14-1	
Graphics File Formats Supported by Excel	
File Type	*Description*
BMP	Windows bitmaps
CDR	CorelDRAW graphics
CGM	Computer Graphics Metafiles
DRW	Micrografx Designer/Draw
DXF	AutoCAD format 2-D
EMF	Windows Enhanced Metafile
EPS	Encapsulated PostScript
GIF	Graphic Interchange Format
HGL	HP Graphics Language
JPG	JPEG File Interchange Format
PCT	Macintosh graphics
PCD	Kodak Photo CD
PCX	Bitmap graphics

File Type	Description
PNG	Portable Network Graphics
TGA	Targa graphics format
TIF	Tagged Interchange Format
WMF	Windows metafile
WPG	WordPerfect graphics

Tip   If you want to use a graphic image for a worksheet's background (similar to wallpaper on the Windows desktop), use the Format⇨Sheet⇨Background command and select a graphics file. The selected graphics file is tiled on the worksheet. It won't be printed, however.

Copying graphics by using the Clipboard

In some cases, you may want to use a graphic image that is not stored in a separate file or is in a file that Excel can't import. For example, you may have a drawing program that uses a file format that Excel doesn't support. You may be able to export the file to a supported format, but it may be easier to load the file into the drawing program and copy the image to the Clipboard. Then you can activate Excel and paste the image to the draw layer.

This capability also is useful if you don't want to copy an entire image. For example, a drawing may be made up of several components, and you may want to use only one element in Excel. In this case, using the Clipboard is the only route.

Suppose that you see a graphic displayed on-screen but you can't select it — it may be part of a program's logo, for example. In this case, you can copy the entire screen to the Clipboard and then paste it into Excel. Most of the time, you don't want the entire screen — just a portion of it. The solution is to capture the entire screen (or window), copy it to the Windows Paint program, and then select the part you want and copy it to Excel. Figure 14-4 demonstrates this technique using Paint. In this case, a window was copied and pasted to Paint.

Use the following keyboard commands as needed:

PrintScreen: Copies the entire screen to the Clipboard

Alt+PrintScreen: Copies the active window to the Clipboard

Modifying pictures

Excel 97   When you insert a picture on a worksheet, you can modify the picture in a number of ways using the Picture toolbar, shown in Figure 14-5. This toolbar appears automatically when you select a picture object. The tools are described in Table 14-2.

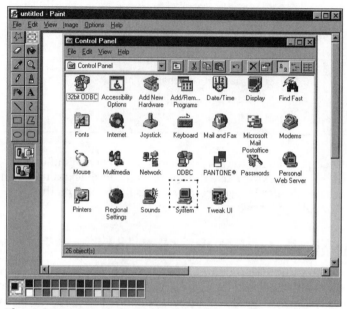

Figure 14-4: The window was captured and pasted to Paint. You can copy the part you want and paste it to Excel.

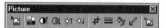

Figure 14-5: The Picture toolbar lets you adjust a picture.

Table 14-2
The Tools on the Picture Toolbar

Tool Name	*What the Tool Does*
Insert Picture from File	Displays the Insert Picture dialog box.
Image Control	Lets you change a picture to gray scale, black and white, or a watermark (semitransparent).
More Contrast	Increases the contrast of the picture.
Less Contrast	Decreases the contrast of the picture.
More Brightness	Increases the brightness of the picture.
Less Brightness	Decreases the brightness of the picture.
Crop	Crops the picture. After clicking on this tool, drag any of the pictures handles to make the picture smaller.

Tool Name	What the Tool Does
Line Style	Selects a border for the picture.
Format Picture	Displays the Format Picture dialog box.
Set Transparent Color	Selects a color that will be transparent. Underlying cell contents appear through the selected transparent color. This option is not available for all types of pictures.
Reset Picture	Returns the picture to its original state.

A word about the draw layer

Every worksheet and chart sheet has what's known as a *draw layer*. This invisible surface is completely independent of the cells on a worksheet (or the chart on a chart sheet). The draw layer can hold graphic images, drawings, embedded charts, OLE objects, and so on.

Objects placed on the draw layer can be moved, resized, copied, and deleted — with no effect on any other elements in the worksheet. Objects on the draw layer have properties that relate to how they are moved and sized when underlying cells are moved and sized. When you right-click on a graphic object and choose Format Object from the shortcut menu, you get a tabbed dialog box (see the accompanying figure). Click on the Properties tab to adjust how the object moves or resizes with its underlying cells. Your choices are as follows:

Move and size with cells: If this option is selected, the object appears to be attached to the cells beneath it. jFor example, if you insert rows above the object, the object moves down. If you increase the column width, the object gets wider.

Move but don't size with cells: If this option is checked, the object moves if rows or columns are inserted, but it never changes its size if you change row heights or column widths.

Don't move or size with cells: This option makes the object completely independent of the underlying cells.

The preceding options control how an object is moved or sized with respect to the underlying cells. Excel also lets you "attach" an object to a cell. In the Edit panel of the Options dialog box, place a check mark next to the check box labeled Cut, Copy, and Sort Objects with Cells. After you do so, graphic objects on the draw layer are attached to the underlying cells.

Because a chart sheet doesn't have cells, objects placed on a chart sheet don't have these options. Such objects do have a property, however, that relates to how the object is sized if the chart size is changed.

Using Excel's Drawing Tools

The discussion so far has focused on using graphics from other sources. If your needs involve simple (or not so simple) graphic shapes, you can use the drawing tools built into Excel to create a variety of graphics.

Excel 97 The drawing features in Excel 97 have been improved significantly. These tools also are available in the other Microsoft Office applications.

The Drawing toolbar

Excel's drawing tools are available from the Drawing toolbar. Drawing objects is one of the few features in Excel that's not available from the menus. Notice that the Standard toolbar has a tool named Drawing. Clicking on this tool toggles the Drawing toolbar on and off. Figure 14-6 shows the Drawing toolbar. As you'll see, there is more to this toolbar than meets the eye.

Figure 14-6: Display the Drawing toolbar to create and modify drawings.

Table 14-3 describes the tools in the Drawing toolbar. The tools are listed in the order in which they appear.

Table 14-3	
The Tools on the Drawing Toolbar	
Tool Name	*What the Tool Does*
Draw	Displays a menu with choices that let you manipulate drawn objects.
Select Objects	Selects one or more graphic objects. If you have several objects and you want to select a group of them, use this tool to drag the outline so that it surrounds all the objects. Click on the button again to return to normal selection mode.
Free Rotate	Lets you freely rotate a drawn object.
AutoShapes	Displays a menu of seven categories of shapes. Drag this menu to create an AutoShapes toolbar. You also can display the AutoShapes toolbar with the Insert⇨Picture⇨AutoShapes command.
Rectangle	Inserts a rectangle or a square.

Tool Name	What the Tool Does
Oval	Inserts an oval or a circle.
Line	Inserts a line.
Arrow	Inserts an arrow.
Text Box	Inserts a free-floating box into which you type text.
WordArt	Displays the WordArt Gallery dialog box, which lets you create attractive titles using text. You also can display this dialog box with the Insert⇨Picture⇨WordArt command.
Fill Color	Lets you select a fill color or fill effect for an object.
Font Color	Lets you select a font color for text objects.
Line Style	Lets you specify the width of the lines in an object.
Dash Style	Lets you specify the style of the lines in an object.
Arrow Style	Lets you specify the arrow style for arrows.
Shadows	Lets you specify the type of shadow for an object and settings for the shadow.
3D Effects	Lets you specify the type of perspective effect for an object and settings for the effect.

Drawing AutoShapes

Drawing objects with the AutoShapes tool is quite intuitive. The AutoShapes tool expands to display the following shape categories:

Lines: Six styles of lines, including arrows and freehand drawing.

Connectors: Nine styles of lines designed to indicate connections between other objects. These objects automatically "snap to" other objects.

Basic Shapes: Thirty-two basic shapes, including standard shapes such as boxes and circles, plus nonstandard shapes such as a smiley face and a heart.

Block Arrows: Twenty-eight arrow shapes.

Flowchart: Twenty-seven shapes suitable for flowchart diagrams.

Stars and Banners: Sixteen stars and banners. Stars are handy for drawing attention to a particular cell.

Callouts: Twenty callouts, suitable for annotating cells.

Click on a tool and then drag in the worksheet to create the shape (the mouse pointer changes shape, reminding you that you're in draw mode). When you release the mouse button, the object is selected and its name appears in the Name box (see Figure 14-7).

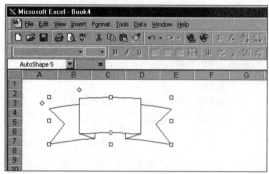

Figure 14-7: This shape was drawn on the worksheet. Its name appears in the Name box.

Formatting AutoShape objects

It should come as no surprise that you can format the AutoShape objects at any time. First, you must select the object. If the object is filled with a color or pattern, you can click anywhere on the object to select it. If the object is not filled, you must click on the object's border.

You can make some modifications using the toolbar buttons — for example, change the fill color. Other modifications require that you use the Format AutoShape dialog box. After selecting one or more objects, you can bring up this dialog box by using any of the following techniques:

✦ Choose the Format⇨AutoShape command.

✦ Press Ctrl+1.

✦ Double-click on the object.

✦ Right-click on the object and choose Format AutoShape from the shortcut menu.

The Format AutoShape dialog box has several tabs, the number of which depends on the type of object and whether it contains text. I discuss each of the tabs in the following sections.

The Colors and Lines tab

Select the Colors and Lines tab to adjust the colors, lines, and arrow used in the object.

There is more to this dialog box than meets the eye, and it can lead to other dialog boxes. For example, click on the Color drop-down list and you can select Fill Effects — which brings up another multi-tabbed dialog box that lets you specify a wide variety of fill effects. Figure 14-8 shows the Fill Effects dialog box.

Excel 97 Excel 97 supports many new types of fill effects. Spend some time experimenting with these effects, and I'm sure you'll be impressed.

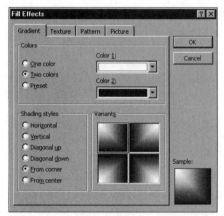

Figure 14-8: The Fill Effects dialog box lets you choose from a variety of gradients, textures, patterns, and pictures.

The Size panel

The Size panel of the Format AutoShape dialog box (shown in Figure 14-9) lets you adjust the size, rotation, and scale of the object. If the object is a picture, you can use the Reset button to return the object to its original dimensions and rotation.

Note Contrary to what you might expect, if you rotate an object that contains text, the text *will not* be rotated along with the object.

You can also change the object's size directly by dragging the object. You can change the rotation directly by clicking on the Free Rotate tool on the Drawing toolbar.

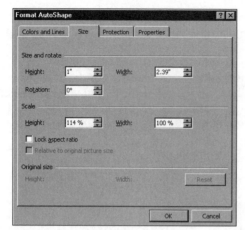

Figure 14-9: The size panel of the Format AutoShape dialog box.

The Protection tab

The Protection tab determines whether the object is "locked." Locking has no effect, however, unless the worksheet is protected and the Objects option is in effect. You can protect the worksheet with the Tools⇨Protection⇨Protect Sheet command.

Tip   Locking an object prevents the object from being moved or resized. After you get all your objects formatted to your satisfactions, it's a good idea to lock all objects and protect the sheet.

The Properties tab

The Properties tab of the Format AutoShape dialog box determines how an object is moved and sized with respect to the underlying cells. (See the sidebar "A word about the draw layer," earlier in this chapter.)

The Font tab

The Font tab appears only if the shape contains text. It should be familiar, because its options are the same as for formatting cells.

The Alignment tab

The Alignment tab appears only if the shape contains text. You can specify the vertical and horizontal alignment of the text and also choose the orientation. Unlike text contained in cells, you cannot specify an angle for the orientation (you're limited to 90 degrees).

If you click on the Automatic size option, the shape's size adjusts to fit the text that it contains.

The Margins tab

The Margins tab appears only if the shape contains text. Use the controls in this panel to adjust the amount of space along the sides of the text.

Changing the stack order of objects

As you add drawing objects to the draw layer of a worksheet, you'll find that objects are "stacked" on top of each other in the order in which you add them. New objects are stacked on top of older objects. Figure 14-10 shows an example of drawing objects stacked on top of one another.

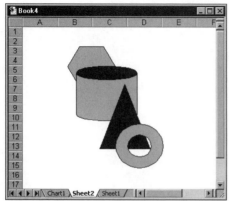

Figure 14-10: These drawing objects are stacked on top of one another.

If you find that an object is obscuring part of another, you can change the order in this stack. Right-click on the object and select Order from the shortcut menu. This leads to a submenu with the following choices:

Bring to Front: Brings the object to the top of the stack.

Send to Back: Sends the object to the bottom of the stack.

Bring Forward: Brings the object one step higher toward the top of the stack.

Send Backward: Sends the object one step lower toward the bottom of the stack.

Grouping objects

Excel lets you combine two or more drawing objects into a single object. This is known as *grouping*. For example, if you create a design that uses four separate drawing objects, you can combine them into a group. Then you can manipulate this group as a single object (move it, resize it, and so on).

To group two or more objects, select all the objects and then right-click. Choose Grouping⇨Group from the shortcut menu.

Later, if you need to modify one of the objects in the group, you can ungroup them by right-clicking and selecting Grouping⇨Ungroup from the shortcut menu. This breaks the object into its original components.

Aligning objects

When you have several drawing objects on a worksheet, you may want to align these objects with each other. You can drag the objects (which isn't very precise), or you can use the automatic alignment options.

Figure 14-11 shows objects before and after they were aligned to the left.

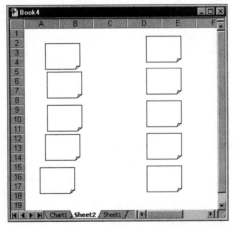

Figure 14-11: The objects on the left are not aligned. Those on the right are aligned to the left.

To align objects, start by selecting them. Then click on the Draw tool on the Drawing toolbar. This tool expands to show a menu. Select the Align or Distribute menu option, followed by any of the six alignment options: Align Left, Align Center, Align Right, Align Top, Align Middle, or Align Bottom.

Note Unfortunately, you cannot specify which object is used as the basis for the alignment. When you're aligning objects to the left, they are always aligned with the left-most object. When you're aligning objects to the top, they are always aligned with the top-most object. Alignment in other directions works the same way.

Spacing objects evenly

Excel 97 Excel can also "distribute" three or more objects such that they are equally spaced horizontally or vertically. Select the objects and then click on the Draw tool on the Drawing toolbar. This tool expands to show a menu. Select the Align or Distribute menu option, followed by either Distribute Horizontally or Distribute Vertically.

Changing the AutoShape defaults

You can change the default settings for the AutoShapes that you draw. For example, if you prefer a particular text color or fill color, you can set these as the defaults for all new AutoShapes that you draw.

To change the default settings, create an object and format it as you like. You can change colors, fill effects, line widths and styles, and shadow or 3D effects. Then select the formatted object, right-click, and select Set AutoShape Defaults from the shortcut menu. You can also access this command from the Draw tool on the Drawing toolbar (this tool expands to show a menu).

Adding shadows and 3D effects

You can apply attractive shadow and 3D effects to AutoShapes (except for those in the Line and Connectors categories). Use the Shadow and 3D tools on the Drawing toolbar to apply these effects.

Note   Shadows and 3D effects are mutually exclusive. In other words, you can apply either a shadow or a 3D effect to an AutoShape — not both.

To apply either of these effects, select an AutoShape that you've drawn on a worksheet and then click on either the Shadow or the 3D tool. The tool expands to show a list of options (see Figure 14-12). Select an option, and it's applied to the selected shape.

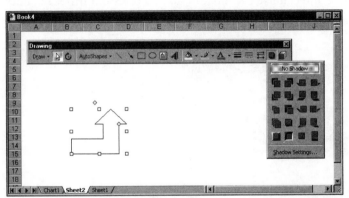

Figure 14-12: Clicking on the Shadow tool displays a list of shadow options.

You can adjust the Shadow or 3D settings by clicking on the appropriate tool and then selecting the Shadow Settings or 3D Settings option. Both these options display a toolbar that lets you fine-tune the effect. You'll find that there are *lots* of options available, and they're all quite straightforward. The best way to get familiar with these effects is to experiment.

Using WordArt

WordArt is an application that's included with Microsoft Office. You can insert a WordArt image by using the WordArt tool on the Drawing toolbar or by selecting the Insert⇨Picture⇨WordArt command. Either method displays the WordArt Gallery dialog box (see Figure 14-13). Select a style and then enter your text in the next dialog box. Click on OK, and the image is inserted in the worksheet.

Figure 14-13: The WordArt Gallery dialog box lets you select a general style for your image.

When you select a WordArt image, Excel displays the WordArt toolbar. Use these tools to modify the WordArt image. You'll find that you have *lots* of flexibility with this tool. In addition, you can use the Shadow and 3D tools to further manipulate the image. Figure 14-14 shows an example of a WordArt image inserted on a worksheet.

Figure 14-14: An example of WordArt.

Drawing Tips

Although drawing objects is quite intuitive, several tips can make this task easier. This section lists some tips and techniques that you should know:

✦ To create an object with the same height and width, press Shift while you draw the object.

✦ To constrain a line or arrow object to angles that are divisible by 15 degrees, press Shift while you draw the object.

✦ To make an object snap to the worksheet row and column gridlines, press the Alt key while you draw the object.

✦ If you press Alt while moving an object, its upper-left corner snaps to the row and column gridlines.

✦ To select multiple objects, press Ctrl while you click on them. Or use the Select Objects tool on the Drawing toolbar to select objects by "lassoing" them.

✦ To select all objects on a worksheet, use the Edit⇨Go To command (or press F5) and then click on the Special button in the Go To dialog box. Choose the Objects option button and click on OK. All objects are selected. Use this technique if you want to delete all objects (select them all and then press Delete).

✦ You can insert text into most of the AutoShapes (the exceptions are the shapes in the Connectors and Lines categories). To add text to a shape, right-click on it and select Add Text from the shortcut menu.

✦ You might find it easier to work with drawing objects if you turn off the worksheet grid line. The snap-to-gridline features work, even if the grid lines aren't visible.

✦ You can control how objects appear on-screen by using the View tab of the Options dialog box. Normally, the Show All option is selected. You can hide all objects by choosing Hide All or display objects as placeholders by choosing Show Placeholders (this may speed things up if you have complex objects that take a long time to redraw).

✦ To copy an object with the mouse, click on it once to select it and then press Ctrl while you drag it.

✦ If an object contains text, you can rotate the text 90 degrees by using the Alignment tab on the Format Object dialog box.

✦ By default, drawn objects are printed along with the worksheet. If you don't want the objects to print, access the Sheet panel of the Page Setup dialog box and select the Draft option. Or right-click on the object, select Format from the shortcut menu, and uncheck the Print Object check box in the Properties panel.

✦ If you want the underlying cell contents to show through a drawn object, access the Colors and Lines tab in the Format dialog box and set the Fill option to No Fill. You can also select the Semi-transparent option, which enables you to choose a fill color *and* have the cell contents show.

A Gallery of Drawing Examples

In this section, I provide you with some examples of using Excel's drawing tools. Perhaps these examples will get your own creative juices flowing.

Calling attention to a cell

The AutoShapes in the Stars and Banners category are useful for calling attention to a particular cell or range to make it stand out from the others. Figure 14-15 shows two examples (one subtle, one more flamboyant) of how you could make one cell's value jump out.

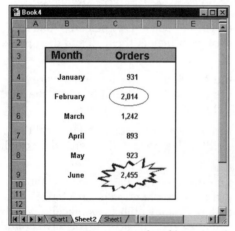

Figure 14-15: Two ways of making a particular cell stand out.

Creating shapes with shadow and 3D effects

Figure 14-16 shows a sample of objects that have various shadow and 3D effects applied. As you can see, the effects can be quite varied.

Figure 14-16: These objects use shadow or 3D effects.

Creating organizational charts

Figure 14-17 shows a simple organizational chart that I created with the AutoShape drawing tools. I used the shapes in the Connectors and Flowchart categories and then added 3D effects. To make the box size consistent, I created one and then made copies of it.

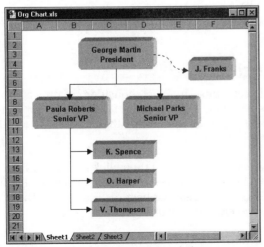

Figure 14-17: This organizational chart was created with Excel's drawing tools.

Tip   You can also create an organizational chart using the Insert⇨Picture⇨ Organization Chart command. This starts the Microsoft Organization Chart application that inserts an OLE object into the worksheet.

Changing the look of cell comments

If a cell contains a cell comment, you can replace the normal comment box with any of the AutoShapes in the Callouts category. Select the cell comment and then click on the Draw tool on the Drawing toolbar. This tool expands to show a menu. Select the Change AutoShape⇨Callouts command, followed by the desired callout shape. Figure 14-18 shows an example of cell comments that use different AutoShapes.

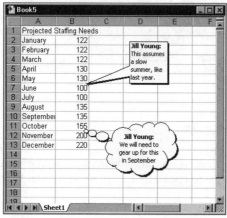

Figure 14-18: These cell comments use different AutoShapes.

Linking text in an object to a cell

As an alternative to typing text directly into an object, consider creating a link to a cell. After doing so, the text displayed in the object will reflect the current contents of the linked cell. Figure 14-19 shows an AutoShape that is linked to a cell. Notice that the edit line displays a formula.

To link an AutoShape to a cell, select the object and then click in the edit line. Enter a simple formula, such as =A1, and press Enter. You can format the text in the shape independent of the format of the cell. For best results, access the shape's Format dialog box and change the following settings:

   ✦ Automatic margins (Margins tab)

   ✦ Automatic size (Alignment tab)

   ✦ Center Horizontal alignment and Center Vertical alignment (Alignment tab)

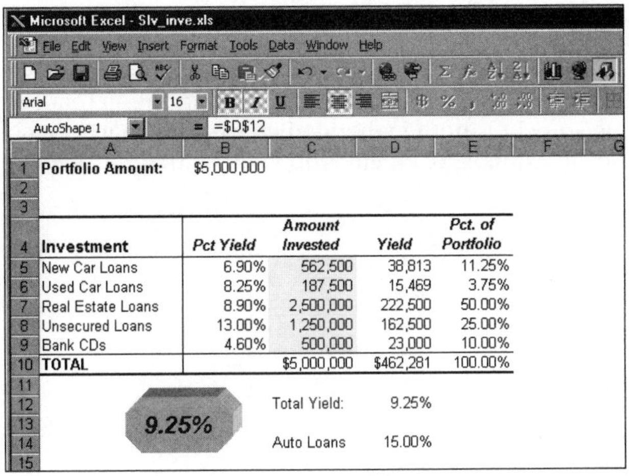

Figure 14-19: The text in the AutoShape is linked to cell D12.

Creating flow diagrams

You also can create flow diagrams using the drawing tools. The shapes in the Connectors and Flowchart categories are most useful. This capability often is useful to describe how a process or system works. Figure 14-20 shows an example of a flow diagram. After creating the diagram, I selected all the objects and grouped them together so that the diagram could be moved as a single unit.

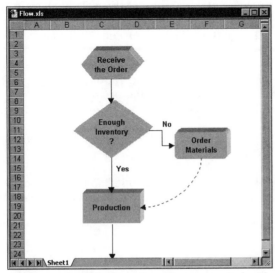

Figure 14-20: This flow diagram was created with Excel's drawing tools.

Annotating a chart

One of the most common uses of the drawing tools is to annotate a chart. For example, you can add descriptive text with an arrow to call attention to a certain data point. This technique works for both embedded charts and charts on chart sheets. Figure 14-21 shows an example of an embedded chart that has been annotated.

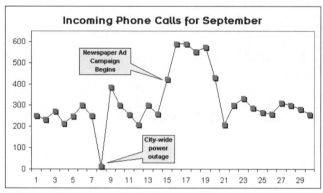

Figure 14-21: Annotating a chart with the drawing tools.

Pasting pictures of cells

One of Excel's best-kept secrets is its ability to copy and paste pictures of cells. You can copy a cell or range and then paste a picture of the cell or range on any worksheet. The picture can be static or linked. With a linked picture, the link is to the cells. In other words, if you change the contents of a cell that's in a picture, the picture changes.

To create a picture of a cell or range, select a range and choose Edit➪Copy. Then press Shift and click on the Edit menu. Choose Paste Picture to create a static picture, or choose Paste Picture Link to paste a linked picture of the selection.

Note If you don't hold down Shift when you select the Edit menu, the Paste Picture and Paste Picture Link commands do not appear.

Figure 14-22 shows an example of a linked picture. I applied some additional formatting to the picture object. Notice that the picture displays a cell reference in the formula bar.

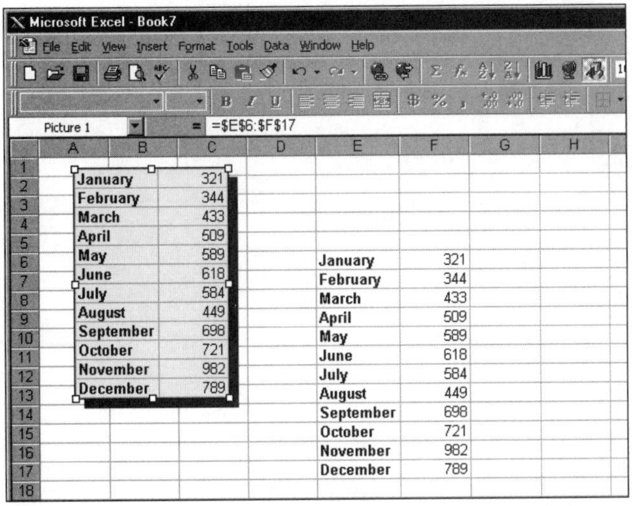

Figure 14-22: This picture is linked to the cells in E6:F17.

Using linked pictures is particularly useful for printing noncontiguous ranges. See "Printing noncontiguous ranges on a single page" in Chapter 12 for more information.

Summary

In this chapter, I cover several types of graphic information you can add to a worksheet's draw layer: imported graphic images, objects you draw using Excel's drawing tools, and other objects such as WordArt or an OLE object using Microsoft's Organization Chart application. Several examples demonstrate some ways you can use these objects in your workbooks.

✦　　✦　　✦

Putting It All Together

The preceding chapters present basic information about how Excel works. But you probably already realize that simply knowing the commands and shortcuts won't help you create successful workbooks. The point of this chapter is to help you tie it all together and provide some pointers and examples to help you develop workbooks that do what you want them to do.

The Audience for Spreadsheets

Before I get too far into this, pause and think about spreadsheets in general. There are many ways to classify spreadsheets, but it's useful to start with two broad categories:

✦ Spreadsheets that you develop for your own use

✦ Spreadsheets that others will use

As you'll see, who the ultimate user of your spreadsheet is (you alone or others) often makes a difference in how you go about developing it and the amount of effort that you put into it.

Developing spreadsheets for yourself

If you're the only person who will ever use a particular spreadsheet, you don't have to be so concerned with issues such as security, ease of use, and error handling as you would be if you were creating the spreadsheet for others. After all, you developed the spreadsheet, and you know how it was designed. If an error occurs, you can simply track down the source and correct the problem.

Quick-and-dirty spreadsheets

Chances are that many of the spreadsheets you develop for your own use are what I call "quick-and-dirty" — usually fairly small and developed to quickly solve a problem or answer a question. Here's an example: You're about to buy a new car, and you want to figure out your monthly payment for various loan amounts. Another example would be that you need to generate a chart showing your company's sales by month, so you quickly enter 12 values, whip off a chart, and paste it into your word processing document.

In this case, you don't really care what the spreadsheet looks like as long as it gives you the correct answer (or in the case of the second example, produces a nice-looking chart). You can probably input the entire model in a few minutes, and you certainly won't take the time to document your work. In many cases, you won't even bother to save the file.

For-your-eyes-only spreadsheets

As the name implies, no one except you, its creator, will ever see or use the spreadsheets that fall into this category. An example would be a file in which you keep information relevant to your income taxes. You open the file whenever a check comes in the mail, you incur an expense that can be justified as business-related, you buy tax-deductible Girl Scout cookies, and so on. Another example is a spreadsheet that you use to keep track of your employees' time records (sick leave, vacation, and such).

Spreadsheets that are for your eyes only differ from the quick-and-dirty ones in that you use them more than once; therefore, you save these spreadsheets to files. Again, though, they're not worth spending a great deal of time on. You may apply some simple formatting, but that's about it (after all, you don't really need to impress yourself — or do you?). Like the quick-and-dirty kind, this type of spreadsheet lacks any type of error detection because you understand how the formulas are set up; you know enough to avoid inputting data that produces erroneous results. If an error does crop up, you immediately know what caused it.

Spreadsheets in this category sometimes increase in sophistication over time. For example, I have an Excel workbook that I use to track my income by source. This workbook was simple when I first set it up, but I tend to add accoutrements to it nearly every time I use it: more summary formulas, better formatting, and even a chart that displays income by month. My latest modification was to add a trend line to the chart to project income based on past trends.

Developing spreadsheets for others

If others will use a spreadsheet that you develop, you need to pay a lot more attention to minor details. Because of this, such a spreadsheet usually takes longer to create than one that only you will see. The amount of extra effort depends, in large part, on the experience level of the other users. A spreadsheet that will be utilized by an inexperienced computer user is often the most difficult to develop, simply because you need to make sure that it's "bulletproof." In other words, you don't want the user to mess things up (erase a formula, for example). In addition, you have to make it perfectly clear how the spreadsheet is to be used. This often means adding more formatting and instructions for the user.

Note As you'll discover in later chapters, you can use Excel as a complete application development environment and create sophisticated applications that may not even look like a normal spreadsheet. Doing so almost always requires using macros and custom interface elements such as buttons, custom toolbars, and custom menus. These topics all are discussed in subsequent chapters.

Characteristics of a Successful Spreadsheet

You create a spreadsheet to accomplish some end result, which could be any of thousands of things. If the spreadsheet is successful, it meets most or all of the following criteria (some of which are appropriate only if the spreadsheet is used by others):

✦ It lets the end user perform a task that he or she probably would not be able to do otherwise — or a task that would take *much* longer to do manually.

✦ It's the appropriate solution to the problem.

Using a spreadsheet isn't always the most suitable approach. For example, you can create an organizational chart with Excel, but if you create org charts for a living, you're better off with a software product designed specifically for that task.

✦ It accomplishes its goal.

This may seem like an obvious prerequisite, but I've seen many spreadsheets that fail to meet this test.

✦ It produces accurate results.

As you may have discovered by now, it's quite easy to create formulas that produce the wrong results. In most cases, no answer is better than an incorrect one.

✦ It doesn't let the user accidentally (or intentionally) delete or modify important components.

Excel has built-in features to help in this area (see "Applying appropriate protection" later in this chapter).

✦ It doesn't let the user enter inappropriate data.

Excel 97's new data-validation feature makes this type of checking easier than ever.

✦ It's laid out clearly so that the user always knows how to proceed.

I've opened far too many spreadsheets and not had a clue as to how to proceed — or even what the purpose of the spreadsheet was.

✦ Its formulas and macros are well documented so that, if necessary, they can be changed.

✦ It is designed so that it can be modified in simple ways without making major changes.

You can create spreadsheets at many different levels, ranging from simple fill-in-the-blank templates to extremely complex applications that utilize custom menus and dialog boxes and may not even look like spreadsheets. The remainder of this chapter focuses on relatively simple spreadsheets — those that can be produced using only the information presented in Part I and Part II of this book.

Uses for Spreadsheets

There are millions of spreadsheets in daily use throughout the world. Many fit into the quick-and-dirty or for-your-eyes-only classifications that I described previously. Of the spreadsheets with lasting value, however, the majority probably fit into one or more of the following broad categories:

✦ Financial or data-analysis models

✦ Reports and presentations

✦ List management worksheets

✦ Workbooks that enable database access

I briefly discuss each of these in the following sections.

Financial or data-analysis models

Before the days of personal computers, large companies relied on mainframe systems to do their financial analysis. Smaller companies used sheets of accounting paper. But things have changed dramatically over the past decade, and now companies of all sizes can use personal computers to perform sophisticated analyses in the blink of an eye.

This category of spreadsheets covers a wide variety of applications, including budgeting, investment analysis, modeling, and statistical data analysis. These applications can range from simple tables of numbers to sophisticated mathematical models designed for "what-if" analyses.

One common type of spreadsheet is a budget spreadsheet. A budget spreadsheet typically has months along the top and budget categories along the left. Each intersecting cell contains a projected expense — for example, telephone expenses for June. Budgets use SUM formulas (and maybe SUBTOTAL formulas) to calculate annual totals and totals for each category. Excel's multisheet feature lets you store budgets for different departments or divisions on separate sheets.

Budget categories often are arranged in hierarchy. For example, there could be a category called Personnel, which is made up of subcategories such as Salary, Benefits, Bonus, and so on (see Figure 15-1). In such a case, you could create additional formulas to calculate category totals. Excel's outlining feature is ideal for this, which is the topic of Chapter 18.

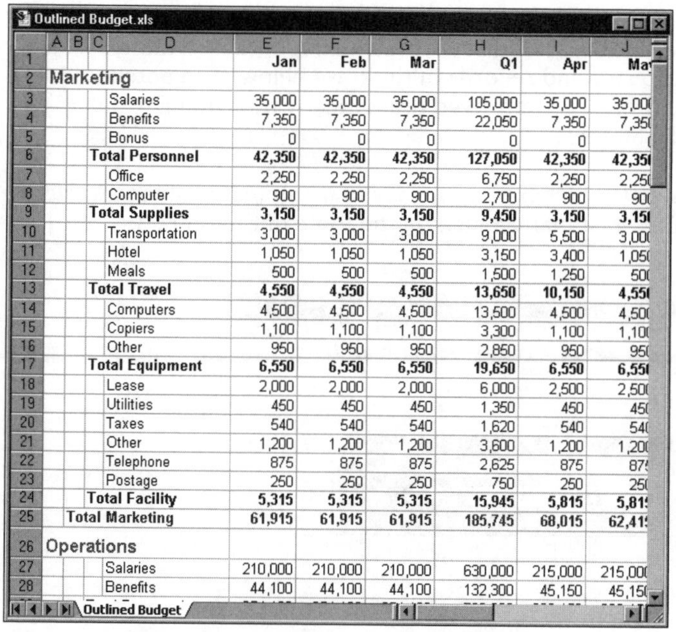
Outlined Budget.xls

	A–D	E	F	G	H	I	J
1		Jan	Feb	Mar	Q1	Apr	Ma
2	Marketing						
3	Salaries	35,000	35,000	35,000	105,000	35,000	35,00
4	Benefits	7,350	7,350	7,350	22,050	7,350	7,35
5	Bonus	0	0	0	0	0	0
6	**Total Personnel**	**42,350**	**42,350**	**42,350**	**127,050**	**42,350**	**42,35**
7	Office	2,250	2,250	2,250	6,750	2,250	2,25
8	Computer	900	900	900	2,700	900	90
9	**Total Supplies**	**3,150**	**3,150**	**3,150**	**9,450**	**3,150**	**3,15**
10	Transportation	3,000	3,000	3,000	9,000	5,500	3,00
11	Hotel	1,050	1,050	1,050	3,150	3,400	1,05
12	Meals	500	500	500	1,500	1,250	50
13	**Total Travel**	**4,550**	**4,550**	**4,550**	**13,650**	**10,150**	**4,55**
14	Computers	4,500	4,500	4,500	13,500	4,500	4,50
15	Copiers	1,100	1,100	1,100	3,300	1,100	1,10
16	Other	950	950	950	2,850	950	95
17	**Total Equipment**	**6,550**	**6,550**	**6,550**	**19,650**	**6,550**	**6,55**
18	Lease	2,000	2,000	2,000	6,000	2,500	2,50
19	Utilities	450	450	450	1,350	450	45
20	Taxes	540	540	540	1,620	540	54
21	Other	1,200	1,200	1,200	3,600	1,200	1,20
22	Telephone	875	875	875	2,625	875	87
23	Postage	250	250	250	750	250	25
24	**Total Facility**	**5,315**	**5,315**	**5,315**	**15,945**	**5,815**	**5,81**
25	**Total Marketing**	**61,915**	**61,915**	**61,915**	**185,745**	**68,015**	**62,41**
26	Operations						
27	Salaries	210,000	210,000	210,000	630,000	215,000	215,00
28	Benefits	44,100	44,100	44,100	132,300	45,150	45,15

Outlined Budget

Figure 15-1: This budget worksheet uses formulas to calculate subtotals within each category.

Another type of financial application is a *what-if model*. A what-if model calculates formulas using assumptions specified in a series of input cells. For example, you can create an amortization spreadsheet that calculates details for a loan based on the loan amount, the interest rate, and the term of the loan. This model would have three input cells. Excel's Scenario Manager is designed to make this type of model easier to handle. I discuss various ways to set up what-if models in Chapter 26.

Reports and presentations

Some spreadsheets are designed primarily for their end result: printed output. These spreadsheets take advantage of Excel's formatting and chart-making features to produce attractive, boardroom-quality output.

Of course, any spreadsheet can produce good quality reports, so spreadsheets in this category often fall into another category as well.

List management

Another common use for spreadsheets is list management. In this usage, a list is essentially a database table stored in a worksheet. A database table consists of field names in the top row and records in the rows below. The potential for list-management applications has improved dramatically now that Excel 97 worksheets have 65,536 rows.

Excel has some handy tools that make it easy to manipulate lists in a variety of ways (see Figure 15-2). List management is the topic of Chapter 23.

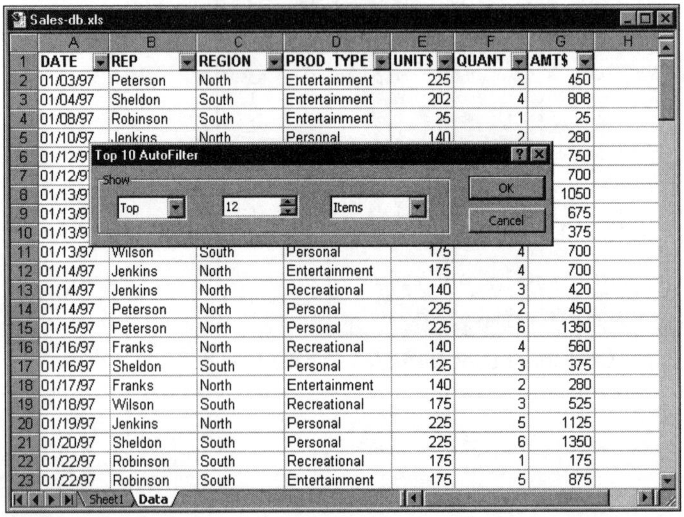

Figure 15-2: Excel makes it easy to work with lists of data.

Database access

Another category of spreadsheets works with data stored in external databases. You can use Excel to query external databases and bring in a subset of the data that meets criteria that you specify. Then you can do what you want with this data, independent of the original database. I discuss this category of spreadsheets in Chapter 24.

Turnkey applications

By a *turnkey application,* I mean a spreadsheet solution that is programmed to work as a stand-alone application. Such an application always requires macros and may involve creating custom menus and custom toolbars.

These applications are large-scale projects designed to be used by a large number of people or over a long period of time. They often interact with other systems (such as a corporate database) and must be very stable. Although this book touches on some elements of developing such applications, they are actually outside this book's scope.

Steps in Creating a Spreadsheet

This section discusses the basic steps you might follow in creating a spreadsheet. I assume that you're creating a workbook that others may use, so you may skip some of these steps if the spreadsheet is for you only. These steps are for relatively simple spreadsheets — those that don't use macros, custom toolbars, or other advanced features. And, of course, these are only basic guidelines. Everyone eventually develops his or her own style, and you may find a method that works better for you. The basic steps are as follows:

1. Think about what you want to accomplish.
2. Consider the audience.
3. Design the workbook layout.
4. Enter data and formulas.
5. Apply appropriate formatting.
6. Test your spreadsheet.
7. Apply protection as necessary.
8. Document your work.

I discuss each of these steps in the following sections.

Developing a plan

If you're like me, when you set out to create a new spreadsheet, you may have a tendency to jump right in and get to work. Tempting as it may be to create something concrete, try to restrain yourself. The end product is almost always better if you take some time to determine exactly what you're trying to accomplish and come up with a plan of action. The time you spend at this stage usually saves you more time later in the project.

Developing a plan for a spreadsheet may involve collecting the following information:

✦ How is the problem currently being addressed? And what's wrong with the current solution?

✦ Is a spreadsheet really the best solution to the problem?

✦ How long will the spreadsheet be used?

✦ How many people will be using it?

✦ What type of output, if any, will be required?

✦ Is there existing data that can be imported?

✦ Will the requirements for this project change over time?

The point here is to attempt to learn as much as possible about the project that you're developing. With that information, you can determine a plan of action — which may even mean not using a spreadsheet for the solution.

Considering the audience

If you'll be the only user of the workbook that you're developing, you can skip this step. But if others will be using the result of your efforts, take some time to find out about these people. Knowing the following information often prevents having to make changes later:

✦ **How experienced are the users?** Can they perform basic operations such as copying, inserting rows, and so on? Don't assume that everyone knows as much as you do.

✦ **What software will they be using?** For example, if you develop your spreadsheet using Excel 97, you need to be aware that it can't be loaded into Excel 95 or earlier versions unless you first save the file in the older format.

✦ **What hardware will they be using?** If your spreadsheet takes 3 minutes to calculate on your Pentium-based system, it may well take 20 minutes on a slower 486 system. Also, be aware of different video modes. If you develop your spreadsheet using a 1024×768 video mode, users with an 800×600 or 640×480 display will have a much smaller viewing area.

✦ **Do you want to allow changes?** Often, you want to make sure that your formulas don't get modified. If so, you'll need to perform some basic protection (see "Applying appropriate protection," later in this chapter).

Designing the workbook layout

An important consideration is how you want to lay out the workbook. Before the days of multisheet workbooks, this was a lot more difficult than it is today. When your file has only a single worksheet, you have to plan it carefully to ensure that making a change doesn't affect something else.

Spreadsheets often consist of distinct blocks of information. In the old days, spreadsheet designers often used a layout like the one shown in Figure 15-3. This example is for a spreadsheet that has three main blocks: an input area, a calculation area, and a report area. This *offset block layout* minimizes the possibility of damage. For example, deleting a column or changing its width affects only one area. If the areas were laid out vertically, this would not be the case.

Because Excel uses multiple worksheets in a file, however, this type of layout is rarely necessary. It's much easier and more efficient to use a separate worksheet for each block. An added advantage is that you can access the various blocks simply by clicking on the tab (which can be named appropriately).

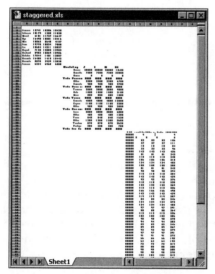

Figure 15-3: This offset block layout is one way to organize a worksheet.

Entering data and formulas

This phase of the spreadsheet development process is often where people begin. But if you've thought through the problem, considered the users, and created an appropriate layout, this phase should go more smoothly than if you jumped right in without the preliminary steps.

The more you know about Excel, the easier this phase is. Formulas are just one part of a spreadsheet. Sometimes you may need to incorporate one or more of the following features (all of which are discussed later in the book):

✦ Workbook consolidation

✦ List management

✦ External databases

✦ Outlining

✦ Data validation

✦ Conditional formatting

✦ Hyperlinks

✦ Statistical analysis

✦ Pivot tables

✦ Scenario management

✦ Solver

✦ Mapping

✦ Interaction with other applications

✦ Custom menus or toolbars (which require macros)

Applying appropriate formatting

Many people prefer to format their work as they go along. If that's not your style, this step must be performed before you unleash your efforts to the end users. As I mentioned in Chapter 11, almost all worksheets benefit from some stylistic formatting. At the very least, you need to adjust the number formats so that the values appear correctly. If the worksheet will be used by others, make sure that any color combinations you use will be visible for those running on a monochrome system (such as a notebook computer).

Of all the basic steps in creating a spreadsheet, formatting is the one with the most variety. Although beauty may be in the eye of the beholder, there are some guidelines that you might want to consider:

✦ **Preformat all numeric cells.** Use number formats appropriate for the numbers and make sure that the columns are wide enough to handle the maximum values. For example, if a cell is designed to hold an interest rate, format it with a percent sign. And if you've created an amortization schedule, make sure that the columns are wide enough to handle large amounts.

✦ **Use only basic fonts.** If others will be using your workbook, stick to the basic TrueType fonts that come with Windows. Otherwise, the fonts may not translate well, and the user may see a string of asterisks rather than a value.

✦ **Don't go overboard with fonts.** As a rule of thumb, never use more than two different typefaces in a single workbook. Usually, one will do just fine (Arial is a good choice). If you use different font sizes, do so sparingly.

✦ **Be careful with color.** Colored text or cell backgrounds can make your workbook much easier to use. For example, if you use a lookup table, you can use color to make it clear where the table's boundaries are. Or you may want to color-code the cells that will accept user input. Overuse of colors makes your spreadsheet look gaudy and unprofessional, however. Also, make sure that color combinations will work if the workbook is opened on a monochrome notebook computer.

✦ **Consider identifying the active area.** Many spreadsheets are set up using only a few cells — the active area. Inexperienced users often scroll away from the active area and get lost. One technique is to hide all rows and columns that aren't used. Or you can apply a color background (such as light gray) to all unused cells. This will make the cells in use very clear.

✦ **Remove extraneous elements.** In some cases, you can simplify things significantly by removing elements that might get in the way or cause the screen to appear more confusing than it is. These elements include automatic page breaks, gridlines, row and column headers, and sheet tabs. These options, which you set in the View panel of the Options dialog box, are saved with the worksheet.

Testing the spreadsheet

Before you actually use your newly created spreadsheet for real work, you'll want to test it thoroughly. This is even more critical if others will be using your spreadsheet. If you've distributed 20 copies of your file and then discover a major error in a formula, you'll have to do a "recall" and send out a corrected copy. Obviously, it's easier to catch the errors before you send out a spreadsheet.

Testing is basically the process of ensuring that the formulas produce correct results under all possible circumstances. There are no rules that I know of for testing a worksheet, so you're pretty much on your own here. I can, however, offer a few guidelines:

✦ **Try extreme input values.** If your worksheet is set up to perform calculations using input cells, spend some time and enter very large or very small
numbers and observe the effects on the formulas. If the user should enter a
percentage, see what happens if you enter a large value. If a positive number
is expected, try entering a negative number. This also is a good way to
ensure that your columns are wide enough.

✦ **Provide data validation.** Although you can't expect your formulas to yield
usable results for invalid entries (garbage in, garbage out), you may want to
use Excel's new data-validation features to ensure that data entered is of the
proper type.

✦ **Use dummy data.** If you have a budget application, for example, try entering
a 1 into each non-formula cell. This is a good way to make sure that all your
SUM formulas refer to the correct ranges. An incorrect formula usually
stands out from the others.

✦ **Get familiar with Excel's auditing tools.** Excel has several useful tools
that can help you track down erroneous formulas. I discuss these tools in
Chapter 31.

Applying appropriate protection

A spreadsheet can be quite fragile. Deleting a single formula often has a ripple
effect and causes other formulas to produce an error value or, even worse,
incorrect results. I've seen cases in which an inexperienced user deleted a critical
formula, panicked, and cemented the mistake by saving the file and reopening it —
only to discover, of course, that the original (good) version had been overwritten.

You can circumvent such problems by using the protection features built into
Excel. There are two general types of protection:

✦ Sheet protection

✦ Workbook protection

Protecting sheets

The Tools➪Protection➪Protect Sheet command displays the dialog box shown in
Figure 15-4.

Figure 15-4: The Protect Sheet dialog box.

This dialog box has three check boxes:

✦ **Contents:** Cells that have their Locked property turned on can't be changed.

✦ **Objects:** Drawing objects (including embedded charts) that have their Locked property turned on can't be selected.

✦ **Scenarios:** Defined scenarios that have their Prevent Changes property turned on can't be changed (see Chapter 26 for a discussion of scenario management).

Note You can provide a password or not in the Protect Sheet dialog box. If you enter a password, the password must be reentered before the sheet can be unprotected. If you don't supply a password, anyone can unprotect the sheet.

By default, all cells have their Locked property turned on. Before protecting a worksheet, you'll normally want to turn the Locked property off for input cells.

You can change the Locked property of a cell or object by accessing its Format dialog box and clicking on the Protection tab. Cells have an additional property: Hidden. This is a bit misleading, because it doesn't actually hide the cell. Rather, it prevents the cell contents from being displayed in the formula bar. You can use the Hidden property to prevent others from seeing your formulas.

Note You can't change a cell's Locked property while the sheet is protected. You must unprotect the sheet to make any changes, and then protect it again.

Protection isn't just for worksheets that others will be using. Many people protect worksheets to prevent themselves from accidentally deleting cells.

Protecting workbooks

The second type of protection is workbook protection. The Tools⇨Protection⇨ Protect Workbook command displays the dialog box shown in Figure 15-5.

Figure 15-5: The Protect Workbook dialog box.

This dialog box has two check boxes:

✦ **Structure:** Protects the workbook window from being moved or resized.

✦ **Windows:** Prevents any of the following changes to a workbook: adding a sheet, deleting a sheet, moving a sheet, renaming a sheet, hiding a sheet, or unhiding a sheet.

Again, you can supply a password or not, depending on the level of protection you need.

Documenting your work

The final step in the spreadsheet-creation process is documenting your work. It's always a good idea to make some notes about the spreadsheet. After all, you may need to modify the spreadsheet later. The elegant formula that you created last week may be completely meaningless when you need to change it in six months. Here are some general tips on documenting your spreadsheets.

Use the Properties dialog box

The File➪Properties command displays the Properties dialog box (the Summary panel is shown in Figure 15-6). You may want to take a few minutes to fill in the missing information and enter some comments in the Comments box.

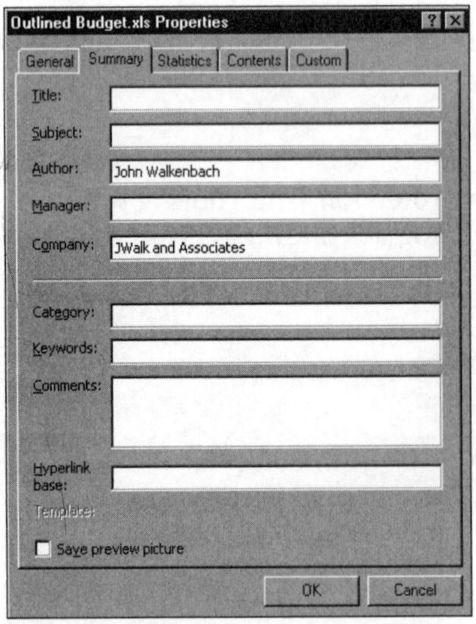

Figure 15-6: The Summary panel of the Properties dialog box.

Use cell comments

As you know, you can document individual cells by using the Insert⇨Comment command. The comment appears when you move the mouse pointer over the cell. If you don't like the idea of seeing the cell comments appear, adjust this setting in the View tab of the Options dialog box. Unfortunately, this setting applies to all workbooks, so if you turn off the note indicator for one workbook, you turn it off for all of them.

Use a separate worksheet

Perhaps the best way to document a workbook is to insert a new worksheet and store your comments there. Some people also like to keep a running tally of any modifications that they made. You can hide the worksheet so that others can't see it.

A Workbook That's Easy to Maintain

One of the cardinal rules of spreadsheeting is that things change. You may have a sales-tracking spreadsheet that you've been using for years, and it works perfectly well. But then you're informed that the company has bought out one of your competitors, and the sales regions will be restructured. Your sales-tracking workbook suddenly no longer applies.

You often can save yourself lots of time by planning for the inevitable changes. There are a few things that you can do to make your worksheets as modifiable as possible:

✦ **Avoid hard-coding values in formulas**. For example, assume that you have formulas that calculate sales commissions using a commission rate of 12.5 percent. Rather than use the value .125 in the formulas, enter it into a cell and use the cell reference. Or use the technique described in Chapter 9 (see "Naming constants") to create a named constant.

✦ **Use names whenever possible.** Cell and range names make your formulas easier to read and more understandable. When the time comes to modify your formulas, you may be able to modify just the range to which a name refers.

✦ **Use simplified formulas.** Beginning users sometimes create formulas that are more complicated than they need to be. Often, this is because they don't know about a particular built-in function. As you gain more experience with Excel, be on the lookout for useful functions that can make your formulas simple and clear. Such formulas are much easier to modify when the time comes.

✦ **Use a flexible layout.** Rather than try to cram everything into a single worksheet, use multiple worksheets. You'll find that this makes expanding much easier, should the need arise.

✦ **Use named styles.** Using named styles makes obtaining consistent formatting much easier if you need to add new data to accommodate a change. I discuss this feature in Chapter 11 (see "Using Named Styles").

✦ **Keep it clean.** It's also a good idea to keep your workbooks clean and free of extraneous information. For example, if the workbook has empty worksheets, remove them. If you created names that you no longer use, delete them. If there's a range of cells that you used to perform a quick calculation (and you no longer need it), delete the range.

When Things Go Wrong

Many types of errors can occur when you work with Excel (or any spreadsheet, for that matter). These range from inconvenient errors that can be easily corrected to disastrous errors that can't.

For example, a formula may return an error value when a certain cell that it uses contains a zero. Normally, you can isolate the problem and correct the formula so that the error doesn't appear anymore (this is an example of an easily corrected error). A potentially disastrous error is when you open a worksheet and Excel reports that it can't read the file. Figure 15-7 shows the message you get. Unless you made a recent backup, you could be in deep trouble. Unfortunately, this type of error (a corrupted file) occurs more often than you might think.

Figure 15-7: When you see an error message like this, you'd better have a recent backup available.

Good testing helps you avoid problems with your formulas. Making modifications to your work, however, may result in a formula no longer working. For example, you may add a new column to the worksheet, and the formulas don't pick up the expanded cell reference. This is an example of when using names could eliminate the need to adjust the formulas.

There will be cases in which you find that a formula just doesn't work as it should. When this happens, try to isolate the problem as simply as possible. I've found that a good way to deal with such formulas is to create a new workbook with a very simplified example of what I'm trying to accomplish. Sometimes, looking at the problem in a different context can shed new light on it.

The only way to prevent disasters — such as a corrupt file — is to develop good backup habits. If a file is important, you should never have only one copy of it. You should get in the habit of making a daily backup on a different storage medium.

Where to Go from Here

This chapter concludes Part II. If you're following the book in sequential-chapter order, you now have enough knowledge to put Excel to good use.

Excel has many more features that may interest you, however. These are covered in the remaining chapters. Even if you're satisfied with what you already know about Excel, I strongly suggest that you at least browse through the remaining chapters. You may see something that can save you hours.

Summary

In this chapter, I distinguish two general categories of spreadsheets: those that you create for yourself only and those that others will use. The approach you take depends on the end user. I also list the characteristics of a successful spreadsheet and discuss basic types of spreadsheets. I discuss the basic steps that you may go through when creating a spreadsheet and cover the features in Excel that let you protect various parts of your work. I conclude with some tips on how to make your spreadsheets easier to maintain and how to handle some common types of errors.

✦   ✦   ✦

Advanced Features

The chapters in this part cover some advanced topics that help you create more powerful spreadsheets. I discuss additional charting techniques, Excel's Microsoft Map feature, worksheet outlines, file linking and consolidation, and array formulas. The final chapter provides information related to using Excel in a workgroup.

Advanced Charting

♦ ♦ ♦ ♦

In This Chapter

Customizing all
aspects of charts

Working with the
data series used in
charts

Creating custom
chart types

Getting the most out
of Excel's 3D charts

Chart-making tricks
and tips

♦ ♦ ♦ ♦

Chapter 13 introduces charting. This chapter takes the
topic to the next level. You learn how to customize
your charts to the max so that they look exactly as you want.
I also share some slick charting tricks that I've picked up
over the years.

Chart Customization: An Overview

Often, the basic chart that Excel creates is good enough. If
you're using a chart to get a better idea of what your data
means, a chart that's based one of the standard chart types
usually does just fine. But if you want to create the most
effective chart possible, you'll probably want to take advantage
of the additional customization techniques available in Excel.

Customizing a chart involves changing its appearance, as well
as possibly adding new elements to it. These changes can be
purely cosmetic (such as changing colors or modifying line
widths) or quite substantial (such as changing the axis scales
or rotating a 3D chart). New elements that you might add
include features such as a data table, a trendline, or error bars.

Note Before you can customize a chart, you must activate it. To
activate a chart on a chart sheet, click on its sheet tab. To
activate an embedded chart, click on the chart's border. To
deactivate an embedded chart, just click anywhere in the
worksheet.

Tip In some cases, you may prefer to work with an embedded
chart in a separate window. For example, if the embedded
chart is larger than the workbook window, it is much easier
to work with if it's in its own window. To display an embedded chart in a window, right-click on the chart's border and
select Chart Window from the shortcut menu.

Here's a partial list of the customizations that you can make to a chart:

✦ Change any colors, patterns, line widths, marker styles, and fonts.

✦ Change the data ranges that the chart uses, add a new chart series, or delete an existing series.

✦ Choose which gridlines to display.

✦ Determine the size and placement of the legend (or delete it altogether).

✦ Determine where the axes cross.

✦ Adjust the axis scales by specifying a maximum and minimum, changing the tick marks and labels, and so on. You also can specify that a scale be represented in logarithmic units.

✦ Add titles for the chart and axes, as well as free-floating text anywhere in the chart.

✦ Add error bars and trendlines to a data series.

✦ Display the data points in reverse order.

✦ Rotate a 3D chart to get a better view or to add impact.

✦ Replace line-chart markers with bitmaps.

Note   It's easy to become overwhelmed with all the chart customization options. However, the more you work with charts, the easier it becomes. Even advanced users tend to experiment a great deal with chart customization, and they rely heavily on trial and error — a technique that I strongly recommend.

Elements of a chart

Before I discuss chart modifications, I need to digress and talk about the various elements of a chart. The number and type of elements in a chart varies with the type of chart — for example, pie charts don't have axes, and only 3D charts have walls and floors.

When a chart is activated, you can select various parts of the chart with which to work. Modifying a chart is similar to everything else you do in Excel: First you make a selection (in this case, select a chart element), and then you issue a command to do something with the selection. Unlike a worksheet selection, with a chart selection you can select only one chart element at a time. The exceptions are elements that consist of multiple parts, such as gridlines. Selecting one gridline selects them all.

You select a chart element by clicking on it. The name of the selected item appears in the Name box. When a chart is activated, you can't access the Name box; it's simply a convenient place for Excel to display the chart element's name.

Excel 97 The Chart toolbar, which is displayed when you select a chart, contains a tool called Chart Objects (see Figure 16-1). This is a drop-down list of all of the named elements in a chart. Rather than selecting a chart element by clicking on it, you can use this list to select the chart element that you want to work with.

Figure 16-1: The Chart Objects tool in the Chart toolbar provides another way to select a chart element.

Tip Yet another way to select a chart element is to use the keyboard. When a chart is activated, press the up arrow or down arrow to cycle through all parts in the chart. When a data series is selected, press the right arrow or left arrow to select individual points in the series.

Table 16-1 lists the various elements of a chart (not all of these parts appear in every chart). You might want to create a chart and practice selecting some of these parts — or use the Chart Objects tool in the Chart toolbar to examine the element names.

Using the Format dialog box

When a chart element is selected, you can access the element's Format dialog box to format or set options for the element. Each chart element has a unique Format dialog box. You can access this dialog box by using any of the following methods:

✦ Select the Format⇨Selected *Part Name* command (the Format menu displays the actual name of the selected part).

✦ Double-click on a chart part.

✦ Press Ctrl+1.

✦ Right-click on the chart element and choose the Format command from the shortcut menu.

Any of these methods displays a tabbed Format dialog box that lets you make many changes to the selected chart element. For example, Figure 16-2 shows the dialog box that appears when the chart's title is selected.

In the sections that follow, I discuss in detail the various types of chart modification.

Table 16-1
Chart Elements

Part	Description
Category Axis	The axis that represents the chart's categories.
Category Title	The title for the category axis.
Chart Area	The chart's background.
Chart Title	The chart's title.
Corners	The corners of 3D charts (except 3D pie charts). Select the corners if you want to rotate a 3D chart using a mouse.
Data Label	A data label for a point in a series. The name is preceded by the series and the point. Example: Series 1 Point 1 Data Label.
Data Labels	Data labels for a series. The name is preceded by the series. Example: Series 1 Data Labels.
Data Table	The chart's data table.
Down-Bars	Down-bars in a stock market chart.
Dropline	A dropline that extends from the data point downward to the axis.
Error Bars	Error bars for a series. The name is preceded by the series. Example: Series 1 Error Bars.
Floor	The floor of a 3D chart.
Gridlines	A chart can have major and minor gridlines for each axis. The element is named using the axis and the type of gridlines. Example: Value Axis Major Gridlines.
High-Low Lines	High-low lines in a stock market chart.
Legend Entry	One of the text entries inside of a legend.
Legend Key	One of the keys inside of a legend.
Legend	The chart's legend.
Plot Area	The chart's plot area — the actual chart, without the legend.
Point	A point in a data series. The name is preceded by the series. Example: Series 1 Point 2.
Series Axis	The axis that represents the chart's series (3D charts only).
Series	A line that connects a series.
Trendline	A trendline for a data series.
Up-Bars	Up-bars in a stock market chart.
Value Axis Title	The title for the value axis.
Value Axis	The axis that represents the chart's values. There also may be a Secondary Value Axis.
Walls	The walls of a 3D chart only (except 3D pie charts).

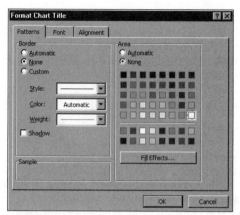

Figure 16-2: The Format dialog box for a chart's title.
Each chart element has its own Format dialog box.

Chart Background Elements

As I mention in the preceding section, a chart is made up of many elements. In this section, I discuss two of those elements: the Chart Area and the Plot Area. These chart items provide a background for other elements in the chart.

The Chart Area

The Chart Area is an object that contains all other elements in the chart. You can think of it as a chart's master background. You can't change the size of the Chart Area. For an embedded chart, it's always the same size as the embedded chart object. For a chart sheet, the Chart Area is always the entire sheet.

Following are some key points about the Chart Area.

✦ The Format Chart Area dialog box contains three tabs: Patterns, Font, and Properties.

✦ The Patterns panel lets you change the Chart Area's color and patterns (including fill effects) and add a border, if you like. The Font panel lets you change the properties of *all fonts used in the chart*. Changing the font won't affect fonts that you have previously changed, however. For example, if you make the chart's title 20-point Arial and then change the font to 8-point Arial in the Format Chart Area dialog box, the title's font is not affected.

✦ The Properties panel lets you specify how the chart is moved and sized with respect to the underlying cells. You also can set the Locked property and specify whether the chart will be printed.

✦ If you delete the Chart Area, you delete the entire chart.

Excel 97 In previous versions of Excel, clicking on an embedded chart selected the chart object. You could then adjust its properties. To actually activate the chart, you had to double-click on it. In Excel 97, clicking on an embedded chart activates the chart contained inside the chart object. You can adjust the chart object's properties by using the Properties tab of the Format dialog box. To select the chart object itself, press Ctrl while you click on the chart. You might want to select the chart object in order to change its name by using the Name box.

The Plot Area

The Chart Area of a chart contains the Plot Area, which is the part of the chart that contains the actual chart. The Plot Area is unlike the Chart Area in that you can resize and reposition the Plot Area. The Format Plot Area dialog box has only one tab: Patterns. This lets you change the color and pattern of the plot area and also adjust its borders.

Tip When a chart element is selected, you'll find that many of the toolbar buttons that you normally use for worksheet formatting also work with the selected chart element. For example, if you select the chart's Plot Area, you can change its color by using the Fill Color tool on the Formatting toolbar. If you select an element that contains text, you can use the Font Color tool to change the color of the text.

Working with Chart Titles

A chart can have as many as five different titles:

- ✦ Chart title
- ✦ Category (X) axis title
- ✦ Value (Y) axis title
- ✦ Second category (X) axis title
- ✦ Second value (Y) axis title

The number of titles that you can use depends on the chart type. For example, a pie chart supports only a chart title because it has no axes.

To add titles to a chart, activate the chart and use the Chart⇨Options command. Excel displays the Chart Options dialog box. Click on the Titles tab and enter text for the title or titles (see Figure 16-3).

Tip The titles that Excel adds are placed in the appropriate position, but you can drag them anywhere.

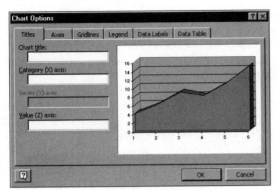

Figure 16-3: The Titles tab of the Chart Options dialog box lets you add titles to a chart.

To modify a chart title's properties, access its Format dialog box. This dialog box has tabs for the following:

> **Patterns:** For changing the background color and borders
>
> **Font:** For changing the font, size, color, and attributes
>
> **Alignment:** For adjusting the vertical and horizontal alignment and orientation

Excel 97 lets you specify an angle for the titles in the Alignment panel.

Tip

Text in a chart is not limited to titles. In fact, you can add free-floating text anywhere you want. To do so, select any part of the chart except a title or data label. Then type the text in the formula bar and press Enter. Excel adds a Text Box AutoShape that contains the text. You can move the Text Box wherever you want it and format it to your liking.

Working with the Legend

If you created your chart with the ChartWizard, you had an option to include a legend. If you change your mind, you can easily delete the legend or add one if it doesn't exist.

To add a legend to your chart, use the Chart⇨Options command and then click on the Legend tab in the Chart Options dialog box. Place a check mark in the Show legend check box. You also can specify where to place the legend using the Placement option buttons.

The quickest way to remove a legend is to select the legend and press Delete. To move a legend, click on it and drag it to the desired location. Or you can use the legend's Format dialog box to position the legend (using the Placement tab).

A chart's legend consists of text and keys. A *key* is a small graphic that corresponds to the chart's series. You can select individual text items within a legend and format them separately using the Format Legend Entry dialog box (which has only a single panel: Font). For example, you may want to make the text bold to draw attention to a particular data series.

Note   You can't use the Chart toolbar's Select Object drop-down list to select a legend entry or legend key. You either must click on the item or select the legend itself, and then press the right arrow until the desired element is selected.

The Legend tool in the Chart toolbar acts as a toggle. Use this button to add a legend if one doesn't exist and to remove the legend if one exists.

Tip   After you move a legend from its default position, you may want to change the size of the plot area to fill in the gap left by the legend. Just select the plot area and drag a border to make it the desired size.

If you didn't include legend text when you originally selected the cells to create the chart, Excel displays *Series 1, Series 2*, and so on in the legend. To add series names, choose the Chart⇨Source Data command and then select the Series tab in the Source Data dialog box (refer to Figure 16-4). Select a series from the Series list box, activate the Name box, and either specify a cell reference that contains the label or directly enter the series name.

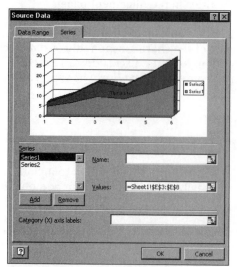

Figure 16-4: Use the Series tab of the Source Data dialog box to change the name of a data series.

Changing Gridlines

Gridlines can help you determine what the chart series represents numerically. Gridlines simply extend the tick marks on the axes. Some charts look better with gridlines; others appear more cluttered. It's up to you to decide whether gridlines can enhance your chart. Sometimes, horizontal gridlines alone are enough, although XY charts often benefit from both horizontal and vertical gridlines.

To add or remove gridlines, use the Chart⇨Options command and select the Gridlines tab. This dialog box is shown in Figure 16-5.

Each axis has two sets of gridlines: major and minor. Major units are the ones displaying a label. Minor units are those between the labels. You can choose which to add or remove by checking or unchecking the appropriate check boxes. If you're working with a true 3D chart, the dialog box has options for three sets of gridlines.

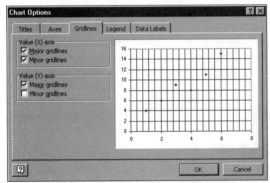

Figure 16-5: The Gridlines panel of the Chart Options dialog box lets you add or remove gridlines from the chart.

To modify the properties of a set of gridlines, select one gridline in the set and access the Format Gridlines dialog box. This dialog has two tabs:

> **Patterns:** Changes the line style, width, and color
>
> **Scale:** Adjusts the scale used on the axis

I discuss scaling in detail in the next section.

Modifying the Axes

Charts vary in the number of axes that they use. Pie and doughnut charts have no axes. All 2D charts have two axes (three, if you use a secondary-value axis; and four if you use a secondary-category axis in an XY chart). True 3D charts have three axes. Excel gives you a great deal of control over these axes. To modify any aspect of an axis, access its Format Axis dialog box. The Format Axis dialog box has five tabs:

Patterns: Change the axis line width, tick marks, and placement of tick-mark labels

Scale: Adjust the minimum and maximum axis values, units for major and minor gridlines, and other properties

Font: Adjust the font used for the axis labels

Number: Adjust the number format for the axis labels

Alignment: Specify the orientation for the axis labels.

Because the axes' properties can dramatically affect the chart's look, I discuss the Patterns and Scale dialog box tabs separately, in the following sections.

Axes patterns

Figure 16-6 shows the Patterns tab of the Format Axis dialog box.

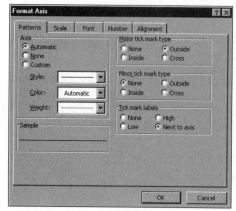

Figure 16-6: The Patterns panel of the Format Axis dialog box.

This panel has four sections:

> **Axis:** This controls the line characteristics of the axis itself (the style, color, and weight of the line).

> **Major tick mark type:** This controls how the major tick marks appear. You can select None (no tick marks), Inside (inside the axis), Outside (outside the axis), or Cross (on both sides of the axis).

> **Minor tick mark type:** This controls how the minor tick marks appear. You can select None (no tick marks), Inside (inside the axis), Outside (outside the axis), or Cross (on both sides of the axis).

> **Tick-mark labels:** This controls where the axis labels appear. Normally, the labels appear next to the axis. You can, however, specify that the labels appear High (at the top of the chart), Low (at the bottom of the chart), or not at all (None). These options are useful when the axis doesn't appear in its normal position at the edge of the plot area.

Note Major tick marks are the axis tick marks that normally have labels next to them. Minor tick marks are between the major tick marks.

Axes scales

Adjusting the scale of a value axis can have a dramatic affect on the chart's appearance. Manipulating the scale in some cases can present a false picture of the data. Figure 16-7 shows two charts that use the same data; the only difference between the charts is that I've adjusted the Minimum value on the value axis scale. In the first chart, the differences are quite apparent. In the second chart, there appears to be little difference between the data points.

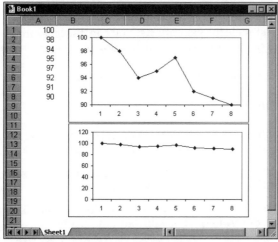

Figure 16-7: These two charts use the same data but different scales.

The actual scale that you use depends on the situation. No hard-and-fast rules exist about scale, except that you should avoid misrepresenting data by manipulating the chart to prove a point that doesn't exist.

If you're preparing several charts that use similarly scaled data, keep the scales the same so that the charts can be compared more easily. The charts in Figure 16-8 show the distribution of responses for a survey. Because the same scale was not used on the value axes, however, comparing the responses across survey items is difficult. All charts in the series should have the same scale.

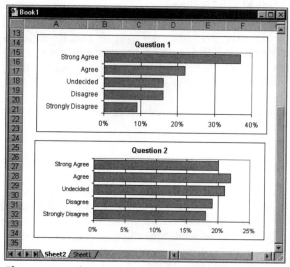

Figure 16-8: These charts use different scales on the value axis, making it difficult to compare the two.

Excel automatically determines the scale for your charts. You can, however, override Excel's choice in the Scale panel of the Format Axis dialog box (see Figure 16-9).

Note   The Scale panel varies slightly depending on which axis is selected.

This dialog box offers the following options:

Mi_nimum: For entering a minimum value for the axis. If the check box is checked, Excel determines this value automatically.

Ma_ximum: For entering a maximum value for the axis. If the check box is checked, Excel determines this value automatically.

Ma_jor unit: For entering the number of units between major tick marks. If the check box is checked, Excel determines this value automatically.

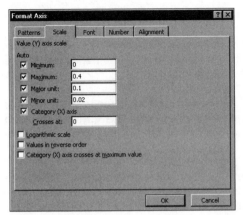

Figure 16-9: The Scale panel of the Format Axis dialog box.

Minor unit: For entering the number of units between minor tick marks. If the check box is checked, Excel determines this value automatically.

Axis Type axis **C**rosses at: For positioning the axes at a different location. By default, it's at the edge of the plot area. The exact wording of this option varies, depending on which axis is selected.

Logarithmic scale: For using a logarithmic scale for the axes. A log scale primarily is useful for scientific applications in which the values to be plotted have an extremely large range. You receive an error message if the scale includes 0 or negative values.

Values in reverse order: For making the scale values extend in the opposite direction. For a value axis, for example, selecting this option displays the smallest scale value at the top and the largest at the bottom (the opposite of how it normally appears).

Axis Type crosses at **m**aximum value: For positioning the axes at the maximum value of the perpendicular axis (normally, the axis is positioned at the minimum value of the perpendicular axis). The exact wording of this option varies, depending on which axis is selected.

Working with Data Series

Every chart is made up of one or more data series. Each series is based on data stored in a worksheet. This data translates into chart columns, lines, pie slices, and so on. In this section, I discuss most of the customizations that you can perform with chart's data series.

To work with a data series, you must first select it. Activate the chart and then click on the data series that you want to select. In a column chart, click on a column; in a line chart, click on a line; and so on. Make sure that you select the entire series and not just a single point. You may find it easier to select the series using the Chart Object tool in the Chart toolbar.

When you select a data series, Excel displays the series name in the Name box (for example, Series 1, or the actual name of the series), and the SERIES formula in the formula bar. A selected data series has a small square on each element of the series.

Many customizations that you perform with a data series use the Format Data Series dialog box, which has as many as seven tabs. The number of tabs varies, depending on the type of chart. For example, a pie chart has four tabs, and a 3D column chart has four tabs. Line and column charts have six tabs, and XY (scatter) charts have seven tabs. The possible tabs in the Format Data Series dialog box are as follows:

> **Axis:** For specifying which value axis to use for the selected data series. This is applicable only if the chart has two value axes.
>
> **Data Labels:** For displaying labels next to each data point.
>
> **Options:** For changing options specific to the chart type.
>
> **Patterns:** For changing the color, pattern, and border style for the data series. For line charts, change the color and style of the data marker in this tab.
>
> **Series Order:** For specifying the order in which the data series are plotted.
>
> **Shape:** For specifying the shape of the columns (in 3D column charts only).
>
> **X Error Bars:** For adding or modifying error bars for the X axis. This is available only for XY charts.
>
> **Y Error Bars**: For adding or modifying error bars for the Y axis.

I discuss many of these dialog box options in the sections that follow.

Deleting a data series

To delete a data series in a chart, select the data series and press the Delete key. The data series is removed from the chart. The data in the worksheet, of course, remains intact.

Note It's possible to delete all data series from a chart. If so, the chart appears empty. It retains its settings, however. Therefore, you can add a data series to an empty chart, and it again looks like a chart.

Adding a new data series to a chart

It's common to need to add another data series to an existing chart. You *could* re-create the chart and include the new data series, but it's usually easier to add the data to the existing chart. Excel provides several ways to add a new data series to a chart:

✦ Activate the chart and select the Chart⇨Source Data command. In the Source Data dialog box, click on the Series tab (see Figure 16-10). Click on the Add button and then specify the data range in the Values box (you can enter the range address or point to it).

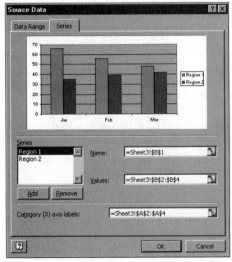

Figure 16-10: Use the Source Data dialog box to add a new data series to a chart.

✦ Select the range to be added and copy it to the Clipboard. Then activate the chart and choose the Edit⇨Paste Special command. Excel responds with the dialog box shown in Figure 16-11. Complete this dialog box to correspond to the data that you selected (or just use Edit⇨Paste and let Excel determine how the data fits into the chart).

✦ Select the range to be added and drag it into the chart. When you release the mouse button, Excel updates the chart with the data you dragged in. This technique works only if the chart is embedded on the worksheet.

Figure 16-11: Using the Paste Special dialog box is one way to add new data to a chart.

Changing data used by a series

Often, you create a chart that uses a particular range of data, and then you extend the range by adding new data points in the worksheet. For example, the previous month's sales data arrives in your office, and you enter the numbers into your sales-tracking worksheet. Or you may delete some of the data points in a range that is plotted; for example, you may not need to plot older information. In either case, you'll find that the chart doesn't update itself automatically. When you add new data to a range, it isn't included in the data series. If you delete data from a range, the chart displays the deleted data as zero values.

In the following sections, I describe a few different ways to change the range used by a data series.

Dragging the range outline

Excel 97 A new feature in Excel 97 makes it very easy to change the data range for a data series. This technique works only for embedded charts. When you select a series, Excel outlines the data range used by that series. You can drag the small dot in the lower-right corner of the range outline to extend or contract the data series. Figure 16-12 shows an example of how this looks. In this figure, the data series needs to be extended to include the data for July. If the chart uses a range for the category axis, you'll also need to extend that range.

You can drag the outline in either direction, so you can use this technique to expand or contract a range used in a data series.

Using the Data Source dialog box

To update the chart to reflect a different data range, activate the chart and select the Chart⇨Source Data command. Click on the Series tab and then select the series from the Series list box. Adjust the range in the Name box (you can edit the range reference or point to the new range).

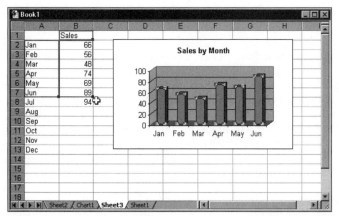

Figure 16-12: To change the range used in a chart's data series, select the data series and drag the small dot at the lower-right corner of the range outline.

Editing the SERIES formula

Every data series in a chart has an associated SERIES formula. This formula appears in the formula bar when you select a data series in a chart (see Figure 16-13). You can edit the range references in the SERIES formula directly. You can even enter a new SERIES formula manually — which adds a new series to the chart (there are, however, easier ways to do this, as described previously).

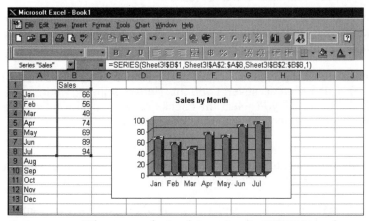

Figure 16-13: When you select a data series, its SERIES formula appears in the formula bar.

A SERIES formula consists of a SERIES function with four arguments. The syntax is as follows:

```
=SERIES(Name_ref,Categories,Values,Plot_order)
```

Excel uses absolute cell references in the SERIES function. To change the data that a series uses, edit the cell references (third argument) in the formula bar. The first and second arguments are optional and may not appear in the SERIES formula. If the series doesn't have a name, the Name_ref argument is missing and Excel uses dummy series names in the legend (Series1, Series2, and so on). If there are no category names, the Categories argument is missing, and Excel uses dummy labels (1, 2, 3, and so on).

Caution If the data series uses category labels, make sure that you adjust the reference for the category labels also. This is the second argument in the SERIES formula.

Using names in SERIES formulas

Perhaps the best way to handle data ranges that change over time is to use named ranges. Create names for the data ranges that you use in the chart and then edit the SERIES formula. Replace each range reference with the corresponding range name.

After making this change, the chart uses the named ranges. If you add new data to the range, just change the definition for the name, and the chart is updated.

Displaying data labels in a chart

Sometimes, you want your chart to display the actual data values for each point. Or you may want to display the category label for each data point. Figure 16-14 shows an example of both these options.

You specify data labels in the Data Labels tab of the Format Data Series dialog box (see Figure 16-15). This panel has several options. Note that not all options are available for all chart types. If you select the check box labeled Show legend key next to Label, each label displays its legend key next to it.

The data labels are linked to the worksheet, so if your data changes, the labels also change. If you would like to override the data label with other text, select the label and enter the new text (or even a cell reference) in the formula bar.

Often, you'll find that the data labels aren't positioned properly — for example, a label may be obscured by another data point. If you select an individual label, you can drag the label to a better location.

Tip   After adding data labels to a series, format the labels by using the Format Data Labels dialog box.

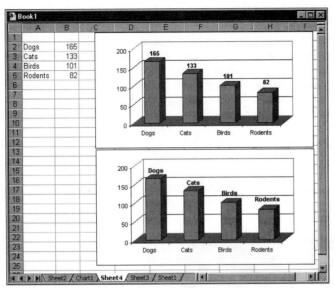

Figure 16-14: The top chart has data labels for each data point; the bottom chart has category labels for each point.

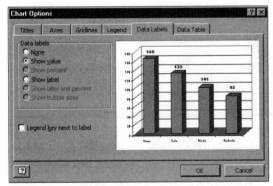

Figure 16-15: The Data Labels panel of the Chart Options dialog box.

As you work with data labels, you may discover that Excel's Data Labels feature leaves a bit to be desired. For example, it would be nice to be able to specify a range of text to be used for the data labels. This would be particularly useful in XY charts in which you want to identify each data point with a particular text item. Unfortunately, this isn't possible. The only way to accomplish this task is to add data labels and then manually edit each label.

Handling missing data

Sometimes, data that you're charting may be missing one or more data points. Excel offers several ways to handle the missing data. You don't control this in the Format Data Series dialog box (as you might expect). Rather, you must select the chart, choose the Tools⇨Options command, and click on the Chart tab, which is shown in Figure 16-16. The reason for putting this setting in the Options dialog box is known only to the Excel design team.

Note A chart must be activated when you select the Tools⇨Options command, or the options in the Chart panel are grayed.

The options that you set apply to the entire active chart, and you can't set a different option for different series in the same chart.

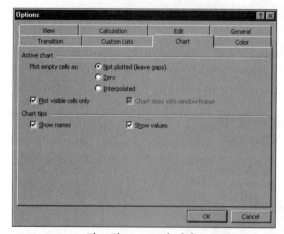

Figure 16-16: The Chart panel of the Options dialog box.

The *options* in the Chart panel for the active chart are as follows:

Not plotted (leave gaps): Missing data is simply ignored, and the data series will have a gap.

Zero: Missing data is treated as zero.

Interpolated: Missing data is calculated using data on either side of the missing point(s). This option is available only for line charts.

Controlling a data series by hiding data

Usually, Excel doesn't plot data that is in a hidden row or column. You can sometimes use this to your advantage, because it's an easy way to control what data appears in the chart. If you're working with outlines or data filtering (both of which use hidden rows), however, you may not like the idea that hidden data is removed from your chart. To override this, activate the chart and select the Tools➪Options command. In the Options dialog box, click on the Chart tab and remove the check mark from the check box labeled Plot visible cells only.

Note The Plot visible cells only setting applies only to the active chart. A chart must be activated when you open the Options dialog box. Otherwise, the option is grayed. This is another example of a setting that shows up in an unexpected dialog box.

Adding error bars

For certain chart types, you can add error bars to your chart. Error bars often are used to indicate "plus or minus" information that reflects uncertainty in the data. Error bars are appropriate only for area, bar, column, line, and XY charts. Click on the Y Error Bars tab in the Format Data Series dialog box to display the options shown in Figure 16-17.

Note A data series in an XY chart can have error bars for both the X values and Y values.

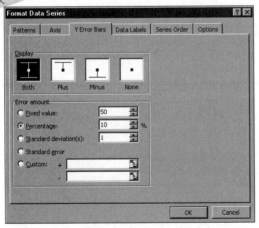

Figure 16-17: The Y Error Bars tab of the Format Data Series dialog box.

Excel enables you to specify several types of error bars:

<u>F</u>ixed value: The error bars are fixed by an amount you specify.

<u>P</u>ercentage: The error bars are a percentage of each value.

<u>S</u>tandard deviation(s): The error bars are in the number of standard-deviation units that you specify (Excel calculates the standard deviation of the data series).

Standard <u>e</u>rror: The error bars are one standard error unit (Excel calculates the standard error of the data series).

<u>C</u>ustom: You set the error bar units for the upper or lower error bars. You can enter either a value or a range reference that holds the error values that you want to plot as error bars.

Figure 16-18 shows a chart with error bars added. After you add error bars, you can access the Format Error Bars dialog box to modify the error bars. For example, you can control the line style and color of the error bars.

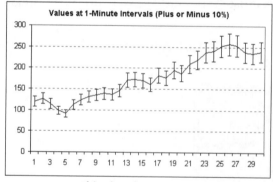

Figure 16-18: This chart has error bars added to the data series.

Adding a trendline

When you're plotting data over time, you may want to plot a trendline that describes the data. A trendline points out general trends in your data. In some cases, you can forecast future data with trendlines. A single series can have more than one trendline.

Excel makes adding a trendline to a chart quite simple. Although you might expect this option to be in the Format Data Series dialog box, it's not. The place to go is the Chart⇨Add Trendline command. This command is available only when a data series is selected. Figure 16-19 shows the Add Trendline dialog box.

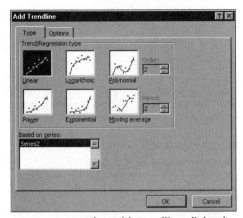

Figure 16-19: The Add Trendline dialog box offers several types of automatic trendlines.

The type of trendline that you choose depends on your data. Linear trends are most common, but some data can be described more effectively with another type. One of the options on the Type tab is Moving average, which is useful for smoothing out "noisy" data. The Moving average option lets you specify the number of data points to be included in each average. For example, if you select 5, Excel averages every five data points.

When you click on the Options tab in the Add Trendline dialog box, Excel displays the options shown in Figure 16-20.

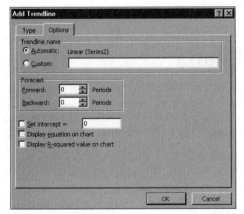

Figure 16-20: The Options tab in the Add Trendline dialog box enables you to smooth or forecast data.

The Options tab lets you specify a name to appear in the legend and the number of periods that you want to forecast. Additional options let you set the intercept value, specify that the equation used for the trendline appear on the chart, and choose whether the R^2 value appears on the chart.

Figure 16-21 shows two charts. The chart on the left depicts a data series without a trendline. The chart on the right is the same chart, but a linear trendline has been added that shows the trend in the data.

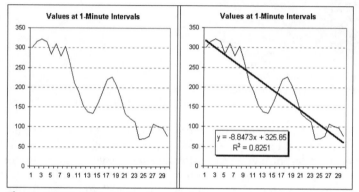

Figure 16-21: Before (chart on the left) and after (chart on the right) adding a linear trendline to a chart.

When Excel inserts a trendline, it may look like a new data series, but it's not. It's a new chart element with a name such as Series 1 Trendline 1. You can double-click on a trendline to change its formatting or change its options.

Creating Combination Charts

A combination chart is a single chart that consists of series that use different chart types. For example, you may have a chart that shows both columns and lines. A combination chart also can use a single type (all columns, for example) but include a second value axis. A combination chart requires at least two data series.

Creating a combination chart simply involves changing one or more of the data series to a different chart type. Select the data series and then choose the Chart⇨ Chart Type command. In the Chart Type dialog box, select the chart type that you want to apply to the selected series. Figure 16-22 shows an example of a combination chart.

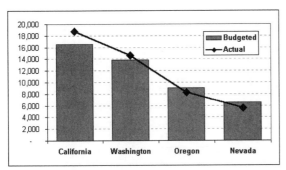

Figure 16-22: This combination chart uses columns and a line.

Note In some cases, you can't combine chart types. For example, you can't combine a 2D chart type with a 3D chart type. If you choose an incompatible chart type for the series, Excel lets you know.

You can't create combination 3D charts, but if you use a 3D column or 3D bar chart, you can change the shape of the columns or bars. Select a series and access the Format Data Series dialog box. Click on the Shape tab and choose the shape for the selected series.

Using Secondary Axes

If you need to plot data series that have drastically different scales, you probably want to use a secondary scale. For example, assume that you want to create a chart that shows monthly sales along with the average amount sold per customer. These two data series use different scales (the average sales values are much smaller than the total sales). Consequently, the average sales data range is virtually invisible in the chart.

The solution is to use a secondary axis for the second data series. Figure 16-23 shows two charts. The first uses a single value axis, and the second data series (a line) is hardly visible. The second chart uses a secondary axis for the second data series — which makes it easy to see.

To specify a secondary axis, select the data series in the chart and then access the Format Data Series dialog box. Click on the Axis tab and choose the Secondary axis option.

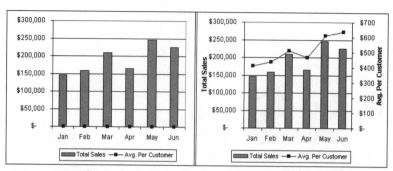

Figure 16-23: These charts show the same data, but the chart on the right uses a secondary axis for the second data series.

Displaying a Data Table

Excel 97 Excel 97 supports data tables — a feature it borrowed from Lotus 1-2-3. A data table displays the chart's data in tabular form, directly in the chart.

To add a data table to a chart, choose the Chart⇨Chart Options command and select the Data Table tab in the Chart Options dialog box. Place a check mark next to the option labeled Show data table. You also can choose to display the legend keys in the data table. Figure 16-24 shows a chart with a data table.

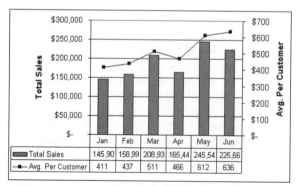

Figure 16-24: This chart includes a data table.

To adjust the formatting or font used in the data table, access the Format Data Table dialog box.

Creating Custom Chart Types

Excel comes with quite a few custom chart types that you can select from the Custom Types tab of the Chart Type dialog box. Each of these custom chart types is simply a standard chart that has been formatted. In fact, you can duplicate any of these custom chart types just by applying the appropriate formatting.

As you might expect, you can create your own custom chart types, called *user-defined* custom chart types.

The first step in designing a custom chart type is to create a chart that's customized the way you want. For example, you can set any of the colors, fill effects, or line styles; change the scales; modify fonts and type sizes; add gridlines; add a formatted title; and even add free-floating text or graphic images.

When you're satisfied with the chart, choose Chart⇨Chart Type to display the Chart Type dialog box. Click on the Custom Types tab and then select the User-defined option. This displays a list of all user-defined custom chart types.

Click on the Add button, which displays the Add Custom Chart Type dialog box as shown in Figure 16-25. Enter a name for the new chart type and a description. Click on OK, and your custom chart type is added to the list.

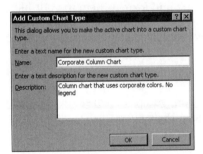

Figure 16-25: The Custom Chart Type dialog box.

Working with 3D Charts

One of the most interesting classes of Excel charts is its 3D charts. Certain situations benefit by the use of 3D charts, because you can depict changes over two different dimensions. Even a simple column chart commands more attention if you present it as a 3D chart. Not all charts that are labeled "3D" are true 3D charts, however. A true 3D chart has three axes. Some of Excel's 3D charts are simply 2D charts with a perspective look to them.

How custom chart types are stored

The custom chart types that you can select from the Chart Types dialog box are stored in a workbook named X18galry.xls, located in the Excel (or Office) folder. If you open X18galry, you can see that it contains only chart sheets — one for each custom chart type.

Also notice that the series formulas for these charts don't refer to actual worksheet ranges. Rather, the series formulas use arrays entered directly into the series formulas. This makes the charts completely independent of any specific worksheet range.

If you create a user-defined custom chart type, it's stored in a file called xlusrgal.xls, also in the Excel folder. Each custom chart type that you create is stored as a chart sheet.

If you want your coworkers to have access to your custom chart types, simply put a copy of your xlusrgal.xls file into their Excel (or Office) folder. By copying the file, you enable everyone in your workgroup to produce consistent-looking charts.

Modifying 3D charts

All 3D charts have a few additional parts that you can customize. For example, most 3D charts have a *floor* and *walls,* and the true 3D charts also have an additional axis. You can select these chart elements and format them to your liking. I don't go into the details here because the formatting options are quite straightforward. Generally, 3D formatting options work just like the other chart elements.

Rotating 3D charts

When you start flirting with the third dimension, you have a great deal of flexibility regarding the viewpoint for your charts. Figure 16-26 shows a 3D column chart that has been rotated to show four different views.

Tip You can rotate a 3D chart in one of the following two ways:

✦ Activate the 3D chart and choose the Chart➪3D View command. The dialog box shown in Figure 16-27 appears. You can make your rotations and perspective changes by clicking on the appropriate controls. The sample that you see in the dialog box is *not* your actual chart. The displayed sample just gives you an idea of the types of changes that you're making. Make the adjustments and choose OK to make them permanent (or click on Apply to apply them to your chart without closing the dialog box).

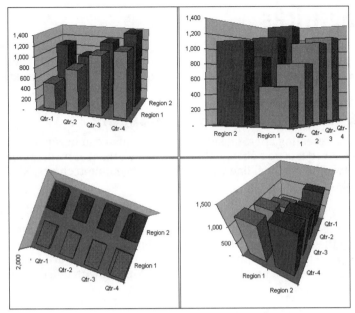

Figure 16-26: Four different views of the same chart.

✦ Rotate the chart in real time by dragging corners with the mouse. Click one of the corners of the chart. Black handles appear, and the word *Corners* appears in the Name box. You can drag one of these black handles and rotate the chart's 3D box to your satisfaction. This method definitely takes some practice. If your chart gets totally messed up, choose Chart➪3D View and then select the Default button to return to the standard 3D view.

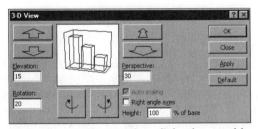

Figure 16-27: The 3D View dialog box enables you to rotate and change the perspective of a 3D chart. You also can drag the chart with the mouse.

Tip   When rotating a 3D chart, hold down the Ctrl key while you drag to see an outline of the entire chart — not just the axes. This technique is helpful because when you drag only the chart's axes, you can easily lose your bearings and end up with a strange-looking chart.

Chart-Making Tricks

In this section, I share chart-making tricks that I've picked up over the years. Some use little-known features; others are undocumented, as far as I can tell. Several tricks let you make charts that you may have considered impossible to create.

Changing a worksheet value by dragging

Excel provides an interesting chart-making feature that also can be somewhat dangerous. This feature lets you change the value in a worksheet by dragging the data markers on two-dimensional line charts, bar charts, column charts, XY charts, and bubble charts.

Here's how it works. Select an individual data point in a chart series (not the entire series) and then drag the point in the direction in which you want to adjust the value. As you drag the data marker, the corresponding value in the worksheet changes to correspond to the data point's new position the chart. Figure 16-28 shows the result of dragging the data points around on an XY chart with five data series.

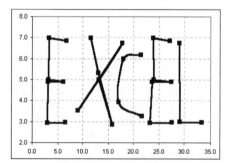

Figure 16-28: This XY chart has five data series.

If the value of a data point you move is the result of a formula, Excel displays the Goal Seek dialog box (I discuss goal seeking in Chapter 27). Use this dialog box to specify the cell that Excel should adjust in order to make the formula produce the result you pointed out on the chart. This technique is useful if you know what a chart should look like and you want to determine the values that will produce the chart. Obviously, this feature also can be dangerous, because you inadvertently can change values that you shouldn't — so be careful.

Unlinking a chart from its data range

A nice thing about charts is that they are linked to data stored in a worksheet. You also can unlink a data series so that it no longer relies on the worksheet data.

To unlink a data series, select the data series and activate the formula bar. Press F9, and the series formula converts its range references to arrays that hold the values (see the formula bar in Figure 16-29). If you unlink all the series in the chart, you create a dead graph that uses no data in a worksheet. If you want, however, you can edit the individual values in the arrays.

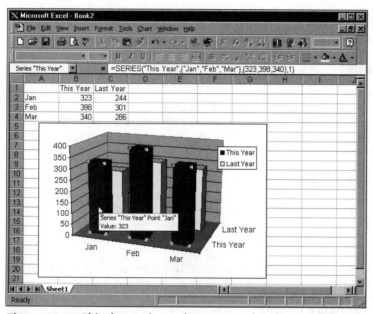

Figure 16-29: This data series no longer uses data in a worksheet.

Creating picture charts

Excel 97 makes it easy to use a pattern, texture, or graphic file for a chart. Figure 16-30 shows an example of a column chart that displays a graphic.

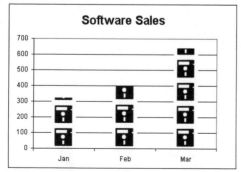

Figure 16-30: This column chart uses a graphic image.

In the following sections, I describe how to create picture charts using two methods.

Using a graphic file to create a picture chart

To convert a data series to pictures, access the chart's Format Data Series dialog box and select the Patterns tab. Click on the Fill Effects button to get the Fill Effects dialog box. Click on the Picture tab and then click on the Select Picture button to locate the graphic file that you want to use.

Note   Use the Fill Effects dialog box to specify some options for the image.

This technique does not work with cylinder, pyramid, cone, or surface charts.

Using the Clipboard to Create a picture chart

This section describes another way to create a picture chart — a method that doesn't require that the image exists in a file. This technique works as long as the image can be copied to the Clipboard.

The first step is to locate the image that you want and copy it to the Clipboard. Generally, simpler images work better. You may want to paste it into Excel first, where you can adjust the size, remove the borders, and add a background color, if desired. Or you can create the image using Excel's drawing tools. In either case, copy the image to the Clipboard.

When the image is on the Clipboard, activate the chart, select the data series, and choose the Edit⇨Paste command. Your chart is converted. You also can paste the image to a single point in the data series, rather than the entire data series. Just select the point before you paste.

This technique also works with data markers in line charts, XY (scatter) charts, or bubble charts. Figure 16-31 shows an example of a line chart that uses a smiley face instead of the normal data markers. I created this graphic using Excel's drawing tools (it's one of the AutoShapes in the Basic Shapes category).

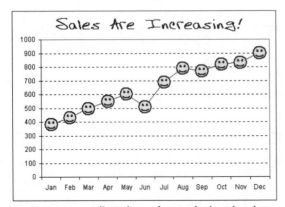

Figure 16-31: A line chart after replacing the data markers with a copied graphic image.

Pasting linked pictures to charts

Another useful charting technique involves pasting linked pictures to a chart. Excel doesn't let you do this directly, but this pasting is possible if you know a few tricks. The technique is useful, for example, if you want your chart to include the data that's used by the chart — and the data table feature isn't flexible enough for you. Figure 16-32 shows an example of a data range pasted to a chart as a linked picture. If the data changes, the changes are reflected in the chart as well as in the linked picture. Notice that the effect is similar to using a data table, but it allows more formatting options.

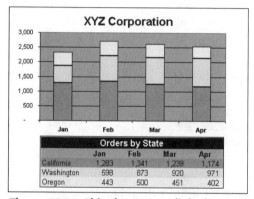

Figure 16-32: This chart uses a linked picture to display the data used in the chart series.

Here are the steps to create the linked picture:

1. Create the chart as usual and format the data range to your liking.

2. Select the data range, press Shift, and select the Edit⟹Copy Picture command. Excel displays a dialog box — accept the default options. This copies the range to the Clipboard as a picture.

3. Activate the chart and paste the Clipboard contents. You'll probably have to resize the plot area to accommodate the pasted image.

4. The image that was pasted is a picture, but not a linked picture. To convert the image to a linked picture, select it and then enter the range reference in the formula bar (or simply point it out). For this example, I entered **=Sheet1!A1:E5**.

The picture is now a linked picture. Changing any of the cells that are used in the chart's SERIES formula is reflected immediately in the linked picture.

Simple Gantt charts

It's not difficult to create a simple Gantt chart using Excel, but it does take some set-up work. *Gantt charts* are used to represent the time required to perform each task in a project. Figure 16-33 shows data that was used to create the Gantt chart in Figure 16-34.

Customer Survey.xls

	A	B	C	D	E
1	Task	Start Date	Duration	End Date	
2	Planning Meeting	01/06/97	1	01/06/97	
3	Develop Questionnaire	01/06/97	5	01/10/97	
4	Print and Mail Questionnaire	01/13/97	8	01/20/97	
5	Receive Responses	01/20/97	14	02/02/97	
6	Data Entry	01/20/97	16	02/04/97	
7	Data Analysis	02/03/97	4	02/06/97	
8	Write Report	02/07/97	9	02/15/97	
9	Distribute Draft Report	02/17/97	1	02/17/97	
10	Solicit Comments	02/18/97	5	02/22/97	
11	Finalize Report	02/24/97	3	02/26/97	
12	Distribute to Board	02/28/97	1	02/28/97	
13	Board Meeting	03/11/97	1	03/11/97	
14					
15					

Sheet1 Sheet4 Sheet2 Sheet5

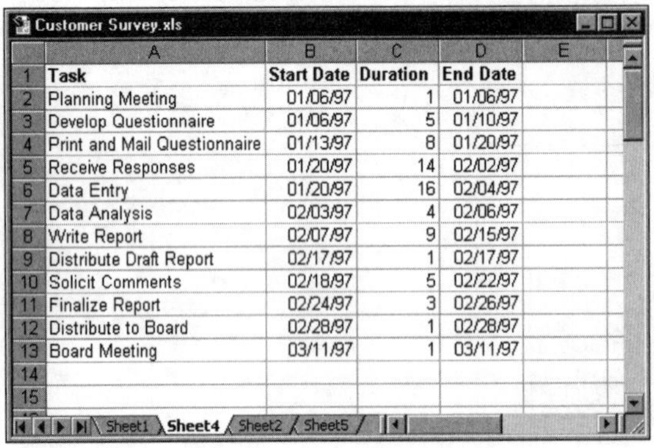

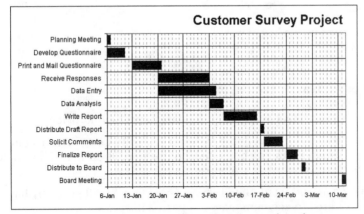

Figure 16-33: Data used in the Gantt chart.

Figure 16-34: You can create a Gantt chart from a bar chart.

Here are the steps to create this chart:

1. Enter the data as shown in Figure 16-33. The formula in cell D2, which was copied to the rows below it, is **=B2+C2-1**.
2. Use the ChartWizare to create a stacked bar chart from the range A2:C13. Use the second sub-type, which is labeled Stacked Bar.

3. In Step 2 of the ChartWizard, select the Columns option. Also, notice that Excel incorrectly uses the first two columns as the Category axis labels.

4. In Step 2 of the ChartWizard, click on the Series tab and add a new data series. Then set the chart's series to the following:

   Series 1: B2:B13

   Series 2: C2:C13

   Category (x) axis labels: A2:A13

5. In Step 3 of the ChartWizard, remove the legend and then click on Finish to create an embedded chart.

6. Adjust the height of the chart so all of the axis labels are visible. You can also accomplish this by using a smaller font size.

7. Access the Format Axis dialog box for the horizontal axis. Adjust the horizontal axis Minimum and Maximum scale values to correspond to the earliest and latest dates in the data (note that you can enter a date into the Minimum or Maximum edit box). You might also want to change the date format for the axis labels.

8. Access the Format Axis dialog box for the vertical axis. In the Scale tab, select the option labeled Categories in reverse order, and also set the option labeled Value (Y) axis crosses at maximum category.

9. Select the first data series and access the Format Data Series dialog box. In the Patterns tab, set Border to None and Area to None. This makes the first data series invisible.

10. Apply other formatting as desired.

Comparative histograms

With a bit of creativity, you can create charts that you may have considered impossible with Excel. For example, Figure 16-35 shows data that was used to create the comparative histogram chart shown in Figure 16-36. Such charts often display population data.

Here's how to create the chart:

1. Enter the data as shown in Figure 16-35. Notice that the values for females are entered as negative values.

2. Select A1:C8 and create a 2D bar chart. Use the sub-type labeled Clustered Bar.

3. Apply the following custom number format to the horizontal axis: **0%;0%;0%**. This custom format eliminates the negative signs in the percentages.

4. Select the vertical axis and access the Format Axis dialog box. Click on the Patterns tab and remove all tick marks. Set the Tick mark labels option to Low. This keeps the axis in the center of the chart but displays the axis labels at the left side.

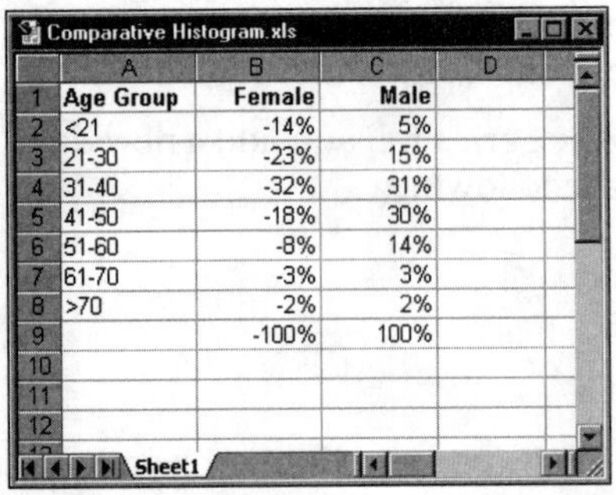

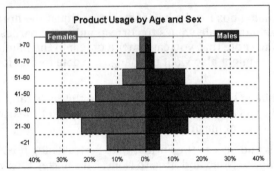

Figure 16-35: Data used in the comparative histogram chart.

Product Usage by Age and Sex

Figure 16-36: Producing this comparative histogram chart requires a few tricks.

5. Select either of the data series and access the Format Data Series dialog box. Click on the Options tab and set the Overlap to 100 and the Gap width to 0.

6. Add two text boxes to the chart (**Females** and **Males**), to substitute for the legend.

7. Apply other formatting as desired.

Summary

This chapter picks up where Chapter 13 left off. I discuss most of the chart customization options in Excel. I demonstrate how to create combination charts and your own custom chart formats — which let you apply a series of customizations with a single command. I also discuss 3D charts and conclude the chapter with several examples that use chart-making tricks.

✦   ✦   ✦

Creating Maps with Microsoft Map

◆ ◆ ◆ ◆

In This Chapter

An overview of creating maps with Microsoft Map, an OLE server application that works with Excel

How to determine which map format is appropriate for your data

How to create and customize a map

How to create a map template

How to convert a map into a static picture

◆ ◆ ◆ ◆

In previous chapters, you saw how you can use a chart to display data in a different — and, usually, more meaningful — way. This chapter explores the topic of mapping and describes how to present geographic information in the form of a map.

Note The mapping feature is not actually part of Excel. Rather, this feature uses an OLE server application named Microsoft Map, which was developed by MapInfo Corporation. You can use this application to insert maps into other Microsoft Office applications. Because the mapping application is not part of Excel, you'll find that the user interface is quite different from that of Excel. When a map is active, Excel's menus and toolbars are replaced with the Microsoft Map menus and toolbars.

Mapping: An Overview

Mapping, like charting, is a tool that visually presents data. People use maps for a variety of purposes, but the common factor in maps is that they work with data that has a basis in geography. If you classify information by state, province, or country, chances are that you can represent the data on a map. For example, if your company sells its products throughout the U.S., it may be useful to show the annual sales by state.

A mapping example

Figure 17-1 shows sales data for a company, with the data categorized by state. To understand this information, you would have to spend a lot of time examining the data.

	A	B	C	D	E
1	State	Product A	Product B	Combined	
2	AK	262,542	0	262,542	
3	AL	92,629	193,254	285,883	
4	AR	19,690	169,615	189,305	
5	AZ	252,523	183,384	435,907	
6	CA	3,692,909	2,135,068	5,827,977	
7	CO	377,034	149,875	526,909	
8	CT	327,585	425,939	753,524	
9	DC	114,492	63,118	177,610	
10	DE	1,233	108,471	109,704	
11	FL	582,033	851,978	1,434,011	
12	GA	408,371	299,702	708,073	
13	HI	43,428	43,378	86,806	
14	IA	128,260	43,378	171,638	
15	ID	0	122,239	122,239	
16	IL	769,711	837,597	1,607,308	
17	IN	262,542	236,633	499,175	
18	KS	116,416	145,927	262,343	
19	KY	39,430	86,757	126,187	
20	LA	96,676	43,378	140,054	
21	MA	656,947	449,627	1,106,574	
22	MD	402,449	609,373	1,011,822	

Figure 17-1: Raw data that shows sales by state.

Figure 17-2 shows the same data displayed in a chart. Although an improvement over the raw-data table, this type of presentation doesn't really work because it has too many data points. In addition, the chart doesn't reveal any information about sales in a particular region.

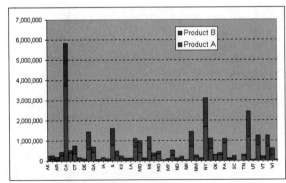

Figure 17-2: The sales data displayed in a chart.

Figure 17-3 shows the sales data presented as a map (it looks even better in color). This presentation uses different colors to represent various sales ranges. Looking at the map, you can see clearly that this company performs much better in some regions than in others.

Note The map in Figure 17-3 might be even more revealing if the sales were represented relative to the population of each state; that is, in per capita sales. You may not have realized it, but this population data is already on your system. When you installed Excel, a workbook containing a variety of population statistics was copied to your hard disk. The workbook is named `Mapstats.xls`, and it is located in the following folder:

```
Program Files\Common Files\Microsoft Shared\Datamap\Data
```

Figure 17-4 shows the contents sheet for this workbook.

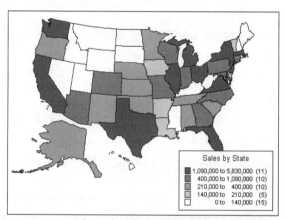

Figure 17-3: The sales data displayed in a map.

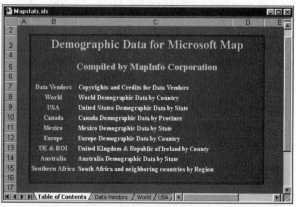

Figure 17-4: The Mapstats workbook contains population statistics that you can use in your maps.

Available maps

The Microsoft Map feature supports a good variety of maps and enables you to create maps in several different formats. A single map can display multiple sets of data, each in a different format. For example, your map can show sales by state and indicate the number of sales offices in each state. In addition, your map can display other accoutrements such as labels and pin markers.

The maps included with Microsoft Map are listed in Table 17-1. As you'll see later, a map can be zoomed to display only a portion of it. Therefore, you can use the Europe map to zoom in on a particular region or country.

Table 17-1 Maps Included with Microsoft Map	
Map	*Description*
Australia	The continent of Australia, by state
Canada	The country of Canada, by province
Europe	The continent of Europe, by country
Mexico	The country of Mexico, by state
North America	The countries of North America (Canada, U.S., Mexico)
U.K. Standard Regions	The countries of the United Kingdom, by region
U.S. in North America	United States (excluding Alaska and Hawaii insets), by state
U.S. with AK and HI Insets	United States (with Alaska and Hawaii insets), by state
World Countries	The world, by country

Tip   If you would like to order additional maps or data from MapInfo, you can contact the company directly or visit its Web site. For information on how to do so, activate a map and click on the Help⇨About command.

Creating a Map

Creating a basic map with Microsoft Map is simple. In almost all cases, however, you'll want to customize the map. In this section, I discuss the basics of mapmaking.

Setting up your data

The Microsoft Map feature works with data stored in a list format (for an example, refer to Figure 17-1). The first column should be names of map regions (such as states or countries). The columns to the right should be data for each area. You can have any number of data columns because you select which columns to use after the map is created.

Creating the map

To create a map, start by selecting the data. This must be one column of area names and at least one column of data. If the columns have descriptive headers, include these in the selection.

Choose the Insert⇨Map command (or click on the Map button the Standard toolbar). Click and drag to specify the location and size of the map or just click to create a map of the default size. Unlike charts, maps must be embedded on a worksheet (there are no separate map sheets).

Microsoft Map analyzes the area labels and generates the appropriate map. If two or more maps are possible (or if you've developed any custom map templates), you get the dialog box shown in Figure 17-5. Select the desired map from this list.

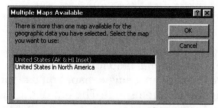

Figure 17-5: If multiple maps are available for your data, you can choose which map to use.

No Insert⇨Map command?

Excel's mapping feature is performed by an OLE server application. The mapping feature is not an integral part of Excel, and it may not be installed on your system. If the Insert menu doesn't have a Map menu item, this means that the mapping feature is not installed.

To install the mapping feature, you need to rerun Excel's Setup program (or the Microsoft Office Setup program) and specify the mapping feature.

Microsoft Map displays the map using the first column of data. It also displays the Microsoft Map Control dialog box, which I discuss later in the chapter. When the map is created, it is activated. Whenever a map is activated, Excel's menus and toolbars are replaced by Microsoft Map's menus and toolbar. When you click outside the map, Excel's user interface is restored. You can reactivate a map by double-clicking on it.

Setting the map format(s)

When a map first appears, the Microsoft Map Control is visible (see Figure 17-6). This dialog box is used to change the format of the selected map. You can use the Show/Hide Map Control tool to toggle the display of this dialog box.

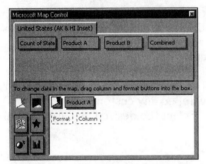

Figure 17-6: The Microsoft Map Control.

By default, you create maps by using the *value-shading* map format. You can change the format or display two or more formats on a single map. You use the Microsoft Map Control dialog box by dragging the items in it. The top of the dialog box displays all available data fields (which correspond to the columns that you selected when you created the map). The bottom part contains the map format information. Six format icons on the left determine the map format (described in the sections that follow). You combine a map format icon with one or more data fields by dragging the icon. For example, you can replace the default map format icon with another one simply by dragging the new icon over the existing one. Some map formats use more than one data field. In such a case, you can drag additional data fields next to the icon.

To change options for a particular map format, either double-click on the format icon or use the Map menu and choose the menu item appropriate for the format that you want to change. In either case, you get a dialog box that's appropriate for the map format.

Following are descriptions (and samples) of each map format supported by Microsoft Map.

Value shading

With this map format, each map region is shaded based on the value of its data. This format is appropriate for data-quantitative information such as sales, population, and so on. Figure 17-7 shows an example of a map formatted with value shading (this map is zoomed to show only part of the U.S.). In this example, the sales are broken down into four ranges, and each sales range is associated with a different shading.

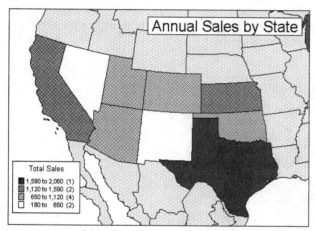

Figure 17-7: This map uses the value-shading format.

You can change the interval ranges in the Value Shading Options dialog box, shown in Figure 17-8. You can specify the number of ranges and the method of defining the ranges — an equal number of areas in each range or an equal spread of values in each range. You also can select a color for the shading. The map displays different variations of the single color that you select. You can choose the summary function used (SUM or AVERAGE). To hide the format from the map, remove the check mark from the Visible check box.

Figure 17-8: The Value Shading Options tab of the Format Properties dialog box.

Category shading

With the *category-shading* format, each map region is colored based on a data value. The map legend has one entry (color) for every value of the data range. Therefore, this format is appropriate for data that has a small number of discrete values. For example, you can use the format to identify states that have a sales office, the number of sales reps in a country, and so on. A common use for this format is to identify the states that make up each sales region. Data need not be numeric. For example, the data can consist of text such as *Yes* and *No*.

Figure 17-9 shows a map that uses category shading to identify states that met the annual sales goal.

Figure 17-9: This map uses the category-shading format.

To change the colors in the categories, use the Category Shading Options dialog box.

Dot density

The *dot-density* map format displays data as a series of dots. Larger values translate into more dots. The dots are placed randomly within a map region. Figure 17-10 shows an example of a map that uses the dot-density format. This map depicts population in the U.K. Each dot represents 100,000 people.

To change the number of units for each dot or to change the dot size, access the Dot Density Options tab of the Format Properties dialog box, which is shown in Figure 17-11.

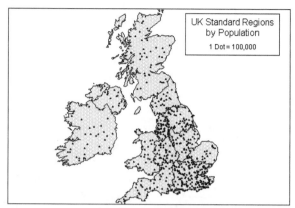

Figure 17-10: A dot-density format map.

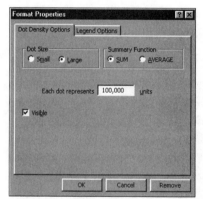

Figure 17-11: The Dot Density Options tab of the Format Properties dialog box.

Graduated symbol

The *graduated-symbol* map format displays a symbol, the size of which is proportional to the area's data value. Figure 17-12 shows an example of this format. I used a Wingdings font character for the symbol. To change the symbol, use the Graduated Symbol Options dialog box. You can select a font, size, and specific character.

Pie chart

The *pie-chart* map format requires at least two columns of data. Maps with this format display a pie chart within each map region. Figure 17-13 shows an example. This map shows a pie chart that depicts the relative sales of three products for each state.

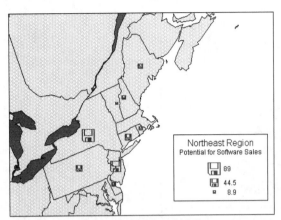

Figure 17-12: A graduated-symbol format map.

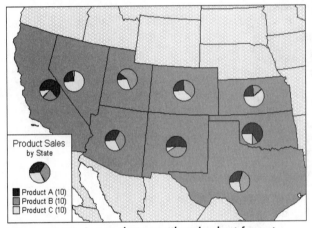

Figure 17-13: A map that uses the pie-chart format.

To change the setting for a pie-chart format map, use the Pie Chart Options tab of the Format Properties dialog box, shown in Figure 17-14. This dialog box lets you select a color for each pie slice. If you choose the Graduated option, the size of each pie is proportional to the sum or average of the data. If you don't use the Graduated option, you also can set the diameter of the pies.

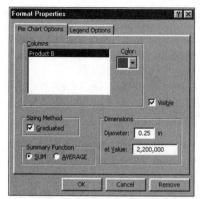

Figure 17-14: The Pie Chart Options tab of the Format Properties dialog box.

Column chart

The *column-chart* map format is similar to the pie-chart format — except that it displays a column chart instead of a pie chart. Figure 17-15 shows an example.

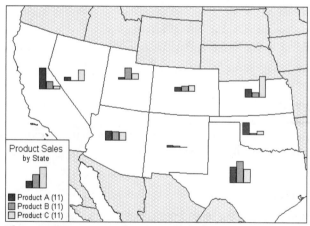

Figure 17-15: A map that uses the column-chart format.

Combining map formats

As I mentioned, a single map can include multiple formats for different data. You do this by stacking groups of icons and data fields in the Microsoft Map Control dialog box. For example, you can display sales as value shading and number of customers as a dot-density map. Each map format has its own legend.

There are no rules for overlaying multiple map types, so some experimentation usually is necessary. Unless the map is very simple, however, you're generally better off using only one or two map types per map; otherwise, the map gets so complicated that the original goal (making the data clear) is lost.

Figure 17-16 shows an example of a map that uses two formats. The value-shading format shows sales broken down into four categories. The graduated-symbol format shows the states that have a sales office.

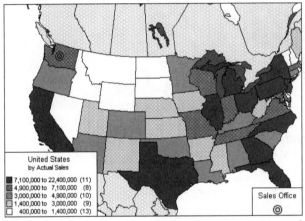

Figure 17-16: An example of a map that uses two map formats.

Customizing Maps

After a map is created, there are a number of customizations that you can make. I describe these customizations in the following sections.

Zooming in and out

Microsoft Map lets you zoom your map in and out. Zooming in displays less of the map, and zooming out displays more (or makes the entire map smaller). The only way to zoom is to use the Zoom Percentage of Map control on the toolbar (no menu commands exist).

To zoom in, select a zoom percentage greater than 100%. To zoom out, select a zoom percentage less than 100%. Before you zoom out, you might want to specify the point that will be the center of the map (use the Center Map toolbar button).

Using the Microsoft Map toolbar

Whenever a map is activated, the Microsoft Map toolbar appears (see the figure in this sidebar). Note that this isn't one of Excel's toolbars; rather, this is a special toolbar that appears only when a map is activated. This toolbar is handy for manipulating and customizing the map.

The tools, from left to right, are as follows:

Select Objects: Turns the mouse pointer into an arrow so you can select objects in the map.

Grabber: Lets you reposition the map within the map window.

Center Map: Lets you specify the center of the map.

Map Labels: Lets you add geography labels or data values in the map.

Add Text: Lets you add free-floating text to the map.

Custom Pin Map: Lets you add pins to the map to indicate specific locations.

Display Entire: Displays the entire (unzoomed) map.

Redraw Map: Redraws the map.

Show/Hide Microsoft Map Control: Toggles the display of the floating Microsoft Map Control dialog box.

Zoom Percentage of Map Help: Provides help for a menu item or toolbar button.

Repositioning a map

You'll find that, after zooming in or out, the map may not be optimally positioned within the map object rectangle. Use the Grabber tool to move the map image within the map object. Just click and drag the map to reposition it.

Adding labels

Usually, a map doesn't have labels to identify areas. You can't automatically add labels to all areas (for example, all states in the U.S.), but you can add individual labels one at a time. You also can insert data values that correspond to a particular map region (such as sales for West Virginia).

Use the Label tool to add labels or data values. When you click on the Label tool, the dialog box shown in Figure 17-17 is displayed. The option button labeled Map feature names refers to labels for the various parts of the map (for example, state names in a U.S. map). When you select the Values from option, you can insert data values from a category in the list box. After closing the dialog box, you can drag the mouse pointer over the map. The label or data value appears when the mouse pointer is over a map region. Just click to place the label or data value and repeat this procedure for each map label or data value that you want to add. Figure 17-18 shows a map with labels and data values added to it.

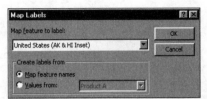

Figure 17-17: The Map Labels dialog box
lets you add labels or data values to your map.

Figure 17-18: This map has labels and data values.

To move a label, click on it and drag it to a new location. You can change the font, size, or color of a label by double-clicking on it. Stretching the label (by dragging a border) also makes the font larger or smaller.

Adding text

Besides the labels described in the preceding section, you can add free-floating text to your map using the Text tool. Just click on the Text tool, click on the area of the map where you want to add text, and enter your text. After text is placed, you can manipulate it like labels.

If you don't like the fact that a map title always has a border around it (and the border can't be removed), delete the title and create your own with the Text tool.

Adding pins to a map

In some cases, you may want to add one or more identifier icons to your map. This is similar in concept to inserting pins in a wall map to identify various places.

Clicking on the Custom Pin Map tool displays a dialog box that asks you to enter a name for a custom pin map (or choose an existing pin map). Enter a descriptive label; you'll be able to bring these same pins into another map (of the same type) later. For example, if you're identifying sales office locations, you can then add the same pins to another map.

When you close the dialog box, the mouse pointer changes to a pushpin. You can place these pins anywhere in your map. When you click on the map to place a pin, you also can enter descriptive text. Double-clicking on a pin lets you change the symbol used to something other than a pin. Figure 17-19 shows a map with pins added to it.

Figure 17-19: This map has pins to identify specific locations.

Modifying the legend

You have a quite a bit of control over the legend in a map. Note that a map displays a separate legend for each map format that it uses. To modify a legend, double-click on it. You get the dialog box shown in Figure 17-20.

Figure 17-20: The Legend Options tab of the Format Properties dialog box.

A legend can be displayed in a compact format or its normal format. A compact format takes up less space, but it doesn't give many details. You also can change the legend's title and subtitle (and enter a different title for a compacted legend). Other buttons let you adjust the font (including size and color) and edit the labels used in the legend.

Tip   To make other changes to the legend — such as changing the number of data ranges used — select the appropriate menu item on the Map menu. For example, to change the number of ranges used in a value-shading map format, select the Map⇨Value Shading Options command.

Adding and removing features

You can add or remove certain features of a map. When you select the Map⇨ Features command, you get a dialog box like the one shown in Figure 17-21. This lists all available features for the selected map. To turn a feature on, place a check mark next to it. To turn a feature off, remove the check mark. The features available vary with the map that you're using. If a feature doesn't appear in the list, you can add it by clicking on the Add button.

Figure 17-21: The Map Features dialog box.

Figure 17-22 shows a North America map with some features added (major cities, major highways, and world oceans) and some features removed (Canada and Mexico).

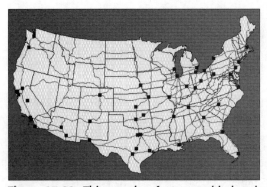

Figure 17-22: This map has features added and removed.

Table 17-2 lists the features available for each map. You can, however, add features from different maps — add world oceans to a North America map, for example.

Table 17-2 Map Features Available	
Map	**Features**
Australia	Airports, Cities, Highways, Major Cities
Canada	Airports, Cities, Forward Sortation Areas, Highways, Lakes, Major Cities
Europe	Airports, Cities, Highways, Major Cities
Mexico	Cities, Highways, Major Cities
U.K.	2-Digit Post Codes, Airports, Cities, Highways, Major Cities, Standard Regions
U.S. in North America	5-Digit Zip Code Centers, Highways, Major Cities, Great Lakes
U.S. (AK & HI Inset)	Airports, Cities, Major Cities
World	Capitals, Countries, Graticule, Oceans

Tip   In some cases, you may want your map to display only specific areas. For example, if your company does business in Missouri, Illinois, Kansas, and Nebraska, you can create a map that shows only these four states. The trick is to create the map and then remove all features from the map using the Map⇨Features command. The map is then limited to those areas that have data. Figure 17-23 shows an example.

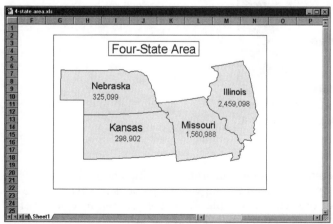

Figure 17-23: This map has all its features removed, leaving only the states for which data is provided.

Plotting U.S. Zip Codes

Besides recognizing geographic place names, Microsoft Map recognizes U.S. five-digit Zip codes, as well. If the data that you select contains multiple geography information (for example, state names and Zip codes), you need to specify which field to use as the geography. Figure 17-24 shows the dialog box that appears to warn you of the existence of multiple geographies.

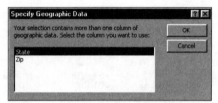

Figure 17-24: This dialog box lets you select the geography to use for your map.

Caution   If you want to create a map that uses Zip codes, make sure that your Zip codes are formatted as values, not as text. Otherwise, they won't be recognized as Zip codes.

Because Zip codes are continually being added, it's possible that Microsoft Map will not recognize all of your Zip codes. If it encounters an unknown Zip code, you get the dialog box shown in Figure 17-25. This gives you the opportunity to change the Zip code to another one. Or you can simply discard that item of data by clicking on the Discard button.

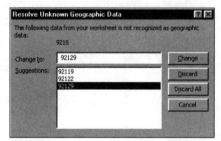

Figure 17-25: Microsoft Map displays this dialog box when it doesn't recognize a geographic name.

Figure 17-26 shows a map that depicts customers by Zip codes. This is a graduated-symbol map (the default format when Zip codes are used as the geography). Note that the symbols are placed on the geographic centers of the Zip codes and don't shade the entire Zip code areas.

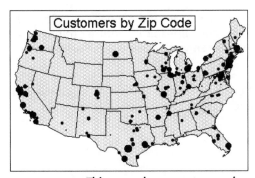

Figure 17-26: This map shows customers by Zip code centers.

Adding More Data to a Map

After you've created a map, you can add additional data to it. Use the Insert⇨Data command to add data from a worksheet range, or use the Insert⇨External Data command to add new data from a database file. Make sure that the data includes geographic labels that match the map to which you're adding data.

Map Templates

As you may have figured out by now, getting a map just right can sometimes take a lot of time. Fortunately, you can save a map template so you can reuse the settings for another map. To do so, create and customize the map and then choose the Map⇨Save Map Template command. You can save a template that includes the following:

✦ The features that you've added or removed

✦ A particular view (zoomed in or out)

✦ Both of the preceding items

Saved templates then appear in the Multiple Maps Available dialog box that is displayed when you create a map.

Converting a Map to a Picture

You'll find that working with maps sometimes can be rather sluggish — a great deal of work goes on behind the scenes. When you finish with your map, you can convert it to a static picture that is no longer linked to the data. To do so, click on the map once to select it (don't double-click on it) and choose Edit⇨Copy. Then select the Edit⇨Paste Special command and choose the Picture option. This creates an unlinked picture of the map. Then you can select the original map object and delete it.

 Caution If you convert a map to a picture, there is no way to link data back to the picture. If any of your data changes or you want to make modifications to the map, you have to re-create the map.

Learning More

The Microsoft Map feature is relatively complex, and it definitely takes time to master. The best way to master it is to simply create some maps and perform customizations. As I mentioned, the user interface is different from Excel's, so you'll have to try some new techniques. Generally, you can find your way around maps by doing the following:

✦ Double-clicking on objects

✦ Right-clicking on objects

✦ Exploring the menus (they change somewhat, depending on the type of map)

✦ Using the Microsoft Map toolbar

Summary

In this chapter, I cover Excel's new Microsoft Map feature — which is actually an OLE server application developed by MapInfo Corporation. I demonstrate how some data is more appropriate for a map than for a chart. I describe the basics of creating and customizing maps and provide an example of each map format.

✦   ✦   ✦

Creating and Using Worksheet Outlines

I f you use a word processor, you may be familiar with the concept of an outline. Most word processors have an outline mode that lets you view only the headings and sub-headings in your document. You can easily expand a heading to show the detail (that is, the text) below it. To write this book, I used the outline feature in my word processor extensively.

Excel also is capable of using outlines, and understanding this feature can make working with certain types of worksheets much easier for you. Outlining is such a great tool that the latest version of Lotus 1-2-3 includes an identical feature.

Introducing Worksheet Outlines

This section introduces you to worksheet outlines and presents an example of how they work. Outlines are most useful for creating summary reports in which you don't want to show all the details. It should go without saying that some worksheets are more suitable for outlines than others. If your worksheet uses hierarchical data with subtotals, it's probably a good candidate for an outline.

An example

The best way to understand how worksheet outlining works is to look at an example. Figure 18-1 shows a simple budget model without an outline. I inserted subtotals to calculate subtotals by region and subtotals by quarter.

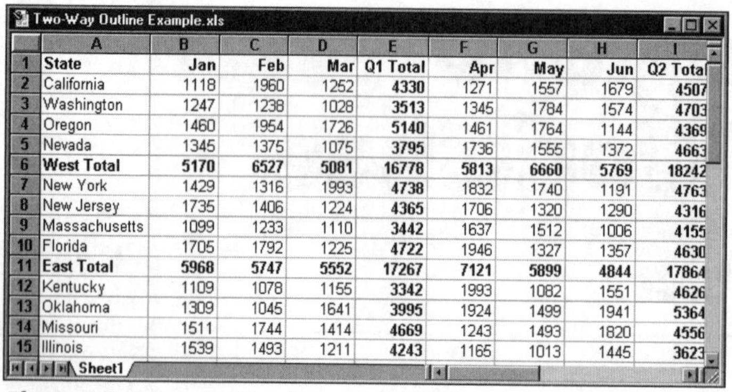

Two-Way Outline Example.xls

	A	B	C	D	E	F	G	H	I
1	State	Jan	Feb	Mar	Q1 Total	Apr	May	Jun	Q2 Total
2	California	1118	1960	1252	4330	1271	1557	1679	4507
3	Washington	1247	1238	1028	3513	1345	1784	1574	4703
4	Oregon	1460	1954	1726	5140	1461	1764	1144	4369
5	Nevada	1345	1375	1075	3795	1736	1555	1372	4663
6	**West Total**	**5170**	**6527**	**5081**	**16778**	**5813**	**6660**	**5769**	**18242**
7	New York	1429	1316	1993	4738	1832	1740	1191	4763
8	New Jersey	1735	1406	1224	4365	1706	1320	1290	4316
9	Massachusetts	1099	1233	1110	3442	1637	1512	1006	4155
10	Florida	1705	1792	1225	4722	1946	1327	1357	4630
11	**East Total**	**5968**	**5747**	**5552**	**17267**	**7121**	**5899**	**4844**	**17864**
12	Kentucky	1109	1078	1155	3342	1993	1082	1551	4626
13	Oklahoma	1309	1045	1641	3995	1924	1499	1941	5364
14	Missouri	1511	1744	1414	4669	1243	1493	1820	4556
15	Illinois	1539	1493	1211	4243	1165	1013	1445	3623

Sheet1

Figure 18-1: A typical budget model with subtotals.

Figure 18-2 shows the same worksheet after I created an outline. Notice that Excel adds a new border to the left of the screen. This border contains controls that let you determine what level to view. This particular outline has three levels: States, Regions (each region is made up of states), and Grand Total (the sum of each region's subtotal). In the figure, the outline is fully expanded so that all data is visible.

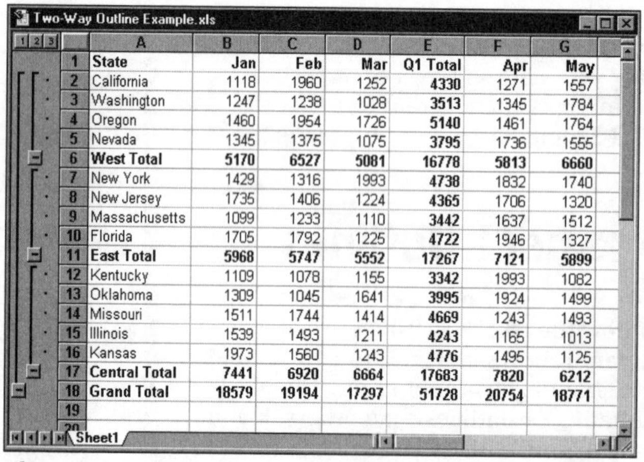

Two-Way Outline Example.xls

	A	B	C	D	E	F	G
1	State	Jan	Feb	Mar	Q1 Total	Apr	May
2	California	1118	1960	1252	4330	1271	1557
3	Washington	1247	1238	1028	3513	1345	1784
4	Oregon	1460	1954	1726	5140	1461	1764
5	Nevada	1345	1375	1075	3795	1736	1555
6	**West Total**	**5170**	**6527**	**5081**	**16778**	**5813**	**6660**
7	New York	1429	1316	1993	4738	1832	1740
8	New Jersey	1735	1406	1224	4365	1706	1320
9	Massachusetts	1099	1233	1110	3442	1637	1512
10	Florida	1705	1792	1225	4722	1946	1327
11	**East Total**	**5968**	**5747**	**5552**	**17267**	**7121**	**5899**
12	Kentucky	1109	1078	1155	3342	1993	1082
13	Oklahoma	1309	1045	1641	3995	1924	1499
14	Missouri	1511	1744	1414	4669	1243	1493
15	Illinois	1539	1493	1211	4243	1165	1013
16	Kansas	1973	1560	1243	4776	1495	1125
17	**Central Total**	**7441**	**6920**	**6664**	**17683**	**7820**	**6212**
18	**Grand Total**	**18579**	**19194**	**17297**	**51728**	**20754**	**18771**
19							
20							

Sheet1

Figure 18-2: The budget model after creating an outline.

Figure 18-3 depicts the outline displayed at the second level. Now the outline shows only the totals for the regions (the detail rows are hidden). You can partially expand the outline to show the detail for a particular region. Collapsing the outline to level 1 would show only the headers and the Grand Total row.

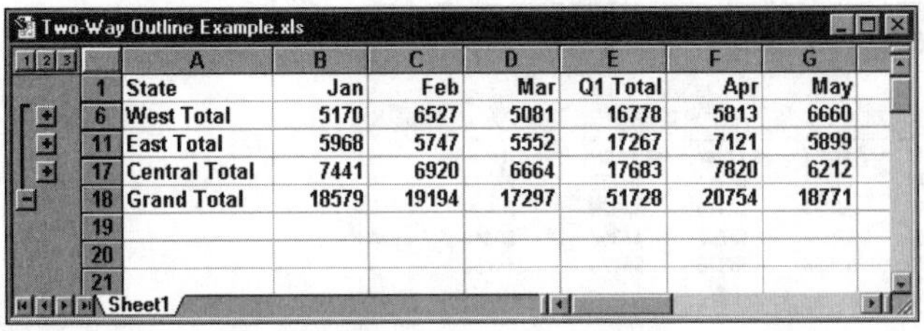

Two-Way Outline Example.xls

	A	B	C	D	E	F	G
1	State	Jan	Feb	Mar	Q1 Total	Apr	May
6	West Total	5170	6527	5081	16778	5813	6660
11	East Total	5968	5747	5552	17267	7121	5899
17	Central Total	7441	6920	6664	17683	7820	6212
18	Grand Total	18579	19194	17297	51728	20754	18771
19							
20							
21							

Sheet1

Figure 18-3: The budget model after collapsing the outline.

Excel can create outlines in both directions. In the preceding examples, the outline was a row (vertical) outline. Figure 18-4 shows the same model after I added a column (horizontal) outline. Now Excel displays another border at the top.

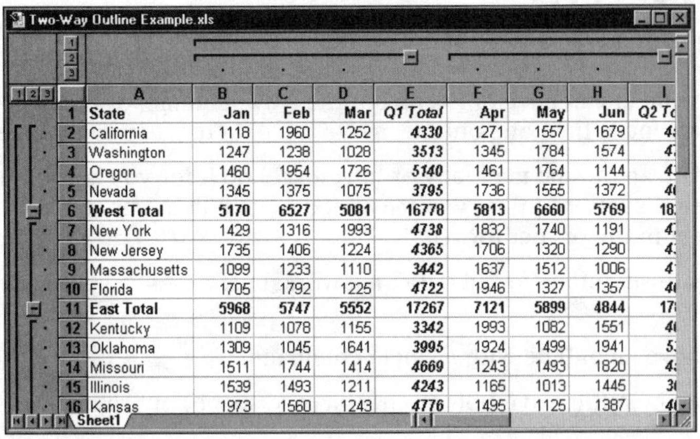

Two-Way Outline Example.xls

	A	B	C	D	E	F	G	H	I
1	State	Jan	Feb	Mar	*Q1 Total*	Apr	May	Jun	*Q2 To*
2	California	1118	1960	1252	***4330***	1271	1557	1679	**4**
3	Washington	1247	1238	1028	***3513***	1345	1784	1574	**4**
4	Oregon	1460	1954	1726	***5140***	1461	1764	1144	**4**
5	Nevada	1345	1375	1075	***3795***	1736	1555	1372	**4**
6	**West Total**	**5170**	**6527**	**5081**	**16778**	**5813**	**6660**	**5769**	**18**
7	New York	1429	1316	1993	***4738***	1832	1740	1191	**4**
8	New Jersey	1735	1406	1224	***4365***	1706	1320	1290	**4**
9	Massachusetts	1099	1233	1110	***3442***	1637	1512	1006	**4**
10	Florida	1705	1792	1225	***4722***	1946	1327	1357	**4**
11	**East Total**	**5968**	**5747**	**5552**	**17267**	**7121**	**5899**	**4844**	**17**
12	Kentucky	1109	1078	1155	***3342***	1993	1082	1551	**4**
13	Oklahoma	1309	1045	1641	***3995***	1924	1499	1941	**5**
14	Missouri	1511	1744	1414	***4669***	1243	1493	1820	**4**
15	Illinois	1539	1493	1211	***4243***	1165	1013	1445	**3**
16	Kansas	1973	1560	1243	***4776***	1495	1125	1387	**4**

Sheet1

Figure 18-4: The budget model after adding a column outline.

If a worksheet has both a row and a column outline, you can work with each independent of the other. For example, you can show the row outline at the second level and the column outline at the first level. Figure 18-5 shows the model with both outlines collapsed at the second level. The result is a nice summary table that gives regional totals by quarter.

Web site

You can download the workbook used in the preceding examples from this book's Web site.

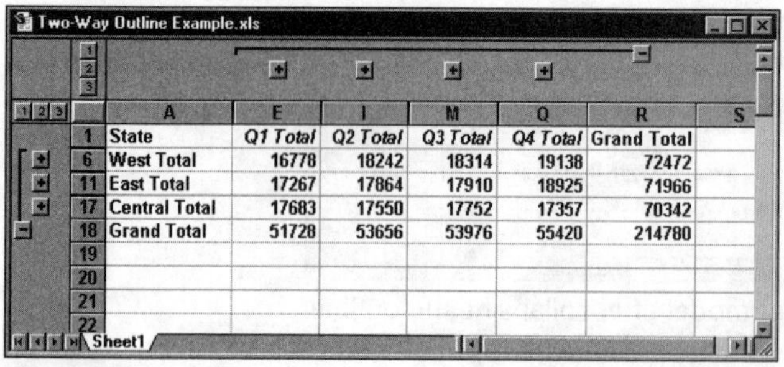
Two-Way Outline Example.xls

	A	E	I	M	Q	R	S
1	State	Q1 Total	Q2 Total	Q3 Total	Q4 Total	Grand Total	
6	West Total	16778	18242	18314	19138	72472	
11	East Total	17267	17864	17910	18925	71966	
17	Central Total	17683	17550	17752	17357	70342	
18	Grand Total	51728	53656	53976	55420	214780	
19							
20							
21							
22							

Sheet1

Figure 18-5: The budget model with both outlines collapsed at the second level.

More about outlines

Following are points to keep in mind about worksheet outlines:

- ✦ A single worksheet can have only one outline (row, column, or both). If you need to create more than one outline, move the data to a new worksheet.
- ✦ You can create an outline manually or have Excel do it for you automatically. If you choose the latter option, you may need to do some preparation to get the worksheet in the proper format.
- ✦ You can create an outline for all data on a worksheet or just a selected data range.
- ✦ You can remove an outline with a single command.
- ✦ You can hide the outline symbols (to free screen space) but retain the outline.
- ✦ You can have up to eight nested levels in an outline.

Cross Reference

Worksheet outlines can be quite useful. But if your main objective is to summarize a large amount of data, you might be better off using a pivot table. A pivot table is much more flexible and doesn't require that you create the subtotal formulas; it does the summarizing for you automatically. I discuss pivot tables in Chapter 25.

Creating an Outline

In this section, you learn the two ways to create an outline: automatically and manually. Before getting into the details, I discuss the first step: getting your data ready for conversion to an outline.

Preparing the data

Before you create an outline, you need to ensure the following:

✦ The data is appropriate for an outline.

✦ The formulas are set up properly.

Determining appropriate data

What type of data is appropriate for an outline? Generally, the data should be arranged in a hierarchy. An example of hierarchical data is a budget that consists of an arrangement such as the following:

Company

    Division

       Department

         Budget Category

          Budget Item

In this case, each budget item (for example, airfare and hotel expenses) is part of a budget category (for example, travel expenses). Each department has its own budget, and the departments are rolled up into divisions. The divisions make up the company. This type of arrangement is well-suited for a row outline — although most of your outlines probably won't have this many levels.

Once created, you can view the information at any level of detail that you desire. An outline is often useful for creating reports for different levels of management. Upper management may want to see only the Division totals. Division managers may want to see totals by department, and each department manager needs to see the full details for his or her department.

As I demonstrated at the beginning of the chapter, time-based information that is rolled up into larger units (such as months and quarters) also is appropriate for a column outline. Column outlines work just like row outlines, however, and the levels need not be time-based.

Setting up the formulas

Before creating an outline, you need to make sure that all the summary formulas are entered correctly and consistently. By consistently, I mean in the same relative location. Generally, formulas that compute summary formulas (such as subtotals) are entered below the data to which they refer. In some cases, however, the summary formulas are entered above the referenced cells. Excel can handle either method, but you must be consistent throughout the range that will be outlined. If the summary formulas aren't consistent, automatic outlining won't produce the results you want.

Note If your summary formulas aren't consistent (that is, some are above and some are below the data), you still can create an outline, but you must do it manually.

Creating an outline automatically

In most cases, the best approach is to let Excel create the outline for you. Excel can do the job in a few seconds, whereas it might take you ten minutes or more.

To have Excel create an outline, move the cell pointer anywhere within the range of data that you're outlining. Then choose the Data⇨Group and Outline⇨Auto Outline command. Excel analyzes the formulas in the range and creates the outline. Depending on the formulas you have, Excel creates a row outline, a column outline, or both.

If the worksheet already has an outline, you're asked whether you want to modify the existing outline. Click on Yes to force Excel to remove the old outline and create a new one.

Note Excel automatically creates an outline when you use the Data⇨Subtotals command. This command inserts subtotal formulas automatically if your data is set up as a list. I discuss this command in Chapter 23 (see "Creating subtotals").

Creating an outline manually

Usually, letting Excel create the outline is the best approach. It's much faster and less error prone. If the outline that Excel creates isn't what you had in mind, however, you can create an outline manually.

When Excel creates a row outline, the summary rows all must be above the data or below the data (they can't be mixed). Similarly, for a column outline, the summary columns all must be to the right of the data or to the left of the data. If your worksheet doesn't meet these requirements, you have two choices:

✦ Rearrange the worksheet so that it does.

✦ Create the outline manually.

Using an outline for text

If you need to present lots of textual information in a workbook — as in user instructions, for example — consider arranging the information in the form of an outline. The accompanying figure shows an example that I developed for one of my shareware products. The user manual is contained on a worksheet, and I created an outline to make locating a specific section easier. I also used a simple macro, attached to a check box, to make it easy for users to expand and collapse the outline.

The workbook shown in the figure is available at this book's Web site.

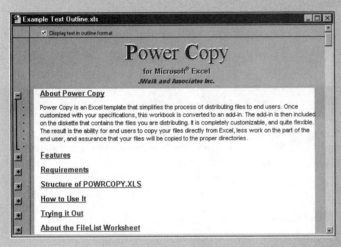

You'll also need to create an outline manually if the range doesn't contain any formulas. You may have imported a file and want to use an outline to display it better. Because Excel uses the formulas to determine how to create the outline, it is not able to make an outline without formulas.

Creating an outline manually consists of creating groups of rows (for row outlines) or groups of columns (for column outlines). To create a group of rows, completely select all the rows that you want included in the group — but do *not* select the row that has the summary formulas. Then choose the Data⇨Group and Outline⇨Group command. Excel displays the outline symbols for the group as it's created. Repeat this for each group that you want to create. When you collapse the outline, rows in the group are hidden. But the summary row, which is not in the group, isn't hidden.

Note If you select a range of cells (rather than entire rows or columns) before creating a group, Excel displays a dialog box asking you what you want to group. It then groups entire rows or columns based on the range that you selected.

You also can select groups of groups. This creates multilevel outlines. When creating multilevel outlines, always start with the innermost groupings and then work your way out. If you group the wrong rows, you can ungroup the group with the Data⇨Group and Outline⇨Ungroup command.

Tip   Excel has toolbar buttons that speed up the process of grouping and ungrouping (see the sidebar "Outlining tools"). You also can use the following keyboard shortcuts:

Alt+Shift+right arrow: Groups selected rows or columns.

Alt+Shift+left arrow: Ungroups selected rows or columns.

Creating outlines manually can be confusing at first. But if you stick with it, you'll become a pro in no time.

Outlining tools

Excel doesn't have a toolbar devoted exclusively to outlining, but it *does* have one that comes close. The Pivot Table toolbar (see accompanying figure) includes four tools that are handy for working with outlines.

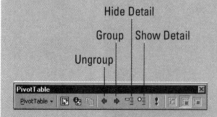

The relevant Pivot Table toolbar buttons are as follows:

Button Name	What It Does
Ungroup	Ungroups selected rows or columns
Group	Groups selected rows or columns
Show Detail	Shows details of selected summary cell
Hide Detail	Hides details of selected summary cell

Using Outlines

In this section, I discuss the basic operations that you can perform with a worksheet outline.

Displaying levels

To display various outline levels, click on the appropriate outline symbol. These symbols consist of buttons with numbers on them (1, 2, and so on) and buttons with either a plus sign (+) or a minus sign (–).

Clicking on the 1 button collapses the outline as small as it will go. Clicking on the 2 button expands it to show one level, and so on. The number of numbered buttons depends on the number of outline levels. Choosing a level number displays the detail for that level, plus any lower levels. To display all levels, click on the highest level number.

You can expand a particular section by clicking on on its + button, or you can collapse a particular section by clicking on on its – button. In short, you have complete control over the details that are exposed or hidden in an outline.

If you prefer, you can use the Hide Detail and Show Detail commands on the Data⇨Group and Outline menu to hide and show details. Or you can use one of the buttons on the Pivot Table toolbar to do the hiding and showing.

Tip
If you find yourself constantly adjusting the outline to show different reports, consider using the Custom Views feature to save a particular view and give it a name. Then you can quickly switch among the named views. Use the View⇨ Custom Views command for this.

Applying styles to an outline

When you create an outline, you can have Excel automatically apply named styles to the summary rows and columns (see Chapter 11 for a discussion of named styles). Excel uses styles with names in the following formats (where *n* corresponds to the outline level):

RowLevel_*n*

ColLevel_*n*

For example, the named style that is applied to the first row level is RowLevel_1.

These styles consist only of formats for the font. Using font variations makes distinguishing various parts of the outline a bit easier. You can, of course, modify the styles any way you want. For example, you can use the Format⇨Style command to change the font size or color for the RowLevel_1 style. After you do so, all the RowLevel_1 cells take on the new formatting. Figure 18-6 shows an outline with the automatic outline styles assigned.

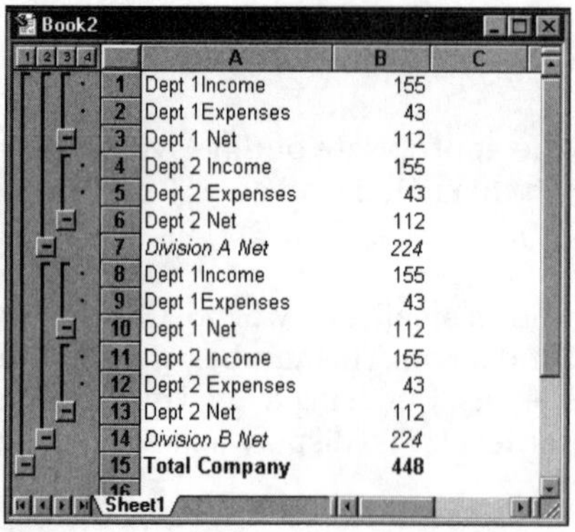

Figure 18-6: This outline has automatic styles.

You can have Excel automatically apply the styles when it creates an outline, or you can apply them after the fact. You control this in the Outline dialog box, shown in Figure 18-7. This dialog box appears when you select the Data⇨Group and Outline⇨Settings command.

Figure 18-7: The Outline dialog box.

If the Automatic Styles check box is checked when you create the outline, Excel automatically applies the styles. To apply styles to an existing outline, select the outline, choose the Data⇨Group and Outline⇨Settings command, and then click on the Apply Styles command. Notice that you also can create an outline using this dialog box.

Tip   You may prefer to use Excel's Format⇨AutoFormat command to format an outline. Several of the AutoFormats use different formatting for summary cells.

Adding data to an outline

You may need to add additional rows or columns to an outline. In some cases, you may be able to insert new rows or columns without disturbing the outline, and the new rows or columns become part of the outline. In other cases, you'll find that the new row or column is not part of the outline. If you created the outline automatically, just select the Data⇨Group and Outline⇨Auto Outline command again. Excel makes you verify that you want to modify the existing outline. If you created the outline manually, you need to make the adjustments manually as well.

Removing an outline

If you decide that you no longer need an outline, you can remove it. Select the Data⇨Group and Outline⇨Clear Outline command. The outline is fully expanded (all hidden rows and columns are unhidden), and the outline symbols disappear. The outline styles remain in effect, however.

Caution Removing an outline can't be undone, so make sure that you really want to remove the outline before selecting this command.

Hiding the outline symbols

The outline symbols displayed when an outline is present take up quite a bit of space (the exact amount depends on the number levels). If you want to see as much as possible on-screen, you can temporarily hide these symbols without removing the outline. There are two ways to do this:

   ♦ Access the Options dialog box, select the View panel, and uncheck the Outline Symbols check box.

   ♦ Press Ctrl+8.

Note When you hide the outline symbols, the outline still is in effect, and the worksheet displays the data at the current outline level. That is, some rows or columns may be hidden.

To redisplay the outline symbols, either place a check mark in the Outline Symbols check box in the Options dialog box or press Ctrl+8.

Tip If you use the Custom Views feature to save named views of your outline, the status of the outline symbols is also saved as part of the view. This lets you name some views with the outline symbols and other views without them.

Creating charts from outlines

A worksheet outline also is a handy way to create summary charts. If you have a large table of data, creating a chart usually produces a confusing mess. But if you create an outline first, then you can collapse the outline and select the summary data for your chart. Figure 18-8 shows a example of a chart created from a collapsed outline. When you expand an outline that has a chart created from it, the chart shows the additional data.

Note If your chart shows all the data in the outline even when it's collapsed, remove the check box from the Plot Visible Cells Only check box in the Chart panel in the Options dialog box.

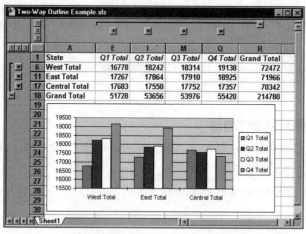

Figure 18-8: This chart was created from the summary cells in an outline.

Summary

This chapter discusses the advantages of creating an outline from worksheet data. It teaches you how to create row outlines and column outlines, either automatically or manually. I also discuss how to use an outline after it is created.

✦   ✦   ✦

Linking and Consolidating Worksheets

I n this chapter, I discuss two procedures common in the world of spreadsheets: linking and consolidation. *Linking* is the process of using references to cells in external workbooks to get data into your worksheet. *Consolidation* combines or summarizes information from two or more worksheets (which can be in multiple workbooks).

Linking Workbooks

With linking, worksheets are linked together such that one depends on the other. The workbook that contains the link formulas (or external reference formulas) is the *dependent* workbook. The workbook that is the source of the information used in the external reference formula is the *source* workbook. It's important to note that the source workbook doesn't need to be open while the dependent workbook is open.

Cross Reference It's also possible to create links to data in other applications, such as a database program or a word processor. This uses a completely different procedure and is the topic of Chapter 29.

Why link workbooks?

When you consider linking workbooks, you might ask yourself the following question: If Workbook A needs to access data in another workbook (Workbook B), why not just enter the data into Workbook A in the first place? In some cases, you can. But the real value of linking is apparent when the source workbook is continually being updated. Creating a link to that workbook means that you'll always have access to the most recent information.

Linking workbooks also can be helpful if you need to consolidate different files. For example, each regional sales manager might store data in a separate workbook. You can create a summary workbook that uses link formulas to retrieve specific data from each workbook and calculate totals across all regions.

Linking also is useful as a way to break up a large model into smaller files. You can create smaller workbook modules that are linked together with a few key external references. Often, this makes your model easier to deal with and uses less memory.

Linking is not without its downside, however. As you'll see later, external reference formulas are somewhat fragile, and it's relatively easy to accidentally sever the links that you create. You can prevent this from happening if you understand how it works. Later in the chapter, I discuss some of the problems that may arise and how to avoid them (see "Potential problems with external reference formulas").

Creating external reference formulas

There are several ways to create an external reference formula:

- ✦ Type the cell references manually. These references can be lengthy, because they include workbook and sheet names (and, possibly, even drive and path information). The advantage of manually typing the cell references is that the source workbook doesn't have to be open.

- ✦ Point to the cell references. If the source workbook is open, you can use the standard pointing techniques to create formulas that use external references.

- ✦ Use the Edit⇨Paste Special command with the Paste Link button. This requires that the source workbook be open.

- ✦ Use Excel's Data⇨Consolidate command. I discuss this method later in the chapter (see "Consolidating worksheets using Data⇨Consolidate").

Understanding the link formula syntax

I touch on the topic of external reference formulas in Chapter 9, and this section takes the concept even further.

The general syntax for an external reference formula is as follows:

```
=[WorkbookName]SheetName!CellAddress
```

The cell address is preceded by the workbook name (in brackets), the worksheet name, and an exclamation point. Here's an example of a formula that uses a cell reference in the Sheet1 worksheet in a workbook named Budget:

```
=[Budget.xls]Sheet1!A1
```

If the workbook name or the sheet name in the reference includes one or more spaces, you must enclose the text in single quotation marks. For example, here's a formula that refers to a cell on Sheet1 in a workbook named Budget For 1997:

```
='[Budget For 1997]Sheet1'!A1
```

When a formula refers to cells in a different workbook, that other workbook doesn't need to be open. If the workbook is closed and not in the current folder, you must add the complete path to the reference. Here's an example:

```
='C:\MSOffice\Excel\Budget Files\[Budget For 1997]Sheet1'!A1
```

Creating a link formula by pointing

As I mentioned, you can directly enter external reference formulas, but doing so can cause errors because you must have every bit of information exactly correct. The easier way is to have Excel build the formula for you. Here's how to do it:

1. Open the source workbook.

2. Activate the cell in the dependent workbook that holds the formula.

3. Begin entering the formula.

4. When you get to the part that requires the external reference, activate the source workbook and select the cell or range.

5. Finish the formula and press Enter.

You'll see that when you point to the cell or range, Excel automatically takes care of the details and creates a syntactically correct external reference. When you point to a cell reference using the procedure oulined in the steps, the cell reference is always an absolute reference (such as $A$1). If you plan to copy the formula to create additional link formulas, you can change the absolute reference to a relative reference by removing the dollar signs.

Note When the source workbook is open, the external reference doesn't include the path to the workbook. If you close the source workbook, the external reference formulas change to display the full path. If you use the File⇨Save As command to save the source workbook with a different name, Excel changes the external references to use the new filename.

Pasting links

The Paste Special command provides another way to create external reference formulas. Here's how to use it:

1. Open the source workbook.

2. Select the cell or range that you want to link and then copy it to the Clipboard.

3. Activate the dependent workbook and select the cell where you want the link formula. If you're pasting a range, just select the upper-left cell.

4. Choose the Edit⇨Paste Special command and click on the Paste Link button.

Excel 97 In previous versions of Excel, this procedure resulted in an *array formula* (a single formula stored in multiple cells). Excel 97 pastes normal formulas that use relative references.

Working with external reference formulas

It's important to understand that a single workbook can have links that refer to any number of different source workbooks. This section discusses what you need to know about working with links.

Creating links to unsaved workbooks

Excel lets you create link formulas to unsaved workbooks and even nonexistent workbooks. Assume that you have two workbooks open and neither has been saved (they have the names Book1 and Book2). If you create a link formula to Book1 in Book2 and then save Book2, Excel displays the dialog box shown in Figure 19-1. Generally, you should avoid this situation. Simply save the source workbook first.

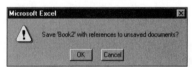

Figure 19-1: This message indicates that the workbook has references to a workbook that hasn't been saved.

You also can create links to documents that don't exist. You might want to do this if you'll be using a source workbook from a colleague, but the file hasn't arrived. When you enter an external reference formula that refers to a nonexistent workbook, Excel displays its File Not Found dialog box, shown in Figure 19-2. If you click on Cancel, the formula retains the workbook name that you entered, but it returns an error. When the source workbook becomes available, the error goes away and the formula displays its proper value.

Opening a workbook with external reference formulas

When you open a workbook that contains one or more external reference formulas, Excel retrieves the current values from the source workbooks and calculates the formulas.

If Excel can't locate a source workbook that's referred to in a link formula, it displays its File Not Found dialog box and prompts you to supply a workbook to use for the source workbook.

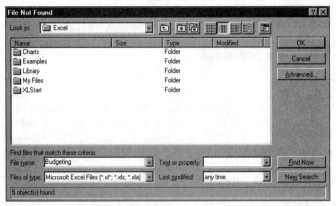

Figure 19-2: When you enter a formula that refers to a nonexistent workbook, Excel displays this dialog box to help you locate the file.

Examining links

If your workbook uses several workbook links, you might want to see a list of source workbooks. To do so, choose the Edit⇨Links command. Excel responds with the Links dialog box, shown in Figure 19-3. This dialog box lists all source workbooks, plus other types of links to other documents (I explain these other types of links in Chapter 29).

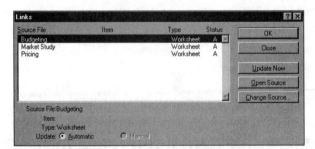

Figure 19-3: The Links dialog box lists all link sources.

Updating links

If you want to ensure that your link formulas have the latest values from their source workbooks, you can force an update. This step might be necessary if you just learned that someone made changes to the source workbook and saved the latest version to your network server.

To update linked formulas with their current value, access the Links dialog box, choose the appropriate source workbook, and click on the Update Now button. Excel updates the link formulas with the latest version of the source workbook.

Note Worksheet links are always set to the Automatic update option in the Links dialog box, and you can't change them to Manual. This means only that the links are updated when the workbook is opened, however. Excel doesn't automatically update links if the source file gets changed.

Changing the link source

There might come a time when you need to change the source workbook for your external references. For example, you might have a worksheet that has links to a workbook named `Preliminary Budget`. Later, you get a finalized version named `Final Budget`.

You *could* change all the cell links manually, or you could simply change the link source. Do this in the Links dialog box. Select the source workbook that you want to change and click on the Change Source button. Excel displays a dialog box that lets you select a new source file. After you select the file, all external reference formulas are updated.

Severing links

If you have external references in a workbook and then decide that you no longer need the links, you can convert the external reference formulas to values, thereby severing the links. To do so, follow these steps:

1. Select the range that contains the external reference formulas and copy it to the Clipboard.

2. Choose the Edit⇨Paste Special command. Excel displays the Paste Special dialog box.

3. Select the Values option and click on OK.

4. Press Esc to cancel cut-copy mode.

All formulas in the selected range are converted to their current values.

Potential problems with external reference formulas

Using external reference formulas can be quite useful, but some risk is involved. In other words, the links may become severed when you don't want them to. In almost every case, you'll be able to reestablish lost links. If you open the workbook and Excel can't locate the file, you're presented with a dialog box that lets you specify the workbook and recreate the links. You also can change the source file using the Change Source button in the Links dialog box. The following sections discuss some pointers that you must keep in mind when using external reference formulas.

Renaming or moving a source workbook

If the source document is renamed or moved to a different folder, Excel won't be able to update the links. You need to use the Links dialog box and specify the new source document.

Using the File⇨Save As command

If both the source workbook and the destination workbook are open, Excel doesn't display the full path in the external reference formulas. If you use the File⇨Save As command to give the source workbook a new name, Excel modifies the external references to use the new workbook name. In some cases, this may be what you want. But in other cases, it may not. Bottom line? Be careful when you use the File⇨Save As command with a workbook that is linked to another workbook.

Modifying a source workbook

If you open a workbook that is a source workbook for another workbook, be extremely careful if the destination workbook is not open at the same time. For example, if you add a new row to the source workbook, the cells all move down one row. When you open the destination workbook, it continues to use the old cell references — which are now invalid.

There are two ways to avoid this problem:

✦ Make sure that the destination workbook is open when you modify the source workbook. If so, Excel adjusts the external references in the destination workbook when you make changes to the source workbook.

✦ Use names rather than cell references in your link formula. This is the safest approach.

Intermediary links

Excel doesn't place many limitations on the complexity of your network of external references. For example, Workbook A can have external references that refer to Workbook B, which can be an external reference that refers to Workbook C. In this case, the value in Workbook A ultimately depends on the value in Workbook C. Workbook B is an intermediary link.

I don't recommend these types of links, but if you must use them, be aware that external reference formulas aren't updated if the workbook isn't open. In the preceding example, assume that Workbooks A and C are open. If you change the value in Workbook C, it won't be reflected in Workbook A because Workbook B (the intermediary link) isn't open.

Consolidating Worksheets

I use the term *consolidation* to refer to a number of operations that involve multiple worksheets or multiple workbook files. In some cases, consolidation involves creating link formulas. Here are two common examples of consolidation:

✦ The budget for each department in your company is stored in a separate worksheet in a single workbook. You need to consolidate the data and create company-wide totals.

✦ Each department head submits his or her budget to you in a separate workbook. Your job is to consolidate these files into a company-wide budget.

Using links to recover data from corrupted files

Sooner or later (with luck, later), it's bound to happen. You attempt to open an Excel workbook, and you get an error telling you that Excel can't access the file. Most of the time, this indicates that the file (somehow) got corrupted. If you're lucky, you have a recent backup that you can fall back on. If you're *very* lucky, you haven't made any changes to the file since it was backed up. But let's assume that you fell a bit behind on your backup procedures, and the dead file is the only version you have.

Although I don't know of any method to fully recover a corrupt file, I'll share with you a method that sometimes lets you recover at least some of the data from worksheets in the file (values, not formulas). Your actual success depends on how badly the file is corrupted.

This technique involves creating an external reference formula that refers to the corrupt file. You'll need to know the names of the worksheets that you want to recover. For example, assume that you have a workbook named Summary Data that can't be opened. Further assume that this workbook is stored in a folder named Sheets on the C drive. This workbook has one sheet, named Sheet1. Here's how to attempt to recover the data from this worksheet:

1. Open a new workbook.

2. In cell A1, enter the following external reference formula:

```
='C:\Sheets\[Summary
Data]Sheet1'!A1
```

If you're lucky, this formula returns the value in cell A1 of Sheet1 in the corrupt file.

3. Copy this formula down and to the right to recover as many values as you can.

4. Convert the external references formulas to values and save the workbook.

If the corrupt file has additional worksheets, repeat these steps for any other worksheets in the workbook (you'll need to know the exact sheet names).

Depending on a number of factors, these tasks can be very difficult or quite easy. The main factor is whether the information is laid out exactly the same in each worksheet. If so, the job is relatively simple (as you'll see shortly).

If the worksheets aren't laid out identically, they may be close enough. In the second example, some budget files submitted to you may be missing categories that aren't used by a particular department. In this case, you can use a handy feature in Excel that matches data by using row and column titles. I discuss this feature later in the chapter (see "Consolidating worksheets using Data➪ Consolidate).

If the worksheets have little or no resemblance to each other, your best bet may be to edit the sheets so that they correspond to one another. In some cases, it may be more efficient to simply reenter the information in a standard format.

You can use any of the following techniques to consolidate information from multiple workbooks:

✦ Use external reference formulas.

✦ Copy the data and use the Paste Special command.

✦ Use Excel's Data⇨Consolidate command.

✦ Use a pivot table. (I discuss this feature in Chapter 25.)

I discuss these methods (with the exception of pivot tables) in the sections that follow.

Consolidating worksheets using formulas

Consolidating with formulas simply involves creating formulas that use references to other worksheets or other workbooks. The primary advantages are the following:

✦ Dynamic updating — if the values in the source worksheets change, the formulas are updated automatically.

✦ The source workbooks don't need to be open when you create the consolidation formulas.

If the worksheets that you are consolidating are in the same workbook — and if all the worksheets are laid out identically — the consolidation task is quite simple. You can just use standard formulas to create the consolidations. For example, to compute the total for cell A1 in worksheets named Sheet2 through Sheet10, enter the following formula:

```
=SUM(Sheet2:Sheet10!A1)
```

You can enter this formula manually or use the multisheet selection technique that I discuss in Chapter 8 (see "Selecting multisheet ranges"). You can then copy this formula to create summary formulas for other cells. Figure 19-4 shows this technique at work.

If the consolidation involves other workbooks, you can use external reference formulas to perform your consolidation. For example, if you want to add the values in cell A1 from Sheet1 in two workbooks (named Region1 and Region2), you can use the following formula:

```
=[Region1.xls]Sheet1!A1+[Region2.xls]Sheet1!A1
```

This formula, of course, can include any number of external references up to the 1,024-character limit for a formula. With many external references, such a formula can be quite lengthy and confusing if you need to edit it.

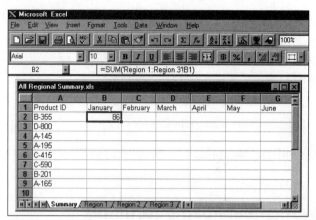

Figure 19-4: Consolidating multiple worksheets by using formulas.

Caution   It's important to remember that Excel expands the references to include the full path — which can increase the length of the formula. Therefore, it's possible that this expansion will exceed the limit and create an invalid formula.

If the worksheets that you're consolidating aren't laid out the same, you can still use formulas — but you'll have to ensure that each formula refers to the correct cell.

Consolidating worksheets using Paste Special

Another method of consolidating information is to use the Edit⇨Paste Special command. This method is applicable only when all the worksheets that you're consolidating are open. The disadvantage — a major disadvantage — is that the consolidation isn't dynamic. In other words, it doesn't generate a formula. So if any data that was consolidated changes, the consolidation is no longer accurate.

This technique takes advantage of the fact that the Paste Special command can perform a mathematical operation when it pastes data from the Clipboard. Figure 19-5 shows the Paste Special dialog box.

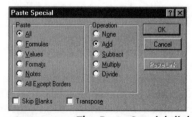

Figure 19-5: The Paste Special dialog box.

Here's how to use this method:

1. Copy the data from the first source range.

2. Activate the destination workbook and select the cell where the consolidation will occur.

3. Select the Edit⇨Paste Special command, click on the Add option, and click on OK.

Repeat these steps for each source range to be consolidated. As you can see, this can be quite error prone and isn't really a good method of consolidating data.

Consolidating worksheets using Data⇨Consolidate

For the ultimate in data consolidation, use Excel's Data⇨Consolidate command. This method is quite flexible, and in some cases it even works if the source worksheets aren't laid out identically. This technique can create consolidations that are *static* (no link formulas) or *dynamic* (with link formulas). The Data⇨ Consolidate command supports the following methods of consolidation:

✦ **By position:** This method is accurate only if the worksheets are laid out identically.

✦ **By category:** Excel uses row and column labels to match data in the source worksheets. Use this option if the data is laid out differently in the source worksheets or if some source worksheets are missing rows or columns.

Figure 19-6 shows the Consolidate dialog box, which appears when you select the Data⇨Consolidate command. Following is a description of the controls in this dialog box.

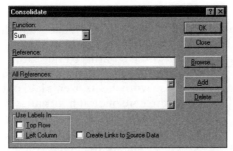

Figure 19-6: The Consolidate dialog box lets you specify ranges to be consolidated.

Function: This is where you specify the type of consolidation. Most of the time you'll use Sum, but you also can select from ten other options: Count, Avg, Max, Min, Product, Count Nums, StdDev (standard deviation), StdDevp (population standard deviation), Var (variance), or Varp (population variance).

Reference: This text box holds a range from a source file that will be consolidated. You can enter the range reference manually or use any standard pointing technique (if the workbook is open). After the range is entered in this box, click on the Add button to add it to the All References list. If you're consolidating by position, don't include labels in the range. If you're consolidating by category, *do* include labels in the range.

All references: This list box contains the list of references that you have added with the Add button.

Use labels in: These check boxes tell Excel to examine the labels in the top row, the left column, or both positions to perform the consolidation. Use these options when you're consolidating by category.

Create links to source data: This option, when selected, creates an outline in the destination worksheet that consists of external references to the destination cells. In addition, it includes summary formulas in the outline. If this option isn't selected, the consolidation won't use formulas.

Browse: This button displays a dialog box that lets you select a workbook to open. It inserts the filename in the Reference box, but you have to supply the range reference.

Add: This button adds the reference in the Reference box to the All References list.

Delete: This button deletes the selected reference from the All References list.

An example

To demonstrate the power of the Data⇨Consolidate command, I'll use a simple example. Figure 19-7 shows three single-sheet workbooks that will be consolidated. These worksheets report product sales for three months. Notice, however, that they don't all report on the same products. In addition, the products aren't even listed in the same order. In other words, these worksheets aren't laid out identically — which would make it difficult to create consolidation formulas.

To consolidate this information, start with a new workbook. The source workbooks can be open or not — it doesn't matter. Following are the steps you take to consolidate the workbooks.

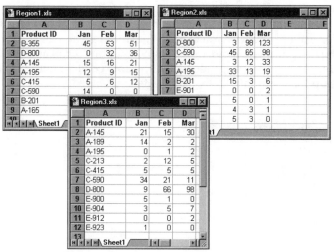

Figure 19-7: Three worksheets to be consolidated.

1. Select the Data⇨Consolidate command. Excel displays its Consolidate dialog box.

2. Select the type of consolidation summary that you want. Use Sum for this example.

3. Enter the reference for the first worksheet to be consolidated. If the workbook is open, you can point to the reference. If it's not open, click on the Browse button to locate the file on disk. The reference must include a range. Use A1:D100. This range is larger than the actual range to be consolidated, but this ensures that the consolidation still works if new rows are added. When the reference in the Reference box is correct, click on Add to add it to the All References list.

4. Enter the reference for the second worksheet. You can simply edit the existing reference by changing Region1 to Region2 and then clicking on Add. This reference is added to the All References list.

5. Enter the reference for the third worksheet. Again, you can simply edit the existing reference by changing Region2 to Region3 and then clicking on Add. This final reference is added to the All References list.

6. Because the worksheets aren't laid out the same, select the Left column and Top row check boxes. This step causes Excel to match the data by using the labels.

7. Select the Create links to source data check box. This causes Excel to create an outline with external references.

8. Click on OK to begin the consolidation.

In seconds, Excel creates the consolidation beginning at the active cell. Figure 19-8 shows the result. Notice that Excel created an outline, which is collapsed to show only the subtotals for each product. If you expand the outline, you can see the details. Examine it further, and you'll discover that each detail cell is an external reference formula that uses the appropriate cell in the source file. Therefore, the destination range is updated automatically if any data is changed.

	A	B	C	D	E	F
1			Jan	Feb	Mar	
3	B-355		45	53	51	
7	D-800		12	196	257	
11	A-145		39	43	84	
13	A-189		14	2	2	
17	A-195		45	23	36	
19	E-901		0	0	2	
21	C-213		2	12	5	
25	C-415		15	11	18	
29	C-590		93	86	109	
32	B-201		19	5	9	
35	E-900		9	4	1	
38	A-165		8	3	1	
40	E-904		3	5	7	
42	E-912		0	0	2	
44	E-923		1	0	0	
45						

Figure 19-8: The result of the consolidation.

More about consolidation

Excel is very flexible when it comes to sources to be consolidated. You can consolidate data from the following:

✦ Workbooks that are open

✦ Workbooks that are closed (you'll have to enter the reference manually — but you can use the Browse button to get the filename part of the reference)

✦ The same workbook in which you're creating the consolidation

And, of course, you can mix and match any of the preceding in a single consolidation.

Excel remembers the references that you entered in the Consolidate dialog box and saves these with the workbook. Therefore, if later you want to refresh a consolidation, you won't have to reenter the references.

If you perform the consolidation by matching labels, be aware that the matches must be exact. For example, *Jan* does not match *January*. The matching isn't case-sensitive, however, so *April* does match *APRIL*. In addition, the labels can be in any order, and they need not be in the same order in all the source ranges.

If you don't choose the Create links to source data check box, Excel doesn't create formulas. This generates a static consolidation. If the data on any of the source worksheets changes, the consolidation doesn't update automatically. To update the summary information, you need to select the destination range and repeat the Data⇨Consolidate command.

Tip If you name the destination range `Consolidate_Area`, you don't need to select it before you update the consolidation. `Consolidate_Area` is a name that has special meaning to Excel.

If you choose the Create links to source data check box, Excel creates an outline. This is a standard worksheet outline, and you can manipulate it using the techniques described in Chapter 18.

Summary

In this chapter, I discuss two important spreadsheet procedures: linking and consolidation. Linking is the process of using references to cells in external workbooks get data for use in your worksheet. Consolidation is the process of combining or summarizing information from two or more worksheets (which can be in multiple workbooks). I cover various methods of linking and consolidation, and I list potential pitfalls.

✦   ✦   ✦

Creating and Using Array Formulas

This chapter introduces a concept that may be new to you: *array formulas*. Understanding this special type of formula may open a whole new world of analytical capability. Working with arrays (rather than with individual cells) requires a different type of mind-set. Some people never quite get the hang of arrays, and others take to this concept quickly. If you're in the former group, don't despair. Using array formulas can be considered an optional skill.

Introducing Arrays

In this chapter I discuss two concepts:

✦ **Array:** A collection of cells or values that is operated on as a group. An array can be stored in cells or be a named constant that consists of multiple elements.

✦ **Array Formula:** A formula that uses one or more arrays either directly or as arguments for a function. An array formula can occupy one or more cells.

If you've ever done any computer programming, you've probably been exposed to arrays. An *array* is a collection of items. Excel's arrays can be one-dimensional or two-dimensional. These dimensions correspond to rows and columns. For example, a one-dimensional array can be a cell range that occupies cells in one row (a horizontal array) or one column (a vertical array). A two-dimensional array occupies cells in one or more rows and columns.

You can perform operations on arrays using array formulas. For example, if you construct an array formula to multiply a five-item vertical array by another five-column vertical array, the result is another five-column vertical array that consists of each element in the first array multiplied by each corresponding element in the second array. Because Excel can fit only one value in a cell, the results of an operation such as this one occupy five cells — and the same array formula is in each of the five cells.

Figure 20-1 illustrates this example. Each cell in the range C1:C5 holds the same formula: {=A1:A5*B1:B5}. The result occupies five cells and contains each element of the first array multiplied by each corresponding element in the second array. The brackets around the formula designate it as an array formula (more about this later in "Entering an array formula").

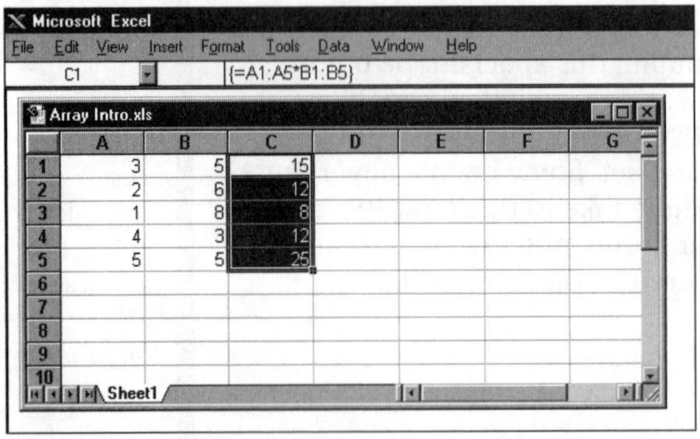

Figure 20-1: A single array formula entered in the range C1:C5 produces results in five cells.

As you will see, arrays have their pros and cons. At the very least, this feature provides an alternative way of doing some operations and is the only way to perform others.

Advantages of array formulas

Some of the advantages of array formulas (as opposed to single-cell formulas) are as follows:

+ They can be much more efficient to work with.

+ They can eliminate the need for intermediary formulas.

+ They can enable you to do things that would otherwise be difficult or impossible.

+ They may use less memory.

Disadvantages of array formulas

This list shows a few disadvantages of array formulas:

✦ Some large arrays can slow your spreadsheet recalculation time to a crawl.

✦ Arrays can make your worksheets more difficult for others to understand.

✦ You must remember to enter an array formula with a special key sequence (Ctrl+Shift+Enter). Otherwise, the result isn't what you expect.

✦ Array formulas cannot be exported to other spreadsheet formats (such as Lotus 1-2-3).

Understanding Arrays

In this section, I present several examples to help clarify this concept. As always, you can get more from this chapter if you follow along on your own computer.

Array formulas versus standard formulas

You can often use a single array formula to substitute for a range of copied formulas. Figure 20-2 shows two examples; the upper worksheet uses standard single-result formulas. The formulas use the SQRT function to calculate the square roots of the values in column A. I entered =**SQRT(A3)** into cell B3 and copied it to the three cells below it. This example uses four different formulas to calculate the results in column B.

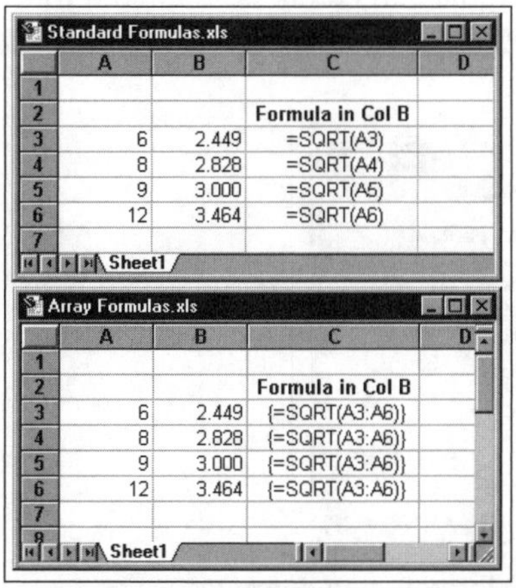

Figure 20-2: These workbooks accomplish the same result, but one uses standard formulas and the other uses an array formula.

The lower workbook uses a single array formula, which is inserted into all four cells. Use the following steps to enter this array formula:

1. Select the range B3:B6.
2. Enter **SQRT(A3:A6)**.
3. Press Ctrl+Shift+Enter to designate the formula as an array formula.

Excel enters the array formula into the three selected cells. It also adds brackets around the formula to indicate that it's an array formula. The key point here is that this example uses only one formula, but the results appear in four different cells because the formula is operating on a four-cell array.

To further demonstrate that this is in fact one formula, try to edit one of the cells in B3:B6. You find that Excel doesn't let you make any changes. To modify an array formula that uses more than one cell, you must select the entire array before editing the formula.

There is virtually no advantage to using an array formula in the preceding example (except perhaps to save the time it takes to copy the formula). The real value of array formulas becomes apparent as you work through this chapter.

An array formula in one cell

Figure 20-3 shows another example. The worksheet on the left uses standard formulas to calculate the average change from the pretest to the posttest. The worksheet on the right also calculates the average changes, but it uses an array formula. This array formula resides in only one cell, because the result is a single value. This is an example of how an array formula can eliminate the need for intermediary formulas. As you can see, it's not necessary to include an additional column to calculate the change in scores.

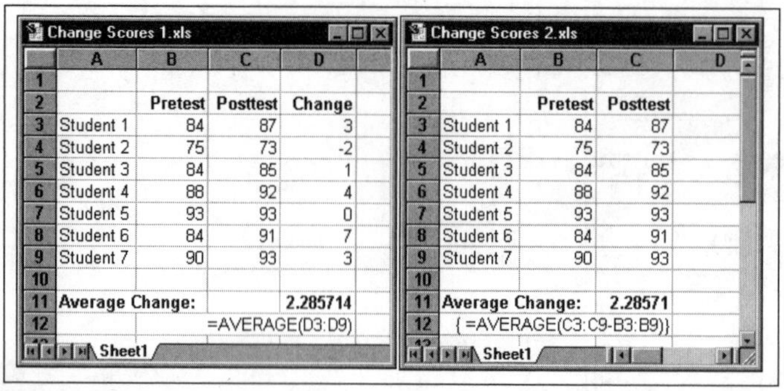

Figure 20-3: Using an array formula to eliminate intermediary formulas.

The formula in cell C11 is as follows:

```
{=AVERAGE(C3:C9-B3:B9)}
```

This array formula operates on two arrays, which are stored in cells. It subtracts each element of B3:B9 from the corresponding element in C3:C9 and produces (in memory) a new seven-element array that holds the result. The AVERAGE function computes the average of the elements in the new array, and the result is displayed in the cell.

"Looping" with arrays

Excel's array feature lets you perform individual operations on each cell in a range — in much the same way as a program language's looping feature enables you to work with elements of an array. For example, assume that you have a range of cells (named `Data`) that contain positive and negative values. You need to compute the average of just the positive values in the range. Figure 20-4 shows an example of this.

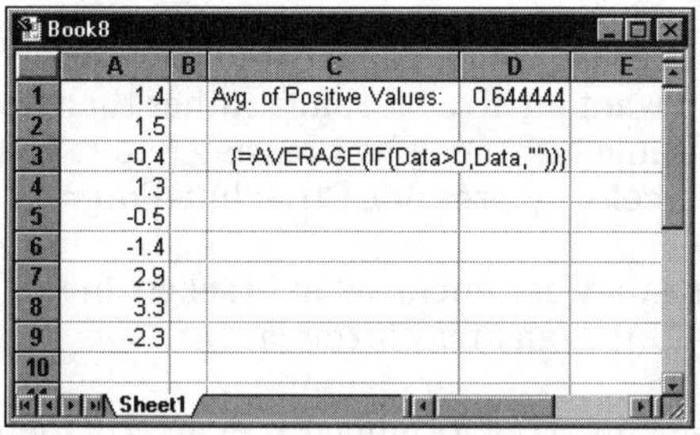

Figure 20-4: You can use an array formula to calculate the average of only the positive values in this range.

One approach is to sort the data and then use the AVERAGE function to calculate the average on only the positive values. A more efficient approach uses the following array formula:

```
={AVERAGE(IF(Data>0,Data,""))}
```

The IF function in this formula checks each element in the input range to see whether it's greater than zero. If so, the IF function returns the value from the input range; otherwise, it returns an empty string. The result is an array that's identical to the input array, except that all nonpositive values are replaced with a null string (the third argument of the IF functions). The AVERAGE function then computes the average of this new array, and the result is displayed in the cell.

The preceding problem can also be solved with the following nonarray formula:

```
=SUMIF(Data,">0",Data)/COUNTIF(Data,">0")
```

Many similar operations cannot be performed with a standard formula, however. For example, to calculate the median of the positive values in a range, an array formula is the only solution.

Later in this chapter, I cover more useful examples that use arrays. But now it's time to provide some rules for how to work with arrays and array formulas.

Working with Arrays

This section deals with the mechanics of selecting arrays and entering and editing array formulas. These procedures are a little different from working with ordinary ranges and formulas.

Entering an array formula

When you enter an array formula into a cell or range, you must follow a special procedure so that Excel knows that you want an array formula rather than a normal formula. You enter a normal formula into a cell by pressing Enter. You enter an array formula into one or more cells by pressing Ctrl+Shift+Enter.

You can identify array formulas because they are enclosed in brackets in the formula bar. For example, {=SQRT(A1:A12)} is an array formula.

Don't enter the brackets when you create an array formula; Excel inserts them for you. If the result of an array formula consists of more than one value, you must select all the cells before you enter the formula. If you fail to do this, only the first result shows.

Editing an array formula

If an array formula occupies multiple cells, you must edit the entire range as though it were a single cell. The key point to remember is that you can't change just one element of an array formula. If you attempt to do so, Excel gives you the messages shown in Figure 20-5.

The following rules apply to multicell array formulas. (If you try to do any of these things, Excel lets you know about it.):

✦ You can't change the contents of any cell that makes up an array formula.

✦ You can't move cells that make up part of an array formula. You can, however, move an entire array formula.

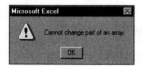

Figure 20-5: Excel's warning message reminds you that you can't edit just one cell of a multicell array.

✦ You can't delete cells that form part of an array formula, but you can delete an entire array.

✦ You can't insert new cells into an array range; this rule includes inserting rows or columns that would add new cells to an array range.

To edit an array formula, select all the cells in the array range and activate the formula bar as usual (click on it or press F2). Excel removes the brackets from the formula while you're editing it. Edit the formula, and then press Ctrl+Shift+Enter to enter the changes. All the cells in the array now reflect your editing changes.

Selecting an array range

You can select an array range manually by using the normal selection procedures. Or, you can use either of the following methods:

✦ Move to any cell in the array range. Select Edit⇨Go To (or press F5), click on the Special button, and then choose the Current Array option. Click on OK to close the dialog box.

✦ Move to any cell in the array range, and press Ctrl+/ to select the entire array.

Formatting arrays

Although you can't change any part of an array formula without changing all parts, you're free to apply formatting to the entire array or to only parts of it.

Using Array Constants

So far, the examples in this chapter have used cell ranges to hold arrays. You can also use constant values as an array. These constants can be entered directly into a formula or defined using the Define Name dialog box. Array constants can be used in array formulas in place of a reference to a range of cells. To use an array constant in an array formula, type the set of values directly into the formula and enclose it in brackets. If you defined a name for the array constant, you can use the name instead.

Array constants can be either one-dimensional or two-dimensional. One-dimensional arrays can be either vertical or horizontal. The elements in a one-dimensional horizontal array are separated by commas. The following example is a one-dimensional horizontal array:

```
{1,2,3,4,5}
```

Because this array constant has five values, it requires five cells (in a row). To enter this array into a range, select a range that consists of one row and five columns. Then enter ={1,2,3,4,5}, and press Ctrl+Shift+Enter.

When you use array constants, you must enter the brackets. Excel doesn't provide them for you. The following example is another horizontal array; it has seven elements:

```
{"Sun","Mon","Tue","Wed","Thu","Fri","Sat"}
```

Figure 20-6 demonstrates how you would create a named array constant using the Define Name dialog box.

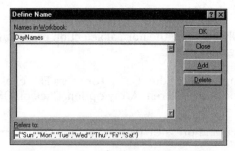

Figure 20-6: Creating an array constant in the Define Name dialog box.

The elements in a one-dimensional vertical array are separated by semicolons. The following is a six-element vertical array:

```
{10;20;30;40;50;60}
```

Another example of a vertical array is as follows; this one has four elements:

```
{"Widgets";"Sprockets";"Do-Dads";"Thing-A-Majigs"}
```

Two-dimensional arrays also separate the elements in a single row with commas and separate the rows with semicolons. The next example is a 3 × 4 array (three rows, each of which occupies four columns):

```
{1,2,3,4;5,6,7,8;9,10,11,12}
```

Figure 20-7 shows how this array appears in a worksheet. First, I created the array constant and named it MyArray. Then I selected A1:D3 and entered **=MyArray**. I pressed Ctrl+Shift+Enter to enter the array formula into the range.

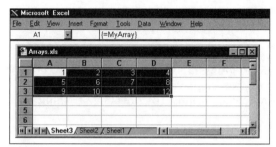

Figure 20-7: An array constant used in a formula.

You can't list cell references, names, or formulas in an array formula in the same way as you list constants. For example, {2*3,3*3,4*3} isn't valid because it lists formulas. {A1,B1,C1} isn't valid either because it lists cell references. Instead, you should use a range reference, such as {A1:C1}.

It's important to keep an array's dimensions in mind when you're performing operations on it. Consider the following array formula:

```
={2,3,4}*{10,11}
```

This formula multiplies a 1×3 array by a 1×2 array. Excel returns an array with three values: 20, 33, and #N/A. Because the second array wasn't large enough, Excel generated #N/A as the third element of the result.

Examples of Using Array Formulas

Perhaps the best way to learn about array formulas is by following examples and adapting them to your own needs. In this section, I present useful examples that give you a good idea of how you can use this feature.

All the examples presented in this section can be found in a workbook that you can download from this book's Web site.

Using an array constant

Figure 20-8 shows a practical example of an array constant. I defined the following constant, named SalesRegions:

```
={"S. California";"Pacific
       NW";"SouthWest";"Central";"SouthEast";"NorthEast"}
```

Because the elements are separated by semicolons, this is a vertical array. I selected A4:A9 and entered **=SalesRegions**; I then pressed Ctrl+Shift+Enter. The worksheet also shows the sales regions displayed horizontally. To do this, I selected A1:F1 and entered the following formula (by pressing Ctrl+Shift+Enter):

```
{=TRANSPOSE(SalesRegions)}
```

The TRANSPOSE function converts a horizontal array to a vertical array (and vice versa).

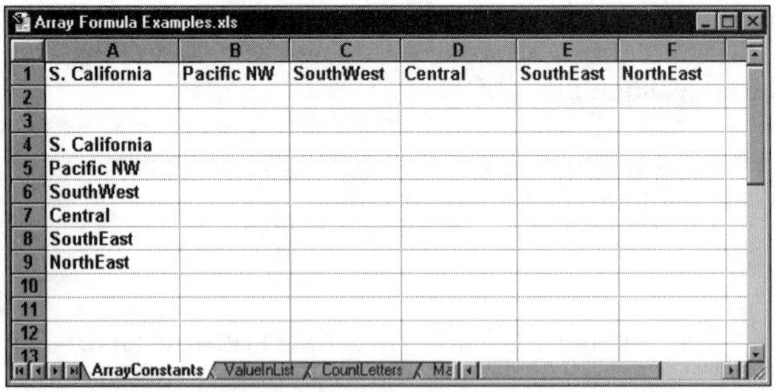

Figure 20-8: Using an array constant to enter the names of sales regions.

The method described is just one way to enter a stored list quickly into a range of cells. Perhaps a better approach is to create a custom list in the Custom Lists panel of the Options dialog box.

Identifying a value in a range

To determine whether a particular value is contained in a range, choose Edit⇨Find. But you also can do this with an array formula. Figure 20-9 shows a worksheet with a list of names (named Names). An array formula in cell E4 checks the name that is entered into cell B1 (named TestValue). If the name exists, it displays the text *Name is in the list*. Otherwise, it displays *Name not found*.

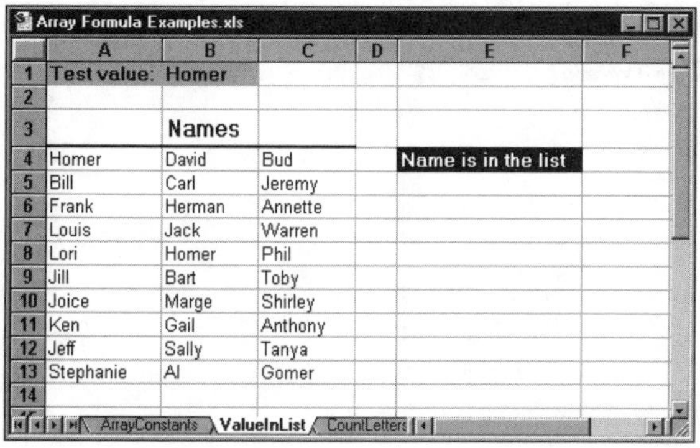

Figure 20-9: Determining whether a range contains a particular value.

The formula in cell E4 is as follows:

```
{=IF(OR(TestValue=Names),"Name is in the list","Name not
        found")}
```

This formula compares `TestValue` to each cell in the range `Names`. It builds a new array that consists of logical TRUE or FALSE values. The OR function returns TRUE if any of the values in the new array is TRUE. The IF function determines which message to display based on the result.

Counting characters in a range

This example demonstrates how to use nested functions in an array formula to loop through each element in the input range. Figure 20-10 shows a worksheet with text entered in a range named `WordList`. The array formula in cell B1 is as follows:

```
{=SUM(LEN(WordList))}
```

This formula is quite straightforward. It creates an array that consists of the length of each word in the `WordList` range. Then it uses the SUM formula to add the values in this new array. You could accomplish this without an array formula by using an additional column of formulas and then summing the results.

Computing maximum and minimum changes

Figure 20-11 shows another example of how an array formula can eliminate the need for intermediary formulas. This worksheet shows two test scores for a group of students. Array formulas compare the two tests and calculate the largest decrease and the largest increase. The formulas are as follows:

```
E3:    {=MIN(C3:C11-B3:B11)}
E4:    {=MAX(C3:C11-B3:B11)}
```

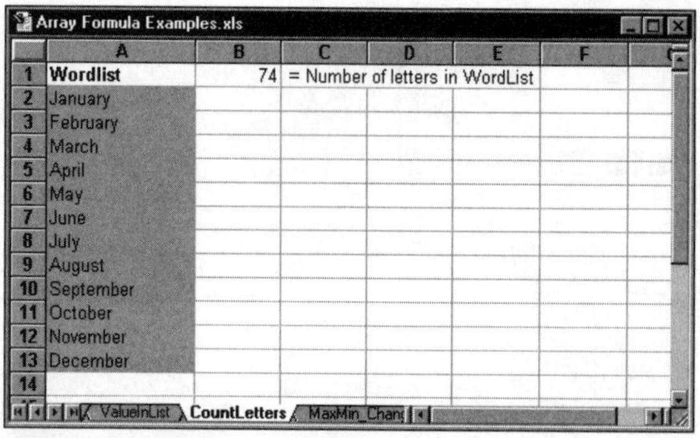
Array Formula Examples.xls

	A	B	C	D	E	F
1	**Wordlist**	74	= Number of letters in WordList			
2	January					
3	February					
4	March					
5	April					
6	May					
7	June					
8	July					
9	August					
10	September					
11	October					
12	November					
13	December					
14						

ValueInList / CountLetters / MaxMin_Chan

Figure 20-10: This array formula counts the number of characters in a range of text.

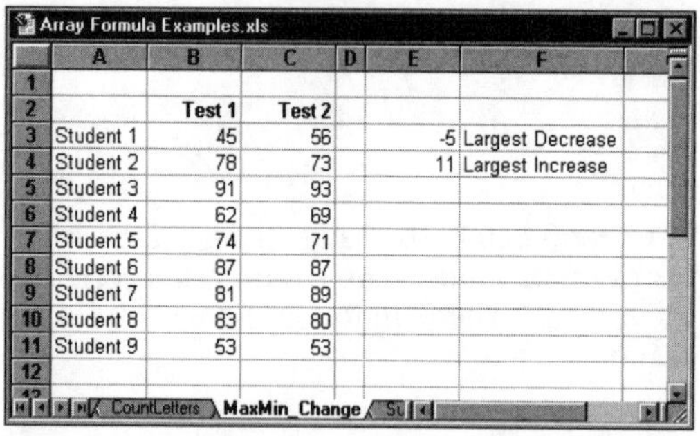
Array Formula Examples.xls

	A	B	C	D	E	F
1						
2		**Test 1**	**Test 2**			
3	Student 1	45	56		-5	Largest Decrease
4	Student 2	78	73		11	Largest Increase
5	Student 3	91	93			
6	Student 4	62	69			
7	Student 5	74	71			
8	Student 6	87	87			
9	Student 7	81	89			
10	Student 8	83	80			
11	Student 9	53	53			
12						

CountLetters / MaxMin_Change / Su

Figure 20-11: Array formulas determine the largest decrease and the largest increase in test scores.

Looping through characters in a cell

The following array formula calculates the sum of the digits in an integer, which is stored in a cell named `Number`:

```
{=SUM(VALUE(MID(Number,ROW($A$1:OFFSET($A$1,LEN(Number)-
     1,0)),1)))}
```

This is a rather complex formula that makes use of an interesting trick. I can break the formula down into its parts so that you can see how it works. (Figure 20-12 shows an example.)

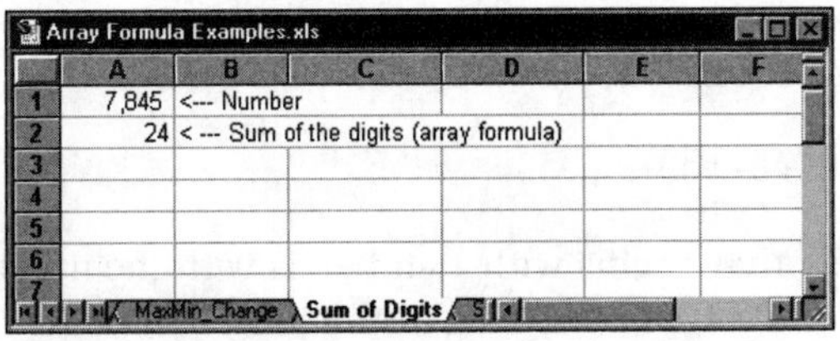

Figure 20-12: An array formula calculates the sum of the digits in a value.

You may be confused by the ROW function (this is the trick). This function is used to generate an array of consecutive integers beginning with 1 and ending with the number of digits in the absolute value of Number.

If Number is 489, then LEN(Number) is 3. The ROW function can then be simplified as:

```
{=ROW($A$1:OFFSET($A$1,3-1,0))}
```

This formula generates an array with three elements: {1,2,3}. This generated array is used as the second argument for the MID function (the third argument is 1). The MID part of the formula, simplified a bit and expressed as values, is:

```
{=MID(489,{1,2,3},1)}
```

This formula generates an array with three elements: {4,8,9}. Simplifying again and adding the SUM function, the formula becomes as follows:

```
{=SUM({4,8,9})}
```

This produces the result of 21.

The following is another version of this formula that also works with negative numbers. I added the ABS function to calculate the absolute value of the result:

```
{=SUM(VALUE(MID(ABS(Number),ROW($A$1:OFFSET($A$1,LEN(ABS(Number))-
    1,0)),1))))}
```

Summing every *n*th digit in a range

The next example can be quite useful. Suppose that you have a range of values and you want to compute the sum of every third value in the list — the first, the fourth, the seventh, and so on. There's no way to accomplish this with a standard formula. The following array formula does the job, however. It assumes that a cell named Nth determines which values to sum, and the range to sum is named Data.

```
{=IF(nth=0,0,SUM(IF(MOD(ROW($A$1:OFFSET($A$1,COUNT(Data)-
    1,0)),nth)=0,Data,0)))}
```

The formula uses the MOD function to determine which values to sum. The first argument for the MOD function is as follows:

```
ROW($A$1:OFFSET($A$1,COUNT(Data)-1,0))
```

This expression generates an array that begins with 1 and ends with the number of cells in the Data range. If the MOD function returns 0, the value is included in the array to sum.

Notice that there's a special case for when Nth is 0 (that is, sum every cell in the range). That's because the MOD function returns an error when its second argument is 0.

This formula has a limitation: It works only when Data consists of a single column of values. That's because it uses the ROW function to determine the element in the array.

Figure 20-13 shows an example that uses the preceding array formula plus a series of intermediary formulas to calculate the result without using an array formula.

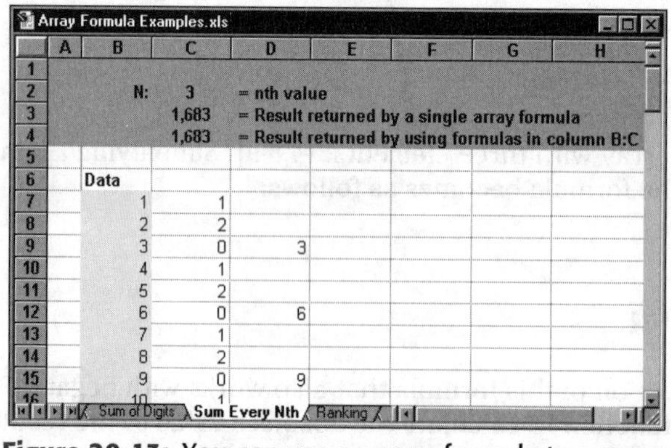

Figure 20-13: You can use an array formula to sum every nth element in a range — or use a series of intermediary formulas (a less-efficient approach).

An alternate method of ranking

It's often desirable to compute rank orders for a range of data. If you have a worksheet with the annual sales figures for 20 salespeople, for example, you may want to know how each person ranks, from highest to lowest.

If you do this sort of thing, you've probably discovered Excel's RANK function. You may have noticed, however, that the ranks produced by this function don't handle ties the way you may like. For example, if two values are tied for third place, they both receive a rank of 3. Many people prefer to assign each an average (or midpoint) of the ranks — that is, a rank of 3.5 for both values tied for third place.

Figure 20-14 shows a worksheet that uses two methods to rank a column of values (named Sales). The first method (column C) uses Excel's RANK function. Column D uses array formulas to compute the ranks. The array formula in cell D2 is as follows:

```
{=IF((SUM(IF(Sales=B2,1)))=1,(SUM(IF(Sales>=B2,1,0))),(SUM(IF(Sales>=B2,1)))-
     ((SUM(IF(Sales=B2,1)))-1)*0.5)}
```

This formula was entered into cell D2 and then copied to the cells below it.

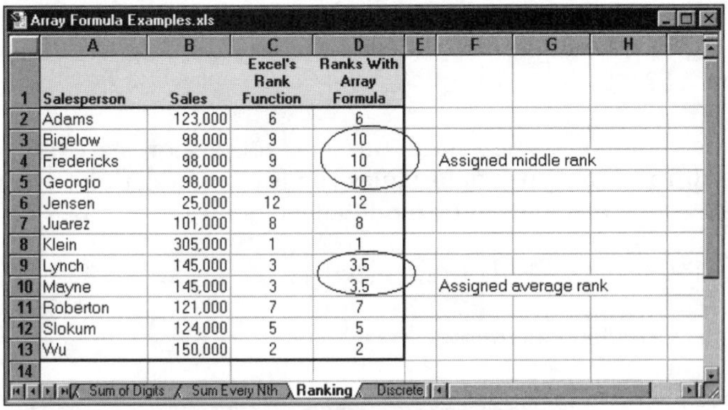

Figure 20-14: Ranking data with Excel's RANK function and with array formulas.

The formula is rather complex, but breaking it down into parts should help you understand how it works.

Frequency distributions

Before Excel 5, the only way to calculate frequency distributions was to use array formulas. Beginning with Excel 5, however, the COUNTIF function provided a more direct way to generate frequency distributions.

Figure 20-15 shows a worksheet with a series of scores in column A that range from 1 to 4. Column D contains array formulas to calculate the frequency of each score. The formula in D6 is as follows:

```
{=SUM(IF(Scores=C3,1))}
```

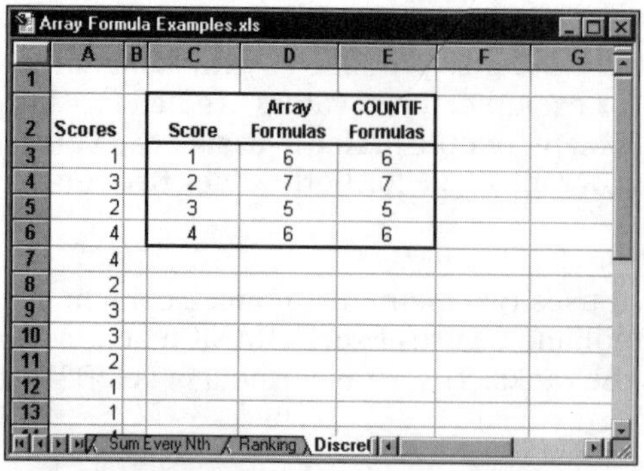

Figure 20-15: Calculating discrete frequency distributions using array formulas and COUNTIF functions.

The corresponding formulas in column E use the COUNTIF function. The formula in E6 is as follows:

```
=COUNTIF(Scores,C3)
```

Both of these methods count specific values. But what if the scores are noninteger values, as in Figure 20-16? Both types of formulas require modification to handle noninteger data. The array formula can be modified as follows:

```
=SUM(IF(Scores>=C3,1))-SUM(IF(Scores>=C4,1))
```

The revised COUNTIF formula is as follows:

```
=COUNTIF(Scores,">="&C3)-COUNTIF(Scores,">="&C4)
```

The array formula requires you to add an additional value in column C so that the last array formula doesn't refer to an empty cell (I added a value of 99).

You also can use the Histogram tool in the Analysis ToolPak to compute distributions (see Chapter 28). An advantage to using arrays or COUNTIF functions, however, is that these procedures are dynamic and display the correct values if you change the input data.

Dynamic crosstabs

In the preceding section, you see that using COUNTIF is a better alternative than using array formulas for calculating frequency distributions. In this section, I demonstrate how to extend these distributions into another dimension and create crosstabs. In this case, an array formula is the only method that can get the job done. This technique lets you create a dynamic crosstab table that is updated automatically whenever the data is changed. Even a pivot table can't do that!

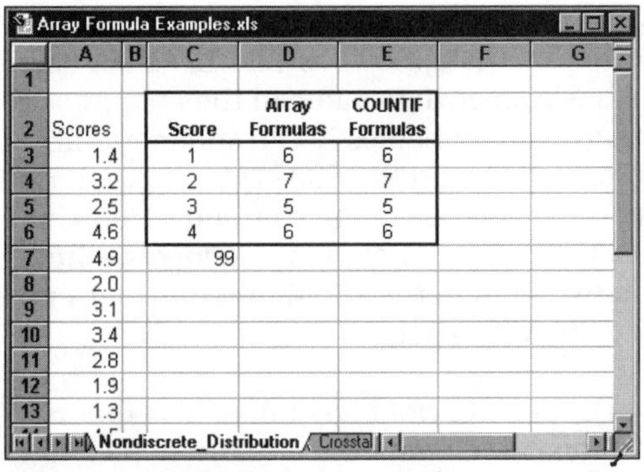

Figure 20-16: Calculating nondiscrete frequency distributions using array formulas and COUNTIF functions.

The worksheet in Figure 20-17 shows a simple expense account listing. Each item consists of the date, the expense category, and the amount spent. Each column of data is a named range, indicated in the first row.

I used array formulas to summarize this information into a handy table that shows the total expenses, by category, for each day. Cell F3 contains the following array formula, which was copied to the remaining 11 cells in the table:

```
{=SUM(IF($E3&F$2=DATES&CATEGORIES,AMOUNTS))}
```

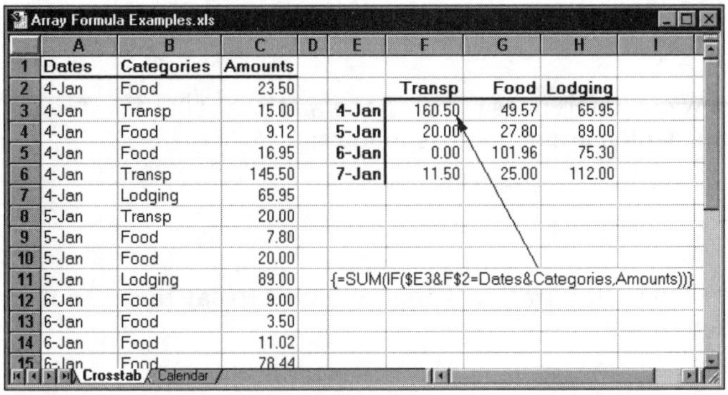

Figure 20-17: You can use array formulas to summarize data like this in a dynamic crosstab table.

These array formulas display the totals for each day, by category.

This formula operates similarly to the more simple one that I demonstrated in the preceding section. This one has a few new twists, however. Rather than count the number of entries, the formula adds the appropriate value in the Amounts range. It does so, however, only if the row and column names in the summary table match the corresponding entries in the DATES and CATEGORIES ranges. It does the comparison by concatenating (using the & operator) the row and column names and comparing the resulting string to the concatenation of the corresponding DATES and CATEGORIES values. If the two match, the =SUM function kicks in and adds the corresponding value in the AMOUNTS range.

This technique can be customized, of course, to hold any number of different categories and any number of dates. You can eliminate the dates, in fact, and substitute people's names, departments, regions, and so on.

You also can cross-tabulate data by creating a pivot table. But, unlike a pivot table, using the procedure described here is completely dynamic (a pivot table must be updated if the data changes). I discuss pivot tables in Chapter 25.

A single-formula calendar

The final array formula example is perhaps the most impressive. Figure 20-18 shows a monthly calendar that is calculated using a single array formula entered in B6:H11. This workbook includes a few additional bells and whistles. For example, you can choose the month and year to display by using dialog box controls that are inserted directly on the worksheet. When you change the month or year, the calendar is updated immediately. The array formula is as follows:

```
{=IF(MONTH(StartDate)<>MONTH(StartDate-StartDOW+Week*7+Weekday-
    1),"",StartDate-StartDOW+Week*7+Weekday-1)}
```

This formula uses a few cell references (StartDate and StartDOW) and two named array constants, which are defined as follows:

```
Week:    ={0;1;2;3;4;5}
Weekday: ={1,2,3,4,5,6,7}
```

I leave it up to you to figure out how this works. Suffice it to say that it took more than a few minutes to develop.

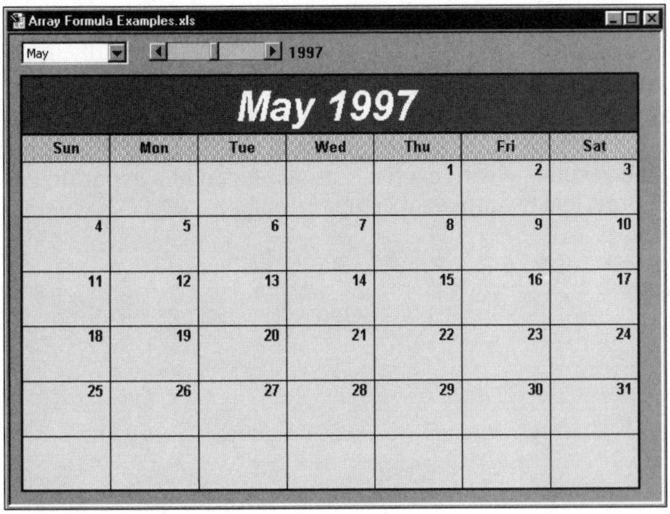

Figure 20-18: This calendar is calculated with a single array formula.

Tips for Array Formulas

If you've followed along in this chapter, you probably understand the advantages of using array formulas. As you gain more experience with arrays, you undoubtedly will discover some disadvantages.

The primary problem with array formulas is that they slow your worksheet's recalculations, especially if you use large arrays. On a faster system, this may not be a problem. But if you have a slower system and speed is of the essence, you should probably avoid using large arrays.

Array formulas are one of the least understood features of Excel. Consequently, if you plan to share a worksheet with someone who may need to make modifications, you should probably avoid using array formulas. Encountering an array formula when you don't know what it is can be confusing.

You may also discover that it's easy to forget to enter an array formula by pressing Ctrl+Shift+Enter. If you edit an existing array, you still must use these keys to complete the edits. Except for logical errors, this problem is probably the most common one that users have with array formulas. If you press Enter by mistake after editing an array formula, just double-click on the cell to get back into Edit mode and then press Ctrl+Shift+Enter.

Summary

This chapter introduces the concept of array formulas. An array formula is a special type of formula that operates on a group of cells. You can write an array formula by entering a single formula that performs an operation multiple inputs and produces multiple results — with each result displayed in a separate cell. I also discuss several practical examples of array formulas.

✦   ✦   ✦

Using Excel in a Workgroup

I f you use Excel on a standalone computer — a PC that's not connected to a network — you can skip this chapter, because it applies only to users who run Excel on a network.

Using Excel on a Network

A computer network, often called a *LAN* (local area network), consists of a group of PCs that are linked. A common type of network uses a client-server model in which one or more PCs on the network are essentially dedicated servers (they store files centrally), and user PCs are clients (they use data in the centrally stored files). Other networks are peer-to-peer networks that don't have a central server. Users on a network can perform the following tasks:

◆ Access files on other systems

◆ Share files with other users

◆ Share resources such as printers and fax modems

◆ Communicate with each other electronically

In many offices, LANs now perform functions that formerly required a mainframe system and dumb terminals. The advantage is that LANs are usually less expensive, easier to expand, more manageable, and more flexible in terms of software availability.

This chapter discusses the Excel features that are designed for network users.

File Reservations

One of the most useful aspects of a network is that users can access files on other systems. The network has one or more file servers attached. A file server stores files that members of a workgroup need to access. A network's file server may contain, for example, files that store customer lists, price lists, and form letters. Keeping these files on a file server has two major advantages:

✦ It eliminates the need to have multiple local copies of the files.

✦ It ensures that the file is always up-to-date; for example, you don't want to be working with an obsolete version of your customer list.

Some software applications are *multiuser* applications. Most database software, for example, lets multiple users work on the same database files. One user may be updating customer records in the database, while another is extracting records. But what if a user is updating a customer record and another user wants to make a change to that same record? Multiuser database software has *record locking* safeguards that are built in to ensure that only one user at a time can modify a particular record.

Excel is not a multiuser application. When you open an Excel file, the entire file is loaded into memory. If the file is accessible to other users, you don't want someone else to be able to open a file that is already open. If the reasons aren't clear, read on.

Note   There is an exception to this that allows multiple users to work on the same workbook. See the next section, "Shared Workbooks."

Assume that your company keeps its sales information in an Excel file that is stored on a network server. Albert wants to add this week's data to the file, so he loads it from the server and begins adding new information. A few minutes later, Betty loads the file to correct some errors that she noticed last week. Albert finishes his work and saves the file. A while later, Betty finishes her corrections and saves the file. Her file overwrites the copy that Albert saved, and his additions are gone.

This scenario *can't happen,* because Excel uses a concept known as *file reservation*. When Albert opens the sales file, he has the reservation for the file. When Betty tries to open the file, Excel informs her that Albert is using the file. If she insists on opening it, the file is opened as *read-only*. In other words, Betty can open the file, but she can't save it under the same name. Figure 21-1 shows the message that Betty receives if she tries to open a file that is in use by someone else.

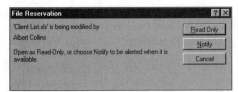

Figure 21-1: The File Reservation dialog box appears if you try to open a file that someone else is using.

Betty has these three choices:

♦ Select Cancel, wait a while, and try again. She may call Albert and ask him when he expects to be finished.

♦ Select Read Only, which lets her open the file but doesn't let her save changes to the same filename.

♦ Select Notify, which opens the file as read-only. Excel pops up a message when Albert is finished using the file.

Figure 21-2 shows the message that Betty receives when the file is available.

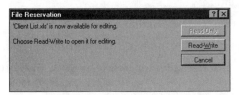

Figure 21-2: The File Reservation dialog box pops up with a new message when the file is available for editing.

Shared Workbooks

Excel also supports a feature known as *shared workbooks*. This feature enables multiple users to work on the same workbook simultaneously. Excel keeps track of the changes and provides appropriate prompts to handle conflict.

Appropriate workbooks for sharing

Although you can designate any workbook as a shared list, this really is not appropriate for all workbooks. The following are examples of workbooks that work well as shared lists:

✦ **Project tracking:** You may have a workbook that contains status information for projects. If multiple people are involved in the project, they can make changes and updates to the parts that are relevant.

✦ **Customer lists:** With such lists, changes usually occur infrequently, but records are added and deleted.

✦ **Consolidations:** You may create a budget workbook in which each department manager is responsible for his or her department's budget. Usually, each department's budget would be on a separate sheet, with one sheet serving as the consolidation sheet.

Limitations of shared workbooks

Shared workbooks have quite a few limitations. If you plan to designate a workbook as shared, be aware that you cannot perform any of the following actions while the workbook is being shared:

✦ Delete worksheets or chart sheets.

✦ Insert or delete a blocks of cells. However, you *can* insert or delete entire rows and columns.

✦ Merge cells.

✦ Define or apply conditional formats.

✦ Set up or change data validation restrictions and messages.

✦ Insert or change charts, pictures, drawings, objects, or hyperlinks.

✦ Assign or modify a password to protect individual worksheets or the entire workbook.

✦ Create or modify pivot tables, scenarios, outlines, or data tables.

✦ Insert automatic subtotals.

✦ Make changes to dialog boxes or menus.

✦ Write, change, view, record, or assign macros. However, you can record operations in a shared workbook into a macro that is stored in another workbook that isn't shared.

Designating a workbook as a shared workbook

To designate a workbook as a shared workbook, select Tools⇨Share Workbook. Excel responds with the dialog box that is shown in Figure 21-3. This dialog box has two tabs: Editing and Advanced. In the Editing tab, select the check box to allow changes by multiple users, and then click on OK. You are then prompted to save the workbook.

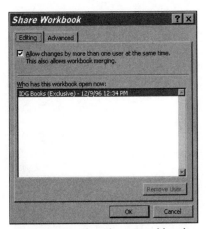

Figure 21-3: The Share Workbook dialog box lets you specify a workbook as a shared workbook.

When a shared workbook is open, the window's title bar displays [Shared]. If you no longer want other users to be able to use the workbook, remove the check mark from the Share Workbook dialog box and save the workbook.

Whenever you're working with a shared workbook, you can find out whether any other users are working on the workbook. Choose Tools⇨Share Workbook, and the Share Workbook dialog box lists the names of the other users who have the file open and the time that the workbook was opened.

Advanced settings

Excel provides a number of other features that are related to shared workbooks. Select Tools⇨Share Workbook and click on the Advanced tab to access these features (see Figure 21-4).

Tracking changes

Excel can keep track of the workbook's changes — something known as *change history*. When you create a shared workbook, the change history feature is turned on automatically. This lets you view information about previous (and perhaps conflicting) changes to the workbook. You can turn off change history by selecting the option labeled Don't keep change history. You can also specify the number of days for which the change history is tracked.

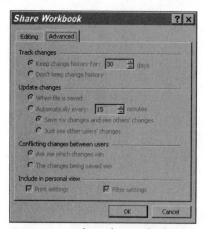

Figure 21-4: The Advanced tab of the Share Workbook dialog box.

Updating changes

While you're working on a shared workbook, you can use the standard File⇨Save command to update the workbook with your changes. The Update changes settings determine what happens when you save a shared workbook. These settings are described as follows:

✦ **When file is saved:** You receive updates from other users when you save your copy of the shared workbook.

✦ **Automatically every:** Lets you specify a time period for receiving updates from other users of the workbook. You can also specify whether your changes are saved or if you just receive the changes from other users.

Conflicting changes between users

As you may expect, multiple users working on the same file can result in some conflicts. For example, assume that you're working on a shared customer database workbook, and another user also has the workbook open. If you and the other user both make a change to the same cell, a conflict occurs. You can specify the manner in which the conflicts are resolved by selecting one of two options in the Advanced tab of the Share Workbook dialog box:

✦ **Ask me which changes win:** If this option is selected, Excel displays a dialog box to let you determine how to settle the conflict.

✦ **The changes being saved win:** If this option is selected, your changes always take precedence.

Include in personal view

The final section of the Advanced tab of the Share Workbook dialog box lets you specify settings that are specific to your view of the shared workbook. You can choose to use your own print settings and your own data-filtering settings. If these check boxes are not selected, you can't save your own print and filter settings.

Mailing and Routing Workbooks

Excel provides a few additional workgroup features. To use these features, your system must have one of the following items installed:

✦ Microsoft Exchange

✦ A mail system that is compatible with MAPI (Messaging Application Programming Interface)

✦ Lotus cc:Mail

✦ A mail system that is compatible with VIM (Vendor Independent Messaging)

The procedures vary depending on the mail system that you have installed. Because of this, discussions in the following sections are general in nature. For specific questions, consult your network administrator.

Mailing a workbook to others

Electronic mail, or e-mail, has seen enormous growth during the past few years, and its use is expected to skyrocket. Consequently, e-mail has become commonplace in many offices; this is not surprising, because it's an efficient means of communication. Unlike a telephone, e-mail doesn't rely on the recipient of the message being available when you want to send the message. Most modern networks have electronic-mail software installed.

In addition to sending messages by e-mail, you can send complete files — including Excel workbooks. Like a growing number of software applications, Excel is *mail-enabled,* which means that you don't have to leave Excel to send a worksheet to someone by e-mail.

To send a copy of your workbook to someone on your network, select File⇨Send To. This command creates an e-mail message with a copy of your workbook attached. It's important to understand that this command sends a *copy* of the workbook. If the recipient makes changes to the notebook, the changes do not appear in your copy of the workbook.

Routing a workbook to others

Excel lets you attach a routing slip to a workbook. This feature enables you to send a copy of a workbook to multiple members of a workgroup. For example, if you're responsible for your department's budget, you may need input from others in the department. You can set up the workbook and then route it to the others so that they can make their respective additions. When the routing is finished, the workbook is returned to you, complete with all the input from the others.

Types of routing

When you route a workbook, you have two options: sequential and simultaneous routing.

Sequential routing enables you to route the workbook sequentially to workgroup members. When the first recipient is finished, the workbook goes to the second recipient. When the second recipient is finished, the workbook goes to the third, and so on. When all recipients have received the workbook, it can be returned to you.

Simultaneous routing enables you to route the workbook to all recipients at once. In this case, you receive a copy of the workbook from each recipient (not just one copy). This type of routing is useful if you want to solicit comments from a group of coworkers, and you want the responses back quickly (you don't want to wait until a single worksheet makes the circuit).

Adding a routing slip

You add a routing slip to a workbook by choosing File⇨Send To. Click on Routing Recipient, and then click on on Address to select the recipients. Click on Route to route the workbook.

Summary

In this chapter, I present a basic overview of computer networks as they relate to Excel. I explain how the concept of a file reservation prevents two users from modifying a workbook simultaneously. Excel's new shared workbook feature, however, lets multiple users work on a single workbook at the same time. I conclude the chapter with a discussion of mailing and routing workbooks.

✦   ✦   ✦

Analyzing Data

T he chapters in Part IV deal with a key topic for most Excel users: data analysis. I give details on importing data, using worksheet tables and external databases, creating pivot tables, doing what-if analysis and goal seeking, understanding the Solver, and using the Analysis ToolPak add-in.

Importing Data from Other Sources

✦ ✦ ✦ ✦

In This Chapter

Sources for data that
you can use in Excel

Various file formats
that Excel can import

How to copy data
from another
application into Excel
using the Windows
Clipboard

How to import text
files into Excel

✦ ✦ ✦ ✦

When you get right down to it, Excel can be described as a tool that manipulates data — the numbers and text that you use in a worksheet. But before you can manipulate data, it must be present in a worksheet. This chapter describes a variety of data-importing techniques.

An Overview of Importing

There are six basic ways to get data into Excel:

- ✦ Enter the data manually by typing values and text into cells
- ✦ Generate data by using formulas or macros
- ✦ Use Query (or a pivot table) to import data from an external database

- ✦ Import data from an HTML document on the Internet
- ✦ Copy data from another application using the Windows Clipboard
- ✦ Import data from another (non-Excel) file

This chapter deals primarily with the last two methods: Clipboard copying and foreign-file importing.

Chapter 29 is somewhat related to this topic. It deals with linking to and from other applications and embedding objects. I discuss querying external databases in Chapter 24 and pivot tables in Chapter 25. Chapter 30 discusses how Excel works with the Internet.

A Few Words about Data

Data is a broad concept that means different things to different people. Data is basically raw information that can come in any number of forms. For example, data can be numbers, text, or a combination. Most of what you do in Excel involves manipulating data in one way or another.

As computers become more commonplace, data is increasingly available in machine-readable formats (otherwise known as *files*). Not too long ago, major data suppliers provided printed reports to their clients. Now, it's not uncommon to be offered a choice of formats: paper or disk.

Data that is stored in files can be in a wide variety of formats. Common file formats for distributing data include Lotus 1-2-3 files (WKS and WK1), dBASE files (DBF), and text files (which come in several varieties). Excel's file format is rather complex and the format tends to change with every new version of Excel. Consequently, the Excel file format is not widely used for the general distribution of data.

As an Excel user, it's important that you understand the types of data that you can access either directly or indirectly.

File Formats Supported by Excel

Rarely does a computer user work with only one application or not interact with people using different applications. Suppose that you're developing a spreadsheet model that uses data from last year's budget, which is stored in your company's mainframe. You can request a printout of the data, of course, and manually enter it into Excel. If the amount of data isn't too large, this route may be the most efficient one. But what if you have hundreds of entries to make? Your mainframe probably can't generate an Excel workbook file, but there's an excellent chance that it can send the report to a text file, which you can then import into an Excel worksheet. You can potentially save yourself several hours of work and virtually eliminate data-entry errors.

As you know, Excel's native file format is an XLS file. In addition, Microsoft included the capability to read other file formats directly. For example, you can open a file that was written by several other spreadsheet products such as Lotus 1-2-3. Table 22-1 lists all the file formats that Excel can read (excluding its own file types).

To open any of these files, choose File⭢Open and select the file type from the drop-down list labeled Files of type (see Figure 22-1). This causes only the files of the selected type to appear in the file list. If the file is a text file, Excel's Text Import Wizard starts up to help you interpret the file. I discuss the Text Import Wizard later in this chapter.

Table 22-1
File Formats Supported by Excel

File Type	Description
Text	Space delimited, tab delimited, and comma delimited
Lotus 1-2-3	Spreadsheet files generated by Lotus 1-2-3 for DOS Release 1.x, Release 2.x, Release 3.x, and 1-2-3 for Windows
Quattro Pro/DOS	Files generated by Novell's Quattro Pro for DOS spreadsheet
Microsoft Works 2.0	Files generated by Microsoft Works 2.0
dBASE	Database files in the DBF format
SYLK	Files generated by Microsoft's Multiplan spreadsheet
Data Interchange Format	Files generated by the VisiCalc spreadsheet
HTML	Files developed for the World Wide Web
Quattro Pro for Windows	Files generated by Novell's Quattro Pro for Windows spreadsheet

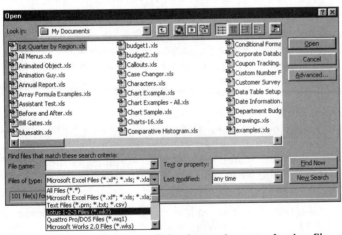

Figure 22-1: Use the Open dialog box to import a foreign file.

It's important to understand, however, that being able to read a file and translating it perfectly are two different matters. In some cases, reading a foreign file into Excel may exhibit one or more of the following problems:

✦ Some formulas aren't translated correctly.

✦ Unsupported functions aren't translated.

✦ Formatting is incorrect.

✦ Column widths are incorrect.

When you open a file that wasn't produced by Excel, examine it carefully to ensure that the data was retrieved correctly.

In the following sections, I discuss the various types of files that Excel can read. I discuss these by file type and list the file extensions that are normally associated with each file type.

If a colleague sends you a file that Excel can't open, don't give up. Simply request that the spreadsheet be saved in a format that Excel *can* read. For example, many applications can save files in 1-2-3 format, and most applications can export to a text file format.

Lotus 1-2-3 spreadsheet files

Lotus spreadsheets come in several flavors:

✦ **WKS files** are single-sheet files used by 1-2-3 Release 1.*x* for DOS. Excel can read and write these files. If you export a workbook to a WKS file, only the active worksheet is saved.

✦ **WK1 files** are single-sheet files used by 1-2-3 Release 2.*x* for DOS. The formatting for these files is stored in ALL files (produced by the Allways add-in) or FM1 files (produced by the WYSIWYG add-in). Excel can read and write all these files. When you save a file to the WK1 format, you can choose which (if any) type of formatting file to generate. If you export a workbook to a WK1 file, only the active worksheet is saved.

✦ **WK3 files** are (potentially) multisheet files generated by 1-2-3 Release 3.*x* for DOS, 1-2-3 Release 4.*x* for DOS, and 1-2-3 Release 1.*x* for Windows. The formatting for these files is stored in FM3 files (produced by the WYSIWYG add-in). Excel can read and write WK3 files with or without the accompanying FM3 file.

✦ **WK4 files** are (potentially) multisheet files generated by 1-2-3 Release 4.*x* for Windows and 1-2-3 Release 5.*x* for Windows (Lotus finally got its act together and eliminated the separate formatting file). Excel can read and write these files.

✦ **123 files** are (potentially) multisheet files generated by 1-2-3 97 for Windows (also known as Release 6). Excel can neither read nor write these files.

If you plan to import or export 1-2-3 files, I urge you to read the online help for general guidelines and specific types of information that may not be translated.

Excel evaluates some formulas differently from 1-2-3. To be assured of complete compatibility when working with an imported 1-2-3 file, choose Tools⇨Options, select the Transition tab, and check the box labeled Transition Formula Evaluation.

Quattro Pro spreadsheet files

Quattro Pro files exist in several versions:

✦ **WQ1 files** are single-sheet files generated by Quattro Pro for DOS Versions 1, 2, 3, and 4. Excel can read and write these files. If you export a workbook to a WQ1 file, only the active worksheet is saved.

✦ **WQ2 files** are (potentially) multisheet files generated by Quattro Pro for DOS Version 5. Excel can neither read nor write this file format.

✦ **WB1 files** are (potentially) multisheet files generated by Quattro Pro for Windows Versions 1 and 5 (there are no Versions 2 through 4). Excel can read (but not write) this file format.

✦ **WB2 files** are (potentially) multisheet files generated by Quattro Pro for Windows Version 6. Excel can neither read nor write this file format.

Database file formats

DBF files are single-table database files generated by dBASE and several other database programs. Excel can read and write DBF files up to and including dBASE 4.

If you have Microsoft Access installed on your system, you can take advantage of a new feature that converts a worksheet list into an Access database file. To use this feature, the Access Links add-in must be installed. Use the Data⇨Convert to Access command.

Excel can't read or write any other database file formats directly. If you install the Query add-in, however, you can use Query to access many other database file formats and then copy or link the data into an Excel worksheet. See Chapter 24 for details.

Text file formats

Text files simply contain data; there's no formatting. Several relatively standard text file formats exist, but there are no standard file extensions.

✦ Each line in *tab-delimited files* consists of fields that are separated by tabs. Excel can read these files, converting each line to a row and each field to a column. Excel also can write these files, using TXT as the default extension.

✦ Each line in *comma-separated files* consists of fields that are separated by commas. Sometimes text is in quotation marks. Excel can read these files, converting each line to a row and each field to a column. Excel can also write these files, using CSV as the default extension.

✦ Each line in *space-delimited filess* consists of fields that are separated by spaces. Excel can read these files, converting each line to a row and each field to a column. Excel also can write these files, using PRN as the default extension.

If you want your exported text file to use a different extension, specify the complete filename and extension in quotation marks. For example, saving a workbook in comma-separated format normally uses the CSV extension. If you want your file to be named output.txt (with a TXT extension), enter **"output.txt"** in the File name box in the Save As dialog box.

When you attempt to load a text file into Excel, the Text Import Wizard kicks in to help you specify how you want the file retrieved. I discuss this in detail later in this chapter.

HTML files

Excel 97 Excel 97 can read (and save) files in HTML (HyperText Markup Language) format. This is the file format that is used on the World Wide Web. Don't expect the imported file to look anything like what the document looks like in a Web browser. For example, graphics are not imported, and the formatting probably doesn't translate well. However, Excel does import the hyperlinks.

Other file formats

✦ DIF (Data Interchange Format) file format was used by VisiCalc. Excel can read and write these files.

✦ SYLK (Symbolic Link) file format was used by MultiPlan. Excel can read and write these files.

These files are rarely encountered. I haven't seen a DIF file in ages, and I've never seen a SYLK file.

Using the Clipboard to Get Data

Another method of getting data into your worksheet is to use the Windows Clipboard. The process involves selecting data from another application and copying the data to the Clipboard. Then you reactivate Excel and paste the information to the worksheet. The exact results that you get can vary quite a bit, depending on the type of data that was copied and the Clipboard formats that it supports. Obviously, you must have a copy of the other application installed on your system.

About the Clipboard

As you probably know, whenever Windows is running, you have access to the Windows Clipboard — an area of your computer's memory that acts as a shared holding area for information that has been cut or copied from an application. The Clipboard works behind the scenes, and you usually aren't aware of it. Whenever you choose Edit⇨Copy or Edit⇨Cut, the selected data is placed on the Clipboard. Like most other Windows applications, Excel can then access the Clipboard data by way of the Edit⇨Paste command.

Data that is pasted from the Clipboard remains on the Clipboard after pasting, so you can use it multiple times. But because the Clipboard can hold only one item at a time, when you copy or cut something else, the old Clipboard contents are replaced.

Windows includes an application called Clipboard Viewer, which displays the contents of the Clipboard. This application may not be installed on your system. If not, you must run the Windows Setup program to install it. You can run Clipboard Viewer to look at what (if anything) is currently on the Clipboard. Figure 22-2 shows the Clipboard Viewer displaying information that was copied from Excel.

Figure 22-2: The Windows Clipboard Viewer application displays the current contents of the Clipboard.

When you copy or cut data to the Clipboard, the source application places one or more formats along with it. Different applications support different Clipboard formats. When you paste Clipboard data into another application, the destination application determines which format it can handle and typically selects the format that either provides the most information or is appropriate for where it is being pasted. In some cases, you can use the Display command in the Clipboard Viewer application to view the Clipboard data in a different format. If you copy a range of cells to the Clipboard, for example, you can display it as a picture, bitmap, palette (the color palette only), text, OEM text, or a DIB bitmap.

The Clipboard format that you select in the Clipboard Viewer doesn't affect how the data is copied. In some cases, however, you can use Excel's Edit⇨Paste Special command to select alternate methods of pasting the data.

Copying data from another Windows application

Copying data from one Windows application to another is quite straightforward. The application that you're copying from is considered the *source application,* and the application that you're copying to is the *destination application.* Use the following steps to copy data from one application into another:

1. Activate the source document window that contains the information you want to copy.

2. Select the information that you want to copy by using the mouse or the keyboard. If Excel is the source application, this information can be a cell, range, chart, or drawing object.

3. Select Edit⇨Copy (or any available shortcut). A copy of the information is sent to the Windows Clipboard.

4. Activate the destination application. If it isn't open, you can start it without affecting the contents of the Clipboard.

5. Move to the appropriate position in the destination application (where you want to paste).

6. Select Edit⇨Paste from the menu in the destination application. If the Clipboard contents aren't appropriate for pasting, the Paste command is grayed (not available).

In the preceding Step 3, you also can select Edit⇨Cut from the source application menu. This step erases the selection from the source application after it's placed on the Clipboard.

Many Windows applications use a common keyboard convention for the Clipboard commands. Generally, this technique is a bit faster than using the menus because these keys are adjacent to each other. The shortcut keys and their equivalents are as follows:

Ctrl+C	Edit⇨Copy
Ctrl+X	Edit⇨Cut
Ctrl+V	Edit⇨Paste

It's important to understand that Windows applications vary in how they respond to data that is pasted from the Clipboard. If the Edit⇨Paste command isn't available (it is grayed on the menu) in the destination application, the application can't accept the information from the Clipboard. If you copy a table from Word for Windows to Excel, the data translates into cells perfectly — complete with formatting. Copying data from other applications may not work as well. For example, you may lose the formatting, or you may end up with all the data in a single column rather than in separate columns. As I discuss later in this chapter, you can use the Convert Text to Columns Wizard to convert this data into columns.

If you plan to do a great deal of copying and pasting, the best advice is to experiment until you understand how the two applications can handle each other's data.

Copying data from a non-Windows application

You also can use the Windows Clipboard with non-Windows applications running in a DOS window. As you may know, you can run non-Windows programs from Windows. You can do this in a window or in full-screen mode (the application takes over the complete screen).

When you're running a non-Windows application in Windows, you can press Alt+Print Screen to copy the entire screen to the Clipboard. The screen contents can then be pasted into a Windows application (including Excel). To copy only part of the screen, you must run the application in a window: press Alt+Enter to toggle between full-screen mode and windowed mode. You can then click on the Control menu, choose Edit⇨Mark, and select text from the window. This window may or may not have a toolbar displayed. If not, right-click on the title bar and select the Toolbar option.

1. Click on the Mark tool, and select the text to be copied.

2. Click on the Copy tool to copy the selected text to the Clipboard.

3. Activate Excel.

4. Select Edit⇨Paste to copy the Clipboard data into your worksheet.

Figure 22-3 shows Quattro Pro running in a DOS window. Some text is selected.

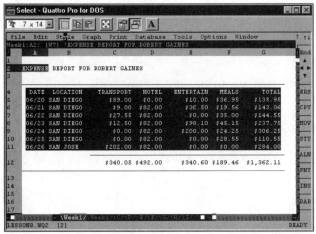

Figure 22-3: Copying data from Quattro Pro for DOS.

If you use this technique and copy to Excel, the information is pasted as text in a single column. In other words, even if the copied information is in the form of neatly formatted columns, it's all pasted into a single column in Excel. But don't fret — you can use Excel's Convert Text to Columns Wizard to convert this data into columns.

You're limited to copying one screen of information at a time. In other words, you can't scroll the DOS application while you're selecting text.

Importing Text Files

Text files (sometimes referred to as ASCII files) are usually considered to be the lowest-common-denominator file type. Such files contain only data, with no formatting. Consequently, most applications are equipped to read and write text files. So, if all else fails, you can probably use a text file to transfer data between two applications that don't support a common file format. Because text files are so commonly used, I devote this entire section to discussing them and explaining how to use Excel's Text Import Wizard.

About text files

It's helpful to think of some text files in terms of a database table. Each line in the text file corresponds to a database record, and each record consists of a number of fields. In Excel, each line (or record) is imported to a separate row, and each field goes into a separate column. Text files come in two types: delimited and nondelimited.

Text files consist of plain text and end-of-line markers. *Delimited* text files use a special character to separate the fields on each line. This character is usually a comma, a space, or a tab (but other delimiters also are used). In addition, text is sometimes (but not always) enclosed in quotation marks.

Nondelimited files don't have a special field separator. Often, however, the fields are a fixed length, which makes it easy to break each line of text into separate columns.

Depending on the font that is used, the fields may not appear to line up, although they actually do. This is because most fonts are not fixed-width fonts. In other words, each character doesn't use the same amount of horizontal space. For best results, it's wise to switch to a fixed-width font when working with text files. Courier New is a good choice; this is the font that Excel uses in its Text Import Wizard dialog box. Figure 22-4 shows the same text displayed in Arial and Courier New fonts.

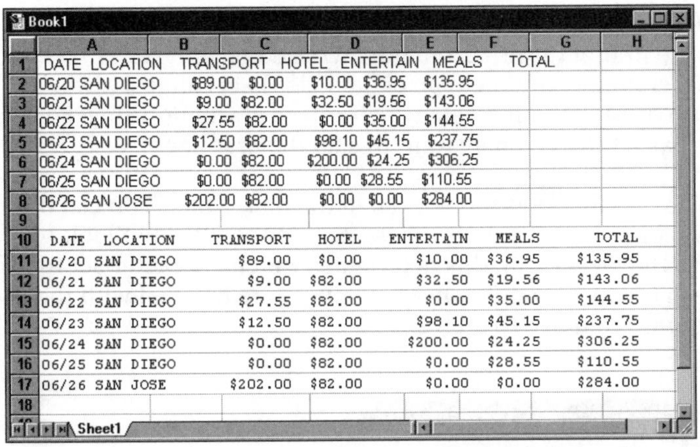

Figure 22-4: The font that is used may obscure columns in a text file.

Excel is quite versatile when it comes to importing text files. If each line of the text file is identically laid out, importing is usually problem-free. But if the line contains mixed information, it may require some additional work before the data is usable. For example, some text files are produced by sending a printed report to a disk file rather than to the printer. These reports often have extra information, such as page headers and footers, titles, summary lines, and so on.

Using the Text Import Wizard

To import a text file into Excel, choose File⇨Open and select Text Files in the drop-down list labeled Files of type. The Open dialog box then displays text files that have an extension of PRN, TXT, or CSV. If the text file that you're importing doesn't have one of these extensions, select the All Files option. Or, you can enter the filename directly in the File name box if you know the file's name.

Excel examines the file. If the file is a tab-delimited or a comma-separated value file, Excel often imports it with no further intervention on your part. If the file can be imported in several different ways, however — or if there are no delimiters — Excel displays its Text Import Wizard. This wizard is a series of interactive dialog boxes in which you specify the information that is needed to break the lines of the text file into columns. You can truly appreciate this time-saving feature only if you have struggled with old data-parsing commands that are used in other spreadsheet programs (and older versions of Excel).

To bypass the Text Import Wizard, press Shift when you click on OK in the Open dialog box. Excel then makes its best guess as to how to import the file.

Text Import Wizard: Step 1 of 3

Figure 22-5 shows the first of three Text Import Wizard dialog boxes. In the Original Data Type section, verify the type of data file (Excel almost always guesses correctly). You also can indicate which row to start importing. For example, if the file has a title, you may want to skip the first line.

Notice that the file is previewed at the bottom of the dialog box. You can use the scroll bars to view more of the file. If the characters in the file don't look right, you may need to change the File Origin; this determines which character set to use (in many cases, it doesn't make any difference). When you're finished with this step, click on the Next button to move to Step 2.

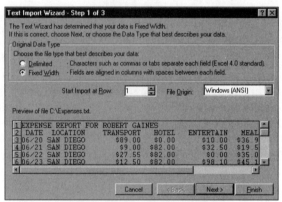

Figure 22-5: Step 1 of the Test Import Wizard.

Text Import Wizard: Step 2 of 3

The dialog box for Step 2 of the Text Import Wizard varies, depending on your choice in the first step. If you selected Delimited, you get the dialog box shown in Figure 22-6. You can specify the type of delimiter, the text qualifier, and whether to treat consecutive delimiters as a single delimiter (this skips empty columns). The Data Preview section displays vertical lines to indicate how the lines are broken up. The preview changes as you make choices in the dialog box.

If you selected fixed width, you get the dialog box shown in Figure 22-7. At this point, Excel attempts to identify the column breaks and displays vertical break lines to represent how the lines are to be broken apart into columns. If Excel guesses wrong, you can move the lines, insert new ones, or delete lines that Excel proposes. Instructions are provided in the dialog box.

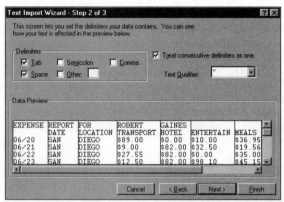

Figure 22-6: Step 2 of the Text Import Wizard (for delimited files).

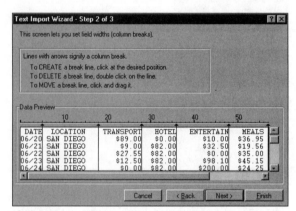

Figure 22-7: Step 2 of the Text Import Wizard (for fixed-width files).

If you're importing a print image file that includes page headers, you can ignore them when you specify the column indicators. Rather, base the columns on the data. When the file is imported, you can then delete the rows that contain the page headers.

When you're satisfied with how the column breaks look, click on Next to move to the final step. Or, you can click on Back to return to Step 1 and change the file type.

Text Import Wizard: Step 3 of 3

Figure 22-8 shows the last of the three Text Import Wizard dialog boxes. In this dialog box, you can select individual columns and specify the formatting to apply (General, Text, or Data). You also can specify columns to skip — they aren't imported. When you're satisfied with the results, click on Finish. Excel creates a new workbook (with one sheet) to hold the imported data.

If the results aren't what you expect, close the workbook and try again (text importing often involves trial and error). Don't forget that you can scroll the Data Preview window to make sure that all the data is converted properly. With some files, however, it's impossible to import all the data properly. In such a case, you may want to import the file as a single column of text and then break lines into columns selectively. The procedure for doing this is discussed in the next section.

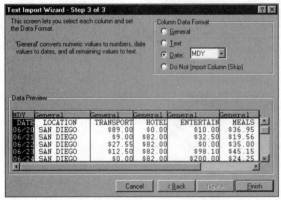

Figure 22-8: Step 3 of the Text Import Wizard.

Using the Text to Columns Wizard

Excel can parse text that is stored in a column. Start by selecting the text (in a single column). Then choose Data⇨Text to Columns. Excel displays the first of three Text to Columns Wizard dialog boxes. These dialog boxes are identical to those used for the Text Import Wizard, except that the title bar text is different.

Unfortunately, you can't use the Data⇨Text to Columns command on a multiple selection; this would be quite handy for parsing imported files with several different layouts. Even worse, you can't use the Edit⇨Repeat command to repeat the Text to Columns command.

Summary

In this chapter, I identify the various sources for getting data into Excel: entering data manually, generating data from formulas or macros, using Query or pivot tables, copying data using the Clipboard, and importing foreign files (including text files) into Excel. The chapter focuses on Clipboard operations and file importing.

✦   ✦   ✦

Working with Lists

Research conducted by Microsoft indicates that one of the most frequent uses for Excel is to manage lists, or *worksheet databases.* This chapter covers list management and demonstrates useful techniques that involve lists.

What Is a List?

A list is essentially an organized collection of information. More specifically, a list consists of a row of headers (descriptive text), followed by additional rows of data, which can be values or text. You may recognize this as a database table — which is exactly what it is. Beginning with Excel 5, Microsoft uses the term *list* to refer to a database stored in a worksheet and the term *database* to refer to a table of information stored in an external file. To avoid confusion, I adhere to Microsoft's terminology.

 **Cross Reference** I cover external database files in Chapter 24.

Figure 23-1 shows an example of a list in a worksheet. This particular list has its headers in row 1 and has 10 rows of data. The list occupies four columns. Notice that the data consists of several different types: text, values, and dates. Column C contains a formula that calculates the monthly salary from the value in column B.

People often refer to the columns in a list as *fields* and to the rows as *records.* Using this terminology, the list shown in the figure has five fields (Name, Annual Salary, Monthly Salary, Location, and Date Hired) and ten records.

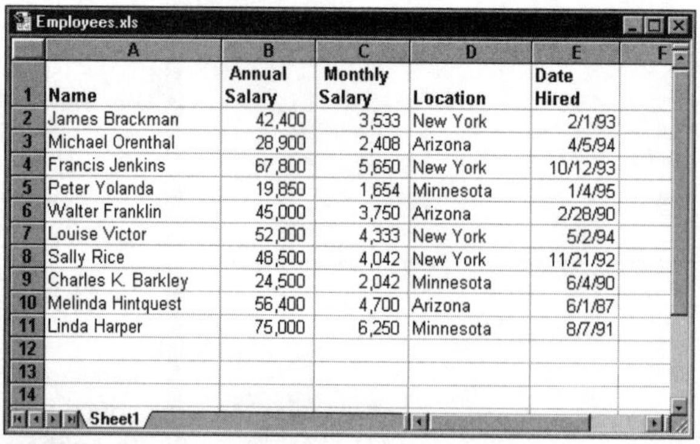

	A	B	C	D	E	F
1	Name	Annual Salary	Monthly Salary	Location	Date Hired	
2	James Brackman	42,400	3,533	New York	2/1/93	
3	Michael Orenthal	28,900	2,408	Arizona	4/5/94	
4	Francis Jenkins	67,800	5,650	New York	10/12/93	
5	Peter Yolanda	19,850	1,654	Minnesota	1/4/95	
6	Walter Franklin	45,000	3,750	Arizona	2/28/90	
7	Louise Victor	52,000	4,333	New York	5/2/94	
8	Sally Rice	48,500	4,042	New York	11/21/92	
9	Charles K. Barkley	24,500	2,042	Minnesota	6/4/90	
10	Melinda Hintquest	56,400	4,700	Arizona	6/1/87	
11	Linda Harper	75,000	6,250	Minnesota	8/7/91	
12						
13						
14						

Figure 23-1: An example of a list.

The size of the lists that you develop in Excel is limited by the size of a single worksheet. In other words, a list can have no more than 256 fields and can consist of no more than 65,535 records (one row contains the field names). A list of this size would require a great deal of memory and even then may not be possible. At the other extreme, a list can consist of a single cell — not very useful, but it's still considered a list.

Excel 97

In previous versions of Excel, a list was limited to 16,383 records.

What Can You Do with a List?

Excel provides several tools to help you manage and manipulate lists. Consequently, people use lists for a wide variety of purposes. For some users, a list is simply a method to keep track of information (for example, customer lists); others use lists to store data that ultimately is to appear in a report. The following are common list operations:

- ✦ Enter data into the list
- ✦ Filter the list to display only the rows that meet a certain criteria
- ✦ Sort the list
- ✦ Insert formulas to calculate subtotals
- ✦ Create formulas to calculate results on the list filtered by certain criteria
- ✦ Create a summary table of the data in the list (this is done using a pivot table; see Chapter 25).

With the exception of the last item, these operations are covered in this chapter.

Designing a List

Although Excel is quite accommodating when it comes to the information that is stored in a list, it pays off to give some initial thought as to how you want to organize your information. The following are some guidelines to keep in mind when creating lists:

✦ Insert descriptive labels (one for each column) in the first row of the list. This is the header row. If the labels are lengthy, consider using the word-wrap format so that you don't have to widen the columns.

✦ Each column should contain the same type of information. For example, don't mix dates and text in a single column.

✦ You can use formulas that perform calculations on other fields in the same record. If you use formulas that refer to cells outside the list, make these absolute references; otherwise, you get unexpected results when you sort the list.

✦ Don't use any empty rows within the list. For list operations, Excel determines the list boundaries automatically, and an empty row signals the end of the list.

✦ For best results, try to keep the list on a worksheet by itself. If this isn't possible, place other information above or below the list. In other words, don't use the cells to the left or the right of a list.

✦ Select <u>W</u>indow⇨<u>F</u>reeze Panes to make sure that the headings are visible when the list is scrolled.

✦ You can preformat entire columns to ensure that the data has the same format. For example, if a column contains dates, format the entire column with the desired date format.

One of the most appealing aspects of spreadsheets is that you can change the layout relatively easily. This, of course, also applies to lists. For example, you may create a list and then decide that it needs another column (field). No problem. Just insert a new column, give it a field name, and your list is expanded. If you've ever used a database management program, you can appreciate how easy this is.

Entering Data into a List

Entering data into a list can be done in three ways:

✦ Manually, using all standard data entry techniques

✦ By importing it or copying it from another file

✦ By using a dialog box

There's really nothing special about entering data into a list. You just navigate through the worksheet and enter the data into the appropriate cells.

Excel has two features that assist with repetitive data entry:

✦ **AutoComplete.** When you begin to type in a cell, Excel scans up and down the column to see whether it recognizes what you're typing. If it finds a match, Excel fills in the rest of the text automatically. Press Enter to make the entry. You can turn this feature on or off in the Edit panel of the Options dialog box.

✦ **Pick Lists.** You can right-click on a cell and select Pick from list from the shortcut menu (see Figure 23-2). Excel displays a list box that shows all entries in the column. Click on the one that you want and it is then entered into the cell (no typing is required).

If you prefer to use a dialog box for your data entry, Excel accommodates you. To bring up a data entry dialog box, move the cell pointer anywhere within the list and choose Data➪Form. Excel determines the extent of your list and displays a dialog box showing each field in the list. Figure 23-3 depicts an example of such a dialog box. Fields that have a formula don't have an edit box.

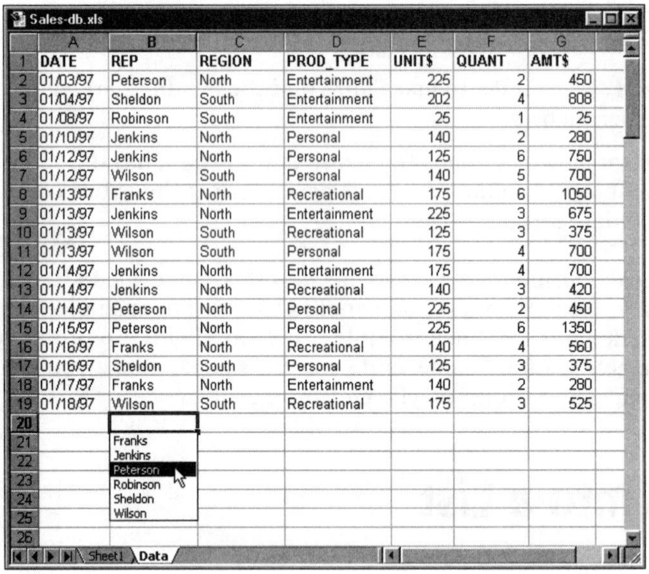

	A	B	C	D	E	F	G
1	DATE	REP	REGION	PROD_TYPE	UNIT$	QUANT	AMT$
2	01/03/97	Peterson	North	Entertainment	225	2	450
3	01/04/97	Sheldon	South	Entertainment	202	4	808
4	01/08/97	Robinson	South	Entertainment	25	1	25
5	01/10/97	Jenkins	North	Personal	140	2	280
6	01/12/97	Jenkins	North	Personal	125	6	750
7	01/12/97	Wilson	South	Personal	140	5	700
8	01/13/97	Franks	North	Recreational	175	6	1050
9	01/13/97	Jenkins	North	Entertainment	225	3	675
10	01/13/97	Wilson	South	Recreational	125	3	375
11	01/13/97	Wilson	South	Personal	175	4	700
12	01/14/97	Jenkins	North	Entertainment	175	4	700
13	01/14/97	Jenkins	North	Recreational	140	3	420
14	01/14/97	Peterson	North	Personal	225	2	450
15	01/15/97	Peterson	North	Personal	225	6	1350
16	01/16/97	Franks	North	Recreational	140	4	560
17	01/16/97	Sheldon	South	Personal	125	3	375
18	01/17/97	Franks	North	Entertainment	140	2	280
19	01/18/97	Wilson	South	Recreational	175	3	525

Figure 23-2: Choosing the Pick from list command on the shortcut menu gives you a list of all items in the current column.

Figure 23-3: The Data⇨Form command gives you a handy data entry dialog box.

Note   If the number of fields exceeds the limit of your display, the dialog box contains two columns of field names. If your list consists of more than 32 fields, however, the Data⇨Form command doesn't work. You must forgo this method of data entry and enter the information directly into the cells.

Entering data with the data form dialog box

When the data form dialog box appears, the first record in the list is displayed. Notice the indicator in the upper-right corner of the dialog box; this indicator tells you which record is selected and the total number of records in the list.

To enter a new record, click on the New button to clear the fields. Then you can enter the new information into the appropriate fields. Use Tab or Shift+Tab to move among the fields. When you click on New (or Close), the data that you entered is appended to the bottom of the list. You also can press Enter, which is equivalent to clicking on the New button. If the list contains any formulas, these are also entered into the new record in the list for you automatically.

Tip   If your list is named Database, Excel automatically extends the range definition to include the new row(s) that you add to the list using the data form dialog box. Note that this works only if the list has the name Database; any other name doesn't work.

Other uses for the data form dialog box

You can use the data form dialog box for more than just data entry. You can edit existing data in the list, view data one record at a time, delete records, and display records that meet certain criteria.

The dialog box contains a number of additional buttons, which are described as follows:

✦ **Delete:** Deletes the displayed record.

✦ **Restore:** Restores any information that you edited. You must click on this button before you click on the New button.

✦ **Find Prev:** Displays the previous record in the list. If you entered a criterion, this button displays the previous record that matches the criterion.

✦ **Find Next:** Displays the next record in the list. If you entered a criterion, this button displays the next record that matches the criterion.

✦ **Criteria:** Clears the fields and lets you enter a criterion upon which to search for records. For example, to locate records that have a salary greater than $50,000, enter **>50000** into the Salary field. Then you can use the Find Next and Find Prev buttons to display the qualifying records.

✦ **Close:** Closes the dialog box (and enters the data that you were entering, if any).

Using Microsoft Access Forms for data entry

If you have Microsoft Access installed on your system, you can use its form creation tools to develop a data entry form for an Excel worksheet. This feature uses the Access Links add-in, which must be loaded. When the add-in is loaded, you have a new command: Data⇨Access Form.

Choosing this command starts Access (if it's not already running) and begins its Form Wizard. Use this tool to create the data entry form. You can then use this form to add data to your Excel worksheet. The worksheet contains a button with the text View Access Form. Click on this button to use the form. Figure 23-4 shows an Access form being used to enter data into an Excel worksheet.

Filtering a List

Filtering a list is the process of hiding all rows in the list except those that meet some criteria that you specify. For example, if you have a list of customers, you can filter the list to show only those who live in New Jersey. Filtering is a common (and very useful) technique. Excel provides two ways to filter a list:

✦ AutoFilter, for simple filtering criteria

✦ Advance Filter, for more complex filtering

I discuss both of these options in the following sections.

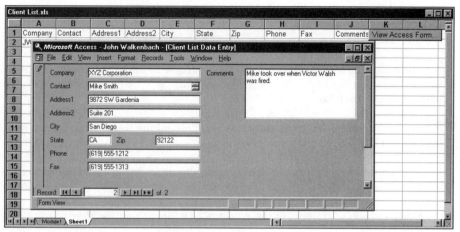

Figure 23-4: This form, developed in Microsoft Access, is being used to enter data into an Excel worksheet.

Autofiltering

To autofilter a list, start by moving the cell pointer anywhere within the list. Then choose Data⇨Filter⇨AutoFilter. Excel analyzes your list and adds drop-down arrows to the field names in the header row, as shown in Figure 23-5.

	A	B	C	D	E	F
	Name	Annual Salary	Monthly Salary	Location	Date Hired	
2	James Brackman	42,400	3,533	New York	2/1/93	
3	Michael Orenthal	28,900	2,408	Arizona	4/5/94	
4	Francis Jenkins	67,800	5,650	New York	10/12/93	
5	Peter Yolanda	19,850	1,654	Minnesota	1/4/95	
6	Walter Franklin	45,000	3,750	Arizona	2/28/90	
7	Louise Victor	52,000	4,333	New York	5/2/94	
8	Sally Rice	48,500	4,042	New York	11/21/92	
9	Charles K. Barkley	24,500	2,042	Minnesota	6/4/90	
10	Melinda Hintquest	56,400	4,700	Arizona	6/1/87	
11	Linda Harper	75,000	6,250	Minnesota	8/7/91	
12	John Daily	87,500	7,292	New York	1/5/93	
13	Elizabeth Becker	89,500	7,458	Arizona	9/29/87	

Figure 23-5: The Data⇨Filter⇨AutoFilter command adds drop-down arrows to the field names in the header row.

When you click on the arrow in one of these drop-down lists, the list expands to show the unique items in that column. Select an item, and Excel hides all rows except those that include the selected item. In other words, the list is filtered by the item that you selected.

After you filter the list, the status bar displays a message that tells you how many rows qualified. In addition, the drop-down arrow changes color to remind you that the list is filtered by a value in that column.

Autofiltering has a limit. Only the first 999 unique items in the column appear in the drop-down list. If your list exceeds this limit, you can use advanced filtering, which is described later.

Excel 97 In previous versions of Excel, only the first 250 unique items were shown in the drop-down list.

Besides showing every item in the column, the drop-down list includes five other items:

✦ **All:** Displays all items in the column. Use this to remove filtering for a column.

✦ **Top 10:** Filters to display the "top 10" items in the list; this is discussed later.

✦ **Custom:** Lets you filter the list by multiple items; this is discussed later.

✦ **Blanks:** Filters the list by showing rows that contain blanks in this column.

✦ **NonBlanks:** Filters the list by showing rows that contain non-blanks in this column.

To display the entire list again, click on the arrow and choose All — the first item in the drop-down list. Or, you can select Data⇨Filter⇨Show All.

To move out of Autofilter mode and remove the drop-down arrows from the field names, choose Data⇨Filter⇨AutoFilter again. This removes the check mark from the AutoFilter menu item and restores the list to its normal state.

Caution If you have any formulas that refer to data in a filtered list, be aware that the formulas don't adjust to use only the visible cells. For example, if a cell contains a formula that sums values in column C, the formula continues to show the sum for *all* the values in column C — not just those in the visible rows. The solution to this is to use database functions, which I describe later in this chapter.

Multicolumn autofiltering

Sometimes you may need to filter a list by values in more than one column. Figure 23-6 shows a list comprised of several fields.

Assume that you want to see the records that show modems sold in February. In other words, you want to filter out all records except those in which the Month field is *Feb* and the Product field is *Modem*.

First, get into Autofilter mode. Then click on the drop-down arrow in the Month field and select *Feb*. This filters the list to show only records with *Feb* in the Month field. Then click on the drop-down arrow in the Product field and select *Modem*. This filters the filtered list — in other words, the list is filtered by values in two columns. Figure 23-7 shows the result.

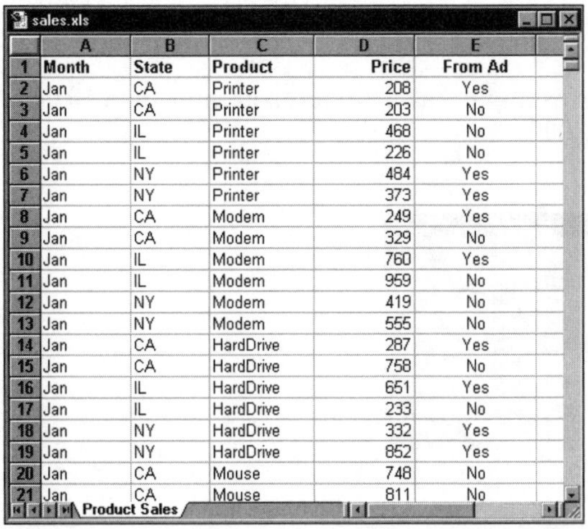

sales.xls

	A	B	C	D	E
1	Month	State	Product	Price	From Ad
2	Jan	CA	Printer	208	Yes
3	Jan	CA	Printer	203	No
4	Jan	IL	Printer	468	No
5	Jan	IL	Printer	226	No
6	Jan	NY	Printer	484	Yes
7	Jan	NY	Printer	373	Yes
8	Jan	CA	Modem	249	Yes
9	Jan	CA	Modem	329	No
10	Jan	IL	Modem	760	Yes
11	Jan	IL	Modem	959	No
12	Jan	NY	Modem	419	No
13	Jan	NY	Modem	555	No
14	Jan	CA	HardDrive	287	Yes
15	Jan	CA	HardDrive	758	No
16	Jan	IL	HardDrive	651	Yes
17	Jan	IL	HardDrive	233	No
18	Jan	NY	HardDrive	332	Yes
19	Jan	NY	HardDrive	852	Yes
20	Jan	CA	Mouse	748	No
21	Jan	CA	Mouse	811	No

Product Sales

Figure 23-6: This list is to be filtered by multiple columns.

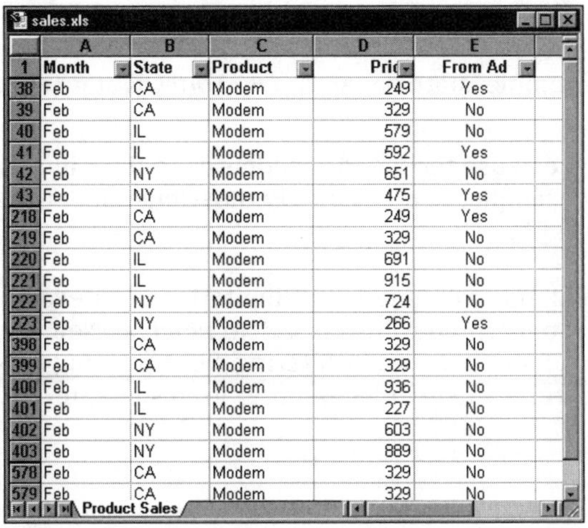

sales.xls

	A	B	C	D	E
1	Month	State	Product	Pric	From Ad
38	Feb	CA	Modem	249	Yes
39	Feb	CA	Modem	329	No
40	Feb	IL	Modem	579	No
41	Feb	IL	Modem	592	Yes
42	Feb	NY	Modem	651	No
43	Feb	NY	Modem	475	Yes
218	Feb	CA	Modem	249	Yes
219	Feb	CA	Modem	329	No
220	Feb	IL	Modem	691	No
221	Feb	IL	Modem	915	No
222	Feb	NY	Modem	724	No
223	Feb	NY	Modem	266	Yes
398	Feb	CA	Modem	329	No
399	Feb	CA	Modem	329	No
400	Feb	IL	Modem	936	No
401	Feb	IL	Modem	227	No
402	Feb	NY	Modem	603	No
403	Feb	NY	Modem	889	No
578	Feb	CA	Modem	329	No
579	Feb	CA	Modem	329	No

Product Sales

Figure 23-7: This list is filtered by values in two columns.

You can filter a list by any number of columns. The drop-down arrows in the columns that have a filter applied are a different color.

Custom autofiltering

Usually, autofiltering involves selecting a single value for one or more columns. If you choose the Custom option in a drop-down list, you gain a bit more flexibility in filtering the list. Selecting the Custom option displays a dialog box like the one shown in Figure 23-8. The Custom AutoFilter dialog box lets you filter in several ways:

✦ **Values above or below a specified value.** For example, sales amounts greater than 10,000.

✦ **Values within a range.** For example, sales amounts greater than 10,000 AND sales amounts less than 50,000.

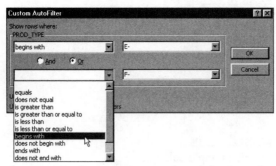

Figure 23-8: The Custom AutoFilter dialog box gives you more filtering options.

✦ **Two discrete values.** For example, state equal to *New York* OR state equal to *New Jersey*.

✦ **Approximate matches.** You can use the * and ? wildcards to filter in a number of other ways. For example, to display only those customers whose last name begins with *B,* use **B***.

Custom autofiltering can be useful, but it definitely has limitations. For example, if you want to filter the list to show only three values in a field (such as New York or New Jersey or Connecticut), you can't do it by autofiltering. Such filtering tasks require the advanced filtering feature, which I discuss later in this chapter.

Top 10 autofiltering

Sometimes you may want to use a filter on numerical fields to show only the highest or lowest values in the list. For example, if you have a list of employees, you may want to identify the 12 employees with the longest tenure. You could use the custom autofilter option, but then you must supply a cutoff date (which you may not know). The solution is to use Top 10 autofiltering.

Top 10 autofiltering is a generic term; it doesn't limit you to the top *10* items. In fact, it doesn't even limit you to the *top* items. When you choose the Top 10 option from a drop-down list, you get the dialog box that is shown in Figure 23-9.

Figure 23-9: The Top 10 AutoFilter gives you more autofilter options.

You can choose either Top or Bottom and specify any number. For example, if you want to see the 12 employees with the longest tenure, choose Bottom and 12. This filters the list and shows the 12 rows with the smallest values in the Date Hired field. You also can choose Percent or Value in this dialog box. For example, you can filter the list to show the Bottom 5 percent of the records.

Charting filtered list data

You can create some interesting multipurpose charts that use data in a filtered list. The technique is useful because only the visible data appears in the chart. When you change the autofilter criteria, the chart updates itself to show only the visible cells.

Note   For this technique to work, select the chart and make sure that the Plot Visible Cells Only option is enabled in the Options dialog box (Chart panel).

Figure 23-10 shows an example of a chart created with an unfiltered list. It shows sales data for three months for each of four sales regions.

Figure 23-11 shows the same chart, but the list was filtered to show only the North sales region. You can apply other filters, and the chart updates automatically. This technique lets a single chart show several different views of the data.

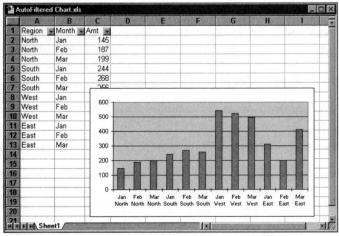

Figure 23-10: This chart was created from an unfiltered list.

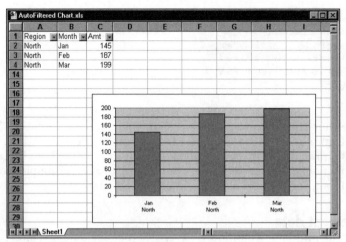

Figure 23-11: The chart from the previous figure, after filtering the list.

Advanced filtering

In many cases, autofiltering does the job. But if you run up against its limitations, you need to use advanced filtering. Advanced filtering is much more flexible than autofiltering, but it takes a bit of up-front work to use it. Advanced filtering provides you with the following capabilities:

✦ You can specify more complex filtering criteria.

✦ You can specify computed filtering criteria.

✦ You can extract a copy of the rows that meet the criteria to another location.

Setting up a criteria range

Before you can use the advanced filtering feature, you must set up a *criteria range*. A criteria range is a designated range on a worksheet that conforms to certain requirements. The criteria range holds the information that Excel uses to filter the list. It must conform to the following specifications:

✦ It consists of at least two rows, and the first row must contain some or all field names from the list.

✦ The other rows consist of your filtering criteria.

Although you can put the criteria range anywhere in the worksheet, it's a good idea not to put it in rows that are used by the list. Because some of these rows are hidden when the list is filtered, you may find that your criteria range is no longer visible after the filtering takes place. Therefore, you should generally place the criteria range above or below the list.

Figure 23-12 shows a criteria range, located in A1:D2, above the list that it uses. Notice that not all field names appear in the criteria range. Fields that aren't used in the selection criteria need not appear in the criteria range.

In this example, the criteria range has only one row of criteria. The fields in each row of the criteria range (except for the header row) are joined with an AND operator. Therefore, the filtered list shows rows in which the Month column equals *January* AND the Type field is *New*. In other words, the list displays only sales to new customers made in January.

To perform the filtering, choose Data⇨Filter⇨Advanced filter. Excel displays the dialog box that is shown in Figure 23-13. Specify the list range and the criteria range, and make sure that the option labeled Filter the List in-place is selected. Click on OK, and the list is filtered by the criteria that you specified.

	A	B	C	D	E	F	G
1	**Month**	**SalesRep**	**Type**	**TotalSale**			
2	January		New				
3							
4							
5							
6	**Month**	**SalesRep**	**Type**	**UnitCost**	**Quantity**	**TotalSale**	
7	March	Wilson	New	175	5	875	
8	March	Wilson	New	140	3	420	
9	February	Franks	Existing	225	1	225	
10	March	Wilson	New	125	5	625	
11	January	Peterson	Existing	225	2	450	
12	March	Sheldon	New	140	2	280	
13	February	Peterson	Existing	225	6	1350	
14	March	Jenkins	Existing	140	2	280	
15	February	Sheldon	New	225	4	900	
16	January	Wilson	New	140	4	560	
17	January	Wilson	New	125	3	375	
18	January	Sheldon	New	225	6	1350	
19	February	Sheldon	New	175	5	875	
20	January	Robinson	New	140	3	420	
21	February	Sheldon	New	125	2	250	
22	March	Sheldon	New	140	6	840	
23	March	Jenkins	Existing	225	3	675	
24	January	Robinson	New	225	2	450	
25	March	Sheldon	New	225	6	1350	
26	February	Wilson	New	140	3	420	

Figure 23-12: A criteria range for a list.

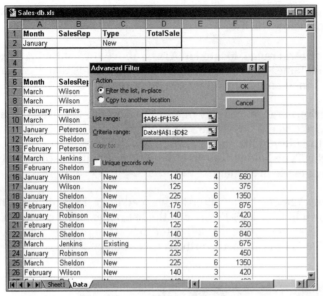

Figure 23-13: The Advanced Filter dialog box.

Multiple criteria

If you use more than one row in the criteria range, the criteria in each row are joined with an OR operator. Figure 23-14 shows a criteria range (A1:D3) with two rows of criteria. In this example, the filtered list shows rows in either of the following:

✦ The Month field is *January* AND the Type field is *New*.

✦ The Month field is *February* AND the Total Sale field is greater than 1000.

This is an example of filtering that could not be done with autofiltering.

A criteria range can have any number of rows, each of which is joined to the others with an OR operator.

Types of criteria

The entries that you make in a criteria range can be either of the following:

✦ **Text or value criteria.** The filtering involves comparisons to a value or string, using operators such as equal (=), greater than (>), not equal to (<>), and so on.

✦ **Computed criteria.** The filtering involves a computation of some sort.

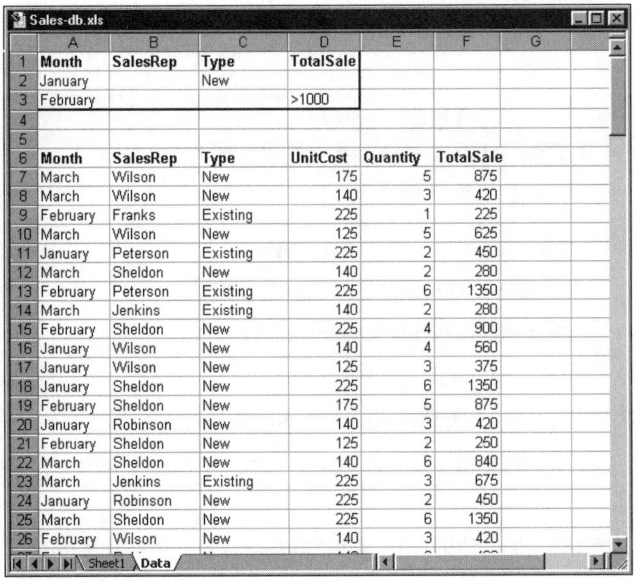

Figure 23-14: This criteria range has two sets of criteria.

Text or value criteria

Table 23-1 lists the comparison operators that you can use with text or value criteria.

Table 23-1	
Comparison Operators	
Operator	*Comparison Type*
=	Equal to
>	Greater than
>=	Greater than or equal to
<	Less than
<=	Less than or equal to
< >	Not equal to

Table 23-2 shows examples of criteria that use strings.

Table 23-2
Examples of String Criteria

Criteria	*Effect*
>K	Text that begins with *L* through *Z*
<>C	All text, except text that begins with *C*
="January"	Text that matches January
Sm*	Text that begins with *Sm*
s*s	Text that begins with *s* and ends with *s*
s?s	Three-letter text that begins with *s* and ends with *s*

Note The text comparisons are not case sensitive. For example, si* matches *Simpson* as well as *sick*.

Computed criteria

Using computed criteria can make your filtering even more powerful. Computed criteria filter the list based one or more calculations. Figure 23-15 shows a simple list that consists of project numbers, start dates, end dates, and resources. Above the list, in range A1:A2, is a criteria range. Notice, however, that this criteria range does not use a field header from the list — it uses a new field header. A computed criteria essentially computes a new field for the list. Therefore, you must supply new field names in the first row of the criteria range.

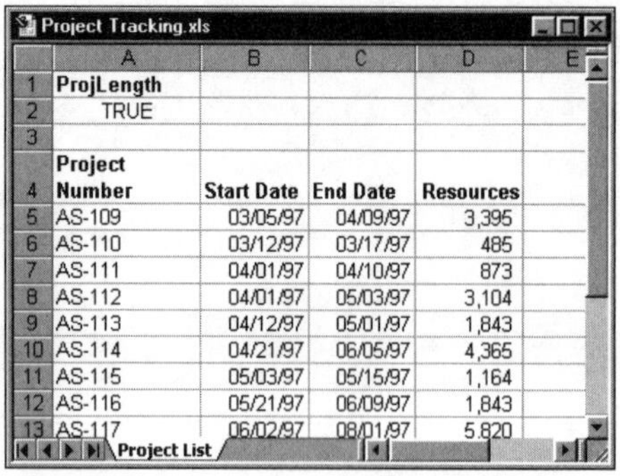
Project Tracking.xls

	A	B	C	D
1	ProjLength			
2	TRUE			
3				
4	Project Number	Start Date	End Date	Resources
5	AS-109	03/05/97	04/09/97	3,395
6	AS-110	03/12/97	03/17/97	485
7	AS-111	04/01/97	04/10/97	873
8	AS-112	04/01/97	05/03/97	3,104
9	AS-113	04/12/97	05/01/97	1,843
10	AS-114	04/21/97	06/05/97	4,365
11	AS-115	05/03/97	05/15/97	1,164
12	AS-116	05/21/97	06/09/97	1,843
13	AS-117	06/02/97	08/01/97	5,820

Project List

Figure 23-15: This list is to be filtered using computed criteria.

Cell A2 contains the following formula:

```
=C5-B5+1>=30
```

This is a logical formula (returns *True* or *False*) that refers to cells in the first row of data in the list; it does *not* refer to the header row. When the list is filtered by this criteria, it shows only rows in which the project length (End Date–Start Date+1) is greater than or equal to 30 days. In other words, the comparison is based on a computation.

Note
You could accomplish the same effect, without using a computed criterion, by adding a new column to the list that contains a formula to calculate the project length. Using a computed criterion, however, eliminates the need to add a new column.

To filter the list to show only the projects that use above average resources, you could use the following computed criteria formula:

```
=D5>AVERAGE(D:D)
```

This filters the list to show only the rows in which the Resources field is greater than the average of the Resources field.

Keep in mind the following items when using computed criteria:

- ✦ Don't use a field name in the criteria range that appears in the list. Create a new field name or just leave the cell blank.

- ✦ You can use any number of computed criteria and mix and match them with noncomputed criteria.

- ✦ Don't pay attention to the values returned by formulas in the criteria range. These refer to the first row of the list.

- ✦ If your computed formula refers to a value outside the list, use an absolute reference rather than a relative reference. For example, use $C$1 rather than C1.

- ✦ Create your computed criteria formulas using the first row of data in the list (not the field names). Make these references relative, not absolute. For example, use C5 rather than $C$5.

Other advanced filtering operations

The Advanced Filter dialog box gives you two other options, which I discuss in the following paragraphs:

- ✦ Copy to Another Location
- ✦ Unique Records Only

Copying qualifying rows

If you choose the Copy to Another Location option in the Advanced Filter dialog box, the qualifying rows are copied to another location in the worksheet or a different worksheet. You specify the location for the copied rows in the Copy to edit box. Note that the list itself is not filtered when you use this option.

Displaying only unique rows

Choosing the option labeled Unique records only hides all duplicate rows that meet the criteria that you specify. If you don't specify a criteria range, this option hides all duplicate rows in the list.

Using Database Functions with Lists

It's important to understand that Excel's worksheet functions don't ignore hidden cells. Therefore, if you have a SUM formula that calculates the total of the values in a column of a list, the formula returns the same value when the list is filtered.

To create formulas that return results based on filtering criteria, you need to use Excel's database worksheet functions. For example, you can create a formula that calculates the sum of values in a list that meets a certain criteria. Set up a criteria range as described previously. Then enter a formula such as the following:

```
=DSUM(ListRange,FieldName,Criteria)
```

In this case, ListRange refers to the list, FieldName refers to the field name cell of the column that is being summed, and Criteria refers to the criteria range.

Excel's database functions are listed in Table 23-3.

<table>
<tr><td colspan="2" align="center">Table 23-3
Excel's Database Worksheet Functions</td></tr>
<tr><td>Function</td><td>Description</td></tr>
<tr><td>DAVERAGE</td><td>Returns the average of selected database entries</td></tr>
<tr><td>DCOUNT</td><td>Counts the cells containing numbers from a specified database and criteria</td></tr>
<tr><td>DCOUNTA</td><td>Counts nonblank cells from a specified database and criteria</td></tr>
<tr><td>DGET</td><td>Extracts from a database a single record that matches the specified criteria</td></tr>
<tr><td>DMAX</td><td>Returns the maximum value from selected database entries</td></tr>
</table>

Function	Description
DMIN	Returns the minimum value from selected database entries
DPRODUCT	Multiplies the values in a particular field of records that match the criteria in a database
DSTDEV	Estimates the standard deviation based on a sample of selected database entries
DSTDEVP	Calculates the standard deviation based on the entire population of selected database entries
DSUM	Adds the numbers in the field column of records in the database that match the criteria
DVAR	Estimates variance based on a sample from selected database entries
DVARP	Calculates variance based on the entire population of selected database entries

Cross Reference Refer to Chapter 10 for general information about using worksheet functions.

Sorting a List

In some cases, the order of the rows in your list doesn't matter. But in other cases, you want the rows to appear in a specific order. For example, in a price list, you may want the rows to appear in alphabetical order by product name. This makes the products easier to locate. Or, if you have a list of accounts receivable information, you may want to sort the list so that the higher amounts appear at the top of the list (in descending order).

Rearranging the order of the rows in a list is called *sorting*. Excel is quite flexible when it comes to sorting lists, and you can often accomplish this task with the click on of a mouse button.

Simple sorting

To quickly sort a list in ascending order, move the cell pointer to the column that you want to sort. Then click on the Sort Ascending button the Standard toolbar. The Sort Descending button works the same way, but it sorts the list in descending order. In both cases, Excel determines the extent of your list and sorts all the rows in the list.

When you sort a filtered list, only the visible rows are sorted. When you remove the filtering from the list, the list is no longer sorted.

Be careful if you sort a list that contains formulas. If the formulas refer to cells in the list that are in the same row, you don't have any problems. But if the formulas refer to cells in other rows in the list or to cells outside the list, the formulas are not correct after the sorting. If formulas in your list refer to cells outside the list, make sure that the formulas use an absolute cell reference.

More complex sorting

Sometimes, you may want to sort by two or more columns. This is relevant to break ties. A tie occurs when rows with duplicate data remain unsorted. Figure 23-16 shows an example of a list. If this list is sorted by Month, the rows for each month are placed together. But you may also want to show the Sales Reps in ascending order within each month. In this case, you would need to sort by two columns (Month and Sales Rep). Figure 23-17 shows the list after sorting by these two columns.

You can use the Sort Ascending and Sort Descending buttons to do this — but you need to do two sorts. First, sort by the Sales Reps column, and then sort by the Month column. As I explain in the next section, Excel provides a way to accomplish multicolumn sorting with a single command.

Excel's sorting rules

Because cells can contain different types of information, you may be curious about how this information is sorted. For an ascending sort, the information appears in the following order:

1. **Values:** Numbers are sorted from smallest negative to largest positive. Dates and times are treated as values. In all cases, the sorting is done using the actual values (not their formatted appearance).

2. **Text:** In alphabetical order, as follows: 0 1 2 3 4 5 6 7 8 9 (space) ! " # $ % & ' ( ) * + , – . / : ; < = > ? @ [\ ] ^ _ ` { | } ~ A B C D E F G H I J K L M N O P Q R S T U V W X Y Z.

By default, sorting is not case sensitive. You can change this, however, in the Sort Options dialog box (described in this chapter).

3. **Logical values:** False comes before True.

4. **Error values:** Error values (such as #VALUE! and #NA) appear in their original order and are not sorted by error type.

5. **Blank cells:** Blanks cells always appear last.

Sorting in descending order reverses this sequence — except that blank cells are *still* sorted last.

Sales-db.xls

	Month	Sales Rep	Type	Unit Cost	Quantity	Total Sale
8	May	Sheldon	Existing	125	1	125
9	January	Sheldon	Existing	175	1	175
10	January	Sheldon	New	140	6	840
11	January	Jenkins	New	225	1	225
12	February	Robinson	New	225	1	225
13	March	Wilson	Existing	125	4	500
14	April	Robinson	Existing	125	2	250
15	February	Sheldon	Existing	175	1	175
16	March	Robinson	Existing	125	1	125
17	May	Jenkins	New	225	3	675
18	April	Jenkins	New	225	2	450
19	February	Wilson	Existing	125	5	625
20	February	Jenkins	New	225	2	450
21	January	Franks	New	225	4	900
22	May	Wilson	New	225	1	225
23	January	Sheldon	New	225	1	225
24	March	Jenkins	New	225	2	450
25	March	Jenkins	Existing	125	5	625
26	April	Peterson	New	140	2	280
27	February	Franks	Existing	175	2	350
28	May	Robinson	New	140	3	420
29	April	Peterson	Existing	175	6	1050
30	February	Robinson	New	225	3	675

SALES-DB

Figure 23-16: This list is unsorted.

Sales-db.xls

	Month	Sales Rep	Type	Unit Cost	Quantity	Total Sale
8	January	Franks	New	225	4	900
9	January	Franks	Existing	175	1	175
10	January	Franks	Existing	175	5	875
11	January	Franks	New	225	1	225
12	January	Franks	Existing	175	1	175
13	January	Franks	Existing	125	3	375
14	January	Jenkins	New	225	1	225
15	January	Jenkins	Existing	125	1	125
16	January	Jenkins	New	140	3	420
17	January	Jenkins	Existing	175	2	350
18	January	Jenkins	New	140	1	140
19	January	Peterson	Existing	125	1	125
20	January	Peterson	Existing	125	3	375
21	January	Peterson	New	140	1	140
22	January	Peterson	New	225	1	225
23	January	Robinson	New	140	2	280
24	January	Robinson	Existing	125	5	625
25	January	Robinson	Existing	175	4	700
26	January	Sheldon	Existing	175	1	175
27	January	Sheldon	New	140	6	840
28	January	Sheldon	New	225	1	225
29	January	Sheldon	Existing	125	2	250
30	January	Sheldon	Existing	175	5	875

SALES-DB

Figure 23-17: The list after sorting on two fields.

The Sort dialog box

If you want to sort by more than one field, choose Data⇨Sort. Excel displays the dialog box that is shown in Figure 23-18. Simply select the first sort field from the drop-down list labeled Sort By, and specify Ascending or Descending order. Then, do the same for the second sort field. If you want to sort by a third field, specify the field in the third section. If the Header Row option is set, the first row (field names) is not affected by the sort. Click on OK, and the list's rows rearrange in a flash.

Figure 23-18: The Sort dialog box lets you sort by up to three columns.

If the sorting didn't occur as you expected, select Edit⇨Undo (or press Ctrl+Z) to undo the sorting.

What if you need to sort your list by more than three fields? It can be done, but it takes an additional step. For example, assume that you want to sort your list by five fields: Field1, Field2, Field3, Field4, and Field5. Start by sorting by Field3, Field4, and Field5. Then resort the list by Field1 and Field2. In other words, sort the three "least important" fields first; they remain in sequence when you do the second sort.

Tip Often, you want to keep the records in their original order but perform a temporary sort just to see how it looks. The solution is to add an additional column to the list with sequential numbers in it (don't use formulas to generate these numbers). Then, after you sort, you can return to the original order by resorting on the field that has the sequential numbers. You can also use Excel's undo feature to return the list to its original order. The advantage of using an additional column is that you can perform other operations while the list is temporarily sorted (and these operations won't be undone when you undo the sort operation).

Sort options

When you click on the Options button in the Sort dialog box, Excel displays the Sort Options dialog, shown in Figure 23-19.

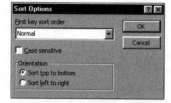

Figure 23-19: The Sort Options dialog gives you some additional sorting options.

These options are described as follows:

✦ **First key sort order:** Lets you specify a custom sort order for the sort (see the next section).

✦ **Case sensitive:** Makes the sorting case sensitive so that uppercase letters appear before lowercase letters in an ascending sort. Normally, sorting ignores the case of letters.

✦ **Orientation:** Enables you to sort by columns rather than by rows (the default).

How Excel identifies a header row

When you use the Data⇨Sort command, there's no need to select the list before you choose the command. That's because Excel examines the active cell position and then determines the list's boundaries for you. In addition, it makes its best guess as to whether the list contains a header row. If the list has a header row, this row is not included in the sorting.

How does this happen? I'm not sure exactly, but the following seems to be Excel's "thought" process:

1. Select the current region. (You can do this manually: press F5, click on the Special button, select the Current Region option, and click on OK.)

2. Examine the first row of the selection.

3. Does the first row contain any blanks? If so, this list has no header row.

4. Does the first row contain text? If so, check the other cells. If they also contain text, this list has no header row.

5. Does the first row contain uppercase text and the list itself contain lowercase or proper case text? If so, this list has a header row.

6. Are the cells in the first row formatted differently from the other cells in the list? If so, this list has a header row.

Knowing this information can help you eliminate incorrect sorting. For example, if you want to sort a range that doesn't have header rows, you need to make sure that Excel doesn't sort the data as if it had header rows. The best solution is to use the Sort Ascending and Sort Descending toolbar buttons only when the data that you're sorting has headers. If there are no headers, select Data⇨Sort and make sure that the No Header Row option is selected.

Using a custom sort order

Normal sorting is done either numerically or alphabetically, depending on the data being sorted. In some cases, however, you may want to sort your data in other ways. For example, if your data consists of month names, you usually want it to appear in month order rather than alphabetically. You can use the Sort Options dialog box to perform such a sort. Select the appropriate list from the drop-down list labled First key sort order. Excel, by default, has four "custom lists," and you can define your own. Excel's custom lists are as follows:

✦ **Abbreviated days:** Sun, Mon, Tue, Wed, Thu, Fri, Sat

✦ **Days:** Sunday, Monday, Tuesday, Wednesday, Thursday, Friday, Saturday

✦ **Abbreviated months:** Jan, Feb, Mar, Apr, May, Jun, Jul, Aug, Sep, Oct, Nov, Dec

✦ **Months:** January, February, March, April, May, June, July, August, September, October, November, December

Note that the abbreviated days and months do not have periods after them. If you use periods for these abbreviations, they are not recognized (and are not sorted correctly).

You may want to create a custom list. For example, your company may have several stores, and you want the stores to be listed in a particular order (not alphabetically). If you create a custom list, sorting puts the items in the order that you specify in the list. You must use the Data⇨Sort command to sort by a custom list (click on the Options button to specify the custom list).

To create a custom list, use the Custom List panel of the Options dialog box, as shown in Figure 23-20. Select the NEW LIST option, and make your entries (in order) in the List Entries box. Or, you can import your custom list from a range of cells by using the Import button.

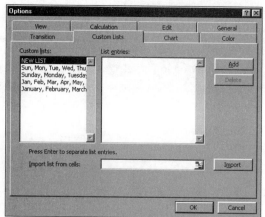

Figure 23-20: Excel lets you create custom sorting lists.

Custom lists also work with the autofill handle in cells. If you enter the first item of a custom list and then drag the cell's autofill handle, Excel fills in the remaining list items automatically.

Sorting non-lists

You can, of course, sort any range in a worksheet — it doesn't have to be a list. You need to be aware of a few things, however. The Sort Ascending and Sort Descending toolbar buttons may assume (erroneously) that the top row is a header row and not include these cells in the sort (see "How Excel identifies a header row" in this chapter).

Therefore, to avoid potential errors when sorting non-lists, don't use these toolbar buttons. Rather, select the entire range, and select Data➪Sort (making sure that you choose the No Header Row option).

Creating Subtotals

The final topic of this chapter is automatic subtotals — a handy feature that can save you a great deal of time. To use this feature, your list must be sorted, because the subtotals are inserted whenever the value in a specified field changes. Figure 23-21 shows an example of a list that's appropriate for subtotals. It was sorted by the Month field.

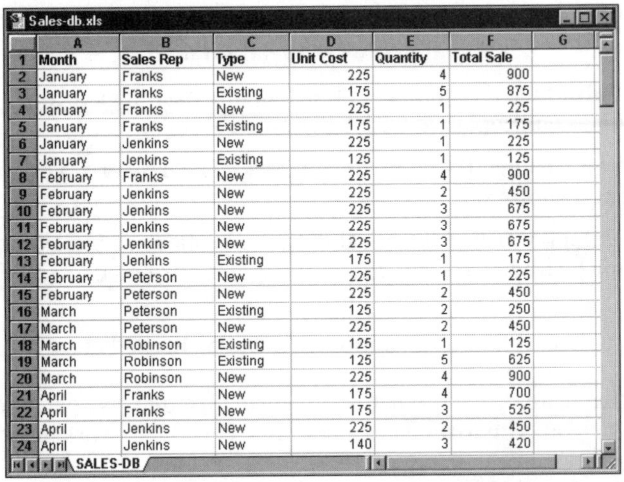

	A	B	C	D	E	F	G
1	Month	Sales Rep	Type	Unit Cost	Quantity	Total Sale	
2	January	Franks	New	225	4	900	
3	January	Franks	Existing	175	5	875	
4	January	Franks	New	225	1	225	
5	January	Franks	Existing	175	1	175	
6	January	Jenkins	New	225	1	225	
7	January	Jenkins	Existing	125	1	125	
8	February	Franks	New	225	4	900	
9	February	Jenkins	New	225	2	450	
10	February	Jenkins	New	225	3	675	
11	February	Jenkins	New	225	3	675	
12	February	Jenkins	New	225	3	675	
13	February	Jenkins	Existing	175	1	175	
14	February	Peterson	New	225	1	225	
15	February	Peterson	New	225	2	450	
16	March	Peterson	Existing	125	2	250	
17	March	Peterson	New	225	2	450	
18	March	Robinson	Existing	125	1	125	
19	March	Robinson	Existing	125	5	625	
20	March	Robinson	New	225	4	900	
21	April	Franks	New	175	4	700	
22	April	Franks	New	175	3	525	
23	April	Jenkins	New	225	2	450	
24	April	Jenkins	New	140	3	420	

Figure 23-21: This list is a good candidate for subtotals, which are inserted at each change of the month.

To insert subtotal formulas into a list automatically, move the cell pointer anywhere in the list and choose Data➪Subtotals. You see the dialog box shown in Figure 23-22.

Figure 23-22: The Subtotal dialog box automatically inserts subtotal formulas into a sorted list.

This dialog box offers the following choices:

✦ **At Each Change in:** This drop-down list displays all fields in your list. The field that you choose must be sorted.

✦ **Use Function:** This gives you a choice of 11 functions. You should normally use Sum (the default).

✦ **Add Subtotal to:** This list box lists all the fields in your list. Place a check mark next to the field or fields that you want to subtotal.

✦ **Replace Current Subtotals:** If this box is checked, any existing subtotal formulas are removed and replaced with the new subtotals.

✦ **Page Break Between Groups:** If this box is checked, Excel inserts a manual page break after each subtotal.

✦ **Summary Below Data:** If this box is checked, the subtotals are placed below the data (the default). Otherwise, the subtotal formulas are placed above the totals.

✦ **Remove All:** This button removes all subtotal formulas in the list.

When you click on OK, Excel analyzes the list and inserts formulas as specified — and creates an outline for you. The formulas all use the SUBTOTAL worksheet function.

When you add subtotals to a filtered list, the subtotals may no longer be accurate when the filter is removed.

Figure 23-23 shows a worksheet after adding subtotals.

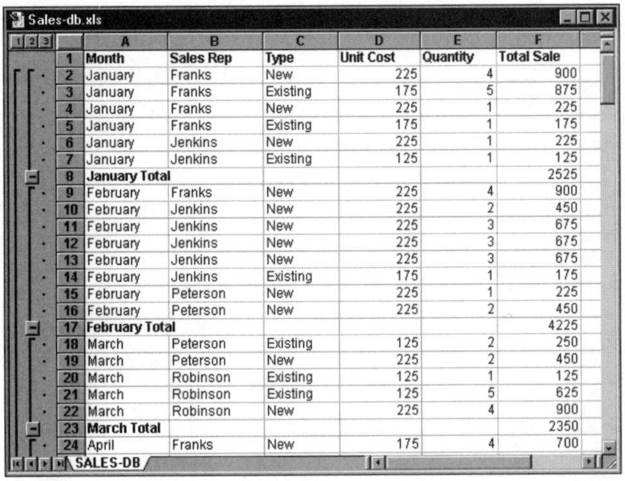

Sales-db.xls

	A	B	C	D	E	F
1	Month	Sales Rep	Type	Unit Cost	Quantity	Total Sale
2	January	Franks	New	225	4	900
3	January	Franks	Existing	175	5	875
4	January	Franks	New	225	1	225
5	January	Franks	Existing	175	1	175
6	January	Jenkins	New	225	1	225
7	January	Jenkins	Existing	125	1	125
8	January Total					2525
9	February	Franks	New	225	4	900
10	February	Jenkins	New	225	2	450
11	February	Jenkins	New	225	3	675
12	February	Jenkins	New	225	3	675
13	February	Jenkins	New	225	3	675
14	February	Jenkins	Existing	175	1	175
15	February	Peterson	New	225	1	225
16	February	Peterson	New	225	2	450
17	February Total					4225
18	March	Peterson	Existing	125	2	250
19	March	Peterson	New	225	2	450
20	March	Robinson	Existing	125	1	125
21	March	Robinson	Existing	125	5	625
22	March	Robinson	New	225	4	900
23	March Total					2350
24	April	Franks	New	175	4	700

SALES-DB

Figure 23-23: Excel added the subtotal formulas automatically – and even created an outline.

Summary

In this chapter, I discuss lists. A list is simply a database table that is stored on a worksheet. The first row of the list (the header row) contains field names, and subsequent rows contain data (records). I offer some pointers on data entry and discuss two ways to filter a list to show only rows that meet certain criteria. Autofiltering is adequate for many tasks, but if your filtering needs are more complex, you need to use advanced filtering. I end the chapter with a discussion of sorting and Excel's automatic subtotal feature.

✦ ✦ ✦

Using External Database Files

◆ ◆ ◆ ◆

In This Chapter

Why you may need to access data that is stored in an external database file

How to use the Query Wizard to create a database query and bring the results into a worksheet

How to use the Microsoft Query application

◆ ◆ ◆ ◆

The preceding chapter described how to work with lists that are stored in a worksheet. Many users find that worksheet lists are sufficient for their data tracking. Others, however, choose to take advantage of the fact that Excel also can access data that is stored in external database files. That's the topic of this chapter.

Why Use External Database Files?

Accessing external database files from Excel is useful when you have the following situations:

◆ The database that you need to work with is very large.

◆ The database is shared with others; that is, other users have access to the database and may need to work with the data at the same time.

◆ You want to work with only a subset of the data — data that meets certain criteria that you specify.

◆ The database is in a format that Excel can't read.

If you need to work with external databases, you may prefer Excel over other database programs. The advantage? After you bring the data into Excel, you can manipulate and format it by using familiar tools.

As you may know, Excel can read some database files directly — specifically, those produced by various versions of dBASE (with a DBF extension). If the database has fewer than 65,535 records and no more than 255 fields, you can load the entire file into a worksheet, memory permitting. Even if you have enough memory to load such a large file, however, Excel's performance would likely be poor.

In many cases, you may not be interested in all the records or fields in the file. Instead, you may want to bring in just the data that meets certain criteria. In other words, you want to *query* the database and load into your worksheet a subset of the external database. Excel makes this type of operation relatively easy.

Note   To perform queries using external databases, Microsoft Query must be installed on your system. If the <u>D</u>ata⇨Get E<u>x</u>ternal Data⇨Create New Query command is not available, Query is not installed. You must rerun the Excel (or Microsoft Office) setup program and install Query.

Excel 97   In previous versions of Excel, using Microsoft Query required that you load an add-in. That is no longer necessary with Excel 97, although the add-in is still included for compatibility purposes.

To work with an external database file from Excel, use the Query application that is included with Excel. The general procedure is as follows:

1. Activate a worksheet.

2. Choose <u>D</u>ata⇨Get E<u>x</u>ternal Data⇨Create New Query. This starts Query.

3. Specify whether you want to use Query directly or use the new Query Wizard.

4. Specify the database that you want to use and then create a query — a list of criteria that determines which records you want.

5. Specify how you want the data that passes your query returned — either to a worksheet or as a pivot table.

You can choose to save the query in a file so that you can reuse it at a later time. This means that it's a simple matter to modify the query or *refresh* it (update it with any changed values). This is particularly useful when the data resides in a shared database that is continually being updated.

Cross Reference   In the next chapter, I discuss pivot tables. You can create a pivot table using data in an external file, and you use Query to retrieve data.

An Example of Using Query

The best way to become familiar with Query is to walk through an example.

The database file

The file that is used in this example is named Budget.dbf. If you want to try this example yourself, you can download this file from this book's Web site.

This database file is a dBASE IV database with a single table that consists of 15,840 records. This file contains the following fields:

✦ **Sort:** A numeric field that holds record sequence numbers.

✦ **Division:** A text field that specifies the company division (this is either Asia, Europe, N. America, Pacific Rim, or S. America).

✦ **Department:** A text field that specifies the department within the division. Each division is organized into the following departments: Accounting, Advertising, Data Processing, Human Resources, Operations, Public Relations, R&D, Sales, Security, Shipping, and Training.

✦ **Category:** A text field that specifies the budget category. The four categories are Compensation, Equipment, Facility, and Supplies & Services.

✦ **Item:** A text field that specifies the budget item. Each budget category has different budget items. For example, the Compensation category includes the following items: Benefits, Bonuses, Commissions, Conferences, Entertainment, Payroll Taxes, Salaries, and Training.

✦ **Month:** A text field that specifies the month (abbreviated as Jan, Feb, and so on).

✦ **Budget:** A numeric field that stores the budgeted amount.

✦ **Actual:** A numeric field that stores the actual amount spent.

✦ **Variance:** A numeric field that stores the difference between the Budget and Actual.

The task

The objective of this exercise is to develop a report that shows the first quarter (January through March) actual compensation expenditures of the training department in the North American division. In other words, the query is to extract records for which the following applies:

✦ The Division is *N. America.*

✦ The Department is *Training.*

✦ The Category is *Compensation.*

✦ The Month is *Jan, Feb,* or *Mar.*

Using Query to get the data

One approach to this task would be to import the entire dBASE file into a worksheet and then choose Data⇨Filter⇨AutoFilter to filter the data as required. This approach would work because the file has fewer than 65,535 records. This isn't always the case. The advantage of using Query is that it imports only the data that's required.

Some database terminology

People who spend their days working with databases seem to have their own special language. The following terms can help you hold your own among a group of database mavens.

External database: A collection of data that is stored in one or more files (not Excel files). Each file of a database holds a single table, and tables are comprised of records and fields.

Field: In a database table, an element of a record that corresponds to a column.

ODBC: An acronym for Open Database Connectivity, a standard developed by Microsoft that uses drivers to access database files in different formats. Microsoft Query comes with drivers for Access, dBASE, FoxPro, Paradox, SQL Server, Excel workbooks, and ASCII text files. ODBC drivers for other databases are available from Microsoft and third-party providers.

Query: To search a database for records that meet specific criteria. This term is also used as a noun; you can write a query, for example.

Record: In a database table, a single element that corresponds to a jrow.

Refresh: To rerun a query to get the latest data. This is applicable when the database contains information that is subject to change, as in a multiuser environment.

Relational database: A database that is stored in more than one table or file. The tables are connected by having one or more common fields (sometimes called the *key* field).

Result set: The data that is returned by a query, usually a subset of the original database. Query returns the result set to your Excel workbook or to a pivot table.

SQL: An acronym for Structured Query Language (usually pronounced *sequel*). Query uses SQL to query data that is stored in ODBC databases.

Table: A record- and field-oriented collection of data. A database consists of one or more tables.

Starting Query

Begin with an empty worksheet. Select Data⇨Get External Data⇨Create new Query, which launches and activates Query (a separate application that Excel starts). Excel continues to run, and you can switch back and forth between Query and Excel if you need to.

Selecting a data source

When Query starts, it displays the Choose Data Source dialog box, as shown in Figure 24-1. This dialog box contains two tabs:

✦ The Databases tab lists the data sources that are known to Query — it may or may not be empty, depending on which data sources are defined on your system.

✦ The Queries tab contains a list of stored queries. Again, this may or may not be empty.

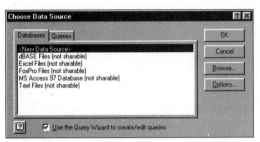

Figure 24-1: The Choose Data Source dialog box.

If you've worked with a database before, it appears in the list of databases. Otherwise, you need to identify the source.

In the Databases tab, select the <New Database Source> option and click on OK. This displays the Create New Data Source dialog box, as shown in Figure 24-2. This dialog box has four parts:

1. Enter a descriptive name for the data source. For this example, the name is Budget Database.

2. Select a driver for the data source by selecting from the list of installed drivers. Because the database file in this example is a dBASE file, select the driver named Microsoft dBASE Driver.

3. The Connect button displays another dialog box that asks for information specific to the driver that you selected in Step 2. For example, you can select the directory where the database is located.

4. Select the default data table that you want to use (this step is optional). If the database requires a password, you can also specify that the password be saved with the Data Source definition.

When you've supplied all the information in the Create New Data Source dialog box, click on OK, and you are returned to the Choose Data Source dialog box — which now displays the data source that you created.

You only have to go through these steps once for each data source. The next time that you access Query, the Budget Database (and any other database sources that you've defined) appears in the Choose Data Source dialog box.

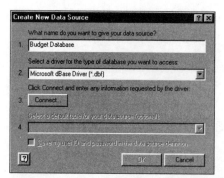

Figure 24-2: The Create New Data Source
dialog box.

Use the Query Wizard?

The Choose Data Source dialog box has a check box at the bottom that lets you
specify whether to use the Query Wizard to create your query. The Query Wizard
walks you through the steps used to create your query, and if you use the Query
Wizard, you don't have to deal directly with Query. I highly recommend using the
Query Wizard — and the examples in this chapter use this tool.

In the Choose Data Sources dialog box, make sure that the Query Wizard checkbox
is checked, and then click on OK to start the Query Wizard.

Query Wizard: Choosing the columns

In the first step of the Query Wizard (see Figure 24-3), select the database columns
that you want to appear in your query.

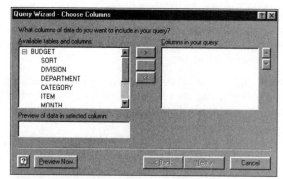

Figure 24-3: In the first step of Query Wizard, you
select the columns to use in your query.

Using the ODBC Manager

Occasionally, you may need to edit data sources — for example, if you move your database files to a new location. You can do this using the ODBC Manager utility. This program is available in the Windows Control Panel (it's called 32-bit ODBC). This utility also lets you add new data sources and remove those that you no longer need.

The columns that you select determine which fields from the database are returned to Excel. Recall that the query for this example involves selecting records based on the following fields: Division, Department, Month, Category, and Actual. You also want to add the Item field. The left panel of the dialog box shows all the available columns. To add a column to the right panel, select the column and click on the > button (or, you can double-click on the column name).

When you're finished adding the columns, the Query Wizard dialog box looks like Figure 24-4.

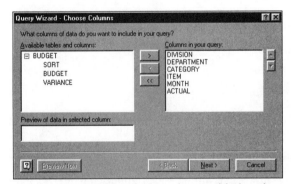

Figure 24-4: Six columns have been added to the query.

If you want to see the data for a particular column, select the column and click on the Preview Now button.

If you accidentally add a column that you don't need, select it in the right panel and click on the < button to remove it.

When you've selected all the columns for the query, click on the Next button.

Query Wizard: Filtering data

In the second Query Wizard dialog box, you specify your record selection criteria — how you want to filter the data. This step is optional. If you want to retrieve all the data, just click on the Next button to proceed.

Figure 24-5 shows the Filter Data dialog box of the Query Wizard.

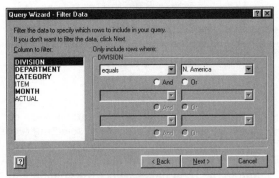

Figure 24-5: In the second step of the Query Wizard, you specify how you want to filter the data.

For the example, not all records are needed. Recall that you're interested only in the records in which one of the following applies:

✦ The Division is *N. America.*

✦ The Department is *Training.*

✦ The Category is *Compensation.*

✦ The Month is *Jan, Feb,* or *Mar.*

The criteria are entered by column. In this case, there are four criteria (one for each of four columns):

1. In the Column to Filter column, select *Division.* In the right panel, select *equals* from the first drop-down list, and select *N. America* from the second drop-down list.

2. In the Column to Filter column, select *Department.* In the right panel, select *equals* from the first drop-down list, and select *Training* from the second drop-down list.

3. In the Column to Filter column, select *Category.* In the right panel, select *equals* from the first drop-down list, and select *Compensation* from the second drop-down list.

4. In the Column to Filter column, select *Month.* In the right panel, select *equals* from the first drop-down list, and select *Jan* from the second drop-down list. Because this column is filtered by multiple values, click on the Or option, and then select *equals* and *Feb* from the drop-down lists in the second row. Finally, select *equals* and *Mar* from the drop-down lists in the second row.

To review the criteria that you've entered, just select the column from the Column to Filter list. The Query Wizard displays the criteria that you entered for the selected column.

When you've entered all the criteria, click on Next.

Query operators

The table below lists and describes the operators that are available when creating a query. These operators give you complete control over which rows are returned.

Operator	What It Does
equals	Field is identical to value
does not equal	Field is not equal to value
is greater than	Field is greater than value
is greater than or equal to	Field is greater than or equal to value
is less than	Field is less than value
is less than or equal to	Field is less than or equal to value
is one of	Field is in a list of values, separated by commas
is not one of	Field is not in a list of values, separated by commas
is between	Field is between two values, separated by commas
is not between	Field is not between two values, separated by commas
begins with	Field begins with the value
does not begin with	Field does not begin with value
ends with	Field ends with value
does not end with	Field does not end with value
contains	Field contains value
does not contain	Field does not contain value
like	Field is like value (using * and ? wildcard characters)
not like	Field is not like value (using * and ? wildcard characters)
is Null	Field is empty
is not Null	Field is not empty

Query Wizard: Sort order

The third step of the query lets you specify how you want the records to be sorted (see Figure 24-6). This step is optional, and you can click on Next to move to the next step if you don't want the data sorted or if you prefer to sort it after it's returned to your worksheet.

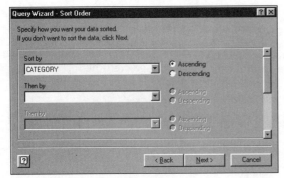

Figure 24-6: In the third step of the Query Wizard, you specify the sort order.

For this example, sort by *Category* in ascending order. You can specify as many sort fields as you like. Click on Next to move on to the next step.

Query Wizard: Finish

The final step of the Query Wizard, shown in Figure 24-7, lets you do the following things:

   ✦ Give the query a name

   ✦ Save it to a file so it can be reused

   ✦ Specify what to do with the data

Normally, you want to return the data to Excel. If you know how to use the Microsoft Query application, you can return the data to Query and examine it or even modify the selection criteria.

If you plan to reuse this query, you should save it to a file. Click on the Save Query button, and you are prompted for a filename. When you've made your choices, click on Finish.

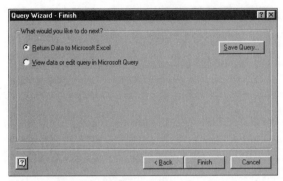

Figure 24-7: The final step of the Query Wizard.

Specifying a location for the data

Figure 24-8 shows the dialog box that appears when you click on the Finish button in the Query Wizard dialog box.

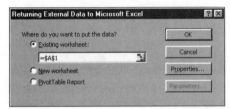

Figure 24-8: Specifying what to do with the data.

You can select from the following choices:

✦ **Existing worksheet.** You can specify the upper-left cell.

✦ **New worksheet.** Excel can insert a new worksheet and insert the data beginning in cell A1.

✦ **Pivot Table Report.** Excel can display its Pivot Table Wizard so that you can specify the layout for a pivot table (see Chapter 25).

Figure 24-9 shows the data that is returned to a worksheet.

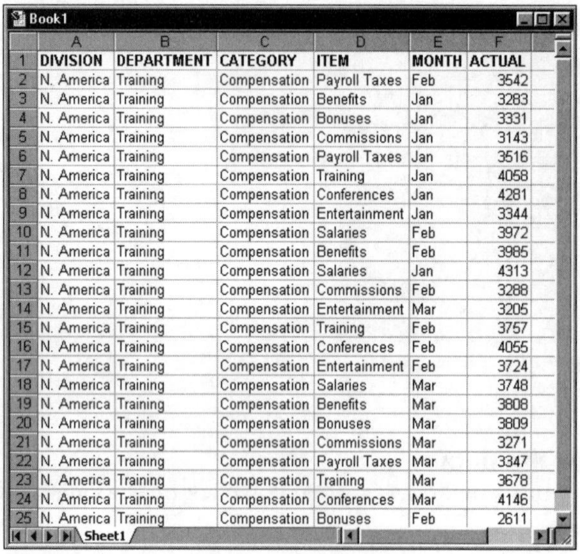

	DIVISION	DEPARTMENT	CATEGORY	ITEM	MONTH	ACTUAL
2	N. America	Training	Compensation	Payroll Taxes	Feb	3542
3	N. America	Training	Compensation	Benefits	Jan	3283
4	N. America	Training	Compensation	Bonuses	Jan	3331
5	N. America	Training	Compensation	Commissions	Jan	3143
6	N. America	Training	Compensation	Payroll Taxes	Jan	3516
7	N. America	Training	Compensation	Training	Jan	4058
8	N. America	Training	Compensation	Conferences	Jan	4281
9	N. America	Training	Compensation	Entertainment	Jan	3344
10	N. America	Training	Compensation	Salaries	Feb	3972
11	N. America	Training	Compensation	Benefits	Feb	3985
12	N. America	Training	Compensation	Salaries	Jan	4313
13	N. America	Training	Compensation	Commissions	Feb	3288
14	N. America	Training	Compensation	Entertainment	Mar	3205
15	N. America	Training	Compensation	Training	Feb	3757
16	N. America	Training	Compensation	Conferences	Feb	4055
17	N. America	Training	Compensation	Entertainment	Feb	3724
18	N. America	Training	Compensation	Salaries	Mar	3748
19	N. America	Training	Compensation	Benefits	Mar	3808
20	N. America	Training	Compensation	Bonuses	Mar	3809
21	N. America	Training	Compensation	Commissions	Mar	3271
22	N. America	Training	Compensation	Payroll Taxes	Mar	3347
23	N. America	Training	Compensation	Training	Mar	3678
24	N. America	Training	Compensation	Conferences	Mar	4146
25	N. America	Training	Compensation	Bonuses	Feb	2611

Figure 24-9: The results of the query.

Working with an External Data Range

Data that is returned from a query is stored in either a worksheet or a pivot table. Data stored in a worksheet is stored in a specially named range known as an *external data range* (Excel creates the name for this range automatically).

In this section, I describe what you can do with the data that's returned from Query and stored in a worksheet.

Adjusting external data range properties

You can adjust various properties of the external data range using the External Data Range Properties dialog box (see Figure 24-10). To bring up this dialog box, the cell pointer must be within the external data range. You can access this dialog box by using any of three methods:

- ✦ Right-click and select Data Range Properties from the shortcut menu.
- ✦ Select Data➪Get External Data➪Data Range Properties.
- ✦ Click on the Data Range properties tool on the External Data toolbar (this toolbar appears automatically when you perform a query).

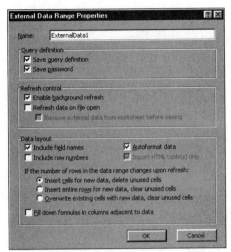

Figure 24-10: The External Data Range Properties dialog box enables you to specify various options for an external data range.

The options in the Data Range Properties dialog box are described below:

✦ **Name:** The name of the external data range. You can change this name or use the default name that Excel creates.

✦ **Query definition:** If Save query definition is checked, the query definition is stored with the external data range (allowing you to refresh the data or edit the query if necessary). If the database requires a password, you can also store the password so that it doesn't need to be entered when the query is refreshed.

✦ **Refresh control:** Determines how and when the data is refreshed.

✦ **Data layout:** Determines how the external data range appears.

The Data Range Properties dialog box has quite a few options. For specific details, click the Help icon in the title bar and then click an option in the dialog box.

Working with an external data range

Data returned from a query can be manipulated just like any other worksheet range. For example, you can sort the data, format it, or create formulas that use the data.

Caution If the query is to be refreshed, you must keep the external data range intact. In other words, do not insert new rows or columns in the external data range. When the query is refreshed, the data is rewritten to the worksheet. For example, you may insert a new row and then create formulas in that new row. When the query is refreshed, those formulas are overwritten.

Refreshing a query

After performing a query, you can save the file and then retrieve it later. The file contains the data that you originally retrieved from the external database. The external database may have changed, however, in the interim.

If the Save query definition option (in the External Data Range Properties dialog box) is checked, then the query definition is saved with the workbook. Simply move the cell pointer anywhere within the external data table in the worksheet, and use one of the following methods to refresh the query:

 ✦ Right-click on and select Refresh Data from the shortcut menu.

 ✦ Select Data⇨Refresh Data.

 ✦ Click on the Refresh Data tool on the External Data toolbar.

Excel launches Query and uses your original query to bring in the current data from the external database.

Tip   If you find that refreshing the query causes undesirable results, use Excel's Undo feature to "unrefresh" the data.

Making multiple queries

A single workbook can hold as many external data ranges as you need. Each is given a unique name, and you can work with each query independently. Excel automatically keeps track of the query that is used to produce each external data range.

Copying or moving a query

After performing a query, you may want to copy or move the external data range. You can do so using normal copy, cut, and paste techniques. However, make sure that you copy or cut the entire external data range — otherwise the underlying query is not copied, and the copied data cannot be refreshed.

Deleting a query

If you decide that you no longer need the data that is returned by a query, you can delete it. To do so, select the entire external data range and choose Edit⇨Delete.

Note   If you simply press Delete, the contents of the cells are erased, but the underlying query remains. This means that you can refresh the query, and the deleted cells appear again.

Changing your query

If you bring the query results into your worksheet and discover that you don't have what you want, you can modify the query. Move the cell pointer anywhere within the external data table in the worksheet, and use one of the following methods to refresh the query:

✦ Right-click on and select Edit Query from the shortcut menu.

✦ Select Data⇨Get External Data⇨Edit Query.

✦ Click on the Edit Query tool on the External Data toolbar.

Excel then launches (or activates) Query, and you can change the original query. When you're finished, choose File⇨Return Data to Microsoft Excel. Excel is reactivated, the modified query is executed, and the external data range is updated.

Using Microsoft Query (Without Query Wizard)

Previous sections in this chapter described how to use the Query Wizard to create a database query. The Query Wizard is essentially a "front end" for Microsoft Query. In some cases, you may want to use Query itself rather than the Query Wizard.

When you select Data⇨Get External Data⇨Create New Query, the Choose Data Source dialog box gives you an option of using the Query Wizard or not. If you choose not to use the Query Wizard, you work directly with Microsoft Query.

Creating a query

Before you can create a query, you must display the Criteria pane. In Query, choose View⇨Criteria. This displays a new pane in the middle of the window. (See Figure 24-11.)

Running Microsoft Query by itself

Normally, you run Query from Excel. But because Query is a standalone application, you also can run it directly. The executable file is named msqry32.exe, and its location can vary (use the Windows Find File feature to locate this program on your system).

If you run Query by itself, you can't return the data to Excel automatically. You can, however, use the Clipboard to copy data from the data pane to any application that you want (including Excel).

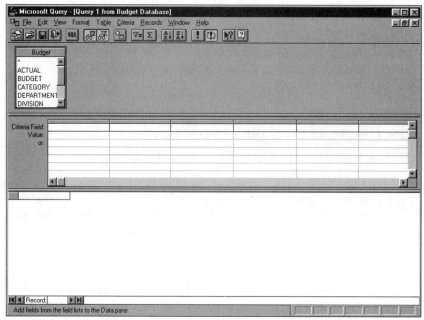

Figure 24-11: Microsoft Query, displaying the Criteria pane.

The Query window has three panes, which are split vertically:

✦ **Tables pane:** The top pane, which holds the data tables for the database. Each data table window has a list of the fields in the table.

✦ **Criteria pane:** The middle pane, which holds the criteria that determine which rows are returned from the query.

✦ **Data pane:** The bottom pane, which holds the data that passes the criteria.

Creating a query consists of the following steps:

1. Drag fields from the Tables pane to the Data pane. You can drag as many fields as you want. These are the columns that are to be returned by the query. You can also double-click on a field instead of dragging it.

2. Enter criteria in the Criteria pane. When you activate this pane, the first row (labeled Criteria field) displays a drop-down list that contains all the field names. Select a field and enter the criteria below. The Data pane is updated automatically. Each row is treated like an OR operator.

3. Choose File⇨Return Data to Microsoft Excel. This executes the query and places the data in a worksheet or pivot table.

Figure 24-12 shows how the query for the example presented earlier in this chapter appears in Query.

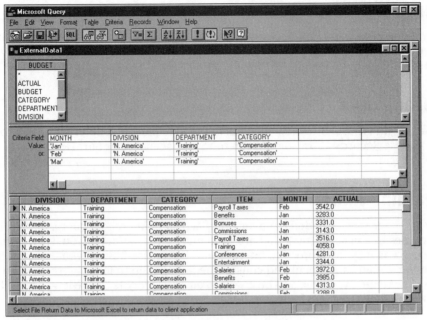

Figure 24-12: The center pane contains a query definition.

Using multiple database tables

The example in this chapter uses only one database table. Some databases, however, use multiple tables. These databases are known as *relational databases,* because the tables are linked by a common field. Query lets you use any number of tables in your queries. To see an example of a relational database, load the sample database (called Northwind Traders) that's provided with Microsoft Query. This particular database has six tables.

Adding and editing records in external database tables

To add, delete, and edit data when using Query, make sure that you choose Records⇨Allow Editing. Of course, you can't edit a database file that's set up as read-only. In any case, you need to be careful with this feature, because your changes are saved to disk as soon as you move the cell pointer out of the record that you're editing (you do not need to choose File⇨Save).

Formatting data

If you don't like the data's appearance in the data pane, you can change the font used by selecting Format⇨Font. Be aware that selective formatting isn't allowed (unlike in Excel); changing the font affects all the data in the data pane.

Sorting data

You may find it useful to view the data in the data pane in a different order. To do so, choose Records⇨Sort (or click on the Sort Ascending or Sort Descending toolbar icon).

Learning more

This chapter isn't intended to cover every aspect of Microsoft Query. Rather, it discusses the basic features that are used most often. In fact, if you use the Query Wizard, you may never need to interact with Query itself. But if you do need to use Query, you can experiment and consult the online Help to learn more. As with anything related to Excel, and best way to master Query is to use it — preferably with data that's meaningful to you.

Summary

In this chapter, I introduce Microsoft Query — a standalone application that can be executed by Excel. Query is used to retrieve data from external database files. You can specify the criteria, and Query returns the data to your Excel worksheet.

✦   ✦   ✦

Analyzing Data with Pivot Tables

In This Chapter

♦ ♦ ♦ ♦

An introduction to Excel's powerful pivot table feature

How to determine whether your data is appropriate for a pivot table

Steps in creating a pivot table

Modifications that you can make after a pivot table is created

Several pivot table examples

♦ ♦ ♦ ♦

Excel provides many data analysis tools, but the pivot table feature may be the most useful overall. Pivot tables are valuable for summarizing information contained in a database, which can be stored in a worksheet or in an external file.

In this chapter, I demonstrate this innovative feature and suggest how you can use it to view your data in ways that you may not have imagined.

What Is a Pivot Table?

A *pivot table* is a dynamic summary of data contained in a database or list. It lets you create frequency distributions and cross-tabulations of several different data dimensions. In addition, you can display subtotals and any level of detail that you desire. But, as I explain later, a pivot table isn't appropriate for all databases.

The best way to understand the concept of a pivot table is to see one. Start with Figure 25-1, which shows the data that is to be used to create the pivot table. This database consists of daily new account information for a three-branch bank. The database tracks the date that each account was opened, the amount, the account type (CD, checking, savings, or IRA), who opened the account (a teller or a new-account representative), the branch at which it was opened, and whether the account was opened by a new customer or an existing customer. The database has 350 records.

This workbook can be downloaded from this book's Web site. It is used in many examples throughout the chapter.

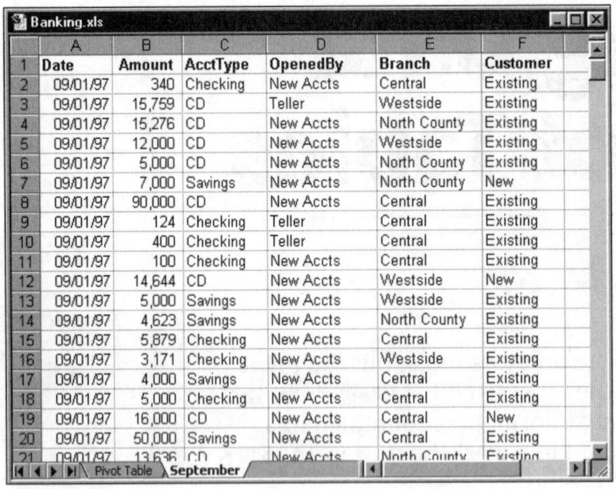
Banking.xls

	A	B	C	D	E	F
1	Date	Amount	AcctType	OpenedBy	Branch	Customer
2	09/01/97	340	Checking	New Accts	Central	Existing
3	09/01/97	15,759	CD	Teller	Westside	Existing
4	09/01/97	15,276	CD	New Accts	North County	Existing
5	09/01/97	12,000	CD	New Accts	Westside	Existing
6	09/01/97	5,000	CD	New Accts	North County	Existing
7	09/01/97	7,000	Savings	New Accts	North County	New
8	09/01/97	90,000	CD	New Accts	Central	Existing
9	09/01/97	124	Checking	Teller	Central	Existing
10	09/01/97	400	Checking	Teller	Central	Existing
11	09/01/97	100	Checking	New Accts	Central	Existing
12	09/01/97	14,644	CD	New Accts	Westside	New
13	09/01/97	5,000	Savings	New Accts	Westside	Existing
14	09/01/97	4,623	Savings	New Accts	North County	Existing
15	09/01/97	5,879	Checking	New Accts	Central	Existing
16	09/01/97	3,171	Checking	New Accts	Westside	Existing
17	09/01/97	4,000	Savings	New Accts	Central	Existing
18	09/01/97	5,000	Checking	New Accts	Central	Existing
19	09/01/97	16,000	CD	New Accts	Central	New
20	09/01/97	50,000	Savings	New Accts	Central	Existing
21	09/01/97	13,636	CD	New Accts	North County	Existing

Figure 25-1: This database is used to create a pivot table.

The bank database contains a lot of information, but it's not all that revealing. In other words, it must be summarized to be useful. Summarizing a database is essentially the process of answering questions about the data. Here are a few questions that may be of interest to the bank's management:

✦ What is the total deposit amount for each branch, broken down by account type?

✦ How many accounts were opened at each branch, broken down by account type?

✦ What's the dollar distribution of the different account types?

✦ What types of accounts do tellers most often open?

✦ How is the Central branch doing compared to the other two branches?

✦ Which branch opens the most accounts for new customers?

You can use a pivot table to answer questions like these. It takes only a few seconds and doesn't require a single formula.

Figure 25-2 depicts a pivot table that was created from the database. It shows the amount of new deposits, broken down by branch and account type. This is one of hundreds of different types of summaries that you can produce from this data.

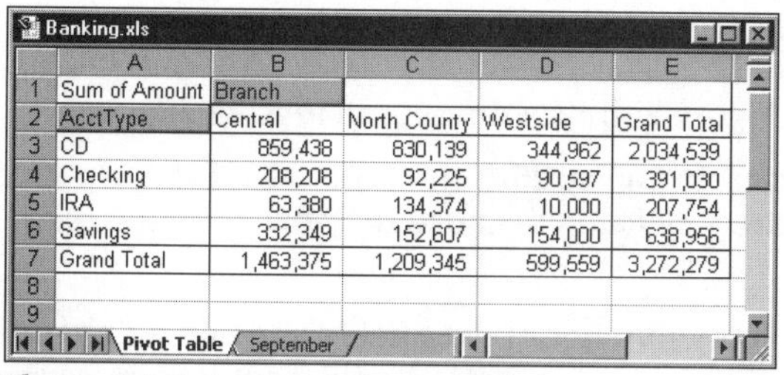

Banking.xls

Sum of Amount	Branch			
AcctType	Central	North County	Westside	Grand Total
CD	859,438	830,139	344,962	2,034,539
Checking	208,208	92,225	90,597	391,030
IRA	63,380	134,374	10,000	207,754
Savings	332,349	152,607	154,000	638,956
Grand Total	1,463,375	1,209,345	599,559	3,272,279

Pivot Table / September

Figure 25-2: A simple pivot table.

Figure 25-3 shows another pivot table that was generated from the bank data. This pivot table uses a page field for the Customer item. In this case, the pivot table displays the data only for New customers. Notice that I also changed the orientation of the table. (Branches are shown in rows and AcctType is shown in columns.)

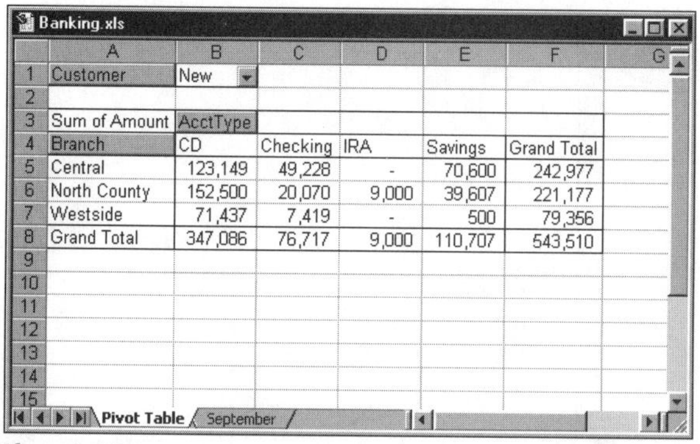

Banking.xls

Customer	New				
Sum of Amount	AcctType				
Branch	CD	Checking	IRA	Savings	Grand Total
Central	123,149	49,228	-	70,600	242,977
North County	152,500	20,070	9,000	39,607	221,177
Westside	71,437	7,419	-	500	79,356
Grand Total	347,086	76,717	9,000	110,707	543,510

Pivot Table / September

Figure 25-3: A pivot table that uses a page field.

Data Appropriate for a Pivot Table

Before I get into the details of pivot tables, it's important to understand the type of data that's relevant to this feature. The data that you're summarizing must be in the form of a database (although there is an exception to this, which I discuss later). The database can be stored in a worksheet (such a database is sometimes known as a table) or in an external database file. Although Excel can convert any database to a pivot table, not all databases benefit.

Generally speaking, fields in a database table can be one of two types:

✦ **Data:** Contains a value. In Figure 25-1, the Amount field is a data field.

✦ **Category:** Describes the data. In Figure 25-1, the Date, AcctType, OpenedBy, and Customer fields are category fields because they describe the data in the Amount field.

A single database table can have any number of data fields and any number of category fields. When you create a pivot table, you usually want to summarize one or more of the data fields. The values in the category fields, on the other hand, appear in the pivot table as rows, columns, or pages.

Exceptions exist, however, and you may find that Excel's pivot table feature is useful even for databases that don't contain actual numerical data fields. The database in Figure 25-4, for example, doesn't contain numerical data fields. But you can create a useful pivot table that counts fields rather than sums them.

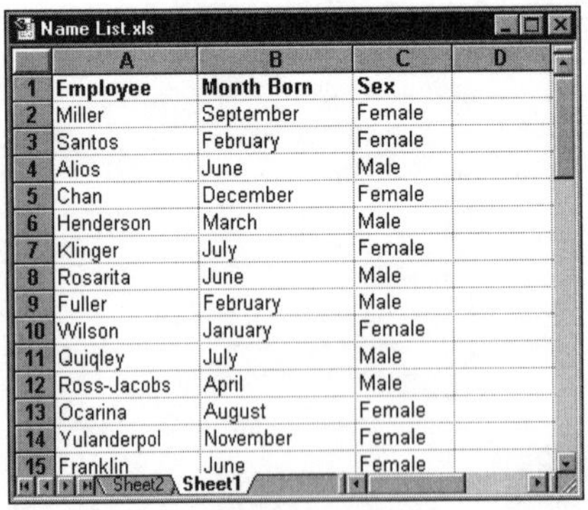

	A	B	C	D
1	Employee	Month Born	Sex	
2	Miller	September	Female	
3	Santos	February	Female	
4	Alios	June	Male	
5	Chan	December	Female	
6	Henderson	March	Male	
7	Klinger	July	Female	
8	Rosarita	June	Male	
9	Fuller	February	Male	
10	Wilson	January	Female	
11	Quigley	July	Male	
12	Ross-Jacobs	April	Male	
13	Ocarina	August	Female	
14	Yulanderpol	November	Female	
15	Franklin	June	Female	

Figure 25-4: This database doesn't have any numerical fields, but it can be used to generate a pivot table.

Figure 25-5 shows a pivot table that was created from this data. In this case, the table cross-tabulates the Month Born field by the Sex field, and the intersecting cells show the count for each combination of city and sex. (Pivot tables can use other summary methods besides summing.)

Pivot table terminology

If you're new to Excel, the concept of a pivot table may be a bit baffling. As far as I know, Microsoft invented the name *pivot table*. It's important to understand the terminology that is used when working with pivot tables. Refer to the accompanying figure to get your bearings.

Column field: A field that has a column orientation in the pivot table. Each item in the field occupies a column. In the figure, Product is a column field, and it has two items (Sprockets and Widgets). Column fields can be nested.

Data area: The cells in a pivot table that contain the summary data. Excel offers several ways to summarize the data (sum, average, count, and so on).

Grand totals: A row or column that displays totals for all cells in a row or column in a pivot table. You can specify that grand totals be calculated for rows, columns, or both (or neither). The pivot table in the figure has grand totals for rows and columns.

Group: A collection of items that are treated as a single item. You can group items manually or automatically (group dates into months, for example).

Item: An element in a field that appears as a row or column header in a pivot table. In the figure, Sprockets and Widgets are items for the Product field. The Year field has three items (1994, 1995, and 1996), and the State field has two items (California and Oregon).

Page field: A field that has a page orientation in the pivot table — similar to a slice of a three-dimensional cube. Only one item at a time in a page field can be displayed at one time. In the figure, Region is a page field that's displaying the West item.

Refresh: To recalculate the pivot table after changes to the source data have been made.

Row field: A field that has a row orientation in the pivot table. Each item in the field occupies a row. Row fields can be nested. In the figure, State and Year are both row fields, and the Year field is nested within the State field.

Source data: The data that is used to create a pivot table. It can be from a worksheet or an external database.

Subtotals: A row or column that displays subtotals for detail cells in a row or column in a pivot table. In the figure, subtotals are calculated for the State field.

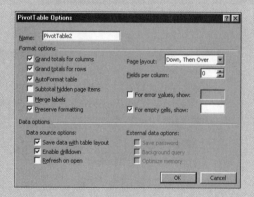

	A	B	C	D	E
1	Count of Employee	Sex			
2	Month Born	Female	Male	Grand Total	
3	January	2	2	4	
4	February	2	2	4	
5	March	0	5	5	
6	April	1	2	3	
7	May	2	0	2	
8	June	3	3	6	
9	July	3	2	5	
10	August	3	2	5	
11	September	4	0	4	
12	October	2	2	4	
13	November	3	1	4	
14	December	2	2	4	
15	Grand Total	27	23	50	

Figure 25-5: This pivot table summarizes non-numeric fields by displaying a count rather than a sum.

Creating a Pivot Table

In this section I walk you through the steps to create a pivot table using the PivotTable Wizard — which is the only way that you can create a pivot table. You access the PivotTable Wizard by choosing Data⇨Pivot Table Report.

Web site I use the banking account workbook, which is available at this book's Web site.

Identifying where the data is located

When you choose Data⇨Pivot Table Report, the first of several dialog boxes appears (see Figure 25-6). In this step, you identify the data source. The possible data sources are described in the following sections.

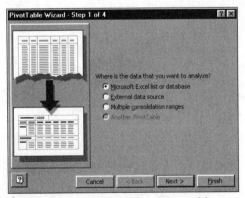

Figure 25-6: The first of four PivotTable Wizard dialog boxes.

Excel list or database

Most of the time, the data that you're analyzing is stored in a worksheet database — which is also known as a list. Databases stored in a worksheet are limited to 65,535 records and 256 fields. It's not efficient to work with a database of this size, however (and memory may not even allow it). The first row in the database should be field names. Other than that, there are no rules. The data can consist of values, text, or formulas.

External data source

If you use the data in an external database for a pivot table, the data is retrieved using Query (a separate application). You can use dBASE files, SQL server data, or other data that your system is set up to access. You are prompted for the data source in Step 2 of the PivotTable Wizard.

Cross Reference I discuss external database access, including Query, in Chapter 24. If you plan to create a pivot table using data in an external database, you should consult Chapter 24 before proceeding.

Multiple consolidation ranges

You also can create a pivot table from multiple tables. This procedure is equivalent to consolidating the information in the tables. But the advantage over other consolidation techniques (discussed in Chapter 19) is that you can work with the consolidated data using all pivot table tools. I present an example of this later in the chapter.

Another pivot table

Excel lets you create a pivot table from an existing pivot table. Actually, this is a bit of a misnomer. The pivot table that you create is based on the *data* that the first pivot table uses (not the pivot table itself). If the active workbook has no pivot tables, this option is grayed.

Tip If you need to create more than one pivot table from the same set of data, it's more efficient (in terms of memory usage) to create the first pivot table and then use that pivot table as the source for subsequent pivot tables.

Specifying the data

To move on to the next step, click on the Next button. Step 2 of the PivotTable Wizard prompts you for the data. The dialog box varies, depending on your choice in the first dialog box. Figure 25-7 shows the dialog box that appears when you select a worksheet database in Step 1.

Tip If the cell pointer is anywhere within the worksheet database when you select Data➪Pivot Table Report, Excel identifies the database range automatically in Step 2 of the PivotTable Wizard.

Figure 25-7: In Step 2, you specify the data range.

You can use the Browse button to open a different worksheet and select a range. To move on to Step 3, click on the Next button.

Setting up the pivot table

The third dialog box of the PivotTable Wizard is shown in Figure 25-8. The fields in the database appear as buttons along the right side of the dialog box. You simply drag the buttons to the appropriate area of the pivot table diagram. The pivot table diagram has four areas:

✦ **Row:** Values in the field appear as row items in the pivot table.

✦ **Column:** Values in the field appear as column items in the pivot table.

✦ **Data:** The field is summarized in the pivot table.

✦ **Page:** Values in the field appear as page items in the pivot table.

You can drag as many field buttons as you want to any of these locations, and you don't have to use all the fields. Fields that aren't used don't appear in the pivot table.

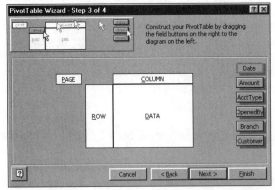

Figure 25-8: In Step 3, you specify the table layout.

When you drag a field button to the Data area, the PivotTable Wizard applies the Sum function if the field has numeric values and the Count function if the field has non-numeric values.

While you're setting up the pivot table in this step, you can double-click on a field button to customize it. You can specify, for example, that a particular field be summarized as a count or other function. You also can specify which items in a field to hide or omit. Be aware, however, that you can customize fields at any time after the pivot table is created.

If you drag a field button to an incorrect location, just drag if off the table diagram to get rid of it.

Figure 25-9 shows how the dialog box looks after I dragged some field buttons to the pivot table diagram. This pivot table displays the sum of the Amount field, broken down by AcctType (as rows) and Customer (as columns). In addition, the Branch field appears as a page field. Click on the Next button to go to the next step.

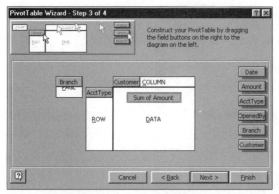

Figure 25-9: The Step 3 PivotTable Wizard dialog box after dragging field buttons to the pivot table diagram.

Pivot table location and options

The dialog box for the final step of the PivotTable Wizard is shown in Figure 25-10. In this step, you specify the location for the pivot table.

Figure 25-10: In Step 4, you specify the pivot table's location.

If you select the New worksheet option, Excel inserts a new worksheet for the pivot table. If you select the Existing worksheet option, the pivot table appears on the current worksheet (you can specify the starting cell location).

You can also click on the Options button to select some options that determine how the table appears. Refer to the sidebar "Pivot table options."

When you click on the Finish button in this dialog box, Excel creates the Pivot Table. Figure 25-11 shows the result of this example.

Notice that the page field displays as a drop-down box. You can choose which item in the page field to display by choosing it from the list. There's also an item called All, which displays all the data.

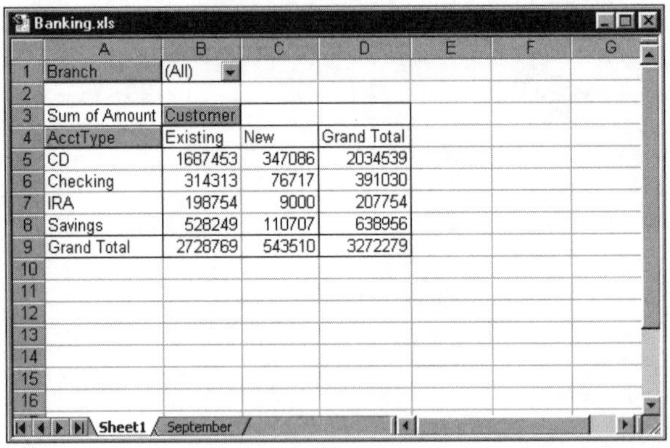

Figure 25-11: The pivot table that is created by the PivotTable Wizard.

Pivot table options

Excel provides plenty of options that determine how your pivot table looks and works. To access these options, click on the Options button in the final step of the PivotTable Wizard. You can also access this dialog box after you create the pivot table. Right-click on any cell in the pivot table, and then select Options from the shortcut menu.

The accompanying figure shows the PivotTable Options dialog box.

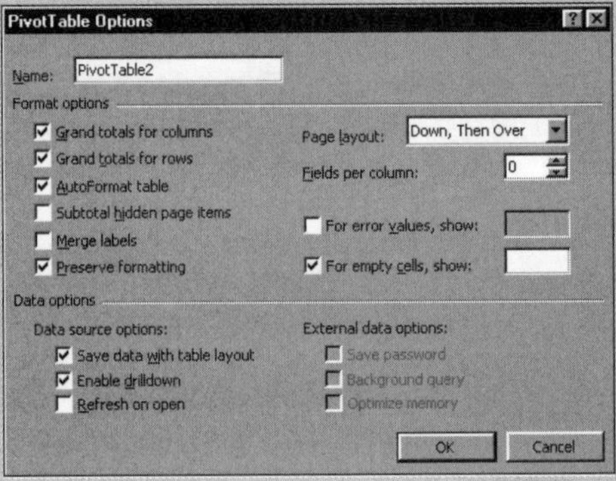

Many of these options are new to Excel 97:

Name: You can provide a name for the pivot table. Excel provides default names in the form of PivotTable1, PivotTable2, and so on.

Grand totals for columns: Check this box if you want Excel to calculate grand totals for items that are displayed in columns.

Grand totals for rows: Check this box if you want Excel to calculate grand totals for items that are displayed in rows.

AutoFormat table: Check this box if you want Excel to apply one of its AutoFormats to the pivot table. Excel uses the AutoFormat even if you re-arrange the table layout.

Subtotal hidden page items: Check this box if you want Excel to include hidden items in the Page fields in the subtotals.

Merge labels: Check this box if you want Excel to merge the cells for outer row and column labels. Doing so may make the table more readable.

Preserve formatting: Check this box if you would like Excel to keep any formatting that you applied when the pivot table is updated.

Page layout: You can specify the order in which you want the page fields to appear.

Fields per column: You can specify the number of page fields to show before starting another row of page fields.

For error values, show: You can specify a value to show for pivot table cells that display an error.

For empty cells, show: You can specify a value to show for pivot table cells that are empty.

Save data with table layout: If this option is checked, Excel stores an additional copy of the data (called a pivot table cache) to allow it to recalculate the table more quickly when you change the layout. If memory is an issue, you should keep this option unchecked (updating is then a bit slower).

Enable drilldown: If checked, you can double-click on a cell in the pivot table to view details.

Refresh on open: If checked, the pivot table is refreshed whenever you open the workbook.

Save password: If you use an external database that requires a password, this option lets you store the password as part of the query so that you don't have to enter it.

Background query: If checked, Excel runs the external database query in the background while you continue your work.

Optimize memory: This option reduces the amount of memory that is used when you refresh an external database query.

Working with Pivot Tables

After you create a pivot table, it's not a static object. You can continue to modify and tweak it until it looks exactly how you want it to look. In this section, I discuss modifications that you can make to a pivot table.

The Pivot Table toolbar is quite useful when working with pivot tables. This toolbar appears automatically when you activate a worksheet that contains a pivot table.

Changing the pivot table structure

Notice that a pivot table, when displayed in a worksheet, includes the field buttons. You can drag any of the field buttons to a new position in the pivot table (this is known as *pivoting*). For example, you can drag a column field to the row position. Excel immediately redisplays the pivot table to reflect your change. You also can change the order of the row fields or the column fields by dragging the buttons. This step affects how the fields are nested and can have a dramatic effect on how the table looks.

Figure 25-12 shows the pivot table that was created in the preceding example but after I made a modification to the table's structure. I dragged the page field button (Branch) to the row position. The pivot table now shows details for each item in the AcctType field for each branch.

Describing how to change the layout of a pivot table is more difficult than doing it. I suggest that you create a pivot table and experiment by dragging field buttons around to see what happens.

Sum of Amount		Customer		
Branch	AcctType	Existing	New	Grand Total
Central	CD	736,289	123,149	859,438
	Checking	158,980	49,228	208,208
	IRA	63,380		63,380
	Savings	261,749	70,600	332,349
Central Total		1,220,398	242,977	1,463,375
North County	CD	677,639	152,500	830,139
	Checking	72,155	20,070	92,225
	IRA	125,374	9,000	134,374
	Savings	113,000	39,607	152,607
North County Total		988,168	221,177	1,209,345
Westside	CD	273,525	71,437	344,962
	Checking	83,178	7,419	90,597
	IRA	10,000		10,000
	Savings	153,500	500	154,000
Westside Total		520,203	79,356	599,559
Grand Total		2,728,769	543,510	3,272,279

Figure 25-12: This pivot table has two row fields.

Note   A pivot table is a special type of range, and (with a few exceptions) you can't make any changes to it. For example, you can't insert or delete rows, edit results, or move cells. If you attempt to do so, Excel displays an appropriate error message.

Removing a field

To remove a field from a pivot table, just click on the field button and drag it away from the pivot table. The field button changes to a button with an X across it (see Figure 25-13). Release the mouse button, and the table is updated to exclude the field.

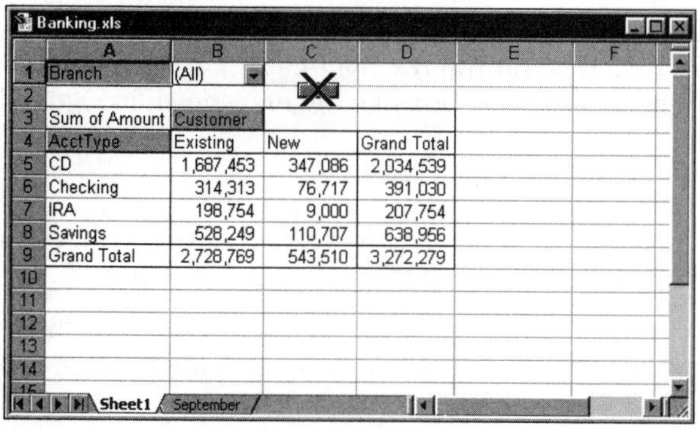

Figure 25-13: Removing a pivot table field by dragging it away.

Adding a new field

To add a new field to the pivot table, move the cell pointer anywhere within the pivot table and choose Data➪Pivot Table Report. Excel displays the third dialog box from the PivotTable Wizard. You can then drag the new field to the desired location in the pivot table diagram. Click on Finish, and Excel updates the pivot table with the new field or fields that you added.

Note   You also can remove fields or change the pivot table's structure from this dialog box.

Refreshing a pivot table

Notice that pivot tables don't contain formulas. Rather, Excel recalculates the pivot table every time you make a change to it. If the source database is large, there may be some delay while this recalculation takes place, but for small databases, the update is virtually instantaneous.

In some cases, you may change the source data. When this happens, the pivot table doesn't get updated automatically. Rather, you must refresh it manually. To refresh a pivot table, you can use any of the following methods:

✦ Choose Data⇨Refresh Data.

✦ Right-click anywhere in the pivot table, and select Refresh Data from the shortcut menu.

✦ Click on the Refresh Data tool on the Pivot Table toolbar.

Customizing a pivot table field

Several options are available for fields within a pivot table. To access these options, simply double-click on a field button (or right-click and select Field from the shortcut menu). Excel displays a dialog box like the one shown in Figure 25-14.

You can modify any of the following items:

✦ **Name:** Changes the name that is displayed on the field button. You can also do this directly by simply editing the cell that holds the field button.

✦ **Orientation:** Changes how the field's items are displayed. You can also take the more direct approach of dragging the field button to another location, as described previously.

✦ **Subtotals:** Lets you change the type of subtotaling that is displayed. Subtotaling is relevant only if you have more than one field displayed as rows or columns. You can make a multiple selection in the list box, which results in more than one line of subtotals. To eliminate subtotals, click on the None option.

✦ **Hide items:** Enables you to hide (not display) one or more items from a field. Click on the specific item names that you want to hide.

Figure 25-14: Double-clicking on a Pivot Table field button displays a dialog box like this one.

Excel 97 Excel 97 includes some additional field options that you can specify by clicking on the Advanced button in the Pivot Table field dialog box. These options let you specify how the field items are sorted and how many items to show (for example, just the top 10).

Formatting a pivot table

When you create a pivot table, the default action is to apply an AutoFormat to the table (you can change this by clicking on the Options button in Step 4). After the pivot table is created, you can always specify a different AutoFormat.

To change the number format for the pivot table data, use the following procedure:

1. Select any cell in the pivot table's data area.

2. Right-click and choose Pivot Table Field from the shortcut menu. Excel displays its Pivot Table Field dialog box.

3. Click on the Number button.

4. Select the number format that you need.

Tip If you want Excel to preserve all the formatting that you perform on individual cells, make sure that the Preserve formatting option is turned on. You do this in the Pivot Table Options dialog box (right-click on a cell, and select Options from the shortcut menu). If this option is not turned on, Excel returns the formats to the default formats when the pivot table is refreshed.

Grouping pivot table items

A handy feature enables you to group specific items in a field. If one of the fields in your database consists of dates, for example, the pivot table displays a separate row or column for every date. You may find it more useful to group the dates into months or quarters and then hide the details. Fortunately, this is easy to do.

Figure 25-15 shows a pivot table that was created with the bank database. It shows total balances for each account type (column field) by the Branch (row field). You've been asked to create a report that compares the Central branch to the other two branches combined. The solution is to create a group that consists of the Westside and North County branches.

To create the group, select the cells to be grouped — in this case, A6:A7. Then choose Data⇨Group and Outline⇨Group (or you can use the Group button on the Pivot Table toolbar). Excel creates a new field called Branch2, and this field has two items: Central and Group1 (see Figure 25-16). At this point, you can remove the Original Branch field (just drag the field button away) and change the names of the field and the items. Figure 25-17 shows the pivot table after making these modifications.

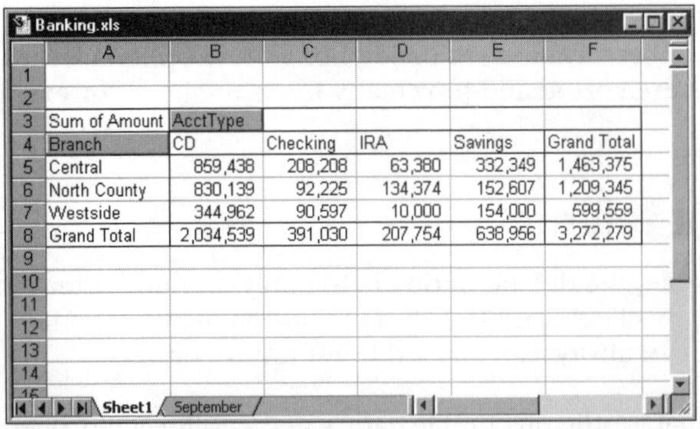

Sum of Amount	AcctType				
Branch	CD	Checking	IRA	Savings	Grand Total
Central	859,438	208,208	63,380	332,349	1,463,375
North County	830,139	92,225	134,374	152,607	1,209,345
Westside	344,962	90,597	10,000	154,000	599,559
Grand Total	2,034,539	391,030	207,754	638,956	3,272,279

Figure 25-15: The North County and Westside branches are to be combined into a group.

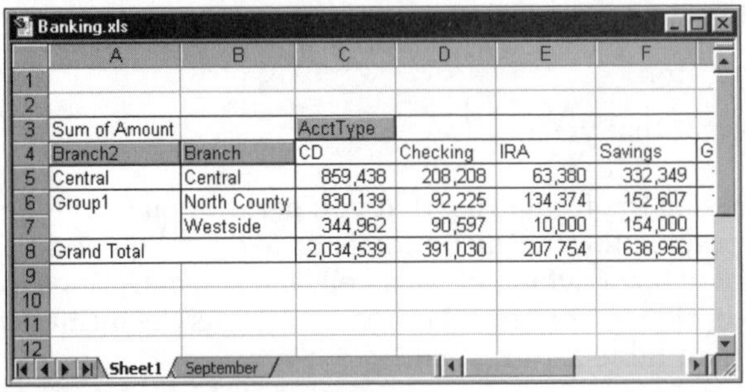

Sum of Amount		AcctType			
Branch2	Branch	CD	Checking	IRA	Savings
Central	Central	859,438	208,208	63,380	332,349
Group1	North County	830,139	92,225	134,374	152,607
	Westside	344,962	90,597	10,000	154,000
Grand Total		2,034,539	391,030	207,754	638,956

Figure 25-16: The pivot table after grouping the North County and Westside branches.

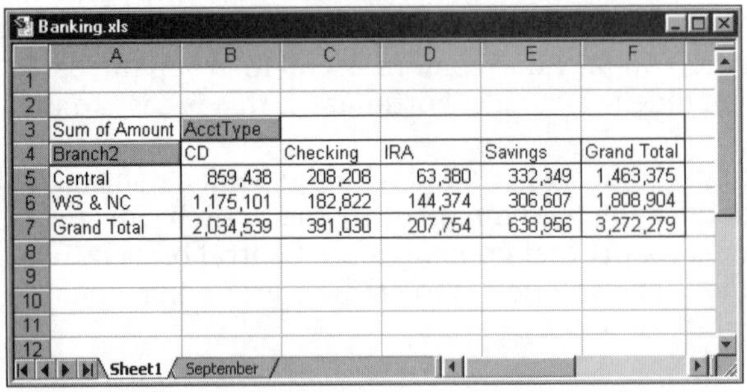

Sum of Amount	AcctType				
Branch2	CD	Checking	IRA	Savings	Grand Total
Central	859,438	208,208	63,380	332,349	1,463,375
WS & NC	1,175,101	182,822	144,374	306,607	1,808,904
Grand Total	2,034,539	391,030	207,754	638,956	3,272,279

Figure 25-17: The pivot table after removing the original Branch field and renaming the new field and items.

Note

The new field name can't be an existing field name. If it is, Excel adds the field to the pivot table. In this example, you can't rename Branch2 to Branch.

Tip

If the items to be grouped are not adjacent to each other, you can make a multiple selection by pressing Ctrl and selecting the items that make up the group.

If the field items to be grouped consist of values, dates, or times, you can let Excel do the grouping for you. Figure 25-18 shows part of another pivot table that I generated from the bank database. This time, I used Amount for the row field and AcctType for the column field. The data area shows the count for each combination. This isn't a useful report because there are so many different items in the Amount field. It can be salvaged, however, by grouping the items into bins.

	A	B	C	D	E	F
	Banking.xls					
1						
2						
3	Count of Amount	AcctType				
4	Amount	CD	Checking	IRA	Savings	Grand Total
5	100	0	16	0	0	16
6	124	0	4	0	0	4
7	133	0	4	0	0	4
8	200	0	3	0	3	6
9	240	0	9	0	0	9
10	245	0	1	0	0	1
11	250	0	0	0	3	3
12	275	0	1	0	0	1
13	340	0	1	0	0	1
14	344	0	3	0	0	3
15	400	0	7	0	0	7
16	500	0	2	0	8	10
17	600	0	0	0	5	5
18	1,000	0	7	0	1	8
19	1,325	0	2	0	0	2
20	1,946	0	2	0	0	2
21	2,000	3	0	6	0	9
22	2,749	0	5	0	0	5

Sheet1 / September /

Figure 25-18: This isn't a useful pivot table because there are too many different items in the Amount field.

To create groups automatically, select any item in the Amount field. Then choose Data➪Group and Outline➪Group. Excel displays the Grouping dialog box that is shown in Figure 25-19. By default, it shows the smallest and largest values — but you can change these to whatever you want. To create groups of $5,000 increments, enter **0** for the Starting at value, **100000** for the Ending at value, and **5000** for the By value (as shown in Figure 25-19). Click on OK, and Excel creates the groups. Figure 25-20 shows the result, which is much more meaningful than the ungrouped data.

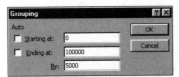

Figure 25-19: The Grouping dialog box instructs Excel to create groups automatically.

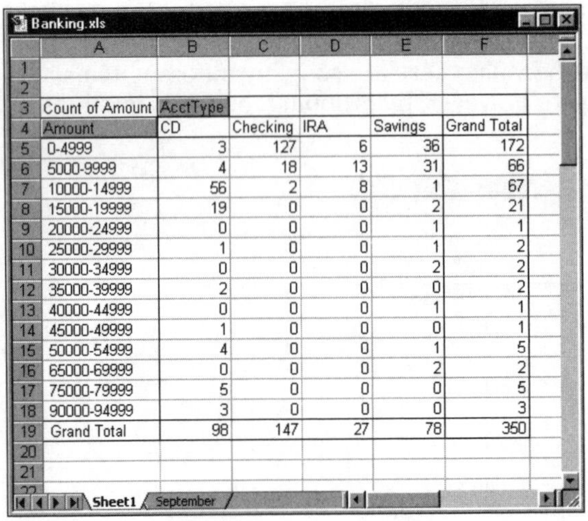

Count of Amount	AcctType				
Amount	CD	Checking	IRA	Savings	Grand Total
0-4999	3	127	6	36	172
5000-9999	4	18	13	31	66
10000-14999	56	2	8	1	67
15000-19999	19	0	0	2	21
20000-24999	0	0	0	1	1
25000-29999	1	0	0	1	2
30000-34999	0	0	0	2	2
35000-39999	2	0	0	0	2
40000-44999	0	0	0	1	1
45000-49999	1	0	0	0	1
50000-54999	4	0	0	1	5
65000-69999	0	0	0	2	2
75000-79999	5	0	0	0	5
90000-94999	3	0	0	0	3
Grand Total	98	147	27	78	350

Figure 25-20: The pivot table after grouping the Amount field items.

Seeing the details

Each cell in the data area of a pivot table represents several records in the source database. You may be interested in seeing exactly which fields contribute to a summary value in the pivot table. Using the banking example, you may want to see a list of the records that make up the total CD accounts in the Central branch. To do so, double-click on the appropriate summary cell in the data area. Excel creates a new worksheet with the records that were used to create the summary. Figure 25-21 shows an example.

Note If double-clicking on a cell doesn't work, make sure that the Enable drilldown option is turned on in the PivotTable Options dialog box (right-click on a pivot table cell and select Options from the shortcut menu).

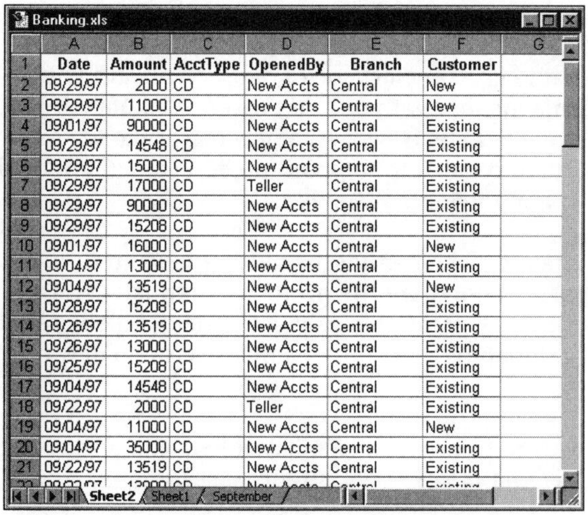

	A	B	C	D	E	F	G
1	Date	Amount	AcctType	OpenedBy	Branch	Customer	
2	09/29/97	2000	CD	New Accts	Central	New	
3	09/29/97	11000	CD	New Accts	Central	New	
4	09/01/97	90000	CD	New Accts	Central	Existing	
5	09/29/97	14548	CD	New Accts	Central	Existing	
6	09/29/97	15000	CD	New Accts	Central	Existing	
7	09/29/97	17000	CD	Teller	Central	Existing	
8	09/29/97	90000	CD	New Accts	Central	Existing	
9	09/29/97	15208	CD	New Accts	Central	Existing	
10	09/01/97	16000	CD	New Accts	Central	New	
11	09/04/97	13000	CD	New Accts	Central	Existing	
12	09/04/97	13519	CD	New Accts	Central	New	
13	09/28/97	15208	CD	New Accts	Central	Existing	
14	09/26/97	13519	CD	New Accts	Central	Existing	
15	09/26/97	13000	CD	New Accts	Central	Existing	
16	09/25/97	15208	CD	New Accts	Central	Existing	
17	09/04/97	14548	CD	New Accts	Central	Existing	
18	09/22/97	2000	CD	Teller	Central	Existing	
19	09/04/97	11000	CD	New Accts	Central	New	
20	09/04/97	35000	CD	New Accts	Central	Existing	
21	09/22/97	13519	CD	New Accts	Central	Existing	

Figure 25-21: Double-clicking on a cell in the data area of a pivot table generates a new worksheet with the underlying data.

Displaying a pivot table on different sheets

If your pivot table is set up to display a field in the Page position, you can see only one slice of the data at a time by using the drop-down list box. Excel has an option, however, that puts each item from a page field on a separate sheet, creating a three-dimensional block of data. To perform this operation, click on the Show Pages button on the Pivot Table toolbar (or right-click and select Show Pages from the shortcut menu). Excel displays the dialog box that is shown in Figure 25-22. This dialog box lists the page fields in your Pivot Table. Select the fields that you want, and Excel inserts enough new sheets to accommodate each item in that field.

Figure 25-22: The Show Pages dialog box lets you display each page field item on a separate worksheet.

Inserting a calculated field into a pivot table

As I noted previously, a pivot table is a special type of data range, and you can't insert new rows or columns. This means that you can't insert formulas to perform calculations with the data in a pivot table. However, a new feature in Excel 97 enables you to create new calculated fields for a pivot table. A calculated field consists of a calculation that can involve other fields.

In the banking example, for instance, assume that management wanted to increase deposits by 15 percent and compare the projected deposits to the current deposits. This can be done by creating a calculated field. Calculated fields must reside in the Data area of the pivot table (you cannot use them in the Page, Row, or Column areas).

The following procedure allows you to create a calculated field that consists of the Amount field multiplied by 1.15 (that is, a 15 percent increase).

1. Move the cell pointer anywhere within the pivot table.

2. Right-click and choose Formulas⇨Calculated Field from the shortcut menu. Excel displays the Insert Calculated Field dialog box, as shown in Figure 25-23.

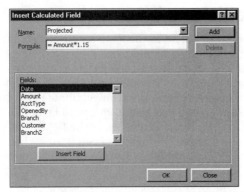

Figure 25-23: The Insert Calculated Field dialog box.

3. Enter a descriptive name for the field, and specify the formula. The formula can use other fields but cannot use worksheet functions. For this example, the name is Projected, and the formula is:

   ```
   =Amount*1.15
   ```

4. Click on Add to add this new field.

5. To create additional calculated fields, repeat Steps 3 and 4. Click on OK to close the dialog box.

After you create the field, it is added to the data area of the pivot table. You can treat it just like any other field, with one exception: It cannot be moved to the page, row, or column area (it must remain in the data area). Figure 25-24 shows a pivot table with a calculated field (called Projected).

	A	B	C	D	E	F
1	Branch	(All)				
2						
3			OpenedBy			
4	Customer	Data	New Accts	Teller	Grand Total	
5	Existing	Sum of Amount	2,279,518	449,251	2,728,769	
6		Sum of Projected	2,621,446	516,639	3,138,084	
7	New	Sum of Amount	541,510	2,000	543,510	
8		Sum of Projected	622,737	2,300	625,037	
9	Total Sum of Amount		2,821,028	451,251	3,272,279	
10	Total Sum of Projected		3,244,182	518,939	3,763,121	
11						
12						
13						
14						
15						

Figure 25-24: This pivot table uses a calculated field.

Tip   The formulas that you develop can also use worksheet functions, but the functions cannot refer to calls or named ranges.

Inserting a calculated item into a pivot table

Excel 97   In the previous section, I explained how to create a calculated field. Excel 97 also lets you create new calculated items for a pivot table field. For example, if you have a field named Months, you can create a calculated item (called Q1, for example) that displays the sum of January, February, and March. You can also do this by grouping the items — but using grouping would hide the individual months and show only the total of the group. Creating a calculated item for quarterly totals shows the total and the individual months. Calculated items must reside in the Page, Row, or Column area of a pivot table (you cannot use calculated items in the Data area).

In the banking example, management may want to look at CD accounts combined with savings accounts. This can be done by creating a calculated item.

To create a calculated item, use these steps:

1. Move the cell pointer to a Row, Column, or Page area of the pivot table. The cell pointer cannot be in the Data area.

2. Right-click and choose Formulas⇨Calculated Item from the shortcut menu. Excel displays the Insert Calculated Item dialog box, as shown in Figure 25-25.

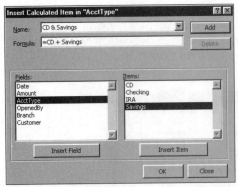

Figure 25-25: The Insert Calculated Item dialog box.

3. Enter a name for the new item, and specify the formula. The formula can use items in other fields but cannot use worksheet functions. For this example, the new item is named **CD & Savings**, and the formula is as follows:

```
=CD + Savings
```

4. Click on Add.

5. Repeat Steps 3 and 4 to create additional items. Click on OK to close the dialog box.

After you create the item, it appears in the pivot table. Figure 25-26 shows the pivot table after adding a calculated item.

	A	B	C	D	E	F
1	Branch	(All)				
2						
3	Sum of Amount	Customer				
4	AcctType	Existing	New	Grand Total		
5	CD	1,687,453	347,086	2,034,539		
6	Checking	314,313	76,717	391,030		
7	IRA	198,754	9,000	207,754		
8	Savings	528,249	110,707	638,956		
9	CD & Savings	2,215,702	457,793	2,673,495		
10	Grand Total	4,944,471	1,001,303	5,945,774		

Figure 25-26: This pivot table uses a calculated item.

Caution If you use a calculated item in your pivot table, you may need to turn off the grand total display to avoid double-counting.

Pivot Table Examples

I firmly believe that the best way to master pivot tables is to work with them — not read about them. The best approach is to use your own data. But if you want to work with some prefab pivot tables, I've developed a few for you to use, and they can be downloaded from this book's Web site. In this section, I describe additional examples of pivot tables to spark your creativity and help you apply some of these techniques to your own data.

Using a pivot table to consolidate sheets

In Chapter 19, I discuss several ways to consolidate data across different worksheets or workbooks. Excel's pivot table feature gives you yet another consolidation option. Figure 25-27 shows three worksheets, each with monthly sales data for a store in a music store chain. The goal is to consolidate this information into a single pivot table. In this example, all the source data is in a single workbook. This situation may not always be the same, however. The data to be consolidated can be in different workbooks.

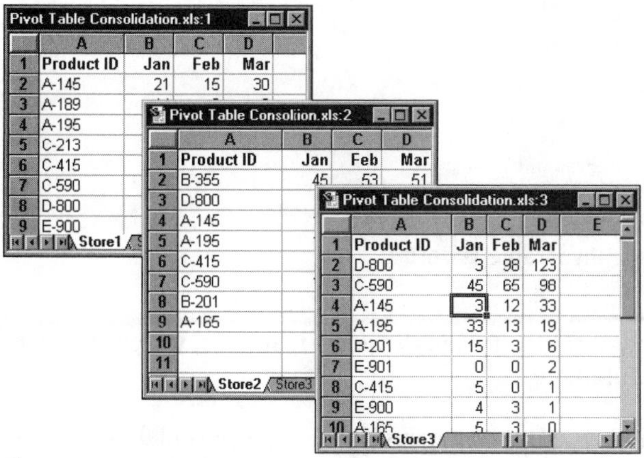

Figure 25-27: These three worksheets are to be consolidated with a pivot table.

The workbook can be downloaded from this book's Web site.

Use the following steps to create this pivot table:

1. Start with a new worksheet named Summary.

2. Choose Data⇨Pivot Table Report to display the PivotTable Wizard.

3. Select the Multiple Consolidation Ranges option, and click on Next.

4. In Step 2a of the PivotTable Wizard, select the option labeled Create a single page field for me. Click on Next.

5. In Step 2b, specify the ranges to be consolidated. The first range is Store1!$A$1:$D$12 (you can enter this directly or point to it). Click on Add to add this range to the All Ranges list.

6. Repeat this for the other two ranges (see Figure 25-28). Click on Next to continue to Step 3.

7. The dialog box in Step 3 of the PivotTable Wizard should look familiar. Notice, however, that it doesn't include actual field names. Rather, it uses generic names such as Row, Column, and Value. You change these names later. Double-click on the button in the data area, and change its function from Sum to Count. Click on Next to continue.

Accept all defaults in Step 4 of the PivotTable Wizard, and click on Finish.

Figure 25-28: Step 2b of the PivotTable Wizard.

Figure 25-29 shows the pivot table. It uses the generic names, which you can change to more meaningful names.

In Step 2a of the PivotTable Wizard, you can choose the option labeled I will create the page fields. Doing so lets you provide an item name for each item in the page field (rather than the generic Item1, Item2, and Item3).

Creating charts from a pivot table

Because a pivot table is just a range in a worksheet, you can create a chart from its data. If you set things up right, the chart changes when you change the pivot table's structure. In general, if you follow these rules, you can produce useful charts from a pivot table:

Page1	(All)			
Sum of Value	Column			
Row	Jan	Feb	Mar	Grand Total
A-145	39	43	84	166
A-165	8	3	1	12
A-189	14	2	2	18
A-195	45	23	36	104
B-201	19	5	9	33
B-355	45	53	51	149
C-213	2	12	5	19
C-415	15	11	18	44
C-590	93	86	109	288
D-800	12	196	257	465
E-900	9	4	1	14
E-901	0	0	2	2
E-904	3	5	7	15
E-912	0	0	2	2
E-923	1	0	0	1
Grand Total	305	443	584	1332

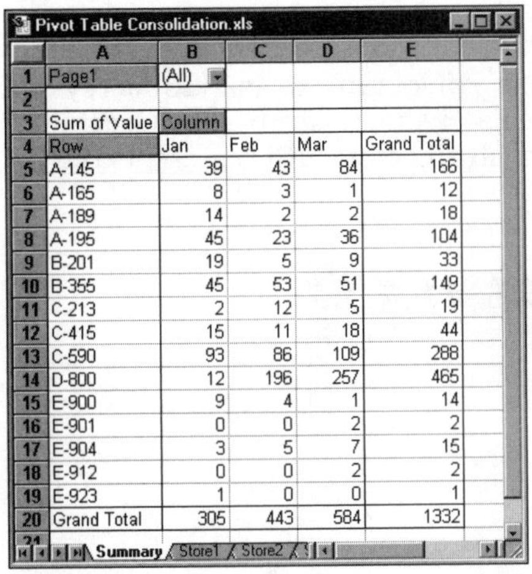

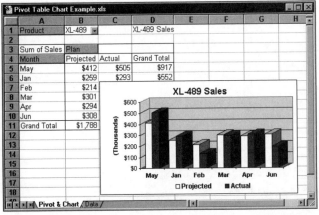

Figure 25-29: This pivot table uses data from three ranges.

- ✦ Don't display subtotals or grand totals. These interrupt the data ranges.
- ✦ Don't use more than two fields for the row position or the column position.
- ✦ Select the entire pivot table (but not the page fields) before you create the chart.

Figure 25-30 shows an example of a chart that was created from a pivot table. This chart is updated whenever I choose a new page field item. Notice that I used a formula for the chart's title, so the chart accurately reflects the data that is depicted.

Web site

The workbook can be downloaded from this book's Web site.

Product	XL-489		XL-489 Sales
Sum of Sales	Plan		
Month	Projected	Actual	Grand Total
May	$412	$505	$917
Jan	$259	$293	$552
Feb	$214		
Mar	$301		
Apr	$294		
Jun	$308		
Grand Total	$1,788		

Figure 25-30: The chart changes based on the pivot table.

Analyzing survey data

In this example, I demonstrate how to use a pivot table to analyze survey data that was obtained via a questionnaire. Figure 25-31 shows part of the raw data typical of that collected from a survey questionnaire. Each record represents the responses for one respondent.

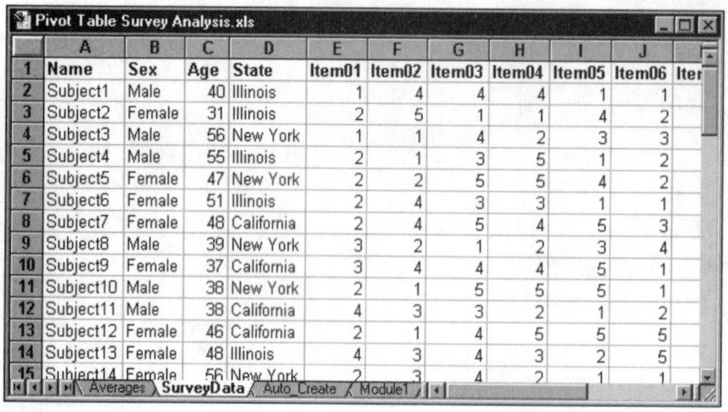
Pivot Table Survey Analysis.xls

	A	B	C	D	E	F	G	H	I	J
1	Name	Sex	Age	State	Item01	Item02	Item03	Item04	Item05	Item06
2	Subject1	Male	40	Illinois	1	4	4	4	1	1
3	Subject2	Female	31	Illinois	2	5	1	1	4	2
4	Subject3	Male	56	New York	1	1	4	2	3	3
5	Subject4	Male	55	Illinois	2	1	3	5	1	2
6	Subject5	Female	47	New York	2	2	5	5	4	2
7	Subject6	Female	51	Illinois	2	4	3	3	1	1
8	Subject7	Female	48	California	2	4	5	4	5	3
9	Subject8	Male	39	New York	3	2	1	2	3	4
10	Subject9	Female	37	California	3	4	4	4	5	1
11	Subject10	Male	38	New York	2	1	5	5	5	1
12	Subject11	Male	38	California	4	3	3	2	1	2
13	Subject12	Female	46	California	2	1	4	5	5	5
14	Subject13	Female	48	Illinois	4	3	4	3	2	5
15	Subject14	Female	56	New York	2	3	4	2	1	1

Averages / SurveyData / Auto_Create / Module1

Figure 25-31: This survey data can be tabulated with a pivot table.

Web site: The workbook used in this example can be downloaded from this book's Web site.

Figure 25-32 show a pivot table that I created to calculate averages for each of the 12 survey items, broken down by sex. Additional page fields make it easy to look at the results by an age group or by a particular state. Or, for a more complex pivot table, you can drag one or both of the page fields to a row or column position.

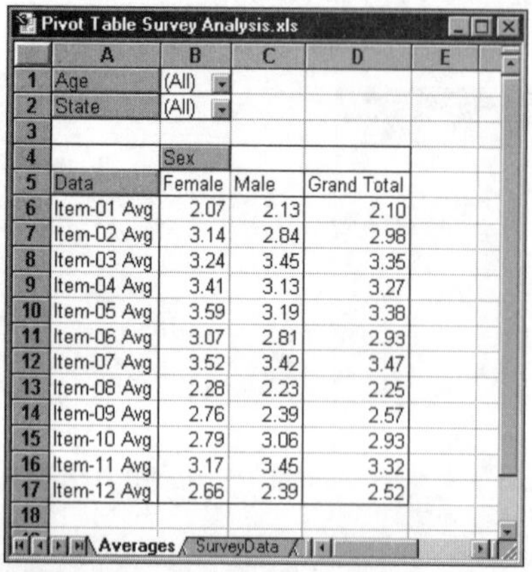
Pivot Table Survey Analysis.xls

	A	B	C	D
1	Age	(All)		
2	State	(All)		
3				
4		Sex		
5	Data	Female	Male	Grand Total
6	Item-01 Avg	2.07	2.13	2.10
7	Item-02 Avg	3.14	2.84	2.98
8	Item-03 Avg	3.24	3.45	3.35
9	Item-04 Avg	3.41	3.13	3.27
10	Item-05 Avg	3.59	3.19	3.38
11	Item-06 Avg	3.07	2.81	2.93
12	Item-07 Avg	3.52	3.42	3.47
13	Item-08 Avg	2.28	2.23	2.25
14	Item-09 Avg	2.76	2.39	2.57
15	Item-10 Avg	2.79	3.06	2.93
16	Item-11 Avg	3.17	3.45	3.32
17	Item-12 Avg	2.66	2.39	2.52
18				

Averages / SurveyData

Figure 25-32: This pivot table calculates averages for each item.

Figure 25-33 shows another sheet in the workbook. This sheet contains 12 separate pivot tables, one for each survey item. Each pivot table displays the frequency of responses and the percentage of responses. Although you could create each table manually, the workbook includes a macro that creates them all in just a few seconds.

Customer geographic analysis

One of the byproducts of creating a pivot table is that you end up with a list of unique entries in a field. Figure 25-34 shows part of a database that tracks customers. The field of interest is the State field (which holds the country in the case of non-U.S. orders). The Type field contains a formula that returns either *Foreign* or *Domestic,* depending on the length of the entry in the State field. The goal of this example is to create a map that shows sales by state.

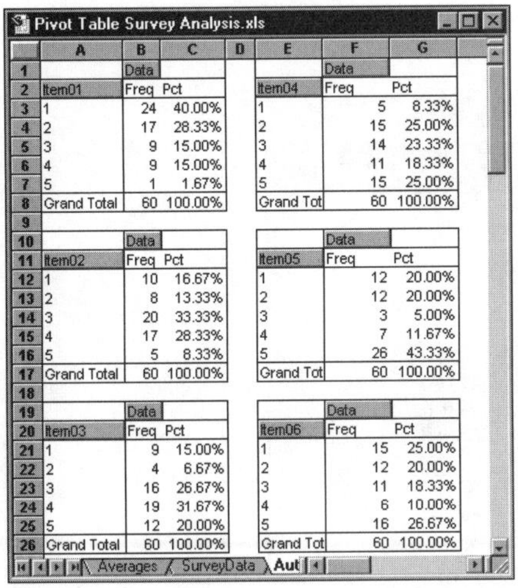
Pivot Table Survey Analysis.xls

	A	B	C	D	E	F	G
1		Data				Data	
2	Item01	Freq	Pct		Item04	Freq	Pct
3	1	24	40.00%		1	5	8.33%
4	2	17	28.33%		2	15	25.00%
5	3	9	15.00%		3	14	23.33%
6	4	9	15.00%		4	11	18.33%
7	5	1	1.67%		5	15	25.00%
8	Grand Total	60	100.00%		Grand Tot	60	100.00%
9							
10		Data				Data	
11	Item02	Freq	Pct		Item05	Freq	Pct
12	1	10	16.67%		1	12	20.00%
13	2	8	13.33%		2	12	20.00%
14	3	20	33.33%		3	3	5.00%
15	4	17	28.33%		4	7	11.67%
16	5	5	8.33%		5	26	43.33%
17	Grand Total	60	100.00%		Grand Tot	60	100.00%
18							
19		Data				Data	
20	Item03	Freq	Pct		Item06	Freq	Pct
21	1	9	15.00%		1	15	25.00%
22	2	4	6.67%		2	12	20.00%
23	3	16	26.67%		3	11	18.33%
24	4	19	31.67%		4	6	10.00%
25	5	12	20.00%		5	16	26.67%
26	Grand Total	60	100.00%		Grand Tot	60	100.00%

Averages / SurveyData / Aut

Figure 25-33: This sheet has 12 pivot tables created by a macro.

Web site

The workbook can be downloaded from this book's Web site.

Figure 25-35 shows a pivot table that I created from this data. It displays the data in terms of total amount, plus a count. I used three page fields to filter the data.

Cross Reference

Figure 25-36 shows the map that I created using Excel's mapping feature (described fully in Chapter 17).

	C	D	E	F	G	H	I
1	City	State	Zip	HowPaid	Amount	Month	Type
56		Canada	L5A 3T5	Card	$49.95	Feb	Foreign
57	Neuendettelesau	Germany		Check	$49.95	Feb	Foreign
58	San Jose	CA	95126-4800	Check	$129.00	Feb	Domestic
59	Montreal Nord, Quebec	Canada	H1G 3L1	Card	$79.95	Feb	Foreign
60	Bellevue	WA	98008-2928	Card	$129.00	Feb	Domestic
61	Austin	TX	78745	Card	$49.95	Feb	Domestic
62	San Antonio	TX	78245	Check	$79.95	Feb	Domestic
63	Fords	NJ	08863	Card	$49.95	Feb	Domestic
64	Solana Beach	CA	92075	Card	$49.95	Feb	Domestic
65	Elkhart	IN	46514	Card	$79.95	Feb	Domestic
66	Omaha	NE	68127	Card	$129.00	Feb	Domestic
67	8036-Barcelona	Spain		Check	$49.95	Feb	Foreign
68	Miami	FL	33122	Card	$79.95	Feb	Domestic
69	Houston	TX	77002	Check	$49.95	Feb	Domestic
70	Great Falls	VA	22066	Check	$129.00	Feb	Domestic
71	Burlington	VT	05402	Check	$49.95	Feb	Domestic
72	Bolingbrook	IL	60440	Check	$49.95	Feb	Domestic

Figure 25-34: This customer database would make a good map, but the data is not in the proper format.

Figure 25-35: This pivot table is perfect input for an Excel map.

Grouping by month and years

The final pivot table example (see Figure 25-37) demonstrates some techniques that involve grouping by dates. The worksheet contains daily pricing data for two years. I created a macro to change the grouping to days, weeks, months, quarters, or years. The macro also changes the range that is used in the chart.

The workbook used in this example can be downloaded from the Web site.

Figure 25-36: This map was created from the data in the pivot table.

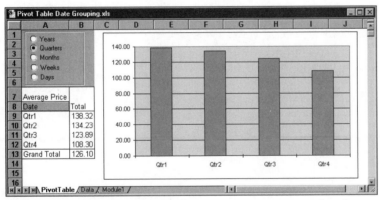

Figure 25-37: Clicking an option button executes a macro that changes the date grouping and updates the chart.

Summary

In this chapter I discuss Excel's pivot table feature. This feature lets you summarize data from a database that can be stored in a worksheet or in an external file. The examples in this chapter demonstrate some useful techniques. The best way to master this feature, however, is to use a database with which you're familiar and experiment until you understand how it works.

✦   ✦   ✦

Performing Spreadsheet What-If Analysis

One of the most appealing aspects of spreadsheet programs — including Excel — is that you can use formulas to create dynamic models that recalculate instantly when you change values in cells to which the formulas refer. When you change values in cells in a systematic manner and observe the effects on specific formula cells, you're performing a type of *what-if* analysis. What-if analysis is the process of asking questions such as, "What if the interest rate on the loan is 8.5 rather than 9.0 percent?" or "What if we raise the prices of our products by five percent?"

If your spreadsheet is set up properly, answering such questions is a matter of plugging in new values and observing the results of the recalculation. Excel provides useful tools to assist you in your what-if endeavors.

A What-If Example

Figure 26-1 shows a spreadsheet that calculates information pertaining to a mortgage loan. The worksheet is divided into two sections: the input cells and the result cells. Column D shows the formulas in column C. With this worksheet, you can easily answer the following what-if questions:

   ◆ What if I can negotiate a lower purchase price on the property?

   ◆ What if the lender requires a 20 percent down payment?

   ◆ What if I can get a 40-year mortgage?

   ◆ What if the interest rate decreases to 7.5 percent?

Hard code values? No way!

The mortgage calculation example, simple as it is, demonstrates an important point about spreadsheet design: You should always set up your worksheet so that you have maximum flexibility to make changes. Perhaps the most fundamental rule of spreadsheet design is:

Do not hard code values in a formula. Rather, store the values in separate cells, and use cell references in the formula.

The term *hard code* refers to the use of actual values, or *constants,* in a formula. In the mortgage loan example, all the formulas use references to cells, not actual values.

You *could* use the value 360, for examplej, for the loan term argument of the PMT function in cell C11. Using a cell reference has two advantages: First, it makes it perfectly clear what values are being used (they aren't buried in the formula). Second, it makes it easier to change the value.

This may not seem like much of an issue when only one formula is involved, but just imagine what would happen if this value were hard coded into several hundred formulas scattered throughout a worksheet.

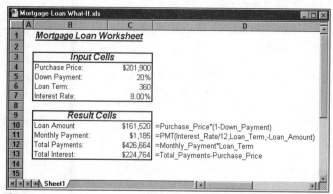

Figure 26-1: This worksheet model uses four input cells to produce the results in the formulas.

You can get the answers by simply plugging in different values in the cells in range C4:C7 and observing the effects in the dependent cells (C10:C13). You can, of course, vary any number of input cells at once.

Types of What-If Analyses

As you may expect, Excel can handle much more sophisticated models than the preceding example. The remainder of this chapter gets into this topic in more depth. To perform what-if analysis using Excel, you have four basic options:

> ✦ **Manual what-if analysis:** Plug in new values and observe the effects on formula cells.
>
> ✦ **Macro-assisted what-if analysis:** Create macros to plug in variables for you.
>
> ✦ **Data tables:** Create a table that displays the results of selected formula cells as one or two input cells are systematically changed.
>
> ✦ **Scenario manager:** Create named scenarios and generate reports that use outlines or pivot tables.

I discuss each of these methods in the following sections.

Manual What-If Analysis

There's not a whole lot to say about this method. In fact, the example that opens this chapter is a good one. It's based on the idea that you have one or more input cells that affect one or more key formulas cells. You change the value in the input cells and see what happens to the formula cells. You may want to print the results or save each scenario to a new workbook. The term *scenario* refers to a specific set of values in one or more input cells.

This is how most people perform what-if analysis. There's certainly nothing wrong with it, but you should be aware of some other techniques.

Macro-Assisted What-If Analysis

Using macros is a slightly more sophisticated form of manual what-if analysis. As I discuss in later chapters, a *macro* is a program that performs a number of operations automatically. Rather than change the input cells manually, you create a macro to do it for you. For example, you may have three macros named BestCase, WorstCase, and MostLikelyCase. Running the BestCase macro enters the appropriate values into the input cells. Executing the WorstCase or MostLikelyCase macros enters other values.

If you understand how to create macros, this technique can be simple to set up. You can attach the macros to buttons so that an inexperienced user can see the results of various scenarios that you've predefined.

Figure 26-2 shows a worksheet that's designed for what-if analysis. It's a simple production model with two input cells: the hourly cost of labor and the unit cost for materials. This company produces three products, and each requires a different number of hours and a different amount of materials to produce. The combined total profit is calculated in cell B17. Management is trying to predict the total profit but is uncertain what the hourly labor cost and material costs are going to be. They've identified three scenarios, as listed in Table 26-1.

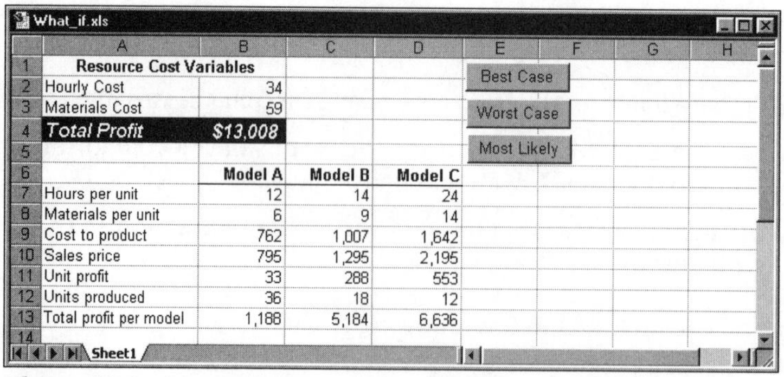

Figure 26-2: This worksheet uses macros to display three different combinations of values for the input cells.

Table 26-1
Three Scenarios for the Production Model

Scenario	Hourly Cost	Materials Cost
Best Case	30	57
Worst Case	38	62
Most Likely Case	34	59

I developed three simple macros and attached one to each of the three buttons on the worksheet. Figure 26-3 shows the VBA macros (also known as subroutines) that are executed when a worksheet button is clicked on. These macros simply place values into the named cells on the worksheet. To change the values that are used in any of the scenarios, you must edit the macros.

Note If you like the idea of instantly displaying a particular scenario, you may be interested in learning about Excel's scenario manager, which I describe later in this chapter. The scenario manager does not require macros.

Creating Data Tables

When you're working with a what-if model, only one scenario at a time can be displayed. But what if you want to compare the results of various scenarios? Here are a few ways to accomplish this:

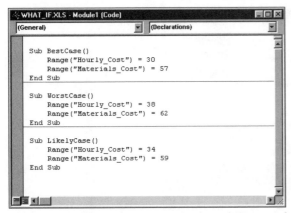

```
WHAT_IF.XLS - Module1 (Code)                              _ □ ×
(General)                    ▼   (Declarations)              ▼

   Sub BestCase()
       Range("Hourly_Cost") = 30
       Range("Materials_Cost") = 57
   End Sub

   Sub WorstCase()
       Range("Hourly_Cost") = 38
       Range("Materials_Cost") = 62
   End Sub

   Sub LikelyCase()
       Range("Hourly_Cost") = 34
       Range("Materials_Cost") = 59
   End Sub
```

Figure 26-3: These macros simply place different values in the input cells in the worksheet.

> ✦ Print multiple copies of the worksheet, each displaying a different scenario.
>
> ✦ Copy the model to other worksheets, and set it up so that each worksheet displays a different scenario.
>
> ✦ Manually create a table that summarizes key formula cells for each scenario.
>
> ✦ Use Excel's Data⇨Table command to create a summary table automatically.

In this section, I discuss the last option — the Data⇨Table command. This command lets you create a handy data table that summarizes formula cells for various values of either of the following:

> ✦ A single input cell
>
> ✦ Various combinations of two input cells

For example, in the production model example, you may want to create a table that shows the total profit for various combinations of hourly cost and materials cost. Figure 26-4 shows a two-input data table that I created, which does just that.

Creating a data table is fairly easy, but it has some limitations. The biggest limitation is that it can deal with only one or two input cells at a time. In other words, you can't create a data table that uses a combination of three or more input cells.

Note The scenario manager, discussed later in this chapter, can produce a report that summarizes any number of input cells and result cells.

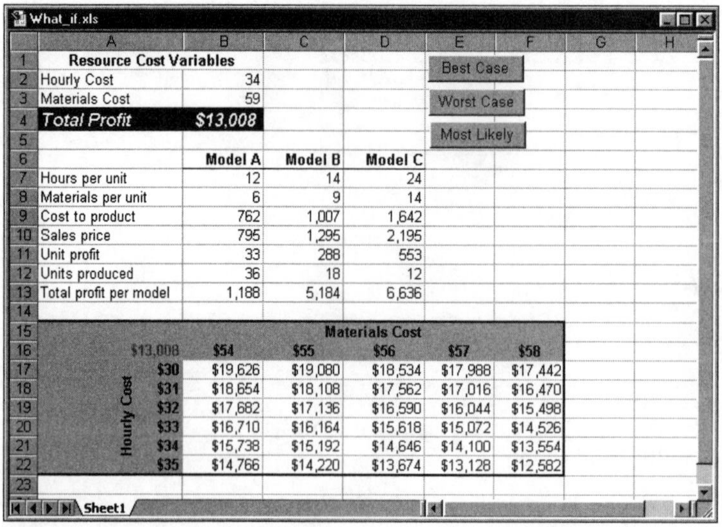

	A	B	C	D
1	Resource Cost Variables			
2	Hourly Cost	34		
3	Materials Cost	59		
4	Total Profit	$13,008		
5				
6		Model A	Model B	Model C
7	Hours per unit	12	14	24
8	Materials per unit	6	9	14
9	Cost to product	762	1,007	1,642
10	Sales price	795	1,295	2,195
11	Unit profit	33	288	553
12	Units produced	36	18	12
13	Total profit per model	1,188	5,184	6,636

		Materials Cost				
	$13,008	$54	$55	$56	$57	$58
Hourly Cost	$30	$19,626	$19,080	$18,534	$17,988	$17,442
	$31	$18,654	$18,108	$17,562	$17,016	$16,470
	$32	$17,682	$17,136	$16,590	$16,044	$15,498
	$33	$16,710	$16,164	$15,618	$15,072	$14,526
	$34	$15,738	$15,192	$14,646	$14,100	$13,554
	$35	$14,766	$14,220	$13,674	$13,128	$12,582

Figure 26-4: This data table summarizes the total profit for various combinations of the input values.

Creating a one-input data table

A one-input data table displays the results of one or more result formulas for multiple values of a single input cell. Figure 26-5 shows the general layout for a one-input data table. The table can be located anywhere in the workbook. The left column contains various values for the single input cell. The top row contains formulas or (more often) references to result formulas that are elsewhere in the worksheet. You can use any number of formula references (including only one). The upper-left cell of the table is not used. Excel calculates the values that result from each level of the input cell and places them under each formula reference.

For this example, I use the mortgage loan worksheet that I referred to earlier in the chapter. It's shown again in Figure 26-6. The goal is to create a table that shows the values of the four formula cells (loan amount, monthly payment, total payments, and total interest) for various interest rates ranging from 7 to 9 percent in 0.25 percent increments.

Figure 26-7 shows how I set up the data table area. Row 2 consists of references to the result formulas in the worksheet. For example, cell F3 contains the formula =C10. Column E has the values of the single-input cell (interest rate) that are to be used in the table. I also add borders to indicate where the calculated values go.

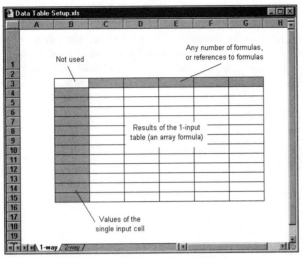

Figure 26-5: How a one-input data table is set up.

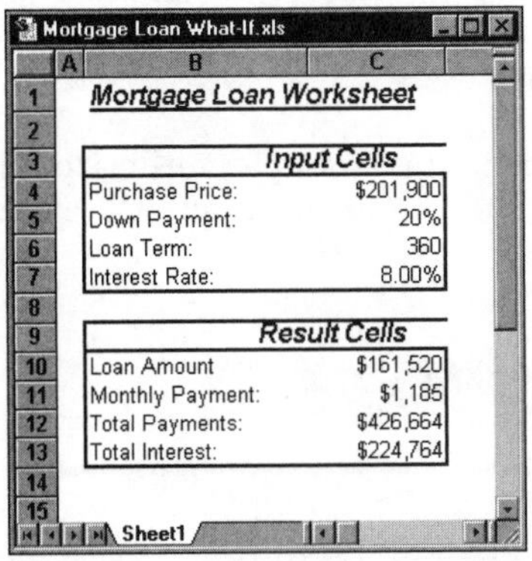

Figure 26-6: This example uses the mortgage loan worksheet to generate a one-input data table.

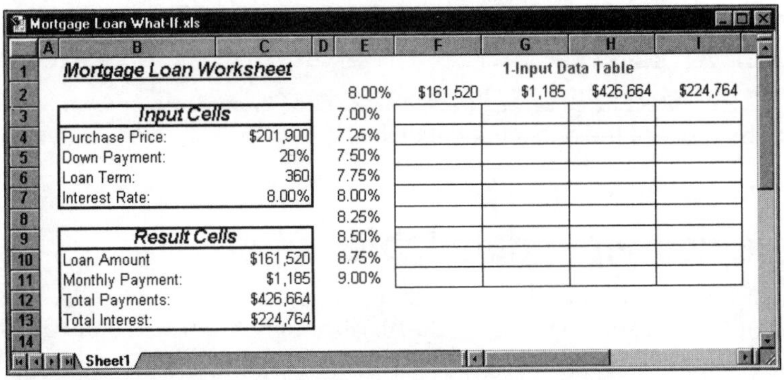

Figure 26-7: Preparing to create a one-input data table.

To create the table, select the range (in this case, E2:I11) and then choose
Data⇨Table. Excel displays the dialog box that is shown in Figure 26-8. You must
specify the worksheet cell that you're using as the input value. Because variables
for the input cell are located in a column in the data table rather than in a row,
you place this cell reference in the text box called Column Input Cell. Enter
Interest_Rate (the name for cell C7), or point to the cell in the worksheet. Leave
the Row Input Cell field blank. Click on OK, and Excel fills in the table with the
appropriate results (see Figure 26-9).

Figure 26-8: The Table dialog box.

If you examine the cells that were entered as a result of this command, notice that
Excel filled in formulas — more specifically, array formulas that use the TABLE
function. As I discuss in Chapter 20, an array formula is a single formula that
produces results in multiple cells. Because it uses formulas, the table that you
produced is updated if you change the cell references in the first row or plug in
different interest rate values in the first column.

Note   A one-input table can be arranged vertically (as in this example) or horizontally. If
the values of the input cell are placed in a row, you enter the input cell reference
in the text box labeled Row Input Cell.

	Mortgage Loan Worksheet				1-Input Data Table			
					8.00%	$161,520	$1,185	$426,664	$224,764
	Input Cells				7.00%	161,520	1,075	386,855	184,955
Purchase Price:	$201,900			7.25%	161,520	1,102	396,666	194,766
Down Payment:	20%			7.50%	161,520	1,129	406,574	204,674
Loan Term:	360			7.75%	161,520	1,157	416,574	214,674
Interest Rate:	8.00%			8.00%	161,520	1,185	426,664	224,764
				8.25%	161,520	1,213	436,840	234,940
	Result Cells			8.50%	161,520	1,242	447,102	245,202
Loan Amount	$161,520			8.75%	161,520	1,271	457,444	255,544
Monthly Payment:	$1,185			9.00%	161,520	1,300	467,866	265,966
Total Payments:	$426,664							
Total Interest:	$224,764							

Figure 26-9: The result of the one-input data table.

Creating a two-input data table

As the name implies, a two-input data table lets you vary *two* input cells. The setup
for this type of table is shown in Figure 26-10. Although it looks similar to a one-
input table, it has one critical difference: A two-input table can show the results of

only one formula at a time. With a one-input table, you can place any number of formulas or references to formulas across the top row of the table. In a two-input table, this top row holds the values for the second input cell. The upper-left cell of the table contains a reference to the single result formula.

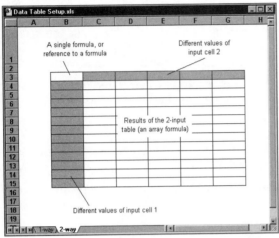

Figure 26-10: How a two-input data table is set up.

In the preceding example, you could create a two-input data table that shows the results of a formula (say, monthly payment) for various combinations of two input cells (such as interest rate and down payment percent). To see the effects on other formulas, you simply create multiple data tables — one for each formula cell that you want to summarize.

I demonstrate a two-input data table with the worksheet that is shown in Figure 26-11. In this example, a company is interested in conducting a direct-mail promotion to sell its product. The worksheet calculates the net profit from the promotion.

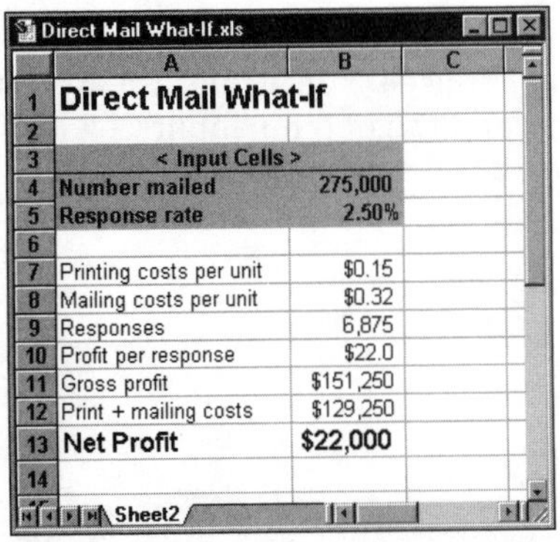

Figure 26-11: This worksheet calculates the net profit from a direct-mail promotion.

This model uses two input cells: the number of promotional pieces mailed and the anticipated response rate. The following items are shown in the results area:

✦ **Printing costs per unit:** The cost to print a single mailer. The unit cost varies with the quantity: $0.20 each for quantities less than 200,000; $0.15 each for quantities of 200,001 through 300,000; and $0.10 each for quantities of more than 300,000. I represent this with the following formula:

```
=IF(Number_mailed<200000,0.2,IF(Number_mailed<300000,0.15,0.1))
```

✦ **Mailing costs per unit:** This is a fixed cost, $0.32 per unit mailed.

✦ **Responses:** This is the number of responses, calculated from the response rate and the number mailed. The formula in this cell is as follows:

```
=Response_rate*Number_mailed
```

✦ **Profit per response:** This is a fixed value. The company knows that it is going to realize a profit of $22 per order.

✦ **Gross profit:** This is a simple formula that multiplies the profit per response by the number of responses:

```
=Profit_per_response*Responses
```

✦ **Print + mailing costs:** This formula calculates the total cost of the promotion:

```
=Number_mailed*(Printing_costs_per_unit+Mailing_costs_per_unit)
```

✦ **Net Profit:** This formula calculates the bottom line — the gross profit minus the printing and mailing costs.

If you plug in values for the two input cells, you see that the net profit varies widely — often going negative to produce a net loss.

I create a two-input data table to summarize the net profit at various combinations of quantity and response rate. Figure 26-12 shows how the table is set up in the range A15:I25.

To create the data table, select the range and choose Data⇨Table. The Row Input Cell is Number_Mailed (the name for cell B4), and the Column Input Cell is Response_Rate (the name for cell B5). Figure 26-13 shows the result of this command.

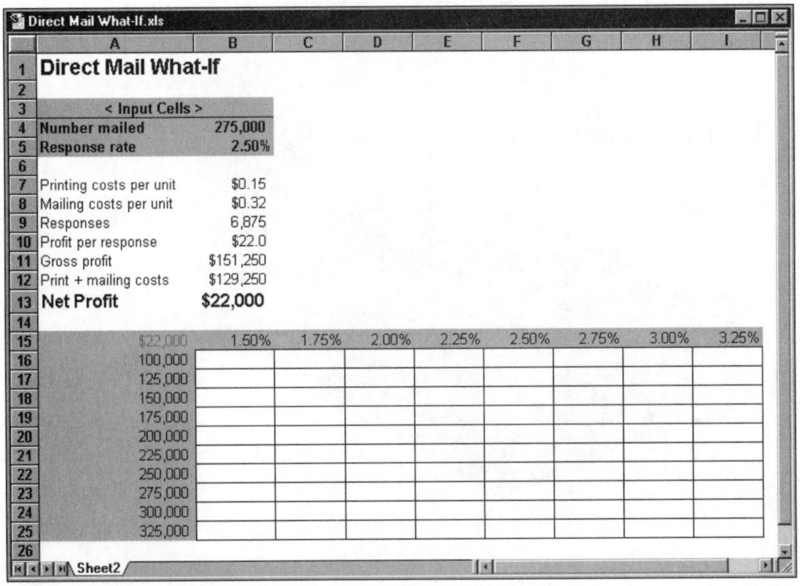

Direct Mail What-If.xls									
	A	**B**	**C**	**D**	**E**	**F**	**G**	**H**	**I**
1	**Direct Mail What-If**								
2									
3	< Input Cells >								
4	Number mailed	275,000							
5	Response rate	2.50%							
6									
7	Printing costs per unit	$0.15							
8	Mailing costs per unit	$0.32							
9	Responses	6,875							
10	Profit per response	$22.0							
11	Gross profit	$151,250							
12	Print + mailing costs	$129,250							
13	**Net Profit**	**$22,000**							
14									
15	$22,000	1.50%	1.75%	2.00%	2.25%	2.50%	2.75%	3.00%	3.25%
16	100,000								
17	125,000								
18	150,000								
19	175,000								
20	200,000								
21	225,000								
22	250,000								
23	275,000								
24	300,000								
25	325,000								
26									

Sheet2

Figure 26-12: Preparing to create a two-input data table.

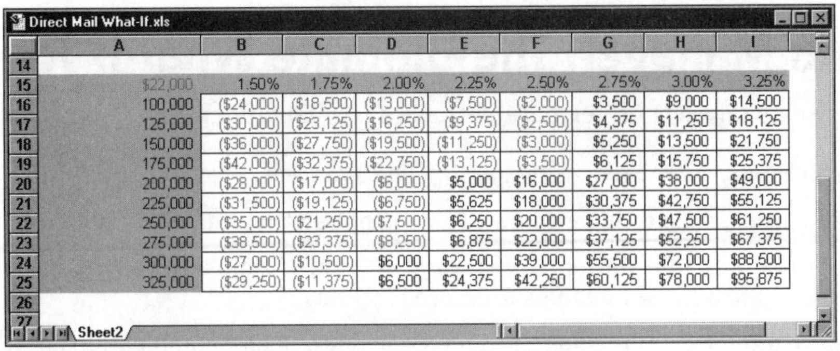

Direct Mail What-If.xls									
	A	**B**	**C**	**D**	**E**	**F**	**G**	**H**	**I**
14									
15	$22,000	1.50%	1.75%	2.00%	2.25%	2.50%	2.75%	3.00%	3.25%
16	100,000	($24,000)	($18,500)	($13,000)	($7,500)	($2,000)	$3,500	$9,000	$14,500
17	125,000	($30,000)	($23,125)	($16,250)	($9,375)	($2,500)	$4,375	$11,250	$18,125
18	150,000	($36,000)	($27,750)	($19,500)	($11,250)	($3,000)	$5,250	$13,500	$21,750
19	175,000	($42,000)	($32,375)	($22,750)	($13,125)	($3,500)	$6,125	$15,750	$25,375
20	200,000	($28,000)	($17,000)	($6,000)	$5,000	$16,000	$27,000	$38,000	$49,000
21	225,000	($31,500)	($19,125)	($6,750)	$5,625	$18,000	$30,375	$42,750	$55,125
22	250,000	($35,000)	($21,250)	($7,500)	$6,250	$20,000	$33,750	$47,500	$61,250
23	275,000	($38,500)	($23,375)	($8,250)	$6,875	$22,000	$37,125	$52,250	$67,375
24	300,000	($27,000)	($10,500)	$6,000	$22,500	$39,000	$55,500	$72,000	$88,500
25	325,000	($29,250)	($11,375)	$6,500	$24,375	$42,250	$60,125	$78,000	$95,875
26									
27									

Sheet2

Figure 26-13: The result of the two-input data table.

Tip   Two-input data tables often make good 3D charts. An example of such a chart for the direct-mail example is shown in Figure 26-14.

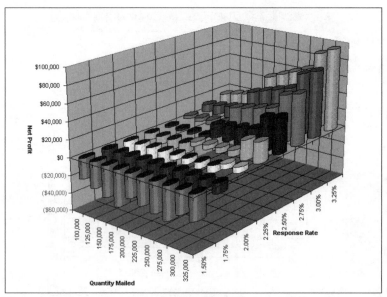

Figure 26-14: Viewing the two-input data table graphically.

Scenario Manager: The Ultimate What-If Tool

Creating data tables is useful, but they have a few limitations:

✦ You can vary only one or two input cells at a time.

✦ The process of setting up a data table is not all that intuitive.

✦ A two-input table shows the results of only one formula cell (although you can create additional tables for more formulas).

✦ More often than not, you're interested in a few select combinations — not an entire table that shows all possible combinations of two input cells.

Excel's scenario manager feature makes it easy to automate your what-if models. You can store different sets of input values (called *changing cells* in the terminology of scenario manager) for any number of variables and give a name to each set. You can then select a set of values by name, and Excel displays the worksheet by using those values. You can also generate a summary report that shows the effect of various combinations of values on any number of result cells. These summary reports can be an outline or a pivot table.

Your sales forecast for the year, for example, may depend on a number of factors. Consequently, you can define three scenarios: best case, worst case, and most likely case. You then can switch to any of these scenarios by selecting the named scenario from a list. Excel substitutes the appropriate input values in your worksheet and recalculates the formulas. This is similar, in some respects, to the macro-assisted what-if technique that I describe earlier. The scenario manager is easier to use, however.

Defining scenarios

To introduce you to the scenario manager, I start with a simple example: the production model that I used earlier.

In this example, I define three scenarios, as depicted in Table 26-2. The Best Case scenario has the lowest hourly cost and materials cost. The Worst Case scenario has high values for both the hourly cost and the materials cost. The third scenario, Most Likely Case, has intermediate values for both of these input cells (this represents the management's best estimate). The managers need to be prepared for the worst case, however — and they are interested in what would happen under the Best Case scenario.

Table 26-2		
Three Scenarios for the Production Model		
Scenario	**Hourly Cost**	**Materials Cost**
Best Case	30	57
Worst Case	38	62
Most Likely Case	34	59

Access the scenario manager by selecting Tools⇨Scenarios. This command brings up the Scenario Manager dialog box, as shown in Figure 26-15.

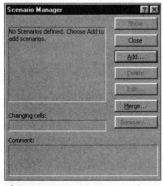

Figure 26-15: The Scenario Manager dialog box lets you assign names to different sets of assumptions.

When you first access this dialog box, it tells you that there are no scenarios defined — which is not too surprising because you're just starting out. As you add named scenarios, they appear in this dialog box.

Tip It's excellent practice to create names for the changing cells, plus all the result cells that you want to examine. Excel uses these names in the dialog boxes and in the reports that it generates. Using names makes it much easier to keep track of what's going on and makes your reports more readable.

To add a scenario, click on the Add button in the Scenario Manager dialog box. Excel displays its Add Scenario dialog box, which is shown in Figure 26-16. This dialog box consists of four parts:

✦ **Scenario name:** The name for the scenario. You can give it any name that you like — preferably something meaningful.

✦ **Changing cells:** The input cells for the scenario. You can enter the cell addresses directly or point to them. Multiple selections are allowed, so the input cells need not be adjacent. Each named scenario can use the same set of changing cells or different changing cells. The number of changing cells for a scenario is limited to 32.

✦ **Comment:** By default, Excel displays who created the scenario and the time that it was created. You can change this text, add new text to it, or delete it.

✦ **Protection:** The two options (preventing changes and hiding a scenario) are in effect only when the worksheet is protected and the Scenario option is chosen in the Protect Sheet dialog box. Protecting a scenario prevents anyone from modifying it; a hidden scenario doesn't appear in the Scenario Manager dialog box.

Figure 26-16: The Add Scenario dialog box lets you create a named scenario.

In this example, define the three scenarios that are listed in the preceding table. The changing cells are `Hourly_Cost` (B4) and `Materials_Cost` (B5).

After you enter the information in the Add Scenario dialog box, click on OK. Excel then displays the Scenario Values dialog box, which is shown in Figure 26-17. This dialog box displays one field for each changing cell that you specified in the previous dialog box. Enter the values for each cell in the scenario. If you click on OK, you return to the Scenario Manager dialog box — which then displays your named scenario in its list. If you have more scenarios to create, click on the Add button to return to the Add Scenario dialog box.

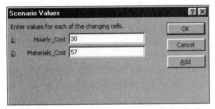

Figure 26-17: You enter the values for the scenario in the Scenario Values dialog box.

Using the Scenarios tool

Excel has a Scenarios tool, which is a drop-down list that shows all the defined scenarios and lets you display a scenario or create a new scenario. Oddly, this useful tool doesn't appear on any of the pre-built toolbars. But, if you use the scenario manager, you may want to add the Scenarios tool to one of your toolbars. You can use the following procedure:

1. Choose Tools➪Customize.

2. In the Customize dialog box, click on the Commands tab.

3. Select the Tools category.

4. In the Commands panel, locate the Scenarios tool and drag it to any toolbar.

5. Click on the Close button.

Refer to Chapter 33 for additional details on customizing toolbars.

Using the Scenarios tool may be more efficient than bringing up the Scenario Manager dialog box to create or view a different scenario.

To create a scenario using the Scenarios tool, enter the scenario's values, select the changing cells, and then enter the name for the scenario in the Scenario drop-down box. To view a named scenario, just choose it from the list. Scenarios that you define in this manner also appear in the Scenario Manager dialog box. So, if you want to perform any operations on your scenarios (add comments, edit values, or generate reports), you need to select Tools➪Scenarios to bring up the Scenario Manager dialog box.

Displaying scenarios

After you define all the scenarios and return to the Scenario Manager dialog box, the dialog box displays the names of your defined scenarios. Select one of the scenarios, and then click on the Show button. Excel inserts the corresponding values into the changing cells, and the worksheet is calculated to show the results for that scenario.

Modifying scenarios

The Edit button in the Scenario Manager dialog box does what you may expect: It lets you edit a scenario (change one or more of the values for the changing cells). Select the scenario that you want to change, click on the Edit button, choose OK to get to the Scenario Values dialog box, and make your changes. Notice that Excel automatically updates the Comments box with new text that indicates when the scenario was modified.

Merging scenarios

In workgroup situations, you may have several people working on a spreadsheet model, and several people may have defined various scenarios. The marketing department, for example, may have its opinion of what the input cells should be, the finance department may have another opinion, and your CEO may have yet another opinion.

Excel makes it easy to merge these various scenarios into a single workbook by using the Merge button in the Scenario Manager dialog box. Clicking on this button displays the dialog box that is shown in Figure 26-18.

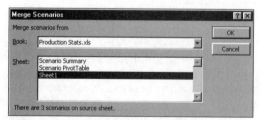

Figure 26-18: The Merge Scenarios dialog box lets you merge scenarios that are defined by others into your workbook.

Before you merge scenarios, make sure that the workbook from which you're merging is open. Then click on the Merge button in the Scenario Manager dialog box. Excel displays its Merge Scenarios dialog box. Choose the workbook that you're merging from the Book drop-down list, and then choose the sheet that has the scenarios defined from the Sheet list box (notice that the dialog box displays the number of scenarios in each sheet as you scroll through the Sheet list box). Click on OK, and you return to the previous dialog box, which now displays the scenario names that were merged from the other workbook.

Generating a scenario report

Now it's time to take the scenario manager through its final feat — generating a summary report. When you click on the Summary button in the Scenario Manager dialog box, Excel displays the Scenario Summary dialog box that is shown in Figure 26-19.

Figure 26-19: The Scenario Summary dialog box lets you choose a report type and specify the result cells in which you're interested.

You have a choice of report types:

Cross
Reference

✦ **Scenario Summary:** The summary report is in the form of an outline.

✦ **Scenario PivotTable:** The summary report is in the form of a pivot table (see Chapter 25).

For simple cases of scenario management, a standard Scenario Summary report is usually sufficient. If you have many scenarios defined with multiple result cells, however, you may find that a pivot table provides more flexibility.

The Scenario Summary dialog box also asks you to specify the result cells (the cells that contain the formulas in which you're interested). For this example, select B15:D15 and B17 (a multiple selection). This makes the report show the profit for each product, plus the total profit.

Excel creates a new worksheet to store the summary table. Figure 26-20 shows the Scenario Summary form of the report, and Figure 26-21 shows the Scenario Pivot Table form. If you gave names to the changing cells and result cells, the table uses these names. Otherwise, it lists the cell references.

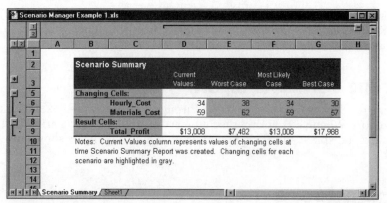

Figure 26-20: A summary report that was produced by the scenario manager.

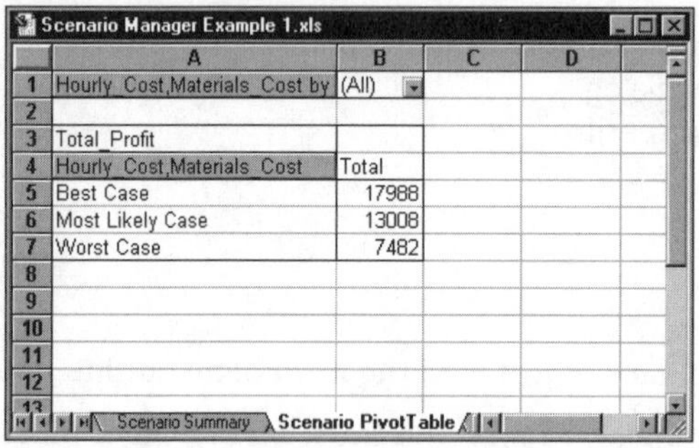

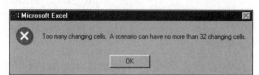

Figure 26-21: A pivot table summary report that was produced by the scenario manager.

Scenario Manager Limitations

As you work with the scenario manager, you may discover its main limitation: a scenario can use no more than 32 changing cells. If you attempt to use more, you get the message that is shown in Figure 26-22.

Figure 26-22: The scenario manager is limited to 32 changing cells.

You can get around this limitation by splitting your scenarios into parts. For example, assume that you have a worksheet with monthly sales projects for three years (36 changing cells). You may want to define various scenarios for these projections. But because the number of changing cells exceeds the 32-cell limit, you can break it down into two or three scenarios — each of which uses a different set of changing cells. For example, you can define a scenario for the first 12 months, another for the second 12 months, and yet another for the third 12 months. Then, to display a particular scenario, you must display all three subscenarios. Writing simple macros makes this easy. The only downside to using this technique is that the summary reports include superfluous information.

Summary

In this chapter, I discuss the concept of spreadsheet what-if analysis. What-if analysis is the process of systematically changing input cells and observing the effects one or more formula cells. You can perform what-if analysis manually by plugging in different values. You also can use macros to automate this process. Excel's data table feature lets you summarize the result of various values of a single input cell or various combinations of two-input cells. The scenario manager feature makes it easy to create scenarios and generate summary reports.

✦   ✦   ✦

Analyzing Data Using Goal Seeking and Solver

◆ ◆ ◆ ◆

In This Chapter

An introduction to goal seeking, which can be viewed as what-if analysis in reverse

How to perform single-cell goal seeking

How Solver extends the concept of goal seeking

Examples of problems that are appropriate for Solver

◆ ◆ ◆ ◆

In the preceding chapter, I discussed what-if analysis — the process of changing input cells to observe the results on other dependent cells. This chapter looks at that process from the opposite perspective: finding the value of one or more input cells that produces a desired result in a formula cell.

What-If Analysis — In Reverse

Consider the following what-if question: "What is the total profit if sales increase by 20 percent?" If your worksheet is set up properly, you can change the value in one cell to see what happens to the profit cell. Goal seeking takes the opposite approach. If you know what a formula result *should* be, Excel can tell you which values of one or more input cells are required to produce that result. In other words, you can ask a question such as, "What sales increase is needed to produce a profit of $1.2 million?" Excel provides two tools that are relevant:

✦ **Goal Seeking:** Determines the value that is required in a single input cell to produce a result that you want in a dependent (formula) cell.

✦ **Solver:** Determines the values that are required in multiple input cells to produce a result that you want. Moreover, because you can specify certain constraints to the problem, you gain significant problem-solving ability.

I discuss both of these procedures in this chapter.

Single-Cell Goal Seeking

Single-cell goal seeking (also known as *backsolving*) is a rather simple concept. Excel determines what value in an input cell produces a desired result in a formula cell. The best way to understand how this works is to walk through an example.

A goal-seeking example

Figure 27-1 shows the mortgage loan worksheet that was used in the preceding chapter. This worksheet has four input cells and four formula cells. I originally used this worksheet for a what-if analysis example, but now I take the opposite approach. Rather than supply different input cell values to look at the calculated formulas, I let Excel determine one of the input values.

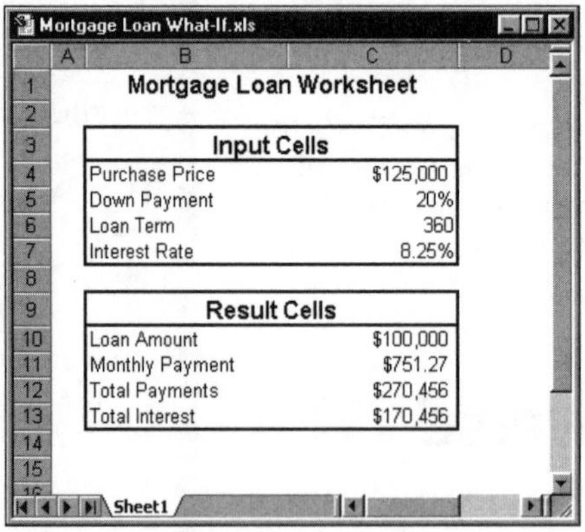

Figure 27-1: This worksheet is a good demonstration of goal seeking.

Assume that you're in the market for a new home and you know that you can afford $1,200 per month in mortgage payments. You also know that a lender can issue a fixed-rate mortgage loan for 8.25 percent, based on an 80 percent loan-to-value (that is, a 20 percent down payment). The question is, "What is the maximum purchase price I can handle?" In other words, what value in cell C4 causes the formula in cell C11 to result in $1,200? One approach is to plug values into cell C4 until C11 displays $1,200. A more efficient approach is to let Excel determine the answer.

To answer this question, select Tools⇨Goal Seek. Excel responds with the dialog box that is shown in Figure 27-2. Completing this dialog box is similar to forming a sentence. You want to set cell C11 to 1200 by changing cell C4. Enter this information in the dialog box by either typing the cell references or by pointing with the mouse. Click on OK to begin the goal-seeking process.

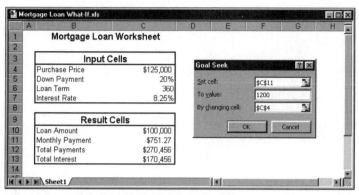

Figure 27-2: The Goal Seek dialog box.

In about a second, Excel announces that it has found the solution and displays the Goal Seek Status box. This box tells you what the target value was and what Excel came up with. In this case, Excel found an exact value. The worksheet now displays the found value in cell C4 ($199,663). As a result of this value, the monthly payment amount is $1,200. At this point, you have two options:

✦ Click on OK to replace the original value with the found value.

✦ Click on Cancel to restore your worksheet to the form it had before you chose Tools⇨Goal Seek.

More about goal seeking

If you think about it, you realize that Excel can't always find a value that produces the result you're looking for — sometimes a solution doesn't exist. In such a case, the Goal Seek Status box informs you of that fact (see Figure 27-3). Other times, however, Excel may report that it can't find a solution, but you're pretty sure that one exists. If that's the case, you can try the following options:

✦ Change the current value of the changing cell to a value closer to the solution, and then reissue the command.

✦ Adjust the Maximum iterations setting in the Calculation panel of the Options dialog box. Increasing the number of iterations makes Excel try more possible solutions.

✦ Double-check your logic, and make sure that the formula cell does indeed depend on the specified changing cell.

Note Like all computer programs, Excel has limited precision. To demonstrate this, enter =A1^2 into cell A1. Then select Tools⇨Goal Seek to find the value in cell A1 that makes the formula return 16. Excel comes up with a value of 4.00002269 — which is close to the square root of 16, but certainly not exact. You can adjust the precision in the Calculation panel of the Options dialog box (make the Maximum change value smaller).

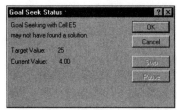

Figure 27-3: When Excel can't find a solution
to your goal-seeking problem, it tells you so.

Note In some cases, multiple values of the input cell produce the same desired result.
For example, the formula =A1^2 returns 16 if cell A1 contains either –4 or +4. If you
use goal seeking when there are two solutions, Excel gives you the solution that
has the same sign as the current value in the cell.

Perhaps the main limitation of the Tools➪Goal Seek command is that it can find
the value for only one input cell. For example, it can't tell you what purchase price
and what down payment percent result in a particular monthly payment. If you
want to change more than one variable at a time, use Solver (which I discuss later
in this chapter).

Graphical goal seeking

Excel provides another way to perform goal seeking — by manipulating a graph.
Figure 27-4 shows a worksheet that projects sales for a startup company. The CFO
knows from experience that companies in this industry can grow exponentially
according to a formula such as this one:

$y*(b^x)$

Table 27-1 lists and describes the variables.

Table 27-1 Variables Used in the Sales Growth Formula	
Variable	*Description*
y	A constant equal to the first year's sales
b	A growth coefficient
x	A variable relating to time

The company managers know that sales during the first year are going to be $250,000, and they want to increase the company's sales to $10 million by the year 2005. The financial modelers want to know the exact growth coefficient that meets this goal. The worksheet that is shown in Figure 27-4 uses formulas to forecast the annual sales using the growth coefficient in cell B1. The worksheet has an embedded chart that plots the annual sales.

The initial guess for the growth coefficient is 1.40. As you can see, this number is too low — it results in sales of only $7.231 million for the year 2005. Although you can select <u>T</u>ools⇨<u>G</u>oal Seek to arrive at the exact coefficient, there's another way to do it.

Double-click on the chart so that you can edit it, and then select the chart series. Now click on the last data column to select only that column in the series. Point to the top of the column, and notice that the mouse pointer changes shape. Drag the column upward, and watch the value change in the small box displayed next to the mouse pointer. When the value is exactly $10 million, release the mouse button.

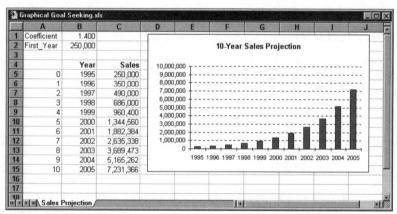

Figure 27-4: This sales projection predicts exponential growth, based on the growth coefficient in cell B1.

Excel responds with the usual Goal Seek dialog box, as shown in Figure 27-5. Notice that two fields are filled in for you. Excel just needs to know which cell to use for the input cell. Specify cell B1 or enter **Coefficient** in the edit box. Excel calculates the value of `Coefficient` that is necessary to produce the result that you pointed out on the chart. If you want to keep that number (which, by the way, is 1.44612554959182), click on OK. Excel replaces the current value of `Coefficient` with the new value, and the chart is updated automatically. You can probably appreciate the fact that it would take quite a while to arrive at this number by plugging in successive approximations.

Figure 27-5: The Goal Seek dialog box appears when you directly manipulate a point on a chart that contains a formula.

You don't want to use this graphical method all the time, because the normal Tools➪Goal Seek command is more efficient. But it does demonstrate another way to approach problems, which is helpful for those who are more visually oriented.

As you may expect, goal seeking can get much more impressive when it's used with complex worksheets that have many dependent cells. In any event, it sure beats trial and error.

Introducing Solver

Excel's goal-seeking feature is a useful tool, but it clearly has limitations. It can solve for only one adjustable cell, for example, and it returns only a single solution. Excel's powerful Solver tool extends this concept in the following ways:

✦ You can specify multiple adjustable cells.

✦ You can specify constraints on the values that the adjustable cells can have.

✦ You can generate a solution that maximizes or minimizes a particular worksheet cell.

✦ You can generate multiple solutions to a problem.

Although goal seeking is a relatively simple operation, using Solver can be much more complicated. In fact, Solver is probably one of the most difficult (and potentially frustrating) features in Excel. I'm the first to admit that Solver isn't for everyone. In fact, most Excel users have no use for this feature. But many users find that having this much power is worth spending the time to learn about it.

Appropriate problems for Solver

Problems that are appropriate for Solver fall into a relatively narrow range. They typically involve situations that meet the following criteria:

✦ A *target cell* depends on other cells and formulas. Typically, you want to maximize or minimize this target cell or set it equal to some value.

✦ The target cell depends on a group of cells (called *changing cells*) that can be adjusted so that they affect the target cell.

✦ The solution must adhere to certain limitations, or *constraints.*

After your worksheet is set up appropriately, you can use Solver to adjust the changing cells and produce the result that you want in your target cell — and simultaneously meet all the constraints that you have defined.

Web site   All the Solver examples in this chapter can be downloaded from this book's Web site.

A simple Solver example

I start with a simple example to introduce Solver and then present some increasingly complex examples to demonstrate what it can do.

Figure 27-6 shows a worksheet that is set up to calculate the profit for three products. Column B shows the number of units of each product, column C shows the profit per unit for each product, and column C contains formulas that calculate the profit for each product by multiplying the units by the profit per unit.

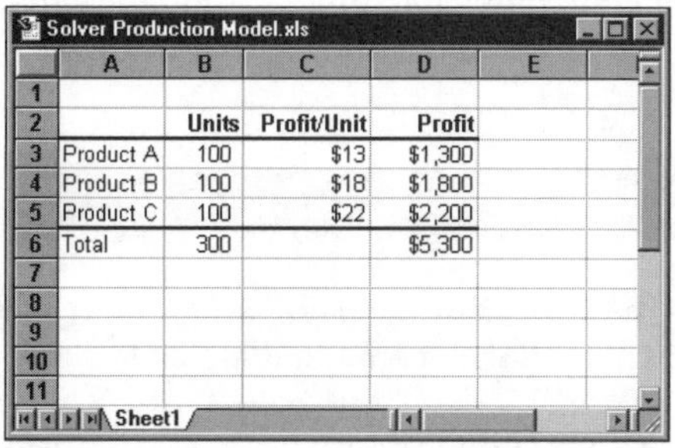

Figure 27-6: Use Solver to determine the number of units to maximize the total profit.

It doesn't take an MBA degree to realize that the greatest profit per unit comes from Product C. Therefore, the logical solution is to produce only Product C. If things were really this simple, you wouldn't need tools such as Solver. As in most situations, this company has some constraints to which it must adhere. These constraints are as follows:

✦ The combined production capacity is 300 total units per day.

✦ The company needs 50 units of Product A to fill an existing order.

✦ The company needs 40 units of Product B to fill an anticipated order.

✦ Because the market for Product C is relatively limited, produce no more than 40 units of this product.

These four constraints make the problem more realistic and challenging. In fact, it's a perfect problem for Solver.

The basic procedure for using Solver is as follows:

1. Set up the worksheet with values and formulas.

2. Bring up the Solver dialog box.

3. Specify the target cell.

4. Specify the changing cells.

5. Specify the constraints.

6. Change the Solver options if necessary.

7. Let Solver solve the problem.

To start Solver, select Tools⇨Solver. Excel displays its Solver Parameters dialog box, as shown in Figure 27-7.

No Tools⇨Solver command?

Solver is an add-in, so it's available only when the add-in is installed. If the Tools menu doesn't show a Solver command, you need to install the add-in before you can use it.

Select Tools⇨Add-Ins. Excel displays its Add-Ins dialog box. Scroll down the list of add-ins, and place a check mark next to the item named Solver Add-In. Click on OK, and Excel installs the add-in and makes the Tools⇨Solver command available.

If Solver Add-In doesn't appear in the list, you need to run Excel's Setup program (or the Setup program for Microsoft Office). Use the Custom option, and specify that Solver be installed. Running Setup again takes only a few minutes.

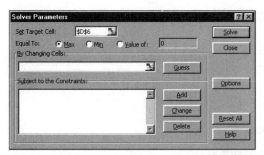

Figure 27-7: The Solver Parameters dialog box.

In this example, the target cell is D6 — the cell that calculates the total profit for three products. Enter (or point to) cell D6 in the Set Target Cell field. Because the objective is to maximize this cell, click on the Max option. Next, specify the changing cells, which are in the range B3:B5.

The next step is to specify the constraints on the problem. The constraints are added one at a time and appear in the box labeled Subject to the Constraints. To add a constraint, click on the Add button. Excel displays the Add Constraint dialog box, which is shown in Figure 27-8. This dialog box has three parts: a cell reference, an operator, and a value. The first constraint is that the total production capacity is 300 units. Enter B6 as the cell reference, choose equal (=) from the drop-down list of operators, and enter 300 as the value. Click on Add to add the remaining constraints. Table 27-2 summarizes the constraints for this problem.

Table 27-2
Constraints Summary

Constraint	Expressed As
Capacity is 300 units	B6=300
At least 50 units of Product A	B3>=50
At least 40 units of Product B	B4>=40
No more than 40 units of Product C	B5<=40

When you've entered the last constraint, click on OK to return to the Solver Parameters dialog box — which now lists the four constraints.

At this point, Solver knows everything about the problem. Click on the Solver button to start the solution process. You can watch the progress on-screen, and Excel soon announces that it has found a solution. The Solver Results dialog box is shown in Figure 27-9.

Figure 27-8: The Add Constraint dialog box.

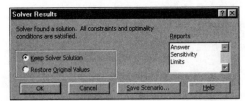

Figure 27-9: Solver displays this dialog box when it finds a solution to the problem.

At this point, you have the following options:

✦ Replace the original changing cell values with the values that Solver found.

✦ Restore the original changing cell values.

✦ Create any or all three reports that describe what Solver did (press Shift to select multiple reports from this list).

✦ Click on the Save Scenario button to save the solution as a scenario so that it can be used by the scenario manager (see Chapter 26).

If you specify any report options, Excel creates each report on a new worksheet, with an appropriate name. Figure 27-10 shows an Answer Report. In the Constraints section of the report, all the constraints except one are *binding,* which means that the constraint was satisfied at its limit, with no more room to change.

This simple example illustrates how Solver works. The fact is, you could probably solve this particular problem manually just as quickly. That, of course, isn't always the case.

More about Solver

Before I present complex examples, I discuss the Solver Options dialog box — one of the more feature-packed dialog boxes in Excel. From this dialog box, you control many aspects of the solution process, as well as load and save model specifications in a worksheet range.

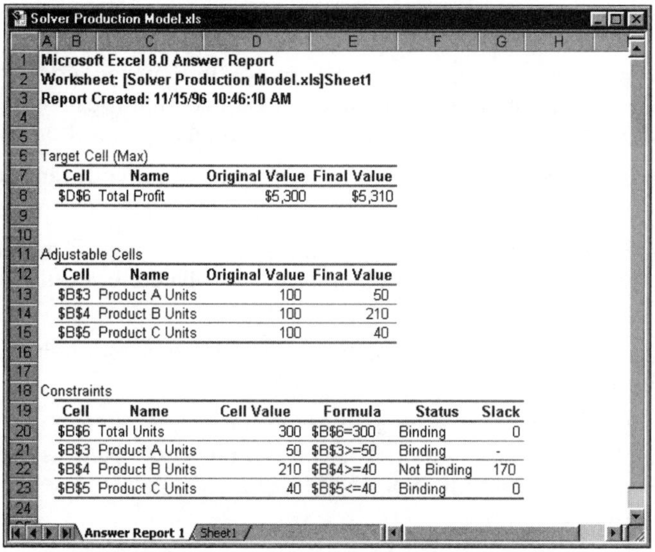

Figure 27-10: One of three reports that Solver can produce.

It's not unusual for Solver to report that it can't find a solution — even when you know that one should exist. Often, you can change one or more of the Solver options and try again. When you choose the Options button in the Solver Parameters dialog box, Excel displays the Solver Options dialog box, as shown in Figure 27-11.

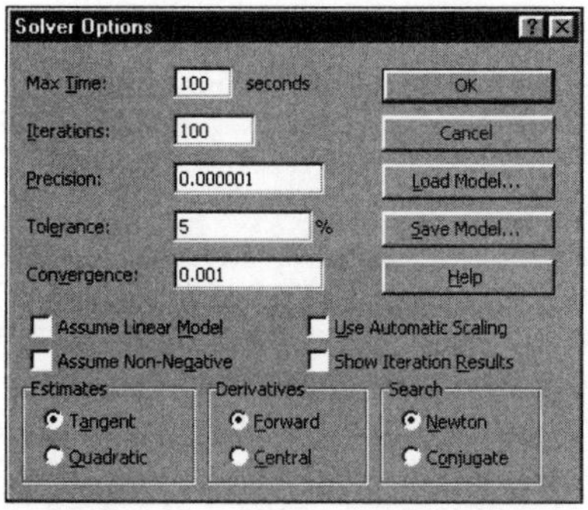

Figure 27-11: You can control many aspects of how Solver solves a problem.

This list describes Solver's options:

✦ **Max Time:** You can specify the maximum amount of time (in seconds) that you want Solver to spend on a problem. If Solver reports that it exceeded the time, you can increase the time that it spends searching for a solution.

✦ **Iterations:** Enter the maximum number of trial solutions that you want Solver to perform.

✦ **Precision:** Specifies how close the Cell Reference and Constraint formulas must be to satisfy a constraint. The problem may be solved more quickly if you specify less precision.

✦ **Tolerance:** The maximum percentage of error allowed for integer solutions (relevant only if there is an integer constraint).

✦ **Assume Linear Model:** Can speed the solution process, but you can use it only if all the relationships in the model are linear. You can't use this option if the adjustable cells are multiplied or divided, or if the problem uses exponents.

✦ **Show Iteration Results:** If this option is set, Solver pauses and displays the results after each iteration.

✦ **Use Automatic Scaling:** Turns on automatic scaling. This is useful when the problem involves large differences in magnitude — when you attempt to maximize a percentage, for example, by varying cells that are very large.

✦ **Estimates, Derivatives, and Search group boxes:** Let you control some technical aspects of the solution. In most cases, you don't need to change these settings.

✦ **Save Model:** Displays the Save Model dialog box, in which you specify a worksheet reference where the model parameters are to be saved.

✦ **Load Model:** Displays the Load Model dialog box, in which you specify a worksheet reference for the model that you want to load.

Usually, you want to save a model only when you're using more than one set of Solver parameters with your worksheet. This is because the first Solver model is saved automatically with your worksheet (using hidden names). If you save additional models, the information is stored in the form of formulas that correspond to the specification that you made (the last cell in the saved range is an array formula that holds the options settings). You can use the Load Model button to save these settings.

Solver Examples

The remainder of this chapter consists of examples of using Solver for various types of problems.

Minimizing shipping costs

This example involves finding alternative options for shipping materials while keeping total shipping costs at a minimum (see Figure 27-12). A company has warehouses in Los Angeles, St. Louis, and Boston. Retail outlets throughout the United States place orders, which then are shipped from one of the warehouses. The object is to meet the product needs of all six retail outlets from available inventory in the warehouses — and keep total shipping charges as low as possible.

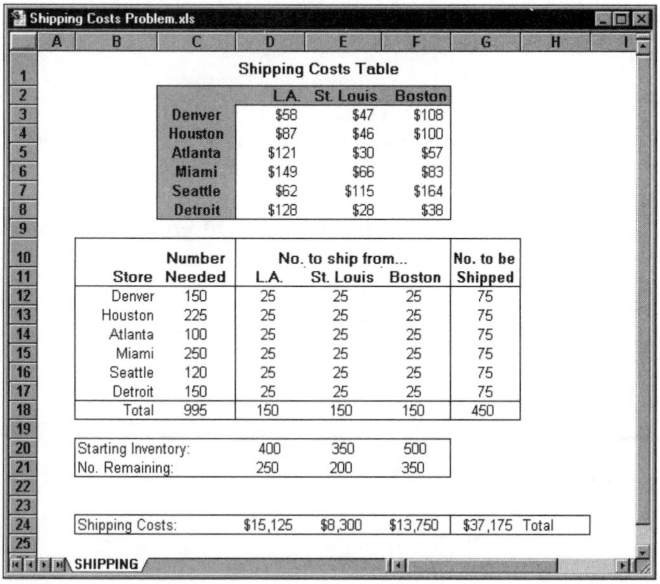

Shipping Costs Problem.xls								
	A	B	C	D	E	F	G	H
1				Shipping Costs Table				
2				L.A.	St. Louis	Boston		
3			Denver	$58	$47	$108		
4			Houston	$87	$46	$100		
5			Atlanta	$121	$30	$57		
6			Miami	$149	$66	$83		
7			Seattle	$62	$115	$164		
8			Detroit	$128	$28	$38		
9								
10			Number	No. to ship from...			No. to be	
11		Store	Needed	L.A.	St. Louis	Boston	Shipped	
12		Denver	150	25	25	25	75	
13		Houston	225	25	25	25	75	
14		Atlanta	100	25	25	25	75	
15		Miami	250	25	25	25	75	
16		Seattle	120	25	25	25	75	
17		Detroit	150	25	25	25	75	
18		Total	995	150	150	150	450	
19								
20		Starting Inventory:		400	350	500		
21		No. Remaining:		250	200	350		
22								
23								
24		Shipping Costs:		$15,125	$8,300	$13,750	$37,175	Total
25								

SHIPPING

Figure 27-12: This worksheet determines the least expensive way to ship products from warehouses to retail outlets.

This workbook is rather complicated, so I explain each part:

✦ **Shipping Costs Table:** This table, at the top of the worksheet, contains per-unit shipping costs from each warehouse to each retail outlet. The cost to ship a unit from Los Angeles to Denver, for example, is $58.

✦ **Product needs of each retail store:** This information is contained in C12:C17. For example, Denver needs 150 units, Houston needs 225, and so on. C18 holds the total needed.

✦ **Number to ship:** The shaded range (D12:F17) holds the adjustable cells that Solver varies (I initialized them all with a value of 25 to give Solver something to start with.) Column G contains formulas that total the number of units to be shipped to each retail outlet.

✦ **Warehouse inventory:** Row 20 contains the amount of inventory at each warehouse, and row 21 contains formulas that subtract the amount shipped (row 18) from the inventory. For example, cell D21 has this formula: =D20–D18.

✦ **Calculated shipping costs:** Row 24 contains formulas that calculate the shipping costs. Cell D24 contains the following formula, which was copied to the two cells to the right:

```
=SUMPRODUCT(D3:D8,D12:D17)
```

This formula calculates the total shipping cost from each warehouse. Cell G24 is the bottom line, the total shipping costs for all orders.

Solver fills in values in the range D12:F17 in such a way that each retail outlet gets the desired number of units *and* the total shipping cost is minimized. In other words, the solution minimizes the value in cell C24 by adjusting the cells in D12:F17, subject to the following constraints:

✦ The number of units needed by each retail outlet must equal the number shipped (in other words, all the orders are filled). These constraints are represented by the following specifications:

```
C12=G12   C14=G14    C16=G16
C13=G13   C15=G15    C17=G17
```

✦ The adjustable cells can't be negative. In other words, shipping a negative number of units makes no sense. These constraints are represented by the following specifications:

```
D12>=0    E12>=0     F12>=0
D13>=0    E13>=0     F13>=0
D14>=0    E14>=0     F14>=0
D15>=0    E15>=0     F15>=0
D16>=0    E16>=0     F16>=0
D17>=0    E17>=0     F17>=0
```

✦ The number of units remaining in each warehouse's inventory must not be negative (that is, they can't ship more than what is available). This is represented by the following constraint specifications:

```
D21>=0    E21>=0     F21>=0
```

Note Before you solve this problem with Solver, you may try your hand at minimizing the shipping cost manually by entering values in D12:F17. Don't forget to make sure that all the constraints are met. This is often a difficult task — and you can better appreciate the power behind Solver.

Setting up the problem is the difficult part. For example, you must enter 27 constraints. When you have specified all the necessary information, click on the Solve button to put Solver to work. This process takes a while, but eventually Solver displays the solution that is shown in Figure 27-13.

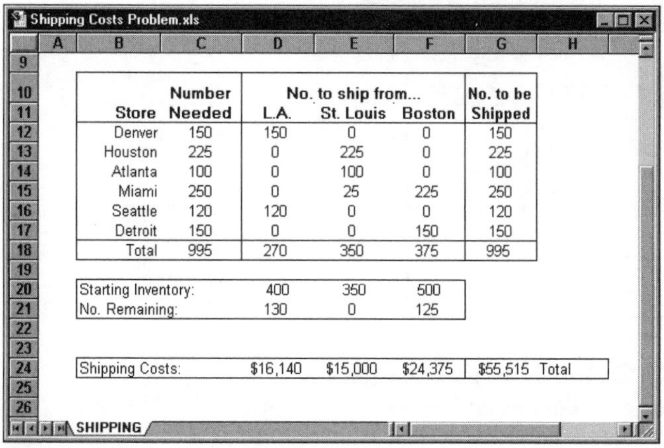

Figure 27-13: The solution that was created by Solver.

The total shipping cost is $55,515, and all the constraints are met. Notice that shipments to Miami come from both St. Louis and Boston.

Scheduling staff

This example deals with staff scheduling. Such problems usually involve determining the minimum number of people that satisfy staffing needs on certain days or times of the day. The constraints typically involve such details as the number of consecutive days or hours that a person can work.

Figure 27-14 shows a worksheet that is set up to analyze a simple staffing problem. The question is, "What is the minimum number of employees required to meet daily staffing needs?" At this company, each person works five consecutive days. As a result, employees begin their five-day workweek on different days of the week.

The key to this problem, as with most Solver problems, is figuring out how to set up the worksheet. This example makes it clear that setting up your worksheet properly is critical to working with Solver. This worksheet is laid out as follows:

- ✦ **Day:** Column B consists of plain text for the days of the week.
- ✦ **Staff Needed:** The values in column C represent the number of employees needed on each day of the week. As you see, staffing needs vary quite a bit by the day of the week.

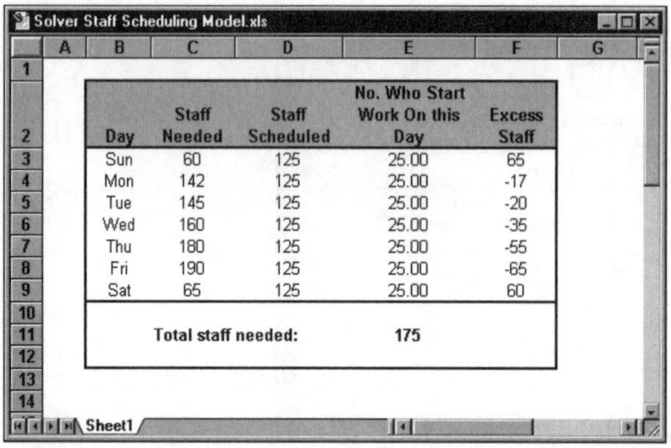
Solver Staff Scheduling Model.xls

Day	Staff Needed	Staff Scheduled	No. Who Start Work On this Day	Excess Staff
Sun	60	125	25.00	65
Mon	142	125	25.00	-17
Tue	145	125	25.00	-20
Wed	160	125	25.00	-35
Thu	180	125	25.00	-55
Fri	190	125	25.00	-65
Sat	65	125	25.00	60
	Total staff needed:		175	

Sheet1

Figure 27-14: This staffing model determines the minimum number of staff members required to meet daily staffing needs.

- ✦ **Staff Schedules:** Column D holds formulas that use the values in column E. Each formula adds the number of people who start on that day to the number of people who started on the preceding four days. Because the week wraps around, you can't use a single formula and copy it. Consequently, each formula in column D is different:

```
D3:    =E3+E9+E8+E7+E6
D4:    =E4+E3+E9+E8+E7
D5:    =E5+E4+E10+E9+E8
D6:    =E6+E5+E4+E10+E9
D7:    =E7+E6+E5+E4+E10
D8:    =E8+E7+E6+E5+E4
D9:    =E9+E8+E7+E6+E5
```

- ✦ **Adjustable Cells:** Column E holds the adjustable cells — the numbers to be determined by Solver. I initialized these cells with a value of 25 to give Solver something to start with. Generally, it's best to initialize the changing cells to values that are as close as possible to the anticipated answer.

✦ **Excess Staff:** Column F contains formulas that subtract the number of staff members needed from the number of staff members scheduled, to determine excess staff. Cell F3 contains =D3 - C3, which was copied to the six cells below it.

✦ **Total Staff Needed:** Cell E11 is a formula that sums the number of people who start on each day. The formula is =SUM(E3:E9). This is the value that Solver minimizes.

This problem, of course, has constraints. The number of people scheduled each day must be greater than or equal to the number of people required. If each value in column F is greater than or equal to 0, the constraints are satisfied.

After the worksheet is set up, select Tools⊃Solver and specify that you want to minimize cell E11 by changing cells E3:E9. Next, click on the Add button to begin adding the following constraints:

```
F3>=0
F4>=0
F5>=0
F6>=0
F7>=0
F8>=0
F9>=0
```

Click on Solve to start the process. The solution that Solver finds, shown in Figure 27-15, indicates that a staff of 188 meets the staffing needs and that no excess staffing exists on any day.

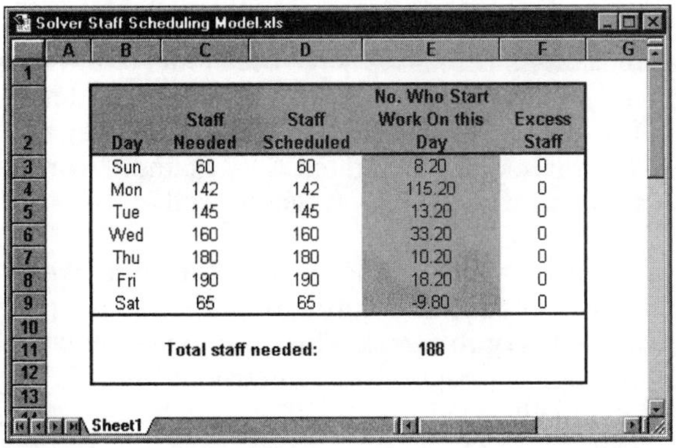

Day	Staff Needed	Staff Scheduled	No. Who Start Work On this Day	Excess Staff
Sun	60	60	8.20	0
Mon	142	142	115.20	0
Tue	145	145	13.20	0
Wed	160	160	33.20	0
Thu	180	180	10.20	0
Fri	190	190	18.20	0
Sat	65	65	-9.80	0
	Total staff needed:		188	

Figure 27-15: This solution that is offered by Solver isn't quite right — you have to add more constraints.

But wait! If you examine the results carefully, you notice that a few things are wrong here:

✦ Solver's solution involves partial people — who are difficult to find. For example, 8.2 people begin their workweek on Sunday.

✦ Even more critical is the suggestion that a negative number of people should begin their workweek on Saturday.

Both these problems are easy to correct by adding more constraints. Fortunately, Solver enables you to limit the solution to integers by using the integer option in the Add Constraint dialog box. This means that you must add another constraint for each cell in E3:E9. Figure 27-16 shows how you can specify an integer constraint. Avoiding the negative people problem requires seven more constraints of the form E3>=0, one for each cell in E3:E9.

These two problems (integer solutions and negative numbers) are quite common when using Solver. They also demonstrate that it's important to check the results rather than to rely only on Solver's solution.

Figure 27-16: With many problems, you have to limit the solution to integers. You can do this by selecting the integer option in the Add Constraint dialog box.

Tip   If you find that adding these constraints is tedious, save the model to a worksheet range. Then you add new constraints to the range in the worksheet (and make sure that you don't overwrite the last cell in this range). Next, run Solver again and load the modified model from the range that you edited. The example workbook (available at this book's Web site) has three Solver ranges stored in it.

After adding these 14 new constraints, run Solver again. This time it arrives at the solution shown in Figure 27-17. Notice that this solution requires 192 people and results in excess staffing on three days of the week. This solution is the best one possible that uses the fewest number of people — and almost certainly is better than what you would arrive at manually.

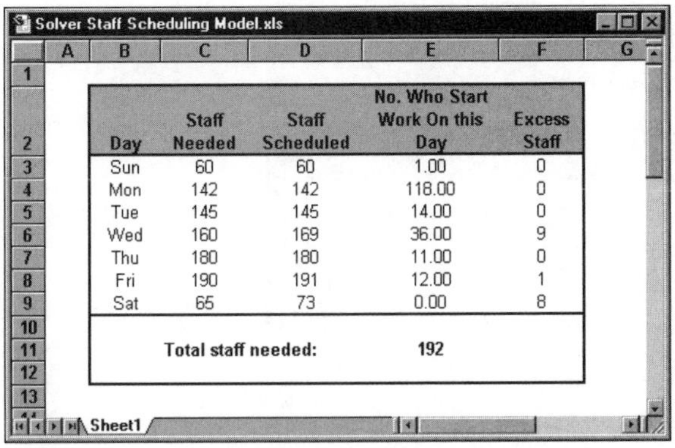

Solver Staff Scheduling Model.xls

Day	Staff Needed	Staff Scheduled	No. Who Start Work On this Day	Excess Staff
Sun	60	60	1.00	0
Mon	142	142	118.00	0
Tue	145	145	14.00	0
Wed	160	169	36.00	9
Thu	180	180	11.00	0
Fri	190	191	12.00	1
Sat	65	73	0.00	8
	Total staff needed:		192	

Figure 27-17: Rerunning Solver after adding more constraints produces a better solution to the staffing model problem.

Allocating resources

The example in this section is a common type of problem that's ideal for Solver. Essentially, problems of this sort involve optimizing the volumes of individual production units that use varying amounts of fixed resources. Figure 27-18 shows an example for a toy company.

This company makes five different toys, which use six different materials in varying amounts. For example, Toy A requires 3 units of blue paint, 2 units of white paint, 1 unit of plastic, 3 units of wood, and 1 unit of glue. Column G shows the current inventory of each type of material. Row 10 shows the unit profit for each toy. The number of toys to make is shown in the range B11:F11 — these are the values that Solver determines. The goal of this example is to determine how to allocate the resources to maximize the total profit (B13). In other words, Solver determines how many units of each toy to make. The constraints in this example are relatively simple:

- ✦ Ensure that production doesn't use more resources than are available. This can be accomplished by specifying that each cell in column F is greater than or equal to zero.
- ✦ Ensure that the quantities produced aren't negative. This can be accomplished by specifying that each cell in row 11 be greater than or equal to zero.

Figure 27-19 shows the results that are produced by Solver. It shows the product mix that generates $12,365 in profit. All resources are used in their entirety, except for glue.

Solver Resource Allocation Model.xls

XYZ Toys Inc.								
	Materials Needed							
Material	Toy A	Toy B	Toy C	Toy D	Toy E	Amt. Avail.	Amt. Used	Amt. Left
Red Paint	0	1	0	1	3	625	500	125
Blue Paint	3	1	0	1	0	640	500	140
White Paint	2	1	2	0	2	1,100	700	400
Plastic	1	5	2	2	1	875	1,100	-225
Wood	3	0	3	5	5	2,200	1,600	600
Glue	1	2	3	2	3	1,500	1,100	400
Unit Profit	$15	$30	$20	$25	$25			
No. to Make	100	100	100	100	100			
Profit	$1,500	$3,000	$2,000	$2,500	$2,500			
Total Profit	$11,500							

Sheet1

Figure 27-18: Using Solver to maximize profit when resources are limited.

Solver Resource Allocation Model.xls

XYZ Toys Inc.								
	Materials Needed							
Material	Toy A	Toy B	Toy C	Toy D	Toy E	Amt. Avail.	Amt. Used	Amt. Left
Red Paint	0	1	0	1	3	625	625	0
Blue Paint	3	1	0	1	0	640	640	0
White Paint	2	1	2	0	2	1,100	1,100	0
Plastic	1	5	2	2	1	875	875	0
Wood	3	0	3	5	5	2,200	2,200	0
Glue	1	2	3	2	3	1,500	1,353	147
Unit Profit	$15	$30	$20	$25	$25			
No. to Make	194	19	158	40	189			
Profit	$2,903	$573	$3,168	$1,008	$4,713			
Total Profit	$12,365							

Sheet1

Figure 27-19: Solver determined how to use the resources to maximize the total profit.

Optimizing an investment portfolio

This example demonstrates how to use Solver to help maximize the return on an investment portfolio. Portfolios consist of several investments, each of which has different yields. In addition, you may have some constraints that involve reducing risk and diversification goals. Without such constraints, a portfolio problem becomes a no-brainer: put all your money in the investment with the highest yield.

This example involves a credit union, a financial institution that takes members' deposits and invests them in loans to other members, bank CDs, and other types of investments. Part of the return on these investments is distributed to the members in the form of dividends, or interest on their deposits. This hypothetical credit union must adhere to some regulations regarding its investments, and the board of directors has imposed some other restrictions. These regulations and restrictions comprise the problem's constraints. Figure 27-20 shows a workbook that is set up for the problem.

The following constraints are the ones to which you must adhere in allocating the $5 million portfolio:

- ✦ The amount that is invested in new-car loans must be at least three times the amount that is invested in used-car loans (used-car loans are riskier investments). This constraint is represented as C5>=C6*3.
- ✦ Car loans should make up at least 15 percent of the portfolio. This constraint is represented as D14>=.15.

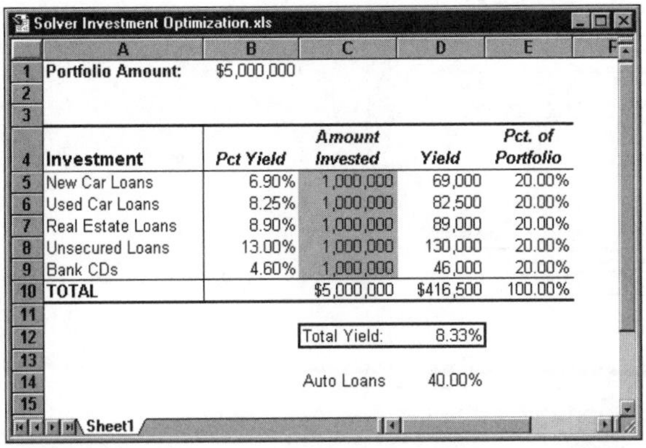

Solver Investment Optimization.xls

	A	B	C	D	E
1	Portfolio Amount:	$5,000,000			
2					
3					
4	Investment	Pct Yield	Amount Invested	Yield	Pct. of Portfolio
5	New Car Loans	6.90%	1,000,000	69,000	20.00%
6	Used Car Loans	8.25%	1,000,000	82,500	20.00%
7	Real Estate Loans	8.90%	1,000,000	89,000	20.00%
8	Unsecured Loans	13.00%	1,000,000	130,000	20.00%
9	Bank CDs	4.60%	1,000,000	46,000	20.00%
10	TOTAL		$5,000,000	$416,500	100.00%
11					
12			Total Yield:	8.33%	
13					
14			Auto Loans	40.00%	
15					

Sheet1

Figure 27-20: This worksheet is set up to maximize a credit union's investments, given some constraints.

- ✦ Unsecured loans should make up no more than 25 percent of the portfolio. This constraint is represented as E8<=.25.
- ✦ At least 10 percent of the portfolio should be in bank CDs. This constraint is represented as E9>=.10.
- ✦ All investments should be positive or zero. In other words, the problem requires five additional constraints to ensure that none of the changing cells go below zero.

The changing cells are C5:C9, and the goal is to maximize the total yield in cell D12. I entered 1,000,000 as starting values in the changing cells. When you run Solver with these parameters, it produces the solution that is shown in Figure 27-21, which has a total yield of 9.25 percent.

In this example, the starting values of the changing cells are very important. For example, if you use smaller numbers as the starting values (such as 10) and rerun Solver, you find that it doesn't do as well. In fact, it produces a total yield of only 8.35 percent. This demonstrates that you can't always trust Solver to arrive at the optimal solution with one try — even when the Solver Results dialog box tells you that *All constraints and optimality conditions are satisfied.* Usually, the best approach is to use starting values that are as close as possible to the final solution.

The best advice? Make sure that you understand Solver well before you entrust it with helping you make major decisions. Try different starting values, and adjust the options to see whether Solver can do better.

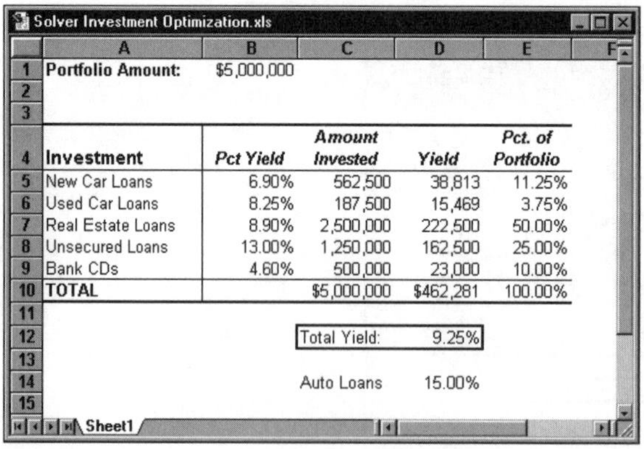

	A	B	C	D	E
1	Portfolio Amount:	$5,000,000			
2					
3					
4	Investment	Pct Yield	Amount Invested	Yield	Pct. of Portfolio
5	New Car Loans	6.90%	562,500	38,813	11.25%
6	Used Car Loans	8.25%	187,500	15,469	3.75%
7	Real Estate Loans	8.90%	2,500,000	222,500	50.00%
8	Unsecured Loans	13.00%	1,250,000	162,500	25.00%
9	Bank CDs	4.60%	500,000	23,000	10.00%
10	TOTAL		$5,000,000	$462,281	100.00%
11					
12			Total Yield:	9.25%	
13					
14			Auto Loans	15.00%	
15					

Figure 27-21: The results of the portfolio optimization.

Summary

In this chapter, I discuss two Excel commands: Tools➪Goal Seek and Tools➪Solver. The latter command is available only if the Solver add-in is installed. Goal seeking is used to determine the value in a single input cell that produces a result that you want in a formula cell. Solver determines values in multiple input cells that produce a result that you want, given certain constraints. Using Solver can be challenging because it has many options, and the result it produces isn't always the best one.

✦ ✦ ✦

Analyzing Data with the Analysis ToolPak

CHAPTER

28

◆ ◆ ◆ ◆

In This Chapter

Introduction to the
Analysis ToolPak
add-in

Descriptions and
examples of the 19
tools in the Analysis
ToolPak

Listing of the 93
worksheet functions
that you can use
when the Analysis
ToolPak is installed

◆ ◆ ◆ ◆

Although spreadsheets such as Excel are designed primarily with business users in mind, these products can be found in other disciplines, including education, research, statistics, and engineering. One way that Excel addresses these nonbusiness users is with its Analysis ToolPak add-in. Many of the features and functions in the Analysis ToolPak are valuable for business applications as well.

The Analysis ToolPak: An Overview

The Analysis ToolPak is an add-in providing analytical capability that is usually not available. The Analysis ToolPak consists of two parts:

◆ 19 analytical procedures

◆ 93 additional worksheet functions

These analysis tools offer many features that may be useful to those in the scientific, engineering, and educational communities — not to mention business users whose needs extend beyond the normal spreadsheet fare.

This section provides a quick overview of the types of analyses that you can perform with the Analysis ToolPak. I discuss each tool in detail later in the chapter.

✦ Analysis of variance (three types)   ✦ Moving average

✦ Correlation   ✦ Random number generation

✦ Covariance   ✦ Rank and percentile

✦ Descriptive statistics   ✦ Regression

✦ Exponential smoothing   ✦ Sampling

✦ F-test   ✦ t-test (three types)

✦ Fourier analysis   ✦ z-test

✦ Histogram

As you can see, the Analysis ToolPak add-in brings a great deal of new functionality to Excel. These procedures have limitations, however, and in some cases, you may prefer to create your own formulas to do some calculations.

Besides the procedures just listed, the Analysis ToolPak provides many additional worksheet functions. These functions cover mathematics, engineering, unit conversions, financial analysis, and dates. These functions are listed at the end of the chapter.

Using the Analysis ToolPak

This section discusses the two components of the Analysis ToolPak: its tools and its functions.

Using the analysis tools

The procedures in the Analysis ToolPak add-in are relatively straightforward. To use of these tools, you select Tools⇨Data Analysis, which displays the dialog box that is shown in Figure 28-1. Then you scroll through the list until you find the analysis tool that you want to use. Click on OK, and you get a new dialog box that's specific to the procedure that you selected.

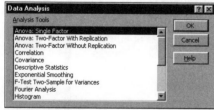

Figure 28-1: The Data Analysis dialog box lets you select the tool in which you're interested.

Making the Analysis ToolPak available

Depending on how Excel was originally installed on your system, you may or may not have access to the Analysis ToolPak. To see whether this add-in is available, select the Tools menu. If the menu displays Data Analysis as an option, you're all set.

If the Tools⇨Data Analysis command is not available on your system, you need to attach the add-in. Select Tools⇨Add-Ins, place a check mark next to the Analysis ToolPak add-in, and click on OK. This makes the Analysis ToolPak available whenever you start Excel. If the Analysis ToolPak doesn't appear in the list of add-ins, you need to rerun the Setup program for Excel (or Microsoft Office) and choose the Custom option. This lets you copy the files that are used by the Analysis ToolPak to your hard drive.

Usually, you need to specify one or more input ranges, plus an output range (one cell is sufficient). Alternatively, you can specify that the results are placed on a new worksheet or in a new workbook. The procedures vary in the amount of additional information that is required. An option that you see in many dialog boxes is whether or not your data range includes labels. If so, you can specify the entire range, including the labels, and indicate to Excel that the first column (or row) contains labels. Excel then uses these labels in the tables that it produces. Most tools also provide different output options that you can select, based on your needs.

Caution   In some cases, the procedures produce their results using formulas. As a result, you can change your data, and the results update automatically. In other procedures, the results are in the form of values, so if you change your data, the results don't reflect your changes. Make sure that you understand what Excel is doing.

Using the Analysis ToolPak functions

After the Analysis ToolPak is installed, you have access to all the additional functions (which are described fully in the online Help system). You access these functions just like any other function, and they appear in the Function Wizard dialog box, intermixed with Excel's standard functions.

Note   If you plan to share worksheets that use these functions, make sure that the other user has access to the add-in functions. If the Analysis ToolPak add-in is not installed, formulas that use any of the Analysis ToolPak functions will return #VALUE.

The Analysis ToolPak Tools

In this section, I describe each tool and provide an example. Space limitations prevent me from discussing every available option in these procedures. I assume that if you need to use some of these advanced analysis tools, you know what you're doing.

Analysis of variance

Analysis of variance is a statistical test that determines whether two or more samples were drawn from the same population. The Analysis ToolPak can perform three types of analysis of variance:

  ✦ **Single-factor:** A one-way analysis of variance, with only one sample for each group of data.

  ✦ **Two-factor with replication:** A two-way analysis of variance, with multiple samples (or replications) for each group of data.

  ✦ **Two-factor without replication:** A two-way analysis of variance, with a single sample (or replication) for each group of data.

Figure 28-2 shows the dialog box for a single-factor analysis of variance. Alpha represents the statistical confidence level for the test.

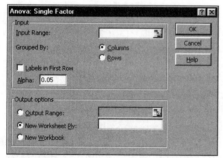

Figure 28-2: Specifying parameters for a single-factor analysis of variance.

The results of an analysis of variance are shown in Figure 28-3. The output for this test consists of the means and variances for each of the four samples, the value of F, the critical value of F, and the significance of F (P-value). Because the probability is greater than the Alpha value, the conclusion is that the samples were drawn from the same population.

	F	G	H	I	J	K	L
1	Anova: Single Factor						
2							
3	SUMMARY						
4	*Groups*	*Count*	*Sum*	*Average*	*Variance*		
5	Low	8	538	67.25	6680.214		
6	Medium	8	578	72.25	7700.214		
7	High	8	636	79.5	9397.714		
8	Control	8	544	68	6845.714		
9							
10							
11	ANOVA						
12	*Source of Variation*	*SS*	*df*	*MS*	*F*	*P-value*	*F crit*
13	Between Groups	757	3	252.3333	0.032959	0.991785	2.946685
14	Within Groups	214367	28	7655.964			
15							

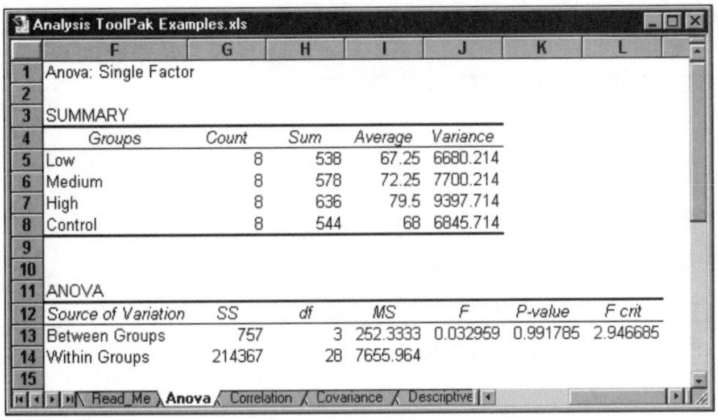

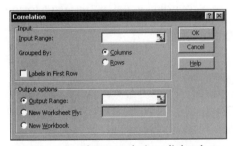

Figure 28-3: The results of the analysis of variance.

Correlation

Correlation is a widely used statistic that measures the degree to which two sets of data vary together. For example, if higher values in one data set are typically associated with higher values in the second data set, the two data sets have a positive correlation. The degree of correlation is expressed as a coefficient that ranges from –1.0 (a perfect negative correlation) to +1.0 (a perfect positive correlation). A correlation coefficient of 0 means that the two variables are not correlated.

The Correlation dialog box is shown in Figure 28-4. Specify the input range, which can include any number of variables arranged in rows or columns.

Figure 28-4: The Correlation dialog box.

Figure 28-5 shows the results of a correlation analysis for eight variables. The output consists of a correlation matrix that shows the correlation coefficient for each variable paired with every other variable.

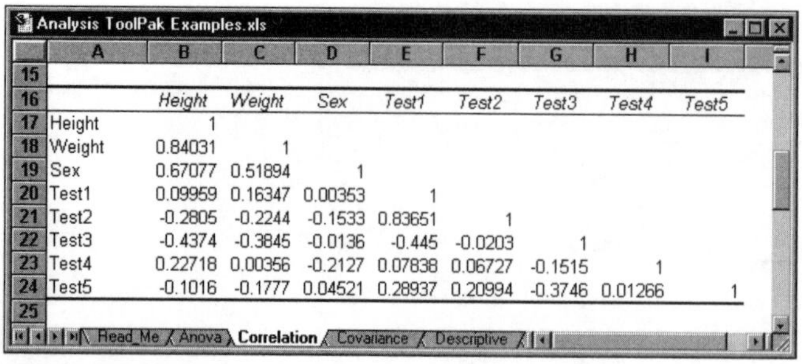

	Height	Weight	Sex	Test1	Test2	Test3	Test4	Test5
Height	1							
Weight	0.84031	1						
Sex	0.67077	0.51894	1					
Test1	0.09959	0.16347	0.00353	1				
Test2	-0.2805	-0.2244	-0.1533	0.83651	1			
Test3	-0.4374	-0.3845	-0.0136	-0.445	-0.0203	1		
Test4	0.22718	0.00356	-0.2127	0.07838	0.06727	-0.1515	1	
Test5	-0.1016	-0.1777	0.04521	0.28937	0.20994	-0.3746	0.01266	1

Figure 28-5: The results of a correlation analysis.

Note Notice that the resulting correlation matrix doesn't use formulas to calculate the results. Therefore, if any data changes, the correlation matrix isn't valid. You can use Excel's CORREL function to create a correlation matrix that is updated automatically.

Covariance

The Covariance tool produces a matrix that is similar to that generated by the Correlation tool. *Covariance* is defined as the average of the product of the deviations of each data point pair from their respective means. Like correlation, this measures the degree to which two variables vary together.

Figure 28-6 shows a covariance matrix. Notice that the values along the diagonal (where the variables are the same) are the variances for the variable.

You can use the COVAR function to create a covariance matrix that uses formulas. The values that are generated by the Analysis ToolPak are *not* the same values that you would get if you used the COVAR function.

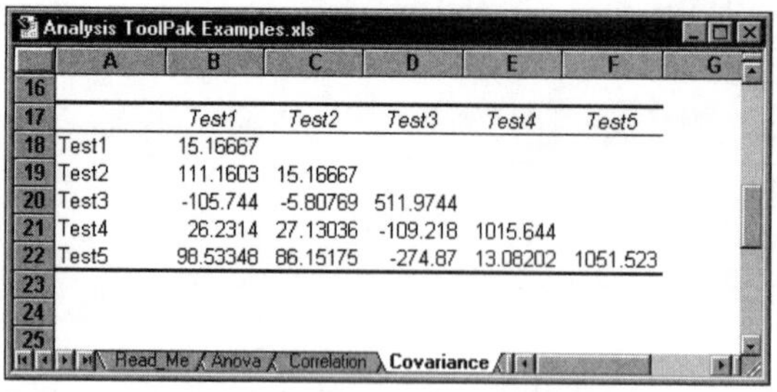

	Test1	Test2	Test3	Test4	Test5
Test1	15.16667				
Test2	111.1603	15.16667			
Test3	-105.744	-5.80769	511.9744		
Test4	26.2314	27.13036	-109.218	1015.644	
Test5	98.53348	86.15175	-274.87	13.08202	1051.523

Figure 28-6: The results of a covariance analysis.

Descriptive statistics

This tool produces a table that describes your data with some standard statistics. It uses the dialog box that is shown in Figure 28-7. The Kth Largest and Kth Smallest option each displays the data value that corresponds to a rank that you specify. For example, if you check Kth Largest and specify a value of 2, the output shows the second-largest value in the input range (the standard output already includes the minimum and maximum values).

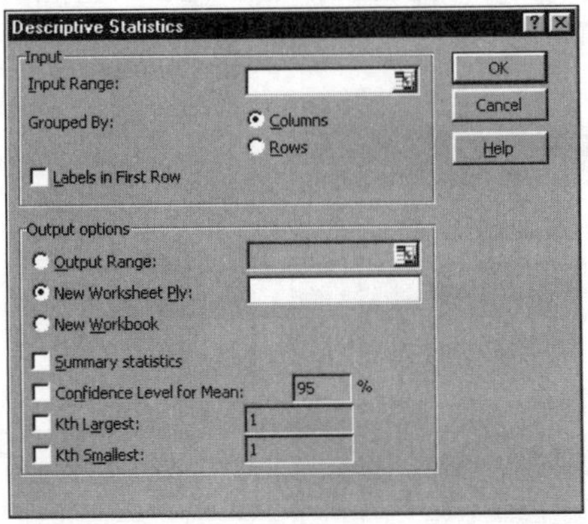

Figure 28-7: The Descriptive Statistics dialog box.

Sample output for the Descriptive Statistics tool is shown in Figure 28-8. This example has three groups. Because the output for this procedure consists of values (not formulas), you should use this procedure only when you're certain that your data isn't going to change; otherwise, you will need to re-execute this procedure. You can generate all these statistics using formulas.

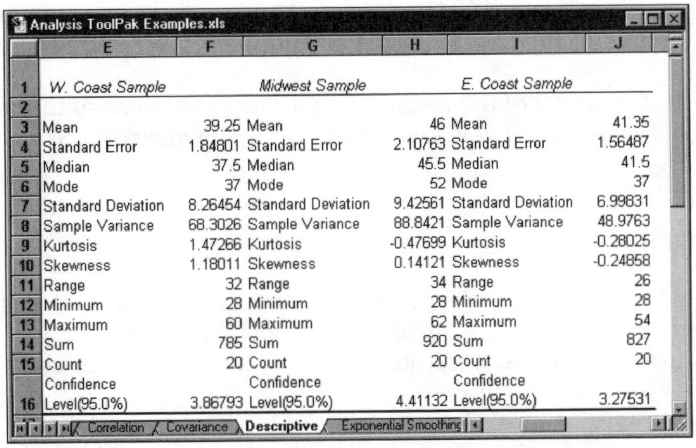

Analysis ToolPak Examples.xls

	E	F	G	H	I	J
1	*W. Coast Sample*		*Midwest Sample*		*E. Coast Sample*	
2						
3	Mean	39.25	Mean	46	Mean	41.35
4	Standard Error	1.84801	Standard Error	2.10763	Standard Error	1.56487
5	Median	37.5	Median	45.5	Median	41.5
6	Mode	37	Mode	52	Mode	37
7	Standard Deviation	8.26454	Standard Deviation	9.42561	Standard Deviation	6.99831
8	Sample Variance	68.3026	Sample Variance	88.8421	Sample Variance	48.9763
9	Kurtosis	1.47266	Kurtosis	-0.47699	Kurtosis	-0.28025
10	Skewness	1.18011	Skewness	0.14121	Skewness	-0.24858
11	Range	32	Range	34	Range	26
12	Minimum	28	Minimum	28	Minimum	28
13	Maximum	60	Maximum	62	Maximum	54
14	Sum	785	Sum	920	Sum	827
15	Count	20	Count	20	Count	20
16	Confidence Level(95.0%)	3.86793	Confidence Level(95.0%)	4.41132	Confidence Level(95.0%)	3.27531

Correlation / Covariance / Descriptive / Exponential Smoothing

Figure 28-8: Output from the Descriptive Statistics tool.

Exponential smoothing

Exponential smoothing is a technique for predicting data that is based on the previous data point and the previously predicted data point. You can specify the *damping factor* (also known as a *smoothing constant*), which can range from 0 to 1. This determines the relative weighting of the previous data point and the previously predicted data point. You also can request standard errors and a chart.

This procedure generates formulas that use the damping factor that you specified. Therefore, if the data changes, the formulas are updated. Figure 28-9 shows sample output from the Exponential Smoothing tool.

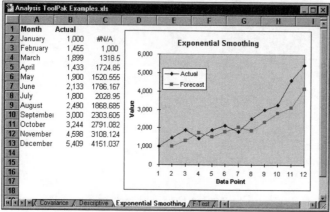

Figure 28-9: Output from the Exponential Smoothing tool.

F-test (two-sample test for variance)

The *F-test* is a commonly used statistical test that lets you compare two population variances. The dialog box for this tool is shown in Figure 28-10.

The output for this test consists of the means and variances for each of the two samples, the value of F, the critical value of F, and the significance of F. Sample output is shown in Figure 28-11.

Fourier analysis

This tool performs a "fast Fourier" transformation a range of data. The range is limited to the following sizes: 1, 2, 4, 8, 16, 32, 64, 128, 256, 512, or 1,024 data points. This procedure accepts and generates complex numbers, which are represented as labels (not values).

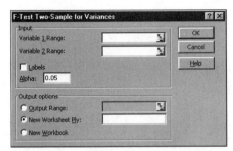

Figure 28-10: The F-Test dialog box.

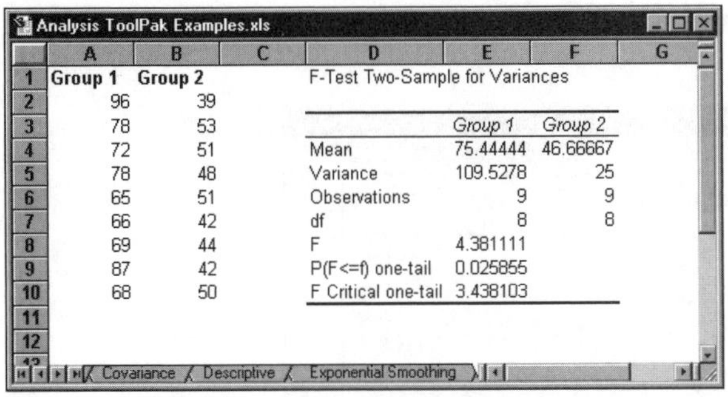

Figure 28-11: Sample output for the F-test.

Histogram

This procedure is useful for producing data distributions and histogram charts. It accepts an input range and a bin range. A *bin* range is a range of values that specifies the limits for each column of the histogram. If you omit the bin range, Excel creates ten equal-interval bins for you. The size of each bin is determined by a formula of the following form:

```
=(MAX(input_range)-MIN(input_range))/10
```

The Histogram dialog box is shown in Figure 28-12. As an option, you can specify that the resulting histogram be sorted by frequency of occurrence in each bin.

If you specify the Pareto (sorted histogram) option, the bin range must consist of values and can't contain formulas. If formulas appear in the bin range, the sorting that is done by Excel doesn't work properly, and your worksheet displays error values.

Figure 28-13 shows a chart that was generated from this procedure. The Histogram tool doesn't use formulas, so if you change any of the input data, you need to repeat the histogram procedure to update the results.

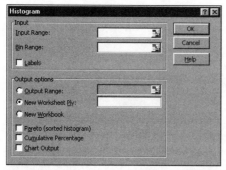

Figure 28-12: The Histogram tool lets you generate distributions and graphical output.

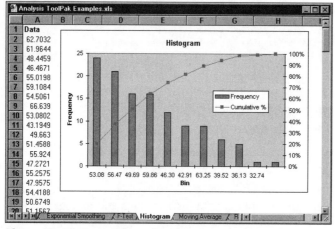

Figure 28-13: Output from the Histogram tool.

Moving average

The Moving Average tool is useful to smooth out a data series that has a lot of variability. This is best done in conjunction with a chart. Excel does the smoothing by computing a moving average of a specified number of values. In many cases, a moving average lets you spot trends that would otherwise be obscured by noise in the data.

Figure 28-14 shows the Moving Average dialog box. You can, of course, specify the number of values to be used for each average. An option in this procedure calculates standard errors and places formulas for these calculations next to the moving average formulas. The standard error values indicate the degree of variability between the actual values and the calculated moving averages. When you exit this dialog box, Excel creates formulas that reference the input range that you specify.

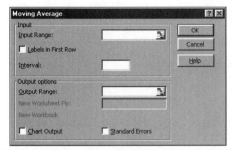

Figure 28-14: The Moving Average dialog box.

Figure 28-15 shows the results of this tool. Notice that the first few cells in the output are #N/A. This is because there aren't enough data points to calculate the average for these initial values.

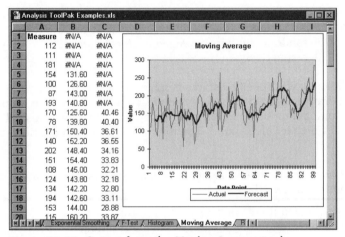

Figure 28-15: Output from the Moving Average tool.

Random number generation

Although Excel contains a built-in function to calculate random numbers, the Random Number Generation tool is much more flexible because you can specify what type of distribution you want the random numbers to have. Figure 28-16 shows the Random Number Generation dialog box. The Parameters box varies depending on the type of distribution that is selected.

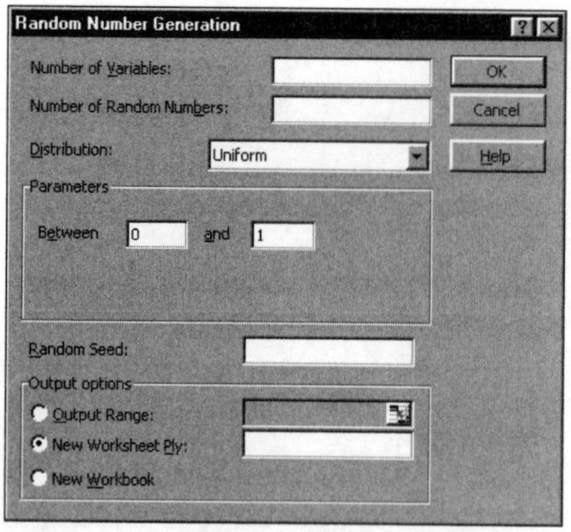

Figure 28-16: This dialog box lets you generate a wide variety of random numbers.

The Number of Variables refers to the number of columns that you want, and the Number of Random Numbers refers to the number of rows that you want. For example, if you want 200 random numbers arranged in 10 columns of 20 rows, you would specify 10 and 20, respectively, in these text boxes.

The Random Seed box lets you specify a starting value that Excel uses in its random number-generating algorithm. Usually, you leave this blank. If you want to generate the same random number sequence, however, you can specify a seed between 1 and 32,767 (integer values only). The following distribution options are available:

✦ **Uniform:** Every random number has an equal chance of being selected. You specify the upper and lower limits.

✦ **Normal:** The random numbers correspond to a normal distribution. You specify the mean and standard deviation of the distribution.

✦ **Bernoulli:** The random numbers are either 0 or 1, determined by the probability of success that you specify.

✦ **Binomial:** This returns random numbers based on a Bernoulli distribution over a specific number of trials, given a probability of success that you specify.

✦ **Poisson:** This option generates values in a Poisson distribution. This is characterized by discrete events that occur in an interval, where the probability of a single occurrence is proportional to the size of the interval. The lambda parameter is the expected number of occurrences in an interval. In a Poisson distribution, lambda is equal to the mean, which also is equal to the variance.

✦ **Patterned:** This option doesn't generate random numbers. Rather, it repeats a series of numbers in steps that you specify.

✦ **Discrete:** This option lets you specify the probability that specific values are chosen. It requires a two-column input range; the first column holds the values and the second column holds the probability of each value being chosen. The sum of the probabilities in the second column must equal 100 percent.

Rank and percentile

This tool creates a table that shows the ordinal and percentile ranking for each value in a range. Figure 28-17 shows the results of this procedure. You can also generate ranks and percentiles using formulas.

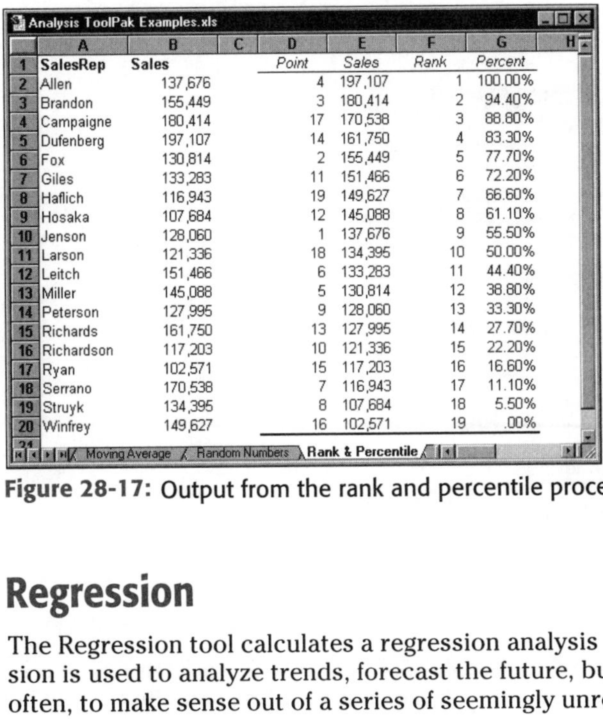

	SalesRep	Sales		Point	Sales	Rank	Percent
2	Allen	137,676		4	197,107	1	100.00%
3	Brandon	155,449		3	180,414	2	94.40%
4	Campaigne	180,414		17	170,538	3	88.80%
5	Dufenberg	197,107		14	161,750	4	83.30%
6	Fox	130,814		2	155,449	5	77.70%
7	Giles	133,283		11	151,466	6	72.20%
8	Haflich	116,943		19	149,627	7	66.60%
9	Hosaka	107,684		12	145,088	8	61.10%
10	Jenson	128,060		1	137,676	9	55.50%
11	Larson	121,336		18	134,395	10	50.00%
12	Leitch	151,466		6	133,283	11	44.40%
13	Miller	145,088		5	130,814	12	38.80%
14	Peterson	127,995		9	128,060	13	33.30%
15	Richards	161,750		13	127,995	14	27.70%
16	Richardson	117,203		10	121,336	15	22.20%
17	Ryan	102,571		15	117,203	16	16.60%
18	Serrano	170,538		7	116,943	17	11.10%
19	Struyk	134,395		8	107,684	18	5.50%
20	Winfrey	149,627		16	102,571	19	.00%

Figure 28-17: Output from the rank and percentile procedure.

Regression

The Regression tool calculates a regression analysis from worksheet data. Regression is used to analyze trends, forecast the future, build predictive models, and often, to make sense out of a series of seemingly unrelated numbers.

Regression analysis lets you determine the extent to which one range of data (the dependent variable) varies as a function of the values of one or more other ranges of data (the independent variables). This relationship is expressed mathematically, using values that are calculated by Excel. You can use these calculations to create a mathematical model of the data and predict the dependent variable using different values of one or more independent variables. This tool can perform simple and multiple linear regressions and automatically calculate and standardize residuals.

Figure 28-18 shows the Regression dialog box. As you see, it offers many options:

✦ **Input Y Range:** The range that contains the dependent variable.

✦ **Input X Range:** One or more ranges that contain independent variables.

✦ **Constant is Zero:** If checked, this forces the regression to have a constant of zero (which means that the regression line passes through the origin; when the X values are 0, the predicted Y value is 0).

✦ **Confidence Level:** The confidence level for the regression.

✦ **Residuals:** These options specify whether to include residuals in the output. Residuals are the differences between observed and predicted values.

✦ **Normal Probability:** This generates a chart for normal probability plots.

The results of a regression analysis are shown in Figure 28-19. If you understand regression analysis, the output from this procedure is familiar.

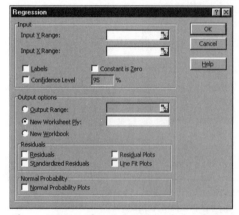

Figure 28-18: The Regression dialog box.

Sampling

The Sampling tool generates a random sample from a range of input values. This is useful for working with a subset of a large database. The Sampling dialog box is shown in Figure 28-20. This procedure has two options: periodic and random. A periodic sample selects every *n*th value from the input range, where *n* equals the period that you specify. With a random sample, you simply specify the size of the sample to be selected, and every value has an equal probability of being chosen.

	F	G	H	I	J	K	L
2	SUMMARY OUTPUT						
3							
4	*Regression Statistics*						
5	Multiple R	0.765099405					
6	R Square	0.585377099					
7	Adjusted R Square	0.530094046					
8	Standard Error	370049.2704					
9	Observations	18					
10							
11	ANOVA						
12		*df*	*SS*	*MS*	*F*	*ignificance F*	
13	Regression	2	2.89997E+12	1.45E+12	10.589	0.001356	
14	Residual	15	2.05405E+12	1.3694E+11			
15	Total	17	4.95401E+12				
16							
17		*Coefficients*	*Standard Error*	*t Stat*	*P-value*	*Lower 95%*	*Upper 95%*
18	Intercept	716434.6615	238757.3324	3.0006813	0.009	207535.1	1225334.2
19	Adv	107.6800943	36.20709499	2.97400535	0.0095	30.50645	184.85374
20	bp Diff	25010.94866	6185.924172	4.04320324	0.0011	11825.96	38195.942
21							

Figure 28-19: Sample output from the Regression tool.

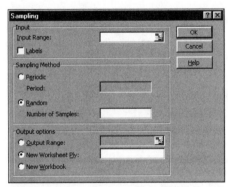

Figure 28-20: The Sampling dialog box is useful for selecting random samples.

t-test

The *t-test* is used to determine whether there is a statistically significant difference between two small samples. The Analysis ToolPak can perform three types of t-tests:

✦ **Paired two-sample for means:** For paired samples in which you have two observations on each subject (such as a pretest and a posttest). The samples must be the same size.

✦ **Two-sample assuming equal variances:** For independent, rather than paired, samples. It assumes equal variances for the two samples.

✦ **Two-sample assuming unequal variances:** For independent, rather than paired, samples. It assumes unequal variances for the two samples.

Figure 28-21 shows the dialog box for the paired two-sample t-test. You specify the significance level (alpha) and the hypothesized difference between the two means (that is, the *null hypothesis*).

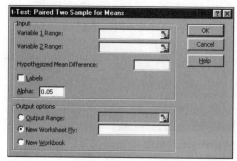

Figure 28-21: The paired t-Test dialog box.

Figure 28-22 shows sample output for the paired t-test. Excel calculates *t* for both a one-tailed and two-tailed test.

	E	F	G	H
1	t-Test: Paired Two Sample for Means			
2				
3		Pretest	Posttest	
4	Mean	69.619048	71.09524	
5	Variance	16.647619	48.79048	
6	Observations	21	21	
7	Pearson Correlation	0.962743		
8	Hypothesized Mean Difference	0		
9	df	20		
10	t Stat	-2.081522		
11	P(T<=t) one-tail	0.0252224		
12	t Critical one-tail	1.724718		
13	P(T<=t) two-tail	0.0504448		
14	t Critical two-tail	2.0859625		
15				

Figure 28-22: Results of a paired t-test.

z-test (two-sample test for means)

The t-test is used for small samples; the z-test is used for larger samples or populations. You must know the variances for both input ranges.

Analysis ToolPak Worksheet Functions

This section lists the worksheet functions that are available in the Analysis ToolPak. For specific information about the arguments required, click on the Help button in the Paste Function dialog box.

Remember, the Analysis ToolPak add-in must be installed to use these functions in your worksheet. If you use any of these functions in a workbook that you distribute to a colleague, make it clear that the workbook requires the Analysis ToolPak.

These functions appear in the Paste Function dialog box in the following categories:

✦ Date & Time

✦ Engineering (a new category that appears when the Analysis ToolPak is installed)

✦ Financial

✦ Information

✦ Math & Trig

Date & Time category

Table 28-1 lists the Analysis ToolPak worksheet functions that are in the Date & Time category.

Table 28-1
Date & Time Category Functions

Function	Purpose
EDATE	Returns the serial number of the date that is the indicated number of months before or after the start date
EOMONTH	Returns the serial number of the last day of the month before or after a specified number of months
NETWORKDAYS	Returns the number of whole workdays between two dates
WEEKNUM	Returns the week number in the year
WORKDAY	Returns the serial number of the date before or after a specified number of workdays
YEARFRAC	Returns the year fraction representing the number of whole days between `start_date` and `end_date`

Engineering category

Table 28-2 lists the Analysis ToolPak worksheet functions that are in the Engineering category. Some of these functions are quite useful for non-engineers as well. For example, the CONVERT function converts a wide variety of measurement units.

Table 28-2 Engineering Category Functions	
Function	**Purpose**
BESSELI	Returns the modified Bessel function In(x)
BESSELJ	Returns the Bessel function Jn(x)
BESSELK	Returns the modified Bessel function Kn(x)
BESSELY	Returns the Bessel function Yn(x)
BIN2DEC	Converts a binary number to decimal
BIN2HEX	Converts a binary number to hexadecimal
BIN2OCT	Converts a binary number to octal
COMPLEX	Converts real and imaginary coefficients into a complex number
CONVERT	Converts a number from one measurement system to another
DEC2BIN	Converts a decimal number to binary
DEC2HEX	Converts a decimal number to hexadecimal
DEC2OCT	Converts a decimal number to octal
DELTA	Tests whether two numbers are equal
ERF	Returns the error function
ERFC	Returns the complementary error function
FACTDOUBLE	Returns the double factorial of a number
GESTEP	Tests whether a number is greater than a threshold value
HEX2BIN	Converts a hexadecimal number to binary
HEX2DEC	Converts a hexadecimal number to decimal
HEX2OCT	Converts a hexadecimal number to octal
IMABS	Returns the absolute value (modulus) of a complex number
IMAGINARY	Returns the imaginary coefficient of a complex number
IMARGUMENT	Returns the argument q, an angle expressed in radians

Function	Purpose
IMCONJUGATE	Returns the complex conjugate of a complex number
IMCOS	Returns the cosine of a complex number
IMDIV	Returns the quotient of two complex numbers
IMEXP	Returns the exponential of a complex number
IMLN	Returns the natural logarithm of a complex number
IMLOG10	Returns the base-10 logarithm of a complex number
IMLOG2	Returns the base-2 logarithm of a complex number
IMPOWER	Returns a complex number raised to an integer power
IMPRODUCT	Returns the product of two complex numbers
IMREAL	Returns the real coefficient of a complex number
IMSIN	Returns the sine of a complex number
IMSQRT	Returns the square root of a complex number
IMSUB	Returns the difference of two complex numbers
IMSUM	Returns the sum of complex numbers
OCT2BIN	Converts an octal number to binary
OCT2DEC	Converts an octal number to decimal
OCT2HEX	Converts an octal number to hexadecimal

Financial category

Table 28-3 lists the Analysis ToolPak worksheet functions that are in the Financial category.

Table 28-3
Financial Category Functions

Function	Purpose
ACCRINT	Returns the accrued interest for a security that pays periodic interest
ACCRINTM	Returns the accrued interest for a security that pays interest at maturity
AMORDEGRC	Returns the prorated linear depreciation of an asset for each accounting period

Table 28-3 *(continued)*

Function	Purpose
AMORLINC	Returns the prorated linear depreciation of an asset for each accounting period
COUPDAYBS	Returns the number of days from the beginning of the coupon period to the settlement date
COUPDAYS	Returns the number of days in the coupon period that contain the settlement date
COUPDAYSNC	Returns the number of days from the settlement date to the next coupon date
COUPNCD	Returns the next coupon date after the settlement date
COUPNUM	Returns the number of coupons payable between the settlement date and maturity date
COUPPCD	Returns the previous coupon date before the settlement date
CUMIPMT	Returns the cumulative interest paid between two periods
CUMPRINC	Returns the cumulative principal paid on a loan between two periods
DISC	Returns the discount rate for a security
DOLLARDE	Converts a dollar price, expressed as a fraction, into a dollar price, expressed as a decimal number
DOLLARFR	Converts a dollar price, expressed as a decimal number, into a dollar price, expressed as a fraction
DURATION	Returns the annual duration of a security with periodic interest payments
EFFECT	Returns the effective annual interest rate
FVSCHEDULE	Returns the future value of an initial principal after applying a series of compound interest rates
INTRATE	Returns the interest rate for a fully invested security
MDURATION	Returns the Macauley modified duration for a security with an assumed par value of $100
NOMINAL	Returns the annual nominal interest rate
ODDFPRICE	Returns the price per $100 face value of a security with an odd first period
ODDFYIELD	Returns the yield of a security with an odd first period
ODDLPRICE	Returns the price per $100 face value of a security with an odd last period

Function	Purpose
ODDLYIELD	Returns the yield of a security with an odd last period
PRICE	Returns the price per $100 face value of a security that pays periodic interest
PRICEDISC	Returns the price per $100 face value of a discounted security
PRICEMAT	Returns the price per $100 face value of a security that pays interest at maturity
RECEIVED	Returns the amount received at maturity for a fully invested security
TBILLEQ	Returns the bond-equivalent yield for a Treasury bill
TBILLPRICE	Returns the price per $100 face value for a Treasury bill
TBILLYIELD	Returns the yield for a Treasury bill
XIRR	Returns the internal rate of return for a schedule of cash flows
XNPV	Returns the net present value for a schedule of cash flows
YIELD	Returns the yield on a security that pays periodic interest
YIELDDISC	Returns the annual yield for a discounted security (for example, a Treasury bill)
YIELDMAT	Returns the annual yield of a security that pays interest at maturity

Information category

Table 28-4 lists the two Analysis ToolPak worksheet functions that are in the Information category.

Table 28-4 Information Category Functions	
Function	**Purpose**
ISEVEN	Returns TRUE if the number is even
ISODD	Returns TRUE if the number is odd

Math & Trig category

Table 28-5 lists the Analysis ToolPak worksheet functions that are in the Math & Trig category.

	Table 28-5 **Math & Trig Category Functions**	
Function	**Purpose**
GCD	Returns the greatest common divisor
LCM	Returns the least common multiple
MROUND	Returns a number rounded to the desired multiple
MULTINOMIAL	Returns the multinomial of a set of numbers
QUOTIENT	Returns the integer portion of a division
RANDBETWEEN	Returns a random number between the numbers that you specify
SERIESSUM	Returns the sum of a power series based on the formula
SQRTPI	Returns the square root of pi

Summary

In this chapter, I discuss the Analysis ToolPak, an add-in that extends the analytical powers of Excel. It includes 19 analytic procedures and 93 new functions. Many of the tools are useful for general business applications, but many are for more specialized uses such as statistical tests.

✦   ✦   ✦

Other Topics

The four chapters in Part V deal with topics that don't fit into the other parts. In Chapter 29, I describe how to share data with other applications by using links. Chapter 30 covers the new Internet features in Excel 97. Chapter 31 describes some techniques that can make your worksheets as accurate as possible. Chapter 32 covers the lighter side of Excel and presents some amusing (and instructive) games.

P A R T

V

✦ ✦ ✦ ✦

In This Part

Chapter 29
Sharing Data with Other Applications

Chapter 30
Excel and the Internet

Chapter 31
Making Your Worksheets Error-Free

Chapter 32
Fun Stuff

✦ ✦ ✦ ✦

Sharing Data with Other Applications

Windows applications are designed to work together. The applications in Microsoft Office are an excellent example. These programs have a common look and feel, and it's quite easy to share data among these applications. In this chapter, I explore some ways that you can make use of other applications while working with Excel, along with ways that you can use Excel while working with other applications.

Sharing Data with Other Windows Applications

Besides importing and exporting files, there are essentially three ways to transfer data to and from other Windows applications:

♦ Copy and paste using the Windows Clipboard. This creates a static copy of the data.

♦ Create a link so that changes in the source data are reflected in the destination document.

♦ Embed an entire object from another application into a document.

In the following sections, I discuss these techniques and present an example for each one.

Using the Windows Clipboard

As you probably know, whenever Windows is running, you have access to the Windows Clipboard — an area of your computer's memory that acts as a shared holding area for information that has been cut or copied from an application. The Clipboard works behind the scenes, and you usually aren't aware of it. Whenever you select Edit⇨Copy or Edit⇨Cut, the selected data is placed on the Clipboard. Like most other Windows applications, Excel can then access the Clipboard data by way of the Edit⇨Paste command (or the Edit⇨Paste Special command).

Note Data that is pasted from the Clipboard remains on the Clipboard after pasting, so you can use it multiple times. But because the Clipboard can hold only one item at a time, when you copy or cut something else, the previous Clipboard contents are replaced.

Copying information from one Windows application to another is quite easy. The application that you're copying from is considered the *source application,* and the application that you're copying to is the *destination application.*

The general steps that are required to copy from one application to another are as follows. These steps apply to copying from Excel to another application and to copying from another application to Excel.

1. Activate the source document window that contains the information that you want to copy.

2. Select the information by using the mouse or the keyboard. If Excel is the source application, this information can be a cell, range, chart, or drawn object.

3. Select Edit⇨Copy. A copy of the information is sent to the Windows Clipboard.

4. Activate the destination application. If the program isn't running, you can start it without affecting the contents of the Clipboard.

5. Move to the appropriate position in the destination application (where you want to paste the copied material).

6. Select Edit⇨Paste from the menu in the destination application. If the Clipboard contents are not appropriate for pasting, the Paste command is grayed (not available).

Note In Step 3 in the preceding steps, you also can select Edit⇨Cut from the source application menu. This step erases your selection from the source application after the selection is placed on the Clipboard.

Note In Step 6 in the preceding steps, you can sometimes select the Edit⇨Paste Special command, which displays a dialog box that presents different pasting options.

If you're copying a graphics image, you may have to resize or crop it. If you're copying text, you may have to reformat it by using tools that are available in the destination application. The information that you copied from the source application remains intact, and a copy remains on the Clipboard until you copy something else.

Figure 29-1 shows an embedded Excel chart. You can easily insert a copy of this chart into a Microsoft Word report. First, select the chart in Excel by clicking on it once. Then copy it to the Clipboard by choosing Edit⇨Copy. Next, activate the Word document into which you want to paste the copy of the chart, and move the insertion point to the place where you want the chart placed. When you select Edit⇨Paste from the Word menubar, the chart is pasted from the Clipboard and appears in your document (see Figure 29-2).

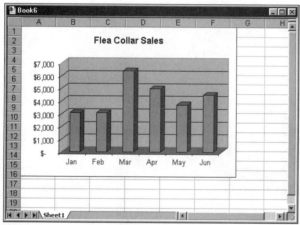

Figure 29-1: An Excel chart ready to be copied into a Word document.

Note It's important to understand that Windows applications vary in the way they respond to data that is pasted from the Clipboard. If the Edit⇨Paste command is not available (is grayed on the menu) in the destination application, the application can't accept the information the Clipboard. If you copy a range of data from Excel to the Clipboard and paste it into Word, Word creates a table when the data is pasted. Other applications may respond differently to this data. If you plan to do a great deal of copying and pasting, the best advice is to experiment until you understand how the two applications can handle each other's data.

An important point here is that this copy-and-paste technique is static. In other words, no link exists between what gets copied from the source application and the destination application. If you're copying from Excel to a word processing document, subsequent changes in your Excel worksheet or charts are *not* reflected in the word processing document. Consequently, you have to repeat the copy-and-paste procedure to update the source document with the changes. The next topic presents a way to get around this limitation.

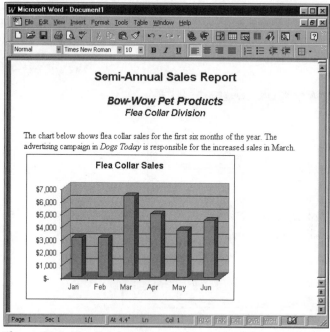

Figure 29-2: The Excel chart copied to a Word document.

Linking Data

If you want to share data that may change, the static copy-and-paste procedure described in the preceding section isn't your best choice. A better solution is to create a dynamic link between the data copied from one Windows application to another. So, if the data changes in the source document, these changes are made automatically in the destination document.

When would you want to use this technique? If you generate proposals using a word processor, for example, you may need to refer to pricing information that is stored in an Excel worksheet. If you set up a link between your word processing document and the Excel worksheet, you can be assured that your proposals always quote the latest prices. Not all Windows applications support dynamic linking, so you must make sure that the application to which you are copying is capable of handling such a link.

Creating links

Setting up a link from one Windows application to another isn't difficult, although the process varies slightly from application to application. The following are the general steps to take:

1. Activate the window in the source application that contains the information that you want to copy.

2. Select the information by using the mouse or the keyboard. If Excel is the server, you can select a cell, range, or entire chart.

3. Select Edit⇨Copy from the source application's menu. A copy of the information is sent to the Windows Clipboard.

4. Activate the destination application. If it isn't open, you can start it without affecting the contents of the Clipboard.

5. Move to the appropriate position in the destination application.

6. Select the appropriate command in the destination application to paste a link. The command varies depending on the application. In Microsoft Office applications, the command is Edit⇨Paste Special.

7. A dialog box will probably appear, letting you specify the type of link that you want to create. The following section provides more details.

More about links

Keep in mind the following when you're using links between two applications:

✦ Not all Windows applications support linking. Furthermore, some programs can be linked *from* but not linked *to.* When in doubt, consult the documentation for the application with which you're dealing.

✦ When you save an Excel file that has a link, the most recent values are saved with the document. When you reopen this document, you are asked whether you want to update the links.

✦ Links can be severed rather easily. If you move the source document to another directory or save it under a different name, for example, the client document is incapable of updating the link. You can usually re-establish the link manually, if you understand how the application manages the links. In Excel, you do this with the Edit⇨Links command, which results in the dialog box that is shown in Figure 29-3.

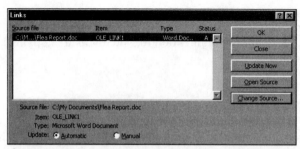

Figure 29-3: The Links dialog box lets you work with links to other applications.

> ✦ You also can use the Edit⇨Links command to break a link. After breaking a link, the data remains but is no longer linked to the source document.
>
> ✦ In Excel, external links are stored in array formulas. If you know what you're doing, you can modify a link by editing the array formula.
>
> ✦ When Excel is running, it responds to link requests from other applications unless you have disabled remote requests. To do this, choose Tools⇨Options, and select the General tab. Select the Ignore other applications check box if you don't want the links to be updated.

Copying Excel Data to Word

One of the most frequently used software combinations is a spreadsheet and a word processor. In this section, I discuss the types of links that you can create using Microsoft Word.

Note   Most information in this section also applies to other word processors, such as Corel's WordPerfect for Windows and Lotus Word Pro. The exact techniques vary, however. I use Word in the examples because readers who acquired Excel as part of the Microsoft Office have Word installed on their systems. If you don't have a word processor installed on your system, you can use the WordPad application that comes with Windows. The manner in which WordPad handles links is very similar to that for Word.

Figure 29-4 shows the Paste Special dialog box from Microsoft Word when a range of data from Excel is on the Clipboard. The result that you get depends on whether the Paste or the Paste link option is selected and on your choice of the type of item to paste. If you select the Paste link option, you can choose to have the information pasted as an icon. If so, you can double-click on this icon to activate the source worksheet.

Pasting without a link

Often, you don't need a link when you copy data. For example, if you're preparing a report in your word processor and you simply want to include a range of data from an Excel worksheet, you probably don't need to create a link.

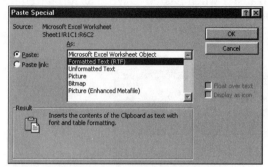

Figure 29-4: The Paste Special dialog box is where you specify the type of link to create.

Table 29-1 describes the effect of choosing the various paste choices when the Paste option is selected — the option that doesn't create a link to the source data.

Table 29-1 Result of Using the Paste Special Command in Word (Paste Option)	
Paste Type	**Result**
Microsoft Excel Worksheet Object	An object that includes the Excel formatting. This creates an embedded object, which I describe in the next section.
Formatted Text (RTF)	A Word table that is formatted as the original Excel range. There is no link to the source. This produces the same result as using Edit⇨Paste.
Unformatted Text	Text (not a table) that corresponds to Word's Normal style. Formatting from Excel is not transferred, and there is no link to the source.
Picture	A picture object that retains the formatting from Excel. There is no link to the source. This usually produces better results than the Bitmap option. Double-clicking on this option lets you edit the picture.
Bitmap	A bitmap object that retains the formatting from Excel. There is no link to the source. Double-clicking on this option lets you edit the bitmap.

Figure 29-5 shows how a copied range from Excel appears in Word using each of the paste special formats.

The pasted data *looks* the same regardless of whether the Paste or Paste link option is selected.

Some Excel formatting does not transfer when pasted to Word as formatted text. For example, Word doesn't support vertical alignment for table cells (you can use Word's paragraph formatting commands to do this).

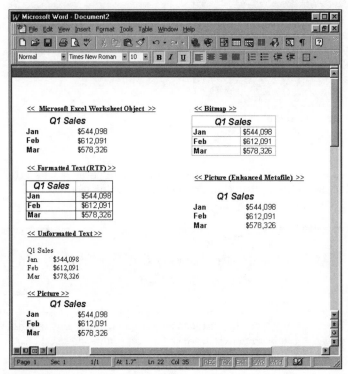

Figure 29-5: Data that is copied from Excel and pasted using various formats.

Pasting with a link

If the data that you're copying is subject to change, you may want to paste a link. If you paste the data using the Paste link option in the Paste Special dialog box, you can make changes to the source document, and the changes appear in the destination application (a few seconds of delay may occur). The best way to test these changes is to display both applications on-screen, make changes to the source document, and watch for them to appear in the destination document.

Table 29-2 describes the effect of choosing the various paste choices in Word's Paste Special dialog box when the Paste link option is selected.

Table 29-2	
Result of Using the Paste Special Command in Word (Paste Link Option)	
Paste Type	*Result*
Microsoft Excel Worksheet Object	A linked object that includes the Excel formatting. Double-click on this option to edit the source data in Excel.
Formatted Text (RTF)	A Word table that is formatted as the original Excel range. Changes in the source are reflected automatically.
Unformatted Text	Text (not a table) that corresponds to Word's Normal style. Formatting from Excel is not transferred. Changes in the source are reflected automatically.
Picture	A picture object that retains the formatting from Excel. Changes in the source are reflected automatically. This usually produces better results than the Bitmap option. Double-click on this option to edit the source data in Excel.
Bitmap	A bitmap object that retains the formatting from Excel. Changes in the source are reflected automatically. Double-click on this option to edit the source data in Excel.

Embedding Objects

Another method of sharing information between Windows applications is to embed an object in the document. This is known as *Object Linking and Embedding* (OLE). This technique lets you insert an object from another program and use the other program's editing tools to manipulate it. The OLE objects can be items such as the ones in this list:

✦ Text documents from other products, such as word processors

✦ Drawings or pictures from other products

✦ Information from special OLE server applications, such as Microsoft Equation

✦ Sound files

✦ Video or animation files

Most of the major Windows applications support OLE. You can embed an object into your document in two ways:

✦ Choose Edit⇨Paste Special, and select the "object" choice (if it's available). If you do this, select the Paste option rather than the Paste link option.

✦ Select Insert⇨Object.

Some applications — such as those in Microsoft Office — can also embed an object by dragging it from one application to another.

The following sections discuss these two methods and provide a few examples using Excel and Word.

Embedding an Excel range in a Word document

In this example, the range shown in Figure 29-6 is embedded in a Word document.

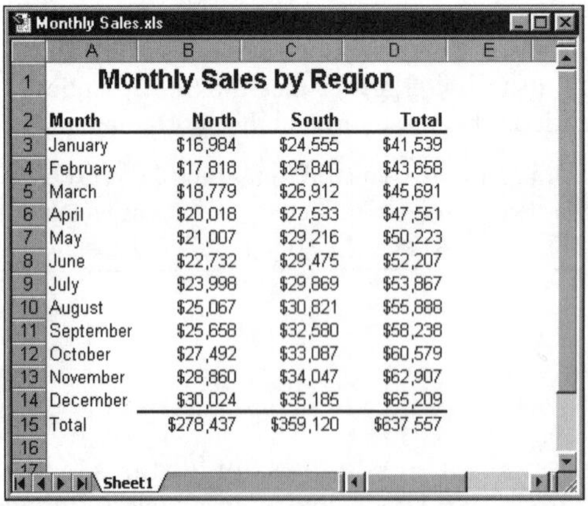

Figure 29-6: This range is to be embedded in a Word document.

To start, select A1:D15 and copy the range to the Clipboard. Then, activate (or start) Word. Move the insertion point to the location in the document where you want the table to be. Choose Word's Edit⇨Paste Special command. Select the Paste option (not Paste link), and choose the Microsoft Excel Worksheet Object format (see Figure 29-7). Click on OK, and the range is pasted to the document.

The pasted object is not a standard Word table. For example, you can't select or format individual cells in the table. Furthermore, it's not linked to the Excel source range. If you change a value in the Excel worksheet, the change does not appear in the embedded object in the Word document.

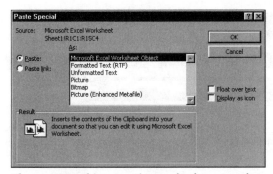

Figure 29-7: This operation embeds an Excel object in a Word document.

If you double-click on the object, however, you notice something unusual: Word's menus and toolbars change to those used by Excel. In addition, the embedded object appears with Excel's familiar row and column borders. In other words, you can edit this object *in place* using Excel's commands. Figure 29-8 shows how this looks. To get back to normal, just click anywhere in the Word document.

Remember that no link is involved here. If you make changes to the embedded object in Word, these changes are not reflected in the original Excel worksheet. The embedded object is completely independent from the original source.

The advantage to this technique is that you have access to all Excel features while you are still in Word. Microsoft's ultimate goal is to allow users to focus on their documents — not on the application that produces the document.

You can accomplish the embedding as described previously by selecting the range in Excel and then dragging it to your Word document. In fact, you can use the Windows desktop as an intermediary storage location. For example, you can drag a range from Excel to the desktop and create a *scrap.* Then, you can drag this scrap into your Word document. The result is an embedded Excel object.

Creating a new Excel object in Word

In the preceding example, a range from an existing Excel worksheet was embedded into a Word document. In this section, I demonstrate how to create a new (empty) Excel object in Word. This may be useful if you're creating a report and need to insert a table of values that doesn't exist in a worksheet. You could insert a normal Word table, but you can take advantage of Excel's formulas and functions to make this task much easier.

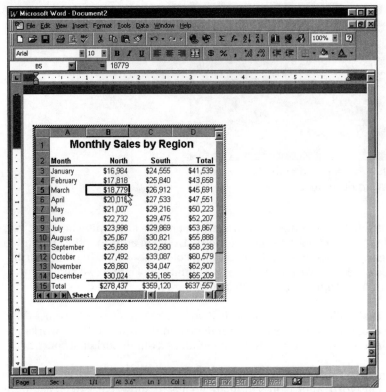

Figure 29-8: Double-clicking on the embedded Excel object lets you edit it in place. Note that Word now displays Excel's menus and toolbars.

To create a new Excel object in a Word document, choose Insert⇨Object. Word responds with the dialog box that is shown in Figure 29-9. The Create New panel lists the types of objects that you can create (this depends on what applications are installed on your system). Choose the Microsoft Excel Worksheet option, and click on OK.

Word inserts an empty Excel worksheet object into the document and activates it for you, as shown in Figure 29-10. You have full access to Excel commands, so you can enter whatever you like into the worksheet object. When you're finished, click anywhere in the document. You can, of course, double-click on this object at any time to make changes or additions.

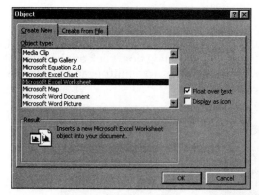

Figure 29-9: Word's Object dialog box lets you create a new object.

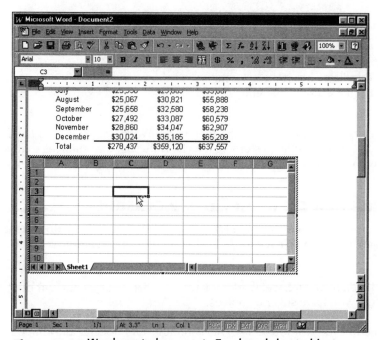

Figure 29-10: Word created an empty Excel worksheet object.

You can change the size of the object while it's activated by dragging the borders. When the object is not activated, you can crop it to display only cells that contain information. To crop an object in Word, press Shift while you drag a border of the object.

Embedding an existing workbook in Word

Yet another option is to embed an existing workbook into a Word document. Use Word's Insert➪Object command. In the Object dialog box, click on the tab labeled Create from File (see Figure 29-11). Click on the Browse button, and locate the Excel workbook that you want to embed.

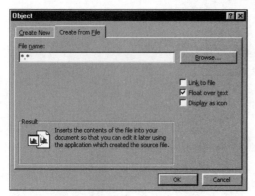

Figure 29-11: This dialog box lets you locate a file to embed in the active document.

A *copy* of the selected workbook is embedded in the Word document. You can double-click on it to make changes or use it as is. Note that any changes that you make to this copy of the document are not reflected in the original workbook.

Embedding objects in an Excel worksheet

The preceding examples involve embedding Excel objects in a Word document. The same procedures can be used for embedding other objects into an Excel worksheet.

For example, if you have an Excel workbook that requires a great amount of explanatory text, you have several choices:

✦ You can enter the text into cells. This is tedious and doesn't allow much formatting.

✦ You can use a text box. This is a good alternative, but it doesn't offer many formatting features.

✦ You can embed a Word document in your worksheet. This gives you full access to all of Word's formatting features.

To embed an empty Word document into an Excel worksheet, choose Excel's Insert⇨Object command. In the Object dialog box, click on the Create New tab and select Microsoft Word Document from the Object type list.

The result is a blank Word document, activated and ready for you to enter text. Notice that Excel's menus and toolbars are replaced with those from Word. You can resize the document as you like, and the words wrap accordingly. Figure 29-12 shows an example of a Word document that is embedded in an Excel worksheet.

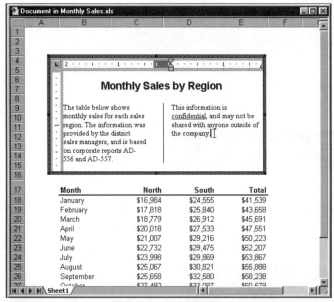

Figure 29-12: A Word document that is embedded in an Excel worksheet. The text on the right is contained in a frame (one of Word's formatting features).

You can embed many other types of objects, including audio clips, video clips, MIDI sequences, and even an entire Microsoft PowerPoint presentation.

When you embed a video clip, the actual file is not stored in the Excel document. Rather, a pointer to the original file is used. If, for some reason, you want to embed the complete video clip file, you can use the Object Packager application. Be aware, however, that video clip files are typically quite large, and the time required to open and save the workbook is lengthy.

Microsoft Office includes a few additional applications that you may find useful. These can all be embedded in Excel documents:

- ✦ **Microsoft Equation:** Lets you create equations. See Figure 29-13 for an example.

- ✦ **Microsoft WordArt:** Lets you modify text in some interesting ways. Figure 29-14 shows an example.

- ✦ **MS Organization Chart:** Lets you create attractive organizational charts, as shown in Figure 29-15.

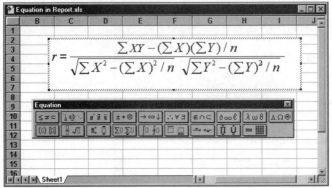

Figure 29-13: This object was created with Microsoft Equation.

Figure 29-14: An example of Microsoft WordArt.

Figure 29-15: An example of an embedded organizational chart.

Using Office Binders

If you have Microsoft Office installed, you may take advantage of its binder feature. A *binder* is a container that can hold documents from different applications: Excel, Word, and PowerPoint.

You may find that a binder is useful when working on a project that involves documents from different applications. For example, you may be preparing a sales presentation that uses charts and tables from Excel, reports and memos from Word, and slides prepared with PowerPoint. You can store all the information in a single file. Another advantage is that you can print the entire binder, and all pages are numbered sequentially.

To use a binder, start the Binder application. You get an empty binder. You then can add existing documents or create new documents in the binder. Figure 29-16 shows a binder that contains Word, Excel, and PowerPoint documents. Consult the online Help for complete details on using this feature.

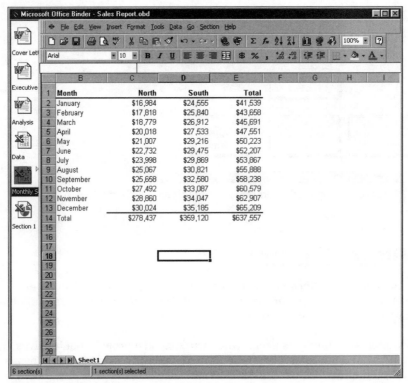

Figure 29-16: An Office binder can hold documents that are produced by different applications.

Summary

In this chapter, I describe techniques that allow you to use data from other applications. These techniques include standard copy and paste using the Windows Clipboard, dynamic linking between applications, and embedding objects. I also note that Microsoft Office has a binder feature that lets you work with documents that are produced by different applications.

✦　　　✦　　　✦

Excel and the Internet

Chances are, you're already involved in the Internet in some way. This technology seems to have taken the world by storm. The World Wide Web (WWW) is probably the most exciting thing happening these days in the world of computing. In fact, the Web reaches well beyond the computer community and has become a pervasive force in our lives. It's quite common to see Web site addresses listed in TV commercials, in magazine ads, and even on billboards.

The applications in Microsoft Office 97 — including Excel — have quite a few new Internet-related features. In this chapter, I provide an introduction to the Internet (for those who have yet to discover this resource) and discuss the new Internet features in Excel 97.

What Is the Internet?

The *Internet,* in a nutshell, is a collection of computers that are located all around the world. These computers are all connected to each other, and they can pass information back and forth. Strange as it may seem, the Internet is essentially a noncommercial system, and no single entity "runs" the Internet.

Most people don't think of the Internet as a collection of computers. Rather, the Internet is a *resource* that contains information — and you use a computer to access that information. The millions of computers that are connected to the Internet simply do the grunt work of passing the information from point A (which could be a computer in Hamburg, Germany) to point B (which could be the computer in your cubicle).

Internet Terminology for newcomers

If you're just starting to explore the Internet, you'll encounter a great deal of new terms (many of them are acronyms). The following is a list of a few common Internet terms and their definitions.

Browser: Software that is designed to download HTML documents, interpret them, and display their contents. You can also use a browser to download files from an FTP site. The two leading Web browsers are Microsoft Internet Explorer and Netscape Navigator.

E-mail: A method of sending messages to others. You may be able to send and receive e-mail only within your company, or you may be able to send and receive e-mail all over the world using the Internet.

FTP: An acronym for File Transfer Protocol. This is one method by which a file is transferred from one computer to another.

FTP site: An area of a computer that contains files that can be downloaded. For example, Microsoft maintains an FTP site that has files that you can download.

HTML document: A computer file that contains information that is usually intended to be read by someone other than its author. The file includes embedded "tags" that describe how the information is displayed and formatted. Browser software is designed to interpret these tags and display the information.

HTTP: An acronym for HyperText Transfer Protocol. This is the method by which documents are transferred over the WWW.

Hyperlink: A clickable object (or text) that opens another document. Most Web pages include hyperlinks to allow the user to jump to another topic or Web site.

Internet: A network of computers throughout the world that can communicate with each other and pass information back and forth.

Intranet: A company-wide network of computers that uses Internet protocols to allow access to information. An intranet can only be accessed by users who have permission.

URL: An acronym for Uniform Resource Locator. A URL uniquely describes an Internet resource such as a WWW document or a file. For example, the URL for the opening page of Microsoft's Web page is `http://www.microsoft.com`.

WWW: The World Wide Web, which is a part of the Internet that supports the transfer of information between computers throughout the world.

WWW site: Also known as a Web site. A collection of HTML documents located on a particular computer. The files on a Web site are available to anyone in the world. For example, Microsoft maintains a Web site that contains information about its products, technical support, and other resources.

What's available on the Internet?

The amount and variety of information that's available on the Internet is simply mind-boggling. You can think of virtually any topic in the world, and there's an excellent chance that there is some information that topic. Not unexpectedly, computer-related information is especially abundant.

So where do you get this information? There are four primary sources for information the Internet:

✦ **Web sites.** The World Wide Web has rapidly become the most popular part of the Internet. There are thousands of Web sites that you can access with your Web browser software. For example, my own Web site (The Spreadsheet Page) has the following URL:

```
http://www.j-walk.com/ss/
```

✦ **FTP sites.** These are computers that have files available for download. You can download these files using Web browser software or other software that is designed specifically to get files from FTP sites. The address for Microsoft's FTP site is:

```
ftp://ftp.microsoft.com
```

✦ **Newsgroups.** These are essentially electronic bulletin boards. People post messages or questions, and others respond to the messages or answer their questions. Thousands of newsgroups are available for just about any topic that you can think of. You need special "news reader" software to read or post messages to a newsgroup (although most Web browsers also include this feature). The address for a newsgroup that deals with Excel (and other spreadsheets) is:

```
news:comp.apps.spreadsheets
```

Figure 30-1 shows the titles of a few messages in this newsgroup.

✦ **Mailing lists.** If you have access to Internet e-mail, you can subscribe to any of several thousand mailing lists that address a broad array of topics. Subscribers send e-mail to the mailing list, and then every other subscriber to the list receives that e-mail. There are two primary mailing lists that deal with Excel (refer to the "Excel Mailing Lists" sidebar for details).

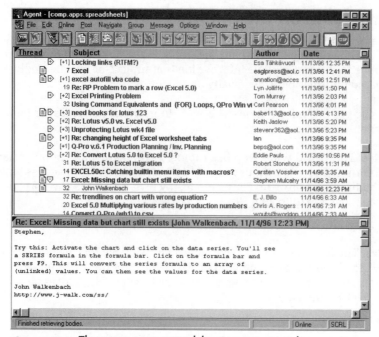

Figure 30-1: The comp.apps.spreadsheets newsgroup is a great source for Excel information.

How do you get on the Internet?

You can access the Internet in a number of ways. Here are some of the most common ways:

✦ **Through your company.** Your company may already be connected to the Internet. If so, just fire up your Web browser and you're there!

✦ **Through an Internet Service Provider (ISP).** Most communities have several companies that can set up an Internet account for you. For a small monthly fee (usually around $20) you can have unlimited (or almost unlimited) access to the Internet.

✦ **Through an online service.** If you subscribe to any of the following online services, you can access the Internet through that service: America Online, CompuServe, Microsoft Network, or Prodigy.

Excel mailing lists

If you like the idea of communicating with other Excel users, you may want to join one of the Excel mailing lists. You can read messages, questions, and answers posted by others and eventually contribute your own messages to the list. If you find that the amount of mail is overwhelming, it's easy to "unsubscribe."

The EXCEL-G mailing list. This mailing list is for Excel users of all levels. To subscribe to the list, send e-mail to:

```
LISTSERV@PEACH.EASE.LSOFT.COM
```

In the body of the message, enter the following:

```
SUB  EXCEL-G  YourFirstName
    YourLastName
```

You'll receive complete instructions via e-mail.

The EXCEL-L mailing list. This mailing list is primarily for Excel developers who discuss more advanced topics. To subscribe to the list, send e-mail to:

```
LISTSERV@PEACH.EASE.LSOFT.COM
```

In the body of the message, enter the following:

```
SUB EXCEL-L YourFirstName
YourLastName
```

You'll receive complete instructions via e-mail.

Where to find out more about the Internet

The best place to find out more about the Internet is — you guessed it — the Internet. A good starting place is the IDG Books Web site. To access it, open the following URL in your Web browser:

```
http://www.idgbooks.com
```

IDG Books Worldwide publishes a number of Internet books for users of all levels, and you can find these listed and described on the IDG Web site.

Excel's Internet Tools

Excel 97 All the features that are discussed in this section are new to Excel 97.

If Excel's Internet features are not available, you need to rerun the Excel (or Microsoft Office) Setup program. Select the Custom option to add these features.

Opening Internet files

Excel can open an HTML file and display it as a worksheet. The HTML file that you open can reside on your local drive, your company's intranet, or the Internet. Excel formats these files as best as it can, but because Excel is not a Web browser, the results are not always that great. For example, if a hyperlink is contained in a paragraph, the paragraph is broken up so that the hyperlink appears in its own cell. Also, graphics are ignored. Nevertheless, imported HTML files contain all the original information and hyperlinks.

To open an HTML file, use Excel's File⇨Open command. In the Open dialog box, select HTML Documents (*.html, *.htm) in the Files of type box. See Figure 30-2.

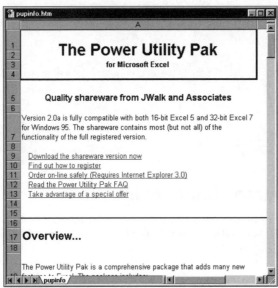

Figure 30-2: Excel 97 can open HTML files — but the results are not always completely satisfactory.

You can save an HTML file as an Excel workbook using the File⇨Save As command. You cannot save the workbook as an HTML file.

The Web toolbar

Use the Web toolbar to move among files (Excel files and HTML documents); this is similar to using a Web browser. You can jump forward or backward among the workbooks and other files that you've visited and add the ones that you may use frequently to a "favorites" list.

Hyperlinks

Hyperlinks are shortcuts that provide a quick way to jump to other workbooks and files. You can jump to files on your own computer, your network, and the Internet and World Wide Web.

Tip   You can also use hyperlinks as a form of bookmarks for a single workbook. For example, if you have a workbook with a number of worksheets, you can create a "contents" page that consists of hyperlinks that activate other sheets in the worksheet.

Inserting a hyperlink

You can create hyperlinks from cell text or graphic objects, such as shapes and pictures. To create a text hyperlink, choose the Insert⇨Hyperlink command (or press Ctrl+K). Excel responds with the dialog box shown in Figure 30-3. Enter the location for the file that you want to link to (you may find it easier to use the Browse button to locate the file). If you want the link to jump to a particular location in the document, specify the location in the bottom part of the dialog box (again, the Browse button will be useful). Click OK, and Excel will create the hyperlink in the active cell.

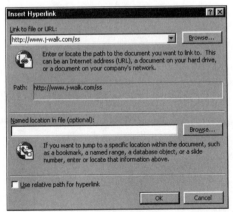

Figure 30-3: The Insert Hyperlink dialog box.

Adding a hyperlink to a graphic object works the same way. Add an object to your worksheet using the Drawing toolbar. Select the object and then choose the Insert⇨Hyperlink command. Specify the required information as outlined in the previous paragraph.

Using hyperlinks

When working with hyperlinks, it's important to keep in mind that Excel attempts to mimic a Web browser. For example, when you click a hyperlink, the hyperlinked document replaces the current document — it takes on the same window size and position. The document that contains the hyperlink is hidden. You can use the Back and Forward buttons on the Web toolbar to activate the documents.

Saving data and charts in HTML format

You can make your Excel data available to users on your intranet or the World Wide Web so that anyone who has a Web browser can view it.

Use the Internet Assistant add-in program to convert worksheet data or charts to HTML Web pages that you can post on the World Wide Web. To save a worksheet in HTML format, select the File⇨Save as HTML command. This displays the Internet Assistant Wizard, a series of four dialog boxes that let you specify several options. Figure 30-4 shows the first of these dialog boxes. You can select various ranges (which are converted into HTML tables) and also select which charts (if any) to export as GIF files.

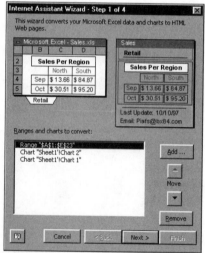

Figure 30-4: The first of four Internet Assistant dialog boxes.

Caution Excel is not an HTML editor. For example, if you open an HTML document using the technique described previously (see "Opening Internet files"), do not use the Internet Assistant to resave the document. If you do so, all of the information will be stored in a table.

Summary

In this chapter, I provide a brief introduction to the Internet and describe a number of Internet tools available in Excel. I explain how to open HTML documents, use the Web toolbar, work with hyperlinks, and save data in HTML format.

✦   ✦   ✦

Making Your Worksheets Error-Free

In This Chapter

An overview of the problems that crop up in spreadsheets

Viewing your formulas

How to trace the relationships between cells in a worksheet

Tools to ensure that your worksheet doesn't contain spelling errors

Techniques that help you understand an unfamiliar workbook

The ultimate goal in developing a spreadsheet solution is to generate accurate results. For simple worksheets, this isn't difficult, and you can usually tell whether the results are correct. But when your worksheets get large or complex, ensuring accuracy becomes more difficult. This chapter provides you with tools and techniques to help you identify and correct errors.

Types of Worksheet Problems

Making a change in a worksheet — even a relatively minor change — may produce a ripple effect that introduces errors in other cells. For example, it's all too easy to accidentally enter a value into a cell that formerly held a formula. This can have a major impact on other formulas, and you may not discover the problem until it's too late. Or you may *never* discover the problem.

An Excel worksheet can have many types of problems. Some problems — such as a formula that returns an error value — are immediately apparent. Other problems are more subtle. For example, if a formula was constructed using faulty logic, it may never return an error value — it simply returns the wrong values. If you're lucky, you can discover the problem and correct it.

Common problems that occur in worksheets are as follows:

+ Incorrect approach to a problem
+ Faulty logic in a formula
+ Formulas that return error values

✦ Circular references

✦ Spelling mistakes

✦ A worksheet is new to you, and you can't figure out how it works

Excel provides tools to help you identify and correct some of these problems. In the remaining sections, I discuss these tools along with others that I've developed.

Formula AutoCorrect

Excel 97 When you enter a formula that has a syntax error, Excel 97 attempts to determine the problem and offers a suggested correction.

For example, if you enter the following formula (which has a syntax error), Excel displays the dialog box that is shown in Figure 31-1:

```
=SUM(A1:A12)/3B
```

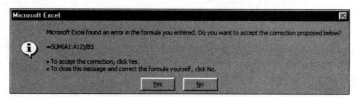

Figure 31-1: Excel can often offer a suggestion to correct a formula.

Caution Be careful about accepting corrections for your formulas. Excel doesn't always guess correctly. For example, I entered the following formula (which has mismatched parentheses):

```
=AVERAGE(SUM(A1:A12,SUM(B1:B12))
```

Excel proposed the following correction to the formula:

```
=AVERAGE(SUM(A1:A12,SUM(B1:B12)))
```

You may be tempted to accept the suggestion without even thinking. In this case, the proposed formula is syntactically correct — but not what I intended.

Tracing Cell Relationships

Excel has several useful tools that help you track down errors and logical flaws in your worksheets. In this section, I discuss the following items:

✦ Go To Special dialog box

✦ Excel's built-in auditing tools

These tools are useful for debugging formulas. As you probably realize by now, the formulas in a worksheet can become complicated and refer (directly or indirectly) to hundreds or thousands of other cells. Trying to isolate a problem in a tangled web of formulas can be frustrating.

Before I discuss the features, there are two concepts with which you should be familiar:

✦ **Cell precedents:** This is applicable only to cells that contain a formula. A formula cell's precedents are all cells that contribute to the formula's result. A *direct precedent* is a cell that is used directly in the formula. An *indirect precedent* is a cell that is not used directly in the formula but is used by a cell that is referred to in the formula.

✦ **Cell dependents:** Formula cells that depend on a particular cell. Again, the formula cell can be a direct dependent or an indirect dependent.

Often, identifying cell precedents for a formula cell sheds light on why the formula isn't working correctly. On the other hand, it's often helpful to know what formula cells depend on a particular cell. For example, if you're about to delete a formula, you may want to check to see if it has any dependents.

The Go To Special dialog box

The Go To Special dialog box can be useful because it lets you specify cells of a certain type that are to be selected. To bring up this dialog box, choose Edit⇨Go To (or press F5). This displays the Go To dialog box. Click on the Special button, which displays the Go To Special dialog box, as shown in Figure 31-2.

Note If you select a range before choosing Edit⇨Go To, the command only looks at the selected cells. If only a single cell is selected, the command operates on the entire worksheet.

You can use this dialog box to select cells of a certain type — which can often be helpful in identifying errors. For example, if you choose the Formulas option, Excel selects all of the cells that contain a formula. If the worksheet is zoomed out to a small size, this can give you a good idea of how the worksheet is organized (see

Figure 31-3). It may also help you spot a common error of a formula that is over-written by a value. If you find a cell that's not selected amid a group of selected formula cells, chances are good that the cell formerly contained a formula, but it was replaced by a value.

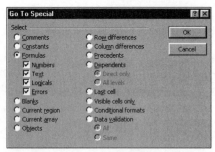

Figure 31-2: The Go To Special dialog box.

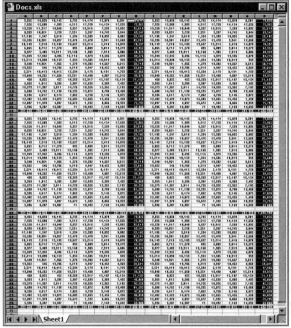

Figure 31-3: Zooming out and selecting all formula cells can give you a good overview of how the worksheet is designed.

You can also use the Go To Special dialog box to identify cell precedents and dependents. In this case, Excel selects all cells that qualify. In either case, you can choose whether to display direct or all levels.

Excel has shortcut keys that you can use to select precedents and dependents. These are listed in Table 31-1.

Table 31-1
Shortcut Keys to Select Precedents and Dependents

Key Combination	What It Selects
Ctrl+[	Direct precedents
Ctrl+Shift+[	All precedents
Ctrl+]	Direct dependents
Ctrl+Shift+]	All dependents

You also can select a formula cell's direct dependents by double-clicking on the cell. This technique, however, works only when the Edit directly in cell option is turned off in the Edit panel of the Options dialog box.

Excel's auditing tools

Excel provides a set of interactive auditing tools that you may find helpful. Access these tools by selecting Tools⇨Auditing (which results in a submenu with additional choices) or by using the Auditing toolbar, as shown in Figure 31-4.

Pay attention to the colors

A new feature in Excel 97 is particularly helpful for debugging formulas. When you edit a cell that contains a formula, Excel color-codes the cell and range references in the formula. The cells and ranges used in the formula are also outlined using corresponding colors. Therefore, you can see at a glance which cells are used in the formulas.

You can also manipulate the colored outline to change the cell or range reference. To change the references that are used, drag the outline's border or drag the outline's fill handle (at the lower-right corner of the outline).

Figure 31-4: The Auditing toolbar.

The tools on the Auditing toolbar, from left to right, are as follows:

✦ **Trace Precedents:** Draws arrows to indicate a formula cell's precedents. Click on this multiple times to see additional levels of precedents.

✦ **Remove Precedent Arrows:** Removes the most recently placed set of precedent arrows.

✦ **Trace Dependents:** Draws arrows to indicate a cell's dependents. Click on this multiple times to see additional levels of dependents.

✦ **Remove Dependent Arrows:** Removes the most recently placed set of dependent arrows.

✦ **Remove All Arrows:** Removes all precedent and dependent arrows from the worksheet.

✦ **Trace Error:** Draws arrows from a cell that contains an error to the cells that may have caused the error.

✦ **New Comment:** Inserts a comment for the active cell. This really doesn't have much to do with auditing. It lets you attach a comment to a cell.

✦ **Circle Invalid Data:** Draws a circle around all of the cells that contain invalid data. This applies only to cells that have validation criteria specified with the Data⇨Validation command.

✦ **Clear Validation Circles:** Removes the circles that are drawn around cells that contain invalid data.

These tools can identify precedents and dependents by drawing arrows (known as cell tracers) on the worksheet. Figure 31-5 shows an example of this. In this case, I selected cell G11 and then clicked on the Trace Precedents toolbar button. Excel drew lines to indicate which cells are used by the formula in G11 (direct precedents).

Figure 31-6 shows what happens when I click on the Trace Precedents button again. This time it adds more lines to show the indirect precedents. The result is a graphical representation of the cells that are used (directly or indirectly) by the formula in cell G11.

Tip   This type of interactive tracing is often more revealing when the worksheet is zoomed out to display a larger area.

The best way to learn about these tools is to use them. Start with a worksheet that has formulas, and experiment with the various buttons on the Auditing toolbar.

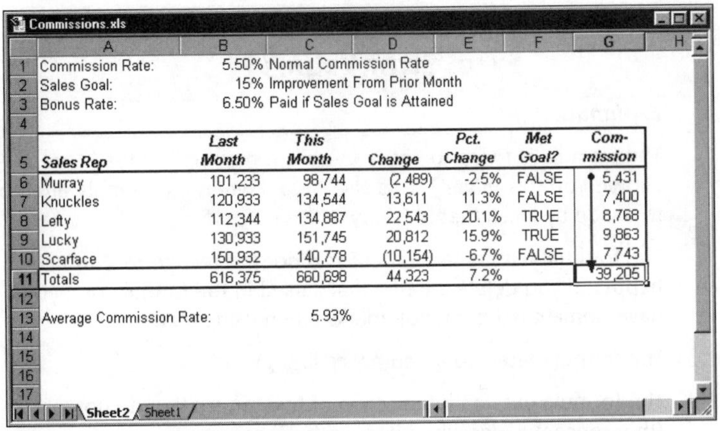

Figure 31-5: Excel draws lines to indicate a cell's precedents.

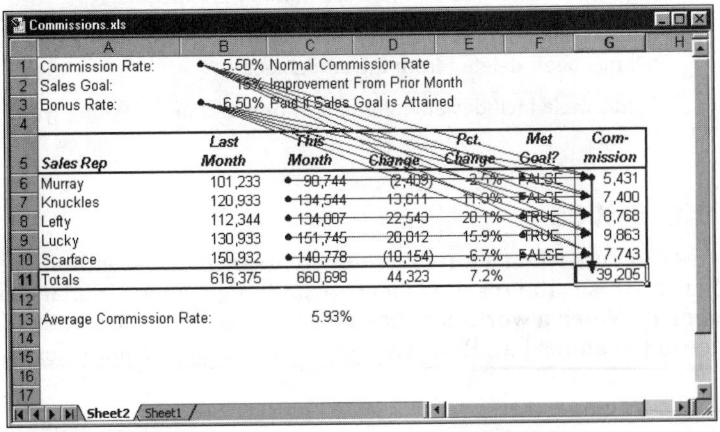

Figure 31-6: Excel draws more lines to indicate the indirect precedents.

Tracing error values

The Trace Error button on the Auditing toolbar helps you identify the cell that is causing an error value to appear. Often, an error in one cell is the result of an error in a precedent cell. Activate a cell that contains an error, and click on the Trace Error button. Excel draws arrows to indicate the error source.

Table 31-2 lists the types of error values that may appear in a cell that has a formula. The Trace Error button works with all these errors.

Table 31-2
Excel Error Values

Error Value	Explanation
#DIV/0!	The formula is trying to divide by zero (an operation that's not allowed on this planet). This also occurs when the formula attempts to divide by a cell that is empty.
#NAME?	The formula uses a name that Excel doesn't recognize. This can happen if you delete a name that's used in the formula or if you have unmatched quotation marks when using text.
#N/A	The formula refers to an empty cell range.
#NULL!	The formula uses an intersection of two ranges that do not intersect (this concept is described later in the chapter).
#NUM!	There is a problem with a value — for example, you specified a negative number where a positive number is expected.
#REF!	The formula refers to a cell that is not valid. This can happen if the cell has been deleted from the worksheet.
#VALUE!	The formula includes an argument or operand of the wrong type.

Circular references

A circular reference occurs when a formula refers to its own cell — either directly or indirectly. Usually, this is the result of an error (although some circular references are intentional). When a worksheet has a circular reference, Excel displays the cell reference in the status bar. Refer to the discussion of circular references in Chapter 9.

Other Auditing Tools

The registered version of the Power Utility Pak includes a utility named Auditing Tools. The dialog box for this utility is shown in Figure 31-7. This utility works with the active worksheet and can generate any or all of the following items:

✦ **Worksheet map:** A color-coded graphical map of the worksheet that shows the type of contents for each cell — value, text, formula, logical value, or error. See Figure 31-8.

✦ **Formula list:** A list of all formulas in the worksheet, including their current value.

✦ **Summary report:** An informative report that includes details about the worksheet, the workbook that it's in, and a list of all defined names.

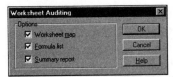

Figure 31-7: The Worksheet Auditing dialog box from the Power Utility Pak.

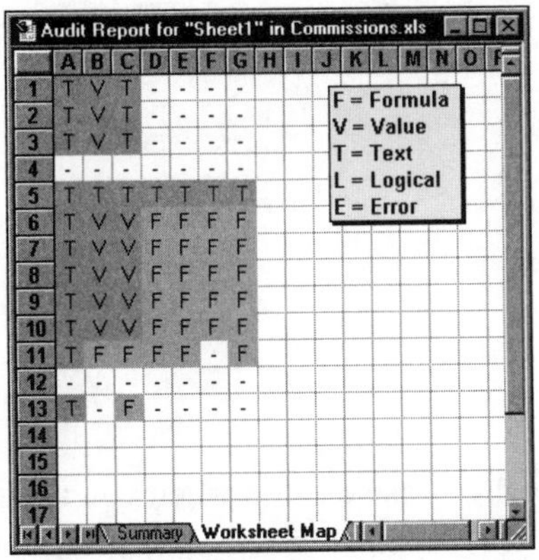

Figure 31-8: This worksheet map was produced by the Auditing Tools utility from the Power Utility Pak.

Note   You can download the shareware version of the Power Utility Pak from this book's Website. Owners of this book can purchase the Power Utility Pak at a significant discount. Use the coupon in the back of the book to order your copy.

Spelling and Word-Related Options

Excel includes several handy tools to help you with the non-numeric problems — those related to spelling and words.

Spell checking

If you use a word processing program, you probably run its spelling checker before printing an important document. Spelling mistakes can be just as embarrassing when they appear in a spreadsheet. Fortunately, Microsoft includes a spelling checker with Excel. You can access the spelling checker using any of these methods:

✦ Select Tools⇨Spelling.

✦ Click on the Spelling button on the Standard toolbar.

✦ Press F7.

You get the Spelling dialog box that is shown in Figure 31-9.

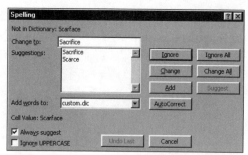

Figure 31-9: The Spelling dialog box.

The extent of the spell checking depends on what was selected when you accessed the dialog box. If a single cell was selected, the entire worksheet is checked; this includes cell contents, notes, text in graphic objects and charts, and page headers and footers. Even the contents of hidden rows and columns are checked. If you select a range of cells, only that range is checked. If you select a group of characters in the formula bar, only those characters are checked.

The Spelling dialog box works similarly to other spelling checkers with which you may be familiar. If Excel encounters a word that isn't in the current dictionary or is misspelled, it offers a list of suggestions. You can respond by clicking on one of the following buttons:

✦ **Ignore:** Ignores the word and continues the spell check.

✦ **Ignore All:** Ignores the word and all subsequent occurrences of it.

✦ **Change:** Changes the word to the selected word in the Change to edit box.

✦ **Change All:** Changes the word to the selected word in the Change to edit box and changes all subsequent occurrences of it without asking.

✦ **Add:** Adds the word to the dictionary.

✦ **Suggest:** Displays a list of replacement words. This button is grayed if the Always suggest check box is checked.

✦ **AutoCorrect:** Adds the misspelled word and its correct spelling to the list of words that are corrected automatically (see the following section). Use this if you frequently misspell a particular word.

Using AutoCorrect

AutoCorrect is a handy feature that automatically corrects common typing mistakes. You also can add words to the list that are corrected automatically. The AutoCorrect dialog box is shown in Figure 31-10. You access this feature by choosing Tools⇨AutoCorrect.

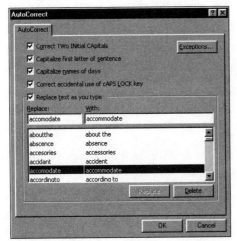

Figure 31-10: The AutoCorrect dialog box.

This dialog box has several options:

✦ **Correct TWo INitial CApitals:** Automatically corrects words with two initial uppercase letters. For example, *BUdget* is converted to *Budget*. This is a common mistake among fast typists. You can click on the Exceptions button to specify a list of exceptions to this rule. For example, my company name is *JWalk and Associates,* so I created an exception for *JWalk.*

✦ **Capitalize first letter of sentence:** Capitalizes the first letter in a sentence.

✦ **Capitalize names of days:** Capitalizes the days of the week. If you enter *monday,* Excel converts it to *Monday.*

✦ **Correct accidental use of cAPS LOCK key:** Corrects errors caused if you accidentally hit the CapsLock key while typing.

✦ **Replace text as you type:** AutoCorrect automatically changes incorrect words as you type them.

Excel includes a long list of AutoCorrect entries for commonly misspelled words. In addition, it has AutoCorrect entries for some symbols. For example, *(c)* is replaced with © and *(r)* is replaced with ®. You can also add your own AutoCorrect entries. For example, if you find that you frequently misspell the word *January* as *Janruary,* you can create an AutoCorrect entry so that it's changed automatically. To create a new AutoCorrect entry, enter the misspelled word in the Replace box and the correctly spelled word in the With box. As I noted previously, you also can do this in the Spelling dialog box.

Tip   You also can use the AutoCorrect feature to create shortcuts for commonly used words or phrases. For example, if you work for a company named Consolidated Data Processing Corporation, you can create an AutoCorrect entry for an abbreviation, such as cdp. Then, whenever you type *cdp,* Excel automatically changes it to *Consolidated Data Processing Corporation.*

Using AutoComplete

AutoComplete automatically finishes a word as soon as it is recognized. For the word to be recognized, it must appear elsewhere in the same column. This is most useful when you're entering a list that contains repeated text in a column. For example, assume that you're entering customer data in a list, and one of the fields is City. Whenever you start typing, Excel searches the other entries in the column. If it finds a match, it completes the entry for you. Press Enter to accept it. If Excel guesses incorrectly, keep typing to ignore the suggestion.

Note   If AutoComplete isn't working, select Tools⇨Options, click on the Edit tab, and check the box labeled Enable AutoComplete for cell values.

You also can display a list of all items in a column by right-clicking and choosing Pick from list from the shortcut menu. Excel then displays a list box of all entries that are in the column (see Figure 31-11). Click on the one that you want, and Excel enters it into the cell for you.

Learning about an Unfamiliar Spreadsheet

When you develop a workbook yourself, you have a thorough understanding of how it's put together. But if you receive an unfamiliar workbook from someone, it may be difficult to understand how it all fits together — especially if it's large.

Usually, the first step is to identify the bottom-line cell or cells. Often, a worksheet is designed to produce results in a single cell or in a range of cells. After you identify this cell or range, you should be able to use the cell-tracing techniques described earlier in this chapter to determine the cell relationships.

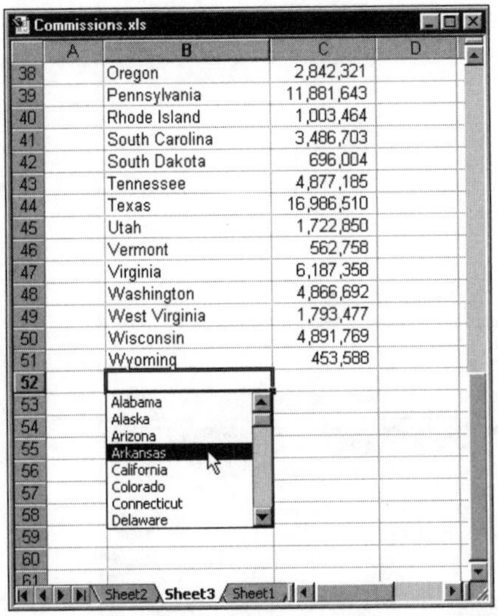

Figure 31-11: Choosing the Pick from list option from the shortcut menu gives you a list of entries from which to choose.

Although every worksheet is different, a few techniques can help you become familiar with an unfamiliar workbook. I discuss these techniques in the following sections.

Zooming out for the big picture

I find that it's often helpful to use Excel's zoom feature to zoom out to get an overview of the worksheet's layout. You can select View⇨Full Screen to see even more of the worksheet. When a workbook is zoomed out, you can use all of the normal commands. For example, you can use the Edit⇨Go To command to select a name range. Or, you can use the options that are available in the Go To Special dialog box (explained previously in this chapter) to select formula cells, constants, or other special cell types.

Viewing formulas

Another way to become familiar with an unfamiliar workbook is to display the formulas rather than the results of the formulas. To do this, select Tools⇨Options, and check the box labeled Formulas in the View panel. You may want to create a new window for the workbook before issuing this command. That way, you can see the formulas in one window and the results in the other.

Figure 31-12 shows an example. The window on the top shows the normal view (formula results). The window on the bottom displays the formulas.

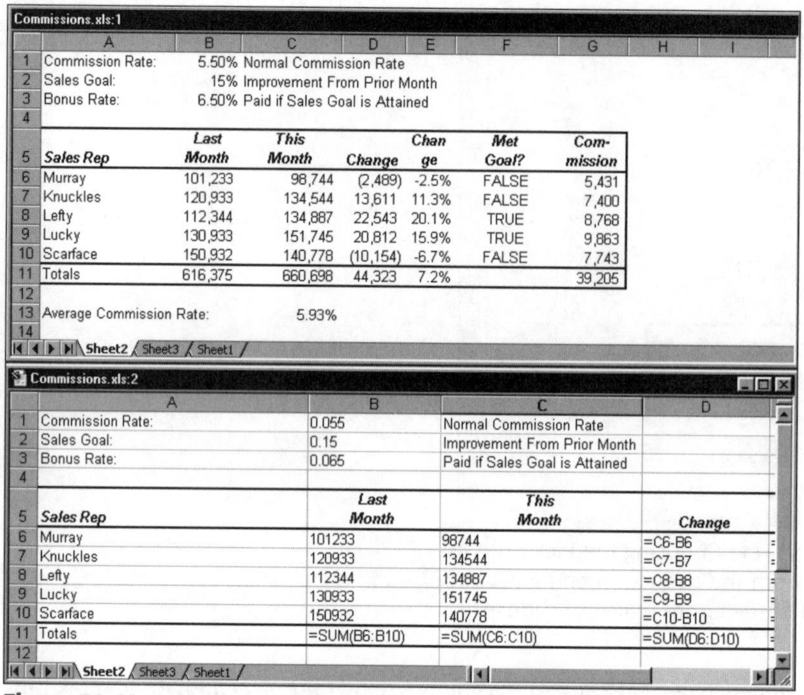

Commissions.xls:1

	A	B	C	D	E	F	G
1	Commission Rate:	5.50%	Normal Commission Rate				
2	Sales Goal:	15%	Improvement From Prior Month				
3	Bonus Rate:	6.50%	Paid if Sales Goal is Attained				
4							
5	*Sales Rep*	*Last Month*	*This Month*	*Change*	*Change*	*Met Goal?*	*Commission*
6	Murray	101,233	98,744	(2,489)	-2.5%	FALSE	5,431
7	Knuckles	120,933	134,544	13,611	11.3%	FALSE	7,400
8	Lefty	112,344	134,887	22,543	20.1%	TRUE	8,768
9	Lucky	130,933	151,745	20,812	15.9%	TRUE	9,863
10	Scarface	150,932	140,778	(10,154)	-6.7%	FALSE	7,743
11	Totals	616,375	660,698	44,323	7.2%		39,205
12							
13	Average Commission Rate:		5.93%				
14							

Sheet2 / Sheet3 / Sheet1

Commissions.xls:2

	A	B	C	D
1	Commission Rate:	0.055	Normal Commission Rate	
2	Sales Goal:	0.15	Improvement From Prior Month	
3	Bonus Rate:	0.065	Paid if Sales Goal is Attained	
4				
5	*Sales Rep*	*Last Month*	*This Month*	*Change*
6	Murray	101233	98744	=C6-B6
7	Knuckles	120933	134544	=C7-B7
8	Lefty	112344	134887	=C8-B8
9	Lucky	130933	151745	=C9-B9
10	Scarface	150932	140778	=C10-B10
11	Totals	=SUM(B6:B10)	=SUM(C6:C10)	=SUM(D6:D10)
12				

Sheet2 / Sheet3 / Sheet1

Figure 31-12: The underlying formulas are shown in the bottom window.

Pasting a list of names

If the worksheet uses named ranges, create a list of the names and their references. To do so, move the cell pointer to an empty area of the worksheet and choose Insert➪Name➪Paste. Excel responds with its Paste Name dialog box. Click on the Paste List button to paste a list of the names and their references into the workbook. Figure 31-13 shows an example.

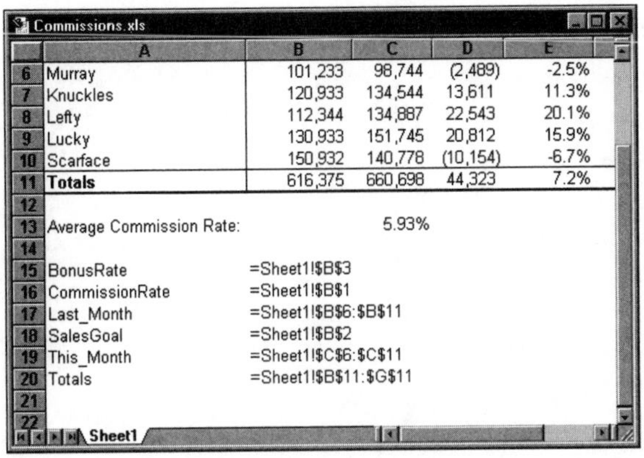

Figure 31-13: Pasting a list of names (in A15:B20) can sometimes help you understand how a worksheet is constructed.

Summary

In this chapter, I discuss tools that can help you make your worksheets error-free. I identify the types of errors that you're likely to encounter. I also cover three tools that Excel provides, which can help you trace the relationships between cells: the Info window, the Go To Special dialog box, and Excel's interactive auditing tools. I go over text-related features, including spell checking, AutoCorrect, and AutoComplete. I conclude the chapter with general tips that can help you understand how an unfamiliar worksheet is put together.

✦ ✦ ✦

Fun Stuff

Although Excel is used primarily for serious applications, many users discover that this product has a lighter side. This chapter is devoted to the less-serious applications of Excel, including games and interesting diversions.

Games

Excel certainly wasn't designed as a platform for games. Nevertheless, I've developed a few games using Excel and have downloaded several others from various online services. I've found that the key ingredient in developing these games is creativity. In almost every case, I had to invent one or more workarounds to compensate for Excel's lack of game-making features. In this section, I show you a few of my own creations.

The examples in this chapter are either available for download at this book's Web site or included with the registered version of my Power Utility Pak (see the coupon at the back of the book).

Tick-Tack-Toe

Although Tick-Tack-Toe is not the most mentally stimulating game, everyone knows how to play it. Figure 32-1 shows the Tick-Tack-Toe game that I developed using Excel. In this implementation, the user plays against the computer. I wrote some formulas and VBA macros to determine the computer's moves, and it plays a reasonably good game — about on par with a three-year-old child. I'm embarrassed to admit that the program has even beaten me a few times (I was distracted).

You can choose who makes the first move (you or the computer) and which marker you want to use (X or O). The winning games and ties are tallied in cells at the bottom of the window.

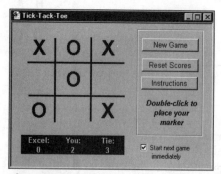

Figure 32-1: My Tick-Tack-Toe game.

Moving Tile puzzle

At some time in your life, you've probably played one of those moving tile puzzles. They come in several variations, but the goal is always the same: rearrange the tiles so that they are in order.

Web site This workbook can be downloaded from this book's Web site.

Figure 32-2 shows a version of this game that I wrote in VBA. When you click on the tile, it appears to move to the empty position. Actually, no movement is taking place. The program is simply changing the text on the buttons and making the button in the empty position invisible.

Figure 32-2: My Moving Tile puzzle.

Hangman

This workbook can be downloaded from this book's Web site.

Hangman is another game that almost everyone has played. Figure 32-3 shows a version that I developed for Excel. The objective is to identify a word by guessing letters. Correctly guessed letters appear in their proper position. Every incorrectly guessed letter adds a new body part to the person being hanged (and the incorrect letters appear at the top). Ten incorrect guesses and the man is hanged — that is, the game is over.

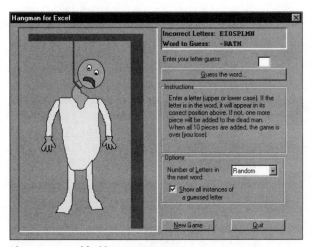

Figure 32-3: My Hangman game.

The workbook includes 1,400 words, ranging in length from 6 to 12 letters. You can choose how many letters you want in the word or have the number of letters determined randomly. In the unlikely event that you get bored with the 1,400 words that are supplied, you can easily add new words to the list without having to make any changes to the macros.

The entire game takes place in a dialog box. This dialog box demonstrates some useful techniques. It contains an edit box, which always has the focus. Entering a letter into the edit box executes a macro, which checks the letter and then clears the edit box for the next letter. The result is that you enter letters without having to press Enter or click on a button. The victim's body parts were created using Excel's drawing tools and are revealed as incorrect letters are guessed.

Trivia Questions

This workbook can be downloaded from this book's Web site.

This isn't really a game — it's a workbook that has more than 1,200 trivia questions and answers, which are grouped into five categories (see Figure 32-4). The workbook provides a way to display the questions and answers. This workbook is designed so that it's very easy to modify. For example, you can add new questions and answers and even add new categories — and you never need to modify any macros. One of the worksheets in this workbook contains instructions for adding new items or categories.

Most of the questions in this workbook were drawn from a public-domain, DOS-based trivia game that I downloaded several years ago. Consequently, some of the answers (especially in the Sports category) may no longer be correct. Play at your own risk.

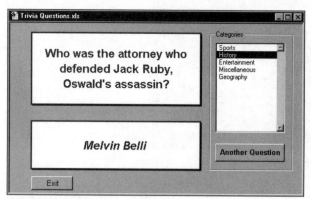

Figure 32-4: This workbook displays random trivia questions from five categories.

Video Poker

Developing my Video Poker game for Excel (see Figure 32-5) was quite a challenge. I was forced to spend many hours performing research at a local casino to perfect this game so that it captures the excitement of a real poker machine. The only problem is that I haven't figured out a way to dispense the winnings. Oh well, maybe in Version 2.0.

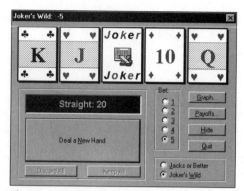

Figure 32-5: My Video Poker game.

My original intention was to use realistic playing-card graphics like those in the Windows Solitaire game. I discovered, however, that Excel insists on storing these graphics as 256-color images — creating a large file. I compromised by developing card images in worksheet cells and using linked pictures. To keep the file size small, I also gave up on my original idea to add sound effects — although this would not be difficult to do.

This version has two games: Joker's Wild (a joker can be used for any card) and Jacks or Better (a pair of jacks or better is required to win). You select which cards to discard by clicking on the card face. You can change the game (or the bet) at any time while playing. You can also request a graph that shows your cumulative winnings (or, more typically, your cumulative losses).

Identifying the various poker hands is done using VBA procedures. The game also has a Hide button that temporarily hides the game. This lets you resume the game when your boss leaves the room.

This game is included with the registered version of the Power Utility Pak. See the coupon in the back of the book for details on how to get your copy.

Dice game

The goal of the Dice game is to obtain a high score by assigning dice rolls to various categories. You get to roll the dice three times on each turn, and you can keep or discard the dice before rolling again.

This game takes place on a worksheet, although it looks like a dialog box. Everything is done using VBA and a few formulas. The dice are created in worksheet cells using Wingdings font characters and are linked picture objects. The game even has an Undo button that lets you change your mind after assigning a roll to a category. This game also has a Hide button that lets you return to work and resume the game later on.

This game is included with the registered version of the Power Utility Pak. See the coupon in the back of the book for details on how to get your copy.

Bomb Hunt

Windows comes with a game called Minesweeper. I developed a version of this game for Excel and named it Bomb Hunt (see Figure 32-6). The goal is to discover the hidden bombs in the grid. Double-clicking on a cell reveals a bomb (you lose) or a number that indicates the number of bombs in the surrounding cells. You use logic to determine where the bombs are located. Like Video Poker and the Dice game, this game includes a Hide button.

This game is included with the registered version of the Power Utility Pak. See the coupon in the back of the book for details on how to get your copy.

Figure 32-6: My Bomb Hunt game.

Symmetrical Pattern Drawing

This workbook can be downloaded from this book's Web site.

I must admit, this program is rather addictive — especially for doodlers. It lets you create colorful symmetrical patterns by using the arrow keys on the keyboard. Figure 32-7 shows an example. As you draw, the drawing is reproduced as mirror images in the other three quadrants. When you move the cursor to the edge of the drawing area, it wraps around and appears on the other side. This workbook is great for passing the time on the telephone when you're put on hold.

The drawing is all done with VBA macros. I used the OnKey method to trap the following key presses: left, right, up, and down. Each of these keystrokes executes a macro that shades a cell. The cells in the drawing area are very tiny, so the shading appears as lines.

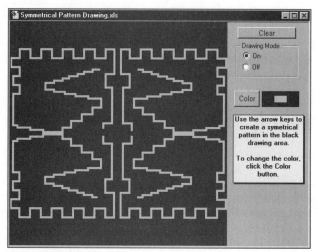

Figure 32-7: My Symmetrical Pattern Drawing worksheet.

For Guitar Players

Web site This workbook can be downloaded from this book's Web site.

If you play guitar, check out this workbook. As you see in Figure 32-8, this workbook has a graphic depiction of a guitar's fret board. It displays the notes (and fret positions) of the selected scale or mode in any key. You can even change the tuning of the guitar, and the formulas recalculate.

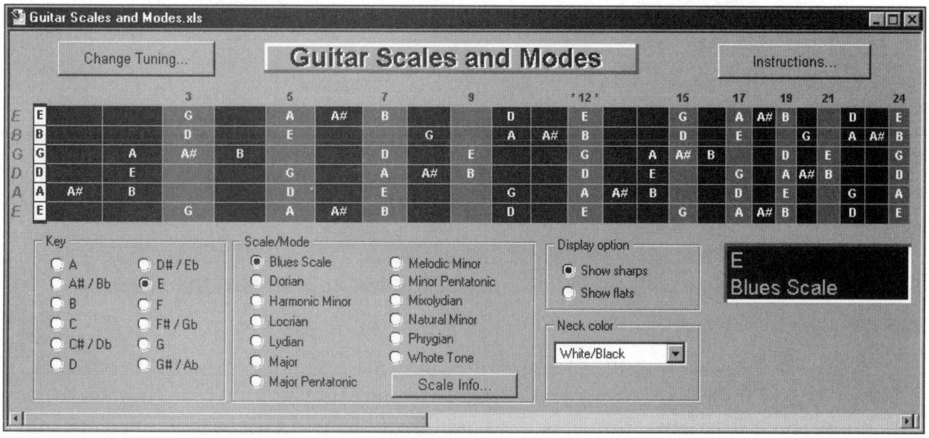

Figure 32-8: My guitar fret board application.

Other options include the choice to display half-notes as sharps or flats, to pop-up information about the selected scale or mode, and to change the color of the guitar neck. This workbook uses formulas to do the calculation, and VBA plays only a minor role. This file was designated a "top pick" on America Online, and I've received positive feedback from fellow pickers all over the world.

An April Fools' Prank

This workbook can be downloaded from this book's Web site.

Here's a good April Fools' trick to play on an office mate (with luck, one with a sense of humor). Set up his or her copy of Excel so that it automatically loads a workbook with macros that reverse the menus. For example, the Insert⇨Macro⇨ Dialog command becomes the Insert⇨Orcam⇨Golaid command. Because the macro that performs this prank is named `Auto_Open`, it is executed whenever the workbook is opened. If the workbook is saved in the victim's XLStart folder, the workbook opens automatically — and Excel's menus look like they're in a strange language. Figure 32-9 shows how this looks.

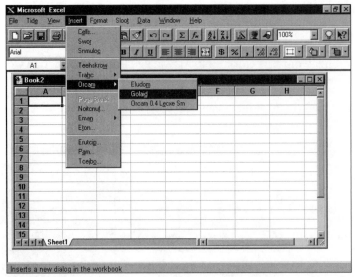

Figure 32-9: Excel with backward menus. The hot keys remain the same.

The routine performs its mischief by calling a custom function that reverses the text in the captions (except for the ellipses), converts the new text to proper case, and maintains the original hot keys. The net effect is a worksheet menu system that works exactly like the original (and is even keystroke compatible) but looks very odd.

Before exiting, the macro routine adds an escape route: A new (legible) menu item to the Pl<u>e</u>h menu (formerly the <u>H</u>elp menu). This new item calls up a macro that returns the menus to normal.

Typing Tutor

This workbook can be downloaded from this book's Web site.

Figure 32-10 shows a dialog box from an application that I developed to help people learn the location of the keys on the keyboard. It was suggested by Colin Anderson, an Internet acquaintance who e-mailed me after reading one of my books. He thought that it would make a good VBA example. I liked the idea so much that I created the Typing Tutor application.

This application has seven lessons, each of which focuses on a different part of the keyboard. Random letters are displayed, and you simply press the corresponding key. The program calculates the latency between when the letter appears and when the keystroke is made. It also determines whether the *proper* keystroke was made.

Figure 32-10: My Typing Tutor application.

I don't make any claims that this actually helps you type better, and I have absolutely no knowledge of typing training. It is likely, however, that you should see some improvement as you work with this program. The results of each lesson (the average latency and the accuracy) are stored in a worksheet database. You can create a chart from this data to plot your progress.

Create Word Search Puzzles

This workbook can be downloaded from this book's Web site.

Most daily newspapers feature a word search puzzle. These puzzles contain words that are hidden in a grid. The words can be vertical, diagonal, horizontal, forwards, or backwards. If you've ever had the urge to create your own word search puzzle, this workbook can make your job a lot easier by doing it for you. You supply the words; the program places them in the grid and fills in the empty squares with random letters. Figure 32-11 shows the puzzle creation sheet plus a sample puzzle that was created with this application.

This is all done with VBA, and randomness plays a major role. Therefore, you can create multiple puzzles using the same words.

Sun Calculations

Several years ago, I downloaded an Excel freeware file that performed some sophisticated calculations regarding the sun. The file included no identifying information, so I don't know who the author is. (If anyone knows, please let me know so that I can give proper credit.) I enhanced this file quite a bit, primarily by improving the user interface.

The program calculates various sun-related items based on a latitude, longitude, and date. It also displays several charts. Figure 32-12 shows an example of this program (the latitude and longitude shown are for San Diego, California). I include a worksheet that has latitudes and longitudes for several other locations — maybe even your hometown.

Making Noise

This workbook can be downloaded from this book's Web site.

If you have a CD-ROM drive installed on your system, you also probably have a sound card. You can embed WAV sound files in your workbooks to add some sound effects. I put together a few sounds effects for your amusement.

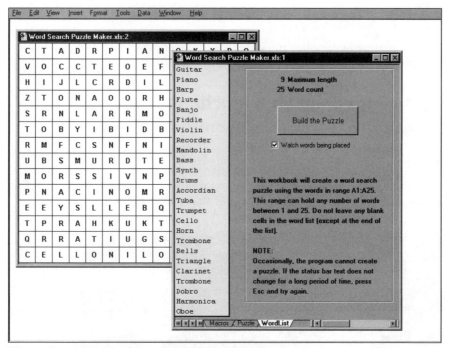

Figure 32-11: My Word Search Puzzle Maker.

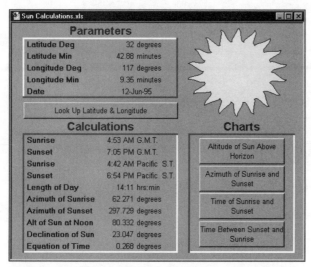

Figure 32-12: This workbook makes sun calculations for any latitude, longitude, and date.

Fun with Charts

Excel's charting feature has the potential to be fun. In this section, I provide examples of some non-serious charting applications.

Plotting trigonometric functions

Web site This workbook can be downloaded from this book's Web site.

Although I don't know too much about trigonometry, I've always enjoyed plotting various trigonometric functions as XY charts. Sometimes you can come up with attractive images. Figure 32-13 shows an example of a trigonometric plot. Clicking on the button changes a random number that makes a new chart.

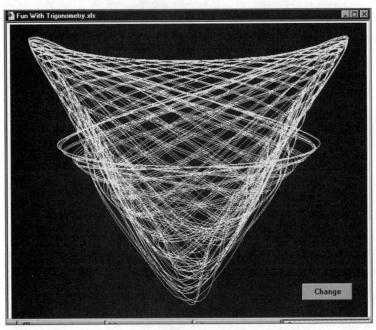

Figure 32-13: This chart plots trigonometric functions.

XY-Sketch

In this workbook, you use the controls to draw an XY chart (see Figure 32-14). Clicking on a directional button adds a new X and Y value to the chart's data range, which is then plotted on the chart. You can change the step size, adjust the color, and choose between smooth and normal lines. I include a multilevel Undo button that successively removes data points that you added.

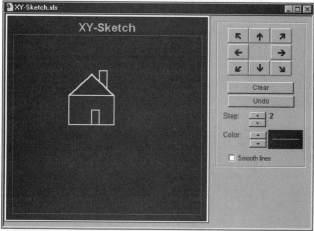

Figure 32-14: My XY-Sketch workbook.

Summary

In this chapter, I present several examples of non-serious applications for Excel. Some of these examples can most likely be adapted and used in more serious applications (well, maybe not).

✦   ✦   ✦

Customizing Excel

Most users find that Excel is a fantastic tool right out of the box. But the designers of this product included many additional capabilities that let you customize Excel in a number of ways. In this part, I discuss a variety of topics, including customizing toolbars and menus, creating custom templates, using VBA macros, and creating custom dialog boxes and add-ins.

◆ ◆ ◆ ◆

In This Part

◆ ◆ ◆

Customizing Toolbars and Menus

✦ ✦ ✦ ✦

In This Chapter

Types of toolbar and
menu customizations
that you can make

How to create
custom toolbars that
contain the tools that
you use most often

How to change the
image that is
displayed on a
toolbar button

✦ ✦ ✦ ✦

You're probably familiar with many of Excel's built-in
toolbars, and you have most likely thoroughly explored
the menu system. Excel lets you modify both toolbars and
menus. In this chapter, I explain how to customize the built-in
toolbars, create new toolbars, and change the menus that
Excel displays. Although many of these customizations are
most useful when you create macros (discussed in subsequent
chapters), even nonmacro users may find these techniques
helpful.

Menu Bar = Toolbar

Excel 97 In Excel 97, there is virtually no distinction between a menu
bar and a toolbar. In fact, the menu bar that you see at the
top of Excel's window is actually a toolbar that is named
Worksheet Menu Bar. As with any toolbar, you can move it to
a new location by dragging it. (See Figure 33-1.)

Many of the menu items display icons in addition to text. This
is a good sign that Excel's menus are not "real" menus. To
further demonstrate that Excel's menu bars are different from
those that are used in other programs, note that if you change
the colors or fonts used for menus (using the Windows Control panel), these changes do not appear in Excel's menus.

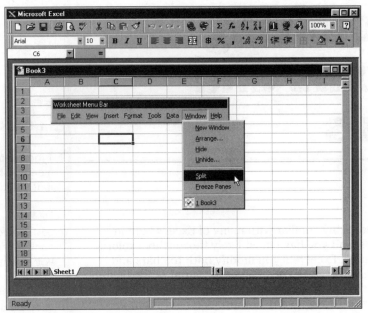

Figure 33-1: Excel's menu bar is actually a toolbar, and you can move it to any location that you want.

Customizing Toolbars

Excel comes with 22 built-in toolbars, and two of these (Worksheet Menu Bar and Chart Menu Bar) serve as menus. Each toolbar consists of one or more "commands." A command can take the form of an icon, text, or both. There are some additional commands that don't appear on any of the prebuilt toolbars.

Many users like to create custom toolbars that contain the commands they use most often.

How Excel keeps track of toolbars

When you start up Excel, it displays the same toolbar configuration that was in effect the last time that you used it. Did you ever wonder how Excel keeps track of this information? When you exit Excel, it updates a file in your Windows folder. This file stores your custom toolbars, as well as information about which toolbars are visible and the on-screen location of each. The file is called `exce18.x1b`.

To restore the toolbars to their previous configuration, select File⇨Open to open this XLB file. This restores your toolbar configuration to the way that it was when you started Excel. You can also make a copy of the XLB file and give it a different name. Doing so lets you store multiple toolbar configurations that you can load at any time.

Types of customizations

The following list is a summary of the types of customizations that you can make when working with toolbars (which also include menu bars):

- ✦ **Move toolbars.** Any toolbar can be moved to another location-screen.
- ✦ **Remove buttons from built-in toolbars.** You may want to do this to eliminate buttons that you never use.
- ✦ **Add buttons to built-in toolbars.** You can add as many buttons as you want to any toolbar.
- ✦ **Create new toolbars.** You can create as many new toolbars as you like, with as many buttons as you like.
- ✦ **Change the functionality of a button.** You do this by attaching your own macro to a built-in toolbar button.
- ✦ **Change the image that appears on any toolbar button.** A rudimentary but functional toolbar button editor is included with Excel.

Shortcut menus

The casual user cannot modify Excel's shortcut menus (the menus that appear when you right-click on an object). Doing so requires the use of macros.

Moving Toolbars

A toolbar can either be *floating* or *docked.* A docked toolbar is fixed in place at the top, bottom, left, or right edge of Excel's workspace. Floating toolbars appear in an "always on top" window.

To move a toolbar, just click on its border and drag it to its new position. If you drag it to one of the edges of Excel's window, it attaches itself to the edge and becomes docked. You can create several layers of docked toolbars. For example, the Standard and Formatting toolbars are (normally) both docked along the upper edge.

If a toolbar is floating, you can change its dimensions by dragging a border. For example, you can transform a horizontal toolbar to a vertical toolbar by dragging one of its corners.

Using the Customize Dialog Box

To make any changes to toolbars, you need to be in what I call "customization mode." In customization mode, the Customize dialog box is displayed, and you can manipulate the toolbars in a number of ways. To get into customization mode, perform either of the following actions:

✦ Select View➪Toolbars➪Customize.

✦ Select Customize from the shortcut menu that appears when you right-click on a toolbar.

Either of these methods displays the Customize dialog box that is shown in Figure 33-2. This dialog box lists all of the available toolbars, including custom toolbars that you have created.

The Customize dialog box has three tabs. I discuss each of these in the following sections.

The Toolbars tab

Figure 33-2 shows the Toolbars tab of the Customize dialog box. In the following sections, I describe how to perform various procedures that involve toolbars.

Figure 33-2: The Customize dialog box.

Hiding or displaying a toolbar

The Toolbars tab displays every toolbar (built-in toolbars and custom toolbars). Add a check mark to display a toolbar; remove the check mark to hide it. The changes take effect immediately.

Creating a new toolbar

Click on the New button, and then enter a name in the New Toolbar dialog box. Excel creates and displays an empty toolbar. You can then add buttons to the new toolbar. See "Adding or Removing Toolbar Buttons" later in this chapter.

Renaming a custom toolbar

Select a custom toolbar from the list, and click on the Rename button. Enter a new name in the Rename Toolbar dialog box. You cannot rename a built-in toolbar.

Deleting a custom toolbar

Select a custom toolbar from the list, and click on the Delete button. You cannot delete a built-in toolbar.

Caution

Deleting a toolbar is one of the few actions that cannot be undone.

Resetting a built-in toolbar

Select a built-in toolbar from the list, and click on the Reset button. The toolbar is restored to its default state. If you've added any custom tools to the toolbar, they are removed. If you've removed any of the default tools, they are restored.

The Reset button is not available when a custom toolbar is selected.

Attaching a toolbar to a workbook

If you create a custom toolbar that you would like to share with someone else, you can "attach" it to a workbook. To attach a custom toolbar to a workbook, click on the Attach button, and you get a new dialog box that lets you select toolbars to attach to a workbook (see Figure 33-3). You can attach any number of toolbars to a workbook.

Figure 33-3: You can attach custom toolbars to a workbook.

A toolbar that's attached to a workbook appears automatically when the workbook is opened, unless the workspace already has a toolbar by the same name.

The toolbar that's stored in the workbook is an exact copy of the toolbar at the time that you attach it. If you modify the toolbar after attaching it, the changed version is not stored in the workbook automatically. You must manually remove the old toolbar and then add the edited toolbar.

The Commands tab

The Commands tab of the Customize dialog box contains a list of every tool that's available. Use this tab when you customize a toolbar. This feature is described later in the chapter (see "Adding or Removing Toolbar Buttons").

The Options tab

Figure 33-4 shows the Options tab of the Customize dialog box. Only three options are available.

Figure 33-4: The Options tab of the Customize dialog box.

Changing the icon size

To change the size of the icons that are used in toolbars, select or unselect the Large icons check box. This optionly affects the images that are in buttons. Buttons that contain only text (such as buttons in a menu) are not changed.

Toggling the ScreenTips display

ScreenTips are the pop-up messages that display the button names when you pause the mouse pointer over a button. If you find the ScreenTips distracting, remove the check mark from the Show ScreenTips on toolbars check box. The status bar still displays a description of the button when you move the mouse pointer over it.

Toolbar autosensing

Normally, Excel displays a particular toolbar automatically when you change contexts; this is called *autosensing*. For example, when you activate a chart, the Chart toolbar appears. When you activate a sheet that contains a pivot table, the PivotTable toolbar appears.

You can easily defeat autosensing by hiding the toolbar. After you do so, Excel no longer displays that toolbar when you switch to its former context. You can restore this automatic behavior, however, by displaying the appropriate toolbar when you're in the appropriate context. Thereafter, Excel reverts to its normal automatic toolbar display when you switch to that context.

Changing the menu animations

When you select a menu, Excel animates the display of the menu that is dropping down. You can select the type of animation that you want:

✦ **Slide:** The menu drops down with a sliding motion.

✦ **Unfold:** The menu unfolds as it drops down.

✦ **Random:** The menu either slides or unfolds randomly.

Adding or Removing Toolbar Buttons

As I noted earlier in this chapter, you can put Excel into customization mode by displaying the Customize dialog box. When Excel is in customization mode, you have access to all of the commands and options in the Customize dialog box. In addition, you're able to perform the following actions:

✦ Reposition a button on a toolbar

✦ Move a button to a different toolbar

✦ Copy a button from one toolbar to another

✦ Add new buttons to a toolbar by using the Commands tab of the Customize dialog box

Moving and copying buttons

When the Customize dialog box is displayed, you can copy and move buttons freely among any visible toolbars. To move a button, drag it to its new location (the new location can be within the current toolbar or on a different toolbar).

To copy a button, press Ctrl while you drag the button to another toolbar. You can also copy a toolbar button within the same toolbar, but there is really no reason to have multiple copies of a button the same toolbar.

Inserting a new button

To add a new button to a toolbar, you use the Commands tab of the Customize dialog box (refer to Figure 33-5).

Figure 33-5: The Commands tab contains a list of every available button.

The buttons are arranged in 16 categories. When you select a category, the buttons in that category appear to the right. To find out what a button does, select it and click on the Description button.

To add a button to a toolbar, locate it in the Commands tab, then click on it and drag it to the toolbar.

Other Toolbar Button Operations

When Excel is in customization mode (that is, the Customize dialog box is displayed), you can right-click on a toolbar button to get a shortcut menu of additional actions for the tool. Figure 33-6 shows the shortcut menu that appears when you right-click on a button in customization mode.

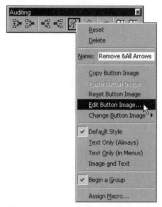

Figure 33-6: In customization mode,
right-clicking on a button displays
this shortcut menu.

These commands are described below. (Note that some of these commands are not available for certain toolbar tools.)

✦ **Reset:** Resets the tool to its original state.

✦ **Delete:** Deletes the tool.

✦ **Name:** Lets you change the name of the tool.

✦ **Copy Button Image:** Makes a copy of the button's image and places it on the Clipboard.

✦ **Paste Button Image:** Pastes the image from the Clipboard to the button.

✦ **Reset Button Image:** Restores the button's original image.

✦ **Edit Button Image:** Lets you edit the button's image using Excel's button editor.

✦ **Change Button Image:** Lets you change the image by selecting from a list of 42 button images.

✦ **Default Style:** Displays the tool using its default style (either text only, or image and text).

✦ **Text Only (Always):** Always displays text (no image) for the tool.

✦ **Text Only (In Menus):** Displays text (no image) if the tool is in a menu bar.

✦ **Image and Text:** Displays the tool's image and text.

✦ **Begin a Group:** Inserts a divider in the toolbar. In a drop-down menu, a separator bar appears as a horizontal line between commands. In a toolbar, a separator bar appears as a vertical line.

✦ **Assign Macro:** Lets you assign a macro that is executed when the button is clicked on.

Creating a Custom Toolbar: An Example

In this section, I walk you through the steps that are used to create a custom toolbar. This toolbar is an enhanced Formatting toolbar that contains many additional formatting tools that aren't found on Excel's built-in Formatting toolbar. You may want to replace the built-in Formatting toolbar with this new custom toolbar.

If you don't want to create this toolbar yourself, you can download a workbook that contains the toolbar from this book's Web site.

Adding the first button

The following steps are required to create this new toolbar and add one button (which has five subcommands):

1. Right-click on any toolbar, and select Customize from the shortcut menu.

    Excel displays its Customize dialog box.

2. Click on the Toolbars tab, and then click on New.

    Excel displays its New Toolbar dialog box.

3. Enter a name for the toolbar: **Custom Formatting**, and click on OK.

    Excel creates a new (empty) toolbar.

4. In the Customize dialog box, click on the Commands tab.

5. In the Categories list, scroll down and select New Menu.

    The New Menu category has only one command (New Menu), which appears in the Commands list.

6. Drag the New Menu command from the Commands list to the new toolbar.

    This creates a menu button in the new toolbar.

7. Right-click on the New Menu button in the new toolbar, and change the name to **Font**.

8. In the Customize dialog box, select Format from the Categories list.

9. Scroll down through the Commands list, and drag the Bold command to the Font button in your new toolbar.

    This step makes the Font button display a submenu (Bold) when the button is clicked on.

10. Repeat Step 9, adding the following buttons from the Format category: Italic, Underline, Font Size, and Font.

At this point, you may want to click on the Close button in the Customize dialog box to try out your new toolbar. The new toolbar contains only one button, but this button expands to show five font-related commands. Figure 33-7 shows the Custom Formatting toolbar at this stage.

Figure 33-7: A new Custom Formatting toolbar after adding a menu button with five commands.

Adding more buttons

If you followed the steps in the previous section, you should understand how toolbar customization works and you can add additional buttons. To finish the toolbar, right-click on a toolbar button and select Customize. Then, add additional tools.

Figure 33-8 shows the final version of the Custom Formatting toolbar, and Table 33-1 describes the tools on this toolbar. This customized toolbar includes all the tools that are on the built-in Formatting toolbar — plus quite a few more (38 tools in all). But because the Custom Formatting toolbar uses five menus (which expand to show more commands), the toolbar takes up a relatively small amount of space.

You can, of course, customize the toolbar any way that you like. The tools that are listed in the table are my preferences. You may prefer to omit tools that you never use — or add other tools that you use frequently.

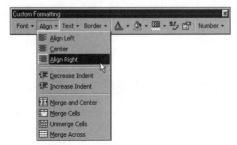

Figure 33-8: The final version of the Custom Formatting toolbar.

Table 33-1
Tools in the Custom Formatting Toolbar

Tool	Subcommands
New Menu (renamed Font)	Bold, Italic, Underline, Font Size, Font
New Menu (renamed Align)	Align Left, Center, Align Right, Decrease Indent, Increase Indent, Merge and Center, Merge Cells, Unmerge Cells, Merge Across
New Menu (renamed Text)	Vertical Text, Rotate Text Up, Rotate Text Down, Angle Text Downward, Angle Text Upward
New Menu (renamed Border)	Clear Border, Apply Outline Borders, Apply Inside Border, Left Border, Right Border, Top Border, Bottom Border, Inside Vertical Border, Inside Horizontal Border, Bottom Double Border
Font Color	(none)
Fill Color	(none)
Pattern	(none)
Clear Formatting	(none)
Format Cells	(none)
New Menu (renamed Number)	Currency Style, Percent Style, Comma Style, Decrease Decimal, Increase Decimal

With two exceptions, all the tools are found in the Formatting category. The Clear Formatting tool is in the Edit category, and the Format Cells tool is in the Built-In Menus category.

Saving the custom toolbar

Excel doesn't have a command to save a toolbar. Rather, the new toolbar is saved when you exit Excel. Refer to the sidebar "How Excel keeps track of toolbars," shown earlier in this chapter.

Changing a Toolbar Button's Image

To change the image that is displayed on a toolbar button, you have several options:

✦ Choose 1 of the 42 images that are provided by Excel.

✦ Modify or create the image using Excel's Button Editor dialog box.

✦ Copy an image from another toolbar button.

I discuss each of these methods in the following sections.

Note

To make any changes to a button image, you must be in toolbar customization mode (the Customize dialog box must be visible). Right-click on any toolbar button, and select Customize from the shortcut menu.

Using a built-in image

To change the image on a toolbar button, right-click on the button and select Change Button Image from the shortcut menu. As you can see in Figure 33-9, this menu expands to show 42 images to choose from. Just click on the image that you want, and the selected button's image changes.

Figure 33-9: You can choose from 42 built-in button images.

Editing a button image

If none of the 42 built-in images suit your tastes, you can edit an existing image or create a new image using Excel's Button Editor.

To begin editing, right-click on the button that you want to edit and then choose Edit Button Image from the shortcut menu. The image appears in the Button Editor dialog box (see Figure 33-10), where you can change individual pixels and shift the entire image up, down, to the left, or to the right. If you've never worked with icons before, you may be surprised at how difficult it is to create attractive images in such a small area.

The Edit Button Image dialog box is straightforward. Just click on a color, and then click on a pixel (or drag across pixels). When it looks good, click on OK. Or, if you don't like what you've done, click on Cancel, and the button keeps its original image.

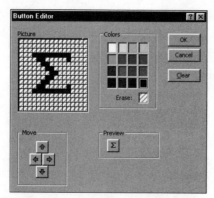

Figure 33-10: The Button Editor dialog box.

Copying another button image

Another way to get a button image on a custom toolbar is to copy it from another toolbar button. Right-click on a toolbar button, and it displays a shortcut menu that lets you copy a button image to the clipboard or paste the Clipboard contents to the selected button.

Summary

In this chapter, I discuss how to modify two components of Excel's user interface: toolbars and menus. Users of all levels can benefit from creating custom toolbars. To create new commands that are executed by toolbar buttons, however, you need to write macros. I also discuss how to change the image that appears on a toolbar button. I introduce Excel's menu editor, which is most useful for macro writers.

✦   ✦   ✦

Using and Creating Templates

This chapter covers one of the most potentially useful features in Excel — template files. Templates can be used for a variety of purposes, ranging from custom "fill-in-the-blanks" workbooks to a way to change Excel's defaults for new workbooks or new worksheets.

An Overview of Templates

A *template* is essentially a model that serves as the basis for something else. If you understand this concept, you may save yourself a great deal of work. For example, you may always use a particular header on your printouts. Consequently, every time that you print a worksheet, you need to select File⇨Page Setup to add your page header. The solution is to modify the template that Excel uses to create a new workbook. In this case, you modify the template file by inserting your header into the template. Save the template file, and then every new workbook that you create has your customized page header.

Excel supports three types of templates:

✦ **The default workbook template:** This is a template that is used as the basis for new workbooks.

✦ **The default worksheet template:** This is a template that is used as the basis for new worksheets that are inserted into a workbook.

✦ **Custom workbook templates:** These are usually ready-to-run workbooks that include formulas. They are usually set up so that a user can simply plug in values and get immediate results. The Spreadsheet Solutions templates (included with Excel) are examples of this type of template.

I discuss each template type in the following sections.

The Default Workbook Template

As you know, every new workbook that you create starts out with some default settings. For example, the workbook's worksheets have gridlines, text appears in Arial 10-point font, values that are entered display in the General number format, and so on. If you're not happy with any of the default workbook settings, you can change them.

Changing the workbook defaults

Making changes to Excel's default workbook is fairly easy to do, and it can save you lots of time in the long run. Take the following steps to change Excel's workbook defaults:

1. Start with a new workbook.

2. Add or delete sheets to give the workbook the desired number of worksheets.

3. Make any other changes that you want to make. These changes can include column widths, named styles, page setup options, and many of the settings that are available in the Options dialog box.

Tip   To change the default formatting for cells, choose Format⇨Style and modify the settings for the Normal style. For example, you can change the default font, size, or number format. Refer to "Using Named Styles" in Chapter 11 for details.

4. When your workbook is set up to your liking, select File⇨Save As.

5. In the Save As dialog box, select Template (*.xlt) from the Save as type box.

6. Enter **book.xlt** for the filename.

7. Save the file in your Excel\Xlstart folder. Or, if you've installed Office 97, save the file in your Office\Xlstart folder.

   You can also save your book.xlt template file in the folder that is specified as an alternate startup folder. You specify an alternate startup folder in the General tab of the Options dialog box.

8. Close the file.

After you've performed the preceding steps, the default new workbook is based on the book.xlt workbook template. You can create a workbook based on your template by using any of the following methods:

✦ Click on the New button on the Standard toolbar.

✦ Press Ctrl+N.

✦ Choose File➪New, and select the Workbook icon in the General tab of the New dialog box (see Figure 34-1).

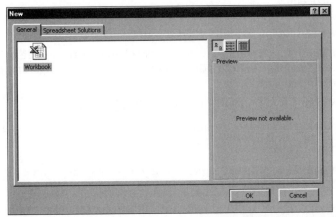

Figure 34-1: After you create a book.xlt template, clicking on the Workbook icon creates a new workbook that is based on your template.

Note Normally, the Xlstart folder does not contain a file named book.xlt. If a file with this name is not present, Excel creates new workbooks using built-in program settings.

Editing the book.xlt template

After you create your book.xlt template, you may discover that you need to change it. You can open the book.xlt template file and edit it just like any other workbook. When you've finished with your edits, save the workbook and close it.

Resetting the default workbook

If you create a book.xlt file and then decide that you would rather use the standard default workbook settings, simply delete the book.xlt template file from the Xlstart folder. Excel then resorts to its built-in default settings for new workbooks.

The Default Worksheet Template

When you insert a new worksheet into a workbook, Excel uses its built-in worksheet defaults for the worksheet. This includes items such as column width, row height, and so on.

Excel 97 Previous versions of Excel also used other sheet templates (dialog.xlt and macro.xlt). These templates are not used in Excel 97.

If you don't like the default settings for a new worksheet, you can change them using the following procedure:

1. Start with a new workbook, deleting all of the sheets except one.

2. Make any changes that you want to make. These changes can include column widths, named styles, page setup options, and many of the settings that are available in the Options dialog box.

3. When your workbook is set up to your liking, select File⇨Save As.

4. In the Save As dialog box, select Template (*.xlt) from the Save as type box.

5. Enter **sheet.xlt** for the filename.

6. Save the file in your Excel\Xlstart folder. Or, if you've installed Office 97, save the file in your Office\Xlstart folder.

   You can also save your book.xlt template file in the folder that is specified as an alternate startup folder. You specify an alternate startup folder in the General tab of the Options dialog box.

7. Close the file.

After performing this procedure, all new sheets that you insert with the Insert⇨Worksheet command are formatted like your sheet.xlt template.

When you right-click on a sheet tab and choose Insert from the shortcut menu, Excel displays its Insert dialog box (which looks just like the New dialog box). If you've created a template named sheet.xlt, you can select it by clicking on the icon labeled Worksheet.

Editing the sheet.xlt template

After you create your sheet.xlt template, you may discover that you need to change it. You can open the sheet.xlt template file and edit it just like any other workbook. After you make your changes, save the file and close it.

Resetting the default new worksheet

If you create a sheet.xlt template and then decide that you would rather use the standard default new worksheet settings, simply delete the sheet.xlt template file from the Xlstart folder. Excel then resorts to its built-in default settings for new worksheets.

Custom Workbook Templates

The book.xlt and sheet.xlt templates that I discussed in the previous section are two special types of templates that determine default settings for new workbooks and new worksheets. In this section, I discuss other types of templates. I refer to these simply as *workbook templates*. A workbook template is simply a workbook that's set up to be used as the basis for a new workbook.

Why use a workbook template? The simple answer is that it saves you from repeating work. Assume that you create a monthly sales report that consists of your company's sales by region, plus several summary calculations and charts. You can create a template file that consists of everything except the input values. Then, when it's time to create your report, you can open a workbook based on the template, fill in the blanks, and you're finished. You could, of course, just use the previous month's workbook and save it with a different name. This is prone to errors, however, because it's easy to forget to use the Save As command and accidentally overwrite the previous month's file.

How templates work

When you create a workbook that is based on a template, Excel creates a copy of the template in memory so that the original template remains intact. The default workbook name is the template name with a number appended. For example, if you create a new workbook based on a template named `Sales Report.xlt`, the workbook's default name is `Sales Report1.xls`. The first time you save a workbook that was created from a template, Excel displays its Save As dialog box so that you can give the template a new name if desired.

Templates that are included with Excel

Excel ships with three workbook templates (called Spreadsheet Solutions templates), which were developed by Village Software. When you select the File⇨New command, you can select one of these templates from the New dialog box. Click on the tab labeled Spreadsheet Solutions to choose a template upon which to base your new workbook (see Figure 34-2). The templates included with Excel 97 are

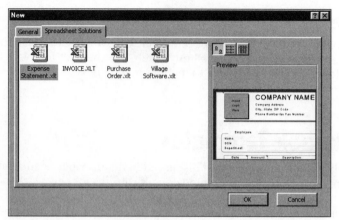

Figure 34-2: You can create a new workbook based on one of the Spreadsheet Solutions templates.

✦ **Expense Statement:** Helps you create expense report forms and a log to track them

✦ **Invoice:** Helps you create invoices

✦ **Purchase Order:** Helps you create purchase orders to send to vendors

Note A fourth template, named Village Software.xlt, describes additional templates that you can obtain from Village Software.

Next, I explain how to create custom workbook templates.

Creating Custom Templates

In this section, I describe how to create workbook templates. It's really quite simple.

A *custom template* is essentially a normal workbook, and it can use any of Excel's features such as charts, formulas, and macros. Usually, a template is set up so that the user can enter values and get immediate results. In other words, most templates include everything but the data — which is entered by the user.

If the template is to be used by novices, you may consider locking all of the cells except the input cells (use the Protection panel of the Format Cells dialog box for this). Then, protect the worksheet by choosing Tools⇨Protection⇨Protect Sheet.

To save the workbook as a template, choose File⇨Save As and select Template (*.xlt) from the drop-down list labeled Save as type. Save the template in your the Microsoft Office\Templates folder (or a folder within that Templates folder).

Where to store your templates

Template files can be stored anywhere. When you open a template file (by selecting File⇨New), you don't actually open the template. Rather, Excel creates a new workbook that's based on the template that you specify. There are some specific locations, however, that make it easier to access your templates:

✦ Your Excel\XLStart folder (or your Office\XLStart folder). If you create a default workbook template (book.xlt) or a default worksheet template (sheet.xlt), you store these templates in this folder.

✦ Your Excel\Templates folder (or your Office\Templates folder). Custom templates that are stored here appear in the New dialog box.

✦ A folder located in your Microsoft Office\Templates folder. If you create a new folder within this folder, its name appears as a tab in the New dialog box. Clicking on the tab displays the templates that are stored in that folder. The accompanying figure shows how the New dialog box looks when there's a new folder (named John's Templates) in the Templates folder.

If you've specified an alternate startup folder (using the General panel of the Options dialog box), templates that are stored in that location also appear in the New dialog box.

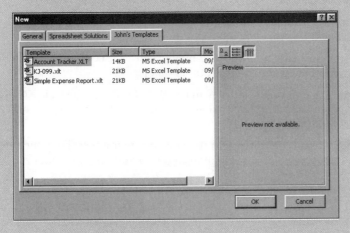

Before saving the template, you may want to specify that the file be saved with a preview image. Select File⇨Properties, and check the box that is labeled Save Preview Picture. That way, the New dialog box displays the preview when the template's icon is selected.

If you later discover that you want to modify the template, choose File⇨Open to open and edit the template (don't use the File⇨New command, which creates a workbook that is based on the template).

Ideas for Creating Templates

In this section, I provide a few ideas that may spark your imagination for creating templates. A partial list of the settings that you can adjust and use in your custom templates is as follows:

✦ **Multiple formatted worksheets.** You can, for example, create a workbook template that has two worksheets: one formatted to print in landscape mode and one formatted to print in portrait mode.

✦ **Workbook properties.** For example, Excel doesn't store a preview picture of your workbook. Select File➪Properties, and change the Save Preview Picture option in the Summary panel.

✦ **Several settings in the View panel of the Options dialog box.** For example, you may not like to see sheet tabs, so you can turn this setting off.

✦ **Color palette.** Use the Color panel of the Options dialog box to create a custom color palette for a workbook.

✦ **Style.** The best approach is to choose Format➪Style and modify the attributes of the Normal style. For example, you can change the font or size, the alignment, and so on.

✦ **Custom number formats.** If you create number formats that you use frequently, these can be stored in a template.

✦ **Column widths and row heights.** You may prefer that columns be wider or narrower, or you may want the rows to be taller.

✦ **Print settings.** Change these settings in the Page Setup dialog box. You can adjust the page orientation, paper size, margins, header and footer, and several other attributes.

✦ **Sheet settings.** These are options in the Options dialog box. They include gridlines, automatic page break display, and row and column headers.

Summary

In this chapter, I introduce the concept of templates. Excel supports three template types: a default workbook template, a default worksheet template, and custom workbook templates. I describe how to create such templates and where to store them. I also discuss the Template Wizard, a tool that helps you create templates that can store data in a central database.

✦   ✦   ✦

Using Visual Basic for Applications (VBA)

◆ ◆ ◆ ◆

In This Chapter

An introduction to VBA macros and why you may want to learn this feature

Distinguishing between two types of VBA macros: subroutines and functions

How to create a simple macro by recording your actions

Using the Personal Macro Workbook to store your macros

Creating more complex VBA subroutines

◆ ◆ ◆ ◆

This chapter is an introduction to the Visual Basic for Applications (VBA) macro language — perhaps the key component for users who want to customize Excel. A complete discussion of VBA would require an entire book. This chapter teaches you how to record macros and create simple macro subroutines. Subsequent chapters expand upon the topics in this chapter.

Introducing VBA Macros

In its broadest sense, a *macro* is a sequence of instructions that automates some aspect of Excel so that you can work more efficiently and with fewer errors. You may create a macro, for example, to format and print your month-end sales report. After the macro is developed and debugged, you can invoke the macro with a single command to perform many time-consuming procedures automatically.

Macros are usually considered to be one of the advanced features of Excel because you must have a pretty thorough understanding of Excel to put them to good use. The truth is that the majority of Excel users have never created a macro and probably never will. If you want to explore one of the most powerful aspects of Excel, however, you should know about macros. This chapter is designed to acquaint you with VBA, which lets you develop simple macros and execute macros that are developed by others.

Are macros for you?

You need not be a power user to create and use simple VBA macros. Casual users can simply turn on Excel's macro recorder: Excel records and then converts your subsequent actions into a VBA macro — which is essentially a program. When you execute this program, Excel performs the actions again.

More advanced users, though, can write code that tells Excel to perform tasks that can't be recorded. For example, you can write procedures that display custom dialog boxes, add new commands to Excel's menus, or process data in a series of workbooks.

VBA: One of two macro languages in Excel

VBA was introduced in Excel 5. Prior to that version, Excel used an entirely different macro system known as XLM (that is, the Excel 4 macro language). VBA is far superior in terms of both power and ease of use. For compatibility reasons, however, the XLM language is still supported in Excel 97. This means that you can load an older Excel file and still execute the macros that are stored in it. However, Excel 97 does not let you record XLM macros — and there's really no reason why you would want to.

What you can do with VBA

VBA is an extremely rich programming language with thousands of uses. Listed below are just a few things that you can do with VBA macros:

✦ **Insert a text string or formula.** If you need to enter your company name into worksheets frequently, you can create a macro to do the typing for you. The AutoCorrect feature can also do this.

✦ **Automate a procedure that you perform frequently.** For example, you may need to prepare a month-end summary. If the task is straightforward, you can develop a macro to do it for you.

✦ **Automate repetitive operations.** If you need to perform the same action in 12 different workbooks, you can record a macro while you perform the task once — and then let the macro repeat your action in the other workbooks.

✦ **Create a custom command.** For example, you can combine several of Excel's menu commands so that they are executed from a single keystroke or from a single mouse click.

✦ **Create a custom toolbar button.** You can customize Excel's toolbars with your own buttons to execute macros that you write.

✦ **Create a simplified "front end" for users who don't know much about Excel.** For example, you can set up a foolproof data entry template.

✦ **Develop a new worksheet function.** Although Excel includes a wide assortment of built-in functions, you can create custom functions that greatly simplify your formulas.

✦ **Create complete, turnkey, macro-driven applications.** Excel macros can display custom dialog boxes and add new commands to the menu bar.

✦ **Create custom add-ins for Excel.** All the add-ins that are shipped with Excel were created with Excel macros. I used VBA exclusively to create my Power Utility Pak.

Two Types of VBA Macros

Before getting into the details of creating macros, it's important to understand a key distinction. A VBA macro (or procedure) can be one of two types: a subroutine or a function. I discuss the difference in the following sections.

VBA subroutines

You can think of a *subroutine macro* as a new command that can be executed by either the user or by another macro. You can have any number of subroutines in an Excel workbook.

Figure 35-1 shows a simple VBA subroutine. When this subroutine is executed, VBA inserts the current date into the active cell, formats it, and then adjusts the column width.

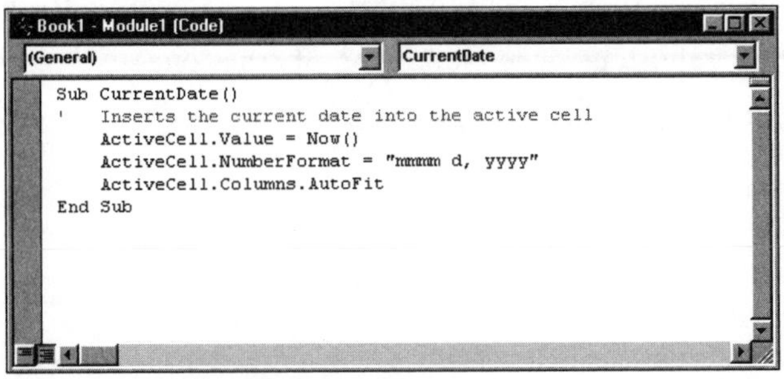

```
Sub CurrentDate()
'   Inserts the current date into the active cell
    ActiveCell.Value = Now()
    ActiveCell.NumberFormat = "mmmm d, yyyy"
    ActiveCell.Columns.AutoFit
End Sub
```

Figure 35-1: A simple VBA subroutine.

Subroutines always start with the keyword *Sub*, the macro's name (every macro must have a unique name), and then a pair of parentheses. (The parentheses are required; they are empty unless the procedure uses one or more arguments.) The *End Sub* statement signals the end of a subroutine. The lines in between comprise the procedure's code.

What's new in Excel 97?

If you've used VBA in Excel 5 or Excel 95, you should be aware that Excel 97 handles VBA very differently than do previous versions of Excel. Listed below are a few of the key areas in which Excel 97 differs from Excel 95.

✦ Excel 97 no longer displays module sheets in a workbook. To view or edit VBA code, you must activate the Visual Basic Editor (Alt+F11 toggles between Excel and the Visual Basic Editor).

✦ Excel 97 makes use of user forms rather than dialog sheets. You create and edit user forms in the Visual Basic Editor. A user form also contains the VBA code that works with the objects in the form. I discuss this feature in Chapter 37.

✦ Excel 97 adds many new objects and methods, providing the macro programmer with a great deal of new capability.

✦ Excel 5 and Excel 95 macros and dialog boxes continue to work in Excel 97. However, the compatibility is not perfect, and you may notice a few problems due to changes.

The subroutine that is shown in Figure 35-1 also includes a comment. Comments are simply notes to yourself and are ignored by VBA. A comment line begins with an apostrophe. You can also put a comment after a statement. In other words, when VBA encounters an apostrophe, it ignores the rest of the text in the line.

You execute a subroutine in any of the following ways:

✦ Choose Tools⇨Macro, and then select the subroutine's name from the list.

✦ Press the subroutine's shortcut key combination (if it has one).

✦ Refer to the subroutine in another VBA procedure.

I discuss subroutines in detail later in this chapter.

VBA functions

The second type of VBA procedure is a function. A *function* always returns a single value (just as a worksheet function always returns a single value). A VBA function can be executed by other VBA procedures or used in worksheet formulas, just as you would use Excel's built-in worksheet functions.

Figure 35-2 shows the listing of a custom worksheet function and shows the function in use in a worksheet. This function is named CubeRoot and requires a single argument. CubeRoot calculates the cube root of its argument. A function looks much like a subroutine. Notice, however, that function procedures begin with the keyword *Function* and end with an *End Function* statement.

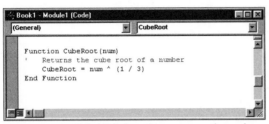

Figure 35-2: This VBA function returns the cube root of its argument.

Creating VBA functions that you use in worksheet formulas can simplify your formulas and let you perform calculations that otherwise may be impossible. I discuss VBA functions in Chapter 36.

Some definitions

VBA newcomers are often overwhelmed by the terminology that is used in VBA. I've put together some key definitions to help you keep the terms straight. These terms cover VBA and user forms (custom dialog boxes) — two important elements that are used in customizing Excel.

Code: VBA instructions that are produced in a module sheet when you record a macro. You also can enter VBA code manually.

Controls: Objects on a user form (or in a worksheet) that you manipulate. Examples include buttons, check boxes, and list boxes.

Function: One of two types of VBA macros that you can create (the other is a subroutine). A function returns a single value. You can use VBA functions in other VBA macros or in your worksheets.

Macro: A set of Excel instructions that are performed automatically. Excel macros can be XLM macros or VBA macros. This book focuses exclusively on VBA macros. VBA macros are also known as *procedures*.

Method: An action that is taken on an object. For example, applying the Clear method to a range object erases the contents of the cells.

Module: A container for VBA code.

Object: An element that you manipulate with VBA. Examples include ranges, charts, drawing objects, and so on.

Procedure: Another name for a macro. A VBA procedure can be a subroutine or a function.

Property: A particular aspect of an object. For example, a range object has properties such as Height, Style, and Name.

Subroutine: One of two types of Visual Basic macros that you can create. The other is a function.

User Form: A container that holds controls for a custom dialog box and holds VBA code to manipulate the controls. (I cover custom dialog boxes in Chapter 36).

VBA: Visual Basic for Applications. The macro language that is available in Excel as well as the other applications in Microsoft Office 97.

VBE: Visual Basic Editor. The window (separate from Excel) that you use to create VBA macros and user forms.

Creating VBA Macros

Excel provides two ways to create macros:

✦ Turn on the macro recorder and record your actions.

✦ Enter the code directly into a module.

In the following sections, I describe both of these methods.

Recording VBA Macros

In this section, I describe the basic steps that you take to record a VBA macro. In most cases, you can record your actions as a macro and then simply replay the macro; you needn't look at the code that's generated. If this is as far as you go with VBA, you don't need to be concerned with the language itself (although a basic understanding of how things work doesn't do any harm).

Recording your actions to create VBA code: The basics

Excel's macro recorder translates your actions into VBA code. To start the macro recorder, choose Tools➪Macro➪Record New Macro. Excel displays the Record Macro dialog box that is shown in Figure 35-3. This dialog box presents several options:

Figure 35-3: The Record Macro dialog box.

✦ **Macro name:** The name of the macro. By default, Excel proposes names such as Macro1, Macro2, and so on.

✦ **Shortcut key:** You can specify a key combination that executes the macro. You can also press Shift when you enter a letter. For example, pressing Shift while you enter the letter H makes the shortcut key combination Ctrl+Shift+H.

✦ **Store macro in:** The location for the macro. Your choices are the current workbook, your Personal Macro Workbook (described later in this chapter), or a new workbook.

✦ **Description:** A description of the macro. By default, Excel inserts the date and your name. You can add additional information if you like.

To begin recording your actions, click on OK. Excel displays the Stop Recording toolbar, which contains two buttons: Stop Recording and Relative Reference. When you're finished recording the macro, choose Tools⇨Macro⇨Stop Recording (or click on the Stop Recording button the toolbar).

Recording your actions always results in a new subroutine procedure. You can't create a function procedure using the macro recorder.

Recording a macro: An example

In this example, I demonstrate how to record a macro that changes the formatting for the current range selection. The macro makes the selected range use Arial 16-point type, boldface, colored red. To create the macro, follow these steps:

1. Enter a value or text into a cell — anything is okay. This gives you something to start with.

2. Select the cell that contains the value or text that you entered in the preceding step.

3. Select Tools⇨Macro⇨Record New Macro. Excel displays the Record Macro dialog box.

4. Enter a new name for the macro to replace the default Macro1 name. A good name is **FormattingMacro**.

5. Assign this macro to the shortcut key Ctrl+Shift+F by entering **F** in the edit box labeled Shortcut key.

6. Click on OK. This closes the Record Macro dialog box. Excel displays a toolbar called Stop Recording.

7. Select Format⇨Cells, and click on the Font tab. Choose Arial font, Bold, and 16-point type, and make the color red. Click on OK to close the Format Cells dialog box.

8. The macro is finished, so click on the Stop Recording button the Stop Recording toolbar (or select Tools⇨Macro⇨Stop Recording).

Examining the macro

The macro was recorded in a new module named Module1. To view the code in this module, you must activate the Visual Basic Editor (VBE). You can activate the VBE in either of two ways:

◆ Press Alt+F11.

◆ Choose Tools⇨Macro⇨Visual Basic Editor.

Figure 35-4 shows the VBE window. Although the module is stored in the Excel workbook, you can view the module only in the Visual Basic Editor window.

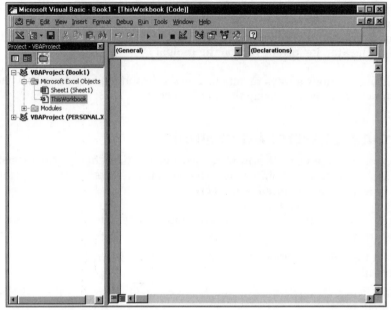

Figure 35-4: The VBE window.

The Project window displays a list of all open workbooks and add-ins. This list is displayed as a tree diagram, which can be expanded or collapsed. The code that you recorded previously is stored in Module1 in the current workbook. When you double-click on Module1, the code in the module is displayed in the Code window.

Figure 35-5 shows the recorded macro, as displayed in the Code window.

Activate the module, and examine the macro. It should consist of the following code:

```
' FormattingMacro Macro
' Macro recorded by John Walkenbach
'
Sub FormattingMacro()
  With Selection.Font
    .Name = "Arial"
    .FontStyle = "Bold"
    .Size = 16
    .Strikethrough = False
    .Superscript = False
    .Subscript = False
    .OutlineFont = False
    .Shadow = False
    .Underline = xlNone
    .ColorIndex = 3
  End With
End Sub
```

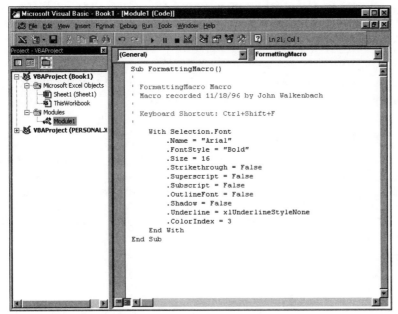

Figure 35-5: The FormattingMacro subroutine was generated by Excel's macro recorder.

The macro recorded is a subroutine (it begins with a Sub statement) that is named FormattingMacro. The statements tell Excel what to do when the macro is executed.

Notice that Excel inserted comments at the top. This is the information that appeared in the Record Macro dialog box. These comment lines (which begin with an apostrophe) aren't really necessary, and deleting them has no effect on how the macro runs.

Note You may notice that the macro recorded some actions that you didn't take. For example, it sets the Strikethrough, Superscript, and Subscript properties to False. This is just a byproduct of the method that Excel uses to translate actions into code. Excel sets the properties for every option in the Font tab of the Format Cells dialog box.

Testing the macro

Before you recorded this macro, you set an option that assigned the macro to the Ctrl+Shift+F shortcut key combination. To test the macro, return to Excel using either of the following methods:

✦ Press Alt+F11.

✦ Click on the View Microsoft Excel button the VBE toolbar.

When Excel is active, activate a worksheet (it can be in the workbook that contains the VBA module or in any other workbook). Select a cell or range, and press Ctrl+Shift+F. The macro immediately changes the formatting of the selected cell(s).

Continue testing the macro with other selections. You'll find that the macro always applies exactly the same formatting.

Editing the macro

Once you record a macro, you can change it (although you must know what you're doing). Assume that you discover that you really wanted to make the text 14-point rather than 16-point. You could re-record the macro. But this is a simple modification, so editing the code is more efficient. Just activate Module1, locate the statement that sets the font size, and change 16 to 14. You can also remove the following lines:

```
.Strikethrough = False
.Superscript = False
.Subscript = False
.OutlineFont = False
.Shadow = False
.Underline = xlNone
```

Removing these lines causes the macro to ignore the properties that are referred to in the statements. For example, if the cell has underlining, the underlining isn't affected by the macro.

The edited macro is as follows:

```
Sub FormattingMacro()
  With Selection.Font
    .Name = "Arial"
    .FontStyle = "Bold"
    .Size = 14
    .ColorIndex = 3
  End With
End Sub
```

Test this new macro, and you see that it performs as it should. Also, notice that it doesn't remove a cell's underlining, which occurred in the original version of the macro.

Another example

In this example, I show you how to record a slightly more complicated VBA macro that converts formulas into values. Converting formulas to values is usually a two-step process:

1. Copy the range to the Clipboard.

2. Choose Edit⇨Paste Special (with the Values option selected) to paste the values over the formulas.

This macro combines these steps into a single command.

Furthermore, you want to be able to access this command by pressing a shortcut key combination (Ctrl+Shift+V). Take the following steps to create this macro:

1. Enter some formulas into a range. Any formula will do.

2. Select the range that contains the formulas.

3. Choose Tools⇨Macro⇨Record New Macro. Excel displays the Record Macro dialog box.

4. Complete the New Macro dialog box so that it looks like Figure 35-6. This assigns the macro the name FormulaConvert. It also gives it a Ctrl+Shift+V shortcut key.

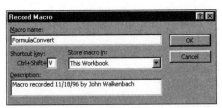

Figure 35-6: How the Record Macro dialog box should look when recording the sample macro.

5. Click on OK to begin recording.

6. With the range still selected, choose Edit⇨Copy to copy the range to the Clipboard.

7. Select Edit⇨Paste Special, click on the Values option, and then click on OK to close the dialog box.

8. Press Esc to cancel paste mode. (Excel removes the moving border around the selected range.)

9. Click on the Stop Recording button (or choose Tools⇨Macro⇨Stop Recording).

To test the macro, activate a worksheet, enter some formulas, and select the formulas. You can execute the macro in two ways:

✦ Press Ctrl+Shift+V.

✦ Choose Tools⇨Macro⇨Macros command, and double-click on the macro name (FormulaConvert).

Excel converts the formulas in the selected range to their values — in a single step instead of two.

Be careful, because you can't undo the conversion of formulas to values. Actually, it's possible to edit the macro so that its results can be undone, but the procedure is beyond the scope of this discussion.

Note The shortcut key combination (Ctrl+Shift+V) is valid only when the workbook is open. When you close the workbook, pressing Ctrl+Shift+V has no effect.

The recorded macro is as follows:

```
' FormulaConvert Macro
' Macro recorded by John Walkenbach
'
' Keyboard Shortcut: Ctrl+Shift+V
'
Sub ConvertFormulas()
  Selection.Copy
  Selection.PasteSpecial Paste:=xlValues, Operation:=xlNone, _
    SkipBlanks:=False, Transpose:=False
  Application.CutCopyMode = False
End Sub
```

Excel added some comment lines that describe the macro. The actual macro begins with the Sub statement. The subroutine has three statements. The first simply copies the selected range. The second statement, which is displayed on two lines (the underscore character means that the statement continues on the next line), pastes the Clipboard contents to the current selection. The second statement has several arguments, representing the options in the Paste Special dialog box. The third statement cancels the moving border around the selected range. (I generated the statement by pressing Esc after the paste operation.)

If you prefer, you can delete the underscore character in the second statement and combine the two lines into one (a VBA statement can be any length). This action may make the macro easier to read.

More about Recording VBA Macros

If you followed along with the preceding examples, you should have a better feel for how to record macros. If you find the VBA code confusing, don't worry — you don't really have to be concerned with it as long as the macro that you record works correctly. If the macro doesn't work, it's often easier to re-record it rather than edit the code.

A good way to learn about what gets recorded is to set up your screen so that you can see the code that is being generated in the Visual Basic Editor windows. Figure 35-7 shows an example of such a setup. While you're recording your actions, make sure that the VBE window is displaying the module in which the code is being recorded (you may have to double-click on the module name in the Project window).

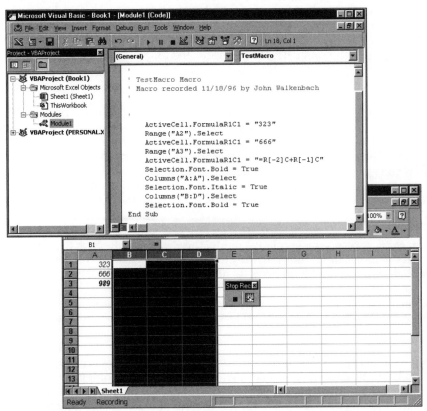

Figure 35-7: This window arrangement lets you see the VBA code as you record your actions.

Absolute versus relative recording

If you're going to work with macros, it's important that you understand the concept of *relative* versus *absolute recording.* Normally, when you record a macro, Excel stores exact references to the cells that you select (that is, it performs absolute recording). If you select the range B1:B10 while you're recording a macro, for example, Excel records this selection as

```
Range("B1:B10").Select
```

This means exactly what it says: "Select the cells in the range B1:B10." When you invoke this macro, the same cells are always selected regardless of where the active cell is located.

You may have noticed that the Stop Recording toolbar has a tool named Relative Recording. When you click on this tool while recording a macro, Excel changes its recording mode from absolute (the default) to relative. When recording in relative mode, selecting a range of cells is translated differently, depending on where the active cell is. For example, if you're recording in relative mode and cell A1 is active, selecting the range B1:B10 generates the following statement:

```
ActiveCell.Offset(0, 1).Range("A1:A10").Select
```

This statement can be translated as "From the active cell, move 0 rows and 1 column, and then treat this new cell as if it were cell A1. Now select what would be A1:A10." In other words, a macro that is recorded in relative mode starts out using the active cell as its base and then stores relative references to this cell. As a result, you get different results depending on the location of the active cell. When you replay this macro, the cells that are selected depend on the active cell. It selects a 10-row-by-1-column range that is offset from the active cell by 0 rows and 1 column.

When Excel is recording in relative mode, the Relative Reference toolbar button appears depressed. To return to absolute recording, click on the Relative Reference button again (and it displays its normal, undepressed state).

Note The recording mode — either absolute or relative — can make a *major* difference in how your macro performs. Therefore, it's important that you understand the distinction.

When you record macros, be careful when you use commands such as Shift+Ctrl+right-arrow key or Shift+Ctrl+down-arrow key (commands that extend the selection to the end of a block of cells). Excel doesn't record this type of command as you may expect. Rather, it records the actual cells that you made in the selection (either in an absolute or relative manner, depending on the mode). When you replay the macro with a different size range, the selection may not be correct (and you may not even realize it).

Storing macros in the Personal Macro Workbook

Most macros that are created by users are designed for use in a specific workbook. But you may want to use some macros in all your work. You can store these general-purpose macros in the Personal Macro Workbook so that they are always available to you. The Personal Macro Workbook is loaded whenever you start Excel. The file, `personal.xls`, is stored in the XlStart folder, which is in your Excel folder.

Note The Personal Macro Workbook is normally in a hidden window (to keep it out of the way).

To record the macro in your Personal Macro Workbook, select the Personal Macro Workbook option in the Record Macro dialog box before you start recording.

If you store macros in the Personal Macro Workbook, you don't have to remember to open the Personal Macro Workbook when you load a workbook that uses macros. When you want to exit, Excel asks whether you want to save changes to the Personal Macro Workbook.

Assigning a macro to a toolbar button

When you record a macro, you can assign it to a shortcut key combination. After you've recorded the macro and tested it, you may want to assign the macro to a toolbar button. You can follow these steps:

1. If the macro is a general-purpose macro that you plan to use in more than one workbook, make sure that the macro is stored in your Personal Macro Workbook.

2. Select View➪Toolbars➪Customize. Excel displays its Customize dialog box.

3. Click on the Toolbars tab in the Customize dialog box, and make sure that the toolbar that is to contain the new button is visible.

4. Click on the Commands tab in the Customize dialog box.

5. Click on the Macros category.

6. In the Commands list, drag the Custom Button icon to the toolbar.

7. Right-click on the toolbar button, and select Assign Macro from the shortcut menu. Excel displays its Assign Macro dialog box.

8. Select the macro name from the list, and click on OK.

9. At this point, you can right-click on the button again to change its name and button image.

10. Click on Close to exit the Customize dialog box.

Writing VBA Code

As I demonstrated in the preceding sections, the easiest way to create a simple macro is to record your actions. To develop more complex macros, however, you have to enter the VBA code manually — in other words, write a program. To save time, you can often combine recording with manual code entry.

Before you can begin writing VBA code, you must have a good understanding of topics such as objects, properties, and methods — and it doesn't hurt to be familiar with common programming constructs such as looping and If-Then statements.

This section is an introduction to VBA programming, which is essential if you want to write (rather than record) VBA macros. This is not intended to be a complete instructional guide. The *Excel 97 For Windows Power Programming with VBA,* 3rd Edition (to be published by IDG Books Worldwide, Inc. in July, 1997) covers all aspects of VBA and advanced spreadsheet application development.

The basics: Entering and editing code

Before you can enter code, you must insert a module into the workbook. If the workbook already has a module sheet, you can use the existing module sheet for your new code.

Use the following steps to insert a new module:

1. Press Alt+F11 to activate the Visual Basic Editor window. The Visual Basic Editor window is separate application, although it works very closely with Excel.

2. The Project window displays a list of all open workbooks and add-ins. Locate the workbook that you are currently working in, and select it (see Figure 35-8).

3. Choose Insert⇨Module. VBA inserts a new (empty) module into the workbook and displays it in the Code window.

A VBA module, which is displayed in the Code window, works like a text editor. You can move through the sheet, select text, insert, copy, cut, paste, and so on.

VBA coding tips

When you enter code in a module sheet, you're free to use indenting and blank lines to make the code more readable (in fact, this is an excellent habit).

After you enter a line of code, it is evaluated for syntax errors. If none are found, the line of code is reformatted, and colors are added to keywords and identifiers. This automatic reformatting adds consistent spaces (before and after an equal sign, for example) and removes extra spaces that aren't needed. If a syntax error is found, you get a pop-up message, and the line is displayed in a different color (red, by default). You need to correct your error before you can execute the macro.

A single statement can be as long as needed. However, you might want to break the statement into two or more lines. To do so, insert a space followed by an underscore(_). The following code, although written as two lines,

is actually a single VBA statement.

```
Sheets("Sheet1").Range("B1").Value = _
Sheets("Sheet1").Range("A1").Value
```

You also can put two or more statements in a single line. You do this by using a colon(:) to separate the statements. The line following consists of three statements.

```
x = 4: y = 6: z = 12
```

You can insert comments freely into your VBA code. The comment indicator is a singe quote character ('). Any text following a single quote is ignored. A comment can be a line by itself, or inserted after a statement. The following examples show two comments.

```
' Assign the values to the variables
Rate = .085   'Rate as of November 16
```

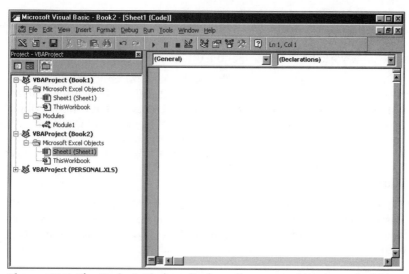

Figure 35-8: The Project window displays all open workbooks and add-ins.

How VBA works

VBA is by far the most complex feature in Excel, and it's easy to get overwhelmed. To set the stage for the details of VBA, here is a concise summary of how VBA works:

✦ You perform actions in VBA by writing (or recording) code in a VBA module sheet and then executing the macro in any number of ways. VBA modules are stored in an Excel workbook, and a workbook can hold any number of VBA modules. To view or edit a VBA module, you must activate the Visual Basic Editor window (press Alt+F11 to toggle between Excel and the VBE window).

✦ A VBA module consists of subroutine procedures. A *subroutine procedure* is basically computer code that performs some action or with objects. The following is an example of a simple subroutine called ShowSum (it adds 1 + 1 and displays the result):

```
Sub ShowSum()
   Sum = 1 + 1
   MsgBox "The answer is " & Sum
End Sub
```

✦ A VBA module also can store function procedures. A *function procedure* returns a single value. A function can be called from another VBA procedure or even used in a worksheet formula. Here's an example of a function named AddTwo (it adds two values, which are supplied as arguments):

```
Function AddTwo(arg1, arg2)
   AddTwo = arg1 + arg2
End Function
```

✦ VBA manipulates objects. Excel provides you with well over 100 objects that you can manipulate. Examples of objects include a workbook, a worksheet, a range on a worksheet, a chart, and a drawn rectangle.

✦ Objects are arranged in a hierarchy, and can act as containers for other objects. For example, Excel itself is an object called Application, and it contains other objects such as Workbook objects. The Workbook object can contain other objects such as Worksheet objects and Chart objects. A Worksheet object can contain objects such as Range objects, PivotTable objects, and so on. The arrangement of these objects is referred to as an *object model*. Excel's object model is depicted in the online Help system (see Figure 35-9).

✦ Like objects form a collection. For example, the Worksheets collection consists of all worksheets in a particular workbook. The CommandBars collection consists of all CommandBar objects (that is, menu bars and toolbars). Collections are objects in themselves.

```
┌──────────────────────────────────────────────────────────────────────┐
│ ? Microsoft Excel Visual Basic                              _ □ ✕      │
├──────────────────────────────────────────────────────────────────────┤
│ Help Topics   Back    Options                                          │
├──────────────────────────────────────────────────────────────────────┤
│  Microsoft Excel Objects                                               │
│     See Also                                                           │
│  ┌──────────────────────────────────────────────────────────────────┐ │
│  │ Application                                                        │ │
│  └──────────────────────────────────────────────────────────────────┘ │
│    ┌ Workbooks (Workbook)                    ┌ AddIns (AddIn)           │
│      ┌ Worksheets (Worksheet)          ▶       AutoCorrect              │
│      ┌ Charts (Chart)                  ▶       Assistant                │
│      ┌ DocumentProperties (DocumentProperty)   Debug                    │
│      ┌ VBProject                               Dialogs (Dialog)         │
│      ┌ CustomViews (CustomView)                CommandBars (CommandBar) │
│      ┌ CommandBar (CommandBar)                 Names (Name)             │
│      ┌ PivotCaches (PivotCache)                Windows (Window)         │
│      ┌ Styles (Style)                            Panes (Pane)           │
│          ┌ Borders (Border)                    WorksheetFunction        │
│          ┌ Font                                RecentFiles (RecentFile) │
│          └ Interior                            FileSearch               │
│      ┌ Windows (Window)                        FileFind                 │
│          └ Panes (Pane)                        VBE                      │
│      ┌ Names (Name)                            ODBCErrors (ODBCError)   │
│      ┌ RoutingSlip                                                      │
│      └ Mailer                             Legend                        │
│                                           □ Object and collection       │
│  ▶ Click red arrow to expand chart        □ Object only                 │
└──────────────────────────────────────────────────────────────────────┘
```

Figure 35-9: A depiction of part of Excel's object model.

✦ You refer to an object by specifying its position in the object hierarchy, using a period as a separator.

For example, you can refer to a workbook named Book1.xls as

```
Application.Workbooks("Book1")
```

This refers to the Book1.xls workbook in the Workbooks collection. The Workbooks collection is contained in the Application object (that is, Excel). Extending this to another level, you can refer to Sheet1 in Book1 as follows:

```
Application.Workbooks("Book1").Worksheets("Sheet1")
```

You can take it to still another level and refer to a specific cell as follows:

```
Application.Workbooks("Book1").Worksheets("Sheet1").Range("A1")
```

✦ If you omit specific references, Excel uses the *active* objects. If Book1 is the active workbook, the preceding reference can be simplified as follows:

```
Worksheets("Sheet1").Range("A1")
```

If you know that Sheet1 is the active sheet, you can simplify the reference even more:

```
Range("A1")
```

✦ Objects have properties. A property can be thought of as a *setting* for an object. For example, a range object has properties such as *Value* and *Name*. A chart object has properties such as *HasTitle* and *Type*. You can use VBA to determine object properties and to change them.

✦ You refer to properties by combining the object with the property, separated by a period. For example, you can refer to the value in cell A1 on Sheet1 as follows:

```
Worksheets("Sheet1").Range("A1").Value
```

✦ You can assign values to variables. To assign the value in cell A1 on Sheet1 to a variable called *Interest*, use the following VBA statement:

```
Interest = Worksheets("Sheet1").Range("A1").Value
```

✦ Objects have methods. A method is an action that is performed with the object. For example, one of the methods for a range object is ClearContents. This method clears the contents of the range.

✦ You specify methods by combining the object with the method, separated by a period. For example, to clear the contents of cell A1, use the following statement:

```
Worksheets("Sheet1").Range("A1:C12").ClearContents
```

✦ VBA also includes all of the constructs of modern programming languages, including arrays, looping, and so on.

Believe it or not, this describes VBA in a nutshell. Now you just have to learn the details, some of which I cover in the rest of this chapter.

Objects and collections

VBA is an object-oriented language. This means that it manipulates *objects,* such as ranges, charts, drawing objects, and so on. These objects are arranged in a hierarchy. The Application object (which is Excel) contains other objects. For example, the Application object contains these objects:

✦ Add-in Assistant

✦ AutoCorrect

✦ Chart

✦ CommandBars

✦ Debug

✦ Dialog

✦ RecentFiles

✦ VBE

✦ Window

✦ Worksheet

✦ WorksheetFunction

✦ Workbook

Most of these objects can contain other objects. For example, a Workbook object can contain the following objects:

✦ Charts (a collection of Chart objects)

✦ Mailer

✦ Names (a collection of Name objects)

✦ PageSetup

✦ RoutingSlip

✦ Styles (a collection of Style objects)

✦ Windows (a collection of Window objects in the workbook)

✦ Worksheets (a collection of Worksheet objects)

Each of these objects, in turn, can contain other objects. A Worksheet object, for example, can contain the following objects:

✦ ChartObjects (a collection of all ChartObject objects)

✦ OLEObjects (a collection of all OLEObject objects)

✦ Outline

✦ PageSetup

✦ PivotTables (a collection of all PivotTable objects)

✦ Range

✦ Scenarios (a collection of all Scenario objects)

✦ Shapes (a collection of all Shape objects)

A *collection* consists of all like objects. For example, the collection of all Workbook objects is known as the Workbooks collection. You can refer to an individual object in a collection by using an index number, or a reference. For example, if a workbook has three worksheets (named Sheet1, Sheet2, and Sheet3), you can refer to the first object in the Worksheets collection in either of these ways:

```
Worksheets(1)
Worksheets("Sheet1")
```

Properties

The objects that you work with have *properties,* which you can think of as attributes. For example, a range object has properties such as Column, Row, Width, and Value. A chart object has properties such as Legend, ChartTitle, and so on. ChartTitle is also an object, with properties such as Font, Orientation, and Text. Excel has many objects, and each has its own set of properties. You can write VBA code to:

✦ Examine an object's current property setting and take some action based on it.

✦ Change an object's property setting.

You refer to a property by placing a period and the property name after the object's name. For example, the following VBA statement sets the Value property of a range named `frequency` to 15 (that is, it causes the number 15 to appear in the range's cells):

```
Range("frequency").Value = 15
```

Some properties are *read-only,* which means that you can examine but can't change the property. For a single-cell range object, the Row and Column properties are read-only properties: You can determine where a cell is (in which row and column), but you can't change the cell's location by changing these properties.

A range object also has a Formula property, which is not read-only; that is, you can insert a formula into a cell by changing its Formula property. The following statement inserts a formula into a cell named `total` by changing the cell's Formula property:

```
Range("total").Formula = "=SUM(A1:A10)"
```

Note Contrary to what you may think, Excel doesn't have a Cell object. When you want to manipulate a single cell, you use the Range object (with only one cell in it).

You need to be aware of the Application object, which is actually Excel, the program. The Application object has several useful properties:

✦ **Application.ActiveWorkbook:** Returns the active workbook (a workbook object) in Excel.

✦ **Application.ActiveSheet:** Returns the active sheet (a sheet object) of the active workbook.

✦ **Application.ActiveCell:** Returns the active cell (a range object) object of the active window.

✦ **Application.Selection:** Returns the object that is currently selected in the active window of the Application object. This can be a range, a chart, a shape, or some other selectable object.

It's important to understand that properties can return objects. In fact, that's exactly what the preceding examples do. The result of **Application.ActiveCell**, for example, is a Range object. Therefore, you can access properties by using a statement such as the following:

```
Application.ActiveCell.Font.Size = 15
```

In this case, **Application.ActiveCell.Font** is an object, and Size is a property of the object. The preceding statement sets the Size property to 15; that is, it causes the font in the currently selected cell to have a size of 15 points.

Tip   Because Application properties are so commonly used, you can omit the object qualifier (Application). For example, to get the row of the active cell, you can use a statement such as the following:

```
ActiveCell.Row
```

There can be many different ways to refer to the same object. Assume that you have a workbook named `Sales.xls` and it's the only workbook open. Furthermore, assume that this workbook has one worksheet named Summary. You can refer to the Summary sheet in any of the following ways:

```
Workbooks("Sales.xls").Worksheets("Summary")
Workbooks(1).Worksheets(1)
Workbooks(1).Sheets(1)
Application.ActiveWorkbook.ActiveSheet
ActiveWorkbook.ActiveSheet
ActiveSheet
```

The method that you use is determined by how much you know about the workspace. For example, if there is more than one workbook open, the second or third method is not reliable. If you want to work with the active sheet (whatever it may be), either of the last three methods would work. To be absolutely sure that you're referring to a specific sheet on a specific workbook, the first method is your best choice.

Methods

Objects also have *methods*. You can think of a method as an action taken with an object. For example, range objects have a Clear method. The following VBA statement clears the range named `total`, an action that is equivalent to selecting the range and then choosing Edit⇨Clear⇨All:

```
Range("total").Clear
```

In VBA code, methods *look* like properties because they are connected to the object with a "dot." However, methods and properties are different concepts.

Variables

Like all programming languages, VBA enables you to work with variables. In VBA (unlike in some languages), you don't need to declare variables explicitly before you use them in your code (although it's definitely a good practice).

In the following example, the value in cell A1 on Sheet1 is assigned to a variable named *rate*:

```
Rate = Worksheets("Sheet1").Range("A1").Value
```

You then can work with the variable *rate* in other parts of your VBA code. Note that the variable *rate* is not a named range. This means that you can't use it as such in a worksheet formula.

Controlling execution

VBA uses many constructs that are found in most other programming languages. These constructs are used to control the flow of execution. In this section, I introduce a few of the more common programming constructs.

The If-Then construct

One of the most important control structures in VBA is the If-Then construct. This common command gives your applications decision-making capability. The basic syntax of the If-Then structure is as follows:

```
If condition Then statements [Else elsestatements]
```

The following is an example (which doesn't use the optional Else clause). This subroutine checks the active cell. If it contains a negative value, the cell's color is changed to red. Otherwise, nothing happens.

```
Sub CheckCell()
   If ActiveCell.Value < 0 Then ActiveCell.Font.ColorIndex = 3
End Sub
```

For-Next loops

For example, you can use a For-Next loop to process a series of items. Its syntax is as follows:

```
For counter = start To end [Step stepval]
      [statements]
      [Exit For]
      [statements]
Next [counter]
```

The following is an example of a For-Next loop:

```
Sub SumSquared()
  Total = 0
  For Num = 1 To 10
    Total = Total + (Num ^ 2)
  Next Num
  MsgBox Total
End Sub
```

This example has one statement between the For statement and the Next statement. This single statement is executed ten times. The variable Num takes on successive values of 1, 2, 3, and so on, up to 10. The variable Total stores the sum of Num squared, added to the previous value of Total. The result is a value that represents the sum of the first ten integers squared. This result is displayed in a message box.

The With-End With construct

Another construct that you encounter if you record macros is the With-End With construct. This is a shortcut way of dealing with several properties or methods of the same object. An example is as follows:

```
Sub AlignCells()
  With Selection
    .HorizontalAlignment = xlCenter
    .VerticalAlignment = xlCenter
    .WrapText = False
    .Orientation = xlHorizontal
  End With
End Sub
```

The following subroutine performs exactly the same operations but doesn't use the With-End With construct:

```
Sub AlignCells()
  Selection.HorizontalAlignment = xlCenter
  Selection.VerticalAlignment = xlCenter
  Selection.WrapText = False
  Selection.Orientation = xlHorizontal
End Sub
```

The Select Case construct

The Select Case construct is useful for choosing among two or more options. The syntax for the Select Case structure is as follows:

```
Select Case testexpression
      [Case expressionlist-n
         [statements-n]] . . .
      [Case Else
         [elsestatements]]
End Select
```

The following example demonstrates the use of a Select Case construct. In this example, the active cell is checked. If its value is less than 0, it's colored red. If it's equal to 0, it's colored blue. If the value is greater than 0, it's colored black.

```
Sub CheckCell()
    Select Case ActiveCell.Value
        Case Is < 0
            ActiveCell.Font.ColorIndex = 3 'Red
        Case 0
            ActiveCell.Font.ColorIndex = 5 'Blue
        Case Is > 0
            ActiveCell.Font.ColorIndex = 1 'Black
    End Select
End Sub
```

Any number of statements can go below each Case statement, and they all get executed if the case is true. If you use only one statement, as in the preceding example, you may want to put the statement on the same line as the Case statement.

A macro that can't be recorded

The following is a VBA macro that can't be recorded because it uses an If-Then structure. This macro enables you to quickly identify cells that exceed a certain value. When you run this macro, it prompts the user for a value. Then it evaluates every cell in the selection. If the cell's value is greater than the value that is entered by the user, the macro makes the cell bold and red.

```
Sub SelectiveFormat()
'This procedure selectively shades cells greater than
'a specified target value
'Get target value from user
    Message = "Change attributes of values greater than or
        equal_to..."
    Target = InputBox(Message)
    Target=Val(Target)

'Evaluate each cell in the selection
    For Each Item In Selection
        If IsNumeric(Item) Then
            If Item.Value >= Target Then
                With Item
                    .Font.Bold = True
                    .Font.ColorIndex = 3 'Red
                End With
            End If
        End If
    Next Item
End Sub
```

Although this macro may look complicated, it's fairly simple when you break it down.

First, the macro assigns text to a variable named Message. It then uses the InputBox function to solicit a value from the user. The InputBox function has a single argument (which is the Message variable), and returns a string — which is assigned to the Target variable. Next, I use the Val function to convert this string to a value.

The For-Next loop checks every cell in the selected range. The first statement within the loop uses the IsNumeric function to determine whether the cell can be evaluated as a number. This is important because a cell without a value would generate an error when the Value property is accessed in the next statement. If the cell is numeric, it is checked against the target value. If it's greater than or equal to the target value, the Bold and ColorIndex properties are changed. Otherwise, nothing happens and the loop is incremented.

After entering this macro, named SelectiveFormat, into a module sheet, you can provide a shortcut key to access it. Choose Tools⇨Macro⇨Macros to display the Macros dialog box. Select the macro from the list, and click on Options. Excel displays a new dialog box (see Figure 35-10) that lets you specify a shortcut key combination to execute the macro.

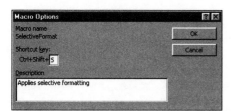

Figure 35-10: You can execute this macro by pressing Ctrl+S.

Figure 35-11 shows the macro in action. Note that you must select the range before you execute the macro.

As macros go, this example is not very good. It's not very flexible, and it doesn't include any error handling. For example, if a nonrange object (such as a graphic object) is selected, the macro halts and displays an error message. To avoid this error message and abort the macro if anything except a range is selected, you can insert the following statement as the first statement in the procedure (directly below the Sub statement):

```
If TypeName(Selection) <> "Range" Then Exit Sub
```

This causes the macro to halt if the selection is not a Range object.

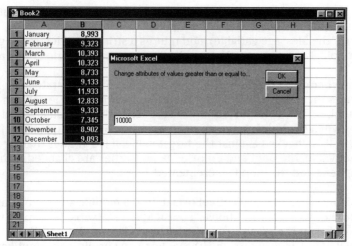

Figure 35-11: The macro uses the InputBox function to prompt the user for a value.

Notice also that the macro is executed even if you click on Cancel in the input box. To avoid this problem, enter the following statement directly above the Target=Val(Target) statement:

```
If Target = "" then Exit Sub
```

This aborts the subroutine if Target is empty.

Note   A much more versatile version of this utility is part of the Power Utility Pak (see Figure 35-12). The shareware version is available from this book's Web site.

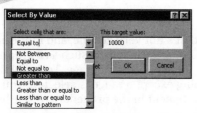

Figure 35-12: The Select By Value utility in the Power Utility Pak is a more versatile version of this macro.

Learning More

This chapter barely scratches the surface of what you can do with VBA. If this is your first exposure to VBA, you're probably a bit overwhelmed by objects, properties, and methods. I don't blame you. If you try to access a property that an object doesn't have, you get a runtime error, and your VBA code grinds to a screeching halt until you correct the problem. Fortunately, there are several good ways to learn about objects, properties, and methods.

Read the rest of the book

This book has three more chapters that are devoted to VBA. Chapter 36 covers VBA functions, Chapter 37 describes custom dialog boxes, and Chapter 38 consists of useful (and informative) VBA examples.

Record your actions

The best way — without question — to become familiar with VBA is to turn on the macro recorder and record actions that you make in Excel. It's even better if the VBA module in which the code is being recorded is visible while you're recording.

Use the online Help system

The main source of detailed information about Excel's objects, methods, and procedures is the online Help system. Help is very thorough and easy to access. When you're in a VBA module, just move the cursor to a property or method and press F1. You get help that describes the word that is under the cursor.

Buy another book

Okay, I promise. This is the last plug for my other book, *Excel 97 For Windows Power Programming With VBA,* 3rd Edition (to be published by IDG Books Worldwide, Inc. in July, 1997). I've received feedback from hundreds of first-edition users who claim that it's the best Excel/VBA book available. You be the judge.

Summary

This chapter introduces VBA, one of two macro languages included with Excel. If you want to learn macro programming, VBA is the language to use. In this chapter, you learn that a VBA module can contain subroutine procedures and function procedures, and that VBA is based on objects, properties, and methods. You also learn how to use the macro recorder to translate your actions into VBA code and write simple code directly in a VBA module. Three other chapters in this book provide additional information about VBA.

✦   ✦   ✦

Creating Custom Worksheet Functions

✦ ✦ ✦ ✦

In This Chapter

An introduction to custom VBA function procedures

How to use custom functions in worksheets and in other VBA procedures

A discussion of function arguments, with examples

Special considerations when debugging custom functions

Using the Function Wizard with custom functions

✦ ✦ ✦ ✦

As I mentioned in the preceding chapter, VBA lets you create two types of procedures: subroutines and functions. This chapter focuses on function procedures.

Overview of VBA Functions

Function procedures that you write in VBA are quite versatile. You can use these functions in two situations:

  ✦ As part of an expression in a different VBA procedure

  ✦ In formulas that you create in a worksheet

In fact, you can use a function procedure anywhere that you can use an Excel worksheet function or a VBA built-in function. Custom functions also appear in the Paste Function dialog box, so they appear to be part of Excel.

Excel contains hundreds of predefined worksheet functions. With so many from which to choose, you may be curious as to why anyone would need to develop additional functions. The main reason is that creating a custom function can greatly simplify your formulas by making them shorter — and shorter formulas are more readable and easier to work with. For example, you can often replace a complex formula with a single function. Another reason is that you can write functions to perform operations that would otherwise be impossible.

Note   This chapter assumes that you are familiar with entering and editing VBA code in the Visual Basic Editor (VBE). Refer to Chapter 35 for an overview of the VBE.

An Introductory Example

The process of creating custom functions is relatively easy once you understand VBA. Without further ado, here's an example of a VBA function procedure.

A custom function

This example function, named *NumSign*, uses one argument. The function returns a text string *Positive* if its argument is greater than zero, *Negative* if the argument is less than zero, and *Zero* if the argument is equal to zero. The function is shown in Figure 36-1.

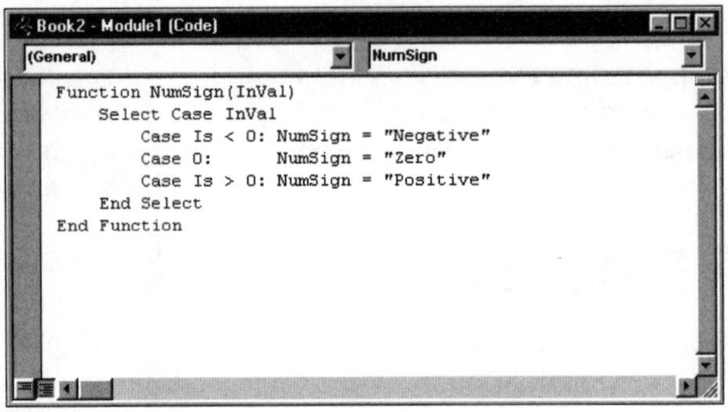

Figure 36-1: A custom function.

You could, of course, accomplish the same effect with the following worksheet formula, which uses a nested IF function:

```
=IF(A1=0,"Zero",IF(A1>0,"Positive","Negative"))
```

Most would agree that the custom function solution is easier to understand and to edit.

Using the function in a worksheet

When you enter a formula that uses the NumSign function, Excel executes the function to get the result (see Figure 36-2). This custom function works just like any built-in worksheet function. You can insert it in a formula by using the normal Insert⇨Function command, which displays the Paste Function dialog box (custom functions are located in the User Defined category). You also can nest custom functions and combine them with other elements in your formulas.

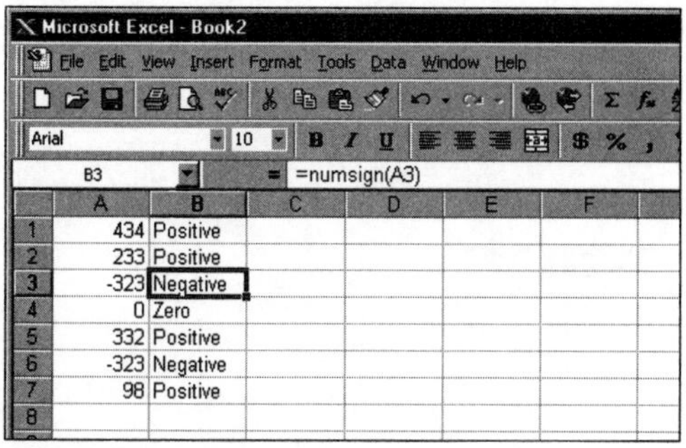

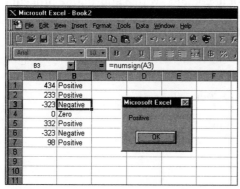

Figure 36-2: Using a custom function in a worksheet formula.

Using the function in a VBA subroutine

The following VBA subroutine procedure, which is defined in the same module as the custom NumSign function, uses the built-in MsgBox function to display the result of the NumSign function:

```
Sub ShowSign()
  CellValue = Sheets("Sheet1").Range("A1").Value
  MsgBox NumSign(CellValue)
End Sub
```

In this example, the variable CellValue contains the value in cell A1 on Sheet1 (this variable could contain any value, not necessarily obtained from a cell). CellValue is then passed to the function as its argument. Figure 36-3 shows the result of executing the NumSign subroutine.

Figure 36-3: Using a custom function in a VBA subroutine.

Analyzing the custom function

In this section, I describe the NumSign function. Here again is the code:

```
Function NumSign(InVal)
  Select Case InVal
    Case Is < 0: NumSign = "Negative"
    Case 0:    NumSign = "Zero"
    Case Is > 0: NumSign = "Positive"
  End Select
End Function
```

Notice that the procedure starts with the keyword *Function* rather than *Sub*, followed by the name of the function (*NumSign*). This custom function uses one argument (*InVal*); the argument's name is enclosed in parentheses. *InVal* is the cell or variable that is to be processed. When the function is used in a worksheet, the argument can be a cell reference (such as A1) or a literal value (such as –123). When the function is used in another procedure, the argument can be a numeric variable, a literal number, or a value that is obtained from a cell.

The NumSign function uses the Select Case construct (described in Chapter 35) to take a different action, depending on the value of InVal. If InVal is less than zero, NumSign is assigned the text *Negative*. If InVal is equal to zero, NumSign is *Zero*. If InVal is greater than zero, NumSign is *Positive*. The value returned by a function is always assigned to the function's name.

The procedure ends with an End Function statement.

About Function Procedures

A custom function procedure has a lot in common with a subroutine procedure, which I cover in the preceding chapter. Function procedures have some important differences, however, which I discuss in this section.

Declaring a function

The syntax for declaring a function is as follows:

```
[Public | Private][Static] Function name [(arglist)][As type]
  [statements]
  [name = expression]
  [Exit Function]
  [statements]
  [name = expression]
End Function
```

These elements are defined as follows:

> **Public** indicates that the function is accessible to all other procedures in all other modules in the workbook. (Optional)
>
> **Private** indicates that the function is accessible only to other procedures in the same module. Private functions can't be used in worksheet formulas and do not appear in the Paste Function dialog box. (Optional)
>
> **Static** indicates that the values of variables declared in the function are preserved between calls, rather than being reset. (Optional)
>
> **Function** is a keyword that indicates the beginning of a function procedure. (Required)
>
> **name** can be any valid variable name. When the function finishes, the single-value result is assigned to the function's name. (Required)
>
> **arglist** is a list (one or more) of variables that represent arguments passed to the function. The arguments are enclosed in parentheses. Use a comma to separate arguments. (Optional)
>
> **type** is the data type that is returned by the function. (Optional)
>
> **statements** are valid VBA statements. (Optional)
>
> **Exit Function** is a statement that causes an immediate exit from the function. (Optional)
>
> **End Function** is a keyword that indicates the end of the function. (Required)

Keep in mind that a value is assigned to the function's name when a function is finished executing.

To create a custom function, follow these steps:

1. Activate the Visual Basic Editor (or press Alt+F11).

2. Select the workbook in the Project window.

3. Choose Insert⇨Module to insert a VBA module (or you can use an existing module).

4. Enter the keyword *Function* followed by the function's name and a list of the arguments (if any) in parentheses.

5. Insert the VBA code that performs the work — and make sure that the variable corresponding to the function's name has the appropriate value (this is the value that the function returns).

6. End the function with an End Function statement.

Function names must adhere to the same rules as variable names, and you can't use a name that looks like a worksheet cell (for example, a function named J21 isn't accepted).

What a function can't do

When you develop a function, you must realize that a function can't perform certain types of actions. For example, you can't develop a function that changes the formatting of a cell (this is something that nearly everyone tries to do — with no luck). In other words, functions are basically passive procedures that return a value. If you attempt to perform an action that is not allowed, the function returns an error.

Executing function procedures

Although there are many ways to execute a *subroutine* procedure, you can execute a function procedure in just two ways:

✦ Call it from another procedure.

✦ Use it in a worksheet formula.

From a procedure

You can call custom functions from a procedure just as you call built-in VBA functions. For example, after you define a function called CalcTax, you can enter a statement like the following one:

```
Tax = CalcTax(Amount, Rate)
```

This statement executes the CalcTax custom function with Amount and Rate as its arguments. The function's result is assigned to the Tax variable.

In a worksheet formula

Using custom function in a worksheet formula is like using built-in functions. You must ensure that Excel can locate the function procedure, however. If the function procedure is in the same workbook, you don't have to do anything special. If the function is defined in a different workbook, you may have to tell Excel where to find the function. There are three ways to do this:

✦ **Precede the function's name with a file reference.** For example, if you want to use a function called CountNames that's defined in a workbook named MyFunctions, you can use a reference such as the following one:

```
=MyFunctions.xls!CountNames(A1:A1000)
```

If you insert the function with the Paste Function dialog box, the workbook reference is inserted automatically.

✦ **Set up a reference to the workbook.** If the custom function is defined in a reference workbook, you don't need to precedethe function name with the workbook name. You establish a reference to another workbook with the Tools⇨References command (which is in the Visual Basic Editor). You'll be presented with a list of references that include all open workbooks. Place a check mark in the item that refers to the workbook that contains the custom function (use the Browse button if the workbook isn't open).

✦ **Create an add-in.** When you create an add-in from a workbook that has function procedures, you don't need to use the file reference when you use one of the functions in a formula; the add-in must be installed, however. I discuss add-ins in Chapter 40.

Notice that your function procedures don't appear in the Macros dialog box when you select Tools⇨Macro. This is because you can't execute a function directly. As a result, you need to do extra, up-front work to test your functions as you're developing them. One approach is to set up a simple subroutine that calls the function. If the function is designed to be used in worksheet formulas, you can enter a simple formula to test it as you're developing the function.

Function Arguments

Keep in mind the following about function procedure arguments:

✦ Arguments can be variables (including arrays), constants, literals, or expressions.

✦ Some functions do not have arguments.

✦ Some functions have a fixed number of required arguments (from 1 to 60).

✦ Some functions have a combination of required and optional arguments.

In the following section, I present a series of examples that demonstrate how to use arguments effectively with functions. Coverage of optional arguments is beyond the scope of this book.

Example: A function with no argument

Like subroutines, functions don't necessarily have to use arguments. Excel, for example, has a few built-in worksheet functions that don't use arguments. These include RAND, TODAY, and NOW.

The following is a simple example of a function that has no arguments. This function returns the UserName property of the Application object. This is the name that appears in the Options dialog box (General tab). This is a simple example, but it can be useful because there is no other way to get the user's name to appear in a worksheet formula

```
Function User()
' Returns the name of the current user
  User = Application.UserName
End Function
```

When you enter the following formula into a worksheet cell, the cell displays the name of the current user:

```
=User()
```

As with Excel's built-in functions, when you use a function with no arguments, you must include a set of empty parentheses.

The following example is a simple subroutine that uses the User custom function as an argument for the MsgBox function. The concatenation operator (&) joins the literal string with the result of the User function.

```
Sub ShowUser()
  MsgBox ("The user is " & User())
End Sub
```

Example: A function with one argument

This section contains a more complex function that is designed for a sales manager who needs to calculate the commissions that are earned by the sales force. The commission rate is based on the amount sold — those who sell more earn a higher commission rate. The function returns the commission amount, based on the sales made (which is the function's only argument — a required argument). The calculations in this example are based on the following table:

Monthly Sales	Commission Rate
0 – $9,999	8.0%
$10,000 – $19,999	10.5%
$20,000 – $39,999	12.0%
$40,000+	14.0%

There are several ways to calculate commissions for various sales amounts that are entered into a worksheet. You could write a formula such as the following one:

```
=IF(AND(A1>=0,A1<=9999.99),A1*0.08,IF(AND(A1>=10000,A1<=19999.99),
    A1*0.105
,IF(AND(A1>=20000,A1<=39999.99),A1*0.12,IF(A1>=40000,A1*0.14,0))))
```

This is not the best approach for a couple of reasons. First, the formula is overly complex and difficult to understand. Second, the values are hard-coded into the formula, making the formula difficult to modify if the commission structure changes.

A better approach is to use a lookup table function to compute the commissions. For example:

```
=VLOOKUP(A1,Table,2)*A1
```

Using the VLOOKUP function requires that you have a table of commission rates set up in your worksheet.

An even better approach is to create a custom function such as the following one:

```
Function Commission(Sales)
' Calculates sales commissions
   Tier1 = 0.08
   Tier2 = 0.105
   Tier3 = 0.12
   Tier4 = 0.14
   Select Case Sales
       Case 0 To 9999.99: Commission = Sales * Tier1
       Case 1000 To 19999.99: Commission = Sales * Tier2
       Case 20000 To 39999.99: Commission = Sales * Tier3
       Case Is >= 40000: Commission = Sales * Tier4
   End Select
End Function
```

After you define the Commission function in a VBA module, you can use it in a worksheet formula or call the function from other VBA procedures.

Entering the following formula into a cell produces a result of 3,000 (the amount, 25,000, qualifies for a commission rate of 12 percent):

```
=Commission(25000)
```

Even if you don't need custom functions in a worksheet, creating function procedures can make your VBA coding much simpler. If your VBA procedure calculates sales commissions, for example, you can use the Commission function and call it from a VBA subroutine. The following is a tiny subroutine that asks the user for a sales amount and then uses the Commission function to calculate the commission due and to display it:

```
Sub CalcComm()
    Sales = InputBox("Enter Sales:")
    MsgBox "The commission is " & Commission(Sales)
End Sub
```

The subroutine starts by displaying an input box that asks for the sales amount. Then the procedure displays a message box with the calculated sales commission for that amount. The Commission function must be available in the active workbook; otherwise, Excel displays a message saying that the function is not defined.

Example: A function with two arguments

This example builds on the previous one. Imagine that the sales manager implements a new policy: The total commission paid is increased by 1 percent for every year that the salesperson has been with the company. I modified the custom Commission function (defined in the preceding section) so that it takes two arguments — both of which are required arguments. Call this new function *Commission2*:

```
Function Commission2(Sales, Years)
'  Calculates sales commissions based on years in service
    Tier1 = 0.08
    Tier2 = 0.105
    Tier3 = 0.12
    Tier4 = 0.14
    Select Case Sales
      Case 0 To 9999.99: Commission2 = Sales * Tier1
      Case 1000 To 19999.99: Commission2 = Sales * Tier2
      Case 20000 To 39999.99: Commission2 = Sales * Tier3
      Case Is >= 40000: Commission2 = Sales * Tier4
    End Select
    Commission2 = Commission2 + (Commission2 * Years / 100)
End Function
```

The modification was quite simple. I just added the second argument (Years) to the Function statement and included an additional computation that adjusts the commission before exiting the function.

The following is an example of how you write a formula by using this function (it assumes that the sales amount is in cell A1, and the number of years that the salesperson has worked is in cell B1):

```
=Commission2(A1,B1)
```

Example: A function with a range argument

The example in this section demonstrates how to use a worksheet range as an argument. Actually, it's not at all tricky; Excel takes care of the details behind the scenes.

Assume that you want to calculate the average of the five largest values in a range named Data. Excel doesn't have a function that can do this, so you can write the following formula:

```
=(LARGE(Data,1)+LARGE(Data,2)+LARGE(Data,3)+LARGE(Data,4)+LARGE
    (Data,5))/5
```

This formula uses Excel's LARGE function, which returns the *n*th largest value in a range. The preceding formula adds the five largest values in the range named `Data` and then divides the result by 5. The formula works fine, but it's rather unwieldy. And what if you decide that you needed to compute the average of the top *six* values? You would need to rewrite the formula — and make sure that all copies of the formula also get updated.

Wouldn't it be easier if Excel had a function named TopAvg? For example, you could use the following (nonexistent) function to compute the average:

```
=TopAvg(Data,5)
```

This is an example of when a custom function can make things much easier for you. The following is a custom VBA function, named *TopAvg*. It returns the average of the top *n* values in a range.

```
Function TopAvg(InRange, Num)
' Returns the average of the highest Num values in InRange
    Sum = 0
    For i = 1 To Num
        Sum = Sum + WorksheetFunction.Large(InRange, i)
    Next i
    TopAvg = Sum / Num
End Function
```

This function takes two arguments: InRange (which is a worksheet range) and Num (the number of values to average). The code starts by initializing the Sum variable to 0. It then uses a For-Next loop to calculate the sum of the *n*th largest values in the range. Note that I used Excel's LARGE function within the loop. You can use an Excel worksheet function in VBA if you precede the function with WorksheetFunction and a period. Finally, TopAvg is assigned the value of Sum divided by Num.

You can use all of Excel's worksheet functions in your VBA procedures *except* those that have equivalents in VBA. For example, VBA has a Rnd function that returns a random number. Therefore, you can't use Excel's RAND function in a VBA procedure.

Debugging Custom Functions

Debugging a function procedure can be a bit more challenging than debugging a subroutine procedure. If you develop a function that is to be used in worksheet formulas, an error in the function procedure simply results in an error display in the formula cell (usually #VALUE!). In other words, you don't receive the normal runtime error message that helps you locate the offending statement. The following are three methods that you may want to use:

✦ **Place MsgBox functions at strategic locations to monitor the value of specific variables.** Fortunately, message boxes in function procedures pop up when the procedure is executed. But make sure that you only have one formula in the worksheet that uses your function, or the message boxes appear for each formula that's evaluated.

✦ **Test the procedure by calling it from a subroutine procedure.** Runtime errors display normally, and you can either fix the problem (if you know it) or jump right into the debugger.

✦ **Set a breakpoint in the function, and then use Excel's debugger to step through the function.** You then can access all the normal debugging tools.

Pasting Custom Functions

Excel's Paste Function dialog box is a handy tool that lets you choose a worksheet function; you even can choose one of your custom worksheet functions. The Formula Palette prompts you for the function's arguments.

Note Function procedures that are defined with the Private keyword do not appear in the Paste Function dialog box.

You also can display a description of your custom function in the Paste Function dialog box. To do so, follow these steps:

1. Create the function in a module using the VBE.

2. Activate Excel.

3. Choose the Tools⇪Macro⇪Macros command.

   Excel displays its Macros dialog box (see Figure 36-4).

Figure 36-4: Excel's Macros dialog box doesn't list functions, so you must enter the function name yourself.

4. In the Macros dialog box, type the name of the function in the box labeled Macro Name. Notice that functions do not normally appear in this dialog box, so you must enter the function name yourself.

5. Click on the Options button.

   Excel displays its Macro Options dialog box. (See Figure 36-5.)

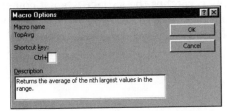

Figure 36-5: Entering a description for a custom function. This description appears in the Paste Function dialog box.

6. Enter a description of the function, and click on OK. The Shortcut key field is irrelevant for functions.

The description that you enter appears in the Paste Function dialog box.

Custom functions are listed under the User Defined category, and there is no straightforward way to create a new function category for your custom functions.

Figure 36-6 shows the Paste Function dialog box, listing the custom functions that are in the User Defined category. In the second Function Wizard dialog box, the user is prompted to enter arguments for a custom function — just as in using a built-in worksheet function.

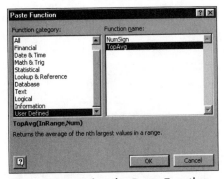

Figure 36-6: Using the Paste Function dialog box to insert a custom function.

When you access a *built-in* function from the Paste Function dialog box, the Formula Palette displays a description of each argument. Unfortunately, you can't provide such descriptions for custom functions.

Learning More

The information in this chapter only scratches the surface when it comes to creating custom functions. It should be enough to get you started, however, if you're interested in this topic. Refer to Chapter 38 for more examples of useful VBA functions. You may be able to use the examples directly or adapt them for your needs.

Summary

In this chapter, you read about how to create and use custom VBA functions. These functions can be used in worksheet formulas and in other VBA procedures. I provide several examples, and you can refer to Chapter 38 for more examples.

✦   ✦   ✦

Creating Custom Dialog Boxes

In This Chapter

Why you may need
to create a custom
dialog box for your
macro

A description of two
simple alternatives to
custom dialog boxes

How to create a
custom dialog box

Several examples of
custom dialog boxes

You can't use Excel very long without being exposed to
dialog boxes. Excel, like most Windows programs, uses
dialog boxes to obtain information, clarify commands, and
display messages. If you develop VBA macros, you can create
your own dialog boxes that work just like those that are built
into Excel. This chapter introduces you to custom dialog
boxes.

Excel 97 introduces a new method for creating custom dialog
boxes. Therefore, the information in this chapter does not
apply to previous versions of Excel.

Why Create Custom Dialog Boxes?

Some macros that you create behave exactly the same every
time you execute them. For example, you may develop a
macro that enters a list of your employees into a worksheet
range. This macro always produces the same result and
requires no additional user input. You may develop other
macros, however, that you want to behave differently under
different circumstances, or that offer some options for the
user. In such cases, the macro may benefit from a custom
dialog box.

The following is an example of a simple macro that makes
each cell in the selected range uppercase (but it skips cells
that have a formula). The subroutine uses VBA's built-in
StrConv function.

```
Sub ChangeCase()
 For Each cell In Selection
 If Not cell.HasFormula Then
 cell.Value = StrConv(cell.Value, vbUpperCase)
 End If
 Next cell
End Sub
```

This macro is useful, but it could be even more useful. For example, it would be nice if the macro could also change the cells to lowercase or initial capitals (only the first letter of each word is uppercase). This modification is not difficult to make. But if you make this change to the macro, you need some method of asking the user what type of change to make to the cells. The solution is to present a dialog box like the one that is shown in Figure 37-1. This dialog box is a user form that was created using the Visual Basic Editor and is displayed by a VBA macro.

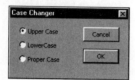

Figure 37-1: A custom dialog box that asks the user for an option.

Another solution would be to develop three macros — one for each type of text case change. Combining these three operations into a single macro and using a dialog box represent a more efficient approach, however. I discuss this example, including how to create the dialog box, later in the chapter.

Custom Dialog Box Alternatives

Although it's not difficult to develop custom dialog boxes, sometimes it's easier to use the tools that are built into VBA. For example, VBA includes two functions (MsgBox and InputBox) that let you display simple dialog boxes without creating a user form in the VBE. These dialog boxes can be customized in some ways, but they certainly don't offer the options that are available in a custom dialog box.

The InputBox function

The InputBox function is useful for obtaining a single input from the user. A simplified version of the function's syntax is as follows:

```
InputBox(prompt[,title][,default])
```

The elements are defined as follows:

> *prompt* is text that is displayed in the input box. (Required)
>
> *title* is the text that appears in the input box's title bar. (Optional)
>
> *default* is the default value. (Optional)

The following is an example of how you can use the InputBox function:

```
Rate = InputBox("Commission rate?","Commission Worksheet")
```

When this VBA statement is executed, Excel displays the dialog box that is shown in Figure 37-2. Notice that this example uses only the first two arguments and does not supply a default value. When the user enters a value and clicks on OK, the value is assigned to the variable *Rate*.

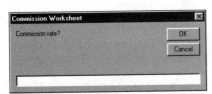

Figure 37-2: This dialog box is displayed by VBA's InputBox function.

VBA's InputBox function always returns a string, so it may be necessary to convert the results to a value. You can use the Val function to convert a string to a value, as follows:

```
Rate = Val(InputBox("Commission rate?","Commission Worksheet"))
```

The MsgBox function

VBA's MsgBox function is a handy way to display information and to solicit simple input from users. I use VBA's MsgBox function in many of this book's examples to display a variable's value. A simplified version of the MsgBox syntax is as follows:

```
MsgBox(prompt[,buttons][,title])
```

The elements are defined as follows:

> *prompt* is text that is displayed in the message box. (Required)
>
> *buttons* is the code for the buttons that are to appear in the message box. (Optional)
>
> *title* is the text that appears in the message box's title bar. (Optional)

You can use the MsgBox function by itself or assign its result to a variable. If you use it by itself, don't include parentheses around the arguments. The following example displays a message and does not return a result:

```
Sub MsgBoxDemo()
 MsgBox "Click OK to continue"
End Sub
```

Figure 37-3 shows how this message box appears.

Figure 37-3: A simple message box,
displayed with VBA's MsgBox function.

To get a response from a message box, you can assign the result of the MsgBox function to a variable. In the following code, I use some built-in constants (described later) to make it easier to work with the values that are returned by MsgBox:

```
Sub GetAnswer()
 Ans = MsgBox("Continue?", vbYesNo)
 Select Case Ans
 Case vbYes
' ...[code if Ans is Yes]...
 Case vbNo
' ...[code if Ans is No]...
 End Select
End Sub
```

When this procedure is executed, the *Ans* variable contains a value that corresponds to vbYes or vbNo. The Select Case statement determines the action to take based on the value of Ans.

You can easily customize your message boxes because of the flexibility of the buttons argument. Table 37-1 lists the built-in constants that you can use for the button argument. You can specify which buttons to display, whether an icon appears, and which button is the default.

Table 37-1
Constants That Are Used in the MsgBox Function

Constant	Value	Description
vbOKOnly	0	Display OK buttonly
vbOKCancel	1	Display OK and Cancel buttons
vbAbortRetryIgnore	2	Display Abort, Retry, and Ignore buttons
vbYesNoCancel	3	Display Yes, No, and Cancel buttons
vbYesNo	4	Display Yes and No buttons
vbRetryCancel	5	Display Retry and Cancel buttons
vbCritical	16	Display Critical Message icon
vbQuestion	32	Display Warning Query icon
vbExclamation	48	Display Warning Message icon
vbInformation	64	Display Information Message icon
vbDefaultButton1	0	First button is default
vbDefaultButton2	256	Second button is default
vbDefaultButton3	512	Third button is default
vbSystemModal	4096	System modal; all applications are suspended until the user responds to the message box

The following example uses a combination of constants to display a message box with a Yes button, a No button (vbYesNo), and a question mark icon (vbQuestion); the second button is designated as the default button (vbDefaultButton2) — which is the button that is executed if the user presses Enter. For simplicity, I assigned these constants to the *Config* variable and then used *Config* as the second argument in the MsgBox function.

```
Sub GetAnswer()
  Config = vbYesNo + vbQuestion + vbDefaultButton2
  Ans = MsgBox("Process the monthly report?", Config)
  If Ans = vbYes Then RunReport
  If Ans = vbNo Then End
End Sub
```

Figure 37-4 shows how this message box appears when the GetAnswer subroutine is executed. If the user clicks on the Yes button (or presses Enter), the routine executes the procedure named RunReport (which is not shown). If the user clicks on the No button, the routine is ended with no action. Because the title argument was omitted in the MsgBox function, Excel uses the default title ("Microsoft Excel").

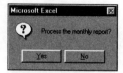

Figure 37-4: The second argument
of the Msgbox function determines
what appears in the message box.

The routine that follows is another example of using the MsgBox function:

```
Sub GetAnswer2()
  Msg = "Do you want to process the monthly report?"
  Msg = Msg & vbLf & vbLf
  Msg = Msg & "Processing the monthly report will take approxi-
         mately "
  Msg = Msg & "15 minutes. It will generate a 30-page report for
         all "
  Msg = Msg & "sales offices for the current month."
  Title = "XYZ Marketing Company"
  Config = vbYesNo + vbQuestion
  Ans = MsgBox(Msg, Config, Title)
  If Ans = vbYes Then RunReport
  If Ans = vbNo Then End
End Sub
```

This example demonstrates an efficient way to specify a longer message in a
message box. I used a variable (Msg) and the concatenation operator (&) to build
the message in a series of statements. In the second statement, vbLF is a constant
that represents a line feed character (using two line feeds inserts a blank line). I
also used the title argument to display a different title in the message box. Figure
37-5 shows how this message box appears when the procedure is executed.

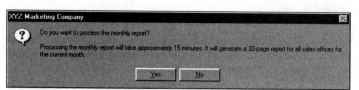

Figure 37-5: A message box with a longer message and a title.

Creating Custom Dialog Boxes: An Overview

The InputBox and MsgBox functions do just fine for many cases, but if you need to
obtain more information, then you need to create a custom dialog box. A custom
dialog box is created on a user form in the Visual Basic Editor.

The following is a list of the general steps that you typically take to create a custom dialog box:

1. Determine exactly how the dialog box is to be used and where it is to fit into your VBA macro.
2. Activate the Visual Basic Editor, and Insert a new user form (select Insert⇨UserForm).
3. Add the appropriate controls to the dialog box.
4. Create a macro to display the dialog box.
5. Create "event-handler" VBA subroutines that are executed when the user manipulates the controls (for example, clicks on the OK button).

I discuss more details in the following sections.

Working with user forms

Excel stores custom dialog boxes on user forms (one dialog box per form). To create a dialog box, you must first insert a new user form in the Visual Basic Editor window.

To activate the Visual Basic Editor, select Tools⇨Macro⇨Visual Basic Editor (or press Alt+F11). Make sure that the current workbook is selected in the Project window, and then select Insert⇨UserForm. The Visual Basic Editor displays an empty form, as shown in Figure 37-6. When you activate a form, the Visual Basic editor displays the Toolbox, which is used to add controls to the dialog box.

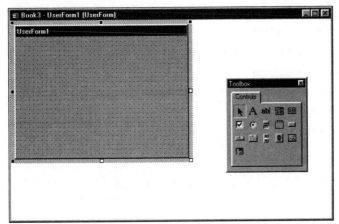

Figure 37-6: An empty form.

Adding controls

The Toolbox, as shown in Figure 37-7, contains a number of ActiveX controls that you can add to your dialog box.

Figure 37-7: The Toolbox contains the controls that you add to your dialog box.

When you move the mouse pointer over a control in the Toolbox, the control's name is displayed. To add a control, click on it and drag it in the form. After adding a control, you can move it or change its size.

Table 37-2 lists the Toolbox controls.

	Table 37-2 **Toolbox Controls**	
Control	*Description*
Select Objects	Lets you select other controls by dragging
Label	Adds a label
TextBox	Adds a text box
ComboBox	Adds a combo box
ListBox	Adds a list box
CheckBox	Adds a check box
OptionButton	Adds an option button
ToggleButton	Adds a toggle button
Frame	Adds a frame (a container for other objects)
CommandButton	Adds a command button
TabStrip	Adds a tab strip
MultiPage	Adds a multipage control (a container for other objects)
ScrollBar	Adds a scroll bar
SpinButton	Adds a spin button
Image	Adds a control that can contain an image
RefEdit	Adds a reference edit control (lets the user select a range)

You can also place these controls directly on your worksheet. Refer to Chapter 38 for details.

Changing the properties of a control

Every control that you add to a user form has a number of properties that determine how the control looks and behaves. You can change some of these properties (such as Height and Width) by clicking on and dragging the controls border. To change other properties, suse the Properties window.

To display the Properties window, select View⇨Properties Window (or press F4). The Properties window displays a list of properties for the selected control (each control has a different set of properties). If you click on the form itself, the Properties window displays properties for the form. Figure 37-8 shows the Properties window for a command button control.

Figure 37-8: The Properties window for a command button control.

To change a property, select the property in the Property window and then enter a new value. Some properties (such as BackColor) let you select a property from a list. The top of the Properties window contains a drop-down list that lets you select a control to work with. You can also click on a control to select it and display its properties.

When you set properties using the Property window, you're setting properties at *design time.* You can also use VBA to change the properties of controls while the dialog box is displayed (that is, at *run time*).

A complete discussion of all the properties is well beyond the scope of this book. To find out about a particular property, select it in the Property window and press F1. The online help for user form controls is extremely thorough.

Handling events

Note When you insert a user form, that form can also hold VBA subroutines to handle the events that are generated by the form. An *event* is something that occurs when the user manipulates a control. For example, clicking on a button is an event. Selecting an item in a list box control is an event. To make a dialog box useful, you must write VBA code to do something when an event occurs.

Event-handler subroutines have names that combine the control with the event. The general form is the controls name, followed by an underscore and the event name. For example, the subroutine that is executed when the user clicks on a button named MyButton is MyButton_Click.

Displaying custom dialog boxes

You also need to write a subroutine to display a custom dialog box. You use the Show method of the Userform object. The following procedure displays the dialog box that is located on the UserForm1 form:

```
Sub ShowDialog()
 UserForm1.Show
End Sub
```

When this subroutine is executed, the dialog box is displayed. What happens next depends on the event-handler subroutines that you create.

A Custom Dialog Box Example

The preceding section is, admittedly, rudimentary. In this section, I demonstrate how to develop a custom dialog box. This example is rather simple. The user form displays a message to the user — something that could be accomplished more easily by using the MsgBox function. However, the custom dialog box gives you a lot more flexibility in terms of formatting and layout of the message.

Creating the dialog box

If you're following along, start with a new workbook. Then follow these steps:

1. Choose Tools⇨Macro⇨Visual Basic Editor (or press Alt+F11) to activate the VBE window.

2. In the VBE window, choose Insert⇨UserForm.

   The VBE adds an empty form name UserForm1 and displays the Toolbox.

3. Press F4 to display the Properties window, and change the following properties of the UserForm object:

Property	Change To
Name	AboutBox
Caption	About This Workbook

4. Use the toolbar to add a Label object to the dialog box.

5. Select the Label object. In the Properties window, enter any text that you want for the label's Caption.

6. In the Properties window, click on the Font property and adjust the font. You can change the typeface, size, and so on. The changes then appear in the form. Figure 37-9 shows an example of a formatted Label control.

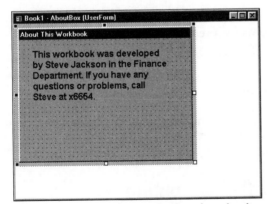

Figure 37-9: A Label control, after changing its Font properties.

7. Add a command button object to the dialog box, and change the following properties for the command button:

Property	Change To
Name	OKButton
Caption	OK
Default	True

8. Make other adjustments so that the form looks good to you. You can change the size of the form, or move or resize the controls.

Testing the dialog box

At this point, the dialog box has all the necessary controls. What's missing is a way to display the dialog box. In this section, I explain how to write a VBA subroutine to display the custom dialog box.

1. Insert a module by selecting Insert➪Module.

2. In the empty module, enter the following code:

```
Sub ShowAboutBox()
 AboutBox.Show
End Sub
```

3. Activate Excel.

4. Choose Tools➪Macro➪Macros (or press Alt+F8).

5. In the Macros dialog box, select ShowAboutBox from the list of macros and click on OK.

   The custom dialog box then appears.

If you click on the OK button, notice that it doesn't close the dialog box as you may expect. This button needs to have an event-handler subroutine. You can dismiss the dialog box by clicking the close button in its title box.

Creating an event-handler subroutine

An event-handler subroutine is executed when an event occurs. In this case, you need a subroutine to handle the Click event that's generated when the user clicks on the OK button.

1. Activate the Visual Basic Editor (pressing Alt+F11 is the fastest way).

2. Activate the AboutBox form by double-clicking on its name in the Project window.

3. Double-click on the OKButton control.

4. VBE activates the module for the user form and inserts some code, as shown in Figure 37-10.

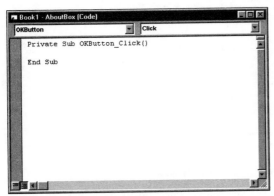

Figure 37-10: The module for the user form.

5. Insert the following statement before the End Sub statement:

```
Unload AboutBox
```

This statement simply dismisses the user form. The complete event-handler subroutine is listed below:

```
Private Sub OKButton_Click()
 Unload AboutBox
End Sub
```

Attaching the macro to a button

In this section, I describe how to attach the ShowAboutBox subroutine to a button object on a worksheet. Follow these steps:

1. Activate Excel.

2. Right-click on any toolbar, and select Forms from the shortcut menu.

   The Forms toolbar is displayed.

3. Click on the Button tool on the Forms toolbar.

4. Drag the Button tool into the worksheet to create a Button object.

   When you release the mouse button, Excel displays its Assign Macro dialog box (see Figure 37-11).

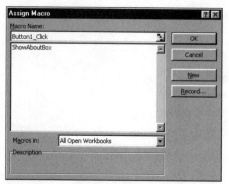

Figure 37-11: The Assign Macro dialog box.

5. Select the ShowAboutBox macro from the list.

6. Click on OK to close the Assign Macro dialog box.

7. Change the caption of the button to **About...**

After you perform these steps, clicking on the button executes the ShowAboutBox subroutine — which displays your custom dialog box.

Another Custom Dialog Box Example

The example in this section is an enhanced version of the ChangeCase example that I presented at the beginning of the chapter. Recall that the original version of this macro changes the text in the selected cells to uppercase characters. This modified version asks the user what type of case change to make: uppercase, lowercase, or initial capitals.

Web site   This workbook is available from this book's Web site.

Creating the dialog box

This dialog box needs one piece of information from the user: the type of change to make to the text. Because only one option can be selected, option buttons controls are appropriate. Follow these steps to create the custom dialog box. Start with an empty workbook:

1. Choose Tools⇨Macro⇨Visual Basic Editor (or press Alt+F11) to activate the VBE window.

2. In the VBE window, choose Insert⇨UserForm.

VBE adds an empty form name UserForm1 and displays the Toolbox.

3. Press F4 to display the Properties window, and change the following properties of the UserForm object:

Property	Change To
Name	CaseChangerDialog
Caption	Case Changer

4. Add a command button object to the dialog box, and change the following properties for the command button:

Property	Change To
Name	OKButton
Caption	OK
Default	True

5. Add another command button object, and change the following properties:

Property	Change To
Name	CancelButton
Caption	Cancel
Cancel	True

6. Add an option button control, and change the following properties (this option is the default, so its Value property should be set to True):

Property	Change To
Name	OptionUpper
Caption	Upper Case
Value	True

7. Add a second option button control, and change the following properties:

Property	Change To
Name	OptionLower
Caption	Lower Case

8. Add an option button control, and change the following properties:

Property	Change To
Name	OptionProper
Caption	Proper Case

9. Adjust the size and position of the controls and the form until your screen resembles Figure 37-12. Make sure that the controls do not overlap.

Tip The Visual Basic Editor provides several useful command to help you size and align the controls. Select the controls that you want to work with, and then choose a command from the Format menu. These commands are fairly self-explanatory, and the online help has complete details.

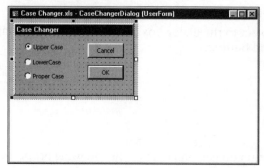

Figure 37-12: The dialog box after adding controls and adjusting some properties.

Testing the dialog box

At this point, the dialog box has all the necessary controls. What's missing is a way to display the dialog box. In this section, I explain how to write a VBA subroutine to display the custom dialog box.

1. Insert a module by selecting Insert⇨Module.

2. In the empty module, enter the following code:

```
Sub ChangeCase()
    CaseChangerDialog.Show
End Sub
```

3. Select Run⇨Sub/User Form (or press F5).

The Excel window is then activated, and the new dialog box is displayed, as shown in Figure 37-13. The options button work, but clicking on the OK and Cancel buttons has no effect. These two buttons need to have event-handler subroutines. Click on the Close button in the title bar to dismiss the dialog box.

Creating event-handler subroutines

In this section, I explain how to create two event-handler subroutines: one to handle the Click event for the CancelButton command button and the other to handle the Click event for the OKButton command button. Event handlers for the option buttons are not necessary. The VBA code can determine which of the three option buttons is selected.

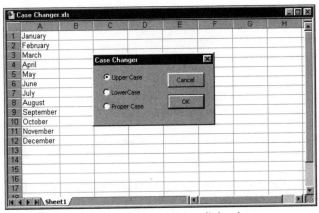

Figure 37-13: Displaying the custom dialog box.

Event-handler subroutines are stored in the form module. To create the subroutine to handle the Click event for the CancelButton, follow these steps:

1. Activate the CaseChangerDialog form by double-clicking on its name in the Project window.

2. Double-click on the CancelButton control.

3. VBE activates the module for the form and inserts some code, as shown in Figure 37-14.

4. Insert the following statement before the End Sub statement:

```
Unload CaseChangerDialog
```

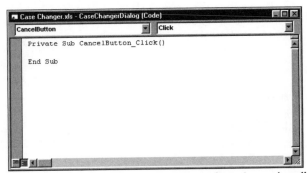

Figure 37-14: VBE sets up an empty subroutine to handle the Click event for the CancelButton control.

That's all there is to it. The following is a listing of the entire subroutine:

```
Private Sub CancelButton_Click()
 Unload CaseChangerDialog
End Sub
```

This subroutine is executed when the CancelButton is clicked on. It consists of a single statement that unloads the CaseChangerDialog form.

The next step is to add the code to handle the Click event for the OKButton control. Follow these steps:

1. Select OKButton from the drop-down list at the top of the module. VBE begins a new subroutine called OKButton_Click.

2. Enter the following code (the first and last statements have already been entered for you by VBE):

```
Private Sub OKButton_Click()
    Application.ScreenUpdating = False
'    Exit if a range is not selected
    If TypeName(Selection) <> "Range" Then Exit Sub
'    Upper case
    If OptionUpper Then
        For Each cell In Selection
        If Not cell.HasFormula Then
            cell.Value = StrConv(cell.Value, vbUpperCase)
        End If
        Next cell
    End If
'    Lower case
    If OptionLower Then
        For Each cell In Selection
        If Not cell.HasFormula Then
            cell.Value = StrConv(cell.Value, vbLowerCase)
        End If
        Next cell
    End If
'    Proper case
    If OptionProper Then
        For Each cell In Selection
        If Not cell.HasFormula Then
            cell.Value = StrConv(cell.Value, bProperCase)
        End If
        Next cell
    End If
Unload CaseChangerDialog
End Sub
```

The macro starts by turning off screen updating (this makes the macro run faster). Next, the code checks the type of the selection. If a range is not selected, the procedure ends. The remainder of the subroutine consists of three separate blocks. Only one block is executed, determined by which option button is selected. The selected option button has a value of True. Finally, the user form is unloaded (dismissed).

Testing the dialog box

To try out the dialog box, follow these steps:

1. Activate Excel.

2. Enter some text into some cells.

3. Select the range with the text.

4. Choose Tools⇨Macro⇨Macros (or press Alt+F8).

5. In the Macros dialog box, select ChangeCase from the list of macros and click on OK. The custom dialog box appears.

6. Make your choice, and click on OK.

Try it with a few more selections. Notice that if you click on Cancel, the dialog box is dismissed and no changes are made.

Making the macro available from a toolbar button

At this point, everything should be working properly. However, there's really no quick and easy way to execute the macro. A good way to execute this macro would be from a toolbar button. You can use the following steps:

1. Right-click on any toolbar, and select Customize from the shortcut menu.

   Excel displays its Customize dialog box.

2. Click on the Commands tab, and select Macros from the Categories list.

3. Click on the Custom Button in the Commands list and drag it to a toolbar.

4. Right-click on the new toolbar button, and select Assign Macro from the shortcut menu.

5. Choose ChangeCase from the list of macros, and click on OK.

   You can also change the button image and add a tool tip by using other commands that are on the shortcut menu.

6. Click on Close to close the Customize dialog box.

After performing the preceding steps, clicking on the toolbar button executes the macro and displays the dialog box.

Note If the workbook that contains the macro is not open, it is opened. You may want to hide the workbook window (select Window⇨Hide) so that it isn't displayed. Another option is to create an add-in. See Chapter 40 for specifics.

More on Creating Custom Dialog Boxes

Creating custom dialog boxes can make your macros much more versatile. You can create custom commands that display dialog boxes that look exactly like those that Excel uses. This section contains some additional information to help you develop custom dialog boxes that work like those that are built into Excel.

Adding accelerator keys

Dialog boxes should not discriminate against those who want to use the keyboard rather than a mouse. All of Excel's dialog boxes work equally well with a mouse and a keyboard, because each control has an associated accelerator key. The user can press Alt plus the accelerator key to work with a specific dialog box control.

It's a good idea to add accelerator keys to your custom dialog boxes. You do this in the Properties window. Enter a character for the Accelerator property.

Obviously, the letter that you enter as the accelerator key must be a letter that is contained in the caption of the object. It can be any letter in the text (not necessarily the first letter). You should ensure that an accelerator key is not duplicated in a dialog box. If you have duplicate accelerator keys, the accelerator key acts on the first control in the "tab order" of the dialog box (explained shortly).

Some controls (such as edit boxes) don't have a caption property. You can assign an accelerator key to a label that describes the control. Pressing the accelerator key then activates the next control in the tab order (which should be the edit box).

Controlling tab order

In the previous section, I refer to a dialog box's *tab order*. When you're working with a dialog box, pressing Tab and Shift+Tab cycles through the dialog box's controls. When you create a custom dialog box, you should make sure that the tab order is correct. Usually, this means that tabbing should move to the controls in a logical sequence.

To view or change the tab order in a custom dialog box, use the Properties window. If the Tab Stop property is True, the selected control is selectable when the user clicks on Tab. Change the value of the TabIndex property. These values range from 0 (first in the tab order) to 1 less than the number of controls that have a TabIndex property. When you change the TabIndex, VBE automatically adjusts the TabIndex of all subsequent controls in the tab order.

Learning More

Mastering custom dialog boxes takes practice. It's a good idea to closely examine the dialog boxes that Excel uses; these are examples of well-designed dialog boxes. You can duplicate nearly every dialog box that Excel uses.

The best way to learn more about creating dialog boxes is by using the online help system.

Summary

In this chapter, I describe how to create dialog boxes and use them with your VBA macros. I also cover two VBA functions — InputBox and MsgBox — which can sometimes take the place of a custom dialog box. The chapter includes several examples to help you understand how to use this feature.

✦   ✦   ✦

Using Dialog Box Controls in Your Worksheet

In Chapter 37, I presented an introduction to custom dialog boxes. If you like the idea of using dialog box controls — but don't like the idea of creating a dialog box — this chapter is for you. I explain how to enhance your worksheet with a variety of interactive controls such as buttons, list boxes, and option buttons.

Why Use Controls on a Worksheet?

The main reason to use dialog box controls on a worksheet is to make it easier for the user to provide input. For example, if you create a model that uses one or more input cells, you can create controls to allow the user to select values for the input cells.

Adding controls to a worksheet requires much less effort than creating a dialog box. In addition, you may not have to create any macros, because you can link a control to a worksheet cell. For example, if you insert a check box control on a worksheet, you can link it to a particular cell. When the check box is selected, the linked cell displays TRUE. When the check box is not selected, the linked cell displays FALSE.

Figure 38-1 shows a simple example that uses option buttons and a scrollbar control.

Figure 38-1: This worksheet uses dialog box controls.

Controls That Are Available to You

Adding controls to a worksheet can be a bit confusing because there are two source for these controls. The controls that you can insert on a worksheet come from two toolbars:

✦ **Forms toolbar:** These controls are insertable objects (and are compatible with Excel 5 and Excel 95).

✦ **Control Toolbox toolbar:** These are ActiveX controls. These controls are the same controls that you insert on a custom dialog box (although not all of these controls are suitable for use on a worksheet). These controls are not compatible with Excel 5 and Excel 95.

To add to the confusion, most of the controls are available on both toolbars. For example, the Forms toolbar and the Control Toolbox toolbar both have a control named List box. However, these are two entirely different controls. In general, the ActiveX controls (those on the Control Toolbox toolbar) provide more flexibility, and you should use those controls. However, if you need to save your workbook so that it can be opened by Excel 5 or Excel 95, you should use the controls that are on the Forms toolbar.

This chapter focuses exclusively on the controls that are available in the Control Toolbox toolbar, as shown in Figure 38-2.

Figure 38-2: The Control Toolbox toolbar.

A description of the buttons in the Control Toolbox appears in Table 38-1.

Table 38-1
Buttons on the Control Toolbox Toolbar

Button	What It Does
Design Mode	Toggles design mode
Properties	Displays the Properties window
View Code	Switches to the Visual Basic Editor so that you can write or edit VBA code for the selected control
Check Box	Inserts a check box control
Text Box	Inserts a text box control
Command Button	Inserts a command button control
Option Button	Inserts an option button control
List Box	Inserts a list box control
Combo Box	Inserts a combo box control
Toggle Button	Inserts a toggle button control
Spin Button	Inserts a spin button control
Scroll Bar	Inserts a scroll bar control
Label	Inserts a label control
Image	Inserts an image control
More Controls	Displays a list of other ActiveX controls that are installed on your system

Using Controls

Adding controls to a worksheet is easy. After you add a control, you can adjust its properties to modify the way that the control looks and works.

Adding a control

To add a control to a worksheet, make sure that the Control Toolbox toolbar is displayed. Then click on the desired control and drag it in the worksheet to create the control. You don't need to be too concerned about the exact size or position because you can modify these properties at any time.

About design mode

When you insert a control, Excel goes into *design mode*. In this mode, you can adjust the properties of any controls on your worksheet, add or edit macros for the control, or change the control's size or position. When Excel is in design mode, you cannot try out the controls. To test the controls, you must exit design mode. You exit design mode by clicking on the Exit Design Mode button on the Control Toolbox toolbar.

Adjusting properties

Every control that you add has a number of properties that determine how it looks and behaves. You can adjust these properties only when Excel is in design mode. When you add a control to a worksheet, Excel enters design mode automatically. If you need to change a control after you've exited design mode, simply click on the Design Mode button on the Control Toolbox toolbar.

To change the properties for a control, select the control and then click on the Properties button on the Control Toolbox toolbar. Excel displays its Properties window, as shown in Figure 38-3. The Properties window has two tabs. The Alphabetic tab displays the properties in alphabetical order. The Categorized tab displays the properties by category. Both tabs show the same properties; only the order is different.

To change a property, select it in the Properties window and then make the change. The manner in which you change a property depends on the property. Some properties display a drop-down list that lets you select from a list of options. Others (such as Font) provide a button that, when clicked on, displays a dialog box. Other properties require you to type the property value. When you change a property, the change takes effect immediately.

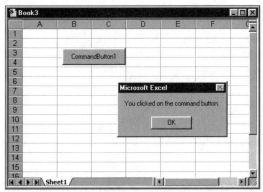

Figure 38-3: The Properties window lets you adjust the properties of a control.

Tip To learn about a particular property, select the property in the Properties window and press F1.

Common properties

Each control has its own unique set of properties. However, many objects share properties. In this section, I describe some of the properties that are common to all or many controls.

Accelerator	The letter underlined in the control's caption.
AutoSize	If True, the control resizes itself automatically based on the text in its caption.
BackColor	The background color of the control.
BackStyle	The style of the background (either transparent or opaque).
Caption	The text that appears on the control.
Value	The controls value.
Left and Top	Values that determine the control's position.
Width and Height	Values that determine the control's width and height.
Visible	If false, the control is hidden.
Name	The name of the control. By default, a control's name is based on the control type. You can change the name to any valid name. However, each control's name must be unique on the worksheet.
Picture	Lets you specify a graphic image to display. The image must be contained in a file (it can't be copied from the Clipboard).

Creating macros for controls

To create a macro for a control, you must use the Visual Basic Editor. The macros are stored on the sheet that contains the control. Each control can have a macro to handle any of its events. For example, a command button control can have a macro for its Click event, its DblClick event, and a number of others.

The easiest way to access the VBA module for a control is to double-click on the control while in design mode. Excel displays the VBE and creates an empty macro for the control's Click event. (See Figure 38-4.)

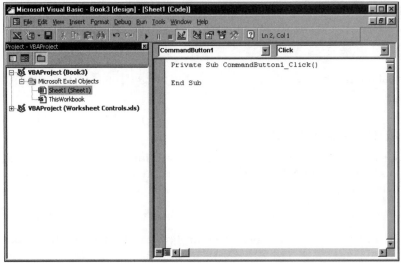

Figure 38-4: Double-clicking on a control in design mode activates the Visual Basic Editor.

The control's name appears in the upper-left portion of the code window, and the event appears in the upper-right. If you want to create a macro that executes when a different event occurs, select the event from the list in the upper-right area.

The following steps demonstrate how to insert a command button and create a simple macro that displays a message when the button is clicked on.

1. Make sure that the Control Toolbox toolbar is displayed.

2. Click on the CommandButton tool in the Control Toolbox.

3. Click and drag in the worksheet to create the button.

4. Double-click on the button. The Visual Basic Editor window is activated, and an empty subroutine is created.

5. Enter the following VBA statement before the End Sub statement:

```
MsgBox "You clicked on the command button."
```

6. Press Alt+F11 to return to Excel.

7. Adjust any other properties for the command button.

8. Click on the Exit Design Mode button in the Control Toolbox toolbar.

After performing the preceding steps, clicking on the command button displays the message box that is shown in Figure 38-5.

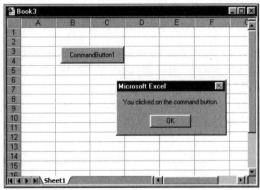

Figure 38-5: This message box is displayed by a simple macro.

The Controls Toolbox Controls

In the sections that follow, I describe the ActiveX controls that are available on the Controls Toolbox toolbar.

Web site This book's Web page contains a file that includes examples of all the ActiveX controls.

Check box control

A check box control is useful for getting a binary choice: yes or no, true or false, on or off, and so on. Figure 38-6 shows some examples of check box controls. Each of these controls displays its value in a cell (in A1:A4).

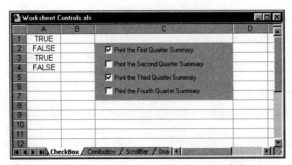

Figure 38-6: Check box controls on a worksheet.

The following is a description of the most useful properties of a check box control:

✦ **Accelerator:** A letter that lets the user change the value of the control using the keyboard. For example, if the accelerator is A, pressing Alt+A changes the value of the check box control.

✦ **LinkedCell:** The worksheet cell that's linked to the check box. The cell displays TRUE if the control is checked or FALSE if the control is not checked.

Combo box control

A combo box control is similar to a list box control. A combo box, however, is a drop-down box, and it displays only one item at a time. Another difference is that the user may be allowed to enter a value that does not appear in the list of items.

Figure 38-7 shows a few combo box controls. One of these controls uses two columns for its ListFill range.

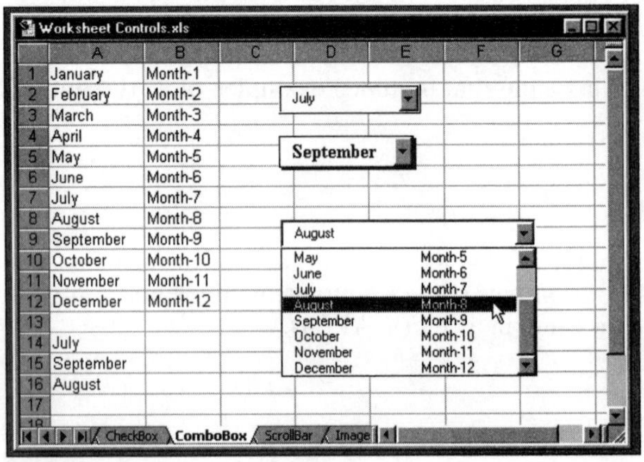

Figure 38-7: ComboBox controls.

The following is a description of the most useful properties of a combo box control:

✦ **BoundColumn:** If the list contains multiple columns, this property determines which column contains the returned value.

✦ **ColumnCount:** The number of columns in the list.

✦ **LinkedCell:** The worksheet cell that displays the selected item.

✦ **ListFillRange:** The worksheet range that contains the list items.

✦ **ListRows:** The number of items to display when the list drops down.

✦ **ListStyle:** Determines the appearance of the list items.

✦ **MultiSelect:** Determines whether the user can select multiple items from the list.

✦ **Style:** Determines whether the control acts like a drop-down list or a combo box. A drop-down list doesn't allow the user to enter a new value.

If you use a multiselect list box, you cannot specify a LinkedCell; you need to write a macro to determine which items are selected.

Command button control

A command button is of no use unless you provide a macro to execute when the button is clicked on. Figure 38-8 shows a worksheet that uses several command buttons. One of these command buttons uses a picture.

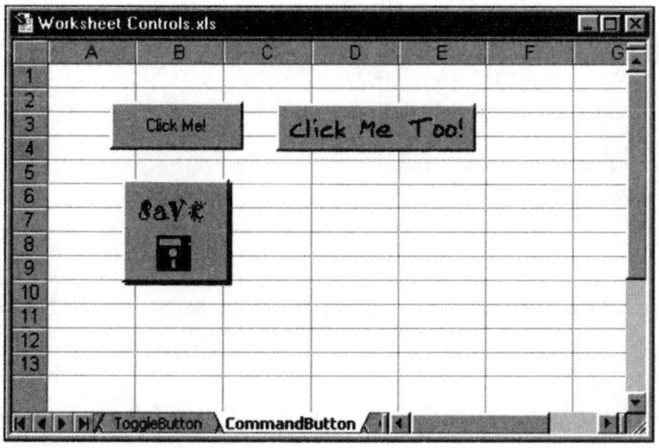

Figure 38-8: Command buttons on a worksheet.

When a button is clicked on, it executes a macro with a name that is made up of the command button's name, an underscore, and the word *Click on*. For example, if a command button is named MyButton, clicking on it executes the macro named MyButton_Click.

Image control

An image control is used to display an image that is contained in a file. This control offers no significant advantages over using standard imported images (as I describe in Chapter 14).

Label control

A label control simply displays text. This is not a useful control for use on worksheets, and a standard TextBox AutoShape gives you more versatility.

List box controls

The list box control presents a list of items, and the user can select an item (or multiple items). Figure 38-9 shows a worksheet with several list box controls. As you can see, you have a great deal of control over the appearance of list box controls. One of the list boxes uses two columns as its ListFill range.

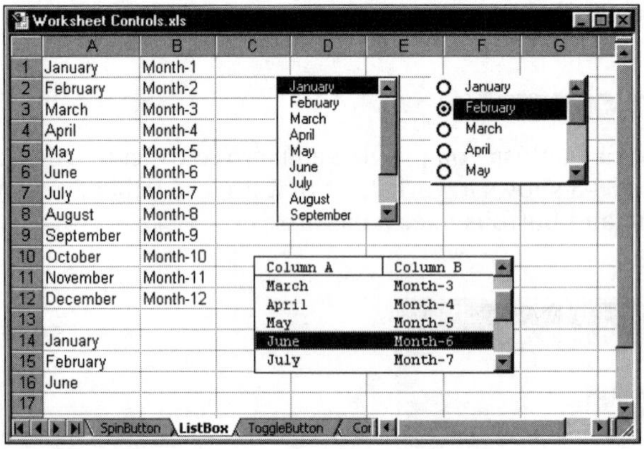

Figure 38-9: List box controls on a worksheet.

You can specify a range that holds the list box items, and this range can consist of multiple columns.

The following is a description of the most useful properties of a list box control:

✦ **BoundColumn:** If the list contains multiple columns, this property determines which column contains the returned value.

✦ **ColumnCount:** The number of columns in the list.

✦ **IntegralHeight:** This is True if the height of the list box adjusts automatically to display full lines of text when the list is scrolled vertically. If False, the list box may display partial lines of text when it is scrolled vertically.

+ **LinkedCell:** The worksheet cell that displays the selected item.

+ **ListFillRange:** The worksheet range that contains the list items.

+ **ListStyle:** Determines the appearance of the list items.

+ **MultiSelect:** Determines whether the user can select multiple items from the list.

If you use a multiselect list box, you cannot specify a LinkedCell; you need to write a macro to determine which items are selected.

Option button controls

Option buttons are useful when the user needs to select from a small number of items. Option buttons are always used in groups of at least two. Figure 38-10 shows two sets of option buttons. One set uses graphic images (set with the Picture property).

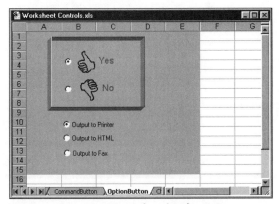

Figure 38-10: Two sets of option buttons.

The following is a description of the most useful properties of an option button control:

+ **Accelerator:** A letter that lets the user select the option by using the keyboard. For example, if the accelerator for an option button is C, pressing Alt+C selects the control.

+ **GroupName:** A name that identifies an option button as being associated with other option buttons with the same GroupName property.

+ **LinkedCell:** The worksheet cell that's linked to the option button. The cell displays TRUE if the control is selected or FALSE if the control is not selected.

> **Note** If your worksheet contains more than one set of option buttons, you *must* change the GroupName property for all option buttons in a particular set. Otherwise, all option buttons become part of the same set.

Scroll bar control

The scroll bar control is similar to a spin button control. The difference is that the user can drag the scroll bar's button to change the control's value in larger increments. Figure 38-11 shows a worksheet with three scroll bar controls. These scroll bars are used to change the color in the rectangle objects. The value of the scroll bars determines the red, green, or blue component of the rectangle's color. This example uses a few simple macros to change the colors.

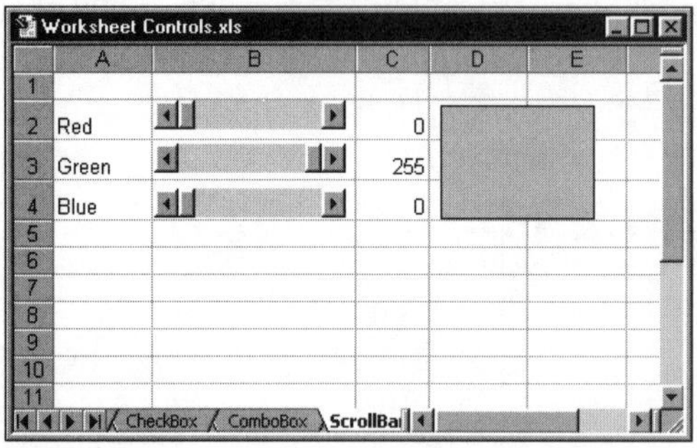

Figure 38-11: This worksheet has several scroll bar controls.

The following is a description of the most useful properties of scroll bar control:

✦ **Value:** The current value of the control.

✦ **Min:** The minimum value for the control.

✦ **Max:** The maximum value for the control.

✦ **LinkedCell:** The worksheet cell that displays the value of the control.

✦ **SmallChange:** The amount that the control's value is changed by a click.

✦ **LargeChange:** The amount that the control's value is changed by clicking on either side of the button.

The scroll bar control is most useful for selecting a value that extends across a wide range of possible values. If you use a linked cell for a spin button, it's important to understand that the worksheet is recalculated every time the value of the control is changed. Therefore, if the user changes the value from 0 to 12, the worksheet gets calculated 12 times. If your worksheet takes a long time to calculate, you may want to reconsider using this control.

Spin button control

The spin button control lets the user select a value by clicking on the control, which has two arrows (one to increase the value and the other to decrease the value). Figure 38-12 shows a worksheet that uses several spin button controls. Each control is linked to the cell to the right. As you can see, a spin button can display either horizontally or vertically.

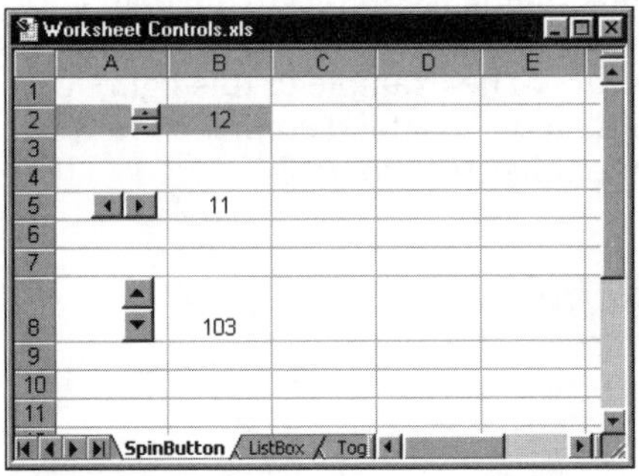

Figure 38-12: Spin button controls in a worksheet.

The following is a description of the most useful properties of a spin button control:

 ✦ **Value:** The current value of the control.

 ✦ **Min:** The minimum value of the control.

 ✦ **Max:** The maximum value of the control.

 ✦ **LinkedCell:** The worksheet cell that displays the value of the control.

 ✦ **SmallChange:** The amount that the control's value is changed by a click. Usually, this property is set to 1, but you can make it any value.

If you use a linked cell for a spin button, it's important to understand that the worksheet is recalculated every time the value of the control is changed. Therefore, if the user changes the value from 0 to 12, the worksheet gets calculated 12 times. If your worksheet takes a long time to calculate, you may want to reconsider using this control.

Text box controls

On the surface, a text box control may not seem useful. After all, it simply contains text — you can usually use worksheet cells to get text input. In fact, text box controls are useful not so much for input control but for output control. Because a text box can have scroll bars, you can use a text box to display a great deal of information in a small area.

Figure 38-13 shows an example of a text box that is used to provide help information. The user can use the scroll bar to read the text. The advantage is that the text uses only a small amount of screen space. The example in this figure uses three controls: the text box, a label control, and a disabled command button control (which provides a backdrop for the other two controls).

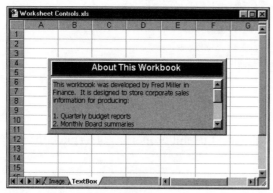

Figure 38-13: This worksheet uses a text box to display help information.

The following is a description of the most useful properties of text box control:

✦ **AutoSize:** Determines whether the control adjusts its size automatically, depending on the amount of text.

✦ **IntegralHeight:** If True, the height of the text box adjusts automatically to display full lines of text when the list is scrolled vertically. If False, the list box may display partial lines of text when it is scrolled vertically.

✦ **MaxLength:** The maximum number of characters allowed in the text box. If 0, there is no limit on the number of characters.

✦ **MultiLine:** If True, the text box can display more than one line of text.

✦ **TextAlign:** Determines how the text is aligned in the text box.

✦ **WordWrap:** Determines if the control allows word wrap.

✦ **ScrollBars:** Determines the type of scroll bars for the control: horizontal, vertical, both, or none.

Toggle button control

A toggle button control has two states: on or off. Clicking on the button toggles between these two states, and the button changes its appearance. Its value is either True (pressed) or False (not pressed). You can often use a toggle button in place of a check box control.

Summary

In this chapter, I describe how to add ActiveX controls to a worksheet and how to use these controls to make it easy for the user to provide data that's used in a worksheet.

✦   ✦   ✦

Creating User-Oriented Applications

My philosophy about learning to write Excel macros
places heavy emphasis on examples. I've found that
a well-thought-out example often communicates a concept
much better than a lengthy description of the underlying
theory. In this book, I chose to avoid a painstaking description of every nuance of VBA. I take this approach for two
reasons. First, space limitations prohibit such a discussion.
But more to the point, the VBA language is described very
well in Excel's online help system.

This chapter consists of several examples that demonstrate
common VBA techniques. You may be able to use some of the
examples directly. But in most cases, you must adapt them to
your own needs. I organize these examples into the following
categories:

✦ Working with ranges

✦ Changing Excel's settings

✦ Working with graphic objects

✦ Working with charts

✦ Learning ways to speed your VBA code

All subroutines and functions in this chapter can be found in
a workbook that can be downloaded from this book's Web site.

Web
site

Working with Ranges

Most of what you do in VBA probably involves worksheet ranges. When you work with range objects, keep the following points in mind:

✦ Your VBA code doesn't need to select a range to do something with the range.

✦ If your code does select a range, its worksheet must be activkZ

✦ The macro recorder doesn't always generate the most efficient code. Often, you can use the recorder to create your macro and then edit the code to make it more efficient.

✦ It's a good idea to use named ranges in your VBA code. For example, a reference such as Range ("Total") is better than Range ("D45"). In the latter case, you would need to modify the macro if you added a row above row 45.

✦ The macro recorder doesn't record keystrokes that are used to select a range. For example, if you record Ctrl+Shift+right-arrow key to select to the end of a row, you find that Excel records the actual range selected.

✦ If you create a macro that loops through each cell in the current range selection, be aware that the user can select entire columns or rows. In most cases, you don't want to loop through every cell in the selection. You need to create a subset of the selection that consists only of nonblank cells.

✦ Be aware that Excel allows multiple selections. For example, you can select a range, press Ctrl, and select another range. You can test for this in your macro and take appropriate actions.

The examples in the following sections demonstrate these points.

Copying a range

Copying a range is a frequent activity in macros. When you turn on the macro recorder and copy a range from A1:A5 to B1:B5, you get a VBA macro like this:

```
Sub CopyRange()
 Range("A1:A5").Select
 Selection.Copy
 Range("B1").Select
 ActiveSheet.Paste
 Application.CutCopyMode = False
End Sub
```

This macro works, but it's not the most efficient way to copy a range. You can accomplish exactly the same result with the following one-line macro:

```
Sub CopyRange2()
 Range("A1:A5").Copy Range("B1")
End Sub
```

This takes advantage of the fact that the Copy method can use an argument that specifies the destination. Information such as this is available in the online help system.

The example demonstrates that the macro recorder doesn't always generate the most efficient code.

As you see, it's not necessary to select an object to work with it. Note that Macro2 doesn't select a range; therefore, the active cell doesn't change when this macro is executed.

Copying a variable-size range

Often, you want to copy a range of cells in which the exact row and column dimensions are unknown.

Figure 39-1 shows a range on a worksheet. This range consists of a number of rows, and the number of rows can change from day to day. Because the exact range address is unknown at any given time, writing a macro to copy the range can be challenging.

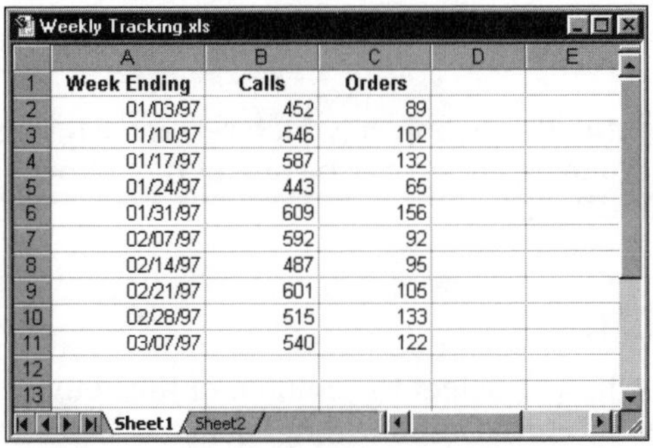

	A	B	C	D	E
1	Week Ending	Calls	Orders		
2	01/03/97	452	89		
3	01/10/97	546	102		
4	01/17/97	587	132		
5	01/24/97	443	65		
6	01/31/97	609	156		
7	02/07/97	592	92		
8	02/14/97	487	95		
9	02/21/97	601	105		
10	02/28/97	515	133		
11	03/07/97	540	122		
12					
13					

Figure 39-1: This range can consist of any number of rows.

The macro that follows demonstrates how to copy this range from Sheet1 to Sheet2 (beginning at cell A1). It uses the CurrentRegion property, which returns a range object that corresponds to the active block of cells. This is equivalent to choosing Edit➪Go To, clicking on the Special button, and selecting the Current Region option.

```
Sub CopyCurrentRegion()
 Range("A1").CurrentRegion.Copy
 Sheets("Sheet2").Select
 Range("A1").Select
 ActiveSheet.Paste
 Sheets("Sheet1").Select
 Application.CutCopyMode = False
End Sub
```

Selecting to the end of a row or column

You've probably gotten into the habit of using key combinations such as
Ctrl+Shift+right-arrow key and Ctrl+Shift+down-arrow key to select from the active
cell to the end of a row or column. You may be surprised to discover that these
types of keystroke combinations do not get recorded by the macro recorder.
Rather, the address of the actual range selected is what gets recorded. As I
describe in the preceding section, you can use the CurrentRegion property to
select an entire block. But suppose you want to select one column from a block
of cells?

Fortunately, VBA can accommodate this type of action. The following VBA subroutine selects the range beginning at the active cell and extending down to the last
cell in the column. When the range is selected, you can do whatever you want with
it — copy it, move it, format it, and so on.

```
Sub SelectDown()
 Range(ActiveCell, ActiveCell.End(xlDown)).Select
End Sub
```

This example uses the End method of the Range object, which returns a Range
object. The End method takes one argument, which can be any of the following
constants: xlUp, xlDown, xlToLeft, or xlToRight.

Selecting a row or column

The macro that follows demonstrates how to select the column of the active cell. It
uses the EntireColumn property, which returns a range that consists of a column.

```
Sub SelectColumn()
 ActiveCell.EntireColumn.Select
End Sub
```

As you may suspect, there's also an EntireRow property that returns a range that
consists of a row.

If you want to perform an operation on all cells in the selected column, you don't
need to select the column. For example, the following subroutine makes all cells
bold in the row that contains the active cell:

```
Sub MakeRowBold()
 ActiveCell.EntireRow.Font.Bold = True
End Sub
```

Moving a range

Moving a range consists of cutting it to the Clipboard and then pasting it to another area. If you record your actions while performing a move operation, the macro recorder generates code as follows:

```
Sub MoveRange()
 Range("A1:C6").Select
 Selection.Cut
 Range("A10").Select
 ActiveSheet.Paste
End Sub
```

As I demonstrate with copying earlier in this chapter, this is not the most efficient way to move a range of cells. In fact, you can do it with a single VBA statement, as follows:

```
Sub MoveRange2()
 Range("A1:C6").Cut Range("A10")
End Sub
```

This takes advantage of the fact that the Cut method can use an argument that specifies the destination.

Looping through a range efficiently

Many macros perform an operation on each cell in a range, or they may perform selective actions based on the content of each cell. These operations usually involve a For-Next loop that processes each cell in the range.

The following example demonstrates how to loop through a range. In this case, the range is the current selection. In this example, *Cell* is a variable name that refers to the cell being processed. Within the For-Next loop, the single statement evaluates the cell and changes its font color if the cell value is negative (vbRed is a built-in constant that represents the color red).

```
Sub ProcessCells()
 For Each Cell In Selection
 If Cell.Value < 0 Then Cell.Font.Color = vbRed
 Next Cell
End Sub
```

The preceding example works, but what if the selection consists of an entire column or an entire range? This is not uncommon, because Excel lets you perform operations on entire columns or rows. But in this case, the macro seems to take forever because it loops through each cell — even those that are blank. What's needed is a way to process only the nonblank cells.

This can be accomplished using the SelectSpecial method. In the following example, the SelectSpecial method is used to create two new objects: the subset of the selection that consists of cells with constants and the subset of the selection that consists of cells with formulas. Each of these subsets is processed, with the net effect of skipping all blank cells.

```
Sub SkipBlanks()
' Ignore errors
 On Error Resume Next

' Process the constants
 Set ConstantCells = Selection.SpecialCells(xlConstants, 23)
 For Each cell In ConstantCells
 If cell.Value > 0 Then cell.Font.Color = vbRed
 Next cell

' Process the formulas
 Set FormulaCells = Selection.SpecialCells(xlFormulas, 23)
 For Each cell In FormulaCells
 If cell.Value > 0 Then cell.Font.Color = vbRed
 Next cell
 End Sub
```

The SkipBlanks subroutine works equally fast, regardless of what is selected. For example, you can select the range, select all columns in the range, select all rows in the range, or even select the entire worksheet. In all of these cases, only the cells that contain constants or values are processed. It's a vast improvement over the ProcessCells subroutine that I presented earlier.

Notice that I used the following statement in the subroutine:

```
On Error Resume Next
```

This statement causes Excel to ignore any errors that occur and to simply process the next statement. This is necessary because the SpecialCells method produces an error if no cells qualify. Normal error checking is resumed when the subroutine ends. To explicitly tell Excel to return to normal error-checking mode, use the following statement:

```
On Error GoTo 0
```

Prompting for a cell value

As I discussed in Chapter 37, you can take advantage of VBA's InputBox function to solicit a value from the user. Figure 39-2 shows an example.

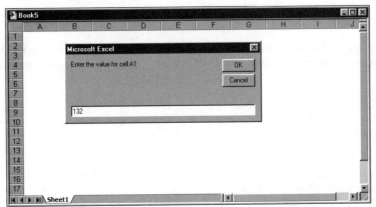

Figure 39-2: Using VBA's InputBox function to get a value from the user.

You can assign this value to a variable and use it in your subroutine. Often, however, you want to place the value into a cell. The following subroutine demonstrates how to ask the user for a value and place it into cell A1 of the active worksheet, using only one statement:

```
Sub GetValue()
  Range("A1").Value = InputBox("Enter the value for cell A1")
End Sub
```

Determining the type of selection

If your macro is designed to work with a range selection, it's important that you determine that a range is actually selected. Otherwise, the macro most likely fails. The following subroutine identifies the type of object that is currently selected:

```
Sub SelectionType()
  MsgBox TypeName(Selection)
End Sub
```

If a Range object is selected, the MsgBox displays *Range*. If your macro is designed to work only with ranges, you can use an If statement to ensure that a range is actually selected. The following is an example that beeps, displays a message, and exits the subroutine if the current selection is not a Range object:

```
Sub CheckSelection()
 If TypeName(Selection) <> "Range" Then
 Beep
 MsgBox "Select a range."
 Exit Sub
 End If
 ' ... [Other statements go here]
End Sub
```

Another way to approach this is to define a custom function that returns True if the selection is a Range object and False otherwise. The following function does just that:

```
Function IsRange(sel) As Boolean
 IsRange = False
 If TypeName(sel) = "Range" Then IsRange = True
End Function
```

If you enter the IsRange function in your module, you can rewrite the CheckSelection subroutine as follows:

```
Sub CheckSelection()
 If IsRange(Selection) Then
 ' ... [Other statements go here]
 Else
 Beep
 MsgBox "Select a range."
 Exit Sub
 End If
End Sub
```

Identifying a multiple selection

As you know, Excel allows you to make a multiple selection by pressing Ctrl while you select objects or ranges. This can cause problems with some macros; for example, you can't copy a multiple selection that consists of nonadjacent ranges. The following macro demonstrates how to determine whether the user has made a multiple selection:

```
Sub MultipleSelection()
 If Selection.Areas.Count > 1 Then
 MsgBox "Multiple selections not allowed."
 Exit Sub
 End If
 ' ... [Other statements go here]
End Sub
```

This example uses the Areas method, which returns a collection of all objects in the selection. The Count property returns the number of objects that are in the collection.

The following is a function that returns True if the selection is a multiple selection:

```
Function IsMultiple(sel) As Boolean
  IsMultiple = False
  If Selection.Areas.Count > 1 Then IsMultiple = True
End Function
```

Changing Excel's Settings

Some of the most useful macros are simple subroutines that change one or more of Excel's settings. For example, it takes quite a few actions to simply change the Recalculation mode from automatic to manual.

This section contains two examples that demonstrate how to change settings in Excel. These examples can be generalized to other operations.

Boolean settings

A Boolean setting is one that is either on or off. For example, you may want to create a macro that turns the row and column headings on and off. If you record your actions while you access the Options dialog box, you find that Excel generates the following code if you turn the headings off:

```
ActiveWindow.DisplayHeadings = False
```

It generates the following code if you turn the headings on:

```
ActiveWindow.DisplayHeadings = True
```

This may lead you to suspect that the heading display requires two macros: one to turn the headings on and one to turn them off. Actually, this isn't true. The following subroutine uses the Not operator to effectively toggle the heading display from True to False and from False to True:

```
Sub ToggleHeadings()
  If TypeName(ActiveSheet) <> "Worksheet" Then Exit Sub
  ActiveWindow.DisplayHeadings = Not
       ActiveWindow.DisplayHeadings
End Sub
```

The first statement ensures that the active sheet is a worksheet; otherwise, an error occurs (chart sheets don't have row and column headers). This technique can be used with any other settings that take on Boolean (True or False) values. For example, you can create macros to toggle sheet tab display, gridlines, and so on.

Non-Boolean settings

For non-Boolean settings, you can use the following Select Case structure. This example toggles the Calculation mode and displays a message indicating the current mode:

```
Sub ToggleCalcMode()
  Select Case Application.Calculation
  Case xlManual
  Application.Calculation = xlAutomatic
  MsgBox "Automatic Calculation Mode"
  Case xlAutomatic
  Application.Calculation = xlManual
  MsgBox "Manual Calculation Mode"
  End Select
End Sub
```

Working with Graphic Objects (Shapes)

As you know, VBA subroutines can work with any type of Excel object, including graphic objects that are embedded on a worksheet's draw layer. This section provides a few examples of using VBA to manipulate graphic objects.

Creating a text box to match a range

The following example creates a text box that is positioned precisely over the selected range of cells. This is useful if you want to make a text box that covers up a range of data.

```
Sub CreateTextBox()
  If TypeName(Selection) <> "Range" Then Exit Sub
  Set RangeSelection = Selection
' Get coordinates of range selection
  SelLeft = Selection.Left
  SelTop = Selection.Top
  SelWidth = Selection.Width
  SelHeight = Selection.Height
' Create a text box

  ActiveSheet.Shapes.AddTextbox(msoTextOrientationHorizontal, _
  SelLeft, SelTop, SelWidth, SelHeight).Select
  RangeSelection.Select
End Sub
```

The macro first checks to make sure that a range is selected. If not, the subroutine is exited with no further action. If a range is selected, the coordinates (Left, Top, Width, and Height) are assigned to four variables. These variables are then used as the arguments for the AddTextbox method of the Shapes collection.

The following is a more sophisticated version of this macro that works with a multiple selection of cells. The subroutine creates a text box for each area in the multiple selection. It uses a For-Next loop to cycle through each area in the range selection. If the range has only one area (not a multiple selection), the For-Next loop is activated only one time.

```
Sub CreateTextBox2()
  If TypeName(Selection) <> "Range" Then Exit Sub
  Set RangeSelection = Selection
  For Each Part In Selection.Areas
' Get coordinates of range selection
  SelLeft = Part.Left
  SelTop = Part.Top
  SelWidth = Part.Width
  SelHeight = Part.Height
' Create a text box

  ActiveSheet.Shapes.AddTextbox(msoTextOrientationHorizontal, _
  SelLeft, SelTop, SelWidth, SelHeight).Select
  Next Part
  RangeSelection.Select
End Sub
```

Drawing attention to a range

The example in this section is a macro that draws an AutoShape around the selected range. Figure 39-3 shows an example.

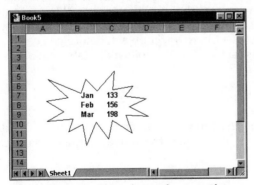

Figure 39-3: A macro draws the AutoShape around a selected range of cells.

```
Sub AddExplosion()
  If TypeName(Selection) <> "Range" Then Exit Sub
  SelLeft = Selection.Left - (Selection.Width * 0.2)
  SelTop = Selection.Top - (Selection.Height * 0.5)
  SelWidth = Selection.Width + (Selection.Width * 0.4)
  SelHeight = Selection.Height + Selection.Height
  ActiveSheet.Shapes.AddShape (msoShapeExplosion1, _
    SelLeft, SelTop, SelWidth, SelHeight).Select
  Selection.ShapeRange.Fill.Visible = msoFalse
End Sub
```

The macro begins by determining the location and size of the shape, using the selected range. The shape needs to be larger than the selected range and must be offset to the left and to the top. Therefore, the macro performs some calculations to determine the left, top, width, and height of the shape. In this example, the shape's height is twice as large as the height of the selection and 40% wider than the width of the selection. I arrived at these calculations by trial and error. In most cases, the shape is drawn in such a way that the contents of the underlying cells are completely visible. In other cases, slight adjustments are required.

After the parameters are calculated, the AutoShape is added to the active sheet. The AutoShape that's drawn by the macro is identified by a constant (msoShapeExplosion1). The final statement makes the shape transparent.

Working with Charts

Manipulating charts with VBA can be confusing, mainly because of the large number of objects involved. To get a feel for this, turn on the macro recorder, create a chart, and perform some routine chart editing. You may be surprised by the amount of code that's generated.

After you understand the objects in a chart, however, you can create some useful macros. This section presents a few macros that deal with charts. When writing macros that manipulate charts, it's important to understand some terminology. An embedded chart on a worksheet is a ChartObject object. Before you can do anything to a ChartObject, you must activate it. The following statement activates the ChartObject named Chart 1.

```
ActiveSheet.ChartObjects("Chart 1").Activate
```

Once activated, you can refer to the chart in your VBA code as the ActiveChart. If the chart is on a separate chart sheet, it becomes the active chart as soon as the chart sheet is activated.

Modifying the chart type

The first example here changes the chart type of every embedded chart on the active sheet. It makes each chart an area chart by adjusting the Type property of the ActiveChart object. A built-in constant, xlArea, represents an area chart.

```
Sub ChartType()
 For Each cht In ActiveSheet.ChartObjects
 cht.Activate
 ActiveChart.Type = xlArea
 Next cht
End Sub
```

The example uses a For-Next loop to cycle through all the ChartObject objects on the active sheet. Within the loop, the chart is activated and then the chart type is assigned a new value.

The following macro performs the same function but works on all chart sheets in the active workbook:

```
Sub ChartType2()
 For Each cht In ThisWorkbook.Charts
 cht.Activate
 ActiveChart.Type = xlArea
 Next cht
End Sub
```

Modifying properties

The following example changes the legend font for all charts that are on the active sheet. It uses a For-Next loop to process all ChartObject objects. I use the On Error statement to ignore the error that occurs if a chart does not have a legend.

```
Sub LegendMod()
 On Error Resume Next
 For Each cht In ActiveSheet.ChartObjects
 cht.Activate
 With ActiveChart.Legend.Font
 .Name = "Arial"
 .FontStyle = "Bold"
 .Size = 8
 End With
 Next cht
End Sub
```

Applying chart formatting

This example applies several different formatting types to the active chart. A chart must be activated before executing this macro. You activate an embedded chart by selecting it. Activate a chart on a chart sheet by activating the chart sheet.

```
Sub ChartMods()
        On Error Resume Next
  ActiveChart.Type = xlArea
  ActiveChart.ChartArea.Font.Name = "Arial"
  ActiveChart.ChartArea.Font.FontStyle = "Regular"
  ActiveChart.ChartArea.Font.Size = 9
  ActiveChart.PlotArea.Interior.ColorIndex = xlNone
  ActiveChart.Axes(xlValue).TickLabels.Font.Bold = True
  ActiveChart.Axes(xlCategory).TickLabels.Font.Bold = True
  ActiveChart.Legend.Position = xlBottom
End Sub
```

I created this macro by recording my actions as I formatted a chart. Then I cleaned up the recorded code by removing irrelevant lines.

VBA Speed Tips

VBA is fast, but it's often not fast enough. This section presents some programming examples that you can use to help speed your macros.

Turning off screen updating

You've probably noticed that, when you execute a macro, you can watch everything that occurs in the macro. Sometimes this is instructive, but after you get the macro working properly, it can be annoying and slow things considerably.

Fortunately, there's a way to disable the normal screen updating that occurs when you execute a macro. Insert the following statement to turn screen updating off:

```
Application.ScreenUpdating = False
```

If, at any point during the macro, you want the user to see the results of the macro, use the following statement to turn screen updating back on:

```
Application.ScreenUpdating = True
```

Preventing alert messages

One of the benefits of using a macro is that you can perform a series of actions automatically. You can start a macro and then get a cup of coffee while Excel does its thing. Some operations cause Excel to display messages that must be attended to, however. For example, if your macro deletes a sheet, you see the message that is shown in the dialog box in Figure 39-4. These types of messages mean that you can't execute your macro unattended.

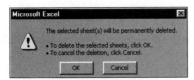

Figure 39-4: You can instruct Excel not to display these types of alerts while a macro is running.

To avoid these alert messages, insert the following VBA statement:

```
Application.DisplayAlerts = False
```

When the subroutine ends, the DisplayAlerts property is automatically reset to True (its normal state).

Simplifying object references

As you probably have discovered, references to objects can get very lengthy — especially if your code refers to an object that's not on the active sheet or in the active workbook. For example, a fully qualified reference to a Range object may look like this:

```
Workbooks("MyBook").Worksheets("Sheet1").Range("IntRate")
```

If your macro uses this range frequently, you may want to create an object variable by using the Set command. For example, to assign this Range object to an object variable named *Rate,* use the following statement:

```
Set Rate= Workbooks("MyBook").Worksheets("Sheet1").
        Range("IntRate")
```

After this variable is defined, you can use the variable *Rate* instead of the lengthy reference.

Besides simplifying your coding, using object variables also speeds your macros quite a bit. I've seen some macros execute twice as fast after creating object variables.

Declaring variable types

Usually, you don't have to worry about the type of data that's assigned to a variable. Excel handles all these details behind the scenes. For example, if you have a variable named *MyVar*, you can assign a number or any type to it. You can even assign a text string to it later in the procedure.

But if you want your procedures to execute as fast as possible, you should tell Excel in advance what type of data is going be assigned to each of your variables. This is known as declaring a variables type.

Table 39-1 lists all the data types that are supported by VBA. This table also lists the number of bytes that each type uses and the approximate range of possible values.

Table 39-1		
Data Types		
Data Type	*Bytes Used*	*Approximate Range of Values*
Byte	1	0 to 255
Boolean	2	True or False
Integer	2	−32,768 to 32,767
Long (long integer)	4	−2,147,483,648 to 2,147,483,647
Single (single-precision floating-point)	4 3.	−3.4E38 to −1.4E−45 for negative values; 1.4E−45 to 4E38 for positive values
Double (double-precision floating-point)	8 1	−1.7E308 to −4.9E−324 for negative values; 4.9E−324 to .7E308 for positive values
Currency (scaled integer)	8	−9.2E14 to 9.2E14
Decimal	14	+/−7.9E28 with no decimal point;
Date	8	January 1, 100 to December 31, 9999
Object	4	Any Object reference
String (variable-length)	10 + string length	0 to approximately 2 billion
String (fixed-length)	Length of string	1 to approximately 65,400
Variant (with numbers)	16	Any numeric value up to the range of a Double
Variant (with characters)	22 + string length	Same range as for variable-length String
User-defined (using Type)	Number required by elements	The range of each element is the same as the range of its data type.

If you don't declare a variable, Excel uses the Variant data type. In general, it's best to use the data type that uses the smallest number of bytes yet can still handle all the data assigned to it. When VBA works with data, execution speed is a function of the number of bytes that VBA has at its disposal. In other words, the fewer bytes that are used by data, the faster VBA can access and manipulate the data.

To declare a variable, use the Dim statement before you use the variable for the first time. For example, to declare the variable *Units* as an integer, use the following statement:

```
Dim Units as Integer
```

To declare the variable *UserName* as a string, use the following statement:

```
Dim UserName as String
```

If you know that *UserName* can never exceed 20 characters, you can declare it as a fixed-length string as follows:

```
Dim UserName as String * 20
```

If you declare a variable within a procedure, the declaration is valid only within that procedure. If you declare a variable outside of any procedures (but before the first procedure), the variable is valid in all procedures in the module.

If you use an object variable (as described previously), you can declare the variable as an object data type. The following is an example:

```
Dim Rate as Range
Set Rate = Workbooks("MyBook").Worksheets("Sheet1").
     Range("IntRate")
```

To force yourself to declare all the variables that you use, insert the following statement at the top of your module:

```
Option Explicit
```

If you use this statement, Excel displays an error message if it encounters a variable that hasn't been declared.

Summary

In this chapter, I present several examples of VBA code that work with ranges, Excel's settings, graphic objects, and charts. In addition, I discuss techniques that you can use to make your VBA macros run faster.

✦　　✦　　✦

Creating Custom Excel Add-Ins

For developers, one of the most useful features in Excel is the capability to create add-ins. In this chapter, I discuss this concept and provide a practical example of creating an add-in.

What Is an Add-In?

Generally speaking, a spreadsheet *add-in* is something that's added to the spreadsheet to give it additional functionality. Excel 97 includes several add-ins, including the Analysis ToolPak, AutoSave, and Solver. Some add-ins (such as the Analysis ToolPak) provide new worksheet functions that can be used in formulas. Usually, the new features blend in well with the original interface, so they appear to be part of the program.

Excel's approach to add-ins is quite powerful, because any knowledgeable Excel user can create add-ins from XLS workbooks. An Excel add-in is basically a different form of an XLS workbook file. Any XLS file can be converted into an add-in, but not every workbook is a good candidate for an add-in. Add-ins are always hidden, so you can't display worksheets or chart sheets that are contained in an add-in. But you can access its VBA subroutines and functions and display dialog boxes that are contained on dialog sheets.

The following are some typical uses for Excel add-ins:

   ✦ **To store one or more custom worksheet functions.**
      When the add-in is loaded, the functions can be used like any built-in worksheet function.

✦ **To store Excel utilities.** VBA is ideal for creating general- purpose utilities that extend the power of Excel. My Power Utility Pak is an example of this.

✦ **To store proprietary macros.** If you don't want end users seeing (or modifying) your macros, store the macros in an add-in. The macros can be used, but they can't be viewed or changed.

As I noted, Excel ships with several useful add-ins (see the sidebar "Add-ins that are included with Excel"), and you can acquire other add-ins from third-party vendors or online services. In addition, Excel includes the tools to let you create your own add-ins. I explain how to do this later in the chapter, but first I need to cover some background.

Working with Add-Ins

The best way to work with add-ins is to use Excel's add-in manager, which you access by selecting <u>T</u>ools⇨Add-<u>I</u>ns. This command displays the dialog box that is shown in Figure 40-1. The list box contains all of the add-ins that Excel knows about. Those that are checked are currently open. You can open and close add-ins from this dialog box by selecting or unselecting the check boxes.

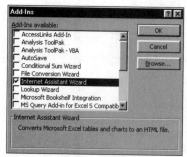

Figure 40-1: The Add-Ins dialog box.

> **Note** Most add-in files can also be opened by selecting <u>F</u>ile⇨<u>O</u>pen. You find that after an add-in is opened, however, you can't choose <u>F</u>ile⇨<u>C</u>lose to close it. The only way to remove the add-in is to exit and restart Excel or to write a macro to close the add-in.

When an add-in is opened, you may or may not notice anything different. In nearly every case, however, some change is made to the menu — either a new menu or one or more new menu items on an existing menu. For example, when you open the Analysis ToolPak add-in, this add-in gives you a new menu item on the <u>T</u>ools menu: <u>D</u>ata Analysis. When you open my Power Utility Pak add-in, you get a new <u>U</u>tilities menu, which is located between the <u>D</u>ata and <u>W</u>indow menus.

Add-ins that are included with Excel

The following is a list of the add-ins that are included with Excel. Depending on how Excel was installed, you may not have access to all these add-ins. To install missing add-ins, rerun Excel's Setup program (or the Microsoft Office Setup program).

Analysis ToolPak: Statistical and engineering tools, plus new worksheet functions.

Analysis ToolPak — VBA: VBA functions for the Analysis ToolPak.

AutoSave: Automatically saves your workbook at a time interval that you specify.

Conditional Sum Wizard: Helps you create formulas that add values based on a condition.

File Conversion Wizard: Converts a group of files to Excel format.

Internet Assistant Wizard: Converts ranges and charts to HTML documents.

Lookup Wizard: Helps you create formulas that look up data in a list.

Microsoft AccessLinks Add-In: Lets you use Microsoft Access forms and reports with Excel worksheets (Access 97 must be installed on your system).

Microsoft Bookshelf Integration: Lets you access Microsoft Bookshelf from Excel.

MS Query Add-In for Excel 5 Compatibility: Works with Microsoft Query to bring external data into a worksheet.

ODBC Add-In: Lets you use ODBC functions to connect to external data sources directly.

Report Manager: Prints reports that consist of a set sequence of views and scenarios.

Solver Add-In: A tool that helps you use a variety of numeric methods for equation solving and optimization.

Template Utilities: Utilities that are used by the Spreadsheet Solutions templates. This is loaded automatically when you use one of these templates.

Template Wizard with Data Tracking: Helps you create custom templates.

Update Add-in Links: Updates links to MS Excel 4.0 add-ins to directly access the new built-in functionality.

Web Form Wizard: Sets up a form on a Web Server to send data to a database.

Why Create Add-Ins?

Most Excel users have no need to create add-ins. But if you develop spreadsheets for others — or if you simply want to get the most out of Excel — you may be interested in pursuing this topic further.

There are several reasons why you may want to convert your XLS application to an add-in:

✦ **To prevent access to your code.** When you distribute an application as an add-in, the end users can't view the sheets in the workbook. If you use proprietary techniques in your VBA code, this can prevent it from being copied.

✦ **To avoid confusion.** If an end user loads your application as an add-in, the file is not visible — and is therefore less likely to confuse novice users or get in the way. Unlike a hidden XLS workbook, an add-in can't be unhidden.

✦ **To simplify access to worksheet functions.** Custom worksheet functions that are stored in an add-in don't require the workbook name qualifier. For example, if you have a custom function named MOVAVG stored in a workbook named `Newfuncs.xls`, you would have to use a syntax such as the following to use this function in a different workbook:

```
=NEWFUNC.XLS!MOVAVG(A1:A50)
```

But if this function is stored in an add-in file that's open, the syntax is much simpler because you don't need to include the file reference:

```
=MOVAVG(A1:A50)
```

✦ **To provide easier access.** After you identify the location of your add-in, it appears in the Add-Ins dialog box, with a friendly name and a description of what it does.

✦ **To permit better control over loading.** Add-ins can be opened automatically when Excel starts, regardless of the directory in which they are stored.

✦ **To omit prompts when unloading.** When an add-in is closed, the user never sees the *Save change in...?* prompt.

Creating an Add-In

Although any workbook can be converted to an add-in, not all workbooks benefit by this. In fact, workbooks that consist only of worksheets (that is, not macros or custom dialog boxes) become unusable because add-ins are hidden.

The only types of workbooks that benefit from conversion to an add-in are those with macros. For example, you may have a workbook that consists of general-purpose macros (subroutines and functions). This type of workbook makes an ideal add-in.

Creating an add-in is quite simple. These steps describe how to create an add-in from a normal workbook file:

1. **Develop your application, and make sure that everything works properly.** Don't forget to include a method to execute the macro or macros. You may want to add a new menu item (I describe how to do this later in the chapter).

2. **Test the application by executing it when a *different* workbook is active.** This simulates its behavior when it's an add-in, because an add-in is never the active workbook. You may find that some references no longer work. For example, the following statement works fine when the code resides in the active workbook but fails when a different workbook is active:

```
Dialogsheets("My Dialog").Show
```

You could qualify the reference with the name of the workbook object, like this:

```
Workbooks("MYWORKBOOK.XLS"). Dialog sheets("My Dialog").Show
```

This method is not recommended because the name of the workbook changes when it's converted to an add-in. The solution is to use the `ThisWorkbook` qualifier, as follows

```
ThisWorkbook.Dialog sheets("My Dialog").Show
```

3. **Select File⇨Summary Info, and enter a brief descriptive title in the Title field and a longer description in the Comments field.** This step is not required, but it makes it easier to use the add-in.

4. **Protect the workbook from viewing.** You do this in the Visual Basic Editor, using the Tools⇨Properties command.

5. **Save the workbook as an XLA file by selecting File⇨Save As.**

After creating the add-in, you need to test it. Select Tools⇨Add-Ins, and use the Browse button in the Add-Ins dialog box to locate the XLA file that you created in Step 5. This installs the add-in. The Add-in dialog box uses the title and description that you provided in Step 3.

Unlike previous versions of Excel, you can continue to modify the macros and user forms in the XLA version of your file, and save your changes in the Visual Basic Editor. In other words, it's not necessary to make changes to the XLS version and then resave the workbook as an add-in.

An Add-In Example

In this section, I discuss the steps that are used in creating a useful add-in. This add-in displays a dialog box (see Figure 40-2) that lets the user quickly change a number of Excel's settings. Although these settings can be changed in the Options dialog box, the add-in makes these changes interactively. For example, if the Grid Lines check box is unselected, the gridlines are removed immediately.

Figure 40-2: This dialog box lets the user change a number of Excel's settings interactively.

Both the XLS and XLA versions of this file are available from this book's Web site.

Setting up the workbook

This workbook consists of one worksheet, which is empty. Although the worksheet is not used, it must be present because every workbook must have at least one sheet.

Use the Visual Basic Editor to insert a VBA module (named Module1) and a user form (named UserForm1). The ThisWorkbook object contains a macro that adds a menu item to the Tools menu when the workbook (add-in) is opened. Another macro removes the menu item when the workbook (add-in) is closed.

Module1

The macro listed below is contained in the Module1 module. This subroutine ensures that a worksheet is active. If so, it displays the dialog box that is contained in UserForm1.

```
Sub ShowToggleSettingsDialog()
   If TypeName(ActiveSheet) <> "Worksheet" Then
     MsgBox "A worksheet must be active.", vbInformation
     Exit Sub
   End If
   UserForm1.Show
End Sub
```

ThisWorkbook

The ThisWorkbook object contains the two subroutines that are listed below:

```
Private Sub Workbook_Open()
   Set NewMenuItem = Application.CommandBars("Worksheet Menu
      Bar") _
     .Controls("Tools").Controls.Add
   With NewMenuItem
     .Caption = "Toggle Settings..."
     .BeginGroup = True
     .OnAction = "ShowToggleSettingsDialog"
   End With
End Sub
```

```
Private Sub Workbook_BeforeClose(Cancel As Boolean)
   On Error Resume Next
   Application.CommandBars("Worksheet Menu
      Bar").Controls("Tools"). _
    Controls("Toggle Settings...").Delete
End Sub
```

The Workbook_Open subroutine adds a menu item (Toggle Settings) to the bottom of the Tools menu on the Worksheet Menu Bar. This subroutine is executed when the workbook (add-in) is opened.

The Workbook_BeforeClose subroutine is executed when the add-in is closed. This subroutine removes the Toggle Settings menu item from the Tools menu.

UserForm1

Figure 40-3 shows the UserForm1 form. This form has ten controls: nine check boxes and one command button. I gave the controls descriptive names and set the Accelerator property so that the controls would display an accelerator key (for keyboard users).

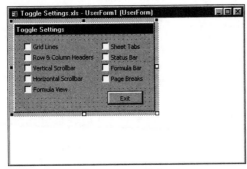

Figure 40-3: The custom dialog box.

The UserForm1 object contains the event-handler subroutines for the objects that are on the form. The following subroutine is executed before the dialog box is displayed:

```
Private Sub UserForm_Initialize()
    cbGridlines = ActiveWindow.DisplayGridlines
    cbHeaders = ActiveWindow.DisplayHeadings
    cbVerticalScrollbar = ActiveWindow.DisplayVerticalScrollBar
    cbHorizontalScrollbar =
        ActiveWindow.DisplayHorizontalScrollBar
    cbFormulaView = ActiveWindow.DisplayFormulas
    cbSheetTabs = ActiveWindow.DisplayWorkbookTabs
    cbStatusBar = Application.DisplayStatusBar
    cbFormulaBar = Application.DisplayFormulaBar
    cbPageBreaks = ActiveSheet.DisplayPageBreaks
End Sub
```

The UserForm_Initialize subroutine adjusts the settings of the check box controls in the dialog box to correspond to the current settings. For example, if the worksheet is displaying gridlines, ActiveWindow.DisplayGridlines returns True. This value is assigned to the cbGridlines check box — which means that the check box is displayed selected.

Each check box also has an event-handler subroutine that is executed when the control is clicked on. These subroutines are listed below. Each subroutine makes the appropriate changes. For example, if the Grid Lines check box is selected, the DisplayGridlines property is set to correspond to the check box.

```
Private Sub cbGridlines_Click on()
    ActiveWindow.DisplayGridlines = cbGridlines
End Sub
Private Sub cbHeaders_Click on()
    ActiveWindow.DisplayHeadings = cbHeaders
End Sub
Private Sub cbVerticalScrollbar_Click on()
    ActiveWindow.DisplayVerticalScrollBar = cbVerticalScrollbar
End Sub
Private Sub cbHorizontalScrollbar_Click on()
    ActiveWindow.DisplayHorizontalScrollBar =
        cbHorizontalScrollbar
End Sub
Private Sub cbFormulaView_Click on()
    ActiveWindow.DisplayFormulas = cbFormulaView
End Sub
Private Sub cbSheetTabs_Click on()
    ActiveWindow.DisplayWorkbookTabs = cbSheetTabs
End Sub
Private Sub cbStatusBar_Click on()
    Application.DisplayStatusBar = cbStatusBar
End Sub
Private Sub cbFormulaBar_Click on()
    Application.DisplayFormulaBar = cbFormulaBar
End Sub
Private Sub cbPageBreaks_Click on()
    ActiveSheet.DisplayPageBreaks = cbPageBreaks
End Sub
```

The UserForm1 object has one additional event-handler subroutine for the Exit button. This subroutine, listed as follows, simply closes the dialog box:

```
Private Sub ExitButton_Click on()
  Unload UserForm1
End Sub
```

Testing the workbook

Before converting this workbook to an add-in, it's necessary to test it. Testing should be done when a different workbook is active to simulate what happens when the workbook is an add-in. Remember, an add-in is never the active sheet.

To test it, I saved the workbook, closed it, and then reopened it. When the workbook was opened, the Workbook_Open subroutine was executed. This subroutine added the new menu item to the Tools menu. Figure 40-4 shows how this looks.

Selecting Tools➪Toggle Setting displays the dialog box that is shown in Figure 40-5.

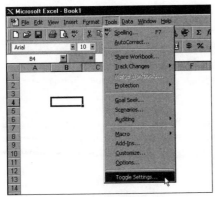

Figure 40-4: The Tools menu displays a new menu item, Toggle Settings.

Figure 40-5: The custom dialog box, in action.

Adding descriptive information

This step is recommended but not necessary. Choose File⇨Properties to bring up the Properties dialog box. Then click on the Summary tab, as shown in Figure 40-6.

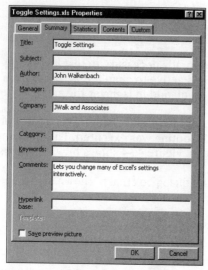

Figure 40-6: Use the Properties dialog box to enter descriptive information about your add-in.

Enter a title for the add-in in the Title field. This is the text that appears in the Add-Ins dialog box. In the Comments field, enter a description. This information appears at the bottom of the Add-Ins dialog box when the add-in is selected.

Protecting the project

One advantage of an add-in is that it can be protected so that others can't see the source code. To protect the project, follow these steps:

1. Activate the Visual Basic Editor.
2. In the Project window, click on the project.
3. Select Tools⇨[project name] Properties.

   VBE displays its Project Properties dialog box.
4. Click on the Protection tab (see Figure 40-7).
5. Select the Lock project for viewing check box.
6. Enter a password (twice) for the project.
7. Click on OK.

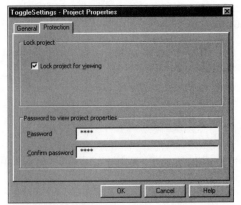

Figure 40-7: The Project Properties dialog box.

Creating the add-in

To save the workbook as an add-in, activate Excel and choose File➪Save As. Select Microsoft Excel Add-In (*.xla) from the Save as Type drop-down list. Enter a name for the add-in file, and click on OK.

Opening the add-in

To avoid confusion, close the XLS workbook before opening the add-in that was created from it. Then select Tools➪Add-Ins. Excel displays its Add-Ins dialog box. Click on the Browse button, and locate the add-in that you just created. After you do so, the Add-Ins dialog box displays the add-in in its list. Notice that the information that you provided in the Properties dialog box appears here (see Figure 40-8). Click on OK to close the dialog box and open the add-in.

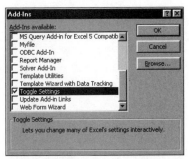

Figure 40-8: The Add-Ins dialog box, with the new add-in selected.

When the add-in is open, the Tools menu displays a new menu item (Toggle Settings) that executes the ShowToggleSettingsDialog subroutine in the add-in.

If you activate the VBE window, you find that the add-in is listed in the Project window. However, you can't make any modifications unless you provide the password.

Summary

In this chapter, I discuss the concept of add-ins — files that add new capabilities to Excel. I explain how to work with add-ins and why you may want to create custom add-ins. I close the chapter with an example of an add-in that makes it easy to toggle a number of Excel's settings.

✦   ✦   ✦

Appendixes

P A R T

VII

◆ ◆ ◆ ◆

In This Part

Appendix A
Using Online Help:
A Primer

Appendix B
Worksheet Func-
tion Reference

Appendix C
Excel's Shortcut
Keys

Appendix D
What's at the
Web Site

◆ ◆ ◆ ◆

Using Online Help: A Primer

Excel's online help system has always been good. But the help available with Excel 97 is better than ever. However, the online help system can be a bit intimidating for beginners, because you can get help in many ways. This appendix assists you in getting the most out of this valuable resource.

Why Online Help?

In the early days of personal computing, software programs usually came bundled with bulky manuals that described how to use the product. Some products included rudimentary help that could be accessed online. Over the years, that situation gradually changed. Now, online help is usually the *primary* source of documentation, which may be augmented by a written manual.

After you become accustomed to it, you'll find that online help (if it's done well) offers many advantages over written manuals:

- ✦ There's no need to lug around a manual — especially important for laptop users who do their work on the road.

- ✦ You don't have to thumb through a separate book, which often has a confusing index.

- ✦ You can search for specific words and then select a topic that's appropriate to your question.

- ✦ In some cases (for example, writing VBA code), you can copy examples from the Help window and paste them into your application.

- ✦ Help sometimes includes embedded buttons that you can click on to go directly to the command that you need.

Types of Help

Excel offers several types of online help:

✦ **Tooltips.** Move the mouse pointer over a toolbar button and the button's name appears.

✦ **Office Assistant.** The animated Office Assistant monitors your actions while you work. If there is a more efficient way of performing an operation, the Assistant can tell you about it.

✦ **Dialog box help.** When a dialog box is displayed, click on the Help button in the title bar (it has a question mark on it) and then click on any part of the dialog box. Excel pops up a description of the selected control. Figure A-1 shows an example.

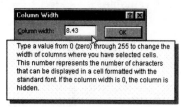

Figure A-1: Getting a description of a dialog box control.

✦ **"What's This" Help.** Press Shift+F1, and the mouse pointer turns into a question mark. You can then click on virtually any part of the screen to get a description of the object.

✦ **1-2-3 help.** The Help⇨Lotus 1-2-3 Help command provides help designed for those who are familiar with 1-2-3's commands.

✦ **Internet-based help.** You can access a variety of Internet resources directly from Excel.

✦ **Detailed help.** This is what's usually considered online help. As you'll see, there are several ways to locate a particular help topic.

Accessing Help

When working with Excel 97, you can access the online help system by using the Help menu, shown in Figure A-2. I describe the various options in the sections that follow.

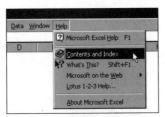

Figure A-2: The Help menu.

Microsoft Excel Help

Selecting this menu item displays the Office Assistant, shown in Figure A-3. Type a brief description of the type of help you're looking for, and the Assistant displays a list of help topics. Chances are, one of these topics will lead to the help you need.

Figure A-3: The Office Assistant.

The information you type doesn't have to be in the form of a question. Rather, you can simply enter one or more keywords that describe the topic. For example, if you want to find out how to turn off gridlines, you can type **gridlines off**.

Tip   You have a great deal of control over the Office Assistant. Right-click on the Assistant and select Options from the shortcut menu. Excel displays the dialog box shown in Figure A-4. The Gallery tab lets you select a new character for the assistant. The Options tab lets you determine how the Assistant behaves. For example, if you find that the Office Assistant is distracting, you can turn off all the options.

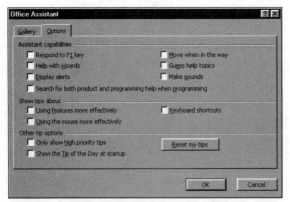

Figure A-4: Use this dialog box to control the Office Assistant's behavior.

Contents and Index

The Help⇨Contents and Index command displays the main Excel help window, which has three tabs. Each of these tabs provides a different way to find the information you need.

Contents tab

The Contents tab is shown in Figure A-5. This panel is arranged as an outline and lets you access general information. When you double-click on a book icon, it expands to show subtopics (each with a Question-Mark icon). Double-click on it again and the subtopics are collapsed. Double-click on a Question-mark icon, and you get a new window that describes the topic.

Figure A-5: The Contents tab.

To return to the original Help Topics dialog box, click on the Help Topics button.

Index tab

Figure A-6 shows the Index panel of the Help Topics dialog box. The topics are arranged alphabetically, much like an index for a book. You can enter the first few letters in the box at the top to quickly scroll to an index entry.

Figure A-6: The Index panel of the Help Topics dialog box.

When you double-click on an index entry, Excel displays a list of all applicable topics in a dialog box. Double-click on a topic to get to the Help Topics window.

Find tab

The Find panel lets you locate help topics that contain a particular word or words. The first time that you access this feature, there will be a slight delay as the index file is created. Figure A-7 shows the Find panel of the Help Topics dialog box. To help you narrow down your search, you can control several options by clicking on the Options button.

Figure A-7: The Find panel of the Help Topics dialog box.

Mastering Help

The information provided in this appendix gets you started using online help. Everyone develops his or her own style for accessing this help, and I urge you to explore this resource. Even if you think you understand a topic in Excel fairly well, you can often discover one or two subtle features that you didn't know about. A thorough understanding of how to use the online help system will definitely make you a more productive Excel user.

Worksheet Function Reference

This appendix contains a complete listing of Excel's worksheet functions. The functions are arranged alphabetically by categories used by the Paste Function dialog box. Some of these functions (indicated in the lists that follow) are available only when a particular add-in is attached.

For more information about a particular function, including its arguments, select the function in the Function Wizard and click on the Help button.

Table B-1
Database Category Functions

Function	What It Does
DAVERAGE	Returns the average of selected database entries
DCOUNT	Counts the cells containing numbers from a specified database and criteria
DCOUNTA	Counts nonblank cells from a specified database and criteria
DGET	Extracts from a database a single record that matches the specified criteria
DMAX	Returns the maximum value from selected database entries
DMIN	Returns the minimum value from selected database entries
DPRODUCT	Multiplies the values in a particular field of records that match the criteria in a database
DSTDEV	Estimates the standard deviation based on a sample of selected database entries
DSTDEVP	Calculates the standard deviation based on the entire population of selected database entries
DSUM	Adds the numbers in the field column of records in the database that match the criteria
DVAR	Estimates variance based on a sample from selected database entries
DVARP	Calculates variance based on the entire population of selected database entries
SQL.OPEN**	Makes a connection to a data source via ODBC
SQL.EXEC.QUERY**	Executes a SQL statement on an SQL.OPEN connection
SQL.BIND**	Specifies where to place SQL.EXEC.QUERY results
SQL.RETRIEVE**	Retrieves SQL.EXEC.QUERY results
SQL.RETRIEVE.TO.FILE**	Retrieves SQL.EXEC.QUERY results to a file
SQL.CLOSE**	Terminates a SQL.OPEN connection
SQL.GET.SCHEMA**	Returns information on a SQL.OPEN connection
SQL.ERROR**	Returns error information SQL* functions
SQL.REQUEST**	Requests a connection and executes a SQL query
QUERYGETDATA***	Gets external data using Microsoft Query
QUERYGETDATADIALOG***	Displays a dialog box to get data using Microsoft Query
QUERYREFRESH***	Updates a data range using Microsoft Query

* Available only when the Analysis ToolPak add-in is attached
** Available only when the ODBC add-in is attached
*** Available only when the MS Query add-in is attached

Table B-2
Date and Time Category Functions

Function	What It Does
DATE	Returns the serial number of a particular date
DATEVALUE	Converts a date in the form of text to a serial number
DAY	Converts a serial number to a day of the month
DAYS360	Calculates the number of days between two dates based on a 360-day year
EDATE*	Returns the serial number of the date that is the indicated number of months before or after the start date
EOMONTH*	Returns the serial number of the last day of the month before or after a specified number of months
HOUR	Converts a serial number to an hour
MINUTE	Converts a serial number to a minute
MONTH	Converts a serial number to a month
NETWORKDAYS*	Returns the number of whole workdays between two dates
NOW	Returns the serial number of the current date and time
SECOND	Converts a serial number to a second
TIME	Returns the serial number of a particular time
TIMEVALUE	Converts a time in the form of text to a serial number
TODAY	Returns the serial number of today's date
WEEKDAY	Converts a serial number to a day of the week
WEEKNUM*	Returns the week number in the year
WORKDAY*	Returns the serial number of the date before or after a specified number of workdays
YEAR	Converts a serial number to a year
YEARFRAC*	Returns the year fraction representing the number of whole days between start_date and end_date

* Available only when the Analysis ToolPak add-in is attached

Table B-3
Engineering Category Functions

Function	What It Does
BESSELI*	Returns the modified Bessel function In(x)
BESSELJ*	Returns the Bessel function Jn(x)
BESSELK*	Returns the modified Bessel function Kn(x)
BESSELY*	Returns the Bessel function Yn(x)
BIN2DEC*	Converts a binary number to decimal
BIN2HEX*	Converts a binary number to hexadecimal
BIN2OCT*	Converts a binary number to octal
COMPLEX*	Converts real and imaginary coefficients into a complex number
CONVERT*	Converts a number from one measurement system to another
DEC2BIN*	Converts a decimal number to binary
DEC2HEX*	Converts a decimal number to hexadecimal
DEC2OCT*	Converts a decimal number to octal
DELTA*	Tests whether two values are equal
ERF*	Returns the error function
ERFC*	Returns the complementary error function
GESTEP*	Tests whether a number is greater than a threshold value
HEX2BIN*	Converts a hexadecimal number to binary
HEX2DEC*	Converts a hexadecimal number to decimal
HEX2OCT*	Converts a hexadecimal number to octal
IMABS*	Returns the absolute value (modulus) of a complex number
IMAGINARY*	Returns the imaginary coefficient of a complex number
IMARGUMENT*	Returns the argument theta, an angle expressed in radians
IMCONJUGATE*	Returns the complex conjugate of a complex number
IMCOS*	Returns the cosine of a complex number
IMDIV*	Returns the quotient of two complex numbers
IMEXP*	Returns the exponential of a complex number
IMLN*	Returns the natural logarithm of a complex number

Function	What It Does
IMLOG10*	Returns the base-10 logarithm of a complex number
IMLOG2*	Returns the base-2 logarithm of a complex number
IMPOWER*	Returns a complex number raised to an integer power
IMPRODUCT*	Returns the product of two complex numbers
IMREAL*	Returns the real coefficient of a complex number
IMSIN*	Returns the sine of a complex number
IMSQRT*	Returns the square root of a complex number
IMSUB*	Returns the difference of two complex numbers
IMSUM*	Returns the sum of complex numbers
OCT2BIN*	Converts an octal number to binary
OCT2DEC*	Converts an octal number to decimal
OCT2HEX*	Converts an octal number to hexadecimal

* Available only when the Analysis ToolPak add-in is attached

Table B-4
Financial Category Functions

Function	What It Does
ACCRINT*	Returns the accrued interest for a security that pays periodic interest
ACCRINTM*	Returns the accrued interest for a security that pays interest at maturity
AMORDEGRC*	Returns the depreciation for each accounting period
AMORLINC*	Returns the depreciation for each accounting period
COUPDAYBS*	Returns the number of days from the beginning of the coupon period to the settlement date
COUPDAYS*	Returns the number of days in the coupon period that contains the settlement date
COUPDAYSNC*	Returns the number of days from the settlement date to the next coupon date
COUPNCD*	Returns the next coupon date after the settlement date
COUPNUM*	Returns the number of coupons payable between the settlement date and maturity date

(continued)

Table B-4 (continued)

Function	What It Does
COUPPCD*	Returns the previous coupon date before the settlement date
CUMIPMT*	Returns the cumulative interest paid between two periods
CUMPRINC*	Returns the cumulative principal paid on a loan between two periods
DB	Returns the depreciation of an asset for a specified period using the fixed-declining balance method
DDB	Returns the depreciation of an asset for a specified period using the double-declining balance method or some other method that you specify
DISC*	Returns the discount rate for a security
DOLLARDE*	Converts a dollar price, expressed as a fraction, into a dollar price, expressed as a decimal number
DOLLARFR*	Converts a dollar price, expressed as a decimal number, into a dollar price, expressed as a fraction
DURATION*	Returns the annual duration of a security with periodic interest payments
EFFECT*	Returns the effective annual interest rate
FV	Returns the future value of an investment
FVSCHEDULE*	Returns the future value of an initial principal after applying a series of compound interest rates
INTRATE*	Returns the interest rate for a fully invested security
IPMT	Returns the interest payment for an investment for a given period
IRR	Returns the internal rate of return for a series of cash flows
MDURATION*	Returns the Macauley modified duration for a security with an assumed par value of $100
MIRR	Returns the internal rate of return where positive and negative cash flows are financed at different rates
NOMINAL*	Returns the annual nominal interest rate
NPER	Returns the number of periods for an investment
NPV	Returns the net present value of an investment based on a series of periodic cash flows and a discount rate
ODDFPRICE*	Returns the price per $100 face value of a security with an odd first period
ODDFYIELD*	Returns the yield of a security with an odd first period
ODDLPRICE*	Returns the price per $100 face value of a security with an odd last period

Function	What It Does
ODDLYIELD*	Returns the yield of a security with an odd last period
PMT	Returns the periodic payment for an annuity
PPMT	Returns the payment on the principal for an investment for a given period
PRICE*	Returns the price per $100 face value of a security that pays periodic interest
PRICEDISC*	Returns the price per $100 face value of a discounted security
PRICEMAT*	Returns the price per $100 face value of a security that pays interest at maturity
PV	Returns the present value of an investment
RATE	Returns the interest rate per period of an annuity
RECEIVED*	Returns the amount received at maturity for a fully invested security
SLN	Returns the straight-line depreciation of an asset for one period
SYD	Returns the sum-of-years' digits depreciation of an asset for a specified period
TBILLEQ*	Returns the bond-equivalent yield for a Treasury bill
TBILLPRICE*	Returns the price per $100 face value for a Treasury bill
TBILLYIELD*	Returns the yield for a Treasury bill
VDB	Returns the depreciation of an asset for a specified or partial period using a declining balance method
XIRR*	Returns the internal rate of return for a schedule of cash flows that is not necessarily periodic
XNPV*	Returns the net present value for a schedule of cash flows that is not necessarily periodic
YIELD*	Returns the yield on a security that pays periodic interest
YIELDDISC*	Returns the annual yield for a discounted security, for example, a Treasury bill
YIELDMAT*	Returns the annual yield of a security that pays interest at maturity

* Available only when the Analysis ToolPak add-in is attached

Table B-5
Information Category Functions

Function	What It Does
CELL	Returns information about the formatting, location, or contents of a cell
COUNTBLANK	Counts the number of blank cells within a range
ERROR.TYPE	Returns a number corresponding to an error type
INFO	Returns information about the current operating environment
ISBLANK	Returns TRUE if the value is blank
ISERR	Returns TRUE if the value is any error value except #N/A
ISERROR	Returns TRUE if the value is any error value
ISEVEN*	Returns TRUE if the number is even
ISLOGICAL	Returns TRUE if the value is a logical value
ISNA	Returns TRUE if the value is the #N/A error value
ISNONTEXT	Returns TRUE if the value is not text
ISNUMBER	Returns TRUE if the value is a number
ISODD*	Returns TRUE if the number is odd
ISREF	Returns TRUE if the value is a reference
ISTEXT	Returns TRUE if the value is text
N	Returns a value converted to a number
NA	Returns the error value #N/A
TYPE	Returns a number indicating the data type of a value

* Available only when the Analysis ToolPak add-in is attached

Table B-6
Logical Category Functions

Function	What It Does
AND	Returns TRUE if all its arguments are TRUE
FALSE	Returns the logical value FALSE
IF	Specifies a logical test to perform
NOT	Reverses the logic of its argument
OR	Returns TRUE if any argument is TRUE
TRUE	Returns the logical value TRUE

Table B-7
Lookup and Reference Category Functions

Function	What It Does
ADDRESS	Returns a reference as text to a single cell in a worksheet
AREAS	Returns the number of areas in a reference
CHOOSE	Chooses a value from a list of values
COLUMN	Returns the column number of a reference
COLUMNS	Returns the number of columns in a reference
HLOOKUP	Looks in the top row of an array and returns the value of the indicated cell
INDEX	Uses an index to choose a value from a reference or array
INDIRECT	Returns a reference indicated by a text value
LOOKUP	Looks up values in a vector or array
MATCH	Looks up values in a reference or array
OFFSET	Returns a reference offset from a given reference
ROW	Returns the row number of a reference
ROWS	Returns the number of rows in a reference
TRANSPOSE	Returns the transpose of an array
VLOOKUP	Looks in the first column of an array and moves across the row to return the value of a cell

Table B-8
Math and Trig Category Functions

Function	What It Does
ABS	Returns the absolute value of a number
ACOS	Returns the arccosine of a number
ACOSH	Returns the inverse hyperbolic cosine of a number
ASIN	Returns the arcsine of a number
ASINH	Returns the inverse hyperbolic sine of a number

(continued)

Table B-8 *(continued)*

Function	What It Does
ATAN	Returns the arctangent of a number
ATAN2	Returns the arctangent from *x* and *y* coordinates
ATANH	Returns the inverse hyperbolic tangent of a number
CEILING	Rounds a number to the nearest integer or to the nearest multiple of significance
COMBIN	Returns the number of combinations for a given number of objects
COS	Returns the cosine of a number
COSH	Returns the hyperbolic cosine of a number
COUNTIF	Counts the number of nonblank cells within a range that meets the given criteria
DEGREES	Converts radians to degrees
EVEN	Rounds a number up to the nearest even integer
EXP	Returns e raised to the power of a given number
FACT	Returns the factorial of a number
FACTDOUBLE	Returns the double factorial of a number
FLOOR	Rounds a number down, toward 0
GCD*	Returns the greatest common divisor
INT	Rounds a number down to the nearest integer
LCM*	Returns the least common multiple
LN	Returns the natural logarithm of a number
LOG	Returns the logarithm of a number to a specified base
LOG10	Returns the base-10 logarithm of a number
MDETERM	Returns the matrix determinant of an array
MINVERSE	Returns the matrix inverse of an array
MMULT	Returns the matrix product of two arrays
MOD	Returns the remainder from division
MROUND*	Returns a number rounded to the desired multiple
MULTINOMIAL*	Returns the multinomial of a set of numbers
ODD	Rounds a number up to the nearest odd integer

Function	What It Does
PI	Returns the value of pi
POWER	Returns the result of a number raised to a power
PRODUCT	Multiplies its arguments
QUOTIENT*	Returns the integer portion of a division
RADIANS	Converts degrees to radians
RAND	Returns a random number between 0 and 1
RANDBETWEEN*	Returns a random number between the numbers that you specify
ROMAN	Converts an Arabic numeral to Roman, as text
ROUND	Rounds a number to a specified number of digits
ROUNDDOWN	Rounds a number down, toward 0
ROUNDUP	Rounds a number up, away from 0
SERIESSUM*	Returns the sum of a power series based on the formula
SIGN	Returns the sign of a number
SIN	Returns the sine of the given angle
SINH	Returns the hyperbolic sine of a number
SQRT	Returns a positive square root
SQRTPI*	Returns the square root of (*number* * pi)
SUBTOTAL	Returns a subtotal in a list or database
SUM	Adds its arguments
SUMIF	Adds the cells specified by a given criteria
SUMPRODUCT	Returns the sum of the products of corresponding array components
SUMSQ	Returns the sum of the squares of the arguments
SUMX2MY2	Returns the sum of the difference of squares of corresponding values in two arrays
SUMX2PY2	Returns the sum of the sum of squares of corresponding values in two arrays
SUMXMY2	Returns the sum of squares of differences of corresponding values in two arrays
TAN	Returns the tangent of a number
TANH	Returns the hyperbolic tangent of a number
TRUNC	Truncates a number to an integer

* Available only when the Analysis ToolPak add-in is attached

Table B-9
Statistical Category Functions

Function	What It Does
AVEDEV	Returns the average of the absolute deviations of data points from their mean
AVERAGE	Returns the average of its arguments
BETADIST	Returns the cumulative beta probability density function
BETAINV	Returns the inverse of the cumulative beta probability density function
BINOMDIST	Returns the individual term binomial distribution probability
CHIDIST	Returns the one-tailed probability of the chi-squared distribution
CHIINV	Returns the inverse of the one-tailed probability of the chi-squared distribution
CHITEST	Returns the test for independence
CONFIDENCE	Returns the confidence interval for a population mean
CORREL	Returns the correlation coefficient between two data sets
COUNT	Counts how many numbers are in the list of arguments
COUNTA	Counts how many values are in the list of arguments
COVAR	Returns covariance, the average of the products of paired deviations
CRITBINOM	Returns the smallest value for which the cumulative binomial distribution is less than or equal to a criterion value
DEVSQ	Returns the sum of squares of deviations
EXPONDIST	Returns the exponential distribution
FDIST	Returns the F probability distribution
FINV	Returns the inverse of the F probability distribution
FISHER	Returns the Fisher transformation
FISHERINV	Returns the inverse of the Fisher transformation
FORECAST	Returns a value along a linear trend
FREQUENCY	Returns a frequency distribution as a vertical array
FTEST	Returns the result of an F-test

Function	What It Does
GAMMADIST	Returns the gamma distribution
GAMMAINV	Returns the inverse of the gamma cumulative distribution
GAMMALN	Returns the natural logarithm of the gamma function, G(x)
GEOMEAN	Returns the geometric mean
GROWTH	Returns values along an exponential trend
HARMEAN	Returns the harmonic mean
HYPGEOMDIST	Returns the hypergeometric distribution
INTERCEPT	Returns the intercept of the linear regression line
KURT	Returns the kurtosis of a data set
LARGE	Returns the kth largest value in a data set
LINEST	Returns the parameters of a linear trend
LOGEST	Returns the parameters of an exponential trend
LOGINV	Returns the inverse of the lognormal distribution
LOGNORMDIST	Returns the cumulative lognormal distribution
MAX	Returns the maximum value in a list of arguments
MEDIAN	Returns the median of the given numbers
MIN	Returns the minimum value in a list of arguments
MODE	Returns the most common value in a data set
NEGBINOMDIST	Returns the negative binomial distribution
NORMDIST	Returns the normal cumulative distribution
NORMINV	Returns the inverse of the normal cumulative distribution
NORMSDIST	Returns the standard normal cumulative distribution
NORMSINV	Returns the inverse of the standard normal cumulative distribution
PEARSON	Returns the Pearson product moment correlation coefficient
PERCENTILE	Returns the kth percentile of values in a range
PERCENTRANK	Returns the percentage rank of a value in a data set
PERMUT	Returns the number of permutations for a given number of objects
POISSON	Returns the Poisson distribution
PROB	Returns the probability that values in a range are between two limits

(continued)

Table B-9 *(continued)*

Function	What It Does
QUARTILE	Returns the quartile of a data set
RANK	Returns the rank of a number in a list of numbers
RSQ	Returns the square of the Pearson product moment correlation coefficient
SKEW	Returns the skewness of a distribution
SLOPE	Returns the slope of the linear regression line
SMALL	Returns the kth smallest value in a data set
STANDARDIZE	Returns a normalized value
STDEV	Estimates standard deviation based on a sample
STDEVP	Calculates standard deviation based on the entire population
STEYX	Returns the standard error of the predicted y-value for each x in the regression
TDIST	Returns the student's t-distribution
TINV	Returns the inverse of the student's t-distribution
TREND	Returns values along a linear trend
TRIMMEAN	Returns the mean of the interior of a data set
TTEST	Returns the probability associated with a student's t-Test
VAR	Estimates variance based on a sample
VARP	Calculates variance based on the entire population
WEIBULL	Returns the Weibull distribution
ZTEST	Returns the two-tailed P-value of a z-test

Table B-10
Text Category Functions

Function	What It Does
CHAR	Returns the character specified by the code number
CLEAN	Removes all nonprintable characters from text
CODE	Returns a numeric code for the first character in a text string

Function	What It Does
CONCATENATE	Joins several text items into one text item
DOLLAR	Converts a number to text, using currency format
EXACT	Checks to see if two text values are identical
FIND	Finds one text value within another (case-sensitive)
FIXED	Formats a number as text with a fixed number of decimals
LEFT	Returns the left-most characters from a text value
LEN	Returns the number of characters in a text string
LOWER	Converts text to lowercase
MID	Returns a specific number of characters from a text string starting at the position that you specify
PROPER	Capitalizes the first letter in each word of a text value
REPLACE	Replaces characters within text
REPT	Repeats text a given number of times
RIGHT	Returns the right-most characters from a text value
SEARCH	Finds one text value within another (not case-sensitive)
SUBSTITUTE	Substitutes new text for old text in a text string
T	Converts its arguments to text
TEXT	Formats a number and converts it to text
TRIM	Removes spaces from text
UPPER	Converts text to uppercase
VALUE	Converts a text argument to a number

Excel's Shortcut Keys

This appendix lists the most useful shortcut keys that are available in Excel. The shortcuts are arranged by context.

The keys listed assume that you are not using the Transition Navigation Keys, which are designed to emulate Lotus 1-2-3. You can select this option in the Transition tab of the Options dialog box.

	Table C-1 Moving Through a Worksheet
Key(s)	**What It Does**
Arrow keys	Move left, right, up, or down one cell
Home	Moves to the beginning of the row
Home*	Moves to the upper-left cell displayed in the window
End*	Moves to the lower-left cell displayed in the window
Arrow keys*	Scrolls left, right, up, or down one cell
PgUp	Moves up one screen
Ctrl+PgUp	Moves to the previous sheet
PgDn	Moves down one screen
Ctrl+PgDn	Moves to the next sheet
Alt+PgUp	Moves one screen to the left
Alt+PgDn	Moves one screen to the right
Ctrl+Home	Moves to the first cell in the worksheet (A1)
Ctrl+End	Moves to the last active cell of the worksheet

(continued)

Table C-1 *(continued)*

Key(s)	What It Does
Ctrl+arrow key	Moves to the edge of a data block. If the cell is blank, moves to the first nonblank cell
Ctrl+Backspace	Scrolls to display the active cell
End, Home	Moves to the last nonempty cell on the worksheet
F5	Prompts for a cell address to go to
F6	Moves to the next pane
Shift+F6	Moves to the previous pane
Ctrl+Tab	Moves to the next window
Ctrl+Shift+Tab	Moves to the previous window

* With Scroll Lock on

Table C-2
Selecting Cells in the Worksheet

Key(s)	What It Does
Shift+arrow key	Expands the selection in the direction indicated
Shift+spacebar	Selects the entire row
Ctrl+spacebar	Selects the entire column
Ctrl+Shift+ spacebar	Selects the entire worksheet
Shift+Home	Expands the selection to the beginning of the current row
Ctrl+*	Selects the block of data surrounding the active cell
F8	Extends the selection as you use navigation keys
Shift+F8	Adds other nonadjacent cells or ranges to the selection; pressing Shift+F8 again ends Add mode
F5	Prompts for a range or range name to select
Ctrl+G	Prompts for a range or range name to select
Ctrl+A	Selects the entire worksheet
Shift+Backspace	Selects the active cell in a range selection

Table C-3
Moving Within a Range Selection

Key(s)	What It Does
Enter	Moves the cell pointer to the next cell down in the selection
Shift+Enter	Moves the cell pointer to the previous cell up in the selection
Tab	Moves the cell pointer to the next cell to the right in the selection
Shift+Tab	Moves the cell pointer to the previous cell to the left in the selection
Ctrl+period (.)	Moves to the next corner of the current cell range
Ctrl+Tab	Moves to the next cell range in a nonadjacent selection
Ctrl+Shift+Tab	Moves to the previous cell range in a nonadjacent selection
Shift+Backspace	Collapses the cell selection to just the active cell

Table C-4
Editing Keys in the Formula Bar

Key(s)	What It Does
F2	Begins editing the active cell
F3	Pastes a name into a formula
Arrow keys	Moves the cursor one character in the direction of the arrow
Home	Moves the cursor to the beginning of the line
Esc	Cancels the editing
End	Moves the cursor to the end of the line
Ctrl+right arrow	Moves the cursor one word to the right
Ctrl+left arrow	Moves the cursor one word to the left
Del	Deletes the character to the right of the cursor
Ctrl+Del	Deletes all characters from the cursor to the end of the line
Backspace	Deletes the character to the left of the cursor

Table C-5
Formatting Keys

Key(s)	What It Does
Ctrl+1	Format⇨[Selected Object]
Ctrl+B	Sets or removes boldface
Ctrl+I	Sets or removes italic
Ctrl+U	Sets or removes underlining
Ctrl+5	Sets or removes strikethrough
Ctrl+Shift+~	Applies the general number format
Ctrl+Shift+!	Applies the comma format with two decimal places
Ctrl+Shift+#	Applies the date format (day, month, year)
Ctrl+Shift+@	Applies the time format (hour, minute, a.m./p.m.)
Ctrl+Shift+$	Applies the currency format with two decimal places
Ctrl+Shift+%	Applies the percent format with no decimal places
Ctrl+Shift+&	Applies border to outline
Ctrl+Shift+_	Removes all borders
Alt+'	Selects Format⇨Style

Table C-6
Other Shortcut Keys

Key(s)	What It Does
Alt+=	Inserts the AutoSum formula
Alt+Backspace	Selects Edit⇨Undo
Ctrl+;	Enters the current date
Ctrl+0 (zero)	Hides columns
Ctrl+1	Displays the Format dialog box for the selected object
Ctrl+6	Cycles among various ways of displaying objects
Ctrl+7	Toggles the display of the standard toolbar
Ctrl+8	Toggles the display of outline symbols
Ctrl+9	Hides rows

Key(s)	What It Does
Ctrl+A	After typing a function name in a formula, displays the Formula Palette
Ctrl+C	Selects Edit⇨Copy
Ctrl+D	Selects Edit⇨Fill Left
Ctrl+Delete	Selects Edit⇨Cut
Ctrl+F	Selects Edit⇨Find
Ctrl+H	Selects Edit⇨Replace
Ctrl+Insert	Selects Edit⇨Copy
Ctrl+K	Selects Insert⇨Hyperlink
Ctrl+N	Selects File⇨New
Ctrl+O	Selects File⇨Open
Ctrl+P	Selects File⇨Print
Ctrl+R	Selects Edit⇨Fill Right
Ctrl+S	Selects File⇨Save
Ctrl+Shift+(	Unhides rows
Ctrl+Shift+)	Unhides columns
Ctrl+Shift+:	Enters the current time
Ctrl+Shift+A	After typing a valid function name in a formula, inserts the argument names and parentheses for the function
Ctrl+V	Selects Edit⇨Paste
Ctrl+X	Selects Edit⇨Cut
Ctrl+Z	Selects Edit⇨Undo
Delete	Selects Edit⇨Clear
Shift+Insert	Selects Edit⇨Paste

Table C-7
Function Keys

Key(s)	What It Does
F1	Displays Help or the Office Assistant
Shift+F1	Displays the What's This cursor
Alt+F1	Inserts a chart sheet
Alt+Shift+ F1	Inserts a new worksheet
F2	Edits the active cell
Shift+F2	Edits a cell comment
Alt+F2	Issues Save As command
Alt+Shift+F2	Issues Save command
F3	Pastes a name into a formula
Shift+F3	Pastes a function into a formula
Ctrl+F3	Defines a name
Ctrl+Shift+F3	Creates names by using row and column labels
F4	Repeats the last action
Shift+F4	Repeats the last Find (Find Next)
Ctrl+F4	Closes the window
Alt+F4	Exits the program
F5	Selects Go To
Shift+F5	Displays the Find dialog box
Ctrl+F5	Restores the window size
F6	Moves to the next pane
Shift+F6	Moves to the previous pane
Ctrl+F6	Moves to the next workbook window
Ctrl+Shift+F6	Moves to the previous workbook window
F7	Issues Spelling command
Ctrl+F7	Moves the window
F8	Extends a selection
Shift+F8	Adds to the selection

Key(s)	What It Does
Ctrl+F8	Resizes the window
Alt+F8	Displays the Macro dialog box
F9	Calculates all sheets in all open workbooks
Shift+F9	Calculates the active worksheet
Ctrl+F9	Minimizes the workbook
F10	Makes the menu bar active
Shift+F10	Displays a shortcut menu
Ctrl+F10	Maximizes or restores the workbook window
F11	Creates a chart
Shift+F11	Inserts a new worksheet
Ctrl+F11	Inserts an Excel 4.0 macro sheet
Alt+F11	Displays Visual Basic Editor
F12	Issues Save As command
Shift+F12	Issues Save command
Ctrl+F12	Issues Open command
Ctrl+Shift+F12	Issues Print command

What's at the Web Site

The sample files described in this book are available for download from this book's Web site. The site also contains the shareware version of the author's Power Utility Pak.

Accessing the Web Site

You can download the sample files via the IDG Books Web site. Your computer must be connected to the Internet, and you must be running a Web browser program such as Microsoft Internet Explorer or Netscape Navigator. Follow these steps to download a file:

1. Point your browser to the following URL:

   ```
   http://www.idgbooks.com
   ```

2. Select the Search Our Site option and type the title of this book into the Search box. A page related to this book appears, with the sample files available to you.

3. Click on the hyperlink to begin downloading the file

Note Most of the files are uncompressed Excel workbooks. Depending on how your browser is configured, the files may be saved to disk or opened immediately in Excel.

File Descriptions

Following are brief descriptions of the example files. Not all chapters have example files.

Chapter 3
```
Hands on example.xls
```

The end-result of the hands-on example.

Chapter 6
```
Custom number formats.xls
```

A workbook that contains a variety of custom number formats.

Chapter 10
```
Amortization.xls
```

A workbook that demonstrates the use of the PMT, PPMT, and IPMT functions to calculate a fixed-interest amortization schedule.

```
Indirect.xls
```

A workbook that uses the INDIRECT function to summarize values contained in other worksheets.

```
Megaformula.xls
```

A workbook that demonstrates the use of a lengthy formula to remove the middle names and middle initials from a list of names.

Chapter 11
```
Formatting.xls
```

A workbook that contains many cell and range formatting examples.

```
Custom styles.xls
```

A workbook that contains examples of custom styles.

Chapter 18
```
Outline.xls
```

A workbook that demonstrates the use of row and column outlining.

Text outline.xls

A workbook that demonstrates the use of an outline to display various levels of text.

Chapter 20

Array examples.xls

A workbook that demonstrates many uses for array formulas.

Chapter 24

Budget.exe (expands to Budget.dbf)

A dBASE file used for the examples in this chapter.

Note This is a large file and has been compressed into a self-extracting executable file. To uncompress the file, double-click on Budget.exe.

Chapter 25

Banking example.xls

A workbook used for several pivot table examples.

Pivot consolidation.exe

Note Pivot consolidation.exe has been compressed into a self-extracting executable file that contains consolidation.xls, file1.xls, file2.xls, and file3.xls. To uncompress the file, double-click on Pivot consolidation.exe. This extracts four files.

Pivot table chart.xls

A workbook that demonstrates charting based on a pivot table.

Survey analysis.xls

A workbook that demonstrates survey data analysis using pivot tables.

Geographic analysis.xls

A workbook that demonstrates geographic analysis using a pivot table.

Pivot table dates.xls

A workbook that demonstrates how to group pivot table data by dates.

Chapter 27

`Shipping costs.xls`

A workbook set up to demonstrate Solver.

`Staff scheduling.xls`

A workbook set up to demonstrate Solver.

`Resource allocation.xls`

A workbook set up to demonstrate Solver.

`Investment portfolio.xls`

A workbook set up to demonstrate Solver.

Chapter 32

`Tick-tack-toe.xls`

An Excel version of a simple game.

`Moving tile.xls`

An Excel version of a simple puzzle.

`Hangman.xls`

An Excel version of the classic word-guessing game.

`Tivia.xls`

A workbook with more than 1,200 trivia questions and answers.

`Pattern drawing.xls`

Create colorful patterns using Excel.

`Guitar scales.xls`

Helps you learn scales and modes on the guitar.

`Menu shenanigans.xls`

A macro that reverses the text in Excel's menus.

Typing tutor.xls

Helps you learn to type.

Word search.xls

Creates word search puzzles.

Sun calculations.xls

Performs sophisticated calculations regarding the sun.

Sound effects.xls

Demonstrates how to play sounds in Excel.

Trigonometric charts.xls

Displays interesting charts that use trigonometric functions.

XY-sketch.xls

Draw simple figures that are actually XY charts.

Chapter 33

Formatting toolbar.xls

A workbook that contains a custom toolbar to assist with formatting.

Chapter 36

function examples.xls

A workbook that contains several examples of custom worksheet functions written in VBA.

Chapter 37

MessageBox.xls

A workbook that contains a simple custom dialog box.

ChangeCase.xls

A workbook that contains a utility (with a custom dialog box) to make it easy to change the case of text in cells.

Chapter 38

```
ActiveX examples.xls
```

A workbook that contains examples of ActiveX controls used on a worksheet.

Chapter 39

```
Range copy.xls
```

VBA macros that demonstrate how to copy a range of cells.

```
Selecting cells.xls
```

VBA macros that demonstrate various ways to select a range of cells.

```
Range move.xls
```

VBA macros that demonstrate how to move a range of cells.

```
Range loop.xls
```

VBA macros that demonstrate how to loop though a range of cells.

```
Prompt for value.xls
```

VBA macros that demonstrate how to prompt for a value and insert the value into a cell.

```
Selection type.xls
```

VBA macros that demonstrate how to determine the type of object that is selected.

```
Create textbox.xls
```

VBA macros that demonstrate how to create a text box.

```
Add explosion.xls
```

VBA macros that demonstrate how to call attention to a particular cell.

```
Chart macros.xls
```

VBA macros that work with chart objects.

Chapter 40

Toggles.xls

A workbook that contains a utility to make it easy to toggle various settings in Excel.

Toggles.xla

The add-in version of Toggles.xls.

Index

A

B

background images for worksheets, 254–255, 323
backing up files, 99–100
backsolving. *See* goal seeking
bar charts, 306–307, 396–397
basic worksheet operations
  adding worksheets, 130–131
  changing column widths and row heights,
     142–143
  changing worksheet's name, 131–132
  creating multiple views, 135–136
  deleting columns and rows, 142
  deleting worksheets, 131
  hiding
    columns and rows, 143–144
    and unhiding worksheets, 133
  inserting columns and rows, 140–142
  making worksheets active, 129–130
  moving worksheets, 132–133
  splitting panes, 137–138
  zooming worksheets, 133–135
bitmap images, 321
Black and white option (Page Setup dialog
     box), 274
blank cells, 510
Bomb Hunt game, 682
book.xlt template, 709
Boolean settings, 805–806
Border panel (Format Cells dialog box), 253
borders
  formatting, 121
  options for, 31
  skipping when pasting, 163
  stylistic formatting with, 251–254
  3D effects with, 254
  in worksheets, 253
Borders tool, 121
bring drawing objects forward, 331
browsers, 652
bubble charts, 314
built-in features
  add-ins, 817
  button images, 705
  format styles, 260
  functions for formulas, 176–177
  toolbars, 69
Button Editor dialog box, 706
buttons
  adding, 699–700, 702–704
  applying styles, 260
  attaching macros to, 729, 771–772, 777–778
  changing images, 704–706
  on Control Toolbox toolbar, 783
  copying, 706
  copying ranges with, 157
  in dialog boxes, 73

editing images for, 705–706
inserting toolbar, 700
number-formatting, 111
option, 73
removing, 699–700
See also toolbars

C

calculated fields and items, 556–559
calculating profit, 593
calculation mode, 185–186
calculator, 198–199
case sensitive sort order, 513
category labels, 381
category shading for maps, 406
Caution icon, 5
cell edit mode, 185
CELL function, 220–221
cell pointer
  entering formulas with, 177–178
  moving after data entry, 123
cell references
  circular, 187–188
  intentional circular, 188–189
  mixed, 182–183
  nonrelative, 183
  in other workbooks, 179–180
  in other worksheets, 179
  to outside cells, 180
  relative and absolute, 180–182
  See also cells
cells, 147–170
  active, 60
  addresses of, 60, 147, 148
  array formulas in single, 450–451
  calling attention to, 336
  changing, 593
  color-coded formula, 665
  comments, 31–32
    adding, 154–155
    documenting spreadsheets with, 357
    in graphic format, 338
    pasting, 162
  copying ranges, 156–157
    to adjacent cells, 159–160
    with menu commands, 158
    to other worksheets, 160
    with shortcut keys and menus, 158
    with toolbar buttons, 157
    using drag and drop, 159
  creating line breaks in, 125
  data entry tips for, 123
  deleting contents of, 155–156
  erasing contents of, 107, 108
  formatting, 30–31, 119–121
    attributes, 120

F

M

The Fun & Easy Way™ to learn about computers and more!

Here's a complete listing of IDG Books' ...For Dummies® titles

Title	Author	ISBN	Price
DATABASE			
Access 2 For Dummies®	by Scott Palmer	ISBN: 1-56884-090-X	$19.95 USA/$26.95 Canada
Access Programming For Dummies®	by Rob Krumm	ISBN: 1-56884-091-8	$19.95 USA/$26.95 Canada
Approach 3 For Windows® For Dummies®	by Doug Lowe	ISBN: 1-56884-233-3	$19.99 USA/$26.99 Canada
dBASE For DOS For Dummies®	by Scott Palmer & Michael Stabler	ISBN: 1-56884-188-4	$19.95 USA/$26.95 Canada
dBASE For Windows® For Dummies®	by Scott Palmer	ISBN: 1-56884-179-5	$19.95 USA/$26.95 Canada
dBASE 5 For Windows® Programming For Dummies®	by Ted Coombs & Jason Coombs	ISBN: 1-56884-215-5	$19.99 USA/$26.99 Canada
FoxPro 2.6 For Windows® For Dummies®	by John Kaufeld	ISBN: 1-56884-187-6	$19.95 USA/$26.95 Canada
Paradox 5 For Windows® For Dummies®	by John Kaufeld	ISBN: 1-56884-185-X	$19.95 USA/$26.95 Canada
DESKTOP PUBLISHING/ILLUSTRATION/GRAPHICS			
CorelDRAW! 5 For Dummies®	by Deke McClelland	ISBN: 1-56884-157-4	$19.95 USA/$26.95 Canada
CorelDRAW! For Dummies®	by Deke McClelland	ISBN: 1-56884-042-X	$19.95 USA/$26.95 Canada
Desktop Publishing & Design For Dummies®	by Roger C. Parker	ISBN: 1-56884-234-1	$19.99 USA/$26.99 Canada
Harvard Graphics 2 For Windows® For Dummies®	by Roger C. Parker	ISBN: 1-56884-092-6	$19.95 USA/$26.95 Canada
PageMaker 5 For Macs® For Dummies®	by Galen Gruman & Deke McClelland	ISBN: 1-56884-178-7	$19.95 USA/$26.95 Canada
PageMaker 5 For Windows® For Dummies®	by Deke McClelland & Galen Gruman	ISBN: 1-56884-160-4	$19.95 USA/$26.95 Canada
Photoshop 3 For Macs® For Dummies®	by Deke McClelland	ISBN: 1-56884-208-2	$19.99 USA/$26.99 Canada
QuarkXPress 3.3 For Dummies®	by Galen Gruman & Barbara Assadi	ISBN: 1-56884-217-1	$19.99 USA/$26.99 Canada
FINANCE/PERSONAL FINANCE/TEST TAKING REFERENCE			
Everyday Math For Dummies™	by Charles Seiter	ISBN: 1-56884-248-1	$14.99 USA/$22.99 Canada
Personal Finance For Dummies™ For Canadians	by Eric Tyson & Tony Martin	ISBN: 1-56884-378-X	$18.99 USA/$24.99 Canada
QuickBooks 3 For Dummies®	by Stephen L. Nelson	ISBN: 1-56884-227-9	$19.99 USA/$26.99 Canada
Quicken 8 For DOS For Dummies,® 2nd Edition	by Stephen L. Nelson	ISBN: 1-56884-210-4	$19.95 USA/$26.95 Canada
Quicken 5 For Macs® For Dummies®	by Stephen L. Nelson	ISBN: 1-56884-211-2	$19.95 USA/$26.95 Canada
Quicken 4 For Windows® For Dummies,® 2nd Edition	by Stephen L. Nelson	ISBN: 1-56884-209-0	$19.95 USA/$26.95 Canada
Taxes For Dummies,™ 1995 Edition	by Eric Tyson & David J. Silverman	ISBN: 1-56884-220-1	$14.99 USA/$20.99 Canada
The GMAT® For Dummies™	by Suzee Vlk, Series Editor	ISBN: 1-56884-376-3	$14.99 USA/$20.99 Canada
The GRE® For Dummies™	by Suzee Vlk, Series Editor	ISBN: 1-56884-375-5	$14.99 USA/$20.99 Canada
Time Management For Dummies™	by Jeffrey J. Mayer	ISBN: 1-56884-360-7	$16.99 USA/$22.99 Canada
TurboTax For Windows® For Dummies®	by Gail A. Helsel, CPA	ISBN: 1-56884-228-7	$19.99 USA/$26.99 Canada
GROUPWARE/INTEGRATED			
ClarisWorks For Macs® For Dummies®	by Frank Higgins	ISBN: 1-56884-363-1	$19.99 USA/$26.99 Canada
Lotus Notes For Dummies®	by Pat Freeland & Stephen Londergan	ISBN: 1-56884-212-0	$19.95 USA/$26.95 Canada
Microsoft® Office 4 For Windows® For Dummies®	by Roger C. Parker	ISBN: 1-56884-183-3	$19.95 USA/$26.95 Canada
Microsoft® Works 3 For Windows® For Dummies®	by David C. Kay	ISBN: 1-56884-214-7	$19.99 USA/$26.99 Canada
SmartSuite 3 For Dummies®	by Jan Weingarten & John Weingarten	ISBN: 1-56884-367-4	$19.99 USA/$26.99 Canada
INTERNET/COMMUNICATIONS/NETWORKING			
America Online® For Dummies,® 2nd Edition	by John Kaufeld	ISBN: 1-56884-933-8	$19.99 USA/$26.99 Canada
CompuServe For Dummies,® 2nd Edition	by Wallace Wang	ISBN: 1-56884-937-0	$19.99 USA/$26.99 Canada
Modems For Dummies,® 2nd Edition	by Tina Rathbone	ISBN: 1-56884-223-6	$19.99 USA/$26.99 Canada
MORE Internet For Dummies®	by John R. Levine & Margaret Levine Young	ISBN: 1-56884-164-7	$19.95 USA/$26.95 Canada
MORE Modems & On-line Services For Dummies®	by Tina Rathbone	ISBN: 1-56884-365-8	$19.99 USA/$26.99 Canada
Mosaic For Dummies,® Windows Edition	by David Angell & Brent Heslop	ISBN: 1-56884-242-2	$19.99 USA/$26.99 Canada
NetWare For Dummies,® 2nd Edition	by Ed Tittel, Deni Connor & Earl Follis	ISBN: 1-56884-369-0	$19.99 USA/$26.99 Canada
Networking For Dummies®	by Doug Lowe	ISBN: 1-56884-079-9	$19.95 USA/$26.95 Canada
PROCOMM PLUS 2 For Windows® For Dummies®	by Wallace Wang	ISBN: 1-56884-219-8	$19.95 USA/$26.95 Canada
TCP/IP For Dummies®	by Marshall Wilensky & Candace Leiden	ISBN: 1-56884-241-4	$19.99 USA/$26.99 Canada

Title	Author	ISBN	Price
The Internet For Macs® For Dummies®, 2nd Edition	by Charles Seiter	ISBN: 1-56884-371-2	$19.99 USA/$26.99 Canada
The Internet For Macs® For Dummies® Starter Kit	by Charles Seiter	ISBN: 1-56884-244-9	$29.99 USA/$39.99 Canada
The Internet For Macs® For Dummies® Starter Kit Bestseller Edition	by Charles Seiter	ISBN: 1-56884-245-7	$39.99 USA/$54.99 Canada
The Internet For Windows® For Dummies® Starter Kit	by John R. Levine & Margaret Levine Young	ISBN: 1-56884-237-6	$34.99 USA/$44.99 Canada
The Internet For Windows® For Dummies® Starter Kit, Bestseller Edition	by John R. Levine & Margaret Levine Young	ISBN: 1-56884-246-5	$39.99 USA/$54.99 Canada

MACINTOSH

Title	Author	ISBN	Price
Mac® Programming For Dummies®	by Dan Parks Sydow	ISBN: 1-56884-173-6	$19.95 USA/$26.95 Canada
Macintosh® System 7.5 For Dummies®	by Bob LeVitus	ISBN: 1-56884-197-3	$19.95 USA/$26.95 Canada
MORE Macs® For Dummies®	by David Pogue	ISBN: 1-56884-087-X	$19.95 USA/$26.95 Canada
PageMaker 5 For Macs® For Dummies®	by Galen Gruman & Deke McClelland	ISBN: 1-56884-178-7	$19.95 USA/$26.95 Canada
QuarkXPress 3.3 For Dummies®	by Galen Gruman & Barbara Assadi	ISBN: 1-56884-217-1	$19.99 USA/$26.99 Canada
Upgrading and Fixing Macs® For Dummies®	by Kearney Rietmann & Frank Higgins	ISBN: 1-56884-189-2	$19.95 USA/$26.95 Canada

MULTIMEDIA

Title	Author	ISBN	Price
Multimedia & CD-ROMs For Dummies®, 2nd Edition	by Andy Rathbone	ISBN: 1-56884-907-9	$19.99 USA/$26.99 Canada
Multimedia & CD-ROMs For Dummies®, Interactive Multimedia Value Pack, 2nd Edition	by Andy Rathbone	ISBN: 1-56884-909-5	$29.99 USA/$39.99 Canada

OPERATING SYSTEMS:

DOS

Title	Author	ISBN	Price
MORE DOS For Dummies®	by Dan Gookin	ISBN: 1-56884-046-2	$19.95 USA/$26.95 Canada
OS/2® Warp For Dummies®, 2nd Edition	by Andy Rathbone	ISBN: 1-56884-205-8	$19.99 USA/$26.99 Canada

UNIX

Title	Author	ISBN	Price
MORE UNIX® For Dummies®	by John R. Levine & Margaret Levine Young	ISBN: 1-56884-361-5	$19.99 USA/$26.99 Canada
UNIX® For Dummies®	by John R. Levine & Margaret Levine Young	ISBN: 1-878058-58-4	$19.95 USA/$26.95 Canada

WINDOWS

Title	Author	ISBN	Price
MORE Windows® For Dummies®, 2nd Edition	by Andy Rathbone	ISBN: 1-56884-048-9	$19.95 USA/$26.95 Canada
Windows® 95 For Dummies®	by Andy Rathbone	ISBN: 1-56884-240-6	$19.99 USA/$26.99 Canada

PCS/HARDWARE

Title	Author	ISBN	Price
Illustrated Computer Dictionary For Dummies®, 2nd Edition	by Dan Gookin & Wallace Wang	ISBN: 1-56884-218-X	$12.95 USA/$16.95 Canada
Upgrading and Fixing PCs For Dummies®, 2nd Edition	by Andy Rathbone	ISBN: 1-56884-903-6	$19.99 USA/$26.99 Canada

PRESENTATION/AUTOCAD

Title	Author	ISBN	Price
AutoCAD For Dummies®	by Bud Smith	ISBN: 1-56884-191-4	$19.95 USA/$26.95 Canada
PowerPoint 4 For Windows® For Dummies®	by Doug Lowe	ISBN: 1-56884-161-2	$16.99 USA/$22.99 Canada

PROGRAMMING

Title	Author	ISBN	Price
Borland C++ For Dummies®	by Michael Hyman	ISBN: 1-56884-162-0	$19.95 USA/$26.95 Canada
C For Dummies®, Volume 1	by Dan Gookin	ISBN: 1-878058-78-9	$19.95 USA/$26.95 Canada
C++ For Dummies®	by Stephen R. Davis	ISBN: 1-56884-163-9	$19.95 USA/$26.95 Canada
Delphi Programming For Dummies®	by Neil Rubenking	ISBN: 1-56884-200-7	$19.99 USA/$26.99 Canada
Mac® Programming For Dummies®	by Dan Parks Sydow	ISBN: 1-56884-173-6	$19.95 USA/$26.95 Canada
PowerBuilder 4 Programming For Dummies®	by Ted Coombs & Jason Coombs	ISBN: 1-56884-325-9	$19.99 USA/$26.99 Canada
QBasic Programming For Dummies®	by Douglas Hergert	ISBN: 1-56884-093-4	$19.95 USA/$26.95 Canada
Visual Basic 3 For Dummies®	by Wallace Wang	ISBN: 1-56884-076-4	$19.95 USA/$26.95 Canada
Visual Basic "X" For Dummies®	by Wallace Wang	ISBN: 1-56884-230-9	$19.99 USA/$26.99 Canada
Visual C++ 2 For Dummies®	by Michael Hyman & Bob Arnson	ISBN: 1-56884-328-3	$19.99 USA/$26.99 Canada
Windows® 95 Programming For Dummies®	by S. Randy Davis	ISBN: 1-56884-327-5	$19.99 USA/$26.99 Canada

SPREADSHEET

Title	Author	ISBN	Price
1-2-3 For Dummies®	by Greg Harvey	ISBN: 1-878058-60-6	$16.95 USA/$22.95 Canada
1-2-3 For Windows® 5 For Dummies®, 2nd Edition	by John Walkenbach	ISBN: 1-56884-216-3	$16.95 USA/$22.95 Canada
Excel 5 For Macs® For Dummies®	by Greg Harvey	ISBN: 1-56884-186-8	$19.95 USA/$26.95 Canada
Excel For Dummies®, 2nd Edition	by Greg Harvey	ISBN: 1-56884-050-0	$16.95 USA/$22.95 Canada
MORE 1-2-3 For DOS For Dummies®	by John Weingarten	ISBN: 1-56884-224-4	$19.99 USA/$26.99 Canada
MORE Excel 5 For Windows® For Dummies®	by Greg Harvey	ISBN: 1-56884-207-4	$19.95 USA/$26.95 Canada
Quattro Pro 6 For Windows® For Dummies®	by John Walkenbach	ISBN: 1-56884-174-4	$19.95 USA/$26.95 Canada
Quattro Pro For DOS For Dummies®	by John Walkenbach	ISBN: 1-56884-023-3	$16.95 USA/$22.95 Canada

UTILITIES

Title	Author	ISBN	Price
Norton Utilities 8 For Dummies®	by Beth Slick	ISBN: 1-56884-166-3	$19.95 USA/$26.95 Canada

VCRS/CAMCORDERS

Title	Author	ISBN	Price
VCRs & Camcorders For Dummies™	by Gordon McComb & Andy Rathbone	ISBN: 1-56884-229-5	$14.99 USA/$20.99 Canada

WORD PROCESSING

Title	Author	ISBN	Price
Ami Pro For Dummies®	by Jim Meade	ISBN: 1-56884-049-7	$19.95 USA/$26.95 Canada
MORE Word For Windows® 6 For Dummies®	by Doug Lowe	ISBN: 1-56884-165-5	$19.95 USA/$26.95 Canada
MORE WordPerfect® 6 For Windows® For Dummies®	by Margaret Levine Young & David C. Kay	ISBN: 1-56884-206-6	$19.95 USA/$26.95 Canada
MORE WordPerfect® 6 For DOS For Dummies®	by Wallace Wang, edited by Dan Gookin	ISBN: 1-56884-047-0	$19.95 USA/$26.95 Canada
Word 6 For Macs® For Dummies®	by Dan Gookin	ISBN: 1-56884-190-6	$19.95 USA/$26.95 Canada
Word For Windows® 6 For Dummies®	by Dan Gookin	ISBN: 1-56884-075-6	$16.95 USA/$22.95 Canada
Word For Windows® For Dummies®	by Dan Gookin & Ray Werner	ISBN: 1-878058-86-X	$16.95 USA/$22.95 Canada
WordPerfect® 6 For DOS For Dummies®	by Dan Gookin	ISBN: 1-878058-77-0	$16.95 USA/$22.95 Canada
WordPerfect® 6.1 For Windows® For Dummies®, 2nd Edition	by Margaret Levine Young & David Kay	ISBN: 1-56884-243-0	$16.95 USA/$22.95 Canada
WordPerfect® For Dummies®	by Dan Gookin	ISBN: 1-878058-52-5	$16.95 USA/$22.95 Canada

For scholastic requests & educational orders please call Educational Sales at 1. 800. 434. 2086

FOR MORE INFO OR TO ORDER, PLEASE CALL ▶ 800. 762. 2974

For volume discounts & special orders please call Corporate Sales, at 415. 655. 3000

Fun, Fast, & Cheap!™

NEW!

The Internet For Macs® For Dummies® Quick Reference

by Charles Seiter

ISBN:1-56884-967-2
$9.99 USA/$12.99 Canada

NEW!

Windows® 95 For Dummies® Quick Reference

by Greg Harvey

ISBN: 1-56884-964-8
$9.99 USA/$12.99 Canada

SUPER STAR

Photoshop 3 For Macs® For Dummies® Quick Reference

by Deke McClelland

ISBN: 1-56884-968-0
$9.99 USA/$12.99 Canada

SUPER STAR

WordPerfect® For DOS For Dummies® Quick Reference

by Greg Harvey

ISBN: 1-56884-009-8
$8.95 USA/$12.95 Canada

Title	Author	ISBN	Price
DATABASE			
Access 2 For Dummies® Quick Reference	by Stuart J. Stuple	ISBN: 1-56884-167-1	$8.95 USA/$11.95 Canada
dBASE 5 For DOS For Dummies® Quick Reference	by Barrie Sosinsky	ISBN: 1-56884-954-0	$9.99 USA/$12.99 Canada
dBASE 5 For Windows® For Dummies® Quick Reference	by Stuart J. Stuple	ISBN: 1-56884-953-2	$9.99 USA/$12.99 Canada
Paradox 5 For Windows® For Dummies® Quick Reference	by Scott Palmer	ISBN: 1-56884-960-5	$9.99 USA/$12.99 Canada
DESKTOP PUBLISHING/ILLUSTRATION/GRAPHICS			
CorelDRAW! 5 For Dummies® Quick Reference	by Raymond E. Werner	ISBN: 1-56884-952-4	$9.99 USA/$12.99 Canada
Harvard Graphics For Windows® For Dummies® Quick Reference	by Raymond E. Werner	ISBN: 1-56884-962-1	$9.99 USA/$12.99 Canada
Photoshop 3 For Macs® For Dummies® Quick Reference	by Deke McClelland	ISBN: 1-56884-968-0	$9.99 USA/$12.99 Canada
FINANCE/PERSONAL FINANCE			
Quicken 4 For Windows® For Dummies® Quick Reference	by Stephen L. Nelson	ISBN: 1-56884-950-8	$9.95 USA/$12.95 Canada
GROUPWARE/INTEGRATED			
Microsoft® Office 4 For Windows® For Dummies® Quick Reference	by Doug Lowe	ISBN: 1-56884-958-3	$9.99 USA/$12.99 Canada
Microsoft® Works 3 For Windows® For Dummies® Quick Reference	by Michael Partington	ISBN: 1-56884-959-1	$9.99 USA/$12.99 Canada
INTERNET/COMMUNICATIONS/NETWORKING			
The Internet For Dummies® Quick Reference	by John R. Levine & Margaret Levine Young	ISBN: 1-56884-168-X	$8.95 USA/$11.95 Canada
MACINTOSH			
Macintosh® System 7.5 For Dummies® Quick Reference	by Stuart J. Stuple	ISBN: 1-56884-956-7	$9.99 USA/$12.99 Canada
OPERATING SYSTEMS:			
DOS			
DOS For Dummies® Quick Reference	by Greg Harvey	ISBN: 1-56884-007-1	$8.95 USA/$11.95 Canada
UNIX			
UNIX® For Dummies® Quick Reference	by John R. Levine & Margaret Levine Young	ISBN: 1-56884-094-2	$8.95 USA/$11.95 Canada
WINDOWS			
Windows® 3.1 For Dummies® Quick Reference, 2nd Edition	by Greg Harvey	ISBN: 1-56884-951-6	$8.95 USA/$11.95 Canada
PCs/HARDWARE			
Memory Management For Dummies® Quick Reference	by Doug Lowe	ISBN: 1-56884-362-3	$9.99 USA/$12.99 Canada
PRESENTATION/AUTOCAD			
AutoCAD For Dummies® Quick Reference	by Ellen Finkelstein	ISBN: 1-56884-198-1	$9.95 USA/$12.95 Canada
SPREADSHEET			
1-2-3 For Dummies® Quick Reference	by John Walkenbach	ISBN: 1-56884-027-6	$8.95 USA/$11.95 Canada
1-2-3 For Windows® 5 For Dummies® Quick Reference	by John Walkenbach	ISBN: 1-56884-957-5	$9.95 USA/$12.95 Canada
Excel For Windows® For Dummies® Quick Reference, 2nd Edition	by John Walkenbach	ISBN: 1-56884-096-9	$8.95 USA/$11.95 Canada
Quattro Pro 6 For Windows® For Dummies® Quick Reference	by Stuart J. Stuple	ISBN: 1-56884-172-8	$9.95 USA/$12.95 Canada
WORD PROCESSING			
Word For Windows® 6 For Dummies® Quick Reference	by George Lynch	ISBN: 1-56884-095-0	$8.95 USA/$11.95 Canada
Word For Windows® For Dummies® Quick Reference	by George Lynch	ISBN: 1-56884-029-2	$8.95 USA/$11.95 Canada
WordPerfect® 6.1 For Windows® For Dummies® Quick Reference, 2nd Edition	by Greg Harvey	ISBN: 1-56884-966-4	$9.99 USA/$12.99/Canada

For scholastic requests & educational orders please call Educational Sales at 1. 800. 434. 2086

FOR MORE INFO OR TO ORDER, PLEASE CALL ▶ 800 762 2974

For volume discounts & special orders please ca Corporate Sales, at 415. 655. 3000

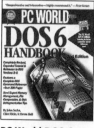

Macworld® Mac® & Power Mac SECRETS™, 2nd Edition

by David Pogue & Joseph Schorr

This is the definitive Mac reference for those who want to become power users! Includes three disks with 9MB of software!

WINNERS 1994-95
TECHNICAL PUBLICATIONS AND ART COMPETITIONS OF THE SOCIETY FOR TECHNICAL COMMUNICATION

ISBN: 1-56884-175-2
$39.95 USA/$54.95 Canada

Includes 3 disks chock full of software.

NEWBRIDGE BOOK CLUB SELECTION

Macworld® Mac® FAQs™

by David Pogue

Written by the hottest Macintosh author around, David Pogue, *Macworld Mac FAQs* gives users the ultimate Mac reference. Hundreds of Mac questions and answers side-by-side, right at your fingertips, and organized into six easy-to-reference sections with lots of sidebars and diagrams.

ISBN: 1-56884-480-8
$19.99 USA/$26.99 Canada

Macworld® System 7.5 Bible, 3rd Edition

by Lon Poole

ISBN: 1-56884-098-5
$29.95 USA/$39.95 Canada

NATIONAL BESTSELLER!

Macworld® ClarisWorks 3.0 Companion, 3rd Edition

by Steven A. Schwartz

ISBN: 1-56884-481-6
$24.99 USA/$34.99 Canada

NATIONAL BESTSELLER!

Macworld® Complete Mac® Handbook Plus Interactive CD, 3rd Edition

by Jim Heid

BMUG SPRING 1995 CHOICE PRODUCT

ISBN: 1-56884-192-2
$39.95 USA/$54.95 Canada

Includes an interactive CD-ROM.

NEWBRIDGE BOOK CLUB SELECTION

Macworld® Ultimate Mac® CD-ROM

by Jim Heid

ISBN: 1-56884-477-8
$19.99 USA/$26.99 Canada

CD-ROM includes version 2.0 of QuickTime, and over 65 MB of the best shareware, freeware, fonts, sounds, and more!

Macworld® Networking Bible, 2nd Edition

by Dave Kosiur & Joel M. Snyder

ISBN: 1-56884-194-9
$29.95 USA/$39.95 Canada

Macworld® Photoshop 3 Bible, 2nd Edition

by Deke McClelland

ISBN: 1-56884-158-2
$39.95 USA/$54.95 Canada

Includes stunning CD-ROM with add-ons, digitized photos and more.

WINNERS 1994-95
TECHNICAL PUBLICATIONS AND ART COMPETITIONS OF THE SOCIETY FOR TECHNICAL COMMUNICATION

NEW!

Macworld® Photoshop 2.5 Bible

by Deke McClelland

ISBN: 1-56884-022-5
$29.95 USA/$39.95 Canada

NATIONAL BESTSELLER!

Macworld® FreeHand 4 Bible

by Deke McClelland

ISBN: 1-56884-170-1
$29.95 USA/$39.95 Canada

Macworld® Illustrator 5.0/5.5 Bible

by Ted Alspach

ISBN: 1-56884-097-7
$39.95 USA/$54.95 Canada

Includes CD-ROM with QuickTime tutorials.

IDG BOOKS WORLDWIDE™

Order Center: **(800) 762-2974** *(8 a.m.–6 p.m., EST, weekdays)*

Quantity	ISBN	Title	Price	Total

Shipping & Handling Charges

	Description	First book	Each additional book	Total
Domestic	Normal	$4.50	$1.50	$
	Two Day Air	$8.50	$2.50	$
	Overnight	$18.00	$3.00	$
International	Surface	$8.00	$8.00	$
	Airmail	$16.00	$16.00	$
	DHL Air	$17.00	$17.00	$

*For large quantities call for shipping & handling charges.
**Prices are subject to change without notice.

Ship to:

Name _____

Company _____

Address _____

City/State/Zip _____

Daytime Phone _____

Payment: ☐ Check to IDG Books Worldwide (US Funds Only)

☐ VISA   ☐ MasterCard   ☐ American Express

Card # _____ Expires _____

Signature _____

Subtotal _____

CA residents add
applicable sales tax _____

IN, MA, and MD
residents add
5% sales tax _____

IL residents add
6.25% sales tax _____

RI residents add
7% sales tax _____

TX residents add
8.25% sales tax _____

Shipping _____

Total _____

Please send this order form to:

**IDG Books Worldwide, Inc.
Attn: Order Entry Dept.
7260 Shadeland Station, Suite 100
Indianapolis, IN 46256**

*Allow up to 3 weeks for delivery.
Thank you!*